Tragic Orphans

The **Institute of Southeast Asian Studies (ISEAS)** was established as an autonomous organization in 1968. It is a regional centre dedicated to the study of socio-political, security and economic trends and developments in Southeast Asia and its wider geostrategic and economic environment. The Institute's research programmes are the Regional Economic Studies (RES, including ASEAN and APEC), Regional Strategic and Political Studies (RSPS), and Regional Social and Cultural Studies (RSCS).

ISEAS Publishing, an established academic press, has issued more than 2,000 books and journals. It is the largest scholarly publisher of research about Southeast Asia from within the region. ISEAS Publishing works with many other academic and trade publishers and distributors to disseminate important research and analyses from and about Southeast Asia to the rest of the world.

CARL VADIVELLA BELLE

Tragic Orphans

INDIANS IN MALAYSIA

ISEAS

INSTITUTE OF SOUTHEAST ASIAN STUDIES

Singapore

First published in Singapore in 2015 by
ISEAS Publishing
Institute of Southeast Asian Studies
30 Heng Mui Keng Terrace
Pasir Panjang
Singapore 119614

E-mail: publish@iseas.edu.sg
Website: <http://bookshop.iseas.edu.sg>

The responsibility for facts and opinions in this publication rests exclusively with the author and his interpretations do not necessarily reflect the views or the policy of the publishers or their supporters.

ISEAS Library Cataloguing-in-Publication Data

Belle, Carl Vadivella.
   Tragic orphans : Indians in Malaysia.
   1. Indians (Asian people)—Malaysia—History.
   I. Title.
   II. Title: Indians in Malaysia
DS595.2 I3B43   2015

ISBN 978-981-4519-03-8 (soft cover)
ISBN 978-981-4620-12-3 (e-book, PDF)

Typeset by Superskill Graphics Pte Ltd
Printed in Singapore by Markono Print Media Pte Ltd

CONTENTS

Reminiscences of UMNO, Razak and Mahathir (Petaling Jaya: Strategic Information and Research Development Centre, 2007), pp. 256–57.

14. In a well-argued study, Andrew Wilford has argued that within current Malay nationalist discourse the Indian represents the "surmounted past", and that the "uncanny Indian" has become a catalytic figure in imagery of the Malay Islamic nationalist which has evolved in the period from 1981 onwards (Andrew C. Wilford, *Cage of Freedom: Tamil Identity and the Ethnic Fetish in Malaysia* [Ann Arbor: The University of Michigan Press, 2006], pp. 446–47).

ACKNOWLEDGEMENTS

The completion of this book would not have been possible without the generous assistance of many people in Malaysia and Singapore. I must first and foremost thank Ambassador K. Kesavapany, former Director of the Institute of Southeast Asian Studies, Singapore, who gave his full encouragement and continuing support for this work. I would also like to thank Mrs Triena Ong, formerly of the Institute, whose support throughout the process of writing was invaluable and who offered much encouragement at crucial points of this work's evolution. Mr Stephen Logan, Mrs Y.L. Lee and other staff at ISEAS provided much needed administrative support.

There were a number of academics and observers whose contributions were both stimulating and helped me to shape my observations and the final direction of this work. These included Dr Ooi Kee Beng, Dr Geoff Wade, the late Mr Barry Wain, Dr Lee Hock Guan, Dr Leon Comber, and others at ISEAS; Dr K. Anbalakan of Universiti Sains Malaysia; Dr S. Nagarajan of Wawasan Open University, whose assistance can only be described as substantial; Dr Haji Mohamad Thalha who shed light on the Indian Muslim experience in Malaysia; Mr Pathmarajah Nagalingam; Dr Gauri Krishnan, National Heritage Board, Singapore; Dr Andrew Wilford, Cornell University, USA; Mr Ismail Kassim, former *Straits Times* Senior Correspondent, Kuala Lumpur; Sri Ramli Ibrahim, Artistic Director, Sutra Dance Theatre; Dr R. Thillainathan, Executive Director of Genting Bhd; Professor P. Ramasamy, Deputy Chief Minister, Penang; Mr Janakey Raman Manickam who supplied me with a copy of his book, *The Malaysian Indian Dilemma*; Mr P. Uthayakumar of Hindraf; Mr J. Terence Netto with whom I shared some illuminating conversations, Mr Liew Chin Tong, MP; Dr S.R. Sivachandralingam of Universiti Malaya; Professor Balachandran Shanmugam; Mr B. Kumaresh; Mr and Mrs Shanmuganathan; Mr V. Chockalingam, who showed me enormous kindness during a visit to Malacca; and Mr Kumar Menon, whose forensic questioning of my assumptions led me to rethink some aspects of my book. I would also wish to acknowledge the kind assistance of the late Puan Sri Janaki Athi Nahappan who shared her recollections of Subhas Chandra Bose and the politics of Indian nationalism; Toh Puan Uma Sambanthan, whose encyclopedic memory, insights, and generosity have over many years greatly enriched my own perspectives; and the late Dr S.M. Ponniah whose observations were always profound. Dr Ooi Cheng Ghee of Penang kindly agreed to allow me to use the photograph which graces the cover of this book. There are also a number of people who specifically requested that their contributions remain unacknowledged, but to whom I am deeply grateful.

With regard to those who assisted me with accommodation and hospitality, I offer my deepest thanks to Mr and Mrs V. Thanapal who for many years have offered me a home away from home during my frequent trips to Malaysia; Mr and Mrs N. Selva; the late Mr N.S. Sundrasekaran and Mrs Sundrasekaran; Mr. K. and Mrs Ah Leng Thuruvan; Mr Kumar and Mrs Nui Menon; Madam V. Jayaladchumy; Mr A. and Mrs Veronica Athimoolmam; and Ms A. Thanam.

I offer my deepest thanks to my wife, Wendy Valli Belle, who has lived with this book for the past three years, who has lived through endless discourses on Indians in Malaysia, and whose support, encouragement, humour, and plain commonsense have been of immeasurable assistance. I dedicate this book, with love, to her.

While many have provided assistance in many fields, the opinions contained in this book, are, of course, my own.

ABBREVIATIONS

ABIM	Angkatan Belia Islam Malaysia (Islamic Youth Force Malaysia)
ACCIN	Allied Coordinating Council of Islamic NGOs
AMCJA	All-Malaya Council for Joint Action
AMRWC	All-Malaya Rubber Workers' Council
API	Angkatan Permuda Insaf (Generation of Aware Youth)
BA	Barisan Alternatif (Alternative Front)
BCE	Before Common Era
BIA	British Indian Army
BMA	British Military Administration
BN	Barisan Nasional (National Front)
CE	Common Era
CIAM	Central Indian Association of Malaya
DAP	Democratic Action Party
EIC	East India Company
EWRF	Education Welfare and Research Foundation
FIO	Federation of Indian Organizations
FMS	Federated Malay States
FRU	Federal Reserve Unit
GATCO	Great Alonioners Trading Corporation
GLU	General Labour Union
HINDRAF	Hindu Rights Action Force
HRP	Human Rights Party
IIL	Indian Independence League
IMP	Independence of Malaya Party
INA	Indian National Army
IPF	Indian Progressive Front
IRRA	International Rubber Regulation Agreement
ISA	Internal Security Act

ITN	Institute Teknologi Negeri (National Technology Institute)
JAKIM	Jabatan Kemajuan Islam Malaysia (Department of Islamic Development)
KMM	Kesatuan Melayu Muda (Malay Youth Movement)
KMT	Kuomintang
KMTM	Kuomintang Malaya
KRIS	Kesatuan Rakyat Istimewa Semananjuang (The Strength of the Special People on the Peninsula/Union of Peninsular Indonesians)
MAJU	Koperasi Belia Majujaya
MAPA	Malaysian Agriculture Producers' Association
MARA	Majlis Amanah Rakyat (People's Trust Council)
McEEU	Malacca Estate Employee's Union
MCA	Malayan/Malaysian Chinese Association
MCP	Malayan Communist Party
MEWU	Malayan Estate Workers Union
MIC	Malayan/Malaysian Indian Congress
MIED	Maju Institute for Educational Development
MNLA	Malayan National Liberation Army
MNP	Malay Nationalist Party
MPABA	Malayan Peoples' Anti-British Army
MPAJA	Malayan Peoples' Anti-Japanese Army
MPIEA	Malayan Planting Industry Employers' Association
MTUC	Malayan/Malaysian Trade Union Congress/Council
NCC	National Consultative Council
NECC	National Economic Consultative Committee
NEP	New Economic Policy
NESA	Syarikat Kerjasama Nesa Pelabagai
NGC	National Goodwill Committee
NGO	non-government organization
NJILU	North Johore Indian Labour Union
NLFCS	National Land and Finance Cooperative Society
NOC	National Operations Council
NSILU	Negri Sembilan Indian Labour Union
NUPW	National Union of Plantation Workers
PAM	Planters' Association of Malaysia
PAP	People's Action Party
PAS	Partai Islam se-Malaysia (Islamic Party of Malaysia)

PEEU	Perak Estate Employees' Union
PMDF	Pan-Malayan Dravidian Federation
PMFTU	Pan-Malayan Federation of Trade Unions
PMGLU	Pan-Malayan General Labour Union
PMIP	Persatuan Islam Se-Melayu (Pan-Malayan Islamic Party)
POW	prisoner of war
PMRWU	Pan-Malayan Rubber Workers' Union
PPP	People's Progressive Party
PR	Pakatan Rakyat (People's Alliance)
PUTERA	Pusat Tenaga Rakyat (Centre of People's Power)
PWUM	Plantation Workers' Union of Malaya
RGA	Rubber Growers' Association
RIAB	Rubber Industry Arbitration Board
SEAC	South East Asian Command
SETWU	Selangor Estate Trade Workers' Union
Sukaham	Suruhanjaya Hak Asai Malaysia (Human Rights Commission of Malaysia)
TUAM	Pan-Malayan Trade Union Advisor
UFMS	Unfederated Malay States
UIAM	Universiti Islam Antarabangsa (International Islamic University)
UMEWU	United Malayan Estates Workers' Union
UMNO	United Malays National Organisation
UPAM	United Planters' Association of Malaysia
VOC	Vereenigd Oost-Indische Compaignie (Dutch East India Company)

INTRODUCTION

Some years ago, while undertaking research in the Oriental and Indian Office Collection Library in London, I uncovered a truly shocking passage contained within the 1957 Federation of Malaya Census Report. Noting that 4 million Indians had been recruited to work in colonial Malaya and that 2.8 million had subsequently returned to India, the report commented: "Much of the 1.2 million net immigration appears to have been wiped out by disease, snakebite, exhaustion and malnutrition, for the Indian population of Malaya numbered only 858,614 of which 62.1 per cent was locally born."[1] The bland matter of fact language cannot begin to disguise the tragedy and horror which lurks behind these raw statistics. Nor does this brief summation of the premature deaths of hundreds of thousands of Indians begin to evaluate the appalling human toll that was exacted in the development of a prosperous colonial economy that enriched many investors and contributed significantly to the wealth of Great Britain. There is no official monument to the nameless Indians who laid the economic and infrastructural foundation upon which the emerging modern Malaysian economy was constructed, but working class Indians will inform you that their legacy is to be found in the railway sleepers and rubber trees of Malaysia; each representing the sacrifice of an Indian life.

Although at that point my energies were directed towards the completion of a doctoral dissertation on the Hindu festival of Thaipusam in Malaysia, my research continued to generate a considerable volume of historical material which I felt cast fresh light on the Indian experience in Malaya/Malaysia. During the fieldwork for my doctorate, I interviewed members of a vanishing generation of Indian Malaysians; people who had been recruited under the kangany system; who had personal experience of the Klang strikes of 1941; who had participated in the wartime politics of Indian nationalism; who had been active in the early years of the

Malayan Indian Congress; and who had known the leading figures who had helped shape contemporary Indian society in Malaysia. Although in recent years there have been a number of historical, political, sociological and anthropological studies of aspects of the Indian experience in Malaysia, an increasing number written from the subaltern perspective, as well as two collections of studies published by the Institute of Southeast Asian Studies, Singapore,[2] there has been no comprehensive general history of Indians in Malaysia since the publication of the two seminal works over forty years ago, namely K.S. Sandhu's *Indians in Malaysia: Some Aspects of their Immigration and Settlement*[3] and S. Arasaratnam's *Indians in Malaysia and Singapore.*[4]

Neither of two recently published works, both of which are general studies of Indians in Malaysia, can be said to constitute the comprehensive history which would complement the works of Sandhu and Arasaratnam. Apart from its detailed discussion of educational issues, I found Muzafar Desmond Tate's *The Malaysian Indians: History, Problems and Future*[5] a slight and disappointing study, incomplete and disjointed.[6] (I subsequently learned that Tate had died before he could revise or edit the work.) Janakey Raman Manickam's far more substantial work, *The Malaysian Indian Dilemma: The Struggles and Agony of the Indian Community in Malaysia,*[7] provides a brief historical overview as an introduction to a thorough and primarily sociological study of contemporary Indian society in Malaysia, coupled with a heartfelt analysis of the immediate problems facing Indian Malaysians.

Much has occurred since the publication of Sandhu's and Arasaratnam's great pioneering studies: the 13 May incident; the introduction of the New Economic Policy (NEP) and the emergence of a substantial Malay middle class; the Mahathir era and the total transformation of the Malaysian economy; the rapid decline of rubber as a vital component of Malaysian exports; the displacement of hundreds of thousands of Indians from the great estates of Malaysia; the unprecedented importance of Islam to the construction of Malay cultural identity; the emergence of Hindu Rights Action Force (Hindraf)/Makkal Sakthi and their impact on the elections of 8 March 2008; and the rise of the influential albeit fractured opposition Pakatan Rakyat (PR). Moreover, many of the established assumptions which informed much of the histories written forty years ago have been challenged and indeed overturned. Thus, for example, on the basis of received scholarship of that time, Sandhu could write of indentured Indian labourers:

> The relegation of these classes to the level of animals in a caste-ridden
> society naturally tended to deprive them of initiative and self-respect,
> and made them a cringing, servile group. These people had neither the
> skill nor the enterprise to rise above the level of manual labour and were
> also willing to accept low wages.[8]

No informed scholar working today would write in this fashion. In the
intervening period scholars have rejected the largely Victorian-created
narratives of an unchanging and immutable hierarchical Indian society,
and have demonstrated that the supposed "inflexibility" of caste was
largely an invention of British orientalist anthropology. Indeed, precolonial
South Indian society was not only extraordinarily diverse but also dynamic
and mobile.

But while this history draws upon the earlier studies of Sandhu and
Arasaratnam, it aims at something more than merely updating these
works. The major point of departure is the exploration of those aspects
of the metropolitan and colonial background which bear directly upon
the Indian experience in Malaysia, as well as discussion of the ideologies
and events which have proven formative in shaping the sort of society in
which Indian Malaysians now find themselves. This book examines the
colonially initiated economic and structural reforms which encouraged,
and in many cases forced, Indians to leave their homeland; demonstrates
the legacy bequeathed by black slavery to schemes of indentured Indian
labour; and reviews the colonial ideologies of "race" which were developed
in British India and later exported to Malaya. The latter not only shaped
Malayan conceptions of "race" in ways that continue to profoundly
influence contemporary Malaysian political and cultural discourse but
also refashioned Indian perceptions of identity in terms of caste, religion,
origins, and culture.

Indian interaction with the Malay Peninsula and indeed the wider
Malay Archipelago has a long and complex history dating back to the
centuries EFH As Rajesh Rai has pointed out, Southeast Asia "is one of the
few regions, if not the only region outside South Asia, where the journey
of Indians has continued from the pre-modern, through the colonial,
and into the contemporary age of globalisation".[9] Indic civilizational
impulses played an important if not dominant role in the formation of
early Malay states and in fashioning indigenous cultural and religious
forms which obtained within the wider Malay world. However, more
recent migrants have overwhelmingly consisted of those recruited to

work as labourers within the colonial economy, a development which denied them opportunities for economic and hence social mobility, and created a framework for postcolonial exclusion. Colonialism left as an unwelcome residue an array of highly negative images of the "coolie immigrant". As P. Uthayakumar has remarked, in modern Malaysia Indian working classes are "to be cast aside socially as the drag [*sic*] with the social stereotypes as labourers, drunks, untrustworthy fellows, black and smelly fellows, dependent and always complaining ... [these are] a few of the stereotypes usually associated with being Indian poor in Malaysia".[10] The continuing Malaysian controversy over the novel *Interlok,* which is perceived to reproduce and perpetuate these demeaning representations, reveals the enduring impact of impressions initially forged by colonial racial ideologies.

An underlying premise of this study is that it is impossible to understand the marginalized status of Indians in Malaysia without reference to the construction and inculcation of theories of "race" in Malaya/Malaysia and the ultimate creation of a Bumiputera (Malay)/non-Bumiputera (non-Malay) "racial" dichotomy which governs Malaysian political, cultural and social life. These ideologies have had an especially marked impact upon the construction of Malay ethnicity. A substantial body of scholarship has documented the dynamic, fluid, and mobile character of pre-colonial indigenous societies, the fact that these societies were not especially ethnicized, and that the emergence of an identifiable ethnicity known as "Malay" is a comparatively recent development.[11] British colonialism imparted ideologies of race, which in the Malayan context consisted, *inter alia*, of a narrative of a weak and backward Malay "race" of tradition-bound subsistence farmers residing in kampungs, who but for British protection would be subjugated by the more enterprising and predacious "immigrants" (primarily the Chinese), who would seize the commanding heights of the economy and usurp political control. The Malay nationalism which emerged following the Pacific war was defensive, driven by a fear of "immigrant" domination, concerned with Malay "backwardness", and obsessed with the recurrent anxiety that Malays might "disappear from this world".[12]

The politics of communalism which have dominated Malayan and Malaysian political, social and cultural life, the continual re-inscription of "racial" boundaries, have not only deepened ethnic divisions but also mandated ethnic mobilization within the political sphere. As a minority ethnic group, lacking an economic base of any substance, Indians have inevitably found themselves disadvantaged in this process. In recent years, inter-ethnic politics have been rendered increasingly problematic by the continuing negotiation of Malay cultural identity and conceptions of self, in particular by the Islamic criticism of *adat* (Malay custom), long held to be a fundamental pillar of "Malayness" and thus what it means to be a Malay, and by changing perceptions of Islam itself.[13] These developments have obvious implications for the future of Malaysia and the type of society it is set to become, but in the interim have impacted disproportionately upon the Indian community.[14]

In this book, I have used the term "Indian" as it is understood in Malaysia, i.e., that it refers to all people who originate from the Indian subcontinent (including Sri Lankans) and who maintain a distinctive civilizational identity which derives inspiration from metropolitan South Asia. I have used the term "Malay world" in a generic sense to refer to the diverse peoples of the Malay Archipelago; that is, the extensive body of islands that fall between Southeast Asia and Australia, but including the Malay Peninsula and incorporating the territories of contemporary Malaysia, Indonesia, the Philippines, Brunei, and East Timor. Although I am aware that the term "Malay" has an application beyond Malaysia, and that this wider usage incorporates Christians and animists as well as Muslims, as well as embracing an extraordinarily wide range of *adat* or custom (some of which would not be recognized as such in Malaysia), in this book "Malay" is generally used, with all its ambiguities, to describe those who are designated as such by the constitutional settlement of 1957.

This book is structured into three basic sections. The first section consists of Chapters 1–4 and provides an overview of the premodern and early modern history of the Malay Peninsula leading to the Melaka Sultanate, the intrusion of European colonialism, the development within British India of colonial ideologies of conceptions of racial and societal hierarchies, and the subsequent imposition of these ideologies upon the Malay Peninsula. The second section, Chapters 5–10, traces the migration of Indians to Malaya throughout the colonial era, and the creation of an incipient Indian social consciousness. Chapter 5 looks at organized black plantation slavery and the inheritance which was passed on to Indian indentured labourers. Chapters 6 and 7 document indentured and assisted labour recruitment, the reforms which disrupted Indian social and economic structures and which encouraged emigration, and conditions under which the Indian workforce laboured. Chapter 8 details other Indian migratory streams, while Chapter 9 traces the evolution of political movements among Indians in pre-war Malaya. Chapter 10 explores the impact of the Japanese occupation, in particular the cohering of ethnic identities and the formative experiences of Indian nationalism. The third section, Chapters 11–16, examines post-Malaya/Malaysia, events leading to Merdeka, the creation of Malaysia, 13 May, the introduction of the NEP, the Mahathir and Abdullah eras, and the UMNO reaction to Hindraf. Each of these chapters provides a preliminary overview of the wider Malayan/Malaysian context before focussing upon the impact of political, societal and cultural developments upon the Indian community. The final chapter furnishes an overview of Prime Minister Najib Razak's 1Malaysia policies, the rapprochement with the Indian community, and the election of May 2013. In the Conclusions I have drawn together the main themes covered within the book.

At this point it is apposite to add a personal note. I was first posted to the Australian High Commission, Kuala Lumpur in 1976 as an employee of the Australian Department of Foreign Affairs. Prior to my departure I was assured that I would find Malaysia a comparatively transparent country, easy to understand and containing no hidden mysteries. My pre-posting programme consisted of a series of rather superficial briefings, many of which were tinctured with the discourses of neocolonialism, and which bore no relationship to the realities of the Malaysia in which I found myself. Indeed, it was only when I stood on the verge of return to Australia in 1979 that I felt that I was beginning to fully comprehend many of the more subtle and recondite nuances of this most complex of societies. Malaysia is a country of astonishing contradictions: an "authoritarian" regime in which people often speak their minds with alarming frankness and which permits a surprising array of scholarly and other opinion; a country whose official religion is Islam but in which Muslim security forces guard non-Muslim religious processions; a society whose official culture is resisted by a multitude of particularistic ethnic and religious impulses; a multi-ethnic society in which communal structures are inscribed within the formal political process but which at the grass-roots level often proves remarkably tolerant and liberal. It is impossible for any historian not to be immediately engaged with such a society. In my case, this engagement has been both encouraged and enriched by the friendliness and hospitality which pervades Malaysian life.

Notes

1. At the time of independence, Indians constituted 12 per cent of Malaya's population (K.J. Ratnam, *Communalism and the Political Process in Malaya* [Kuala Lumpur and Singapore: University of Malaya Press, 1965], p. 1). By 2000 the Indian component of the population of Malaysia had fallen to 7.8 per cent (Saw Swee-Hock, "Population Trends and Patterns in Multiracial Malaysia", in *Malaysia: Recent Trends and Challenges*, edited by Saw Swee-Hock and K. Kesavapany [Singapore: Institute of Southeast Asian Studies, 2006], p. 16), and by 2010 to 7.4 per cent (P. Uthayakumar, *Marginalization of the Indians in Malaysia*, paper emailed to the author on 6 April 2010).

2. K.S. Sandhu and A. Mani, eds., *Indian Communities in Southeast Asia* (Singapore: Institute of Southeast Asian Studies, 1993); K. Kesavapany, A.Mani, and P. Ramasamy, *Rising India and Indian Communities in East Asia* (Singapore: Institute of Southeast Asian Studies, 2006).

3. K.S. Sandhu, *Indians in Malaya: Some Aspects of their Immigration and Settlement 1786–1957* (Cambridge: Cambridge University Press, 1969).

4. Sinnappah Arasaratnam, *Indians in Malaysia and Singapore* (London: Oxford University Press, 1970).

5. Muzafar Desmond Tate, *The Malaysian Indians: History, Problems and Future* (Petaling Jaya: Strategic Information and Research Development, 2008).

6. See Carl Vadivella Belle, "Malaysian Indians: An Incomplete History", *Malaysiakini*, 25 June 2009 <http://www.malaysiakini.com/opinions/107202> (accessed 26 June 2009).

7. Janakey Raman Manickam, *The Malaysian Indian Dilemma: The Struggles and Agony of the Indian Community in Malaysia*, 2nd ed. (Klang: Janakey Raman Manickam, 2010).

8. Sandhu, *Indians in Malaya*, p. 57.

9. Rajesh Rai, "Positioning the Indian Diaspora: The Southeast Asian Experience", in *Tracing an Indian Diaspora: Contexts, Memories and Representations*, edited by Parvati Raghuram, Ajaya Kumar Sahoo, Brij Maharaj, and Dave Sangha (New Delhi: Sage, 2008), p. 29.

10. Uthayakumar, *Marginalization of the Indians*.

11. See for example, Alberto Gomes, "Ethnicisation of the Orang Asli: A Case Study of the Semai", in *Multiethnic Malaysia: Past, Present and Future*, edited by Lim Teck Ghee, Alberto Gomes, and Azly Rahman (Petaling Jaya: Strategic Information and Research Development Centre, 2009), p. 302.

12. Anthony Milner, *The Malays* (Chichester: Wiley Blackwell, 2011), p. 16. Milner's work is a multifaceted study of the subject of "Malayness" and a detailed consideration of Malay ethnicity.

13. See for example, Ahmad Mustapha Hassan, *The Unmaking of Malaysia: Insider's*

1

THE MALAY PENINSULA
Early History, Melaka and the Colonial Setting

For countless centuries the Malay Peninsula was a major locus for maritime trade conducted between West and East Asia. The Peninsula was strategically situated at the crossroads of the principal South and East Asian maritime routes, lying between two major subcontinents (India and China) and two great oceans (Indian and Pacific). The international trade route between China and India and thence to West Asia and Europe passed through the Strait of Melaka, and the Riau-Lingga Archipelago (south of contemporary Singapore), regarded as the only known safe route between East and West Asia.[1] The centrality of the Malay Peninsula was underscored by the seasonal pattern of the monsoons. While between January and April the northwest monsoons were favourable to traders from China, between July and November the prevailing southwest monsoons brought traders from the Indian subcontinent. The pivotal location of the Strait of Melaka led to the early establishment of trading entrepôts on the Malay Peninsula and in Sumatra.[2] Trade networks reached as far as the African coast, Arabia, and the Persian Gulf and thence to Europe.[3]

Trade between India and the Malay Peninsula dates back to prehistoric times. Verifiable sources indicate that there were systematic exchanges between India, Southeast Asia, and China in the first millennium EFH, and that throughout this period, India and Southeast Asia became important trading partners.[4] However, the earliest documented Indian links can be traced to the period of the great Indian Emperor Ashoka (circa 268–233 EFH).[5] Later Indian traders and adventurers visited the Peninsula in search of gold.[6] Indeed contemporary Indian sources, both Hindu texts and Buddhist *Jatakas*, refer to the Malay Peninsula as the Golden Khersonese or "land of gold" (in Sanskrit, *Suvarnabhumi*).[7]

The increasing volume of Indian maritime trade with Southeast Asia in the closing centuries EFH had a powerful impact on indigenous political and social structures. The consequent Indianization of Southeast Asia was to reshape and leave a permanent imprint upon local cultures, societies, languages and religious beliefs.[8]

Early Indian trade within the Malay Peninsula and Sumatra was conducted through local chieftains and chieftaincies. Most scholars accept that the processes of Indianization commenced in the earliest years FH[9] and became more pronounced following the rise of the Gupta dynasty. (It is widely held that the Malay/Malaysian term *"keling"* as a generic descriptor for South Indians is derived from the prominent Gupta port Kalinga, from which many Southeast Asian–based cargoes were dispatched.) This adumbrated a political and administrative regime which became a model for the entire region.[10] The development of East-West trade led to the transformation of commercial centres into established political units within the Malay Archipelago and on the Malay Peninsula.[11] Small Indianized states began appearing in Southeast Asia from the first century FH Two of the earliest trading centres appear to have been Langkasuka, an Indianized Buddhist kingdom which was established about 100 FH in the region of modern day Pattani,[12] and the settlement in Kedah, which was known by the Sanskrit name of *Kataha* and the Chinese name of *Chieh-cha*.[13]

The influence of Indian traders extended well beyond the commercial sphere and introduced new religious forms as well as systems of social and political organization. While Buddhism was the main religion of Indian traders, the rise of the Gupta Empire, which had adopted a state religion based upon pre-Buddhist Vedic traditions and rituals, encouraged the spread of a rival Vaisnavite trade network and the use of Sanskrit as the official language.[14] Traders were followed into the new states by Brahmans who possessed the necessary skills of writing, organization and administration.[15] The Brahmans intermarried with the families of local chiefs and thus exercised a powerful influence on the future shape of Southeast Asian polities. As Tan Ta Sen observes:

> Indianization was seen as an expansion of an organized culture that was founded upon the Indian conception of royalty, was characterized by Hindu or Buddhist cults, the theology of the *Puranas*, and the observance of the *Dharmasastras*, and expressed itself in the Sanskrit language.[16]

In keeping with Hindu notions of royalty, Brahman priests would have elevated the local chiefs by employment of the *vratyastatoma*, a rite which admitted foreigners into the received orthodox community. The newly anointed kings, now known by the titles of *raja* or *maharaja*, could thus claim to hold the Hindu rank of *Ksatriya* or regal/warrior caste.[17]

Most historians aver that Indian civilizational mores remained the province of the elite, especially the aristocracy, and that the general population continued to preserve an autochthonous culture structured around animism and ancestor cults.[18] However, Indian influences helped shape indigenous crafts and modes of artistic expression, as well as providing a system of writing, an expanded vocabulary (containing both Sanskrit and Tamil words),[19] a new lunar/solar calendar, administrative and legal structures, and a sense of social rank, influenced by notions of caste.[20] In addition, the classic epics of Hindu cosmology, the *Puranas*, the *Ramayana* and the *Mahabharata*, became integrated within the culture of the Malay Archipelago, and many generalist Hindu and Buddhist elements penetrated local belief systems and modes of organization.[21] The processes of Indianization, predominantly South Indian, were "overwhelmingly peaceful".[22]

While China and Southeast Asia had enjoyed close connections for centuries, the introduction of Buddhism in the third century FH and the trading ethos associated with the religion, promoted more frequent exchanges among China, Southeast Asia, and India. Chinese pilgrims made their way to and from India, the land in which Buddhism had originated, often in the process stimulating scholarship in the Peninsular and Sumatran ports in which they broke their voyages.[23] From the third century onwards, various Southeast Asian principalities sent tribute missions to China. Recognition of China's overlordship proved beneficial to the states involved. Not only did this establish a trading relationship between the state and China, but it also accorded recognition to the rulers of these states and to their designated agents.[24]

China's renewed interest in Southeast Asia under the Tang Dynasty (618–907) fuelled the movement of international trade and led to a regrouping of Malay maritime polities. During this period, Peninsular Malay states increasingly fell under the direction of the powerful Buddhist kingdom of Srivijaya.[25] The first official record of Srivijaya appears in the groups of inscriptions discovered in Sumatra which reveal the existence of a Buddhist kingdom in Palembang in 683–686, which had recently conquered the hinterland of Jambi.[26] In the final quarter of the seventh century, Srivijaya strengthened its position as one of the leading transit points for ships sailing between China and South Asia.[27] In subsequent years, Srivijaya expanded its control to both sides of the Strait of Melaka and to much of the Malay Peninsula.[28] The kingdom established diplomatic relations with both China and Chola India.[29]

It was throughout the period of the Srivijaya Empire that the common cultural features emerged of what might be regarded as an incipient Melayu (Malay) ethnicity. From the seventh century onwards, Srivijaya linked together most of the political units of the Melaka Strait, both in Sumatra and in the Malay Peninsula, in the process creating a broad accepted culture which incorporated language, institutions and an overlapping and interchangeable series of cultural forms. Leonard Andaya contends that an overarching sense of shared ethnicity originated in Southwest Sumatra and was later bequeathed to other parts of the region, most notably Melaka, Aceh and Johor.[30]

Later developments in both China and India did much to promote trade in Southeast Asia. The Song Dynasty of China, founded in 960, adopted a much more aggressive trade policy.[31] Within India, the rise of the Chola Kingdom, which from 985 onwards had expanded from its core region on the Kaveri delta to control all of South India and much of Central India, as well as the offshore islands of Sri Lanka and the Maldives, fostered wide-ranging trade networks between Arabia and India, Southeast Asia and China.[32] Indeed, Chola kings took a personal interest in trade and, in addition to repealing harbour tolls and other imposts, encouraged trade missions and related maritime expeditions.[33] The establishment of maritime trade between Song China and Chola India not only involved the states of Southeast Asia as active participants, but also led to the decline of the land routes which had hitherto borne the bulk of East Asian–South Asian trade.[34] Trade between India and China also produced extensive diplomatic, cultural and religious exchanges between the two subcontinents and intensified Indian influences within Southeast Asia.[35]

Given the ostensibly close ties between the Chola kingdom and Srivijaya, it is thus surprising to discover that in 1017 and again in 1025 the South Indian king Rajendra Chola launched attacks on Srivijaya. The latter was a more extensive action which targeted fourteen major port cities in Sumatra and along the Malay Peninsula.[36] There appear to have been two major factors which led to these attacks, namely,

1. Persistent attempts to obstruct Chola trade with China.[37]
2. The exaction of excessive imposts and other levies upon Chola ships transiting the Srivijaya controlled Melaka Strait.[38]

An additional expedition was conducted against Srivijaya in 1077 by King Kulottunga I.[39] In the years immediately following the final raid, the capital of Srivijaya was moved from Pelambang to Jambi.[40]

The raids resulted in Chola domination of direct trade between South India and China.[41] The Chola kingdom also developed an extensive trading network, and South Indian trade guilds were established in ports in Burma, Srivijaya (both along the Malay Peninsula and in Sumatra), and Java.[42]

The intrusion of Mongol forces in the late thirteenth century fractured the established political order and resulted in a fundamental rearrangement of the geopolitics of the Malay Archipelago. The decline of the Srivijaya Empire was accompanied by the Siamese occupation of much of the Malay Peninsula and the rise of Majapahit, the last of the great Indianized empires of the Archipelago.[43]

MELAKA

The establishment of Melaka as a Malay kingdom is credited to Parameswara, originally a Hindu prince of Srivijaya and resident in Palembang, which had become a vassal state of Majapahit.[44] In 1378, the Emperor Hongwu, founder emperor of the Ming dynasty, sent envoys to install the prince as king of Srivijaya. Majapahit viewed this action as a challenge to its authority and overlordship of Palembang, and in the ensuing affray the envoys were killed.[45] Parameswara was forced to flee to Temasek (site of current day Singapore) where after a few years reign he was driven out by the Siamese kingdom of Ayutthaya.[46] After sojourns in both Muar and Bertam, Parameswara arrived in Melaka in about 1400. Melaka, a settlement of about 2,000 people and founded by Bugis "piratical adventurers", was regarded as a Siamese dependency.[47]

From the outset of his rule, Parameswara recognized that the continued existence of his fledgling state was threatened by both the Majapahit and the Siamese kingdom, the latter claiming overlordship of the entire Malay Peninsula. He therefore sought to forge an alliance with China, the region's great power.[48] Parameswara's initiative coincided with a renewed Chinese interest in trade with Southeast Asia. Following Emperor Yongle's accession to power in 1402, he ordered that a series of missions be despatched to foreign states to advise them of his succession.[49] In 1405, the Emperor appointed Admiral Zheng He (Cheng Ho) to extend friendship and trade relations to Indian Ocean states and to organize these states into a tributary relationship with China.[50] Between 1405 and his death in 1433, Zheng He undertook a series of voyages that concentrated on Southeast Asia but which extended as far as India and Africa.[51] These voyages, and the armada which Zheng He commanded — consisting at times of a force of some 30,000 men and 300 armed ships[52] — not only successfully projected Chinese military, diplomatic and commercial interests but also enforced widespread recognition of Ming China as the region's dominant power.[53]

The first Chinese reference to Melaka is in 1403, the year Emperor Yongle sent a mission under eunuch Ya Chi'ing to visit the state.[54] This expedition probably reached Melaka in 1404. In 1405 Parameswara reciprocated by sending an envoy to the Ming Court. The official reception of this envoy signified formal Ming acceptance of Melaka as an independent kingdom. On 11 November 1405, Melaka was granted the status of a tributary state and was endowed with the Emperor's inscription, thus officially gaining Chinese protection.[55] In 1409 Zheng He visited Melaka with an armada of forty-eight ships. He bore official tablets which confirmed Melaka and its environs as a kingdom in the sight of Ming China.[56] Ming warnings to the Siamese ensured that Melaka was henceforth free of the risk of encroachment.[57] Melaka's need for Chinese patronage was complemented by China's need for a strategically located base which would command a safe sea route to India. Zheng He duly established his Southeast Asian headquarters in Melaka, thus making the state central to his regional operations.[58] In this way, the actions of Ming China, and in particular the visits of Zheng He, not only protected the fledgling state but also elevated it to a position of regional prominence, in the process recasting the religio-political configuration of the fifteenth century Malay Archipelago.[59]

Melaka made abundant use of its strategic location to regulate trade passing through the Strait, and indeed from 1434 to 1511 it became the largest and most influential trading centre within Southeast Asia.[60] By the time the close relationship with China was discontinued after 1435, when Ming China abandoned Yongle's trade policies and focused state energies on the renewed Mongol threat on its northern boundaries, Melaka had attained the status of a great regional political power, one which was capable of withstanding Siamese pressure.[61]

The astonishing rise of Melaka was fuelled by the rapid expansion of trade throughout Southeast Asia from the late fourteenth century onwards. This was based firstly upon the post-Crusade "spice orgy" which engulfed Europe, and secondly the trade generated by Ming China and associated with a complex trading network reaching beyond Southeast Asia and India to Europe.[62] Melaka was both cosmopolitan and pluralistic and housed resident colonies of traders, including Indian Muslims, South Indian Hindus, Bengalis, Gujaratis, Parsees, Chinese, Arabs and representatives of all the diverse ethnic groups of the Malay Archipelago.[63] Contemporary records reveal that in 1500 Melaka's population was approaching 100,000, and the Sultanate possessed a merchant fleet of one hundred junks, thus, according to Anthony Reid, achieving a more than comparable status with the great Mediterranean port of Venice.[64] At the height of its powers, the Melaka Sultanate exercised suzerainty over the entire Peninsula, extending as far north as Pattani and incorporating parts of Eastern Sumatra.[65]

ISLAM

Arab Muslim traders established their presence in Southeast Asia between the eighth and ninth centuries. The newcomers often worked in partnership with Indian and Chinese and Southeast Asian traders and provided a crucial link between Asian producers and European markets.[66] In the ninth century, Baghdad, capital of the powerful Islamic Abbasid Dynasty, became the greatest commercial centre of the Middle East. Throughout this period, Arab merchants established trading enclaves in a number of Asian commercial centres.[67] With the advent of the Crusades and the later severe impact of the Mongol conquests and the consequent decline and ultimate collapse of the Abbasid Dynasty, Middle Eastern trade became concentrated in the hands of the Fatimid Dynasty of Egypt. The subsequent relocation of trading activities from the Persian Gulf to the Red Sea increased the centrality of the Malabar Coast to intra-Asian trading routes.[68] Arab traders, mainly from Hadramaut in Yemen, established an

enduring presence in the Indian Ocean. Intermarriage with locals, leading
to absorption in the Malay world, created a kinship network which, while
especially concentrated in the Strait of Melaka, stretched from the Hejaz
to Sulawesi.[69] Following the decline of the Srivijaya Empire, Arab traders
exercised virtual control over the spice trade.[70] Aceh embraced Islam in
1204, while Samudera-Pasai became Muslim in 1292 and Terengganu
followed in 1303.[71] However, while Islam became firmly established in
these locations, in other states its advance was checked by strong cultural
resistance from Hindu courts.[72]

While the *Malay Annals* assert that Parameswara converted to Islam,[73]
Ming records suggest that it was the Raja's son Megat Iskandar Shah who
made Melaka a Muslim state.[74] In 1413, Megat Iskandar had married a
princess from the Islamic state of Pasai and had converted to Islam. Raja
Parameswara, the founding ruler of Melaka, died in 1414 and was succeeded
by his son.[75] Following his accession to the throne, Melaka formally adopted
Islam as its state religion and became a Muslim sultanate rather than a
Hindu kingdom.[76]

However, while Megat Iskandar's conversion may have been prompted
by religious convictions, as in other parts of the Archipelago, acceptance
of Islam was at least partially spurred by pragmatic politico-commercial
considerations, in particular recognition of the economic power of Arab
traders and their near monopoly of spice routes.[77] But, while Arab traders
not only dominated the complex network which underpinned the spice
trade, they also offered access to superior technology, including advanced
maritime proficiency and weaponry far superior to that available within
the contemporary Malay world.[78]

The Melaka Sultanate became a focal point for the dissemination
of Islamic thought and scholarship throughout the Archipelago. The
Sultanate became a noted centre of theological speculation, learned debate
and mysticism, especially under the patronage of Sultans Mansur Syah
(1456–1477) and Mahmud Syah (1488–1511).[79] During the post-Mongol
period, Islam made rapid progress throughout the Malay Archipelago.[80]
Apart from isolated enclaves, Islam was to become the common heritage
of the Malay world. The religion encouraged commercial and intellectual
pursuits and was well suited to the needs of the maritime traders of the
Archipelago. Malay, used as a lingua franca, and Jawi Malay, written
in Arabic script, became the media of intellectual creativity in religion,
philosophy, history and literature.[81]

The school of Islam promulgated in Melaka was that of Shafi'i, which followed the philosophical path enunciated by Muhammad ash-Shafi'i (died 820) who had taught in Baghdad and Cairo.[82] Shafi'i had argued that the *Sunna*, the collection of readings which claim to recount Muhammad's words and deeds, as well as those of the Prophet's earliest followers known as the Companions, comprised the wellspring of *fiqh* or Islamic jurisprudence.[83] At the heart of Shafi'i's teachings is the philosophical quest of plumbing the essentialist "premises" (*illa*) of the Qur'an, in the process eschewing literalist and formulaic interpretations, the application of which might not necessarily obtain within localized cultures. While maintaining the sanctity and inviolability of core Islamic values and principles, the Shafi'i school emphasized the need for community consensus in interpretation and application of *fiqh*.[84]

But the region was also greatly influenced by the mystical form of Islam known as Sufism, which was introduced by initiates of the Sufi order.[85] At the basis of Sufism is the *tariqah* (*tarakat* in Malay), the "long and arduous path of spiritual self-reflection ... the mystical journey that leads the Sufi away from external reality of religion and toward the divine reality — the *only* reality — of God".[86] The Sufist thus necessarily resists the imposition of centralized forms of religion in favour of, under the direction of an appropriately qualified preceptor, a measured and disciplined individual path.[87]

Megat Iskandar Shah's transformation of Melaka into an Islamic state set a pattern for sultanate rule which was to become a model for statecraft throughout the Peninsula. However, while Islam was to establish itself as the major regional religion, it remained grafted upon an indigenous culture which for over a millennium had been permeated by Indic concepts of religion, statecraft and social organization.[88] The *Sejarah Melayu* clearly demonstrates the continued tolerated coexistence and acceptance of these seemingly disparate strands of Malay culture.[89] Indeed, Islam was rapidly and seamlessly synthesized with the ruling ideologies which had long prevailed in the Malay world. Nearly all indigenous chronicles took considerable trouble to highlight the continuity (and hence legitimacy) obtaining between the new Islamic polities and the earlier dynasties. Although rajas became sultans, in effect the pre-existing Hindu/Buddhist rituals and precepts remained largely unchallenged. Instead of being blessed by Indra, King of the Gods, sultans were regarded as caliphs, representatives of Allah on Earth.[90] Most of the Malay states retained pre-Islamic traditions surrounding courtly ritual and the other paraphernalia associated with aristocratic life, as well as the *daulat* (aura of sovereignty) which constituted the ruler's major claim to the throne. Hindu practices lingered on in the use of Sanskrit words for titles of rank and formal codes of address. The social hierarchy, based upon vertical bonding, which lay at the core of Southeast Asian polities, the definition of self, which rested upon the individual's social distance from the sultan, remained largely unaffected by the adoption of Islam.[91]

At the popular level, Islam became intertwined with long-established and deeply embedded Indic and animist beliefs, traditions and social relations which endured as a substratum of Malay *adat* (custom).[92] Thus, to select some random examples, Indic influences could be observed in numerous rituals and observances, including Malay weddings[93] and the practice of *silat* (a Malay form of self-defence), while kris belts often contained motifs depicting Garuda (the mythical avian mount of Vishnu). Both animist and Indic influences were found in the practices of local healers (*bomohs* and *pawangs*).[94]

Melaka was to build upon the ethnic forms — language, institutions, and cultural norms — established throughout the period of Srivijaya dominance, and which were embraced by communities within Sumatra as well as parts of Java and other diverse regions within the Malay Archipelago.[95] On the eve of the intrusion of European colonial powers, the Melaka Sultanate was a confident, outward looking and vibrant polity, a state which rejoiced in the "exuberant diversity"[96] which typified the Southeast Asia of that era. This easy cosmopolitanism had been informed by a plethora of cultural influences and religious forms which over the centuries had become deeply entrenched within Sumatra and the Malay Peninsula and which had profoundly shaped the outlook of the local populations.

CONCLUSIONS

Over many centuries, the premodern Malay Archipelago, and in particular the regions adjacent to the Melaka Strait, forged dynamic trading and cultural relationships with various Indian polities and China. Indic traders and scholars introduced concepts of statecraft and political organization as well as religious and cultural forms, all of which deeply permeated indigenous culture. The founder of the Melaka kingdom, Parameswara, was a Hindu prince who originated from Pelambang and who sought and obtained tributary status from Ming China. The protection provided by China, especially the presence of the armada of Admiral Zheng He, enabled Melaka to resist Siamese pressure and to develop as a formidable regional power. Parameswara's son, Megat Iskandar, converted to Islam and, following his accession to the throne, made Melaka a Muslim sultanate. The school of Islam adopted by Melaka was that of Shafi'i, which emphasized community consensus in interpreting Islam and thus permitted considerable latitude in observing *adat* inherited from the pre-Islamic Archipelago. Islam in Southeast Asia was also deeply tinctured with Sufism which emphasized personal mysticism and direct experience of the Divine and often blended with pre-existing religious forms. The Melaka Sultanate derived legitimacy from its immediate predecessor, the great kingdom of Srivijaya, and retained many of the Indic influences and modes of social and political organization which had informed this polity. The Melaka Sultanate, in common with earlier Melayu entities, was a cosmopolitan and confident state that demonstrated a readiness as well as an actual capacity to accommodate a diversity of peoples.

Notes

1. Leonard Andaya, *Leaves of the Same Tree: Trade and Ethnicity in the Straits of Melaka* (Honolulu: University of Hawai'i Press, 2008), p. 2; Carl A. Trocki, *Prince of Pirates: The Temenggongs and the Development of Johor and Singapore 1784–1855*, 2nd ed. (Singapore: NUS Press, 2007), p. 16.
2. Johannes Widido, "A Celebration of Diversity: Zheng He and the Origin of the Pre-Colonial Coastal Urban Pattern in Southeast Asia", in *Admiral Zheng He and Southeast Asia*, edited by Leo Suryadinata (Singapore: Institute of Southeast Asian Studies, 2005), p. 94; G. Coedes (trans. Susan Brown Cowling), *The Indianized States of Southeast Asia*, 3rd ed. (Canberra: Australian National University Press, 1975), p. 3.
3. Coedes, *Indianized States*, p. 3.
4. Andaya, *Leaves of the Same Tree*, p. 24.
5. Burton Stein, *A History of India* (London: Blackwell, 1998), pp. 6–7, 78.
6. Coedes, *Indianized States*, p. 20; Tan Ta Sen, *Cheng Ho and Islam in Southeast Asia* (Singapore: Institute of Southeast Asian Studies, 2009), p. 132.
7. Tan, *Cheng Ho and Islam*, p. 134; Samuel S. Dhoraisingam, *Peranakan Indians of Singapore and Melaka: Indian Babas and Nonyas — Chitty Melaka* (Singapore: Institute of Southeast Asian Studies, 2006), p. 2; V. Nadarajan, *Bujang Valley: The Wonder that was Ancient Kedah* (Sungai Petani: Dato V. Nadarajan, 2011), p. 17.
8. Arun Mahizhnan, "Indian Interactions in East Asia", in *Rising Indian and Indian*

Communities in East Asia, edited by K. Kesavapany, A. Mani and P. Ramasamy (Singapore: Institute of Southeast Asian Studies, 2008), p. 158.

9. M.C. Ricklefs et al., *A New History of Southeast Asia* (London: Palgrave Macmillan, 2010), p. 20.
10. Andaya, *Leaves of the Same Tree*, p. 27.
11. Coedes, *Indianized States*, p. 24.
12. Ibid., p. 36; Dhoraisingam, *Peranakan Indians*, p. 2; Nicholas Tarling, *Southeast Asia: Past and Present* (Melbourne: Cheshire, 1966), p. 11.
13. Coedes, *Indianized States*, p. 36; Balaji Sadasivan, *The Dancing Girl: A History of Early India* (Singapore: Institute of Southeast Asian Studies, 2011), p. 129.
14. Andaya, *Leaves of the Same Tree*, p. 27.
15. Tarling, *Southeast Asia*, p. 25.
16. Tan, *Cheng Ho and Islam*, pp. 134–35.
17. Coedes, *Indianized States*, p. 24.
18. Tan, *Cheng Ho and Islam*, p. 140.
19. Pradeep Kapur has noted that the continuing influences of Sanskrit and Pali are readily discerned in all the major languages of Southeast Asia, and the names of several cities and at least one country (Singapore) are derived from Sanskrit (Pradeep K. Kapur, "Indian's Engagement with Asia", in *Rising India and Indian Communities in East Asia*, edited by K. Kesavapany, A. Mani and P. Ramasamy (Singapore: Institute of Southeast Asian Studies, 2008), p. 90.
20. Coedes, *Indianized States*, p. 33; Tarling, *Southeast Asia*, p. 25.
21. Gordon P. Means, *Political Islam in Southeast Asia* (Boulder, CO: Rienner, 2009), pp. 20–21; Coedes, *Indianized States*, p. 33.
22. Coedes, *Indianized States*, p. 34.
23. Ricklefs et al., *A New History*, pp. 117–18.
24. Ibid.
25. O.W. Wolters, *The Fall of Srivijaya in Malay History* (London: Lund Humphries, 1970), p. 2; Hermann Kulke, "The Naval Expeditions of the Cholas in the Context of Asian History", in *Nagapattinam to Suvarnadwipa: Reflections on the Chola Naval Expeditions to Southeast Asia*, edited by Hermann Kulke, K. Kesavapany and Vijya Sakhuja (Singapore: Institute of Southeast Asian Studies, 2009), p. 5.
26. Coedes, *Indianized States*, p. 5.
27. Tan Ta Sen, "Did Zheng He Set out to Colonize Southeast Asia?", in *Admiral Zheng He and Southeast Asia*, edited by Leo Suryadinata (Singapore: International Zheng He Society/ Institute of Southeast Asian Studies, 2005), p. 65.
28. Coedes, *Indianized States*, p. 84.
29. Kulke, "The Naval Expeditions of the Cholas", pp. 5–6.
30. Andaya, *Leaves of the Same Tree*, p. 61.
31. Kulke, "The Naval Expeditions of the Cholas", pp. 5–6.

32. Hema Devare, "Cultural Implications of the Chola Maritime Fabric Trade with Southeast Asia", in *Nagapattinam to Suvarnadwipa: Reflections on the Chola Expeditions to Southeast Asia*, edited by Hermann Kulke, J. Kesavapany and Vijay Sakhuja (Singapore: Institute of Southeast Asian Studies, 2009), p. 181.

33. R. Champakalakshmi, *Trade, Ideology and Urbanization: South India 300 BC to AD 1300* (New Delhi: Oxford University Press, 1996), p. 51.

34. Kulke, "The Naval Expeditions of the Cholas", p. 9.

35. Tan, *Did Zheng He Set Out to Colonize Southeast Asia*, p. 74; Devare, *Cultural Implications*, p. 181.

36. Kulke, "The Naval Expeditions of the Cholas", p. 9.

37. Risha Lee, "Rethinking Community: The Indic Carvings of Quanzhou", in *Nagapattinam to Suvarnadwipa: Reflections on the Chola Naval Expeditions to Southeast Asia*, edited by Hermann Kulke, K. Kesavapany and Vijay Sakhuja (Singapore: Institute of Southeast Asian Studies, 2009), p. 244; Kulke, *The Naval Expeditions of the Cholas*, p. 8; Tansen Sen, "The Military Campaigns of Rajendra Chola and the Chola-Srivijaya-China Triangle", in *Nagapattinam to Suvarnadwipa: Reflections on the Chola Expeditions to Southeast Asia*, edited by Hermann Kulke, K. Kesavapany and Vijay Sukhuja (Singapore: Institute of Southeast Asian Studies, 2009), p. 69.

38. Vijay Sakhuja and Sangeeta Sakhuja, "Rajendra Chola I's Naval Expedition to Southeast Asia: A Nautical Perspective", in *Nagapattinam to Suvarnadwipa: Reflections on the Chola Naval Expeditions to Southeast Asia*, edited by Hermann Kulke, K. Kesavapany, and Vijay Sakhuja (Singapore: Institute of Southeast Asian Studies, 2009), p. 79.

39. Sen, "Military Campaigns of Rajendra Chola", p. 70.

40. Wolters, *The Fall of Srivijaya*, p. 142.

41. Sakhuja and Sakhuja, "Rajendra Chola I's Naval Expedition", p. 80.

42. Champakalakshmi, *Trade, Ideology and Urbanization*, p. 222.

43. Coedes, *Indianized States*, pp. 200–201.

44. Tan, *Cheng Ho and Islam*, p. 175.

45. Ibid., pp. 175–76.

46. Widido, "A Celebration of Diversity", p. 114; Coedes, *Indianized States*, p. 245.

47. Widido, "A Celebration of Diversity", p. 114.

48. Tan, *Cheng Ho and Islam*, p. 176.

49. Wang Gungwu, "The Opening of Relations between China and Malacca 1403–05", in *Admiral Zheng He and Southeast Asia*, edited by Leo Suryadinata (Singapore: International Zheng He Society/Institute of Southeast Asian Studies, 2005), p. 2.

50. Widido, "A Celebration of Diversity", pp. 94–95; Tan Ta Sen, *Did Zheng He Set Out*, p. 44.

51. Widido, "A Celebration of Diversity", pp. 96–97.

52. Ricklefs et al., *A New History*, p. 119.

53. Tan, *Cheng Ho and Islam*, pp. 160–61.
54. Wang, "The Opening of Relations", p. 2.
55. Ibid. pp. 12–15; Tan Ta Sen, *Zheng He*, pp. 51–53.
56. Widido, "A Celebration of Diversity", p. 115.
57. Wang, "The Opening of Relations", p. 2.
58. Ibid., p. 18; Tan Ta Sen, *Cheng Ho and Islam*, p. 155.
59. Tan, *Cheng Ho and Islam*, p. 155.
60. Ibid., pp. 176–77.
61. Ricklefs et al., *A New History*, p. 120; Wang, *The Opening of Relations*, p. 19; Coedes, *Indianized States*, p. 246.
62. Anthony Reid, *Charting the Shape of Early Modern Southeast Asia* (Singapore: Institute of Southeast Asian Studies, 2000), p. 19.
63. Tarling, *Southeast Asia*, p. 32.
64. Reid, *Charting the Shape*, p. 220.
65. Tan, *Cheng Ho and Islam*, p. 180.
66. Means, *Political Islam*, p. 2.
67. Tan, *Cheng Ho and Islam*, pp. 157–58.
68. Kulke, "The Naval Expedition of the Cholas", p. 2.
69. Ho Engseng, "Before Parochialism: Diasporic Arabs Cast in Creole Waters", in *Arabs, Politics, Trade and Islam in Southeast Asia*, edited by Huub De Jonge and Nico Kaptein (Leiden: KLTV Press, 2003), pp. 15–16.
70. Coedes, *Indianized States*, p. 244.
71. Tan, *Cheng Ho and Islam*, p. 152.
72. Ibid., p. 168.
73. Ahmad Fauzi Abdul Hamid, *Islamic Education in Malaysia*, Monograph No. 18 (Singapore: S. Rajaratnam School of International Studies, 2010), p. 13.
74. Tan, *Cheng Ho and Islam*, p. 178.
75. Ibid., pp. 177–79.
76. Widido, "A Celebration of Diversity", p. 114.
77. Tarling, *Southeast Asia*, p. 30; Wolters, *The Fall of Srivijaya*, p. 160.
78. Means, *Political Islam*, p. 21.
79. Ahmad Fauzi, *Islamic Education*, p. 13.
80. Tan Yeok Song, "Chinese Element in the Islamization of Southeast Asia: A Study of the Story of Najai Gede Pinatah, The Great Lady of Gresik", in *Admiral Zheng He and Southeast Asia*, edited by Leo Suryadinata (Singapore: International Zheng He Society/Institute of Southeast Asian Studies, 2005), p. 70.
81. Reid, *Charting the Shape*, pp. 222–23; Ricklefs et al., *A New History*, p. 83.
82. Means, *Political Islam*, p. 13.
83. Reza Aslan, *No God but God: The Origins, Evolution and Future of Islam* (London: William Heinemann, 2005), pp. 163–65.
84. Means, *Political Islam*, p. 22.

85. Reid, *Charting the Shape*, p. 19.
86. Aslan, *No God but God*, p. 206.
87. Ibid.; Reid, *Charting the Shape*, pp. 22–23.
88. Richard Allen, *Malaysia: Prospect and Retrospect* (London: Oxford University Press, 1968), p. 17. The precariousness of Islam as a state religion was shown by an attempted restoration of Hinduism under Parameswarar Deva Syah (1445–46), who was deposed and killed after a coup that placed his Muslim half-brother Sultan Muzaffar on the throne (Ricklefs et al., *A New History*, p. 111).
89. Andaya, *Leaves of the Same Tree*, p. 137.
90. John Funston, *Malay Politics in Malaysia: A Study of UMNO and PAS* (Kuala Lumpur: Heinemann Educational Books (Asia, 1980), p. 25; Means, *Political Islam*, p. 22.
91. Reid, *Charting the Shape*, pp. 29–30.
92. Judith Nagata, *The Reflowering of Malaysian Islam: Modern Religious Radicals and their Roots* (Vancouver: University of British Columbia Press, 1984), pp. 34–35; Richard Windstedt, *The Malays: A Cultural History* (London: Routledge and Kegan Paul, 1963), pp. 166–68.
93. Anthony Milner, *The Malays* (Chichester: Wiley Blackwell, 2011), pp. 24–25.
94. Nagata, *The Reflowering of Malaysian Islam*, pp. 34–35; Windstedt, *The Malays*, pp. 166–68.
95. Andaya, *Leaves of the Same Tree*, p. 81.
96. Reid, *Charting the Shape*, p. 39.

2

EUROPEAN COLONIALISM
AND THE MALAY PENINSULA

PORTUGUESE COLONIALISM

The power of the Melaka Sultanate, and ultimately that of the entire Malay Archipelago, was to be challenged and subsequently broken by the arrival of European colonial powers. Portugal was the first European power to establish a colony on the Malay Peninsula. The Portuguese, like later Europeans, were aware that the Strait of Melaka was an essential sea route for the conduct of east-west trade, especially that between China, the Malay Archipelago and Europe.[1] They also knew that that the wealthy and flourishing state was the hub of a vast trading network and that, among other things, it was the principal emporium of the spices (nutmeg, cloves and cinnamon) which were in such high demand in Europe. The capture of Melaka would wrest this commerce from Muslim control, in the process undermining the trading economies of Cairo and Mecca. Moreover, it would force Venetian merchants to purchase their spices from Portugal at prices determined by the Portuguese.[2]

In 1509, a Portuguese fleet, consisting of four or five ships, and commanded by Diego Lopes de Sequiera, arrived in Melaka. De Sequiera attempted to strike a trading agreement with the Melaka Court, but met with Malay opposition, largely inspired by Arab and Indian Muslim traders who were aware of the reputation of the Catholic Portuguese as "fanatical" enemies of Islam.[3] A botched Melaka attack failed to destroy the Portuguese expedition, and although several of de Sequiera's men were captured, the main body of his force successfully put to sea.[4]

Having failed to negotiate their way into Melaka, the Portuguese now resorted to military measures. A Portuguese invasion force, consisting of eighteen ships and 1,200 men, including Malabar Muslim auxiliaries, and commanded by Alfonso de Albuquerque, returned to Melaka in 1511.[5] Albuquerque's key objectives were the destruction of the Melaka Sultanate both as a major Malay trading power and as a celebrated centre for the study and diffusion of Islam.[6] Albuquerque faced a Melaka that was rent by internal divisions; between Sultan Mahmud and his son, and between merchants who remained loyal to the Sultan and those who supported the Portuguese. Fighting continued for several months before the Portuguese could finally claim victory.[7]

Ironically the seizure of Melaka, regarded as a major prize by the Portuguese,[8] was to lead to its decline. The newcomers ran Melaka as a "factory-fort" with the intention of imposing a monopoly mercantilist system and eliminating all Muslim competition.[9] The levying of excessive tolls and other imposts, coupled with trading practices weighted in favour of Portuguese merchants, led to Asian traders, especially Muslim traders, who had been the mainstay of Melaka's prosperity, eschewing the port.[10]

The Portuguese willingness to use force, the rigidity of their rule, and the cruelty that accompanied it, created deep suspicions throughout the Malay Archipelago.[11] While Portuguese intermarriage with the local population led to the permanent establishment of Catholicism on the Peninsula, Portuguese pro-Christian policies, and more particularly the activities of Catholic missionaries, hardened Muslim resistance to the colonizers and actually contributed to the further spread of Islam within the Archipelago.[12]

DUTCH COLONIALISM

Trading patterns in Southeast Asia were fundamentally reshaped following the arrival of Dutch and English vessels towards the beginning of the seventeenth century. While the North European traders were initially regarded as just another factor within the overall complexity of Southeast Asian maritime trade, their greater efficiency and determination to establish and maintain monopolies had a major impact upon rival powers.[13] The capacity of the newcomers' shipping exceeded that of the Asian traders of the region, and their vigorous pursuit of pepper and spices resulted in Europe displacing China as the major market for Southeast Asian produce.[14]

The rise of the Dutch as a commercial and trading power was followed by more aggressive penetration into Southeast Asia. Dutch rivalry with the Portuguese led to an initial, albeit unsuccessful, attack on Melaka in 1607. The Dutch East India Company (Vereenigd Oost-Indische Compagnie [VOC]) established a base at Jakarta (renamed Batavia in 1619), and embarked upon a vigorous campaign of expansion within the region.[15] In 1633 the Dutch blockaded Melaka and mounted a siege of the port in 1640. Aided by Johor forces, the Dutch finally forced the Portuguese surrender in 1641.[16]

The Dutch did little to revive the fortunes of Melaka. Trade through the port never approached anything near the levels which had been common during the halcyon years of the Melaka Sultanate. Batavia, rather than Melaka, was chosen as the Dutch administrative centre for the entire Archipelago, and the VOC insisted that the Chinese junk trade be directed through this port.[17] The Dutch also regulated the movement of trade through the Strait of Melaka to their advantage and attempted to eliminate all competition within their sphere of control.[18] However, in one significant respect, Dutch administration differed from the Portuguese. While the Dutch were Christians and supported the establishment and the activities of the Dutch Reformed Church, they practised religious toleration and did not seek to suppress Islam or any other religion within the territories falling under their control.[19]

The thoroughness with which the Dutch monopoly was enforced was to have a dramatic impact upon the political, economic and social structures of the Malay Archipelago. The most obvious outcome was the destruction of the local trading classes. The island trade networks, largely frequented by Middle Eastern, Indian and Malay traders, passed under Dutch control.[20] While the Portuguese had discovered the Southeast Asian sea lanes dominated by Javanese junks, by the 1670s these had virtually disappeared and few Javanese worked as seafarers.[21] Malay involvement in long-distance trading began an abrupt decline.[22] The suppression of local trade also led to the atrophy of the hitherto influential indigenous mercantile classes and the decay of the vital urban centres which had formerly operated as thriving ports.[23] Local industries either disappeared or stagnated, held at or below the technological levels they had attained prior to the arrival of the Dutch. Denied access to trade and commerce, locals were increasingly forced into a reactive agricultural economy in which low capital returns discouraged either incentive or innovation.[24] The very processes of colonial exploitation promoted the formation and enrichment of a collaborative elite, who were also noted for their ostentatious consumption of the array of imported goods and services produced by the colonial metropolis.[25]

BRITISH COLONIALISM

From 1760 until the first decade of the twentieth century, a more acquisitive European imperialism fuelled by great-power rivalry was to result in the colonization of almost the entire Southeast Asian region from Burma to the Indo-Chinese peninsula. The paramount power throughout this period was Britain, which possessed industrial muscle, a formidable navy, and which, among its extensive possessions, had India and its vast resources — both human and material — which it could mobilize to further its interests. Indeed, so prominent was the Indian role in advancing British objectives in Asia that Nicholas Tarling contends that "in a sense the new British empire in Southeast Asia was an Indian empire. Indian wealth supported the country traders, Lascars manned their ships, Indian revenues helped to finance the British administrations".[26] Following the defeat of Napoleonic France in 1815, Britain's dominance in both India and Southeast Asia was largely unchallenged.[27]

Penang

Given the extensive East India Company (EIC) trade between India and China, it was only a matter of time before the British sought a port on the Malay Peninsula which would serve as a maritime base for shipping plying routes between the two subcontinents.

Captain Francis Light, acting on behalf of the EIC, negotiated an agreement with the Sultan of Kedah for the cession of the island of Penang. The Sultan was anxious to conclude a treaty with a recognized power which would strengthen his hold on his insecure throne.[28] Captain Light subsequently anchored at Penang on 15 July 1786 and hoisted the British flag on 11 August 1786.[29] In 1791, an attempted attack by the Sultan to reclaim the island was easily dispersed by Light, and a subsequent treaty was signed between the EIC and the Sultan.[30] In 1800 the EIC negotiated the cession of a narrow strip of mainland Kedah comprising about 300 square miles adjacent to the island of Penang, which was named Province Wellesley after Marquis Wellesley, the Governor-General of India.[31] For this transaction the Sultan was paid 800 pounds.[32] In 1805, somewhat surprisingly, Penang was made a full presidency of the EIC, thus placing it on the same administrative footing as the great subcontinental presidencies — Madras, Bombay and Calcutta — of British India.[33]

Singapore

Singapore was first established as a British settlement in 1819. During the Napoleonic wars, the British seized Dutch possessions in the Malay Archipelago. An EIC functionary, Sir Stamford Raffles, who had been appointed Lieutenant-Governor of Java, initially failed in his attempts to persuade the company to retain Singapore, which he believed would prove an incomparable strategic and commercial asset. However, in 1816, during his tenure as Lieutenant-Governor of Bencoolen, an EIC settlement in West Sumatra, Raffles won approval from the Marquis of Hastings, EIC Governor-General, for the siting of a new settlement at the foot of the Melaka Strait which the Company believed would act as a counter to Dutch influence within the region.[34] In 1819 Raffles negotiated an agreement for the release of the island of Singapore with a Malay chief known as Abdul Rahman, Temenggong Sri Maharaja, a high official from the former Johor Court, then located at Riau on the island of Bentan.[35]

The agreement was viewed by the Temenggong as an opportunity to enter a close and privileged relationship with an important European power. However, the vague provisions of the settlement were interpreted in radically different ways by each of the interested parties. Between 1819 and 7 June 1823, when a new agreement was reached, the right to govern Singapore was claimed by three competing authorities. In addition to the EIC, both the Temenggong and his rival Sultan Hussain continued to regard Singapore as their own state, a mere variation of a typical Malay maritime polity.[36] However, to Raffles, Singapore was an entirely new entity, a trading settlement which was destined to become an integral outpost of the EIC and to form the basis for a dynamic company presence within the Malay Archipelago. The inevitable power struggle ended with a new agreement, whereby the chiefs surrendered their rights to port duties and their shares in revenue farms, as well as relinquishing all authority over Singapore Island.[37] Following Raffles' replacement as Resident by John Crawfurd, a further treaty was negotiated. The treaty, dated 3 August 1824, forced the Temenggong and the Sultan to make a complete cession of Singapore and adjacent islands to the EIC and thus forgo any claim to royal status or exercise of power in Singapore. In exchange the EIC provided the Temenggong with a cash settlement.[38] Singapore quickly eclipsed Riau as a regional port, drawing both local and Chinese trade and becoming a focus of the British Indian opium trade.[39]

Melaka and the Straits Settlements

Melaka was first taken by British forces in 1795 during the wars with revolutionary France, but was restored to Dutch authority in 1818, three years after the conclusion of the Napoleonic Wars. Under the terms of the Anglo–Dutch Treaty of London on 17 March 1824, the Dutch formally recognized British interests in the Malay Peninsula. This included the permanent cession of Melaka to the EIC. In return the British rescinded all interest in the islands south of Singapore, agreed not to enter treaties with indigenous rulers in Sumatra, and to withdraw from their settlement on Bencoolen.[40] The emergence of Penang and Singapore had a dramatic impact upon Melaka's standing as a trading centre, and the port began a precipitous decline.[41]

In 1826 Melaka and Singapore became dependencies of the Presidency of Penang. In 1829 the EIC reduced Penang to the status of a Residency. From 1832 the Malayan territories were collectively described as the "Straits Settlements" and were ruled from India.[42] In 1858, following the convulsions of the Great Rebellion (Indian Mutiny), the Settlements were removed from EIC rule and placed under the control of the India Office. Agitation among the Straits Settlements business community finally led to a transfer of governance from the India Office to the Colonial Office. This took effect on 1 April 1867, and Sir Harry St. George Ord was appointed as the first Governor.[43]

The Straits Settlements were unique economic entities; free ports which levied no customs duties. While this practice had no precedent in Asia, it also ran counter to conventional Western doctrine.[44] During this period,

Singapore and Penang developed as flourishing entrepôts, as important bases for European business concerns, as well as magnets for Chinese immigrants who became revenue farmers, merchants, entrepreneurs, and artisans.[45] The prosperity of Penang also drew large numbers of indigenous migrants, including Malays from other parts of the Peninsula as well as settlers from Sumatra.[46] Other immigrants included Chulias (Indian Muslims), locally based merchants (mainly from neighbouring Kedah), and Bugis traders from the Moluccas.[47]

Peninsular Malaya

In 1826 the British signed a treaty with Siam which implicitly acknowledged the three northern Malay states — Kedah (which incorporated the territory which was to later become the state of Perlis), Kelantan and Terengganu — as falling within the Siamese sphere of influence. The Peninsula to the south of these states was recognized by both parties as a British sphere of influence.[48] This treaty thus provided the British with a free hand to move into these territories if and when it considered this course of action either necessary or desirable.

Formal British intervention was preceded by chronic instability within the Malay states, which included piracy, lawlessness and dynastic clashes, especially disputes over succession. From the 1840s onwards, chiefs in the Malay states began to exploit tin resources. The reduction of protection for tin mines in Cornwall, and the general inability of British mines to meet increasing demand, provided considerable opportunities for local enterprises. Tin mines operated in a number of localities within the Malay states, including the Larut and Kinta districts of Perak, as well as in districts adjacent to the new settlement of Kuala Lumpur in Selangor, and Seremban in Sungei Ujong (a Minangkabau polity which was later to become a constituent unit of the state of Negeri Sembilan).[49] Malay chiefs relied heavily on the use of Chinese immigrant labour in the mining and transport of tin, and by the 1850s there were over 40,000 Chinese in Perak alone.[50] But tin mining activities produced imbalances of power among Malay chiefs. The internecine disputes and struggles, together with major clashes between the two secret societies into which the Chinese miners were organized, resulted in the so-called Larut Wars, which were followed by shifting alliances and repeated hostilities between combined Malay and Chinese factions in other parts of Perak.[51] By the 1870s law and order within Perak had all but collapsed, the state trembled on the edge of civil war, and the tin trade was all but paralysed.[52] Similar wars broke out in Selangor and by 1873 the town of Kuala Lumpur had been devastated.[53]

The incessant round of disturbances in Selangor and Perak, which raged largely unabated between 1861 and 1873, created serious disruptions in the supply of tin and frequently brought the industry to a standstill. As early as 1867, British and Chinese merchants based in the Straits Settlements were clamouring for Colonial Office intervention.[54] By 1873, despite the strictures of Lord Kimberly, the Liberal Colonial Secretary, the Straits Settlements had become inextricably entangled in the political affairs of the Malay states.[55] On 4 November 1873 Major-General Sir Andrew Clarke, the new Governor-General, arrived in Singapore under official instructions to put an end to the disorder.[56]

Intervention in the Malay states was to be justified by the ideology of "good government";[57] the need to "protect and advance the sovereign Malay rulers and their peoples".[58] This ideology necessarily portrayed the Malay states in wholly negative terms: as despotic, antiquated, hopelessly disorganized, and incapable of either managing an economy or guarding the welfare of their own inhabitants.[59] It was the "inferiority" of the Malay "race" and their inability to cope with the processes of modernization, in particular the incapacity of the chiefs to provide effective government, that formed the basis on which the policy towards the Malay states was ostensibly moulded. The need to halt "outrage and bloodshed" meant that extending British control was nothing less than a "matter of imperial duty and moral obligation".[60] Moreover, good government, under close British supervision, would maximize exploitation of natural resources (a task in which the Malay chiefs were alleged to have conspicuously failed), thus promoting economic development within the Malay states. Overall, then, the assumption of British control was presented as a necessary intervention; purportedly the triumph of an advanced or higher form of civilization over an inferior one.[61]

Although the continued disorder and the concomitant disruption of British trade in tin, a commodity vital to British industrial expansion, were the immediate pretexts for British intervention,[62] there were underlying and more compelling considerations. These included British fear of European colonization of the Malay Peninsula, most particularly that of Germany, France or the Netherlands;[63] growing awareness of the strategic significance of Singapore, especially in the wake of the opening of the Suez Canal (1869) and the development of telegraphic links between London and Singapore (1871);[64] changing perceptions of the potential of

Malayan trade;[65] and mounting pressure from within the Straits Settlements trading communities for firm British control and the establishment of orderly conditions within the Malay states as a necessary precondition for investment and development of those states.[66]

The Perak succession disputes of 1873, and the widespread and often savage encounters between the mixed Malay-Chinese followers of rival claimants, precipitated British intervention.[67] In 1874, Sir Andrew Clarke invited Malay chiefs to meet him at Pangkor, an island lying off the coast of the Perak estuary. Under the terms of the resultant Pangkor Engagement (1874), Sultan Abdullah agreed to accept the appointment of a British Resident to the court of Perak. The Resident would be charged with "advising" the Sultan on all matters other than those involving Malay religion (i.e., Islam) and custom (*adat*).[68]

After the first British Resident to Perak, James Birch, an officious, high-handed and insensitive man,[69] was murdered on 1 November 1875, a mixed force of British and Indian troops were dispatched to restore order. British retribution against Malay dissidents clearly signalled that although the term "Advisor" had implied guidance, it actually stood for British overlordship.[70] Following the Perak war, the "advised" rulers offered little opposition to the increasing demands made by residents.[71]

The residency system imposed in Perak was extended to Selangor and Sungei Ujong (a constituent state of Negeri Sembilan) in 1874, to Pahang in 1888, and to the whole of Negeri Sembilan in 1889.[72] These four states — Perak, Selangor, Pahang and Negeri Sembilan — were grouped together as the Federated Malay States (FMS) in November 1896, with the capital in Kuala Lumpur (in Selangor), and under the direction of a Resident-General. He, in turn, was responsible to a High Commissioner who also occupied the position of Governor of the Straits Settlements.[73]

In 1909 the British signed an agreement with Siam by which, in return for a loan to construct a railway line and the loss of some extra-territorial rights, the Protectorates of Perlis, Kedah, Terengganu, and Kelantan were transferred to British administration.[74] In 1910 the British concluded agreements with the respective sultanates.[75] Residents were successively appointed — to Kelantan (1910), Terengganu (1919), Kedah (1923) and Perlis (1930) — and introduced a succession of reforms which gradually but inexorably tightened British direction over the internal affairs of all four states.[76]

Johor

The modern state of Johor was founded by Temenggong Daing Ibrahim who, following his accession to the throne in 1825, was to become a close ally of Britain. In 1841 he was recognized as Temenggong of Johor, and British acknowledgement of his full claim to the state was extended in 1855.[77] Under his leadership Johor followed a different trajectory to that of other Peninsular Malay states of that period.

The Temenggong's Johor represented a new model for Malay states. While the administration was vested in a "tightly knit" group of Malay court officials headed by an autocratic Sultan,[78] the prosperity of the state was generated by Chinese agricultural *taukehs*. Over time the rising Chinese mercantile class displaced the dwindling body of indigenous traders.[79] But the sultanate itself represented a departure from the monarchies which had ruled the traditional Malay polities. The former bonds which had sustained the sultans — intricate patterns of kinship, carefully wrought lines of personal loyalty, networks of economic ties — were replaced with a new system of inflexible written contracts transplanted from British administrative practice and which overrode the traditional structures. This form of contractual agreement, of formally constituted authority, was to be replicated under the residency system within every Malay state.[80] The nexus forged in Johor — that of Malay political authority coupled with Chinese enterprise and wealth — was to carry over into other Malay states and ultimately into independent Malaya.[81]

Throughout this period the British retained close relations with Johor. In 1885, as the sole remaining independent Malay state, Johor, agreed in principle to accept a British Advisor. However, twenty-nine years was to elapse until the appointment was made. In April 1895 Sultan Abu Bakar turned Johor into a constitutional monarchy.[82] On 12 May 1914, Sultan Ibrahim finally signed an agreement which preceded the appointment of a General Advisor, making it the last Malay state to accept British overlordship.[83]

The five Malay states — the four ex-Siamese protectorates, together with Johor — were known as the Unfederated Malay States (UFMS).[84] The unwieldy division of British colonial control in Malaya into three politico-administrative systems, namely the direct rule over the Straits Settlements and indirect rule under the nominal aegis of the Sultans in the FMS and UFMS — was to remain in place, interrupted only by the years of Japanese Occupation and the hiatus of the post-war Malayan Union, until the Federation of Malaya Agreement of 1948. However, it should be noted that under the treaties concluded between the British and the Sultans, each state remained a legally sovereign and independent kingdom, even if in practice these qualities were largely fictitious.[85] This vital fact, often forgotten under the reality of British rule, was to resurface in unexpected ways after World War II.

THE BRITISH COLONIAL ECONOMY: AN OVERVIEW

British control of the Straits Settlements had naturally focused upon entrepôt trade, but the EIC also encouraged the development of commercial agriculture as an additional source of revenue.[86] Sugar estates were established in Penang, Province Wellesley and Melaka. Initially, Chinese capitalists were also involved in sugar production, but by 1838 the industry was largely controlled by European business houses and their agents.[87] Other crops included gambier and pepper (both dominated by Chinese interests, particularly in Singapore) and spices, especially nutmeg.[88]

The extension of British control over the Malay Peninsula was followed by the rapid development of a full colonial economy based on large-scale plantation agriculture and extraction industries, the latter predominantly involving tin mining. The development and management of the Malayan economy was principally driven by British and European individuals and firms and, to a lesser extent, by an emerging and flourishing Chinese business class. The British administration embarked upon major infrastructure projects designed to ensure the easy exploitation of resources and to promote the development of commerce and trade. These included public works such as ports, roads, railways, coastal shipping, municipal works, and communications.[89] As in India, the government replaced local customary land laws with British systems of tenure.[90]

The colonial administrations took measures to ensure that British and, to a lesser extent, European capital enjoyed precedence in attaining access to all profitable sectors of the emerging Malayan economy. Thus, for example, contracts for the construction of railways, which began in 1884, were routinely handed to British firms. The major beneficiaries were British steel and iron companies, British financiers who raised the necessary loans to underwrite the project, and British agricultural and mining interests which were provided with cheap transport. By 1931, 1,700 kilometres of track had been laid at a total cost of $233 million.[91]

Similarly, with the advent of the rubber boom, the colonial regime offered major land concessions to European enterprises, in the process confiscating extensive tracts of abandoned land and placing restrictions on Chinese tapioca and gambier plantations. Large parcels of agricultural land were alienated for European concerns and offered on a ninety-year lease, of which the first twenty-five years were rent free. In allocating land, the colonial administration also gave European businesses precedence in securing properties which offered road frontage.[92]

Agriculture

While sugar remained an important estate crop, during the 1880s it was rapidly overtaken by coffee. In the 1870s and 1880s, the European plantation coffee industry in Ceylon was all but annihilated by the fungus *Hemileia vastarix*.[93] As a consequence, many planters moved their operations to Malaya, and from the 1880s onwards extensive coffee plantations were established in Perak, Selangor and Negeri Sembilan.[94] However, following a boom in the 1890s, coffee entered a period of rapid decline.[95]

Rubber was to replace coffee as the most important agricultural commodity in Malaya. *Hevea brasiliensis* was transplanted from its Amazonian homeland to Malaya via the Kew Gardens, London, in 1877, when experimental plantings were established in Singapore and Kuala Kangsar.[96] But although these plantings were successful, rubber did not make much of an impact in Malaya until the failure of the lucrative coffee plantations in the 1890s provided the stimulus for a large-scale conversion to rubber.[97] This process accelerated during the early years of the twentieth century with the rapid growth of the automobile industry and increasing applications of rubber in the manufacture of clothing, footwear, electrical and medical equipment, and household goods and furniture. New methods of tapping greatly improved productivity and reduced overheads, thus enhancing returns to investors.[98]

The growth and development of the rubber industry was a phenomenal success. Rubber soon eclipsed all other commodities as Malaya's major export. By 1922, 1.4 million acres were dedicated to rubber cultivation. In 1930 this had increased to 1.9 million acres, and by 1941, at the outbreak of the Pacific War, it had expanded to 3.4 million acres. Of this figure, 2.1 million acres was held by 2,500 estates employing a labour force of about 325,000. Although Europeans owned only 1,000 of these estates, these accounted for 75 per cent of estate acreage and employed approximately

260,000 people.[99] Rubber became the single most remunerative colonial export within the British Empire. John Drabble estimates that "Between 1935 and 1937, it [rubber] provided one-fifth to one-quarter of total domestic exports from the colonies, and between 1937 and 1941 the aggregate value of rubber exports (US$590 million) almost equalled that of British domestic industry exports to the United States (US$620 million)."[100]

While rubber was the key to Malayan prosperity, the British administration made efforts, with varying rates of success, to promote diversification into other agricultural products, including palm oil, tea, and pineapple.[101] In 1941 the overall structure of the Malayan colonial agricultural economy was as follows:

Rubber:	3,422,649 acres
Coconut:	600,000 acres
Palm oil:	75,000 acres
Coffee:	20,000 acres
Tea:	7,000 acres.[102]

Tin Mining

Initially tin mining was largely controlled by Chinese interests. Chinese tin miners found it increasingly difficult to compete with the highly mechanized and capital-intensive European enterprises.[103] European and British pre-eminence swelled as easily accessed tin deposits were worked out. Chinese firms were generally unable to raise the large amounts of capital required to fund dredge mining. But, in addition, the colonial administration adopted a policy of reserving for European firms the considerable tracts of low-yielding land that were regarded as suitable for this enterprise.[104] While in 1900 Chinese-run mines had accounted for ninety per cent of the FMS's output, by 1929 this had declined to twenty-nine per cent.[105] Until the 1960s, tin mining remained largely under the control of European firms.[106]

Labour

With the "Forward Movement" into the Malay states, the colonial regime was confronted with the dual problem of a superabundance of exploitable land coupled with a chronic shortage of available labour. The establishment of a thriving colonial economy was based on a reliable supply of cheap and easily managed labour.[107] The British encouraged immigration from other parts of the Malay Archipelago, but made every attempt to ensure that the newcomers were excluded from the modern sectors of the colonial economy and restricted to the production of food.[108] Labour was recruited to work in the plantations, mines, and public utilities which comprised the more dynamic sectors of the economy. Labour was largely of immigrant origin, consisting mainly of Chinese and Indian coolie labour with a Javanese admixture. As far as possible the British regulated the flow of migrants to meet the demands of the colonial economy. During the nineteenth century most of this labour was channelled through the Straits Settlements which became a "labour emporium" supplying workers not only to Malaya but also to neighbouring countries.[109]

The British colonial economy in Malay was extraordinarily successful, though there were serious downturns in the rubber industry in the early 1920s (created by slackening of demand following the conclusion of World War I), and again throughout the Great Depression of 1929–33.[110] On the eve of the Japanese invasion of 1941–42, Malaya was one of the richest colonies in the British Empire. Trade generated by Malaya exceeded that of Britain's combined African possessions and was over half that of British India.[111] Malaya was the UK's most remunerative source of U.S. dollars, and in 1938 accounted for half the world's tin and a "great proportion" of the world's rubber.[112]

CONCLUSIONS

European colonialism disrupted and fundamentally reshaped the political processes and economic dynamics which had hitherto obtained throughout the Malay Archipelago. The imposition of foreign rule, the enforcement of trade monopolies, and the suppression of long-established networks of commerce, and in the case of the Portuguese, the introduction of religious fanaticism, collectively re-ordered societal and economic structures. Domestic economies were now subject to the demands of colonialism, and in particular the imperatives of European markets, and foreign merchants and their agents largely displaced indigenous traders. Colonial restrictions on indigenous mercantile activity preceded a decline in local commerce, which was henceforth largely directed into agriculture.

British involvement on the Malay Peninsula was initially spurred by strategic considerations, but was rapidly overtaken by commercial and imperial imperatives. The British "Forward Movement" into the Malay states initially justified itself by the ideology of "good government", in particular by the supposed inability of local rulers to provide stable governance. In reality, British actions were designed not only to forestall the intervention of other European colonial powers, but also to secure supplies of tin which were required for the metropolitan economy. The British administration appointed advisors to the Malay courts but maintained a façade of indigenous control, leaving ruling structures *in situ* and assigning the management of Islam and *adat* to sultans. In Johor the ruling elite forged a symbiotic alliance with Chinese merchants which linked Malay political control with Chinese enterprise and wealth, thus foreshadowing future patterns of interethnic cooperation.

The British colonial economy, based in mining and tropical agriculture, was supported by an ambitious programme of infrastructural development. The labour required to work in the colonial economy was largely imported from China and India; the indigenous Malays together with the immigrants from the adjacent Archipelago were excluded from the more dynamic sectors of the colonial economy and were, as far as possible, confined to the production of food. Indirect rule created the illusion of an Anglo–Malay partnership and fostered the myth that the British were in Malaya to assist the sultans in the administration of their states.

Notes

1. Nordin Hussin, *Trade and Society in the Straits of Melaka: Dutch Melaka and English Penang, 1780–1830* (Singapore: NUS Press, 2007), p. 13.
2. Balaji Sadasivan, *The Dancing Girl: A History of Early India* (Singapore: Institute of Southeast Asian Studies, 2009), p. 203.
3. Anthony Reid, *Charting the Shape of Early Modern Southeast Asia* (Singapore: Institute of Southeast Asian Studies, 2000), pp. 166–67.
4. J. Kennedy, *A History of Malaya* (London: Macmillan, 1970), pp. 22–23; S. Dhoraisingam, *Peranakan Indians of Singapore and Melaka: Indian Babas and Nonyas — Chitty Melaka* (Singapore: Institute of Southeast Asian Studies, 2006), p. 8.
5. Kennedy, *A History of Malaya*, pp. 25–26; Ricklefs et al., *A New History of Southeast Asia* (London: Palgrave Macmillan, 2010), p. 112.
6. Dhoraisingam, *Peranakan Indians*, pp. 8–9.
7. Ricklefs et al., *A New History*, p. 128.
8. Kennedy, *A History of Malaya*, p. 27.
9. Gordon P. Means, *Political Islam in Southeast Asia* (Boulder, CO: Rienner, 2009), p. 32.

10. Kennedy, *A History of Malaya*, p. 30; Tan Ta Sen, *Cheng Ho and Islam in Southeast Asia* (Singapore: Institute of Southeast Asian Studies, 2009), p. 209.
11. Means, *Political Islam*, p. 32.
12. Nicholas Tarling, *Southeast Asia: Past and Present* (Melbourne: Cheshire, 1966), p. 43.
13. Reid, *Charting the Shape*, p. 56.
14. Ibid., p. 92.
15. Kennedy, *A History of Malaya*, p. 39.
16. Means, *Political Islam*, p. 39; Tarling, *Southeast Asia*, p. 50.
17. Nordin, *Trade and Society*, p. 11.
18. Ibid., p. 25.
19. Ibid., p. 217.
20. Wazir Jahan Karim, "The Affairs of the Bogeyman: Migration and Class across Borders", in *Multiethnic Malaysia: Past Present and Future*, edited by Lim Teck Ghee, Alberto Gomes, and Azly Rahman (Petaling Jaya: Strategic Information and Research Development Centre, 2009), p. 410.
21. Reid, *Charting the Shape*, p. 56.
22. Nordin, *Trade and Society*, p. 340.
23. Reid, *Charting the Shape*, p. 228.
24. Ibid., pp. 229–32.
25. Wazir, "The Affairs of the Bogeyman", p. 410.
26. Tarling, *Southeast Asia*, p. 105.
27. Ibid., p. 101.
28. Geoffrey Dutton, *Founder of a City: The Life of Colonel William Light* (Adelaide: Rigby, 1984), p. 4.
29. Sir Frank Swettenham, *British Malaya: An Account of the Origin and Progress of British Influence in Malaya* (London: Allen and Unwin, 1948), pp. 34–35.
30. Kennedy, *A History of Malaya*, p. 79.
31. Tarling, *Southeast Asia*, p. 133.
32. George Bilainkin, *Hail Penang! Being a Narrative of Comedies and Tragedies in a Tropical Outpost among Europeans, Chinese, Malays and Indians* (Penang: Areca Books, 2010), p. 238.
33. Kennedy, *A History of Malaya*, p. 79.
34. Tarling, *Southeast Asia*, pp. 115–16.
35. Carl A. Trocki, *Prince of Pirates: The Temenggongs and the Development of Johor and Singapore 1784–1855*, 2nd ed. (Singapore: NUS Press, 2007), p. 21.
36. Ibid., pp. 61–62.
37. Ibid.
38. Ibid., pp. 65–67.
39. Ibid., p. 65.
40. Ibid., p. 67.
41. Nordin, *Trade and Society*, p. 63.

42. Swettenham, *British Malaya*, p. 78.

43. Tarling, *Southeast Asia*, p. 178; Trocki, *Prince of Pirates*, p. 154.

44. Ricklefs et al., *A New History*, p. 201.

45. Tarling, *Southeast Asia*, p. 178.

46. Nordin, *Trade and Society*, p. 307.

47. Ibid., pp. 26–28.

48. R.S. Milne and Dianne K. Mauzy, *Politics and Government in Malaysia* (Singapore: Federal, 1978), p. 12.

49. Tarling, *Southeast Asia*, p. 179.

50. Lawrence James, *The Rise and Fall of the British Empire* (London: Abacus, 1998), p. 247.

51. Tarling, *Southeast Asia*, p. 279.

52. Collin Abraham, *The Naked Social Order: The Roots of Racial Polarisation in Malaya* (Subang Jaya: Pelanduk, 2004), pp. 28–29.

53. J.M. Gullick, *The Story of Kuala Lumpur 1857–1939* (Singapore: Eastern Universities Press, 1983), p. 23.

54. Milne and Mauzy, *Politics and Government in Malaysia*, p. 14.

55. James, *The Rise and Fall*, p. 247.

56. Swettenham, *British Malaya*, p. 173.

57. Abraham, *The Naked Social Order*, pp. 30–31.

58. Michael R. Stenson, *Class, Race and Colonialism in West Malaysia: The Indian Case* (St. Lucia: University of Queensland Press, 1980), p. 14.

59. Reid, *Charting the Shape*, p. 237.

60. Abraham, *The Naked Social Order*, p. 37.

61. Ibid., p. 33.

62. Malcolm Caldwell, "The British 'Forward Movement' 1874–1914", in *Malaya: The Making of a Neo-Colony*, edited by Mohamad Amin and Malcolm Caldwell (Nottingham: Spokesman, 1977), pp. 13, 18–19.

63. James, *The Rise and Fall*, p. 245.

64. Trocki, *Prince of Pirates*, p. 190.

65. Caldwell, "The British 'Forward Movement'", pp. 18–19.

66. Kennedy, *A History of Malaya*, p. 156; Abraham, *The Naked Social Order*, pp. 27–29.

67. Kennedy, *A History of Malaya*, p. 156.

68. Means, *Political Islam*, pp. 46–47.

69. Ibid.

70. Shaharuddin Ma'aruf, *Malay Ideas on Development: From Feudal Lord to Capitalism* (Singapore: Times Book International, 1998), pp. 44–45.

71. Tarling, *Southeast Asia*, p. 181.

72. Ricklefs et al., *A New History*, p. 176.

73. Swettenham, *British Malaya*, p. 272.

74. Tarling, *Southeast Asia*, p. 156.
75. Ibid., p. 138.
76. Ricklefs et al., *A New History*, p. 176.
77. Trocki, *Prince of Pirates*, pp. 83–85.
78. Ibid., p. 162.
79. Ibid., p. 119.
80. Ibid., p. 186.
81. Ibid., p. 201.
82. Ooi Kee Beng, *The Reluctant Politician: Tun Dr Ismail and His Time* (Singapore: Institute of Southeast Asian Studies, 2006), p. 13.
83. Ibid.; Trocki, *Prince of Pirates*, p. 161.
84. Margaret Shennan, *Out in the Midday Sun: The British in Malaya 1880–1960* (London: John Murray, 2004), p. 134.
85. Ricklefs et al., *A New History*, p. 116.
86. Ibid., p. 202.
87. P. Ramasamy, *Plantation Labour, Unions, Capital and the State in Peninsular Malaysia* (New York: Oxford University Press, 1994), p. 8.
88. Ricklefs et al., *A New History*, p. 202.
89. Ibid., p. 204.
90. Ibid.
91. Amarjit Kaur, "Working on the Railway: Indian Workers in Malaya 1880–1957", in *The Underside of Malaysian History: Pullers, Prostitutes, Plantation Workers*, edited by Peter J. Rimmer and Lisa M. Allen (Singapore: Singapore University Press, 1990), pp. 100–101.
92. Ramasamy, *Plantation Labour*, pp. 23–24.
93. Hugh Tinker, *A New System of Slavery: The Export of Indian Labour Overseas 1830–1920* (London: Oxford University Press, 1974), p. 33.
94. J. Norman Parmer, *Colonial Labor Policy and Administration: A History of Labor in the Rubber Industry in Malaya, 1910–1941* (New York: Augustin, 1960), p. 8.
95. Ramasamy, *Plantation Labour*, p. 8.
96. Kennedy, *A History of Malaya*, pp. 202–3.
97. Parmer, *Colonial Labor Policy*, p. 8.
98. Kennedy, *A History of Malaya*, p. 204.
99. Parmer, *Colonial Labor Policy*, p. 8.
100. John Drabble, "Politics of Survival: European Reactions in Malaya to Rubber Smallholders in the Interwar Years", in *The Underside of Malayan History: Pullers, Prostitutes, Plantation Workers*, edited by Peter J. Rimmer and Lisa M. Allen (Singapore: Singapore University Press, 1990), p. 71.
101. Virginia Thompson, *Post-Mortem on Malaya* (New York: Macmillan, 1943), p. 109.

102. Major G. St. J. Orde-Brown, *Report on Labour Conditions in Ceylon, Mauritius and Malaya 1942–1943* (Parliamentary Papers [HC], IX-659, Oriental and India Office Collection, London).

103. Francis Loh Kok Wah, "From Tin Mine Coolies to Agricultural Squatters: Socio-Economic Change in the Kinta District During the Inter-War Years", in *The Underside of Malaysian History: Pullers, Prostitutes, Plantation Workers*, edited by Peter J. Rimmer and Lisa J. Allen (Singapore: Singapore University Press, 1990), p. 73.

104. J.M. Gullick, *The Story of Kuala Lumpur*, p. 121.

105. Ricklefs et al., *A New History*, p. 242.

106. Gullick, *The Story of Kuala Lumpur*, p. 121.

107. Amarjit Kaur, "Tappers and Weeders: South Indian Plantation Workers in Peninsular Malaysia, 1880–1970", *Journal of South Asian Studies* 21 (1998): 76.

108. Joel S. Kahn, *Other Malays: Nationalism and Cosmopolitanism in the Modern Malay World* (Singapore: Asian Studies Association of Australia in association with Singapore University Press and NIAS Press, 2006), p. 89.

109. Parmer, *Colonial Labor Policy*, p. 16.

110. Ibid., pp. 9–10.

111. Khong Kim Hoong, *Merdeka! British Rule and the Struggle for Independence in Malaya 1945–1957* (Kuala Lumpur: Insan, 1984), p. 9.

112. Bilainkin, *Hail Penang!*, p. 236.

3

INDIA AND THE DEVELOPMENT OF BRITISH IDEOLOGIES OF EMPIRE

British colonialism in Malaya imported specific ideologies of governance to administer their new colonial possessions. These ideologies, developed by British theorists in reaction to the Great Rebellion (Indian Mutiny) of 1857–58, were incorporated into the formal structures of British imperialism. Later chapters will explore how significant aspects of these ideologies, in particular those pertaining to the concept of "race", were applied in colonial Malaya, and how in certain respects these continue to resonate within the racial policies of contemporary Malaysia.

In the period leading to the Great Rebellion, the British, through the agency of the East India Company (EIC), adopted an aggressive policy of reform based on an amalgam of three dominant ideologies, namely:

1. The philosophical utilitarianism of, among others, James Mill and his son John Stuart Mill, Jeremy Bentham and Baron Thomas Macaulay.[1]
2. Evangelical Protestantism, seen as the principal factor underlying and sustaining the elevated character of the British ruling classes. The 1813 reform of the East India Company Act provided missionaries with the freedom to proselytize in India.[2]

3. In the 1840s, free trade, portrayed as the dynamic upholding British pre-eminence and global power.[3]

The reform programme comprised nothing less than "an ideological offensive against the foundations of Indian life".[4] It was assumed that under the benevolent and wise guidance of British rule — and liberated from the tyrannies of idolatry and false religions, superstition and meaningless traditions representing the dead hand of antiquity — Indians would naturally aspire to and attain the same level of civilization as post-Enlightenment Britain. This civilizing role was to become the imperial mission; a great enterprise in which British rulers would envisage themselves not so much as conquerors, but as emancipators.[5]

The Great Rebellion thus came as a profound shock to all levels of British society in both India and metropolitan Britain. The mutineers had not only rejected the British as rulers but had also, in imperial terms, launched a direct onslaught on the entire Victorian world view and had disparaged some of the Victorians' most cherished values. At its deepest level, the Rebellion challenged the very precepts which had informed the entire nineteenth-century imperial project.[6] The mutineer's vehement repudiation of a "benevolent" British rule indicated, to the British at least, that the Indians were incapable of appreciating or ingesting the great and ennobling gifts that they had offered them and that efforts to uplift them were therefore both misplaced and destined to fail.[7]

The immediate aftermath of the Rebellion was the termination of the power of the EIC and the substitution of direct British rule. The Government of India Act 1858 appointed a Cabinet Minister as Secretary of State for India and provided him with an Advisory Council of fifteen members. The office of the Governor-General was abolished and replaced with that of Viceroy, who would be assisted by an appointed Supreme Council. The EIC military was absorbed by the Crown.[8] In her proclamation foreshadowing the passage of the India Act, Queen Victoria "promised that the government would treat all its subjects equally, uphold the rights of princes, and respect all religions of India".[9] The Queen's statement marked a number of major shifts of policy towards the governance of India.

Firstly, the agenda of ambitious reform, promoted with such enthusiasm, and such little regard for the feelings, traditions or fears of the subject population, was largely abandoned. The optimistic and far-reaching programme designed to reshape India was replaced by a regime driven by benevolent and condescending paternalism. A new orthodoxy emerged; that in terms of historical development, India as a society was equivalent to England of the early Middle Ages and that as a consequence Indians "preferred" to be ruled as a feudal entity.[10]

Secondly, the position of the traditional Indian rulers, perceived as threatened in the years leading to the Rebellion, was now guaranteed. The British recognized that indirect rule provided a welcome buffer between colonial authority and those ultimately governed within the princely states.[11] The majority of Indian rulers had remained loyal to the British throughout the Mutiny. In recognition of their service, Viceroy Canning held durbars at which native princes were confirmed in their ranks and titles and presented with rewards.[12]

Thirdly, the British quickly decided that the process of sound administration and governmental stability required that local elites be incorporated at appropriate levels within the overall structures of the local government.[13] Acting upon the assumption that the societal structures of metropolitan Britain were both analagous and replicable within India, the administration decided that some of the reliable collaborative elites would be the large landowners, "men of property ... power and influence" who allegedly comprised the traditional aristocracy of India. This stratum of society would not only prove dependable in upholding British rule, but could also be relied upon to fulfil key roles such as revenue collection and dispensation of justice.[14]

This co-option would be perpetuated through the establishment of select schools modelled on the great English public schools. There the sons of the elite would be inculcated with the ethos of British public school values, especially those derived from the quintessentially British agency of the games field.[15] Rajkumar College, the "Indian Eton", opened in 1870, was charged with educating the sons of Indian princes.[16] This was followed by the prestigious Mayo College (1875), as well a number of other exclusive establishments.[17]

As we have noted, the Rebellion convinced British rulers that Indians as a society were incapable of improvement. This, coupled with new racial ideologies developed within Britain and the Raj (discussed later in this chapter), produced the doctrine of *prestige* which was to henceforth inform the administration of the Empire. Essentially a defensive posture, prestige emphasized the intrinsic and ascendant "difference" — the social, political, and moral distance of the British from their subject populations.[18] The key ingredients of this doctrine consisted of loyalty and conformity to the disciplines and codes of behaviour conferred by race; the upholding of status (or "form"); the maintenance of public dignity; and adherence to Christianity, the "European" religion, a putative lofty and elevated spiritual tradition and a badge of pre-eminence, not to be shared with the world.[19]

British prestige was fostered through increasingly elaborate and authoritative displays of layered ceremonial grandeur. In 1876, Disraeli, the Prime Minister, introduced the Imperial Titles Act which formally declared Queen Victoria Empress of India. This proclamation was intended to symbolize both the permanence of the British presence in India,[20] and the British crown as the legitimate successor to the great empire of the Mughals. British pageantry reached its pinnacle with the Coronation Durbar of 1911.[21]

In complying with the constant demands imposed by prestige, the British ruling classes became hidebound, secure in their own infallible judgements and increasingly incapable of any intimate understanding of the societies they ruled. The constant pressures placed upon white men to maintain the edifice of overlordship continually perverted the fabric of everyday life and forced people into acts of irrationality. The inflexibility and remoteness of the British proved a major handicap in understanding and responding to shifts in native attitudes, in particular the rise of twentieth-century nationalism.[22]

The underside of prestige, which belied the British myth of invincibility, was the powerful legacy of fear, loathing, and paranoia left by the Rebellion.[23] Henceforth, any outbreak of unrest, any attempt to reduce the demarcated distance between ruled and rulers, and any disturbance to the status quo were likely to be interpreted as a threat to British prestige.[24] Official reactions were immediate, and often disproportionate, brutal, and indiscriminate.[25]

BRITISH RACIAL IDEOLOGIES

The most far-reaching ideological impact of the Rebellion (reinforced by the subsequent Jamaica revolt of 1865) was the development of complex ideologies of race, the legacy of which continues to resonate throughout much of the postcolonial world. These ideologies would be used to simultaneously enable the British to "know" India (in British terms) but, more importantly, to explain the inherent and irredeemable "inferiority" of Indians and their innate biological incapacity to recognize or absorb the fruits of British civilization. These racial beliefs would be employed to justify the continuation and expansion of British (and by extension, European) rule over non-Europeans. They would also be used to define "the Other" in terms of his/her perceived social and political distance from the British ruling class.

While European racial theorists had long conflated the issues of race and biology, it was only with the publication of Charles Darwin's *Origin of Species by Natural Selection* in 1859 that these rather inchoate theories appeared to receive a solid scientific undergirding. For the first time, science encased the concept of race in terms of biological inevitability. Race, it seemed, was all-encompassing, "the prime determinant of all important traits of body and soul, character and personality of human beings and nations".[26] Social Darwinism, as the theory became known, implied the linear development of man, an evolutionary advance from primitive and degraded to civilized and cultivated, a maturation propelled by "progress" (defined in strictly European terms), as the dynamic agent of human history, and the survival of the fittest, pushed to the limit, as the dominant principle of human organization.[27] Since a people's racial characteristics ineluctably predetermined its culture and capabilities, it was possible to systematically assess and rank each society within the framework of an exhaustive human taxonomy. The upper echelons of this table of humanity were necessarily occupied by the white races. Thus, Social Darwinism could be invoked not only to explain European ascendency, but also to catalogue the many backwardnesses of inferior races, and in particular their inability to comprehend, let alone grasp, the benefits wrought by a higher civilization.[28]

The Victorians' ethnocentrism placed them at the unassailable summit of the human racial and cultural hierarchy. Indeed, judged in terms of material, scientific, and intellectual achievements, Anglo-Saxons could be reckoned as a "super-race".[29] It followed that other races and cultures could only be assessed and evaluated in terms of British criteria, and in particular according to the benchmarks established by British technology, law, religion and philosophy. All other races, including fellow Europeans, were axiomatically inferior, and non-Europeans were seen as hopelessly immature and even childlike.[30] But Social Darwinism, anointed with the formidable imprimatur of Victorian scientism, not only explained British and European supremacy, but also invested the conquest of technologically backward non-European people with a moral purpose. For, applied wisely, the benevolent rule of Europe would uplift the degraded races of the world. European domination was therefore "natural, inevitable, ordered by (the) different endowments granted by a Creator, and beneficial to all mankind".[31]

But Social Darwinism not only explained the progress of mankind, it also warned of the dangers of degeneration. Degeneration, a morbid deviation from the racial archetype, manifested itself in a brutish survival known as "atavism".[32] Degeneration not only explained "stationary" or backward societies[33] but also served as a warning of the deleterious effects of careless or promiscuous breeding, and what this might imply for the future of any given society. Theories of degeneration melded with the nineteenth-century European historiography which highlighted the extent of Asian decline. The discovery of the temple-building civilizations of Angkor, Pegan, Champa, and Java, together with archaeological evidence that suggested that current-day India was little but a poor echo of a great and ancient Hindu power, led European scholars to draw parallels with the decline and collapse of the glorious empires of Greece and Rome. Asian powers, it was asserted, had once been great and powerful, but had degenerated into sterile and stagnant oriental despotisms.[34] These Asian examples, it was asserted, served as a warning to the great European powers of the dangers of complacency, and the need to maintain racial homogeneity, as well as the purity of the bloodlines of the ruling classes.[35]

In the early twentieth century, the emerging disciplines of genetics and heredity were to steer Social Darwinism into increasingly murky and indeed sinister waters.[36] John Gray has commented that "The peculiar achievement of Enlightenment racism was to give genocide the blessing of science and civilization. Mass murder could be justified by faux-Darwinian ideas of the survival of the fittest and the destruction of entire peoples could be welcomed as part of the advance of the species."[37] These views seemed to have gained the imprimatur of Darwin himself. In his 1871 work, *The Descent of Man and Selection in Relation to Sex,* Darwin not only assumed the superiority of northern and western European white human beings over all other shades of humanity,[38] but also had written that "The civilized races of man will almost certainly exterminate, and replace the savage races throughout the world."[39] He had also appeared to condone acts of genocide perpetrated by British colonists, such as the annihilation of Tasmanian Aborigines, preferring to view these actions as part of the evolutionary process.[40]

But Social Darwinism was not just a racial ideology. As David Cannadine has demonstrated, Social Darwinism was both invested and supplemented with considerations of class.[41] This was a time of increasing anxiety for the hereditary aristocratic elites of Britain. Economic and social changes were challenging the traditional order. Between 1873 and 1896, Britain experienced a prolonged agricultural depression, largely fuelled by imports of cheap corn from Australia and North America, together with the advent of refrigerated shipping which promoted foreign competition within the British meat market.[42] During this period, many of the great estates which had sustained the aristocracy became unprofitable, and the once axiomatic nexus between land ownership and political and economic power was increasingly threatened.[43] Between 1886 and 1914, a total of 246 new titles were created, of which 70 were drawn from the so-called plutocratic class representing the increasingly powerful world of industry, trade, and commerce.[44] Upper class insecurities assumed various modes of expression,[45] but became ever more insistent on the maintenance of social hierarchies governed by both class and race.[46] These considerations were expressed in the form of a metropolitan-peripheral analogy. Thus, members of the working class in overcrowded British industrial towns were likened in terms of their character and their behaviour to the non-whites within the Empire. Similarly, an additional factor which weighed against the "natives" of Empire was that they were viewed as the overseas peers of the lowest classes of British society.[47] Thus, prominent political and economic analyst Walter Bagehot commented that:

> If men differ in anything they differ in their forms and the delicacies of their moral intuitions ... we need not go as far as the savages to learn that lesson; we need only talk to the English poor or to our servants, and we shall be taught that very completely. The lower classes in civilized countries, *like all classes in uncivilized countries* [emphasis added] are clearly wanting in the nicer part of those feelings which taken together, we call the sense of morality.[48]

As the Victorian period progressed, elite social formations increasingly employed the language of racialized class, and in particular that habitually attached to the British underclass, to describe the colonial "Other".[49]

RACIALIZED INDIA

The British wasted no time in applying the lessons of these new racial ideologies to their subject populations. Census operations, which began in India in 1872, allowed for the accumulation of vast quantities of data which enumerated the population according to a variety of social criteria.[50]

Between 1868 and 1875, the administration published an eight-volume work entitled *Peoples of India* complete with commentaries on the many different groups they now ruled.[51] The full cumbersome apparatus of Victorian Social Darwinism transformed this state into a complete Indian bio-racial taxonomy which ordered India both vertically and horizontally into a series of overlapping classificatory systems revolving about notions of caste, religion, and primary race. These systems enabled the British to exactly locate the cultural and racial status of any individual within the overall structure of what was perceived as the timeless, unchanging Indian social hierarchy.[52] The taxonomy also emphasized the "otherness" of India, a society whose peoples could only be "known" according to categories which permitted the development and maintenance of colonial authority, and which thus underscored the intrinsic social and racial distance of Indian society from that of metropolitan Britain.[53]

We will explore aspects of British racial policy in so far as it affected South India in later chapters. In the interim we should note that most scholars now accept that India was the proving ground for theories of imperial rule and that the ideologies and policies formulated and applied in the Raj were exported to other parts of the Empire.[54] The dominant ideologies which developed in response to the challenges of the Rebellion — an imperial nationalism composed of monarchism, militarism, and Social Darwinism through which the British delineated their own unique superiority — were vigorously promoted through British and Empire media until the late 1950s, by which time the Empire was becoming a forsaken cause.[55]

CONCLUSIONS

The Great Rebellion led to a major reassessment of the fundamental policies which had directed British colonial rule in India. The initial casualty was the ambitious programme of reform which had sought the transformation, if not the extirpation, of indigenous social, political and religious cultures.[56] The British government not only replaced EIC rule with direct British control but also introduced new ideologies of governance. These included indirect rule, the incorporation of local elites into the structures of colonial administration, and the doctrine of prestige, constituting a studied colonial remoteness from the subject population. However, the most powerful ideology was that of Social Darwinism, a racial world view which appeared to be scientifically based and which not only posited the demonstrable civilizational superiority of white and especially British races, but also supposedly invested their rule over lesser races with moral purpose. These ideologies, developed in India, were to consistently inform British rule in other parts of the Empire.

Notes

1. Eric Stokes, *The English Utilitarians and India* (Oxford: Oxford University Press, 1959), pp. 48–50.
2. Gauri Viswanathan, *The Masks of Conquest: Literary Study and British Rule in India* (New York: Columbia University Press, 1989), p. 38.
3. Stokes, *The English Utilitarians*, pp. 40–48.
4. Michael Edwardes, *The Red Year: The Indian Rebellion of 1857* (London: Cardinal, 1975), p. 18.
5. Lawrence James, *Raj: The Making and Unmaking of British India* (London: Little, Brown and Company, 1997), p. 151.
6. Ibid., pp. 295–97.
7. Ibid.
8. Richard Holmes, *Sahib: The British Soldier in India* (London: Michael Joseph, 1994), p. 80.
9. James, *Raj*, p. 293.
10. Maria Misra, *Vishnu's Crowded Temple: India since the Great Rebellion* (London: Allen Lane, 2007), pp. 10–11.
11. Edwardes, *The Red Year*, p. 151.
12. Ibid.; Cannadine, *Ornamentalism: How the British Saw Their Empire* (London: Penguin, 2001), pp. 43–44; V.G. Kiernan, *The Lords of Humankind: European Attitudes Towards the Outside World in an Imperial Age* (Harmondsworth: Penguin Books, 1972), pp. 54–55.
13. Edwardes, *The Red Year*, p. 150.
14. Cannadine, *Ornamentalism*, pp. 43–44; Misra, *Vishnu's Crowded Temple*, p. 12.
15. J.A. Mangan, *The Games Ethic and Imperialism: Aspects of the Diffusion of an Ideal* (Harmondsworth: Viking, 1986), pp. 33–43.
16. Holmes, *Sahib*, p. 83.
17. Misra, *Vishnu's Crowded Temple*, p. 14.
18. Kiernan, *The Lords of Humankind*, pp. 56–57.
19. Thomas R. Metcalf, *Ideologies of the Raj* (Cambridge: Cambridge University Press, 1977), p. 90; Christine Bolt, *Victorian Attitudes Towards Race* (London: Routledge and Kegan Paul, 1971), p. 165.
20. Holmes, *Sahib*, p. 82.

21. Cannadine, *Ornamentalism*, p. 57.

22. Kiernan, *The Lords of Humankind*, p. 325.

23. Ibid., p. 49.

24. Vyvyen Brendon, *Children of the Raj* (London: Weidenfeld and Nicholson, 2005), p. 241.

25. Kiernan, *The Lords of Humankind*, p. 159.

26. Bolt, *Victorian Attitudes towards Race*, p. 9.

27. Ibid., p. 11; Charles Hirschmann, "The Making of Race in Colonial Malaya: Political Economy and Racial Ideology", *Journal of Asian Studies* 46, no. 3 (1987): 341.

28. Arthur Hermann, *The Idea of Decline in Western History* (New York: The Free Press, 1997), pp. 109–14; Hirschmann, *The Making of Race*, p. 341.

29. Lawrence James, *The Rise and Fall of the British Empire* (London: Abacus, 1998), pp. 197–98.

30. Hermann, *The Idea of Decline*, pp. 265–66; Mangan, *The Games Ethic*, pp. 111–12.

31. Hirschmann, "The Making of Race", p. 341.

32. Hermann, *The Idea of Decline*, p. 129.

33. Bolt, *Victorian Attitudes Towards Race*, pp. 21–24.

34. Anthony Reid, *Charting the Shape of Early Modern Southeast Asia* (Singapore: Institute of Southeast Asian Studies, 2000), pp. 238–39.

35. Robin Gilmour, *The Idea of the Gentleman in the Victorian Novel* (London: George Allen and Unwin, 1981), p. 87; Esme Wingfield-Stratford, *The Victorian Sunset* (London: George Rutledge and Sons Ltd., 1932), p. 34.

36. Eric Johnson and Karl-Heinz Reuband, *What We Knew: Terror, Mass Murder and Everyday Life in Nazi Germany* (London: John Murray, 2005), p. 337.

37. John Gray, *Black Mass: Apocalyptic Religion and the Death of Utopia* (London: Allen Lane, 2007), p. 62.

38. A.N. Wilson, *After the Victorians: The World Our Parents Knew* (London: Arrow Books, 2006), p. 104.

39. Rajiv Malhotra and Aravindan Neelakandan, *Breaking India: Western Interventions in Dravidian and Dalit Faultlines* (New Delhi: Amaryllis, 2011), p. 31.

40. Wilson, *After the Victorians*, pp. 375–76.

41. Cannadine, *Ornamentalism*, pp. 5–6.

42. Andrew Thompson, *The Empire Strikes Back? The Impact of Imperialism on Britain from the Mid-Nineteenth Century* (Harlow: Pearson Longman, 2005), p. 12; Juliet Nicolson, *The Perfect Summer: Dancing into Shadow in 1911* (London: John Murray, 2007), p. 139.

43. Angela Lambert, *Unquiet Souls: The Indian Summer of the British Aristocracy* (London: Papermac, 1985), p. 137.

44. Wingfield-Stratford, *The Victorian Sunset*, p. 291; A.N. Wilson, *The Victorians* (London: Hutchinson, 2002), p. 583.

45. Many leading eugenicists were troubled by the supposed threat to civilization posed by the "lower classes" at home. Thus William Inge, Dean of St. Pauls, would warn "the urban proletariat may cripple our civilization as it destroyed that of ancient Rome" further claiming that "these degenerates have no survival value" (Marek Kohn, *A Reason for Everything: Natural Selection and the English Imagination* [London: Faber and Faber, 2004], p. 98).

46. Cannadine, *Ornamentalism*, p. 43.

47. Ibid., pp. 5–6.

48. Lambert, *Unquiet Souls*, p. 143.

49. Thompson, *The Empire Strikes Back?*, p. 40.

50. Peter Van der Veer, *Religious Nationalisms: Hindus and Muslims in India* (Berkeley: University of California Press, 1994), p. 19.

51. Thompson, *The Empire Strikes Back?*, p. 26.

52. Ibid.

53. Metcalf, *Ideologies of the Raj*, p. 141.

54. Ibid., p. 215.

55. John M. McKenzie, *Propaganda and Empire: The Manipulation of British Public Opinion 1880–1960* (Manchester: Manchester University Press, 1985), p. 2.

56. Viswanathan, *The Masks of Conquest*, pp. 16–17; Stokes, *The English Utilitarians*, pp. 45–46.

4

BRITISH GOVERNANCE OF MALAYA

This chapter will explore how the ideologies of rule developed in British India, namely British prestige; indirect rule; incorporation of elites into the formal structures of administration; and racial ideologies built around the principles of Social Darwinism and the tenets of Victorian anthropology, were reproduced within colonial Malaya.

PRESTIGE

As with other parts of the Empire, British society was shaped by the doctrine of prestige. This manifested as an inherent sense of superiority characterized by aloofness and social distance from the subject population. The British adopted a number of strategies to emphasize their difference in racial terms from those they ruled. The most obvious of these were levels of income and patterns of consumption. The Governor and Residents of the Federated Malay States (FMS) and Unfederated Malay States (UFMS) were representatives of the British sovereign and as such lived in a style which was intended to reflect the majesty and dignity of the Crown. High officials occupied grand residences and were served by numerous officials and full households of servants.[1] But even among lower ranks, the British administration took every precaution to ensure that "white" prestige was not challenged. Salaries and wages, including those of the lowest paid workers, were fixed at rates which ensured that even working class Europeans could enjoy, and more importantly be seen to enjoy, a standard of living conspicuously higher and largely unattainable by all but a handful of the Asian population.[2]

While, in general, anything less than total acquiescence to British rule was viewed by the administration as rank insubordination, the imposition of a strict racial hierarchy in colonial Malaya was nowhere near as inflexible or absolute as it had become in the British Raj. There were elites among all communities, most particularly the Malay aristocracy and the Chinese business classes, whose sensitivities had to be taken into account, and who would effectively resist any attempts by Europeans to introduce complete racial segregation.[3] Thus, the establishment of whites-only compartments within the Malayan railways, begun in 1904, was withdrawn in 1915 against a background of Asian resentment, having in the interim caused great offence to the Chinese population.[4]

European Malaya was intellectually conformist and insular and was organized into a rigid social hierarchy based on rank, status and class.[5] Over the years, the notion of prestige based on the social distance between rulers and ruled became an obsession.[6] However, this was driven in part by a constant and barely disguised sense of unease, the legacy of the Great Rebellion (Indian Mutiny) of 1857, so that even the slightest challenge — or perceived challenge — to white supremacy was greeted with disproportionate alarm. Thus, the Police Report into a strike at Batu Arang in 1936 assumed near apoplectic tones:

> The Federated Malay States had passed the most serious crisis in its history. It was within an ace of dissolving into temporary chaos as a result of communist intrigue. Had the organization not been crushed ... this country with its European women and children living in scattered bungalows on estates, would have been in serious danger of being overrun by angry and desperate Chinese mobs.[7]

As we will see, the self-enclosed and complacent world of British prestige, together with the myth of British invincibility, was to be irrevocably shattered by the invading Japanese army of 1941, with a force sufficient to destroy forever the ideological assumptions upon which the British Empire had been built and sustained.

INDIRECT RULE

We have seen that the British appointed Resident Advisors to all Malay states, whether FMS or UFMS, as they fell under colonial control. While the residency system was ostensibly based on the assumption that the Resident was more a benevolent mentor to the Sultan than an actual ruler, the 1875 deposition of the Sultan of Perak had shown that the proffered "advice" was in fact mandatory and would be backed by force if necessary.

Under the system of indirect rule, the territorial integrity of the sultanates was respected and the Malay aristocracy was furnished with generous pensions — in theory to replace forgone revenue, but in practice well in excess of precolonial incomes.[8] The conciliatory diplomacy of early colonial administrators forged a generally harmonious relationship with the Malay rulers, who experienced little difficulty in adjusting to British rule.[9] The full façade of the sultanates was retained. The sultans each presided over their territorial administrations, though real power resided with the residents. Henceforth, the Malay aristocracy was to largely occupy itself with effusive displays of pomp and majesty.[10]

Indeed, the need to maintain the authority and prestige of the rulers was constantly reiterated as a cardinal point of British policy in Malaya.[11] As in India, the British encouraged the sultans to provide an outward show of grandeur which underscored their dominion. Following Federation in 1896, the sultans held a biennial durbar which was noted for its ostentatious splendour. The rulers were accompanied by impressive retinues and the durbar was studded with elaborate ceremonials which were enacted in the presence of large crowds.[12]

Under the system of indirect rule, the sultans were charged with responsibility for all matters affecting Islam and *adat*. The net impact of these and other measures was to destroy the traditional lines of authority which hitherto prevailed upon the Malay Peninsula, in particular the localized power exercised by the territorial chiefs and the *penghulu* (village headman).[13]

The rulers of the precolonial sultanates had combined a generic political authority with leadership in religious and cultural affairs. However, religion was not directly administered by the sultan, and there was no state religion per se.[14] Following the Pangkor Treaty, an elaborate bureaucratic machinery was established in various sultanates with the aim of bringing Islam under the formal control of the rulers. A *Majlis Agama Islam dan Adat Isti'adat Melayu* (Council of Islamic Religion and Malay Customs) was founded. This oversighted a *Jabatan Hal-Ehwal Agama Islam* (Department of Islamic Religious Affairs). These new organizations consolidated within themselves the formal apparatus of Islamic administration, including the right to issue *fatwa* (legal edits) and *tauliah* (the letter of authority to qualified religious teachers), as well as the appointment of *ulama* who were overwhelmingly drawn from the aristocratic class.[15] The new arrangements not only created a state religion but also welded "a nascent religious establishment and a traditional elite ... to colonial officialdom".[16]

The land reforms introduced by the British also enhanced the power of the sultanates and the feudal hold of the rulers over the Malay peasantry. The British introduction of the Torrens system of land title vested full control of lands with the sultans. This reorganization represented a major extension of the sultan's political authority.[17] In addition, the British provided the sultans with efficient state administrations, thus maximizing the collection of revenues which in turn furnished the rulers with incomes well in excess of those received in the era preceding British rule.[18] The net effect of these measures was to embellish and consolidate the sultan's power in a form of authoritarian religious administration much more extensive than anything previously known in the Peninsula.[19] But this power derived from and was ultimately dependent upon the formal structures of British colonialism.[20]

Indirect rule had distinct advantages for the colonial power. Not only did it obviate the necessity for the cumbersome (and expensive) apparatus of direct colonial administration, but it also perpetuated the illusion that the nexus between the indigenous population and their traditional rulers remained intact. In addition, it preserved the mirage of Malay political sovereignty and the fiction of an Anglo–Malay partnership with Malays holding a privileged position.[21] Thus, Sir Hugh Clifford, Governor of the Straits Settlements, between 1927 and 1930 could make the following claim, breathtaking in its sophistry: "this is a Malay country, and we came here at the invitation of their Highnesses, the Malay Rulers, and it is our duty to help the Malays rule their own country".[22] As in India, indirect rule also inserted a cushioning layer between the colonial authorities and those whom they ultimately governed.

CO-OPTION OF ELITES

As we have noted, the residency system made the sultan the focal point of administration and centralized power within the states. However, within the Malay states, male members of the aristocracy were offered prestigious positions within the new and extended state administrations.[23] This not only ensconced Malay elites within the structures of British rule, but also, by making them dependent upon British patronage, ensured a reliable and compliant administration within each state.[24]

In 1905 the English-medium Malay College, known locally as "The Eton of the East", was established in Kuala Kangsar, the royal town of Perak, with the express aim of educating the sons of the Malay aristocracy.[25] The curriculum and ethos of the school was designed to familiarize and inculcate students with the value system of British colonialism and the British Empire. The rationale of the college was, in the words of the Inspector of Malay Schools for the FMS (1903–6), to mould "At best ... an Asiatic governing class rather than Asiatic races capable of self-government."[26] The graduates of the school would be equipped to occupy middle-level positions in the colonial bureaucracy. This self-replicating system would permanently enmesh local elites as partners — albeit junior partners — within the British colonial structure.[27]

Co-option was also followed, albeit to a lesser extent, with regard to Chinese and Indian elites. Within the Straits Settlements, which had a Chinese majority population, the British appointed influential members of the Chinese community to the Legislative Council. As will be discussed in Chapter 9, this strategy was also adopted in relation to Indian and Ceylonese (Sri Lankan) elites. Chinese (and Indians) were later admitted to the lower echelons of the Straits Settlements Civil Service.[28]

RACIAL IDEOLOGIES

British Social Darwinism introduced a new, powerful and potentially disruptive ideology into the politics of interethnic relations in the Malay Peninsula. Charles Hirschman argues that in the prolonged period prior to the advent of British imperialism, ethnic accommodation had been determined by the economic imperatives required to develop and maintain long-distance trade networks among the culturally disparate ethnic groups of Southeast Asia. While this did not preclude conflict, friction or ethnocentrism (i.e., the belief in the superiority of one's own people and culture), it did not embrace any racial ideology which stressed a doctrine of inherent difference between ethnic groups.[29] Historically, Malays had shown themselves flexible on matters relating to ethnicity and had erected no racial barriers in their dealings with outsiders.[30] Malay rulers had been prepared to enter alliances with European powers in order to conduct military campaigns against rival sultanates or other European forces.[31] Examples of ethnic accommodation within Malay society had included the absorption of Bugis settlers into the Malay aristocracy, and the easy interaction with Chinese and Indian communities which had resulted in the development of Baba cultures, that is, specifically localized Chinese and Indian cultures which had assumed elements of Malay culture, including food, dress and language.[32] In the northern state of Kelantan, Malays had acquired the Hakka dialect in order to conduct trade with communities of immigrant Chinese who had been established in the region since the Ming period and had become acculturated within the Malay kingdom.[33]

The contours of indigenous ethnicity were now challenged on two fronts: firstly, by large-scale colonially sponsored immigration of ethnic groups whose culture seemingly had little in common with that of the Malays and, secondly, by a steady stream of immigration from the Malay Archipelago of people whose culture overlapped in significant respects with that of indigenous Malays, and which was to make a substantial contribution to refashioning the local cultures of the Malay Peninsula.[34]

The processes of racial categorization of the many ethnicities and sub-ethnicities within British Malaya were formalized through the agency of censuses, which successively collapsed the fluid diversity of Malaya's population into three major and bounded "races".[35] While the censuses of 1881–91 used the term "nationalities" to head ethnic categories, the term "race" made its first appeared in the 1891 census within the instructions for enumerators.[36] The 1891 Straits Settlements census was the first to develop the generic division of Malays (Malays and other natives of the Archipelago), Chinese and Indians (Tamils and other races of India).[37] By 1901 the term "nationalities" had been changed to "race". Over the years the censuses inexorably subsumed the entire multiple ethnicities resident in the Malay states and the Straits Settlements under the rubric of three major racial groupings, each of which was subsequently crystallized into a distinct and delineated "race".[38]

British Social Darwinism did not just formulate racial groupings; it also erected a complex racial hierarchy in Malaya. This racial ideology not only justified British rule, but also ascribed socio-biological characteristics to each of the component "races" now under their control. The assumptions which underlay Social Darwinism led British administrators to draw complacent racial profiles and often reductive caricatures of the cultures and outlooks of those they now ruled. The British ruling classes naturally placed themselves at the apex of the hierarchy. The British saw themselves as intrinsically superior to all Asians. They had no doubt that their higher level of civilization uniquely equipped them to develop Malaya economically, and to bring the multifarious benefits of social and cultural progress, including sound and just rule, to the backward races of the region.[39] They entertained no illusions as to the lowly status of their colonial subjects.[40] The Malays, largely because of the supposed reluctance to work for wages in the colonial economy, especially in the plantation sector, were typecast as backward, lazy, and inferior.[41] Thus, for example, the 1909 Sanderson Report (see Chapter 6) would comment, "All the information which we have observed ... is to the effect that the native population is not characterised by any aptitude for steady work and conditions in which they live are not of a kind to compel them to it. By some observers the Malayan has been described as incorrigibly idle."[42] However, in the later colonial period, these same qualities, their imagined love of leisure, and their supposed unwillingness to emulate the putative squalid money grubbing of the Chinese and Indian immigrants earned them the rather patronizing sobriquet "nature's gentlemen"; people of discernment and character.[43] While the Chinese were admired for their capacity for hard work and economic success, they were also viewed as incapable of governing themselves,[44] and as greedy, avaricious, and duplicitous.[45] The Indians were welcomed as cheap and docile labour, tractable, servile, and easily managed, but were also regarded as dissipated, superstitious, and childlike.[46] Eurasians were considered to have absorbed the worst features of both Europeans and Asians, without inheriting any of the better qualities. They were depicted as being devoid of vigour and unreliable, dishonest and faithless.[47]

The characteristics imputed to the respective races could also be used to stipulate the range of vocational roles each was to occupy within the structure of colonial Malaya.[48] While some commentators have argued that ethnic separatism was a by-product of the occupational specialization which accompanied the development of the colonial economy,[49] there is no doubt that interethnic isolation was both exacerbated and deliberately fostered by the racial policies adopted by the British.[50]

MALAY SOCIETY UNDER COLONIALISM

The British made an early decision to exclude Malays from the modern sectors of the colonial economy. The official rationale was that the

Malays were too feckless and disinclined for any form of manual labour to be of any real worth in the plantations or mines.[51] Instead the British intended that the Malays should be shepherded into peasant agriculture, thus providing Malaya with cheap food and reducing dependency on imported foodstuffs.[52] The colonialists actively promoted immigration from the wider Archipelago and offered cash grants to intending settlers to open and cultivate new plots of land.[53] Throughout the nineteenth century there was substantial immigration from Java and Sumatra, and in the early decades of the twentieth century this was supplemented by immigration from the Riau Archipelago and Kalimantan.[54] By 1939 some forty per cent of Peninsular "Malays" were first-generation settlers.[55]

Many Malays proved reluctant to acquiesce in their colonially allocated role as small-scale paddy rice cultivators. Malays proved adroit as smallholder rubber producers and were more than competitive against the larger-scale British enterprises.[56] Malay producers quickly adapted both to cash cropping and to urban commerce.[57] To counter Malay competition and to restrict their mobility and versatility, the British introduced a series of measures designed to force Malays into food production, and thereby insulate them from the developing colonial economy. These policies were both rationalized and portrayed as necessary to "preserve" a "traditional" Malay kampung-based society, and to protect Malay land from acquisition by predatory Chinese and Indian immigrants.[58]

Neither the colonial administration nor the Malay aristocracy evinced any particular wish to reform or uplift Malay society as a whole. The policy of isolating Malays from the dynamic sectors of the colonial economy denied them the opportunity of participating in commercial or industrial undertakings. At the same time, the lack of funding for agriculture prevented peasant producers from developing a modern or innovative agricultural sector.[59] Moreover, the colonial administration made little attempt to provide the Malays with any form of comprehensive education; indeed, such education as was offered aimed at nothing greater than preserving the Malays as a self-respecting peasantry.[60] An elementary vernacular education was introduced in the 1870s. Any form of English education was eschewed. According to Sir Frank Swettenham, it was feared that this might give Malays ideas above their allotted station, and make them "unfit for the duties of life and ... discontent with anything like manual labour".[61]

British attempts to exclude the diverse groups of people, newly categorized as "Malay", from the colonial economy, coupled with Malay recognition of, and refusal to submit to, the hardships and harsh and oppressive conditions which obtained within the colonially managed plantation and extraction economy, were to give rise to and reinforce a number of pejorative myths about the Malays as a "race".[62] But for the purposes of sustaining British colonial interests and eliminating Malay enterprise as a threat to those interests, it was necessary to ensure that the colonial narratives which portrayed Malaya as a society composed of a traditional and fixed race of kampung-dwelling subsistence farmers, backward, incapable of innovation, and living in constant peril of being overwhelmed by the more hardworking and ingenious immigrants which now flooded the Peninsula, were accepted by the Malays themselves.[63] The myth of the unchanging and tradition-bound Malay peasant, backward and hamstrung by a fatalistic and feudal culture, was to become as engrained in British colonial folklore as other ideological constructions of subject peoples in other colonies — for example the supposedly static and timeless hierarchies of village India. And, as in India, it was the colonialist images of society which became embedded within nationalist discourse, so that narratives of reform and liberation refracted the portrayals of indigenous society originally inculcated by the colonial power itself.

CHINESE SOCIETY IN COLONIAL MALAYA

While China had long traded with Southeast Asia, and Chinese settlements had existed within the region for centuries,[64] the economic development which followed the full colonization of Malaya stimulated an increased flow of Chinese immigration, which intensified in the 1880s with the discovery of the rich Kinta tin fields in Perak.[65] Between 1881 and 1900 some two million immigrants arrived from China to work in Perak, Selangor, Negeri Sembilan, and Pahang.[66]

The fresh wave of Chinese migrants, known as *Laukeh* or "new guests" (Babas were known as *Sinkeh* or "old guests"),[67] strongly identified with the cultural norms they had left in mainland China. As a result they attempted to reproduce within Malaya "known" traditional and essentially grass-roots social structures, including lineage groups (based on village affiliations), customary religions, voluntary associations or *Huay-Kuan* consisting of dialect or territorial associations, trade guilds, clan/surname associations, and secret societies.[68] All of these traditional organizations, though moulded to fit local conditions, continued to influence the political and cultural life of Malayan Chinese.[69]

The British managed the Chinese communities through a system of indirect rule. Community leaders known as "*Kapitan Cina*" (Captain China) were appointed who answered directly to the colonial authorities. These officials exercised absolute control over their respective communities.[70] From the 1920s onwards, a series of measures were introduced by the colonial administration to restrict the influx of Chinese, to quell political activism within the Chinese community, and to reduce Chinese competition within the tin industry. These measures collectively served to antagonize the Chinese community and to increase the fervour of Chinese nationalists.[71]

Although by the late 1930s the Chinese *Laukeh* were well established in Malaya, the continued emphasis on Chinese affairs and in maintaining Chinese cultural traditions had created a community which was in general socially, culturally and politically distant from other ethnic communities.[72] Chinese distinctiveness was reinforced by the nationalist ideologies of Sun Yat Sen who emphasized the supposed biological, civilizational, and hence "racial" unity of the Chinese, including the diasporic Nanyang communities — communities which had hitherto offered primary allegiance to dialect and clan groups.[73] These ideologies were given wide circulation in Malaya following Sun's visit to Singapore in 1900.[74] *Laukeh* political activity largely centred upon two main and mutually antagonistic political parties, the Kuomintang Malaya (KMTM) and the Malayan Communist Party (MCP). Both modelled themselves on their metropolitan parent parties, not only in matters of ideology, but also in organizational structures and internal procedures.[75] In 1937 the outbreak of war between Japan and China elicited a powerful surge of Sino-centric nationalism among all segments of the Chinese community — *Baba* and *Laukeh*; KMTM and MCP.[76] These impulses found expression in the newly formed National Salvation Movement, which dedicated itself to raising funds to support the Chinese government.[77]

ETHNIC COMPARTMENTALIZATION IN COLONIAL MALAYA

The racial compartmentalization of colonial Malaya was generally effective. The 1931 census revealed that the Malay population was concentrated in areas of smallholdings and had been "nourished by fresh immigration from the Archipelago"; the Chinese were to be found in the mining areas around Kuala Lumpur and the Kinta Valley, as well as in the urban areas and the Straits Settlements, whereas the Indians were grouped on the estates and around public utilities.[78] Such a diverse and ethnically compartmentalized population was easily managed. As Rehman Rashid points out: "The British were famous for turning to their administrative advantage the social divisions of the lands they colonized, and they kept the races at just the right distance to have the disparate elements of Malaya work in remote harmony."[79]

The imperial racial ideology also provided a justificatory rationale for the British presence in Malaya, a rationale which claimed responsibility for nothing less than the cultural and economic survival of the Malays as a "race". According to British observers, unless restrained by a diligent colonial administration, the industriousness of the immigrant races would result in their rapid economic and cultural domination of Malaya to the exclusion of the Malays. The Malays, seen as culturally and intellectually backward, their weaknesses so pronounced that it had led to their exclusion from the modern sectors of the colonial economy, required the guidance and security provided by a benevolent power, a power which would guarantee their welfare against the predations of unscrupulous outsiders.[80] The British were in Malaya to supply that protection. To underscore their self-anointed role, the British encouraged the belief that irrespective of the length of their stay, the Chinese and Indian immigrants would never belong in Malaya. Moreover, their status as transients made them ineligible to claim even the most rudimentary political or social privileges which might be extended to the Malays.[81] The politics of race, as enunciated by the British, also justified the ruling structures the British had put in place. For, given the backwardness of the Malays, and the impermanence of the immigrants, it was necessary to restrict full participation in the politics and administration of Malaya to the Malay aristocrats and their British advisors.[82]

SIGNS OF CHANGE

Although the British had managed to establish a stable colonial regime based on the quiescence of its subject population and judicious manipulation of ethnic and sub-ethnic groups, by the late 1930s there were signs of restiveness within all communities. In 1936, serious strikes broke out among the Chinese workers in Batu Arang, Sungei Besi and Tong San mines in Selangor.[83] These were followed by strikes among

Singapore labourers later in the year, and among Chinese estate workers in 1937.[84] The militancy spread to Indian workers who struck on a number of estates in 1941. As will be discussed in Chapter 9, these latter strikes were suppressed with considerable violence, resulting in several deaths. The mass of Malays remained politically quiescent, continued to define themselves in terms of their traditional relationships to the sultans, and indeed entertained little concept of themselves as members of a broader ethnic community. However, discourses advocating social, political and religious reform, and expressing profound resentment at the intrusions of immigrant communities into *Tanah Melayu* (the Land of the Malays), had begun to make headway among English-educated intellectuals.[85] More perceptive Malay observers could scarcely fail to note that while elements of the Chinese community had acquired considerable wealth, many Malays, excluded from the colonial economy, eked out an impoverished and often precarious livelihood.[86]

These developments were as yet isolated stirrings which bespoke of an incipient political consciousness within the various communities, but forecast no direct challenge to colonial rule. To this time, the various ethnic groups within Malaya had remained fragmented and lacked the self-reflexivity and wider communal allegiances to mount unified action. By the late 1930s, the sense of ethnic separatism, in particular the Malay/Chinese dichotomy, had begun to develop its own momentum, encouraged by official British colonialist discourses, but independent of it.[87] Ethnically charged movements of reform, many of which were to oppose colonialism, were to be galvanized and given shape by the experiences of the Japanese occupation.

CONCLUSIONS

The British implemented ideologies of rule developed in the wake of the Great Rebellion of 1857–58; namely, the prestige of the British as colonial rulers, indirect rule, the incorporation of local elites into the formal structures of administration, and Social Darwinist ideologies of "race". The processes of indirect rule not only strengthened the sultan's authority over his subjects, but also introduced new modes of religious control.

The British ideologies of race not only collapsed multiple ethnicities into three bounded races, each with their own ascribed and inherent characteristics, but also established a justification for colonial rule which emphasized the "backwardness" of Malays and the concomitant need for protection from the supposedly superior organizational skills of the thrusting immigrant races. The depiction of Malays as a rather timid race of feudal kampung-dwellers engaged in subsistence agriculture as opposed to the enterprising, innovative and acquisitive Chinese, established a framework for future Sino–Malay suspicion, rivalry and discord.

British narratives of race were reinforced by developments within the broader Chinese and Malay communities. Chinese nationalist and political currents — the nationalist ideologies of Sun Yat Sen and the new political movements — duplicated those of the Chinese metropolis. The 1937 Chinese–Japanese war generated an outpouring of Sino-centric nationalism. Until World War II, Malay political loyalties were in the main localized and focused upon the sultanates. However, Malay intellectuals generated a diversity of largely reactive responses to the challenges of British colonialism, and the concomitant immigration of large numbers of Chinese and Indians. These discourses increasingly drew attention to the "threat" posed by the Chinese and echoed colonial narratives which highlighted Malay traditionalism, backwardness, and feudalism. Although still inchoate and fluid, the Sino–Malay dichotomy, greatly magnified by colonial racial policies and the ethnic "compartmentalization" which characterized the colonial economy, had developed its own momentum.

In the following chapters we will turn our attention to the migration of Indians to Malaya, the society from which they originated, and their struggles to establish a political presence in the country.

Notes

1. David Cannadine, *Ornamentalism: How the British saw their Empire* (London: Penguin, 2001), p. 125.
2. John G. Butcher, *The British in Malaya 1880–1941: The Social History of a European Community in Southeast Asia* (Kuala Lumpur: Oxford University Press, 1979), p. 109; J.M. Gullick, *The Story of Kuala Lumpur 1857–1939* (Singapore: Eastern Universities Press, 1983), p. 125.
3. Butcher, *The British in Malaya*, p. 105.
4. Gullick, *The Story of Kuala Lumpur*, p. 127.
5. Kate Caffrey, *Out in the Midday Sun: Singapore 1941–45* (London: Andre Deutsch, 1974), p. 142.
6. Gullick, *The Story of Kuala Lumpur*, p. 129.
7. Ibid., p. 174.
8. Gordon P. Means, *Political Islam in Southeast Asia* (Boulder, CO: Rienner, 2009), p. 50.

9. Shaharuddin Ma'aruf, *Malay Ideas on Development: From Feudal Lord to Capitalism* (Singapore: Times Books International, 1998), pp. 46–47.

10. Malcolm Caldwell, "The British 'Forward Movement' 1874–1914", in *Malaya: The Making of a Neo-Colony*, edited by Mohamed Amin and Malcolm Caldwell (Nottingham: Spokesman, 1977), p. 26.

11. Brigadier-General Sir Samuel Wilson, Permanent Undersecretary of State for the Colonies, *Report: Visit to Malaya, 1933* (CMD. 4276, Oriental and India Office Collection, London).

12. Cannadine, *Ornamentalism*, p. 64.

13. Collin Abraham, *The Naked Social Order: The Roots of Racial Polarisation in Malaya* (Subang Jaya: Pelanduk, 2004), p. 121.

14. Ibid.

15. Ahmad Fauzi Abdul Hamid, *Islamic Education in Malaysia*, Monograph No. 18 (Singapore: S. Rajaratnam School of International Studies, 2010), p. 48.

16. Ibid.

17. Caldwell, "The British 'Forward Movement' ", p. 26.

18. Ibid.

19. Michael Morgan, "The Rise and Fall of Malayan Trade Unionism 1945–1950", in *Malaya: The Making of a Neo-Colony*, edited by Mohamad Amin and Malcolm Caldwell (Nottingham: Spokesman, 1977), p. 150.

20. Abraham, *The Naked Social Order*, p. 22.

21. John Funston, *Malay Politics in Malaysia: A Study of UMNO and PAS* (Kuala Lumpur: Heinemann Educational Books (Asia), 1980), p. 25.

22. Patrick Keith, *Ousted!* (Singapore: Media Masters, 2005), pp. 138–40.

23. Funston, *Malay Politics*, p. 25.

24. M.C. Ricklefs et al., *A New History of Southeast Asia* (London: Palgrave Macmillan, 2010), p. 215.

25. Ahmad Fauzi, *Islamic Education in Malaysia*, p. 19.

26. Caldwell, "The British 'Forward Movement' ", p. 27.

27. Butcher, *The British in Malaya*, pp. 9, 108.

28. Cheah Boon Kheng, "Race and Ethnic Relations in Colonial Malaya during the 1920s and 1930s", in *Multiethnic Malaysia: Past, Present and Future*, edited by Lim Teck Ghee, Alberto Gomes and Azly Rahman (Petaling Jaya: Strategic Information and Research Development Centre, 2009), p. 35.

29. Charles Hirschmann, "The Making of Race in Colonial Malaya during the 1920s and 1930s", *Sociological Forum* 1, no. 2 (Spring 1986): 337.

30. Alberto Gomes, "Ethnicisation of the Orang Asli", in *Multiethnic Malaysia: Past, Present and Future*, edited by Lim Teck Ghee, Alberto Gomes, and Azly Rahman (Petaling Jaya: Strategic Information and Research Development Centre, 2009), p. 301; Leonard Y. Andaya, *Leaves of the Same Tree: Trade and Ethnicity in the Straits of Melaka* (Honolulu: University of Hawai'i Press), p. 13.

31. Hirschmann, "The Making of Race", p. 337.
32. John R. Clammer, "Ethnic Processes in Urban Melaka", in *Ethnicity and Ethnic Relations in Malaysia*, edited by Raymond L.M. Lee (Northern Illinois University, Center for Southeast Asian Studies, 1986), p. 57.
33. Robert L. Winzeler, "Overseas Chinese Power, Social Organization and Ethnicity in Southeast Asia: An East Coast Malayan Example", in *Ethnicity and Ethnic Relations in Malaysia*, edited by Raymond L.M. Lee (Northern Illinois University, Center for Southeast Asian Studies, 1986), pp. 128–44.
34. Charles Hirschmann, "The Meaning and Measurement of Ethnicity in Malaysia: A Study of Census Classifications", *Journal of Asian Studies* 46, no. 3 (August 1987): 558–59.
35. Gomes, "Ethnicisation of the Orang Asli", p. 301.
36. Hirschmann, "The Meaning and Measurement of Ethnicity in Malaysia", p. 561.
37. Ibid., p. 563.
38. Ibid.
39. Margaret Shennan, *Out in the Midday Sun: The British in Malaya 1880–1960* (London: John Murray, 2004), p. 31.
40. Hirschmann, "The Making of Race", p. 349.
41. Abraham, *The Naked Social Order*, p. 51.
42. *Emigration from India to the Crown Colonies and Protectorates (Report of the Sanderson Committee) 1910* (Parliamentary Paper [HC] 1910 XXVII I, Oriental and India Office Collection, London).
43. J. Victor Morais, *Hussein Onn: A Tryst with Destiny* (Singapore: Times Books International, 1981), p. 152; Sheila Nair, "Colonialism, Nationalism, Ethnicity: Constructing Identity and Difference", in *Multiethnic Malaysia: Past, Present and Future*, edited by Lim Teck Ghee, Alberto Gomes, and Azly Rahman (Petaling Jaya: Strategic Information and Research Centre, 2009), p. 86.
44. George Bilainkin, *Hail Penang! Being a Narrative of Comedies and Tragedies in a Tropical Outpost among Europeans, Chinese, Malays, and Indians* (Penang: Areca Books, 2009), p. 247.
45. Hirschmann, "The Making of Race", p. 346.
46. Henri Fauconnier, "The Soul of Malaya", in *Where Monsoons Meet: The Story of Malaya in the Form of an Anthology*, edited by Donald Moore (London: Harap, 1956), p. 20; Leopold Ainsworth, *The Confessions of a Planter in Malaya: A Chronicle of Life and Adventure in the Jungle* (London: Witherby, 1933), pp. 55–56.
47. Bilainkin, *Hail Penang!*, p. 109; Shennan, *Out in the Midday Sun*, p. 69.
48. Selvakumaran Ramachandran, *Indian Plantation Labour in Malaysia* (Kuala Lumpur: S. Abdul Majeed, 1994), pp. 40–41.
49. Khoo Kay Kim, "The Emergence of Plural Communities in the Malay Peninsula before 1874", in *Multiethnic Malaysia: Past Present and Future*, edited by Lim Teck

Ghee, Alberto Gomes, and Azly Rahman (Petaling Jaya: Strategic Information and Research Development Centre, 2009), p. 21.

50. Michael R. Stenson, *Class, Race and Colonialism in West Malaysia: The Indian Case* (St. Lucia: University of Queensland Press, 1980), p. 29.

51. Frank Swettenham, *British Malaya: An Account of the Origins and Progress of British Influence in Malaya* (London: Allen and Unwin, 1943), p. 146.

52. P. Ramasamy, *Plantation Labour, Unions, Capital and the State in Peninsular Malaysia* (New York: Oxford University Press, 1994), p. 7.

53. Joel S. Kahn, *Other Malays: Nationalism and Cosmopolitanism in the Modern Malay World* (Singapore: Asian Studies Association of Australia in association with Singapore University Press and NIAS Press, 2006), p. 39.

54. Ibid., pp. 31–34; Abu Talib Ahmad, *The Malay Muslims, Islam and the Rising Sun: 1941–1945* (Kuala Lumpur: MBRAS, 2003), p. 17.

55. Anthony Milner, *The Malays* (Chichester: Wiley-Blackwell, 2011), p. 147.

56. John Drabble, "The Politics of Survival: European Reactions in Malaya to Rubber Smallholders in the Interwar Years", in the *The Underside of Malayan History: Pullers, Prostitutes, Plantation Workers*, edited by Peter J. Rimmer and Lisan M. Allen (Singapore: Singapore University Press, 1990), p. 51.

57. Malcolm Caldwell, "War, Boom and Depression" in *Malaya: The Making of a Neo-Colony*, edited by Mohamad Amin and Malcolm Caldwell (Nottingham: Spokesman, 1977), p. 39; Kahn, *Other Malays*, p. 57.

58. Abraham, *The Naked Social Order*, p. 150.

59. Cheah, "Race and Ethnic Relations", p. 43.

60. Gullick, *The Story of Kuala Lumpur*, p. 161; Caldwell, *The British "Forward Movement"*, p. 27.

61. Ricklefs et al., *A New History*, p. 179; Shaharuddin, *Malay Ideas on Development*, p. 57.

62. Ramasamy, *Plantation Labour*, p. 19; Syed Hussein Alatas, *The Myth of the Lazy Native* (London: Cass, 1977), p. 95.

63. Abraham, *The Naked Social Order*, p. 56.

64. Ricklefs et al., *A New History*, p. 120.

65. Francis Loh Kok Wah, *Beyond the Tin Mines: Coolies, Squatters and the New Villages in the Kinta Valley Malaysia c1880–1980* (Singapore: Oxford University Press, 1988), p. 8.

66. Milner, *The Malays*, p. 109

67. Heng Peng Koon, *Chinese Politics in Malaysia: A History of the Malaysian Chinese Association* (Singapore: Oxford University Press, 1988), p. 9.

68. Raj K. Vasil, *Tan Chee Khoon; An Elder Statesman* (Petaling Jaya: Pelanduk, 1987), p. 4.

69. Heng, *Chinese Politics in Malaya*, pp. 12–19.

70. Ricklefs et al., *A New History*, p. 179; R.S. Milne and Diane K. Mauzy, *Politics and Government in Malaysia* (Singapore: Federal, 1978), p. 20.

71. Abraham, *The Naked Social Order*, p. 342.
72. Heng, *Chinese Politics in Malaysia*, p. 11; Wang Gungwu, "Memories of War: World War II in Malaysia", in *War and Memory in Malaysia and Singapore*, edited by Patricia Lim Pui Huen and Diana Wong (Singapore: Institute of Southeast Asian Studies, 2000), p. 15.
73. Abraham, *The Naked Social Order*, p. 376.
74. Ricklefs et al., *A New History*, p. 271.
75. Heng, *Chinese Politics in Malaya*, p. 20.
76. Huang Jianli , "Remembering World War II: Legacies of the War Fought in China" in *Legacies of World War II in South and East Asia*, edited by David Koh Wee Hock (Singapore: Institute of Southeast Asian Studies, 2007), p. 124.
77. Heng, *Chinese Politics in Malaysia*, p. 30.
78. Virginia Thompson, *Post-Mortem on Malaya* (New York: Macmillan, 1943), p. 20.
79. Rehman Rashid, *A Malaysian Journey* (Petaling Jaya: Rehman Rashid, 1993), p. 28.
80. Hirschmann, *The Meaning and Measurement of Ethnicity*, p. 570.
81. Richard Allen, *Malaysia: Prospect and Retrospect* (London: Oxford University Press, 1968), pp. 276–77.
82. Collin Abraham, "Manipulation and Management of Racial and Ethnic Groups in Colonial Malaya: A Case Study in Ideological Domination and Control", in *Ethnicity and Ethnic Relations in Malaysia*, edited by Raymond L.M. Lee (Northern Illinois University: Center for Asian Studies, 1986), pp. 2–3.
83. Aloysius Chin, *The Communist Party of Malaya: The Inside Story* (Kuala Lumpur: Vinpress, 1995), pp. 23–24.
84. Ibid., p. 24.
85. K.J. Ratnam, *Communalism and the Political Process in Malaysia* (Kuala Lumpur and Singapore: University of Malaya Press, 1965), pp. 13–16; Shaharuddin, *Malay Ideas on Development*, p. 91.
86. Kah Senh Loh et al., *The University Socialist Club and the Contest for Malaya: Tangled Strands of Modernity* (Amsterdam: University Press, 2012), p. 52.
87. Milner, *The Malays*, p. 12.

5

SLAVERY AND INDENTURED LABOUR

This chapter will examine European conceptions of the institution of slavery, the crucial role played by slavery in the development of Iberian and North European colonialism, its ultimate abolition in the British Empire, and its replacement by Indian indentured labour. The latter sections will highlight the linkages and similarities between slavery and indentured labour, in particular the all-encompassing regime under which labourers toiled, and the unremitting severity with which it was enforced. It will also demonstrate how class and race were deployed by the plantation industry to simultaneously justify indentured labour and to stigmatize and tyrannize those entrapped within the system.

The late medieval era coincided with an unprecedented expansion of European power and subsequent control of substantial areas of the globe. In the period following the Renaissance, Europeans increasingly sought the produce of the tropics which could not be cultivated in the northern latitudes. During the subsequent mercantile expansion, Europeans secured a commanding role in the purchase, transport, and marketing of tropical goods. The conquest of the New World provided European powers with the opportunity to acquire their own colonies and to develop trading economies based on the supervised production of commodities which were in demand in Europe.¹ Initially this trade revolved about the procurement and sale of spices, but later expanded to include sugar, chocolate, tobacco and cotton. However, the profitability of the new economy depended upon the maintenance of low-price structures. This necessarily required the deployment of a disciplined and easily controlled workforce which was paid low wages or, preferably, none at all.²

The Iberian colonization of the Americas was driven by a voracious appetite for territorial expansion and colonial settlement and was accompanied by a total disregard for the cultures and welfare of subject peoples.³ Enslavement of the indigenous populations having been thwarted by a Papal Bull of 1537 which declared the American Indians "full people",⁴ the Iberians turned to African slaves. Medieval Christians were able to call upon Biblical exegesis to justify the enslavement of black Africans. Thus, while St Paul had sanctioned the principle of slave ownership (in I Corinthians), Noah's cursing of Ham and his descendants to eternal servitude (in Genesis) legitimized the subjection of designated branches of humanity. Biblical scholarship clearly identified Hamitic groups as those who possessed dark skins, while Biblical genealogies appeared to locate Ham and his descendants in the land of Cush (Cush meaning black), in the geographical areas later known as North Africa and the Horn.⁵ This viewpoint thus not only upheld the doctrinal principle underlying slavery, but also stipulated that clearly identifiable groups, bearers of a Biblically ascribed and hereditary inferiority, had been assigned the role of permanent enslavement. The legal structure which supported slavery in medieval Europe was inherited from Roman law.⁶

The European transatlantic trade in African slaves⁷ was initiated by the Portuguese in the mid-fifteenth century and was virtually monopolized by them for the next 150 years.⁸ Throughout the period 1650–1720, Iberian domination of the slave trade was first challenged and then superseded by the emergence of the powerful North European economies, primarily those of the British, French and Dutch. The rising economies of northern Europe had developed around the principles of consumerism, and resulted in the creation of entrepreneurial and professional classes. This new wealth was based upon important innovations in the management of tropical agriculture and trade, and in particular the production of agricultural commodities within a "closed" or "total" plantation environment.⁹

The British colony of Barbados was settled in 1627 with the express intention of cultivating tobacco, but it was sugar, initially planted in 1643, which not only saved the colony financially but also transformed the economy of the West Indies. By the 1660s a string of West Indian islands — St Kitts, Antigua, Nevis, Montserrat, and Jamaica (wrested from Spain in 1655) — had been planted with sugar to meet the requirements of an expanding domestic market.[10] While entire categories of "white" labour — Irish rebels, Scottish captives, beggars and vagrants — were transported to the American colonies and to the West Indies to serve as indentured labourers,[11] from the 1650s onwards the workforce increasingly consisted of black African slaves.[12]

By 1700 the term "plantation" had gained common currency within Britain. A plantation was understood as an overseas settlement in which involuntary labour cultivated tropical crops, and by extension an estate producing such commodities through the mobilization of black slaves.[13] But this rather bland description fails to convey the revolutionary approaches the plantation system introduced to the management and organization of tropical agriculture. The new methods concentrated production by the integration of a range of tasks (cultivation, processing and transportation), as well as the simplification and repetition of processes which had hitherto been regarded as differentiated and hence separate. These innovations resulted in the consolidation of labour on estates and helped streamline management. In addition, the sedulous invigilation and harsh governance of labour maintained an active and alert workforce, thereby intensifying output. The "completion" and "perfection" of the slave plantation in the British Caribbean in the last decade of the seventeenth century introduced a new form of slavery by transforming the plantation into a "total" environment, a self-contained unit with its own subculture, language, ruler and regulations and customs, and existing almost entirely independent of the state. The plantation system greatly increased the profitability of colonial economies.[14] Nevertheless, planters lived in a state of constant wariness and maintained their authority over slaves by the infliction of merciless punishments for the slightest infractions. The 1696 Barbadian Code, which described black slaves as "barbarous, wild, savage natives", placed them beyond the bounds of the laws to which white civil society was subject and prescribed dire penalties for even minor transgressions.[15]

The slave trade continued unabated throughout the eighteenth century, with Britain increasingly assuming a leading role. The severity of plantation life with its incessant brutality resulted in low birth rates and high death rates, so much so that the labour force required continual replenishment.[16]

While in the first decade of the eighteenth century British traders supplied 12,000 of the 31,000 slaves shipped annually by the major trading nations, over the following years British traders annually transported in excess of 23,000 slaves. In the 1790s, the British navy having disposed of French competition, Britain's slave traders were procuring 45,000 black African slaves per annum, and had claimed sixty per cent of the total slave trade.[17] It is estimated that from 1517 to 1840, twenty-two million slaves were shipped from Africa to the Americas.[18] The slave trade not only sustained the West Indian economy,[19] but also transformed Bristol, Glasgow and Liverpool into major ports and thriving cities,[20] and more importantly generated the wealth which funded the Industrial Revolution in Britain.[21]

Movements agitating for the abolition of slavery gained momentum throughout the 1770s.[22] The American War of Independence proved the catalyst which galvanized British public opinion in support of the Abolitionist cause. Following the "inexplicable" British defeat at the hands of colonists, Abolitionists argued that God had punished them not only because of their corruption and their presumptuousness but also because they had made war on fellow Protestants. Moreover, a nation which treated heathens for gain rather than inculcating them in the Christian faith would not be permitted to progress. Given these circumstances, the abolition of slavery could be viewed as a national act of atonement which would serve to redeem the nation.[23] However, Abolition was not intended to disrupt existing racial and social hierarchies, and it was anticipated that once freed, black slaves would remain pliable to the needs of propertied authority, and content with their lot at the very base of the social order.[24] The evangelicals who spearheaded Abolitionism were adamant that moral "improvements" should not disturb the existing balance of society, and within Britain the prominent Abolitionist William Wilberforce, together with the influential Anglican Clapham Sect leadership, strongly supported the maintenance of a low-wage structure for all workers, irrespective of race, and the immediate suppression of any action by workers to protect their wages or their jobs.[25]

The British government outlawed British involvement in the slave trade in May 1807 when it legislated that no British ship was permitted to clear port with a cargo of slaves.[26] However, it was not until 1833 that the House of Commons abolished slavery itself.[27] The Emancipation Act decreed that children under the age of six years would be freed from 1 August 1834, the 120th anniversary of the Hanoverian Succession. All above that age would enter a transitory period of six years, as unpaid apprentices, before attaining freedom.[28] A payment of twenty million pounds to Caribbean planters was voted as compensation for loss of labour.[29] In fact, emancipation was extended to all slaves, numbering 750,000 in the West Indies, on 1 August 1838.[30]

THE INTRODUCTION OF INDENTURE

In her influential study, *Involuntary Labour Since the Abolition of Slavery*, W. Kloosterboer observes that "the abolition of slavery did not mean an end to compulsory labour, other forms having evolved whenever this seems advantageous from an economic point of view". Thus, if voluntary labour, that is, where no external compulsion is exerted, is not available, compulsory labour, that is, labour where the worker cannot withdraw without being liable to punishment, whether in the form of serfdom, debt slavery or contract labour under penal or legislative sanction, will necessarily take its place.[31] The veracity of Kloosterboer's thesis will become obvious with the examination of colonially sponsored Indian labour schemes in Malaya.

In succeeding paragraphs and in the following chapter, I will argue that the indenture of Indian labour in colonial Malaya replaced black African slavery with a system of "virtual slavery" which rested on a punitive framework of legally sanctioned compulsion and which incorporated many of the most brutal aspects of slavery. I shall also argue that while modified to some extent by the different conditions which prevailed in colonial Malaya, the plantation culture in Malaya reproduced the worst aspects of the slave-based plantocracy of the West Indies, namely:

1. A system of legally sanctioned forced labour which involved excessive and disproportionate punishment for all transgressors.
2. A tied plantation system under the absolute control of the planter, which consisted of self-enclosed sub-units, socially isolated and largely insulated from the outside world, governed by its own rules and regulations, and responding to its own cultural norms.
3. A social hierarchy grossly exaggerated and distorted by qualification of race, religion and class.

As we have seen, the European demand for tropical goods, and indeed the profitability of the entire plantation industry, rested upon low production costs which were in turn dependent upon minimal outlays on labour. The sanguine British anticipation that black African slaves would remain on the plantations as "free labour" proved mistaken; most slaves who could leave did so.[32] The ability of newly manumitted slaves to find alternative employment and means of support resulted in an escalation of wages costs in former slave-reliant economies.[33] With the dismantling of the institution of slavery, British and European plantation owners were compelled to look elsewhere for a cheap and easily disciplined workforce. Even before the abolition of slavery, the sugar planters of Mauritius (which had come under British control in 1810), had contemplated the advantages of Indian labour which was perceived as "diligent, docile, obedient, everything that the (African) blacks were not".[34] Indeed, both the Dutch and French Empires had experimented with Indian slavery. Throughout the eighteenth century the Dutch had procured between 26,000 and 28,000 Indian slaves who laboured in various Dutch colonies, including Batavia, Ceylon, Melaka and the Cape.[35] The French had utilized Indian slave labour in both Mauritius and Reunion and between 1770 and 1810 (when Mauritius fell under British control) had imported between 15,000 and 18,000 Indians to work as slave labour upon the sugar plantations.[36] Mauritius planters believed that Indians could be persuaded to work in the sugar plantations for negligible wages and for total costs little greater than those expended on African slaves. With the enforced termination of slavery, planters now pressed for a dependable supply of Indian labour to replace the workforce they had lost.[37]

The British government was quick to respond to the demands of the influential and economically crucial agricultural sector. The East India Company subsequently requested the Law Commission to provide a legislative framework for overseeing and managing Indian emigration. Act V of 1837 laid down a number of conditions attendant upon the recruitment and employment of Indian labour. This act specified that:

1. An intending emigrant had to appear before an officer designated by the Government of India together with an immigration agent who was required to produce a written statement of the terms of contract.
2. The length of the service was fixed at five years, though this could be renewed for a further five years.
3. The emigrant was to be repatriated to the point of departure.
4. Vessels carrying emigrants would be required to meet specified standards, including a guaranteed volume of space for each emigrant

and provision for an adequate diet. Each ship was required to carry a medical man to meet health needs.

The Superintendent of Police was designated responsible for enforcing the provisions of the act. A further legislative measure, ACT XXX11 of 1837, extended the scheme from Calcutta to other points of embarkation.[38]

Within Britain, Lord Glenelg, the Colonial Secretary, authorized the drafting of complementary legislation to regulate the terms under which indentured labourers could be recruited to work in Mauritius. The resultant legislation, Ordinance 6 of 1838, served as a template for the recruitment of Indian indentured labour to work in other locations within the British Empire and in other selected destinations.[39]

The approval of the recruitment of indentured "coolie" labour[40] to meet the needs of the Mauritius sugar industry was followed by a series of similar agreements with other British colonies. Indian workers were induced to take up employment in most parts of the British Empire, including colonies in the Caribbean and Africa, as well as Ceylon, Burma, Malaya, and Fiji. In addition, Britain negotiated agreements with the French and Dutch authorities to supply Indian labour to selected colonies within both Empires. Thus began a mass migration of Indian "coolie" labour in which, between 1834 and 1938, some 30,192,000 Indians would leave their homelands, of whom 24,104,000 would return.[41]

The first Indians to be exploited as indentured labourers were recruited from among the Dhangars of Chota Nagpur. These initial intakes suffered "appalling" mortality rates.[42] Later, recruiting agencies were to seek labour from other and more accessible parts of the subcontinent. These were transhipped from the ports of Calcutta, Madras, and Bombay, each of which was designated as an official point of embarkation.[43]

Initially, the deployment of Indian indentured labour was designed as an interim measure, as a means of meeting the immediate labour shortfall created by the emancipation of slaves, most of whom, as we have seen, vacated the plantations immediately they were liberated. However, the supply of indentured Indian labour proved cheap, convenient, and administratively straightforward, and both colonial authorities and the plantation industry came to view Indian labour as a long-term and reliable replacement for lost slaves; a source of labour which would meet the growing demands of the developing economies of the expanding European empires.[44] Indenture was thus viewed as a system which would prove beneficial to all involved. The Government of India was convinced that indentured labour would provide the poor of India with the opportunity to enter gainful waged employment, at the same time removing an unwanted and cumbersome surplus population from India, while colonial governments would receive a reliable, servile and inexpensive workforce.[45]

It is important to note that Ordinance 6 was enacted a mere four years after the abolition of slavery and the slave ideal remained a fixed point of reference in both the planters' and the colonial officials' collective outlook. Indeed, this legislation was modelled upon and contained the residual elements of laws pertaining to slavery.[46] Indentured labourers thus toiled within a system which had been devised as an alternative to slavery and which perpetuated many of its worst abuses. The "total" environment of the slave plantation was reproduced, enclosing and subjugating the Indian workforce. Their lives were minutely ordered by the same crushing regime which had oppressed African slaves, with its intense and integrated task load; its stringent and unremitting supervision; the inflexibility of contractual arrangements; immediate and severe punishments for actual and suspected infractions, including those which might reasonably be viewed as minor; the absence of adequate legal or workplace protection; and official indifference to the physical, cultural, or social welfare of the workforce.[47]

Perhaps the most pernicious aspect of indenture was the rigidity of the contractual agreement signed by the labourer, and the willingness of planters, supported by the full weight of colonial law, to enforce it. The contract agreement, usually committing the labourer to work for five years (but sometimes as long as eight or even ten years), was signed by the indentured worker prior to departure from India. The contract was totally binding and the labourer had no means to terminate it or even vary the conditions under which he/she lived and worked. Any actual (or even alleged) breach of contract rendered the labourer liable to prosecution (often resulting in an extension of the term of indenture). Lydia Potts tersely notes that "to all intents and purposes such contracts meant enslavement."[48]

Such an arrangement suited the plantation industry whose outlook towards labour had been habituated by nearly two centuries of black slavery. In 1909, reporting to the Parliamentary Committee established to investigate the operations of indentured labour schemes, C.P. David, a Member of the Trinidad Legislative Council, observed that, the value to the planter, of Indian labour, consists rather in the state of indenture than anything else — what he wants is an indentured labourer — not so much a labourer as an indentured labourer ... someone who is bound to him for five years, and liable to be committed to prison for disobeying orders.[49]

Scholars have generally agreed that the subjugation and exploitation of others is frequently justified on the grounds of their intrinsic inferiority, the "slavish nature" of those condemned to servitude. Thus, for example, during the early Mediterranean slave trade, which included fair skinned Slavs and Celts, "Rufus" (red head) became a common name for slaves, and red hair was a sign of inherent slavishness.[50] We have noted that the supposed inferiority of black skin, the signifier of a hereditary Biblical curse, justified the enslavement of black Africans. As had been the case with African slaves, the position of Indian workers was worsened by the racial and religious contempt of their employers and the colonial authorities. Indian labourers were denigrated as "unclean and ignorant beings ... semi barbarous heathens who were naturally prone to crime".[51] Thus, those who were brutalized were perceived as nothing more than superstitious idol worshippers, wretched menials, drawn from the very societal base of an inferior racial species, abject creatures who could be motivated only by the threat or enforcement of savage discipline, and thus were fully deserving of the harsh treatment they received.[52]

CONCLUSIONS

Indentured Indian labour inherited both its structure and the exploitative conditions of employment from the long centuries of black African slavery which preceded it. Slavery was not only instrumental in the creation of an enormously lucrative tropical plantation economy, but also comprised the foundation upon which the emerging metropolitan economies of Iberia and Northern Europe were constructed.

British slave plantations in the Americas, and in particular those in the West Indies, streamlined and consolidated methods of agricultural production. The plantation economy created a series of socially isolated and total environments, each of which developed its own distinct subculture, including language, regulations, and customs. Those who toiled in such localities were subject to unremitting invigilation coupled with immediate and disproportionate punishment for the most minor breaches of discipline.

The modes of transport to the Americas and the subsequent harsh work regime led to a high mortality among the slave population.

With the abolition of black slavery, European employers sought an alternative low-waged workforce. Indians were viewed as an ideal replacement. Many of the key features of the plantation environment were to remain unchanged throughout the period of indentured Indian labour. The legislation which governed Indian recruitment and terms of employment was modelled upon and contained many of the key elements which had regulated slavery. Ordinance 6 of 1838 reproduced the regime of compulsion and punishment which had been the dominant feature of the slave plantations.

Chapter 6 will examine the recruitment of Indian indentured labour to Malaya and the conditions under which the workforce was employed.

Notes

1. Hugh Tinker, *A New System of Slavery: The Export of Indian Labour Overseas 1830–1920* (London: Oxford University Press, 1974), p. 20.
2. Ibid., pp. 21–22.
3. Robin Blackburn, *The Making of New World Slavery: From the Baroque to the Modern 1497–1800* (London: Verso, 1997), pp. 45, 63, 83.
4. Lydia Potts (trans. Terry Bond), *The World Labour Market: A History of Migration* (London: Zed Books, 1990), p. 16.
5. Blackburn, *The Making of New World Slavery*, p. 65; Rajiv Malhotra and Aravindan Neelakandan, *Breaking India: Western Interventions in Dravidian and Dalit Faultlines* (New Delhi: Amaryllis, 2011), pp. 39–40.
6. Blackburn, *The Making of New World Slavery*, p. 76.
7. Robin Blackburn points out that Muslims were also permitted to buy and sell slaves provided that those who were thus bonded were infidels or had been at the time of their enslavement. The Muslim world also employed the curse of Noah as a justification for black slavery (Blackburn, *The Making of New World Slavery*, pp. 79–82).
8. Blackburn, *The Making of New World Slavery*, p. 97.
9. Ibid., p. 187.
10. James, *The Rise and Fall of the British Empire* (London: Abacus, 1998), p. 17.
11. Ibid., pp. 10, 20.
12. Ibid., p. 20.
13. Blackburn, *The Making of New World Slavery*, p. 309.
14. Ibid.
15. James, *The Rise and Fall*, p. 41.

16. Ibid., p. 23.
17. Linda Colley, *Britons: Forging the Nation 1707–1837* (New Haven: Yale University Press, 1992), p. 352.
18. Malhotra and Aravindan, *Breaking India*, p. 41.
19. James, *The Rise and Fall of the British Empire*, p. 21.
20. Colley, *Britons*, p. 352.
21. Blackburn, *The Making of New World Slavery*, p. 502.
22. James, *The Rise and Fall of the British Empire*, p. 185.
23. Colley, *Britons*, pp. 353–54.
24. David Cannadine, *Ornamentalism: How the British Saw Their Empire* (London: Penguin, 2001), p. 14.
25. Jerry White, *London in the Nineteenth Century* (London: Cape, 2007), p. 430.
26. Tinker, *A New System of Slavery*, p. 1.
27. James, *The Rise and Fall of the British Empire*, p. 186.
28. Colley, *Britons*, p. 356.
29. Tinker, *A New System of Slavery*, p. 1.
30. Colley, *Britons*, p. 356.
31. W. Kloosterboer, *Involuntary Labour Since the Abolition of Slavery* (Leiden: Brill, 1960), pp. 1–2.
32. Tinker, *A New System of Slavery*, p. 17.
33. M.D. North-Coombs, "From Slavery to Indenture: Forced Labour in the Political Economy of Mauritius 1824–1867", in *Indentured Labour in the British Empire 1834–1920*, edited by Kay Saunders (London: Croom Helm, 1984), p. 84.
34. Hugh Tinker, "Into Servitude: Indian Labour in the Sugar Industry", in *International Labour Migration: Historical Perspectives*, edited by Shula Marks and Peter Richardson (London: Maurice Temple Smith, 1984), p. 78.
35. Marina Carter, "Indians and the Colonial Diaspora", in *Rising India and Indian Communities in East Asia*, edited by K. Kesavapany, A. Mani and P. Ramasamy (Singapore: Institute of Southeast Asian Studies, 2008), p. 13.
36. Ibid.
37. Tinker, *A New System of Slavery*, p. 18.
38. Ibid., p. 64.
39. Ibid., p. 17.
40. Hugh Tinker claims that the term "coolie" originated in the late eighteenth century, and was a pejorative designation which "ceased to have any connection with any group or race: it was used to describe those at the lowest level of the industrial labour market." (Tinker, *A New System of Slavery*, pp. 42-43).
41. Potts, *The World Labour Market*, p. 70.
42. Tinker, *A New System of Slavery*, p. 45.
43. Ibid.

44. Shula Marks and Peter Richardson, "Introduction" in *International Labour Migration" Historical Perspectives*, edited by Shula Marks and Peter Richardson (London: Maurice Temple Smith, 1984), p. 9. Often the link between slavery and indentured labour was made explicit by colonial observers. Thus, for example, writing in 1884, the British Consul in Paramaribo remarked that "The Surinam planters have found in the meek Hindu a ready substitution for the negro slave he lost." (Brij Maharaj, "Introduction: 'A New Form of Slavery' — Indentured Diaspora", in *Tracing an Indian Diaspora: Contexts, Memories, Representations*, edited by Parvati Raghuram, Ajaya Kumar Sahoo, Brij Maharaj and Dave Sangha [New Delhi: Sage, 2008, p. 23]).

45. Tinker, *Into Servitude*, p. 79.

46. Ibid.

47. Klosterboer, *Involuntary Labour*, p. 42.

48. Potts, *The World Labour Market*, p. 85.

49. Marianne D. Ramesar, "Indentured Labour in Trinidad 1880–1917", in *Indentured Labour in the British Empire 1834–1920*, edited by Kay Saunders (London: Croom Helm, 1984), p. 67.

50. Thomas R. Trautmann, *Aryans and British India* (Berkeley: University of California Press, 1997), p. 225.

51. North-Coombs, *From Slavery to Indenture*, p. 80.

52. Jan Breman, *Taming the Coolie Beast: Plantation, Society and the Colonial Order in Southeast Asia* (Delhi: Oxford University Press, 1989), p. 174.

6

INDIAN INDENTURED LABOUR IN MALAYA

We have already noted that British control over the Straits Settlements and the FMS was followed by economic exploitation of its new possessions. The Malayan colonies were not only viewed as suppliers of raw materials and potential producers of tropical commodities which could be profitably retailed on the world market, but also as consumers of British-manufactured goods. The colonial authorities encouraged commercial plantation agriculture over every other form of enterprise. Early commercial agriculture concentrated upon the production of spices and pepper, but from the 1820s onwards, exports of both commodities were increasingly eclipsed by sugar. Sugar plantations, with their ceaseless demands for labour, were largely concentrated in Penang and Province Wellesley.[1] Other plantations diversified into the cultivation of tapioca and coconuts. Throughout the 1870s, coffee and gambier estates were developed in Perak, Selangor and Negeri Sembilan. After the turn of the century, rubber production dominated the Malayan plantation industry. Later, the plantation economy widened to include the production of palm oil, tea and pineapple.[2]

We also observed that British penetration of Malaya was supported by an ambitious programme of infrastructure development designed to promote and enhance economic activity. Successive colonial administrations embarked on a series of far-ranging projects which included capital works, the construction of ports, roads and railways, reticulated water supplies (at least to major towns and cities), and (later) the provision of an electricity grid and a telecommunications network.[3]

The development of a viable colonial economy was dependent on ready access to a pool of cheap, pliable, and easily managed labour. As observed in Chapter 4, the Malays were not interested in hiring themselves for plantation or infrastructure labour and, in fact, the British made repeated attempts to insulate the Malays from the emerging colonial economy. Having thus ruled out indigenous labour, and after early and unsuccessful experiments with African slave labour,[4] the British broadened their search to tap Chinese, Indian and Javanese coolie sources.[5]

While the system of indentured labour furnished the majority of the Indian workforce in Malaya between 1844 and 1910, some of the earliest Indian labour was supplied by convicts. Between 1790 and 1860 approximately 80,000 Indian convicts were dispatched to various colonial destinations, not only to the Straits Settlements but also to Burma and Mauritius.[6] Transportation to Penang began in 1790.[7] By 1800, 130 Indian convicts were working in Penang, with the number increasing to 722 by 1805.[8] The paucity of relevant records means that the exact number of those transported is impossible to gauge, but it appears that about 200 convicts arrived in the Straits Settlements each year and that a total of 15,000 convicts were shipped from India. The convicts consisted of a cross section of Indian society, and included members of most castes, including Brahmans. While the majority of transportees were criminals, sentenced for such offences as *dacoity* (organized banditry), thuggee, robbery, murder and "professional poisoning", a minority were political prisoners. The latter included Sikhs who had fought against the British in an attempt to restore the Sikh Empire, and after 1857, ex-Mutineers.[9] Although some women convicts were sent to the Straits Settlements, the convict population was overwhelmingly male.[10] The transportees were dispatched on ships known as *jatha junaza* ("living tombs") an appellation which may have referred either to the high death rates experienced among convicts during the passage to Malaya or to the horror of crossing the dark seas (*kale pani*) to an unknown land.[11] Transportation ceased in 1860 when public resistance in the Straits Settlements forced its abandonment. The last remaining convicts serving out their sentences in the Settlements were finally removed to the Andaman Islands in 1873.[12]

Indian labour immigration to the Straits Settlements began almost immediately following the establishment of the British port of Penang. In 1787 Captain Francis Light requested that the Governor-General dispatch one hundred coolies to the island, as the price of labour was "enormous".[13] Seven years later, Light indicated that the Tamil population stood at 1,000.[14]

It is clear that there were intakes of Indian coolie labour before 1823, that is, some years prior to the formal inauguration of indenture in the British Parliamentary legislation of 1836. These labourers were employed on European-owned and -managed tapioca, coconut and sugar estates in Penang and Province Wellesley. Indian labour was certainly sought for sugar production; the cultivation of sugar required a substantial and disciplined workforce which could only be guaranteed by the procurement of long-term contractual labour.[15] In 1844, the Indian population of Province Wellesley numbered approximately 1,805.[16] While statistical data covering the earliest years of Indian indentured labour are both sketchy and unreliable, after 1844, far more detailed records are available. In his seminal study, *Indians in Malaya: Some Aspects of their Immigration and Settlement 1786–1957*, Kernial Singh Sandhu estimates that a total of 250,000 indentured labourers were recruited to work in Malaya between 1844 and 1910.[17]

Apart from a few hundred labourers from Bengal, the majority of the labour force was of South Indian origin. The colonial preference for South Indian labour over that from other parts of the subcontinent was informed by an official perspective which viewed the "Madrassi" as an inferior, somewhat contemptible specimen, timid and tractable, less expensive to keep and far more easily led than his fellow countrymen.[18] The Parliamentary Paper, *Emigration from India to the Crown Colonies and Protectorates* (henceforth referred to as the Sanderson Report), published in 1910 in the very twilight of indenture within Malaya, reflected this viewpoint with the contention that "the Indian indentured labourer ... is, if properly treated, perfectly docile and easily managed".[19] Indeed, this representation of the South Indian as an inherently lesser species of humanity, subservient and willingly dominated, was to colour the British outlook throughout the entire colonial era. This ideology enabled the colonial administration and employers as a group to conveniently dismiss examples of Indian assertion and organization as uncharacteristic and temporary aberrations, the result of extraneous agitation which had implanted seeds of discontent among an impressionable and easily led labour force.[20]

Over time, South Indian labour came to be viewed as a stabilizing influence within the overall structure of the Malayan colonial economy. The "cringingly servile" Tamil was portrayed both as an alternative and as a counterweight to the Chinese worker whose industriousness and resourcefulness were potentially undermined by his perceived troublesome qualities, namely ambition, assertiveness and deviousness.[21] Speaking in 1884, Sir Frederick Weld, Governor of the Straits Settlements, was merely echoing a long-held colonial shibboleth when he advocated the immigration of "peaceful and easily governed Indians" to offset the possible dangers posed by "the preponderance of any one eastern nationality" (i.e., the Chinese).[22]

In the main, Indian indentured labourers consisted of adult males aged between fifteen and forty-five.[23] The largest labour flows were drawn from the districts of Tanjore, Trichinopoly and Madras, with lesser flows originating from Salem and Coimbatore.[24] While a majority of those who served indentures were agricultural labourers, more than one-third were drawn from the ranks of weavers, oil millers and related occupations. Women and children comprised a small percentage of total immigration. Rarely did they constitute more than twenty per cent and ten per cent, respectively, of annual intakes, frequently significantly less.[25] Although the colonial authorities attempted to redress this imbalance with the passage of Act XIII of 1864 which stipulated that the female proportion of indentured migration was to be fixed at twenty-five per cent of the overall intake, in practice this made little difference to the general composition of the total labour force, and the target figure was seldom achieved.[26] Most female indentured labourers were abandoned wives or widows, many of whom were found by recruiters in a "pitiable state".[27]

The migration which provided Malaya and much of the British Empire with Indian labour was overwhelmingly the result of push rather than pull factors and was most often resorted to by desperate people who were living under intolerable conditions. In the following paragraphs we will turn our attention to the changing circumstances within South India which generated this outflow.

THE SOUTH INDIAN ECONOMY AND INDENTURED LABOUR

Throughout the nineteenth century, major structural changes in the Indian economy produced a large underclass which was perennially subject to impoverishment and the grim threat of destitution. Along with other British tropical colonies, India was in the process of being forcibly enmeshed within a London centred "global" economy, a liberal capitalist regime governed by "the theological application of the sacred principles of Smith, Bentham and Mill".[28] In the early nineteenth century, in its incessant search for revenue, the East India Company (EIC) sought to achieve control over the resources controlled by the *palaiyakkarars* ("little kings") of South India. The Permanent Settlement of 1803–5 granted titles over land to the *palaiyakkarars* and their kin, thus converting them into a class of *zamindars* (or landlords), who were subject to the powers of the colonial state. Land control was conditional on the payment of assessed revenue to the state. The result was a major increase in the power of the *zamindars,* who by the end of the nineteenth century had acquired approximately forty per cent of the cultivated land within the Madras Presidency.[29]

The early reforms were followed during the 1820s and 1830s by the *ryotwari* settlement which, in effect, granted tenures of land to better-off peasants at the expense of smaller landholders, tenants and other agricultural labourers. The British aimed to promote titled landholders into a thriving class of commercial farmers who would make a substantial contribution to EIC coffers.[30] Acting in accordance with what the Company perceived as the established caste hierarchy ordered by the "pure" *varna* (caste) system, the EIC appointed Brahmans and Vaisyas as revenue collectors and assessors. In collaboration with EIC officials, these functionaries re-ordered customary land arrangements, granting inalienable land tenure to "higher" castes. The longstanding traditional loose joint sinecures of land ownership were abolished, consolidating the power of well-off peasants at the expense of the small *mirasdas* (traditional owners of land in the village community) and the *payakars* and *vilkudis* (traditional tenant cultivators with hereditary rights of occupancy).[31]

However, as Mytheli Sreenivas has demonstrated, these reforms also fundamentally struck at the pattern of relationships which had traditionally existed within household and kin networks. South Indian households had customarily provided for non-kin dependents who worked and lived with families. State policies, structured upon revenue generation, now strictly defined a household in terms of blood-kin ties; that is, as a biological family which occupied a fixed residence. The ritual bonds which had linked family and dependents were replaced with legally enforceable covenants which were wholly defined in terms of economic ties and contractual obligations.[32]

But these reforms also had implications for extended kin relationships. Because landholders could obtain greater returns from leasing land to lower-class cultivators than from land managed by kinsmen, many large landowners sought to force their kin from uneconomic land tenures, thus rupturing the system of wider kin-based landholdings which had hitherto obtained throughout much of India.[33]

The social dislocation wrought by reform of Indian landholdings in accordance with the principles of English law was further aggravated by additional measures which fell heavily upon agricultural labourers, sharecroppers and poorer peasants. These included the transfer of common lands from village communities to the state under whose jurisdiction they were transformed into taxable private property or state monopolies; the removal of forests from communal control and their subsequent separation from the agrarian village economy; and the abolition of common water rights, and their enshrinement, along with land titles, as private property. The latter measure was coupled with the wanton neglect and in many cases outright abandonment of the great precolonial irrigation works which had provided assured supplies of water to all landholders.[34]

The revenue-driven system of land tenure introduced by the EIC and continually added to by succeeding administrations placed a cumbersome and ever-increasing burden upon Indian agrarian society. By the 1890s, this had reduced most agricultural labourers and peasant smallholders to insurmountable poverty. Most were chronically indebted to financiers and rich landowners, many accruing debts so substantial as to blight the lives of succeeding generations.[35]

However, the most serious impact of these rural reforms was the almost total loss of food security among poorer sections of South Indian agrarian society. Traditionally, wages of "attached" labour were paid in kind and were regulated by long-established custom.[36] In the years following the Great Rebellion, the traditional system of household and grain reserves which had operated in accordance with complex networks of patrimonial operations were increasingly displaced by merchant inventories and the cash nexus. Traditionally, the Indian rural poor had recourse to three safeguards in times of famine and economic distress, namely (1) domestic hoards of grains, (2) family ornaments, and (3) credit with the village moneylender who was also the grain dealer. The introduction of a cash economy, and especially the commodification of grain, served to destroy the village-level exchanges and reciprocities which had hitherto accommodated the disadvantaged during periods of crisis, leaving the poor without defence in times of need.[37] In general, the agricultural labourer earned sufficient to provide for himself and his family. However, any savings that he might glean in years of good harvests would be lost in lean years. From 1875 onwards the wages of the poor tended to decline in real terms. This not only reduced the purchasing power, but also the concomitant ability to make provision for unforseen emergencies.[38] In 1893 the precipitous decline in the incomes of the rural poor was greatly exacerbated by the imposition upon India of the International Gold Standard which resulted in the depreciation and thus the vitiation of the purchasing power of the rupee.[39] The deteriorating standing of poorer sections of agrarian South India was aggravated by rapid population growth. Between 1802 and 1901, the population of the Madras Presidency increased by 300 per cent, in some districts forcing pressure on land and increasing prices beyond the reach of peasants.[40]

The full impact of these changes was more starkly revealed during the severe famines which intermittently wracked the Madras Presidency throughout the last forty years of the nineteenth century. While there were no instances of severe or widespread famine throughout the period 1834–65, intense and far-reaching famines occurred in 1865–66, 1876–78 (this was the worst famine of the nineteenth century and covered the entire Madras Presidency claiming five million lives), 1896–97, and 1898–1900. The latter had an especially punitive impact on Telegu districts, and indeed for the first time in recorded memory, the Godavari River ran dry.[41] The new economy was based upon the retail and export of grain, which meant that throughout famines, the price of foodstuffs, untrammelled by any form of control, floated beyond the reach of those marginalized by structural reforms.[42] Indeed, eighty per cent of all deaths due to famine throughout this period occurred within the poorest twenty per cent of the population.[43] The immense suffering which accompanied the famines was greatly magnified by the Government of India's unflinching rejection of any suggestion of controls either on the price or movement of grains. Thus, in 1877–78, at the very peak of the famine in South India, Indian grain merchants exported 6.4 million hundred weight (or approximately 310,000 tonnes) of wheat to Europe.[44] This was coupled with a callous refusal to implement appropriate relief measures to assist the impoverished lest it create a culture of dependence among those groups, that is, lower castes and the landless, who were already suspected of habitual laziness and even thievery.[45] The misery of the poor was magnified by the insistence of courts that debt collection be rigidly enforced throughout famines.[46]

The famines served to reinforce the structural changes to agriculture and land tenure enacted by the colonial regime, thus worsening the plight of the poor. Caste divisions became more pronounced, peasant indebtedness became more entrenched, alienation of land increased sharply, and merchants and moneylenders acquired a greater share of available land.[47] The rural indigent, traumatized by the fear of starvation and bludgeoned by serious debt, and shorn of their former independence and traditional rights, had now been relegated to the status of an acquiescent and malleable underclass.[48]

It was the fear or experience of famine and prolonged privation which provoked the migration of the majority of indentured labourers.[49] There was a strong correlation between poor harvests and recruitment peaks, especially among depressed and lower castes left exposed to the perils of the new economy.[50] Indeed, the major flows of coolie labour consisted of landless agricultural labourers originating from the most famine-afflicted and overpopulated Tamil districts, but also included Telegu and Malayalee migrants.[51] It has also been suggested that the periods of famine were also exploited by the British authorities to encourage the major outflows of coolie labour.[52] Certainly, the overtly Malthusian approach towards the provision of famine relief and the wilful disregard of the welfare of indigent Indians proved a major inducement to migration.[53]

THE RECRUITMENT OF INDENTURED LABOUR

Although some indentured labourers were recruited after reading advertisements which spoke of the good and indeed "comfortable" conditions they would experience in Malaya,[54] the majority were recruited by means of personal approach. These were usually through the agency of a tout known as an *arkatia* (or *arkati*, in Tamil *aal kati;* literally one who identifies people) who made it his business to seek out those in financial or social difficulty. He generally regaled likely candidates with highly flavoured accounts of life in Malaya, which coruscated with the glowing prospects the subject might reasonably anticipate should he/she choose to emigrate. These stories invariably inflated the wages the labourer could expect to receive and the favourable circumstances under which he/she could expect to work. The *arkatias* often obtained an easy psychological dominance over potential recruits — who, as we have noted, were often the hopeless and disoriented victims of socio-economic dislocation and famine — by seeming to work on their behalf and to take a keen interest in their welfare. To those who were destitute, indenture could easily be portrayed as a pathway to prosperity. As one emigration officer remarked, "In most cases the recruiter finds the coolie absolutely on the brink of starvation and he takes him in and feeds him and explains to him the terms of service ... under such conditions our terms of service are absolute wealth."[55] However, if necessary, *arkatias* were often prepared to employ underhand measures, including fraud, deception, and even violence to secure the acquiescence of those they had targeted. The *arkatia* was legally able to recruit any individual who had attained the age of ten years, and children were especially susceptible to his advances.[56] The *arkatia's* main recruiting grounds were markets, caravanserais, railway stations, bazaars and temples.[57] He would also frequent noted pilgrimage sites in the hope of ensnaring travellers who had exhausted their funds.[58]

Most recruits had little inkling of the new way of life they were about to enter. The majority were simple folk without much experience of the world beyond their village boundaries. Many were recruited in a state of demoralization, having been cast adrift by the asperities of the new economy imposed on South India, and having been exposed to the grinding hunger of famine. Few had even a rudimentary understanding of the alien environment to which they were now committed, or the rigid terms of service which would govern every aspect of their lives.[59] Indeed, the District Magistrate of Ghazipur was to note in 1871:

> The *arkatias* entice the villagers with a wonderful account of the place for which emigrants are wanted, and bring their victims long distances ... on arrival at the sub-depot, the intending migrants are told the exact facts of their prospects, and on hearing them decline to proceed ... the wretched coolie may be a hundred miles from his home, and finding that he has the option of returning penniless ... [or] ... emigrating, chooses the latter alternative; but it is not voluntary emigration.[60]

This ignorance of the basic terms and structure of bonded labour remained unchanged through the entire period of indenture. In 1909, a year prior to the dismantling of indenture within Malaya, the Sanderson Committee observed that "it seems doubtful whether the majority of immigrants leaving India fully realize the conditions of the new life before them or start with the deliberate intention of making for themselves a home in a new country".[61]

Having registered recruits with local District Magistrates, the *arkatias* now arranged for transport to depots located in the major disembarkation ports (for emigrating Indians, these ports were Madras and Nagapattinam). The journey from the interior to the port was often made by foot. These depots were little more than primitive transit camps, encircled by high walls which prevented the escape of disillusioned or opportunist labourers, and which were designed to hold up to two shiploads of coolies for up to three weeks while they waited for embarkation. The conditions at the depot were very basic, devoid of separate facilities for men and women, and without adequate provision for washing and cooking.[62] The depot, and the sea voyage which followed, often exposed coolies to a range of diseases, including cholera, typhoid and dysentery.[63]

In theory, all coolies were required to pass a medical examination prior to embarkation, but this was often perfunctory. As Tinker remarks, "Almost everything combined to ensure that a coolie who was not suffering from an obvious malfunction or displaying a disease would pass the doctor."[64] Coolies emaciated and chronically ill-nourished upon recruitment were "fattened up" immediately prior to their examination, while the "pitiable" women were often re-clothed and generally rendered more presentable before inspection.[65] Medical examination of women was cursory at the best of times; the authorities did not wish to apply too stringently any measure which might discourage female emigration. In any case, medical personnel were only required to certify that the coolie was sufficiently fit to undertake the sea voyage; they were not charged with assessing his/her suitability for plantation labour. Thus, many coolies who were ill-prepared for the hardships of indenture bypassed any form of rigorous medical scrutiny.[66] Indeed, evidence presented before the Sanderson Committee revealed that many recruits did not possess the physical fitness necessary to discharge the duties expected of them, while a considerable number of those drawn from famine districts did not survive long after their arrival in Malaya.[67]

Following the medical examination, labourers were issued with standard clothing which bore little resemblance to the traditional village dress to which they had been accustomed.[68] The ship voyage itself stripped the coolie of the trappings of his/her background. Indeed, the prospect of a sea voyage struck terror into many coolies. He/she was surrounded by strangers; fellow emigrants who hailed from different districts and whose caste mannerisms were usually vastly different from his/her own, and with whom he/she had little in common. The fear of loss of caste occasioned by the crossing of the *kale pani* (black waters) was widespread among Hindus, and some refused food throughout the entire voyage in an attempt to retain caste.[69] Facilities aboard the ship were spartan, and crews — frequently European — were at best indifferent, and at worst actively hostile towards their human cargoes. The coolie often suffered from extremes of homesickness and depression which were, in many cases, compounded by seasickness. All voyages were accompanied by the omnipresent threat of epidemics, usually cholera. Although after the first voyages the Indian authorities insisted that a surgeon be appointed to each ship to uphold basic standards of medical welfare, these were seldom met.[70] Many recruits arrived in Malaya debilitated by the voyage and in particular by the unaccustomed food provided on the ship.[71] However, the worst aspect of the voyage appears to have been the abject realization that the coolie had henceforth lost the identity and ascribed status he/she had enjoyed as a member of a village community.[72]

Upon arrival in Malaya, each labourer was bonded to his/her employer. Most recruits had little comprehension of the indenture agreement they were required to sign, or the harshness of the contractual obligations which they would be required to fulfil. They had no knowledge of the legislative ordinance which authorized the signing of the contract of indenture, which was written in English and covered twenty-four pages. No Tamil translation was made available.[73] But in any case, the overwhelming majority of coolies were illiterate, and even the literate among their number had limited familiarity with English. The agreements which they signed, or more often than not endorsed with a thumbprint, represented an act of trust.[74] Following their arrival, recruits were detained until they had signed the contract. The original was then held by the planter.[75]

The labourer was then assigned to a "ganger" (usually known as a *tindal* or *mondal*), representing the planter. *Tindals* (drivers) were employed as a cushioning layer between management and the labour force and were often known for their petty corruption and their readiness to abuse their powers.[76]

Until 1908 — a mere two years prior to the termination of indenture — the emigrant was required to repay the cost of the passage from India, which was generally between four to five pounds (although in practice he/she was often charged more), together with any other advances he/she had incurred, plus whatever dues the *tindal* could extract. The coolie thus commenced his/her working life deeply indebted to his/her employer. This financial obligation, often augmented by the cumulative addition of other forms of expenditure, was frequently, albeit subtly, encouraged by the employer. Because the labourer could not be released from his indenture until he/she had discharged all monies owing to the employer, debt could be used as a medium to extend the period of service.[77]

Theoretically, the system of indenture was devised as one of mutual reciprocity between employer and labourer. The coolies signed a contract which stated that in return for a designated volume of labour over a stipulated period of time, employers would guarantee to provide the labourer with regular work at reasonable wages, as well as housing and free medical attention.[78] In practice, indenture worked almost exclusively to the benefit of employers. The conditions upon estates were unremittingly harsh and were enforced with the total support of the colonial and administrative apparatus. Penal sanctions contained within the terms of the indenture agreement deprived the labourer of any personal freedom for the entire life of the contract.[79] Indentured workers faced criminal (rather than civil) liability for even minor breaches of contract — for such "crimes" as "deception", negligence, carelessness, or even impertinence.[80] Failure to discharge a full day's labour (often expressed in terms of completion of a series of set tasks rather than hours to be worked) could result in loss of pay or extension of the period of indenture. Planters had many ways of prolonging indenture — by invoking penalties for sickness and absence, by the application of "joint and several" contracts which held all members of a gang responsible for the misdemeanours or failings of any member of that gang, and by the imposition of collective penalties in the case of absconders.[81] The full rigour of the law was applied against "offending" coolie labour. European magistrates could be expected to side with employers and inevitably found against the claims of indentured labourers.[82] Indeed, a labourer who left the estate to lodge a complaint with a protector or a magistrate might instead find himself charged with unlawful absenteeism.[83] The terms of indenture were so crushing as to lead one planter, a commentator who could scarcely be considered sympathetic to Indian labourers, to describe the plantation labour force as "to all intents and purposes comprised of slaves conveniently camouflaged under the 'officially approved' sounding title of indentured labour".[84]

As we have noted, the general racial contempt European planters felt for Indians as people drawn from a "lower" racial stock, and a "backward" civilization, was magnified by issues of class. Indian labourers were additionally depreciated as the "dregs of their country: low born, even criminal".[85] Their standing as the despicable rejects of a primitive racial grouping could be used to condone the daily regime of casual violence and relentless discipline which often characterized the plantation environment. Punishment for actual or even suspected infractions was severe and frequently instantaneous, and often consisted of whipping or flogging.[86] The "confessions" of one planter make it clear that even driving a car into the midst of workers was a justifiable reprisal again "scum ... [who had dared] ... to resent my actions".[87] One of the most common manifestations of European contempt for their Tamil labour was the widespread practice of exercising seigneurial control over indentured women.[88] However, this was justified on the grounds that all Tamil women who had sunk so low as to consent to the terms of indenture were supposedly of irredeemable character and thus of habitually lax morality.[89]

The conditions under which coolies lived were substandard and manifestly inadequate. Labourers were lodged in barrack-like structures known as "lines", so-called because they consisted of extended rows of housing divided into small compartments. Coolie lines were often little more than overcrowded and poorly ventilated "squalid hovels" of mud and attap. Up to ten coolies, and sometimes more, might be squeezed together within each cubicle. Under these conditions, the personal space allocated to each labourer was extremely limited.[90] The labourers were housed indiscriminately without any regard for pre-existing loyalties of caste or regional origin. Basic sanitation amenities were neglected, thus contributing to the outbreak of disease. Although planters were required to make provision for the medical care of the indentured labour force under their charge, in most cases this was either inadequate or non-existent.[91]

The substandard living conditions contributed to high mortality rates among the indentured workforce. As late as 1905, the average death rate on all estates was 11.6 per cent,[92] though some estates registered much greater figures.[93] Many labourers arrived in Malaya in poor physical condition, the result of near starvation and poverty in India prior to embarkation. This was compounded by the psychological traumas of removal from a known environment, the strains of a sea voyage, and arrival in an alien setting which lacked the familiar reference points of caste, custom and kinship. Some labourers found it quite impossible to adapt to the new circumstances in which they now found themselves; chronic depression compounded by a sense of loss and betrayal vitiated their ability to adapt to their new surroundings.[94] Indeed, the Sanderson Report recorded cases where labourers died of "homesickness", especially in workplaces where they were denied contact with others from their own district of origin.[95]

However, the main cause of premature death was the high incidence of sickness and disease. Sickness was easily contracted among a workforce which was constantly malnourished and which was compelled to subsist on a diet which was both deficient in content and insufficiently varied to meet basic nutritional requirements.[96] Wages, which were paid in arrears,[97] were insufficient to cover the costs of basic dietary requirements. Many labourers consumed rice rations intended to last a month within a fortnight, and subsisted thereafter on unripe fruits, sugar cane and whatever other food which might be fortuitously garnered.[98]

The sparseness of diet was aggravated by an oppressive work regime. Coolies were not paid on a per diem basis but rather according to the fulfilment of an allotted schedule of tasks. This set routine was usually excessive and would have proven beyond the capabilities of a fit, healthy, and well-fed labourer. As a consequence, many coolies worked long hours in a vain attempt to meet daily task-loads that were regarded by employers as "routine".[99] Most were thus both overworked and underpaid.[100] In addition, most estates and labour camps, especially those adjacent to the jungle, were plagued with constant and extreme levels of morbidity. The Sanderson Committee was advised that death rates among labourers employed on road and railway projects, most of which were located in jungle settings, were significantly greater than those recorded in the estate sector. Most sickness-related deaths were attributed to malaria, cholera, "bowel complaints" (i.e., dysentery), and phthisis.[101] Hookworm and related parasitical infections were also very prevalent.[102]

However, while colonial officials were prepared to concede that socio-economic factors might have played a role in the acute incidence of disease among the indentured workforce, they were more likely to attribute the high death rates to racial and cultural factors. Colonial narratives stressed the putative congenital "inferiority" of Indians, the "inherited vulnerability" of Indian labourers, and the "poor physique" of the Indian coolie. In addition, they drew attention to the reluctance of the (already impoverished) Indian workers to spend money on additional food or in acquiring mosquito netting.[103]

Other labourers died as a result of murder and suicide, both common phenomena on estates. The majority of these cases had their genesis in quarrels over women.[104] Indeed, the comparatively small proportion of indentured females created major problems among the entire workforce. Upon arrival at the workplace, females were housed indiscriminately with males.[105] This negligent approach to the welfare and safety of women appears consistent with the official perspective which regarded all indentured females as of "low character", prostitutes, or women of the inferior classes among whom the "habits of honesty and decency are non-existent".[106] The Selangor Journal of 1894 reported that "The Tamil coolie is most philosophical in this respect; a young unmarried woman is not objecting in the least to residing with a family, or even having to share her quarters, if necessary, with quite a number of the opposite sex."[107] The reality was somewhat different; in effect, no indentured woman was safe from the attentions of predatory males. Some women made depot marriages while still in India to provide themselves with a male protector in Malaya.[108] Hindu marriages were not recognized by the colonial authorities, and Hindu wives were thus denied any legal protection that might have been provided to them had their marital status been officially acknowledged.[109] While some married women might have earned a small independent income as cooks for the men with whom they shared accommodation,[110] the inability of married couples to secure family accommodation exposed women to the threats, cajolery or blandishments offered by unaccompanied males.[111] Under these conditions, men of low standing often lost their wives to those of higher station or to authority figures.[112] Abuse of young women appears to have been widespread, and many found themselves directly recruited into prostitution.[113]

The grinding regime endured by the indentured workforce — a round of never-ending work, stringent conditions of service, an enervating climate, brutal discipline, low pay, exposure to sickness, and malnutrition — helped spawn a plethora of problems which included uncontrolled gambling, drug abuse and alcoholism. With regard to the latter, the Sanderson Report noted that the Indian labourer habitually drank alcohol of poor quality, unlike the "wholesome" whisky consumed by the planter.[114] Desertion from estates was also a frequent occurrence despite the imposition of heavy penalties on those convicted of absconding.[115] In providing evidence before the Sanderson Committee, colonial official Sir Walter Egerton asserted that estates and workplaces with poor health records were subject to "frequent desertion of the able-bodied".[116] Thus, for example, in 1880, nearly twelve per cent of the total labour force employed upon the sugar and tapioca estates in Province Wellesley deserted their posts.[117]

Given this bleak backdrop, it is surprising to discover that a handful of workers not only survived their period of indenture, but against all odds succeeded in remitting a portion of their earnings to India.[118]

REGULATION OF INDENTURED LABOUR

In general, colonial officials adopted a policy of non-interference in the management of indenture. Recruits were regarded as "free labour"; that is, workers who had voluntarily signed a legal contract to work in Malaya. Thus, government oversight was to be kept to a minimum, and the terms and conditions of that contract were to be determined by (supposedly) free and open negotiations between employers and employees. Indeed, colonial officials congratulated themselves on the putative success of the scheme which was attributed to the unambitious nature of the coolie and his/her assumed satisfaction at receiving regular wages in a climate far healthier than that found in his/her homeland.[119]

Attempts to regulate or overhaul the system of indenture were largely ad hoc and generally ineffective. In the early years of indenture, there was no pressure on the Government of India to control labour flows, or to insist upon the enforcement of minimum standards of welfare and protection of the indentured workforce. Few colonies submitted regular reports on their Indian populations, and the Indian government remained ignorant of the appalling abuses perpetrated upon indentured labourers living abroad.[120]

In the case of Malaya, the position of the indentured workforce was complicated by the fact that the major port of disembarkation was Penang. Until 1867 the Straits Settlements were administered directly by India and were hence regarded as internal territories rather than separate colonies with which covenants on the management of indentured labour needed to be negotiated. Thus, the Straits Settlements were not subject to the Act XIII of 1864 passed by the Indian government which aimed to regulate recruitment and conveyance of indentured labourers to external colonies. The act specified that all recruiters had to be licensed and follow prescribed rules; that the duties of the Protector were clearly delineated; that agents were to be paid a salary rather than commissions; that the treatment of emigrants on the voyage to the colony was to be properly managed; and that females had to comprise at least twenty-five per cent of the intake.[121] Apart from regulations enacted in 1857 and 1859 to control overcrowding on ships, and the standardization of "joint and several" contacts for all indentured labourers mandated by the India Act XIII of 1859, agreements reached between the Government of India and receiving colonies excluded Malaya.[122] However, this did not prevent the Indian government from temporarily ceasing the flow of indentured labour to the Straits Settlements after repeated reports of habitual ill-treatment of Indian coolies. This hiatus lasted from its imposition in 1864 until 1867 when the Colonial Office assumed administrative responsibility for the Straits Settlements and resumed the supply of indentured labour.[123] (However, this measure appears to have had little practical impact. Official statistics reveal a continuous flow of indentured labour throughout those years.[124])

In 1876 negotiations between the Government of India and the Straits Settlements regarding the management of Indian indentured labour were finalized and codified in the Straits Settlements Ordinance No. 1 (also known as the Indian Immigrants Protection Ordinance of 1876 or the Indian Act No. 5 of 1877). This ordinance specified that the labourer would agree to work for a given employer for a set period of years and to repay all expenses incurred in his/her recruitment. In return the employer agreed to provide the initial outlay for the recruit's voyage to Malaya and to pay the labourer wages of twelve cents per day. Other conditions stipulated that:

1. The employer was not to deduct more than one dollar per month in recouping advances made to or on behalf of the employee.
2. The employer would supply the labourer with rice and other agreed items at "proper prices" and that the cost of these items would be deducted from the employee's wages.
3. Employees would be required to work for no more than six days per week or more than ten hours in any working day (however, this definition of "work" excluded a range of tasks such as care of animals, maintenance of machinery, and cleaning of premises, all of which could be used to extend a labourer's working hours, and which he/she could be required to perform on his/her rest day).
4. Employees had the right to request a magistrate to annul a contract if the payment of wages fell more than four months in arrears, or if an employer was found guilty of maltreatment.
5. An employee absent from work would not only forfeit his/her day's pay, but would be fined fifty cents for each working day lost (in other

words more than 400 per cent of his/her daily wages), and those absent for a week or longer could be jailed and sentenced to "rigorous punishment".

6.   Severe punishment would be meted out for disobedience or desertion.[125]

However, the act was regarded as unsatisfactory by both the planters and the government, and in 1881, following vigorous representations by the planters lobby, the act was repealed.[126]

In general, the working conditions experienced by Indian indentured labourers deteriorated after the repeal. In 1882 a Labour Contracts Ordinance extended the scope of the "joint and several" agreement to cover entire workforces; thus if a single labourer failed to complete his/her allotted tasks, the remainder of the coolies employed in that estate/workplace could be rendered liable.[127]

Further discussions in 1877 between the Government of India and the Straits Settlements led to the appointment of an officer from each of the governments to assist in oversight of the management of indentured labour — the Madras Presidency appointed a Protector of Emigrants and the Straits Settlements appointed an Emigration Agent in Nagapattinam.[128] This agreement did little in practical terms for the welfare of coolie labour. It was essentially a superficial gesture designed to mollify the limited criticism of indenture mounted by Indian reformers and British humanitarians without impairing or impeding the underlying structure of the indenture system. As Tinker records, by the 1870s, "an uneasy balance had evolved between the Indian Government, Whitehall and the various importing colonies in which the plantation industry was enabled to draw upon a pool of cheap labour with the minimum of restrictions and the maximum of leverage against its workers".[129]

In 1884 the Straits Settlements enacted the Indian Immigration Ordinance (Straits Settlements Ordinance No. 5 of 1884) which supplanted legislation remaining from the period when the Settlements had been ruled from India and was designed to remove the restrictions on the migration of Indian labour to Malaya.[130] The new legislation empowered the Straits Settlements agent to register and grant recruitment licences to individuals who were thereby authorized to obtain South Indian workers on three-year contracts.[131] The act also decreed that labourers were not permitted to sign any contract until arrival in the Straits Settlements.[132] The legislation also set wages at twelve cents per day. However, employers were also granted extraordinary punitive powers which allowed them to deduct wages for even trivial breaches of workplace regulations.[133]

In the years after 1884 the Malayan authorities introduced measures to encourage further Indian immigration. These included subsidising shipping owned by the British India Steam Navigation Company with the aim of providing cheaper fares; appointing government inspectors to ensure that standards of accommodation were satisfactory; and appointing a medical officer to ensure that all intending emigrants met minimum health criteria.[134]

In 1890, following reports of high mortality among indentured Indians, a Labour Commission was established by the Governor, Sir Frederick Dickson. The Commission was charged with the formulation of measures which would stimulate the flow of Indian immigrants.[135] The Commission, largely representing the views of coffee and rubber planters, was highly critical of the indenture system, and advanced two major recommendations, namely:

1. That the government should establish a comprehensive system of planning and management of Indian immigration.
2. That working conditions in Malaya should be improved so that they compared favourably to those of other countries in which Indian labour was employed.

In 1892, despite the vigorous and sustained opposition of the sugar planting lobby, the government enacted an ordinance which aimed at upgrading the regulatory framework which administered the recruitment and employment of Indian labour. However, this ordinance was never enforced.[136]

A further bill was introduced in 1898 which attempted to reform labourers' conditions of employment. Later the same year, this bill became law. The period of indenture was enforced and minimum wages were established. The bill also stipulated that amenities on estates be upgraded and foreshadowed a more comprehensive inspectorial service to oversight this legislation.[137] It should be emphasized that neither the 1892 ordinance nor the 1898 bill were fuelled by humanitarian impulses or by genuine concerns about the welfare of labourers; both measures formed part of an overall strategy designed with the express intention of increasing the numbers of Indian indentured labourers who were prepared to migrate to Malaya.[138]

The abuse and coercion of Indian indentured labour within and beyond the British Empire was finally placed on the Indian nationalist agenda largely because of the indefatigable work of the barrister Mohandas K. Gandhi. Gandhi, who commenced a legal career in South Africa in 1893, quickly discovered that the Indian coolie population comprised a subjugated underclass which was treated with open disdain by the European community.[139] His activism was spurred by personal experience of racial discrimination accompanied by violence.[140] During his twenty years in South Africa, Gandhi, whose advocacy of Indian causes earned him the sobriquet "the coolie lawyer", succeeded in elevating the plight of Indian labour in South Africa to a major political issue.[141] His incessant efforts on behalf of the Indian community, especially those who had suffered ill usage and violence at the hands of Europeans, gained increasing attention not only throughout South Africa but also in India and Britain.[142] Coincidentally, Lord Curzon, Viceroy of India between 1898 and 1905, became the first head of state to query the putative benefits of indentured labour. He considered that wherever Indian workers had migrated they had become oppressed and tyrannized menials, "the helots of the British Empire".[143] The inveterate maltreatment of Indian workers within the colonies, coupled with the typecasting of indentured labour as an inferior and lesser species of humanity, rapidly became a major political concern among Indian nationalists, both within India and abroad.[144] Unfortunately, as Marina Carter has pointed out, Indian nationalists accepted at face value these pejorative colonial stereotypes, thus helping to perpetuate a demeaning image of the coolie immigrant, henceforth to be portrayed, in the words of prominent nationalist Gopal Krishna Gokhale, as "simple, ignorant, illiterate, resourceless".[145]

It was against this backdrop that the British government in 1909 appointed a Committee of Inquiry (the Sanderson Committee) to review and make recommendations on the operations of the indentured labour system. However, the Committee was handicapped by institutional constraints which curbed its ability to thoroughly investigate the major issues surrounding indenture. These were:

1. Membership was drawn from the ranks of the government or from the planting industry. There was no attempt to recruit Indians or those

who might query the system or expose the abuses which accompanied all phases of indenture from recruitment to employment on the estates and in the workplaces.

2. The Committee undertook no actual site visits or fieldwork and was thus unable to conduct inspections of estates or working environments.

3. The decision to conduct all hearings in London meant that evidence tendered to the Committee was overwhelmingly provided by colonial officials, representatives of employing bodies, and planters rather than by Indian workers or their representatives. Only two Indians — one of whom was a Christian (and thus atypical of the workforce which was almost exclusively Hindu in composition) — were examined by the Committee.[146]

Given these circumstances, the Sanderson Committee could never have been expected to produce a report that was either accurate or impartial. Not surprisingly, the draft conclusions of the Inquiry were generally supportive of the system of indentured labour. However, the final report did note several issues of concern, including the high mortality rates among Indian labourers, the inadequacy of education for children of Indian immigrants, and the need to promote the immigration of females "of good character".[147]

The Sanderson Report also made other observations which reflected changing patterns of behaviour among Indian labourers and those who recruited them. Firstly, it noted that upon expiration of their contracts, rather than choosing repatriation to India, an increasing number of Indian labourers were opting to remain in Malaya. Secondly, it observed that while sugar planters advocated the continuation of indentured labour, upon which, it was claimed, the sugar industry was dependent, both coffee and rubber planters called for its abolition. Finally, the Committee noted the declining proportion of indentured recruits within total labour intakes (in 1907 only 5,499 indentured labourers arrived in Malaya, compared to 24,709 under other forms of recruitment).[148]

Indenture was finally abandoned, not because of any humanitarian or moral concerns, nor due to the pressures of Indian nationalists, but rather as a result of the imperatives which accompanied the rubber boom. The decades leading to World War I witnessed an unprecedented demand for rubber. This led to the conversion of many estates which had previously grown coffee and sugar, and clearing and planting of thousands of acres of

Malayan jungle. Quite simply, the huge demand for labour could not be met through the cumbersome apparatus of indenture.[149] Indenture had always been the final resort of those who had been forced to the fringes of Indian society, those who had exhausted all other options; and since its inception the system had failed to provide a regular and reliable workforce.[150] The higher wages paid by the rubber industry now suddenly made emigration attractive to a far wider range of workers. As we shall see, the rubber industry permitted planters a great selectivity in recruitment and allowed the prospect of a more robust and committed workforce.

Although there was significant pressure within Malaya for the continuation of indentured labour, principally from sugar estates; from older estates where "voluntary" labour was impossible to retain, either because of health concerns or substandard conditions; or from new estates planning to establish the nucleus of an Indian labour force, it was clear that the days of indenture were now numbered.[151] As from 1 January 1909, all Indians migrating to Malaya travelled "free". On 11 March 1910, the Colonial Office advised Sir John Anderson, Governor of the FMS, that the system of indenture could no longer be defended. Indenture was subsequently terminated in the FMS on 30 June 1910, and employers were advised that all existing contracts would expire in 1913.[152]

CONCLUSIONS

Between the 1830s and 1909, some 250,000 Indian indentured labourers, overwhelmingly recruited from the Madras Presidency, arrived in Malaya. Recruitment was stimulated by the introduction of administrative reforms and the imposition of a global economy which *inter alia* abolished hereditary rights of the agricultural workforce, impoverished many agricultural workers, and destroyed food security in the Tamil countryside. Severe famines swept South India throughout the second half of the nineteenth century. In most cases, indenture was grasped at by the indigent as a means of survival.

In Chapter 5 it was shown that the regulations governing indenture were conceived out of the vestiges of black slavery and that in many respects indenture perpetuated slavery's worst features. Those recruited into indenture were subject to an exploitative regime of ceaseless toil enforced by a repressive legal framework and the constant threat of disciplinary violence. Workers were underpaid, malnourished, inadequately housed, and subject to disease and a wide range of social problems. While Indian nationalists took up the cause of indentured labourers, they did so in such a way as to inculcate and perpetuate a portrayal of the indentured workforce as simple, ignorant, illiterate and resourceless coolies.

Although in 1875, in an attempt to stimulate increased Indian emigration to the colonies, Lord Salisbury, the British secretary of state for India, had pledged that once Indian indentured labours had fulfilled their contractual obligations, they would share "privileges no whit inferior to that of any class of Her Majesty's subjects" — a promise never honoured[153] — indenture was to ultimately fail as a reliable source. In Malaya this was to be largely replaced by the kangany system of recruitment, which will be the subject of the next chapter.

Notes

1. Ravindra K. Jain, "South Indian Labour 1840–1930: Asylum, Stability and Involution", in *Indentured Labour in the British Empire*, edited by Kay Saunders (London: Croom Helm, 1984), pp. 160–61.
2. J. Kennedy, *A History of Malaya* (London: Macmillan, 1970), p. 208.
3. Kernial Singh Sandhu, *Indians in Malaya: Some Aspects of their Immigration and Settlement* (Cambridge: Cambridge University Press, 1969), pp. 48–50.
4. Ibid., p. 53.
5. Ibid., pp. 53–54.
6. Marina Carter, "Indians and the Colonial Diaspora", in *Rising India and Indian Communities in East Asia*, edited by K. Kesavapany, A. Mani and P. Ramasamy (Singapore: Institute of Southeast Asian Studies, 2008), p. 13.
7. Kernial Singh Sandhu, "Tamils and Other Indian Convicts in the Straits Settlements 1790–1873", in *International Conference Seminar of Tamil Studies* (Kuala Lumpur: 1966), pp. 198–99.
8. Nordin Hussin, *Trade and Ideology in the Straits of Melaka: Dutch Melaka and English Penang* (Singapore: NUS Press, 2007), p. 240.
9. Sandhu, "Tamils and Other Indian Convicts", pp. 199–200; Tan Sri Dato Seri Darshan Singh, *Sikh Community in Malaysia* (Petaling Jaya: MPH Publishing, 2009), p. 40.
10. Sandhu, "Tamils and Other Indian Convicts", pp. 199–200.
11. Ibid., pp. 197–98.
12. Ibid., p. 202.
13. Jain, "South Indian Labour", p. 158.
14. Ibid., p. 160.
15. Ibid., p. 160–61.

16. Khoo Kay Kim, "The Emergence of Plural Communities in the Malay Peninsula before 1874", in *Multiethnic Malaysia: Past, Present and Future*, edited by Lim Teck Ghee, Alberto Gomes, and Azly Rahman (Petaling Jaya: Strategic Information and Research Development Centre, 2009), p. 16.

17. Sandhu, *Indians in Malaya*, p. 81.

18. Ibid., p. 56.

19. *Emigration from India to the Crown Colonies and Protectorates (Report of the Sanderson Committee)* Parliamentary Paper (HC) 1910, 27 (Oriental and India Office Collection, London).

20. See, for example, Peter Elphick, *Singapore, The Pregnable Fortress* (London: Coronet Books, 1995), p. 72; Margaret Shennan, *Out in the Midday Sun: The British in Malaya 1880–1960* (London: Murray, 2004), p. 308.

21. Collin Abraham, "Manipulation and Management of Racial and Ethnic Groups in Colonial Malaysia: A Case Study of Ideological Domination and Control", in *Ethnicity and Ethnic Relations in Malaysia*, edited by Raymond M. Lee (Center for Southeast Asian Studies: Northern Illinois University, 1986), pp. 10–11.

22. J. Norman Parmer, *Colonial Labor Policy and Administration: A History of Labor in the Rubber Plantation Industry* (New York: Augustin, 1960), p. 19.

23. Sandhu, *Indians in Malaya*, p. 82.

24. Sinnappah Arasaratnam, *Indians in Malaysia and Singapore* (London: Oxford University Press, 1970), p. 15.

25. Sandhu, *Indians in Malaya*, p. 82.

26. Hugh Tinker, *A New System of Slavery: The Export of Indian Labour Overseas 1830–1920* (London: Oxford University Press, 1974), pp. 104–5.

27. Ibid.

28. Mike Davis, *Late Victorian Holocausts: El Nino Famines and the Making of the Third World* (London: Verso, 2001), p. 9.

29. Mytheli Sreenivas, *Wives, Widows and Concubines: The Conjugal Family Ideal in Colonial India* (Bloomington: Indiana University Press, 2008), pp. 18–19.

30. Maria Misra, *Vishnu's Crowded Temple: India since the Great Rebellion* (London: Allen Lane, 2007), p. 18.

31. Jain, "South Indian Labour", p. 168; Misra, *Vishnu's Crowded Temple*, pp. 18–19.

32. Sreenivas, *Wives, Widows and Concubines*, p. 26.

33. Ibid., p. 27.

34. Davis, *Late Victorian Holocausts*, pp. 326–28.

35. Misra, *Vishnu's Crowded Temple*, p. 18; Jain, *South Indian Labour*, p. 168.

36. Dharma Kumar, *Land and Caste in South India: Agricultural Labour in the Madras Presidency during the Nineteenth Century* (London: Cambridge University Press, 1965), p. 161.

37. Davis, *Late Victorian Holocausts*, p. 10.

38. Kumar, *Land and Caste*, p. 161.

39. Davis, *Late Victorian Holocausts*, pp. 302–3.

40. Kumar, *Land and Caste*, p. 192.

41. Davis, *Late Victorian Holocausts*, p. 158; Kumar, *Land and Caste*, p. 104.

42. Davis, *Late Victorian Holocausts*, p. 206.

43. Ibid., p. 32.

44. Ibid.

45. Ibid., p. 147. During the 1876–1878 famine, the viceroy Lord Lytton ordered that "there is to be no interference of any kind on the part of the Government of reducing the price of food" and in his letters to the Indian officer he denounced any concern over famine victims as "humanitarian hysterics" (Davis, *Late Victorian Holocausts*, p. 31).

46. Ibid., p. 206.

47. Ibid.

48. Ibid.

49. Tinker, *A New System of Slavery*, pp. 118–19.

50. Kumar, *Land and Caste*, p. 59.

51. Tinker, *A New System of Slavery*, p. 54.

52. Davis, *Late Victorian Holocausts*, p. 122.

53. Ibid., pp. 37–38.

54. Shanthini Pillai, *Colonial Visions, Postcolonial Revisions: Images of the Indian Diaspora in Malaysia* (Newcastle: Cambridge Scholars Publishing, 2007), pp. 7–8.

55. Tinker, *A New System of Slavery*, p. 119.

56. Marina Carter and Khal Torabully, *Coolitude: An Anthology of the Indian Labour Diaspora* (London, Anthem Press, 2002), p. 24.

57. Tinker, *A New System of Slavery*, pp. 122–29.

58. Carter and Torabully, *Coolitude*, p. 24.

59. Tinker, *A New System of Slavery*, p. 117.

60. Carter and Torabully, *Coolitude*, p. 51.

61. *Report of the Sanderson Committee*.

62. Tinker, *A New System of Slavery*, pp. 130–33.

63. Ibid., p. 117.

64. Ibid., p. 139.

65. Ibid., p. 130.

66. Ibid., pp. 134–39.

67. *Report of the Sanderson Committee*.

68. Tinker, *A New System of Slavery*, p. 141.

69. Carter and Torabully, *Coolitude*, p. 37.

70. Hugh Tinker, "Into Servitude: Indian Labour in the Sugar Industry", in *International Labour Migration: Historical Perspectives*, edited by Shula Marks and Peter Richardson (London: Temple Smith, 1984), p. 79.

71. Tinker, *A New System of Slavery*, p. 181.

72. Ibid., p. 155.

73. Pillai, *Colonial Visions*, pp. 8–9.

74. Carter and Torabully, *Coolitude*, p. 121.

75. Pillai, *Colonial Visions*, p. 9.

76. Tinker, *A New System of Slavery*, p. 180.

77. Ibid.

78. W. Kloosterboer, *Involuntary Labour since the Abolition of Slavery* (Leiden: Brill, 1960), p. 8.

79. Jain, "South Indian Labour", p. 161.

80. Ibid., pp. 164–65.

81. Sandhu, *Indians in Malaya*, p. 84.

82. Kloosterboer, *Involuntary Labour*, pp. 12–13.

83. Ibid., p. 12.

84. Leopold Ainsworth, *The Confessions of a Planter in Malaya: A Chronicle of Life and Adventure in the Jungle* (London: Witherby, 1933), pp. 46–47.

85. Tinker, *A New System of Slavery*, pp. 220–21.

86. Selvakumaran Ramachandran, *Indian Plantation Labour in Malaysia* (Kuala Lumpur: S. Abdul Majeed, 1994), p. 57.

87. Ainsworth, *Confessions of a Planter*, p. 186.

88. Tinker, *A New System of Slavery*, p. 222.

89. Carter and Torabully, *Coolitude*, p. 60.

90. Tinker, *A New System of Slavery*, p. 208.

91. Ibid., p. 199.

92. Ibid.

93. Jain, "South Indian Labour", p. 169.

94. Tinker, *A New System of Slavery*, p. 181.

95. *Report of the Sanderson Committee*.

96. Jain, "South Indian Labour", p. 167.

97. Arasaratnam, *Indians in Malaysia and Singapore*, pp. 13–14.

98. Jain, "South Indian Labour", pp. 166–67.

99. *Report of the Sanderson Committee*.

100. Tinker, *A New System of Slavery*, p. 181.

101. *Report of the Sanderson Committee*.

102. J. Norman Parmer, "Health in the Federated Malay States in the 1920s", in *The Underside of Malaysian History: Pullers, Prostitutes, Plantation Workers*, edited by Peter J. Rimmer and Lisa M. Allen (Singapore: Singapore University Press, 1990), p. 181.

103. Leonore Manderson, "Colonial Health and Public Health in Early Twentieth Century Malaya", in *The Underside of Malaysian History: Pullers, Prostitutes, Plantation Workers*, edited by Peter J. Rimmer and Lisa M. Allen (Singapore: Singapore University Press, 1990), pp. 198–99.

104. Tinker, *A New System of Slavery*, pp. 200–202.

105. Jain, "South Indian Labour", p. 164.

106. *Report of the Sanderson Committee.*

107. Jain, "South Indian Labour", p. 164.

108. Carter and Torabully, *Coolitude*, p. 43.

109. Tinker, *A New System of Slavery*, p. 201.

110. Khoo, *The Emergence of Plural Communities*, p. 21.

111. Lydia Potts (trans. Terry Bond), *The World Labour Market: A History of Migration* (London: Zed Books, 1990), p. 83.

112. Tinker, *A New System of Slavery*, p. 202.

113. Arasaratnam, *Indians in Malaysia and Singapore*, pp. 13–14.

114. *Report of the Sanderson Committee.*

115. Jain, "South Indian Labour", p. 169.

116. *Report of the Sanderson Committee.*

117. P. Ramasamy, *Plantation Labour, Unions, Capital and the State in Peninsular Malaysia* (New York: Oxford University Press, 1994), p. 39.

118. Tinker, *A New System of Slavery*, pp. 208–9.

119. Carter and Torabully, *Coolitude*, p. 53.

120. Tinker, *A New System of Slavery*, p. 103.

121. Ibid., p. 116.

122. Jain, "South Indian Labour", p. 161; Ramasamy, *Plantation Labour*, p. 24.

123. Arasaratnam, *Indians in Malaysia and Singapore*, p. 12.

124. Sandhu, *Indians in Malaya*, p. 311.

125. Ramasamy, *Plantation Labour*, pp. 24–25, 166.

126. Ibid., p. 25; Amarjit Kaur, "Working on the Railway: Indian Workers in Malaya 1880–1957", in *The Underside of Malaysian History: Pullers, Prostitutes, Plantation Workers*, edited by Peter J. Rimmer and Lisa M. Allen (Singapore: Singapore University Press, 1990), p. 104.

127. Jain, "South Indian Labour", p. 166.

128. Ramasamy, *Plantation Labour*, p. 25.

129. Tinker, *A New System of Slavery*, p. 115.

130. Parmer, *Colonial Labor Policy*, p. 18.

131. Kaur, *Working on the Railway*, p. 104.

132. Ramasamy, *Plantation Labour*, p. 25.

133. Ibid., p. 31.

134. Ibid, p. 25.

135. Parmer, *Colonial Labor Policy*, p. 20.

136. Ramasamy, *Plantation Labour*, p. 25; Parmer, *Colonial Labor Policy*, p. 20.

137. Parmer, *Colonial Labor Policy*, pp. 24–26.

138. Ibid., p. 20.

139. Mohandas K. Gandhi (trans. Mahadev Desai), *An Autobiography: The Story of my Experiments with Truth* (London: Penguin, 1983), p. 103.

140. Ibid., p. 110.

141. Ibid.

142. Ved Mehta, *Mahatma Gandhi and His Apostles* (Harmondsworth: Penguin Books, 1976), p. 106.

143. Tinker, *A New System of Slavery*, p. 288.

144. Arasaratnam, *Indians in Malaysia and Singapore*, p. 21.

145. Carter, "Indians and the Colonial Diaspora", p. 17.

146. Tinker, *A New System of Slavery*, p. 305.

147. *Report of the Sanderson Committee.*

148. Ibid.

149. Tinker, *A New System of Slavery*, p. 315.

150. Jain, "South Indian Labour", p. 169.

151. Parmer, *Colonial Labor Policy*, p. 49.

152. Tinker, *A New System of Slavery*, p. 315.

153. Henry Srebrnik, "Indian Fijians Marooned Without Land and Power in a South Pacific Archipelago", in *Tracing an Indian Diaspora: Contexts, Memories, Representations*, edited by Parvati Raghuram, Ajaya Kumar Sahoo, Brij Maharaj and Dave Sangha (New Delhi: Sage, 2008), p. 78.

7

KANGANY LABOUR IN MALAYA

In Chapter 6 we noted that the form of recruitment known as the "kangany system" had become firmly established in Malayan plantations well before the abolition of indenture in 1910. The Sanderson Report of that year had commented that an increasing proportion of the estate workforce was being recruited under the kangany system, and had observed that this form of recruitment generally produced a more reliable and stable workforce than that obtained under indenture. The Committee had also commented that while kangany labour was popular with coffee and rubber planters, sugar planters were resolutely opposed to the system.[1]

Kangany recruitment entered Malaya via Ceylon where it had been successfully used to procure labour for European-owned coffee estates. While a handful of Malayan planters had experimented with kangany labour in the early 1860s, the system did not achieve broad acceptance until the establishment of coffee plantations in the 1880s and 1890s.[2] The introduction of rubber to the Peninsula in the 1890s coincided with a protracted downturn in coffee prices, and encouraged many coffee planters to convert their estates to the new crop with the consequence that rubber rapidly became the leading plantation crop in Malaya. In 1909–10 rubber entered a prolonged boom period.[3] Rubber estates were invariably staffed by kangany labour.[4] Until the abandonment of indenture, the two systems of immigration — indenture and kangany — ran parallel, with coffee and rubber planters importing kangany labour and sugar planters preferring indentured labour.[5]

What was the kangany system? The term originates from the Tamil *kankani*, meaning owner or foreman. It is a word that connotes some degree of power and respect.[6] Kanganies were "coolies of standing" who not only recruited labour to work on estates, but as field foremen ("headmen") undertook to supervise those whom they had recruited.[7] The kangany came from a non-Brahman "clean" (that is, non-polluting) caste, almost always drawn from the *Vanniyar*, *Kallar* or *Goundar* castes,[8] and preferably headed a large family. He was a man who enjoyed a reputation for probity and fairness in his dealings, and who thus could be expected to command respect within his home *taluk* (district). He was charged with the task of recruiting in his own *taluk*, thus selecting a workforce comprised of people whose customs and traditions he understood.[9]

Prior to 1907, when the Tamil Fund Ordinance was enacted,[10] the recruitment of kangany labour was a three-way process conducted largely free of government controls, and involving the Malayan employer, the coolie he had appointed as kangany, and thus as a direct agent of the planter, and the Indian villagers who had agreed to work in Malaya. The system was subject to major abuses. Frequently recruits found it impossible to repay the advances expended by kanganies. The Indian Immigration Department Report of 1904 highlighted the problem:

> The recovery of passage money and advances from free labourers is left by some estate managers to their *mandors*. It is the seed of an evil system. The *mandors*, more often men recruited from the coolie ranks, keep accounts and recover money from the labourers on the pay day. They charge interest. The *mandors* are made responsible to the managers for whatever money has been spent on the labourers. This is a vicious system. The *mandors* generally do not keep the labourers under them informed of the state of their accounts.[11]

After 1907, when the kangany system was accorded official recognition, the mode of operation was as follows:

> A Malayan employer who required labour would obtain a blank kangany licence from the Labour Department. He would inscribe the licence with the kangany's name, the number of labourers that the kangany was permitted to recruit, the rates of pay the workforce would receive upon

arrival in Malaya, and finally the commission which would accrue to the kangany. The licence would be registered firstly by the Malayan Deputy Controller of Labour in Penang [in later years an additional office was opened in Port Swettenham], and then upon arrival in either Madras or Negapatam [Nagapattinam] by the Agent of the Government of India. The employer would pay the cost of the kangany's return passage and advance reasonable expenses to sustain him during his visit.[12]

The kangany was empowered to pay for the labourer's passage to Malaya and for designated expenses associated with recruitment.[13] As we have noted, he was also paid a commission for every labourer he recruited. Each kangany was permitted to sign on no more than twenty workers, all of whom (in theory) had been enlisted within the neighbourhood of the kangany's home village. Recruits were paraded before the village headman who was required to certify that there was no objection to their departure for Malaya.[14] The kangany would organize a farewell party in the village and complete other formalities such as settling emigrant's debts and allocating gifts to those left behind.[15]

The village/district phase of recruitment now complete, the kangany would arrange travel for the labourers and accompany them to a transit camp in Avani (near Madras) or Nagapattinam where they were to be medically cleared prior to boarding the steamship which would convey them to Malaya.[16] In general, the medical examinations were far less cursory than those conducted upon indentured labourers, and the rates of rejection were significantly higher. In 1922, the main grounds for failure to meet the requisite medical standards were listed as physical unfitness, improper recruitment, "being other than an agricultural labourer", as well as other factors such as recruitment from districts suffering plague or from areas subject to political or communal disturbances.[17]

However, while medical inspections may have been more rigorous, conditions on the voyage and the mandatory one-week period of quarantine upon arrival in Malaya[18] remained largely unchanged from the indenture era. Accommodation on shipping and in quarantine depots was crowded, unhealthy and unsanitary. Both steamship companies and the receiving authorities in Malaya were accused of negligence and failure to observe specified standards. Serious outbreaks of cholera occurred in the Penang depot in 1900 and in the Port Swettenham depot in 1919.[19]

The kangany system offered many advantages over indenture in procuring labour. For a start, the costs associated with recruiting and transporting labour were considerably lower. The commission paid to the kangany proved much cheaper than the charges levied by the professional firms which had recruited indentured labour. Moreover, the fact that kangany labour was considered "free" meant that it did not — initially at least — arouse the intense levels of Indian nationalist animosity which had surrounded the final years of indenture. This led to a more relaxed official attitude towards kangany recruitment, and thus greater cooperation in all phases of the enlistment and emigration processes. The fact that the kangany was well known and trusted in the district in which he operated promoted a greater readiness among villagers to volunteer to labour in Malaya.[20] However, the kangany occasionally encountered difficulties from higher caste villagers who, worried about losing their supply of labour, attempted to hinder his activities.[21] In general, his good standing led to a significant increase in the number of labourers who were prepared to migrate with their wives and children. This resulted in the relocation of whole families, and in some cases entire lineages, to the estates of Malaya.[22] However, the most attractive aspect from the planter's viewpoint was that the kangany exercised far greater care in the selection of labour than had been possible under indenture, thus producing a more reliable, skilled and stable workforce.[23] Moroever, the ties of common origin between kangany and labourer — those of district, and often of village and even extended kin lineage — promoted an inferential patron–client relationship between kangany and labourer which in practice made the kangany system every bit as exploitative and binding as that of indenture.[24]

The most irksome aspect of kangany recruitment, at least from the employer's perspective, was the poaching of labour, a practice known as "crimping". In theory, the labourer was "free" upon arrival and not obligated to work at any specified workplace until he/she had formally signed a contract. The offer of better wages and conditions might induce a labourer to agree to join a workplace other than that for which he/she had been recruited. The practice of crimping newly recruited workers, thus producing potentially serious shortfalls of labour within affected estates, was a constant anxiety among planters.[25]

While in the earliest phases of kangany recruitment, Indian nationalist criticisms were less trenchant or sustained than those which had been directed against indenture, Indian observers were quick to highlight perceived social ills and injuries. Kanganies were accused of forging signatures and exploiting family quarrels to gain dominance over potential recruits.[26] In particular, kanganies were charged with preying upon the gullible and vulnerable within the community. Thus, in 1912, the newspaper *Amrita Bazar Patrika* inveighed against the system in the following terms: "The recruiting kanganies ... generally belong to the lowest class ... the kanganies are easily believed by the simpletons, because he shines like a tin-god clothed in gorgeous velvat [*sic*] coat and lace turban and be-decked with costly jewels in his fingers."[27] Indian nationalism, a dynamic and expanding force in the early decades of the twentieth century, became increasingly censorious of the laissez-faire liberalism which informed British social and economic policies towards India and colonial issues generally. Indian critics queried the putative benefits of emigration and stressed the social and psychological impact of emigration upon labourers. Malayan recruiting policies were ever more frequently targeted by the Indian National Congress, which was a growing and increasingly assertive power within Indian political forums.[28]

The kangany system was to remain in operation until the Government of India finally banned the migration of assisted labour in 1938. Kangany recruitment produced a far greater flow and a more consistent supply of labour than that achieved under indenture. On the basis of available official data, Sandhu has estimated that between 1865 and 1938, 1,116,717 Indian emigrants arrived in Malaya under kangany auspices. The figure represents sixty-two per cent of the total assisted labour migration, nearly forty-four per cent of all labour, and almost twenty-eight per cent of total Indian migration into Malaya up until Merdeka in 1957.[29] Unlike indentured migration, recruitment under the kangany system proved more responsive to actual labour demand in Malaya. Indeed, by increasing or decreasing the number of kangany licences and/or the amount of recruitment allowance advanced to kanganies, the Malayan authorities were able to manipulate and control the volume of immigration to accord with changing labour market requirements.[30] The kangany system also appears to have functioned far more independently of social and economic conditions within India.[31]

Throughout the years leading to World War II, the flow of kangany labour was augmented by two additional migratory streams, namely independent assisted and non-assisted workers. The former comprised those labourers who had volunteered, independent of the kangany system, to enter contractual employment in Malaya, and to whom the Indian Immigration Committee extended financial and other forms of support.[32] The number of independent assisted migrants rose substantially in the 1920s, and by 1925 accounted for twenty-eight per cent of the total number of labourers whose passage to Malaya was funded through the Committee.[33] Throughout the 1930s, independent assisted labour consistently accounted for about thirty per cent of total labour immigration.[34] The movement of independent assisted labourers ended in 1938, when the Indian Government banned all forms of assisted emigration to Malaya.[35] Non-assisted migrants were those who funded their own travel to Malaya and who sought work after arrival. The latter were not encouraged by the Committee, which was reluctant to endorse any form of migration which might threaten the primacy of kangany recruitment. Despite the lack of official support, there was a steady flow of non-assisted migrants from the 1890s onwards.[36] In the early 1930s, the Malayan government noted a sharp increase in the numbers of non-assisted labourers, with the annual intakes rising from 10,000 in 1931 to 22,000 in 1934. The Malayan Controller of Labour, C.D. Ahearne, suggests that this increase was due to the desire of better circumstanced workers to avoid the week's quarantine which was imposed upon all assisted labourers following their arrival in Malaya.[37]

There was a further category of Indian labour available to Malayan employers. This consisted of former indentured labourers and their locally born children. These workers had shown their capabilities in the field and had adjusted physically and culturally to the Malayan plantation milieu. Moreover, their services were readily accessible and did not require the costly and time-consuming outlays which were associated with kangany recruitment. Yet employers proved unwilling to engage them. This was because these labourers were perceived as self-willed and assertive, potential loose cannons who might disrupt the culture of dependence and subservience the planters valued within their workforce.[38]

By 1940, a total of 218,000 Indian workers, comprising sixty-two per cent of the total plantation workforce, were employed within the rubber estates.[39] Within the public sector, Indian labour predominated in the Public Works Department (15,157 employees), the Municipalities, Town Boards and Sanitary Boards (14,481 employees), the railways (7,819 employees), and the Singapore-based Admiralty, Air and War Departments (4,877 employees). A further 6,711 Indians worked in other miscellaneous government departments.[40]

IMMIGRATION MACHINERY

Elaborate machinery was set up to regulate the flow and management of kangany recruited labour. This represented the interests of those bodies considered vitally concerned with the issue of assisted migration, namely (1) employers, (2) the Malayan administration, and (3) the Government of India. The labourers themselves had no representation nor were they directly consulted.

The first association of European planters within Malaya was inaugurated in Selangor in 1893. Parallel associations were founded in Negeri Sembilan and Perak. In 1897, these three bodies combined to form the United Planters' Association. In 1907 the Association linked with several fledgling planters' groups to create a new peak organization, the Planters' Association of Malaysia (PAM). The Rubber Growers Association (RGA) was founded in 1907. The RGA and PAM later coalesced to form the influential United Planters' Association of Malaysia (UPAM). The dominant concern of all these bodies was the supply and management of plantation labour.[41] Indeed, as early as 1906, planters' associations had urged the government to develop a central labour body which would oversight the importation of Indian and Javanese labour.[42] The planters were to play a considerable role in all aspects of labour policy throughout the remainder of the colonial period.[43]

Under pressure to increase the supply of labour, the Malayan authorities appointed an Indian Immigration Committee in March 1907. This consisted of three government officers and five European planters (drawn from the PAM). The Committee was charged with investigating and advising on all aspects of Indian immigration with the aim of overhauling recruitment procedures and creating a pan-Malayan apparatus capable of regulating and directing the supply of South Indian labour. The Committee's findings were subsequently embodied in the Tamil Immigration Fund Ordinance enacted in the Straits Settlements in September 1907. The Ordinance established a legal and administrative framework for the importation of Indian labour and formally empowered the Indian Immigration Committee to manage the Immigration Fund, and thus to oversight and finance the immigration of Indian labourers recruited from the Madras Presidency.[44] The Fund would be required to cover the costs associated with fares, food, medical attention and steamship passages of incoming labour, and to pay for the repatriation of those workers whose contracts had expired and who wished to return to India.[45] The Fund was to be underwritten by a contribution of assessments paid by each employer. These assessments were levied according to a formula based upon the number of Indians engaged and work performed on each employer's estate. The process also ensured that costs associated with the establishment and maintenance of the Fund were distributed fairly and proportionately among all employers of Indian labour.[46]

The Ordinance also set forth other measures for the regulation of Indian immigration. The kangany system was formally recognized and a number of controls imposed. The Ordinance decreed that a kangany had to be a member of the South Indian labouring class who had been employed in the workplace for which he was recruiting for at least three months. He now required a licence which was issued in Malaya and endorsed in India by the Malayan Emigration Officer at Madras or Nagapattinam. He was also obliged to clear recruits with the village *munsif*.[47] The Ordinance further allowed for the appointment of a Malayan government officer to serve in South India and to oversight the entire process of migration from the Madras Presidency. This officer was to be known as the Emigration Commissioner.[48]

The Ordinance sought to underscore four basic principles which were to guide the administration and regulation of kangany and assisted Indian immigration. These were:

1.   To ensure that each employer of Indian labour bore a fair share of the cost of importation.
2.   To prevent the deduction of large amounts from labourers' wages to recoup recruiting expenses.
3.   To attract more labourers by assuring the prospect of good wages.
4.   To prevent malpractices by recruiters and kanganies in India.[49]

Subsequent legislation relating to the passage and control of Indian immigrant labour was merely designed to refine the operational aspect of the Ordinance without losing sight of or modifying these basic principles.

Between 1907 and 1938 the Indian Immigration Committee and the Indian Immigration Fund were used as quasi-official instruments for the centralized supply of labour to estates.[50] The Committee's principal means of regulating labour flows lay in its power to increase or decrease the issuing of kangany licences.[51]

In 1912 the newly formed Labour Department assumed full responsibility for the oversight of Indian immigration, as well as the management of Indian labour in Malaya.[52] It was announced that all officers down to the assistant level, all of whom were British, would spend a year in South India learning Tamil and Telegu and studying South Indian culture.[53] The officer in charge of the new department was to be known as the Protector of Labour, though later this position was retitled Controller of Labour, Straits Settlements and FMS. In 1912, the Indian Immigration Department was incorporated into the new Department of Labour.[54]

One of the Department's first tasks was the preparation of the Labour Code of 1912. This comprehensive legislation consolidated all the labour laws that that been hitherto passed piecemeal by State Councils of the FMS.[55] Part VIII of the Code enabled the government to impose certain minimum standards relating to living conditions in the estates and made specific mention of housing, medical, and hospital facilities and health and sanitary arrangements.[56] The UPAM opposed provisions of the Code. It had wanted the implementation of measures to curtail crimping, a repeal of the Code's interdiction on "truck" (i.e., the ability of employers to make deductions to labourers' wages), and a drastic reduction of the Controller's power to remove workers from sites considered unsafe for employment.[57]

Further legislation aimed at managing Indian labour in Malaya followed major reforms within India. In 1897 the Government of India had removed all controls over the emigration of Indians departing for Malaya. In 1917, reacting to pressures exerted by Indian nationalists, the Madras authorities suggested that the government create a legislative framework which laid down the terms and conditions under which Indian labourers were to be recruited and employed. The Montague-Chelmsford reforms of 1918–19 placed the regulation of immigration in the hands of India's central legislature, and an Emigration Bill was introduced to the Indian Legislative Assembly in March 1921. This Bill permanently prohibited Indian indentured emigration and created structures designed to protect Indians residing abroad. Despite the objections of the Malayan High Commissioner, the Bill became law in 1922.[58] The Emigration Act of 1922 established a standing Emigration Committee to advise the Government on issues relating to emigration. The Committee drew membership from both Houses.[59] The Committee subsequently introduced a number of key measures, the most significant of which were:

1. The appointment of an Indian civil servant to serve in Malaya as an Agent of the Government of India. He was specifically charged with reporting upon and promoting the welfare of the workforce. The Agent

would be based in Kuala Lumpur but would have the authority to visit all workplaces where Indian labour was employed, as well as points of disembarkation and immigration reception facilities.[60] This appointment was strenuously opposed in Malaya on the grounds that it would undermine the authority of the Labour Department and disrupt the efficient administration of the estate labour forces.

2. A Malayan Indian was to be appointed to the Indian Immigration Committee. This measure created disquiet among Malayan planters who believed that the appointee might prove militant and hence troublesome.[61]

3. The regulation of the proportion of male/female emigrants with the stipulation that the number of males of age eighteen or over and unaccompanied by a wife, must not exceed one in every five persons in any one year. The Indian Government also aimed to increase the number of women among the migrant population in the interests of a "healthier married life".[62] This condition was also opposed by the plantation industry on the grounds that that it might prove cumbersome and thus disrupt the processes of labour recruitment.[63]

The Act also included a number of minor provisions regarding recruitment, among which was a clause which forbade the operation of emigration agents in pilgrimage centres during times of pilgrimage, or at places where festivals were being conducted.[64]

In the negotiations leading to the Emigration Act of 1922, the Indian Government suggested that a standard wage be struck and that the authority to determine such a wage be fixed in law.[65] Despite the virulent opposition of the UPAM, the Malayan government accepted this approach. The Labour Code of 1923 empowered the Indian Immigration Committee, with its planter majority, to prescribe standard wage rates.[66] Although the Government of India had argued that a reasonable wage should not only allow a labourer to live in "tolerable" comfort but also allow him/her to meet contingencies (such as sickness), as well as to make provision for old age, the Committee, which held its first hearing on 9 February 1924, interpreted standard wages as minimum wages.[67] It subsequently established two rates of pay, namely:

1. A lower rate for non-key areas, which were regarded as well-located, in a healthy environment, and subject to low prices, and

2. Conversely, a higher rate for non-key areas, which were regarded
    as less accessible, in unhealthy environments, and subject to higher
    prices.[68]

The Committee set a daily rate of pay at thirty-five cents for males and
twenty-seven cents for females. Between 1924 and 1930, the Committee
was to establish standard wages on no less than seven occasions.[69]

Apart from the issue of wage fixing, the Labour Code of 1923 introduced
a number of changes to the conditions of service under which Indian
labourers were employed. These included free repatriation of workers
who had fulfilled their contracts; the abolition of penalties for some minor
labour-related offences; the prohibition of child labour (i.e., children under
the age of seven years);[70] the establishment of estate nurseries; schools
for labourers' children; payment of maternity benefits; and the direction
that employers must provide twenty-four days' work per month to all
employees. The Code also allowed for the free repatriation of any Indian
labourer who within a year of his arrival was found to be suffering chronic
ill health or was subject to unjust treatment by an employer. These measures
were considered necessary to anticipate the challenges seen as implicit in
the Emigration Act.[71]

Throughout the boom periods, many employers found illicit means
of tying recalcitrant labour to particular estates, thus countermanding the
freedom of movement which was supposedly an enshrined right under
the kangany system. These measures included the employment of Sikh
watchmen to deter departures from the plantations, delayed payment of
wages, the refusal to accept a notice to quit, the use of the kangany to
bring refractory labourers into line, and in collusion with other employers,
agreement to hire only employees who arrived on their estates with
certificates/statements indicating that they had been freely discharged
from the workplace of prior employment.[72]

However, while measures to retain workers were rigidly observed,
during downturns employers showed almost indecent eagerness to retrench
labour considered surplus. During the period till 1938, the rubber industry
suffered two prolonged slumps, both of which brought attendant hardship
to the Indian workforce. The first recession, that of 1920–22, followed
closely on the ending of World War I and the concomitant collapse of the
demand for rubber, while the second (1930–34) was a consequence of the
Great Depression.

In 1920 the price of rubber tumbled from three shillings to nine pence per pound. In response the plantations reduced their labour forces to minimum levels. Despite government concern at the possible permanent loss of labour which would once again be required when conditions improved, some labourers, faced with the spectre of prolonged unemployment, chose repatriation. Departures from Malaya totalled 60,000 in 1921.[73] While some jobless labourers were directed to relief camps, many others were simply cast adrift to experience the hardships of destitution. The Malacca Agricultural Board in 1922 outlined the distress suffered by these workers:

> Many estates on instructions from agents or directors discharged their coolies to reduce expenses and were later told to increase their force and resume tapping. These coolies, being out of work for long spells, wandered about like ill-fed and helpless children, sleeping on road sides with the result they became malarious and anemic [sic] and when re-employed had to go to hospital to be re-conditioned. It was a most expensive and disastrous economy for an industry employing labour of so dependent a type, *encumbered as Tamils are, by wives and children* [emphasis added].[74]

The Depression of 1929–33 led to a protracted collapse of rubber prices and widespread retrenchment of Indian labour. In 1929 rubber had retailed at thirty-eight cents per pound. By April 1930 this had plummeted to twenty-four cents per pound, and by September, the following year the price had halved. It was not until May 1931 that the price bottomed out at ten cents per pound.[75] The planting community responded with a sustained campaign to reduce production costs.[76] The Indian Immigration Committee held a wage inquiry in July 1930 and determined upon a substantial reduction of wages based upon the industry's "ability to pay".[77] On 5 August 1930, per diem wages for "non-key area" workers were reduced to forty cents for men, thirty-two cents for women and sixteen cents for children over the age of ten years. Consistent with the wage fixing formula devised in 1923, a margin in pay rates was retained for "key area" workers.[78] In addition, the Controller of Labour introduced the option of part-time work for part-time wages, though on many plantations these part-time wages were paid only on fulfilment of the customary day's work.[79]

However, the Indian Immigration Committee's primary method of dealing with the large number of Indians unemployed throughout the Depression was a policy of swingeing retrenchments coupled with aggressive repatriation.[80] The colonial authorities did not wish to be left with the responsibility of caring for unemployed workers and their families and were quick to offer surplus labour and their dependents free passage back to India. In addition, returnees would receive a modest repatriation allowance drawn from the Tamil Immigration Fund.[81] Thus in 1930, 66,079 Indians (labourers and their dependents) were repatriated, while in 1931 and 1932 the figures were 69,661 and 57,535, respectively.[82]

This policy represented a major shift on the part of the Malayan government which had previously sought to maintain a stable workforce within the Peninsula.[83] The government's repatriation policy was attacked by planters who were opposed to any mass exodus that might remove the leverage provided by a reserve pool of labour which could always be used to hold down wages and erode conditions. Indeed, the planters feared that the loss of so many workers could well create a tight labour market which might actually result in higher wages.[84]

In 1934, following the Depression, the Indian Government allowed the resumption of emigration on a limited scale.[85] The Malayan government also encouraged the influx of independent immigration to quickly boost the available workforce.[86] Wages, which had been cut sharply during the Depression, were gradually increased until 1937, when there was a further reduction.[87]

By the mid-1930s the emigration of Indian labour to British colonies and the conditions under which they were employed were the subjects of renewed and bitter attacks of Indian nationalists, in both India and Malaya. In 1936, responding to these pressures, the Indian Government sent the Honourable V.S. Srinivas Sastri, leader of the moderates in the Indian National Congress, to investigate and report upon the social and economic conditions of Indian labour in Malaya and to recommend upon the feasibility and desirability of prolonging the system of assisted immigration.[88] Sastri undertook his tour in December 1936. While in Malaya, Sastri mainly consulted with government officials and employers rather than the rank and file of the labouring classes.[89] In reading his report, it appears clear that Sastri allowed these official perspectives to cloud his judgement and to tincture many of his final conclusions. Thus, while Sastri found little evidence of abuse within the system in his report for 1938, claiming that "No complaints were made to me of any case of physical violence or compulsion, and in one case only did I have any evidence of the use of abusive language",[90] the Agent for the Government of India pointedly noted that the 1937 report of the Labour Department recorded thirty-five complaints by labourers of alleged assaults perpetrated by managers or assistant managers in 1936 (i.e., the year of the Sastri visit) and further observed that this figure had risen to fifty-three alleged assaults in 1937.[91] While Sastri's 1937 report listed a number of concerns, he was generally satisfied with the procedures relating to the immigration and reception of Indian labourers and the overall conditions under which they worked in Malaya. However, he expressed serious reservations about kangany recruitment, and he was deeply troubled by the lack of Indian representation on the Indian Immigration Committee.[92] He also considered that wages paid to estate labour were insufficient to meet basic needs, and that if there was no general increase in wages levels, then the system of assisted labour should be abolished.[93] Although Sastri had served with distinction in the Indian Civil Service, Malayan critics found his report superficial, timid, and jejune.[94] Other reactions to the Sastri Report will be discussed in Chapter 9.

In 1938, following a further downturn in rubber prices, there was yet another threat to cut the wages of Indian labourers. On 30 March 1938, the UPAM recommended that the wages of Indian labourers be reduced by five cents a day.[95] The announcement met with sustained criticism among Indian nationalists, and the newly formed Central Indian Association of Malaya (CIAM) cabled the Government of India urging the immediate cessation of assisted emigration.[96] On 15 June 1938, the Indian Government, acting on the Sastri wage recommendations,[97] and under intense pressure from Indian nationalists, including Gandhi, placed a ban on assisted emigration to Malaya.[98]

Although throughout 1938, some 30,000 labourers, including minors, had been repatriated to India[99] (despite official evidence that demonstrated that forced repatriation led to acute social and psychological problems among returnees[100]), the Malayan government and the UPAM argued strongly for the lifting of the ban, especially after the outbreak of war in 1939 which greatly increased world demand for rubber.[101] Negotiations continued unsuccessfully up until the Japanese invasion in late 1941, but always foundered on the crucial issue of wage levels of plantation labour.[102] The latter period coincided with increasing industrial unrest and growing militancy among the Indian workforce. These matters will be examined in Chapter 9.

KANGANY LABOUR: ESTATE ORGANIZATION

The organizational structure of plantations during the period of kangany recruitment was as depicted in Figure 7.1.

It can be seen from this outline that the kangany occupied a relatively modest rank within the overall plantation hierarchy. However, in practice, the kangany filled a pivotal role that was critical to the functioning of the estate. His position as an intermediary between the tiers of management and the bulk of the labour force allowed to him to amass considerable power and influence within the estate setting.[103] Indeed, in their 1917 report on Indian labour management, N.G. Marjoribanks and Ahmad Tambi Marrakayar warned estate managers to learn the language of their workforce lest subordinates, most particularly kanganies, gain undue ascendancy over their labour.[104]

From the outset the kangany's relationship with his recruited labour was one of implied if not actual superiority. It was he who had persuaded

FIGURE 7.1
Plantation Organizational Structure during Kangany Recruitment Period

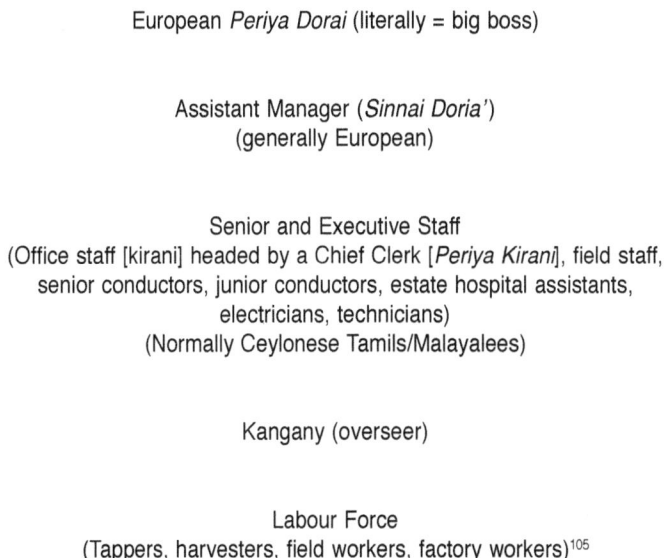

European *Periya Dorai* (literally = big boss)

Assistant Manager (*Sinnai Doria'*)
(generally European)

Senior and Executive Staff
(Office staff [kirani] headed by a Chief Clerk [*Periya Kirani*], field staff, senior conductors, junior conductors, estate hospital assistants, electricians, technicians)
(Normally Ceylonese Tamils/Malayalees)

Kangany (overseer)

Labour Force
(Tappers, harvesters, field workers, factory workers)[105]

the labourer to leave his village and the familiarity of his surroundings and to work in a strange environment abroad. The kangany had undertaken to pay for and guide him through the mysteries of health and quarantine formalities and to initiate him into the work regime which awaited him at his destination. Within the plantation setting, the kangany was an authority figure who shared his culture and background, and who was familiar with his village customs, religious beliefs, and patterns of thought: "a visible link between the world he now inhabited and that he had left behind".[106] In times of difficulty, it was to him that the labourer turned for guidance in matters related to work, finances, social adjustment, or even personal issues of a more sensitive nature. Within the workplace, the kangany would oversee the labourer's daily routine and would, where necessary, negotiate on his behalf with his superior staff (who, as may be seen from the organizational chart, were more often than not of different ethnicity, caste and frequently religion[107]). When considered necessary, the kangany was also empowered to enforce disciplinary measures and impose punishment upon workers.[108] In a myriad of ways, then, the labourer was made aware of his total dependence on the kangany for his and his family's well-being. In such circumstances, the kangany–labourer relationship resembled that of patron and client, engendering the inferential subordination and acquiescence of the latter.

One of the major outcomes of the kangany system was the development of estates which were discrete and self-enclosed sub-cultural units constructed around the remembered mores of the ancestral village. The recruitment of labourers and families from the same areas tended to reproduce social relations based on shared beliefs, traditions and behavioural patterns, and family and lineage structures.[109] In this sense, the network of indebtedness and obligations spun around the kangany acted as a centripetal social force which introduced far greater stability and coherence within the South Indian plantation workforce than that provided by indenture.[110]

The self-referentiality of estate culture was reinforced by their absolute hierarchical control which impacted upon almost every aspect of the labourer's life. Bayly and Harper have described the rubber plantation as "one of the most all-encompassing labour regimes on earth".[111] There was a marked, indeed insurmountable social division between the *Periya Dorai*, the intermediary Asian *kirani*, and the workforce. The estate was dominated by the *Dorai*, supreme despot of his little world, whose word remained unchallenged, and who was addressed by the workforce as "our mother and father".[112] His house, large and well-appointed, always commanded the most prominent location on the estate.[113] The Asian management staff invariably deferred to the *Dorai's* authority, indeed "their loyalty verged on servility".[114] The *kirani* were invariably of a different class and ethnicity to the workforce, from whom they maintained their professional and social distance. Their living quarters, while not as palatial as those of the *Dorai*, were manifestly more spacious and comfortable than those of the workforce, and were usually sited some distance from the coolie lines.[115] Discipline was harsh and usually instantaneous. Disturbances among labourers, mainly over failure to receive wages, ill-treatment and poor facilities, were met with immediate reprisals.[116] Earlier in this chapter it was noted that the Labour Department Report of 1938 recorded a mere thirty-five complaints for alleged assault by a manager or an assistant manager throughout 1937, rising to fifty-three in 1938. However, the testimony presented to this writer over the course of numerous interviews suggests that reported cases represented but a small proportion of actual incidents and that disciplinary violence as a mode of control over and intimidation of the workforce was both habitual and ubiquitous.

While the awareness of collective identity may have helped to accustom labourers to particular estates and assisted in the creation of a more constant and reliable workforce, the culture of dependency was to produce other, often more negative outcomes. The sub-cultural autonomy of individual plantations imposed psychological and personal barriers that restricted freedom of movement, thus limiting opportunities for social and economic mobility. Thus, while in 1915 desertions among Indian labourers involved 29.05 per cent of the workforce,[117] by 1937 Sastri would comment on the general stasis of estate labour, noting that even when coolies were offered better employment elsewhere, they were deterred from moving by the "binding associations" formed on plantations.[118] Continued reliance upon others vitiated employee confidence and self-sufficiency among workers, and inculcated subservience and lack of ambition and self-worth.[119] The greatest legacy of the kangany system was the fragmentation of the plantation workforce into socially as well as geographically isolated component units fissured by primal loyalties of caste, village, and regional and linguistic origin. Given this backdrop, Indian labourers could not be expected to develop any broader social consciousness, generic cultural awareness, or unity of purpose.[120]

COMPOSITION OF THE KANGANY WORKFORCE AND RELATED SOCIAL ISSUES

Approximately ninety per cent of those recruited under the kangany system were Tamils, but intakes also included Telegus and Malayalees. At the peak period of recruitment, especially throughout the rubber booms, demand for labour could not be met from Tamil sources alone, and recruiting extended to other parts of the Madras Presidency.[121] The majority of Tamils recruited were drawn from the principal districts adjoining or close to the ports of Madras and Nagapattinam, especially North and South Arcot, Trinchinopoly, Tanjore, Salem, Chingleput and Ramnad.[122] However, recruiting within the Tamil country was not restricted to these districts and some migration occurred from nearly all Tamil *taluks*.[123]

Caste

The caste composition of kangany recruitment differed essentially from that of indentured labourers, whom as we have noted, were drawn overwhelmingly from the lowest castes.[124] Approximately one-third of kangany migrants were drawn from the so-called "untouchable" castes of Paraiyar, Chakkiliyar, and Pallar (officially known after 1922 as Adi Dravidas or "first Dravidians".[125]) Other major caste groups included Vellalar, Gounder, Ambalakkarar, Kallar, and Vanniyar.[126] Several of these groups, especially the Vellalar, Goundar, and Vanniyar, were drawn from higher Tamil caste groups. This migration produced a more variegated Indian community within Malayan estates and towns, and a greater spread of social behaviour and belief structures than had been evidenced under indenture.[127]

Ravindra Jain has argued that the estate environment in Malaya mitigated caste differences. He states that:

> The levelling process, involving so many ascribed distinctions, which is an essential part of the caste system, was affected on the Malayan estates because of the common identity of all residents of the labour lines as a 'sub-proletariat'... caste distinctions had begun to decline by the late 1920s, but the resilience of kinship bonds in the form of 'kindred-around-kanganies' remained a salient feature of labourers' social structure.[128]

The general softening of institutionalized caste was also noted by contemporary observers. Writing in 1935, J.M. Baron, Acting Controller of the Department of Labour, noted that Adi Dravidas had been admitted to the opening of the new Mariamman Temple in Penang and instanced this as a new spirit of social tolerance. However, in the same report he advised that at least one Province Wellesley estate "caste labourers" complained that Adi Dravidas did not display "the same respectful inferiority as in India".[129] In 1936, C.E. Wilson noted that while caste distinctions had receded, it was still necessary to provide "caste men" with separate lines of accommodation on all workplaces. Wilson forecast that caste would vanish in Malaya and optimistically suggested that "a piped water supply spells death to caste".[130] However, the abatement of caste distinctions did not lead to the abandonment or obliteration of caste within Malayan/ Malaysian Indian society. (It has been my observation, and that of most scholars, that in important social domains, caste distinctions remain both obvious and potentially contentious.)

Male/Female Immigration

The low proportion of females within the immigrant workforce had been considered a major problem throughout the entire period of indentured labour. In 1920 the Government of India turned its attention to this issue.[131] We have seen that the 1922 Emigration Act, which, *inter alia*, aimed at substantially increasing the number of women within migrant intakes, reflected that concern. The encouragement of female migrants also served the interests of the new plantation industries, especially rubber, which required a more settled and long-term labour force. It was recognized that this could only be achieved by actively adopting measures which would stabilize the balance between the sexes.[132] Female labourers received wages which, on average, were seventy-eighty per cent of those paid to male labourers, though male/female differentials tended to equalize when women were paid on the basis of actual productivity.[133]

As late as 1891 the female/male ratio was a mere eighteen females per thousand males. We have noted that the kangany system elicited a greater flow of families and indeed entire lineages. The proportion of females within the general population increased steadily after the cessation of indentured labour and the adoption of kangany recruitment. The following figures expressed as a ratio of females per thousand males demonstrates this increase:

1901: 171, 1911: 308, 1921: 406, 1931: 482, 1947: 687.[134]

The proportion of the Indian population which was Malayan born rose commensurately in the wake of increased female immigration. Thus, while in 1911 local-born comprised a mere 12 per cent of the Indian community, by 1931 this had risen to 21.1 per cent. In 1947, the locally born component of the population had increased to 49.8 per cent, or just under one-half of the community.[135]

However, the pronounced and continuing imbalance between the sexes made the establishment of settled family life within the Malayan context extremely difficult. Disputes over women accounted for a high proportion of the crime as well as many of the social disturbances within the plantation workforce.[136] Contentious issues, often resulting in violence, included marital infidelity, the enticement of married women, and prostitution. On many estates, these problems were exacerbated by the seigneurial (and deeply resented) presumptions of "delinquent" European planters who regularly used their positions to entice or cajole the women under their charge.[137]

One of the greatest barriers to settled family life in Malaya was the refusal of colonial authorities to recognize Hindu marriages.[138] This meant that couples who had married according to Hindu custom had no legal recognition and therefore no recourse to law in the event of the birth of children, separation, or the death of one partner. This problem was only partially resolved with the passage of the Hindu Registration Enactment within the FMS in 1924. However, in general, only "educated" Hindus bothered to register; registrants were required to pay a fee of $2 (close to a weekly wage for the average labourer), and in 1927, out of 1,506 marriages, only 74 were formally registered.[139] Most labourers continued to believe that the religious ceremony bestowed full marital status within the sight of the community and that registration was therefore unnecessary. This view was consistent with custom; registration of marriage was unknown in India.[140] However, the absence of proof of valid marriage made cases of enticement and other legal issues involving family matters difficult, if not impossible, to arbitrate.[141]

Health and Welfare

The overall impression of the Indian labour force in the period leading to the Japanese invasion of December 1941 is that of a community beset by major social problems, including poor health, a high incidence of alcoholism, accommodated in substandard housing, and constrained by a lack of education.

We have noted the high, sometimes extreme mortality rate among Indian indentured labourers in Malaya. Throughout the entire period of kangany labour, the Indian mortality rate continued to exceed that of other communities.[142] In 1911, the year after the abolition of indenture, the death rate of Indian labourers was 62.9 per 1,000 people. Colonial authorities made efforts to improve health upon estates and in workplaces, and each of the Labour Codes of 1912, 1918, and 1923 successively prescribed more comprehensive minimum standards of health care and prophylaxis, though these measures were loosely enforced. However, even with these modest measures, the mortality rate showed a substantial decline, and by 1923 stood at 14.5 per 1,000 people. It was not until 1929 that births exceeded deaths.[143]

As noted in Chapter 6, while European commentators attributed the high mortality rate among the Indian labour force to such factors as genetic disposition and inherited vulnerability,[144] the simple fact was that Malaya was an unhealthy environment and an extensive range of tropical diseases were prevalent within the wider community. The processes of development which accompanied the growth of the colonial economy, including the massive clearing of jungle for estates, the expansion of mining, and the inauguration of public works projects, disrupted existing ecological checks and balances, thus contributing to the spread of diseases.[145] One of the most obvious factors which contributed to the high death rate was the close proximity of many estates and utilities (e.g., railways), to known "unhealthy" areas, particularly jungle where malaria was common and the risk of contracting other tropical diseases was greatly increased.[146] Malaria claimed the lives of more than 200,000 people within the period 1908–20 and took a similar number of victims throughout the 1920s.[147] Hookworm was the most pernicious of parasites found in Malaya, and after a year's residence, the incidence of ankylostomiasis ran at between 75 and 85 per cent of all new intakes. Venereal diseases, mainly linked to prostitution, infected about 80 per cent of the adult population. Tuberculosis was also a major cause of deaths on estates and in workplaces.[148] Overall mortality was boosted by the high frequency of suicide among Indian labourers, which was often spurred by disputes over women, and normally took the form of hanging, poisoning, drowning or throat cutting.[149]

The excessive rate of Indian infant mortality, which averaged 195.62 between 1910 and 1920, prompted the government to pass legislation requiring employers to establish workplace crèches, but no figures are available to indicate how many actually complied with this directive. Medical facilities on estates were generally sparse. In 1925, out of a total of 1,304 estates comprising 100 acres or greater, only 167 possessed hospitals. Most of these were frugally equipped and poorly staffed — indeed, the officers in charge of 86 of these had no medical qualifications to speak of.[150] On the eve of the Pacific War, a government report commented that hospitals remained sub-standard, especially those on smaller estates.[151]

A further factor contributing to the high death rate among the Indian workforce was the poor and inadequate diet which lowered the resistance of workers and their families to serious illness. Reports submitted by the Agents of the Government of India consistently refer to the widespread incidence of "subnutrition" among the Indian workforce and their families.[152] In 1940, Indian Agent, S. Dutt, commented on the inadequacies of the diet of the average labourer and his family, which generally consisted of rice supplemented by small quantities of pulses and vegetables, but lacking milk, eggs, meat (or similar protein), fish, and green vegetables. Dutt attributed the poor health of Tamils, including the high incidence of rickets among children, to a continuous lack of access to nourishing food, especially that containing vitamin A.[153]

Social Problems

Although there was evidence of considerable gambling among the labourers,[154] the greatest social problem within the Indian community was the high incidence of alcoholism, a phenomenon so common that it led to the Indian labourer being typecast by the other ethnic communities as "an inveterate drunkard".[155] Alcoholism took the form of habitual consumption of toddy, a fermented drink gathered from palm trees. Sale of most other forms of alcohol — arack, samsu, and foreign liquors — to Indian labourers was prohibited by law.[156] This restriction provided toddy suppliers with a near monopoly on the retail of alcohol to Indian consumers. Toddy shops were provided on virtually all estates and often returned handsome profits to the estate management.[157] Many Indian observers believed that the toddy shops were a cheap and convenient means of maintaining social control over the labour force and that the government, which levied a forty per cent tax on all toddy sales, and which thus received substantial revenue, which by 1935 amounted to $2 million per annum, had little or no interest in addressing the problem.[158]

The easy availability of toddy was of major concern to Government of India agents, and their reports repeatedly refer to the deleterious impact of its consumption. Thus, Rao Sahib M. Kunhiraman wrote in 1931:

> Toddy drink is a newly acquired habit to many of the Indian labourers in Malaya. This needless temptation provided in estates at their very doors is the real reason for this... Where the toddy shops were a little further away from the labourers' lines there were many total abstainers and occasional drinkers, whereas the location of toddy shops close to their lines has converted almost the whole labour force into habitual drinkers.[159]

The problem of toddy related alcoholism attracted the attention of the Government of India, which raised the matter with the Singapore and Malayan colonial administration on several occasions. In 1939, Sir Girja Shankar Bajpai, Secretary to the Government of India, advised the Colonial Secretary, Singapore, that the "toddy question" on Malayan estates was considered a major problem by the Indian Government. The government recommended that "toddy shops on estates be closed and Government toddy and liquor shops be sited as far as possible from places where Indian labour is employed".[160]

The restriction of toddy distribution and consumption was also vigorously pursued by Indian social and political reform movements. However, many who advocated tighter controls did not want total prohibition; they feared that a complete ban on toddy might lead to labourers consuming the far more potent, and occasionally lethal, illicitly distilled samsu. The combined pressures wrought by the Indian Government, its agents, and reform movements in Malaya were to no avail; toddy shops remained firmly implanted on estates and in close proximity to urban workplaces.[161]

Education

Another issue of concern to Indian reformers was that of education. Although the Labour Code of 1923 mandated the provision of a nursery and a school in all workplaces/estates where there were ten or more resident children of school age (defined as aged six to twelve years[162]), evidence indicates that the education of Tamil children was accorded a very low priority by employers and government authorities. In 1929 regulations governing the organization and administration of Tamil estate schools were drawn up and circulated to all estates. These recommended that payments of grants-of-aid be extended on the basis of specified criteria, including average attendance figures and the number of examinations sat within the school.[163] Under the Labour Code, employers were required to appoint and pay teachers and to supply and equip premises. However, educational facilities were often basic, the teachers were unqualified (many were estate clerks, kanganies or literate labourers), and the educational content was largely worthless. In many cases the estate school was housed in a disused shed or storeroom, and the entire educational experience amounted to little more than a period of child minding.[164]

Despite the obvious inadequacy of estate schools, the colonial authorities continued to assert that education provided to plantation children was of "a standard suited to their needs",[165] and that literacy among Tamils in Malaya was significantly higher than that in the Madras Presidency. In 1933, responding to criticisms, the Malayan government pointed out that the literacy rate among Indians as shown by the 1931 census report was 245 per 1,000 in the FMS and 376 per 1,000 in the Straits Settlements, as compared with 92 per 1,000 in the Madras Presidency.[166] However, the reports of the Agent of the Government of India suggest that little effort was expended on the education of estate children. In 1936, K.A. Mukundan describes the standard of schooling as poor, with inferior accommodation, insufficient equipment, unqualified and untrained teachers, and no compulsion for children to attend school.[167] Although in 1937 colonial authorities initiated a scheme for training Tamil teachers,[168] the 1939 report indicates that Tamil teachers remained seriously unqualified and that of 917 teachers employed in estate schools only 129 had received any training.[169]

Moreover, the harsh realities of estate life did not encourage many labourers to invest in the education of their children or to demand adequate facilities and qualified teachers. In most cases the employee's world view did not extend beyond the boundaries of the plantations. Few workers had an understanding of the role of education in pursuing social or economic opportunities, but in any case children were needed on the payroll at the earliest age possible to supplement family incomes. And indeed most children fulfilled the required educational formalities demanded of them and left school to take up employment as soon as they reached the age when they might legally do so.[170] Only a small minority of children completed the six years of primary education offered in estate schools, and because all secondary education was offered in English, almost none progressed beyond primary level.[171]

Housing

After 1912, housing standards for kangany labourers were enforceable by law. This resulted in the erection of "lines" — long buildings, generally of timber and plank construction, roofed with attap, and divided into a series of very basic dwellings.[172] The "coolie" lines were generally sited adjacent to the plantation factory. This area was the hub of social life on the estate. The accommodation provided on some plantations reinforced pre-existing village, caste and kinship loyalties, but upon other estates replaced them with the new ties of neighbourhood.[173] The "lines" imposed regulated and standardized living conditions upon estate labour, thus permitting none of the variations which might have been found in villages of origin.[174] The 1912 legislation also required the provision of proper cement drains, a piped water supply and communal latrines.[175] This was also a belated acknowledgement of the fact that inadequate sanitation and the improper disposal of sullage wastes had contributed to the high rates of morbidity upon estates. In 1935 the Labour Department and Health authorities condemned "lines" structures as unfit for estate or utility labour, after which there was a tendency to construct cottage type buildings.[176] However, despite this stricture, many plantations and workplaces retained "lines" style living quarters well into the Mahathir era.

CONCLUSIONS

The kangany system marked a change in the mode of recruitment, though in practice it was just as binding and exploitative as indenture. The kangany was a "coolie of standing" who recruited within his home district in South India. This form of recruitment produced a more variegated workforce, including representatives of higher castes as well as a greater number of family groups and indeed entire lineages. The kangany was pivotal to the operation of the estate labour force and formed a crucial link between management and workers. Kangany recruitment was supplemented by other flows of Indian labour immigration — assisted and non-assisted — both making significant contributions to the overall Indian labour force.

By 1940, 218,000 Indian workers were employed within the plantation sector, and Indian labour was also concentrated within the public utilities.

A formal structure of immigration machinery was established to manage the importation and repatriation of Indian labour. Registration of wages and conditions of employment were entrusted to the Labour Department. In 1922, responding to pressure from the Government of India, the Malayan administration acquiesced in the appointment of an Indian Agent and Indian representatives on the Indian Immigration Committee. However, this made little difference to the general welfare of Indian labourers and their dependents. Workers were viewed as merely instrumental within the production process, and employers were quick to retrench labour throughout economic downturns.

Indian labourers suffered a range of social problems, including inadequate nutrition, a high incidence of alcoholism, deficient housing and limited educational opportunities. Moreover, the total and enclosed environment of estates fragmented the workforce into socially as well as geographically isolated sub-units, thus militating against the formation of wider political or ethnic consciousness among Indian workers. In 1938, following foreshadowed cuts to wages, the Government of India banned the recruitment of all forms of assisted labour to Malaya.

The wretched circumstances surrounding the recruitment and employment of the Indian workforce were to leave an unexpected and enduring legacy. In Chapter 6, we noted that a feature of slavery was the vilification and dehumanization of the workforce both in terms of class and "race", and how the "slavish nature" of those forced to labour was viewed as justification for both their bondage and their ill-treatment. This same mindset moulded official and planter perceptions of the Indian workforce. Those who laboured to generate much of the wealth of the Malayan economy were viewed as the very dregs of an inferior and degraded race, the worthless scourings of a subjugated colony. This contempt for the Indian workforce, often echoed by middle- and upper-class Indians, was to persist throughout the entire colonial era, and many commentators (including the author) would contend continued to obtain well beyond colonialism. As Hugh Tinker has commented: "With the formal termination of indenture and other kinds of servitude, there came no end to the unequal treatment of Indians. They arrived as coolies, and in many people's eyes they are itinerant coolies still. For slavery is both a system and an attitude of mind. Both the system and the attitude are with us still."[177]

Notes

1. *Emigration from India to the Crown Colonies and Protectorates (Report of the Sanderson Committee), 1910* (Parliamentary Paper [HC] [1910] XXVII I, Oriental and India Office Collection, London).
2. Kernial Singh Sandhu, *Indians in Malaya: Some Aspects of their Immigration and Settlement, 1786–1957* (Cambridge: Cambridge University Press, 1969), p. 89.
3. J. Norman Parmer, *Colonial Labor Policy and Administration: A History of Labor in the Rubber Plantation Industry in Malaya 1910–1941* (New York: Augustin, 1960), p. 5.
4. Ibid., p. 21.
5. Sinnappah Arasaratnam, *Indians in Malaysia and Singapore* (London: Oxford University Press, 1970), p. 16.
6. Ravindra K. Jain, "South Indian Labour in Malaya 1840–1920: Asylum, Stability and Involution", in *Indentured Labour in the British Empire 1834–1920*, edited by Kay Saunders (London: Croom Helm, 1984), p. 170.
7. Parmer, *Colonial Labor Policy*, p. 21.
8. P. Ramasamy, *Plantation Labour, Unions, Capital and the State in Peninsular Malaysia* (New York: Oxford University Press, 1994), p. 39.
9. Arasaratnam, *Indians in Malaysia and Singapore*, pp. 16–17.
10. Parmer, *Colonial Labor Policy*, pp. 38–39.
11. Khoo Kay Kim, "The Emergence of Plural Communities in the Malay Peninsula before 1874", in *Multiethnic Malaysia: Past, Present and Future*, edited by Lim Teck Ghee, Alberto Gomes, and Azly Rahman (Petaling Jaya: Strategic Information and Research Development Centre, 2009), p. 21.
12. Sandhu, *Indians in Malaya*, p. 90.
13. Parmer, *Colonial Labor Policy*, p. 22.
14. Jain, "South Indian Labour", p. 172.
15. Arasaratnam, *Indians in Malaysia and Singapore*, p. 16.
16. Ibid.
17. Parmer, *Colonial Labor Policy*, pp. 52–53.
18. George Bilainkin, *Hail Penang! Being a Narrative of Comedies and Tragedies in a Tropical Outpost, among Europeans, Chinese, Malays and Indians* (Penang: Areca Books, 2010), p. 125.
19. Parmer, *Colonial Labor Policy*, p. 57.
20. Selvakumaran Ramachandran, *Indian Plantation Labour in Malaysia* (Kuala Lumpur: S. Abdul Majeed, 1994), p. 59.
21. *Report of the Sanderson Committee*.
22. Arasaratnam, *Indians in Malaysia and Singapore*, p. 16.
23. Ibid.
24. Collin Abraham, *The Naked Social Order: The Roots of Racial Polarisation in Malaysia* (Subang Jaya: Pelanduk, 2004), pp. 230–31.

25. Arasaratnam, *Indians in Malaysia and Singapore*, p. 17.
26. Parmer, *Colonial Labor Policy*, p. 57.
27. Ibid., p. 62.
28. Arasaratnam, *Indians in Malaysia and Singapore*, pp. 21–22.
29. Sandhu, *Indians in Malaya*, p. 96.
30. Jain, "South Indian Labour", p. 172.
31. Sandhu, *Indians in Malaya*, p. 97.
32. Parmer, *Colonial Labor Policy*, p. 54.
33. Ibid., p. 56.
34. Sandhu, *Indians in Malaya*, p. 109.
35. Ibid., p. 57.
36. Ibid. Amarjit Kaur places the total number who arrived as assisted labourers (including kangany labourers) up until 1941 at 1,910,820, while 811,598 arrived unassisted (Amarjit Kaur, "Tappers and Weeders: South Indian Workers in Peninsular Malaysia, 1880–1970", *Journal of South Asian Studies* 21 (1998): 86.
37. C.D. Ahearne, Controller of Labour, Malaya, *Annual Report of the Labour Department, Malaya, 1934* (Kuala Lumpur: Government Press, 1935).
38. Jain, "South Indian Labour", p. 173.
39. Colin Barlow, "Changes in the Economic Position of Workers on Rubber Estates and Small Holdings in Peninsular Malaysia 1910–1985", in *The Underside of Malaysian History: Pullers, Prostitutes, Plantation Workers*, edited by Peter J. Rimmer and Lisa M. Allen (Singapore: Singapore University Press, 1990), p. 26.
40. S. Dutt, *Annual Report of the Government of India, 1940* (Calcutta: Government of India Press, 1941).
41. Parmer, *Colonial Labor Policy*, p. 12.
42. Ibid., p. 38.
43. Ibid., p. 12.
44. Ibid., pp. 38–39.
45. Jain, "South Indian Labour", p. 171.
46. Arasaratnam, *Indians in Malaysia and Singapore*, p. 18.
47. Ibid., pp. 18–19.
48. Parmer, *Colonial Labor Policy*, p. 50.
49. Jain, "South Indian Labour", p. 171.
50. Ibid.
51. Parmer, *Colonial Labor Policy*, pp. 40–41.
52. Ibid., p. 131.
53. Ibid., p. 133.
54. Ibid., pp. 131–32.
55. Arasaratnam, *Indians In Malaysia and Singapore*, p. 53.
56. Ibid., p. 54.
57. Ramasamy, *Plantation Labour*, pp. 41–42.

58. Parmer, *Colonial Labor Policy*, p. 69.
59. Arasaratnam, *Indians in Malaysia and Singapore*, p. 23.
60. Kaur, *Tappers and Weeders*, p. 91.
61. Parmer, *Colonial Labor Policy*, p. 73.
62. Ibid., p. 72.
63. Ibid., pp. 72–73.
64. *Indian Immigration Rules, 1923, and Special Rules Applicable to Ceylon and Malaya* (File V/27/821/6, Oriental and India Office Collection, London).
65. Arasaratnam, *Indians in Malaysia and Singapore*, p. 59.
66. Ibid.; Ramasamy, *Plantation Labour*, p. 32.
67. Ramasamy, *Plantation Labour*, p. 32.
68. Kaur, *Tappers and Weeders*, p. 92.
69. Ramasamy, *Plantation Labour*, p. 32.
70. Charles Gamba, *The Origins of Trade Unionism in Malaya: A Study in Colonial Labour Unrest* (Singapore: Eastern Universities Press, 1962), p. 259.
71. Arasaratnam, *Indians in Malaysia and Singapore*, pp. 54–56; Ramasamy, *Plantation Labour*, p. 46.
72. Parmer, *Colonial Labor Policy*, p. 150.
73. Ibid., p. 230.
74. Ibid.
75. Ramasamy, *Plantation Labour*, p. 35.
76. Parmer, *Colonial Labor Policy*, pp. 196–200.
77. Ibid., p. 190.
78. Ramasamy, *Plantation Labor*, p. 35.
79. Parmer, *Colonial Labor Policy*, pp. 196–200.
80. Ibid., p. 233.
81. Selvakumaran, *Indian Plantation Labour*, p. 66.
82. Sandhu, *Indians in Malaya*, p. 69.
83. Ibid.
84. Ibid., p. 67.
85. Parmer, *Colonial Labor Policy*, p. 207.
86. Selvakumaran, *Indian Plantation Labour*, p. 68.
87. Parmer, *Colonial Labor Policy*, p. 73.
88. Selvakumaran, *Indian Plantation Labour*, p. 68.
89. It is unclear as to the exact methodology Sastri adopted in planning and conducting his review, in particular whether he visited locations selected or suggested by others, or whether his visits included estates/workplaces he himself chose to visit.
90. The Right Honourable V.S. Sastri, *Report: Conditions of Indian Labour in Malaya, 1937* (Calcutta: Government of India Press, 1937).
91. C.S. Venkatachar, *Report of the Agent of the Government of India in British Malaya for the year 1937* (Calcutta: Government of India Press, 1938).

92. Sastri, *Conditions of Indian Labour*.

93. Ibid.

94. Michael R. Stenson, *Class, Race and Colonialism in West Malaysia: The Indian Case* (St. Lucia: University of Queensland Press, 1980), pp. 46–47.

95. Ramasamy, *Plantation Labour*, p. 36.

96. Parmer, *Colonial Labor Policy*, p. 207.

97. Sandhu, *Indians in Malaya*, p. 107.

98. Ibid., p. 112.

99. Ramasamy, *Plantation Labour*, p. 36.

100. C.E. Wilson, Controller of Labour, Malaya, *Annual Report of the Labour Department Malaya, 1938* (Kuala Lumpur: Government Press, 1939).

101. Parmer, *Colonial Labor Policy*, pp. 213–15.

102. Ibid.

103. Arasaratnam, *Indians in Malaysia and Singapore*, p. 16.

104. N.G. Marjoribanks and A.K.G. Ahmad Tambi Marrakayar, *Report on Indian Labour Emigrating to Ceylon and Malaya, 1917* (File V/27/820/12, Oriental and India Office Collection, London).

105. Workers were employed divided into the following categories: (1) rubber tappers, invariably male, who tapped rubber and collected latex which they transported to plantation factories. Rubber tapping was regarded as a skilled occupation; (2) field workers, who were engaged in a wide variety of tasks on the estates, the main one of which was weeding. Most field workers were female; (3) factory workers who were engaged in preparing latex or liquid rubber for preliminary moulding. Both field and factory workers were classified as unskilled labour (Kaur, *Tappers and Weeders*, p. 93).

106. Sinnappah Arasaratnam, "Malaysian Indians: The Formation of an Incipient Society", in *Indian Communities in Southeast Asia*, edited by K.S. Sandhu and A. Mani (Singapore: Institute of Southeast Asian Studies, 1993), p. 194.

107. Selvakumaran, *Indian Plantation Labour*, pp. 59–60.

108. Ramasamy, *Plantation Labour*, p. 40.

109. Stenson, *Class, Race and Colonialism*, pp. 24–25.

110. Jain, "South Indian Labour", p. 174.

111. Christopher Bayly and Tim Harper, *Forgotten Wars: The End of Britain's Asian Empire* (London: Penguin Books, 2008), p. 384.

112. Ibid., p. 335. The absolute authority enjoyed by the *Periya Dorai* is demonstrated in the following passage: "We tyrannize over them with unconscious egoism and they reply to our condescension by a blind admiration.... The coolies believed in my justice. I could say to one of them, 'You will come to the bungalow tomorrow with a rattan and I will thrash you.' He came and I thrashed him" (Henri Fauconnier, "The Soul of Malaya", in *Where Monsoons Meet: The Story of Malaya in the Form of an Anthology*, edited by Donald Moore (London: Harap, 1956), p. 203).

113. Abraham, *The Naked Social Order*, p. 275.

114. Ramasamy, *Plantation Labour*, p. 20.

115. Bayly and Harper, *Forgotten Wars*, pp. 344–45.

116. Abraham, *The Naked Social Order*, pp. 275, 291; Shanthini Pillai, *Colonial Visions, Post-Colonial Revisions: Images of the Indian Diaspora in Malaysia* (Newcastle: Cambridge Scholars Publishing, 2007), p. 28.

117. Ramasamy, *Plantation Labour*, p. 43.

118. Sastri, *Conditions of Indian Labour.*

119. Stenson, *Class, Race and Colonialism*, pp. 24–25.

120. Ibid., p. 26; Abraham, *The Naked Social Order*, p. 256.

121. Arasaratnam, *Indians in Malaysia and Singapore*, p. 24.

122. Sandhu, *Indians in Malaya*, p. 99.

123. Ibid., p. 164.

124. Jain, "South Indian Labour".

125. Nicholas Dirks, *Castes of Mind: Colonialism and the Making of Modern India* (Princeton, NJ: Princeton University Press, 2001), p. 241.

126. Arasaratnam, *Indians in Malaysia and Singapore*, pp. 25–26.

127. Ibid.

128. Jain, "South Indian Labour", p. 177.

129. J.M. Baron, *Annual Report of the Labour Department Malaya, 1935* (Kuala Lumpur: Government Press, 1936).

130. C.E. Wilson, *Annual Report of the Labour Department, Malaya, 1936* (Kuala Lumpur: Government Press, 1937).

131. Arasaratnam, *Indians in Malaysia and Singapore*, p. 32.

132. Ibid.

133. Parmer, *Colonial Labor Policy*, p. 197.

134. Arasaratnam, *Indians in Malaysia and Singapore*, p. 32.

135. Ibid.

136. R. Subbaya, *Annual Report of the Agent of the Government of India in British Malaya, 1930* (Calcutta: Government of India Press, 1931).

137. Arasaratnam, *Indians in Malaysia and Singapore*, p. 68. Planter/Periya Dorai, Henri Fauconnier convinced himself that exercising seigneurial rights over the wives of Tamil labourers troubled husbands "no more than men of ancient days who gladly gave their wives to a god with taste for mortal women" (Fauconnier, *The Soul of Malaya*, p. 202). The easy and complacent assumptions which underlie Fauconnier's implied self-deification are disputed by subaltern testimony. As we will see in Chapter 9, one of the demands of the 1941 strikers in the Klang Valley was an end to management molestation of women.

138. Arasaratnam, *Indians in Malaysia and Singapore*, p. 68.

139. R. Subbaya, *Annual Report of the Agent of the Government of India in British Malaya, 1928* (Calcutta: Government of India Press, 1929).

140. Arasaratnam, *Indians in Malaysia and Singapore*, pp. 68–69.

141. R. Subbaya, *Annual Report of the Agent of the Government of India in British Malaya, 1929* (Calcutta: Government of India Press, 1930).

142. Ibid.

143. Stenson, *Class, Race and Colonialism*, p. 21.

144. Leonore Manderson, "Colonial Mentality and Public Health in the Early Twentieth Century Malaya", in *The Underside of Malaysian History: Pullers, Prostitutes, Plantation Workers*, edited by Peter J. Rimmer and Lisa M. Allen (Singapore: Singapore University Press, 1990), p. 198.

145. J. Norman Parmer, "Health in the Federated Malay States in the 1920s", in *The Underside of Malaysian History: Pullers, Prostitutes, Plantation Workers*, edited by Peter J. Rimmer and Lisa M. Allen (Singapore: Singapore University Press, 1990), p. 179.

146. Subbaya, *Annual Report, 1929*.

147. Parmer, "Health in the Federated Malay States", p. 179.

148. Ibid., pp. 181–82.

149. Subbaya, *Annual Report, 1930*.

150. Parmer, "Health in the Federated Malay States", pp. 183–85.

151. Major G. St. J. Orde, *Labour Conditions in Ceylon, Mauritius and Malaya 1942–1943* (Parliamentary Paper [HC] 1942–1943 IX 659, Oriental and India Office Collection, London).

152. K.A. Mukundan, *Annual Report of the Agent of the Government of India in British Malaya, 1935* (Calcutta: Government of India Press, 1936).

153. Dutt, *Annual Report, 1940*.

154. *Annual Report of the Agent of the Government of India in British Malaya, 1926* (Calcutta: Government of India Press, 1927).

155. Arasaratnam, *Indians in Malaysia and Singapore*, p. 70.

156. *Annual Report, 1926*.

157. Ibid.

158. Arasaratnam, *Indians in Malaysia and Singapore*, pp. 69–70.

159. Rao Sahib M. Kunhiraman, *Annual Report of the Agent of the Government of India in British Malaya, 1931* (Calcutta: Government of India Press, 1932).

160. Sir Girja Shankar Bajpai, Secretary to the Government of India, *Memorandum to the Honourable Colonial Secretary Singapore, 1938* (Memorandum No. f.44/38, L&O, 1938, Oriental and India Office Collection, London).

161. Amarjit Kaur, "Working on the Railway: Indian Workers in Malaya 1880–1957", in *The Underside of History: Pullers, Prostitutes, Plantation Workers*, edited by Peter J. Rimmer and Lisa M. Allen (Singapore: Singapore University Press, 1990), p. 119.

162. T. Marimuthu, "The Plantation School as an Agent of Social Reproduction", in *Indian Communities in Southeast Asia*, edited by K.S. Sandhu and A. Mani (Singapore: Institute of Southeast Asian Studies, 1993), p. 468; Muzafar

Desmond Tate, *The Malaysian Indians: History, Problems and Future* (Petaling Jaya: Strategic Information Research Development Centre, 2008), p. 161.

163. Tate, *The Malaysian Indians*, p. 163.

164. Ibid., p. 162.

165. *Annual Report of the Labour Department, Federated Malay States, For the Year 1933* (Kuala Lumpur: Government Press, 1934).

166. Ibid.

167. Mukundan, *Annual Report, 1936*.

168. Tate, *The Malaysian Indians*, p. 163.

169. C.S. Venkatachar, *Report of the Agent of the Government of India in British Malaya for the Year 1939* (Calcutta: Government of India Press, 1940).

170. Mukandan, *Annual Report, 1935*.

171. Tate, *The Malaysian Indians*, p. 162.

172. Arasaratnam, *Indians in Malaysia and Singapore*, p. 163.

173. Ravindra K. Jain, *South Indians on the Plantation Frontier in Malaya* (New Haven and London: Yale University Press, 1970), p. 276.

174. Ibid., p. 12.

175. Arasaratnam, *Indians in Malaysia and Singapore*, p. 64.

176. Ibid.

177. Hugh Tinker, *A New System of Slavery: The Export of Indian Labour Overseas 1830–1920* (London: Oxford University Press, 1974), p. 383. This attitude exists elsewhere in relation to the Indian diaspora. Henry Srebrnik points out that in Fiji, ethnic Fijians refer to the Indians as *kaisi* (slaves/coolies), and *villagai* (outsiders), and as unwelcome guests rather than co-sharers of a modern nation (Henry Srebrnik, "Indo-Fijians: Marooned without Land and Power in a South Pacific Archipelago", in *Tracing an Indian Diaspora: Contexts, Memories, Representations*, edited by Parvati Raghuram, Ajaya Kumar Sahoo, Brij Maharaj and Dave Sangha (New Delhi: Sage Publications, 2008), p. 91).

8

OTHER INDIAN IMMIGRATION

British rule in Malaya inaugurated a period of rapid economic and political change. The colonial authorities set about the process of providing the physical structure and administrative apparatus necessary to support a colonial economy and to encourage commercial enterprise. Both government and commercial sectors required the support of a trained English-speaking workforce which possessed a range of specialist skills and expertise. This was not immediately available in Malaya, among either the indigenous Malays or the immigrant labouring communities, and thus had to be imported from abroad. India was a fertile recruiting ground for the required skilled manpower.[1] The expansion of the Malayan economy also attracted other groups — merchants, financiers, and skilled labour — which saw personal and professional advantages in working in colonial Malaya. By 1927 the Agent of the Government of India could report that Indians "other than labourers" resident in Malaya included the following diverse groups: professional and clerical classes of "Madrassi" Tamils and Malayalees; Sikhs and North Indian "Muhammadans" who had, in the main, been recruited to serve in the military and police; Chettiar merchants; South Indian "Muhammadans" who were largely engaged in small to medium business enterprises; and an entrepreneurial/business class from the Bombay Presidency which established an array of medium to large merchant houses.[2] The Agent did not list Ceylonese Tamils who were at that point not officially recognized as Indians by the colonial authorities.

CHITTY MELAKA

We noted in Chapter 1 that Indian Hindu and Muslim merchants had a lengthy history of trade and cultural interaction with Malayan polities and that they comprised established communities within the cosmopolitan Melaka Sultanate. In 1510, on the eve of the Portuguese conquest of Melaka, there were an estimated 1,000 Gujaratis and approximately 3,000 other Indians (mainly Tamils, Bengalis, Parsis, and Malayalees) resident in the city. The Indian communities lived in enclaves known as *vira pattanas* and collectively comprised a prosperous and respected mercantile class.[3] The Portuguese administrator, Tome Pires, observed that the South Indian Hindu merchants, known as *klings*, were active as traders and controlled the bulk of commerce conducted between Melaka and South India.[4]

Hindu communities based in Melaka intermarried with local communities, including Malays, Batak, Javanese, as well as *Nonya* (acculturated) Chinese.[5] With the fall of the powerful South Indian Vijayanagara kingdom, the longstanding trading links between the community and South India were ineluctably ruptured. Thereafter most of the community moved into agriculture or crafts. Over time the *Peranakan* (locally born) Indians of Melaka, more commonly known as Chitty Melaka (according to Samuel Dhoraisingam, the term is derived from the Gujarati word *setji* or merchant[6]), lost their hereditary languages and adopted local cultural forms, including dress, food and language.[7] However, the Chitty Melaka remained overwhelmingly steadfast in their adherence to their religious beliefs and maintained observation of Saivite Hindu rituals and festivals.[8] The community continues to reside as a recognized entity within contemporary Melaka.

CEYLON (JAFFNA) TAMILS

Ceylonese Tamils, often known in Malaya as "Jaffna" Tamils, largely because of their district of origin, were extensively recruited by British officials to fill technical and civil service positions within the Malay states. They were to play a vital role within the colonial administration.[9] The Jaffna

Tamils had attended a superior network of secondary schools established by Christian missionaries and had acquired a high level of both spoken and written proficiency in English. The first batch arrived in Malaya in the 1890s and was mainly employed in the service departments of the colonial administration, especially the railways (most station masters were Jaffna Tamils), postal services, accounts divisions, and the Treasury.[10] They were also recruited to serve in middle-level management within the plantations and were appointed to various commercial enterprises.[11] Jaffna Tamils were also prominent in medical delivery and worked in middle-ranking positions on estates and within the junior medical service (which was open to non-Europeans). Following the establishment of the FMS and Straits Medical School in Singapore in 1904, a number trained as medical doctors.[12] By 1921 more than 50 per cent of subordinate officers in the government services were Jaffna Tamils, and by 1930, this figure had reached 65.3 per cent.[13] In 1947 there were approximately 23,000 Jaffna Tamils in Malaya.[14] Until World War II, this community was largely male, but throughout the 1930s there was a gradual increase in the proportion of females as well as established families.[15]

The Ceylon Tamils did not view themselves as Indian, even though after 1928 they were included in the population for representational purposes.[16] In 1902 they formed the Selangor Ceylon Tamils Association (SCTA) (a majority of Jaffna Tamils were stationed in this state), to advance their political and other interests in Malaya.[17] They were aware of their status as an educated middle-class community which held an array of responsible and secure appointments within the colonial economy.[18] They consequently made every effort to heighten their own distinct cultural identity, to develop their own organizations, to concern themselves with issues and problems pertinent to their own community, and to maintain social distance from the various Indian communities.[19] Determined to bolster the standing of the community among succeeding generations, they ensured that their children were educated in English-medium schools.[20]

The Jaffna Tamils were also acutely aware of the caste differences — whether actual or imagined — which separated them from the mass of Indian society within Malaya. Most Jaffna Tamils in Malaya belonged to the Vellalar caste, a "clean" caste, by tradition landlords, independent farmers and holders of political office, and had a long history of exercising authority over lower caste "coolie" labour.[21] Moreover, their language and customs differed significantly from those of mainland Tamils and they followed great tradition and philosophical Hinduism and eschewed the "village" Hinduism which predominated among Indians in Malaya.[22] They were thus emphatic in maintaining their inherent difference and remoteness from the impoverished and depressed Indian labouring classes, especially Indian Tamils.[23]

Their self-imposed social and political isolation created occasional resentment among elements of the broader Indian community.[24] On the estates the perceived exclusivity of the Ceylonese *kirani* resulted in the charge that they were so closely allied to, or identified with, the plantation managements that they might be considered "black Europeans".[25] They were often regarded by Indian groups as self-regarding and nepotistic, and generally inclined to disregard the welfare of the general Indian community and that of their co-religionists.[26]

The anomalous position of Ceylon Tamils also attracted the attention of the Indian government which deprecated the British habit of appointing members of the community to deliberative and consultative bodies as representatives of the wider Indian population.[27]

CHETTIARS

The Nattukottai Chettiyars, more commonly known in Malaya/Malaysia as the Chettiars (or more occasionally as Chetties), are a Tamil caste of businessmen and financiers who comprise one of the principal banking and trading communities of India.[28] The Chettiars, whose ancestral villages lie in a region known as Chettinad ("Land of the Chettiars") within the Ramnad and Pudukkottai districts south of Chennai,[29] have a lengthy tradition of mobility in seeking and fostering commercial enterprise, and are prepared to endure great austerities in pursuit of fresh business openings.[30] They also have a prolonged history of extensive contacts with Southeast Asian traders and merchants which preceded European colonialism by many centuries.[31]

As a community which exploited the opportunities provided by the expansion of Western maritime trading networks in Southeast Asia, the Chettiars were quick to take advantage of the possibilities offered by the British acquisition of South and Southeast Asian colonies.[32] They established moneylending and banking facilities in Ceylon (1805), Malaya and Singapore (1824), and Burma (1854), and maintained lodges (*kittingi*) at all the main seaports in colonial Southeast Asia.[33] Their extension of credit and moneylending facilities were to finance many commercial enterprises in these colonies, including tea plantations in Ceylon and the massive expansion of the rice industry in Burma.[34] Generally, the Chettiars sent selected males from the home base to manage their branch lodges while their wives and children remained at home in India. Small groups would reside and work within these lodges, living according to a regime which was noted for its austerity, tradition and self-discipline.[35] After a certain period, usually two years, these agents would return to their ancestral homes to be succeeded by other members of their clan.[36]

Within Malaya, Chettiar moneylenders provided credit to European entrepreneurs, Chinese speculators, and Indian hawkers and peddlers. They extended their operations beyond the FMS and lent money in the UFMS to royalty, nobles and peasants. By the 1930s the Chettiars were represented in all major cities and towns within the FMS.[37] From the 1920s onwards, the Chettiars began purchasing land and property and investing in rubber.[38] By 1933 the Agent of the Government of India could report that:

> The South Indian Nattukottai Chettiar community has invested considerable capital in Malaya on rubber estates, house property, etc., and generally do moneylending and banking business in all the important towns. The credit facilities rendered by them, often at a considerable risk to their own capital, supply a real need to traders and businessmen. The Chettiars have now well-organized chambers of commerce to protect their interests.[39]

In 1935 two Chettiar banks — the Chettinad Bank and the Bank of Chettinad — were established.[40]

Throughout the Depression, the Chettiars acquired significant parcels of land and properties through the forfeiture of mortgages, especially from Malay smallholders in the FMS, to whom they had lent a total of $125 million.[41] Following representations from the Sultan of Perak, the colonial authorities passed the Small Holdings (Restrictions of Sale) Bill in 1931, which was designed to exclude the properties of Malay peasantry from foreclosures induced by Indian moneylenders. This bill was followed by the Malay Reservations Act of 1933 which effectively ensured land reservations against sale or escheat and in effect prevented the disposal of Malay reservation land to non-Malays.[42]

The debate on these two bills focussed public attention on the role of Chettiars within Malaya. Sinnappah Arasaratnam has argued that the lack of general Indian support for the Chettiars highlighted their social isolation from the broader Indian community. He comments that:

It is significant that other Indian groups did not come to the support of the Chettyar [*sic*] in their struggle against these acts. The Chettyar were generally an introvert group, separatist in outlook, having their own exclusive organizations and religious institutions, and leading an isolated social life ... it is significant that the two Chinese members of Council supported the Chettyar and the most strenuous fight on their behalf was put up by Mr E.S. Shearn, an unofficial European member. The Chettyar seem to have presented their case through him rather than through the Indian member.[43]

However, this argument fails to convince. The fact is that at the time these bills were passed into law, there was no generic Indian organization or pressure group to which the Chettiars might have appealed. As will be shown in the following chapter, at this juncture the Indian population remained fragmented, riven by distrust and suspicion, and was incapable of mounting a campaign in defence of the interests of any of its component sub-communities.[44] Moreover, as we shall see, appointed Indian representatives to legislative bodies were distinguished only by their pronounced ineffectiveness and their exaggerated reluctance to pursue issues which might have brought them into conflict — whether real or imagined — with the colonial administration.[45]

While the Chettiars followed specialist occupations, largely lived their own, generally frugal, social lives, and were closely tied to India, they genuinely identified with the broader Indian community in Malaya.[46] They followed great tradition *Agamic* Hinduism and were recognized for their generosity and donations to religious, educational, and cultural projects, thus continuing in Malaya the philanthropic sponsorship for which they had become known in South India.[47]

SIKHS

Sikhs comprised the largest body of North Indians who migrated to Malaya. Sikhs were sought for employment in occupations connected with security: soldiers, watchmen, caretakers and policemen. The latter was a vocation which held little attraction within Malaya; Malays, South Indians and Chinese had shown an equal reluctance to enter the ranks of the colonial police.[48]

We noted in Chapter 6 that Sikhs were among the convicts transported to Malaya. The first independent Sikh migrants were police and military recruits who arrived in 1873. Following the Larut Wars in Northern Perak, Ngah Ibrahim, the Malay Chieftain of Larut, commissioned a Captain T.C. Speedy to recruit a paramilitary force to maintain order. Speedy, who had served with the Punjabi Sikhs in the British Indian Army (BIA) during the Great Rebellion of 1857–58, recruited a force of 110 Sikhs.[49] Later that year, the first Perak police force, known as the Perak Army Police, was formed. By 1877, this contained about 300 Sikhs.[50] In 1884, the Perak Army Police mutated into the first Battalion Perak Sikhs which in 1896 was replaced, in turn, by the Malay States Guides, which until its disbandment in 1919 was largely made up of Sikh personnel.[51]

In 1882 Sikhs were recruited to serve as police in British North Borneo and later in Sarawak where they also worked as prison warders.[52] They were also recruited, generally by British officials who had served in India, to fill various positions within the railways.[53] Sikhs were well represented among railway police and as guards.[54] However, they also worked in other government departments, as well as taking more menial positions such as bullock cart drivers, dairy farmers and mining labourers. Others moved into business and became moneylenders, traders, and merchants, especially in the importation of textiles.[55]

The Sikh community was quick to establish cultural and religious institutions in Malaya. Between 1881 and 1890, gurdwaras (Sikh temples) were constructed in Penang, Kuala Lumpur, Ipoh, Kuala Kangsar and Taiping.[56] Socio-religious organizations such as the Khalsa Diwan Malaya and Guru Kalgidhar Diwan Malaya were founded, respectively, in Taiping (1903) and Selangor (1920).[57] A Punjabi newspaper, *Pardesi Khalsa Sewak*, the first of several such papers, began publication in September 1918.[58]

Sikhs who had migrated to Malaya usually returned to the Punjab to fetch their wives and families.[59] The community, which placed great store upon education, enjoyed considerable social mobility.[60]

SOUTH INDIAN PROFESSIONAL, CLERICAL AND TECHNICAL MIGRANTS

The rapid expansion of the colonial economy was accompanied by a demand for English-educated personnel to fill a range of professional, technical and clerical positions. The dearth of qualified personnel in Malaya coincided with serious unemployment among the salaried classes in South India. The sudden expansion of higher education in India had also produced an oversupply of graduates.[61] Under these circumstances, Malayan employers found little difficulty in recruiting a well-trained workforce from Indian sources.[62] Indeed, many of those selected for these positions were grateful for the opportunity to pursue vocations in the more dynamic but less-crowded and less-competitive Malayan employment market.[63]

Malayalees began arriving in Malaya prior to the end of the nineteenth century. Most originated from the Travencore, Cochin, and Malabar districts of what is now the modern-day state of Kerala. Malayalees, many of whom were Syrian Christians, tended to concentrate in European firms and plantations, in the latter occupying middle-management positions.[64] Young educated Indian Tamils migrated throughout the early years of the twentieth century and were recruited into government departments and private firms, initially within the Straits Settlements and later into commercial enterprises within the FMS of Selangor, Perak, and Negeri Sembilan. This cohort also included some professionally qualified appointees and others who established independent premises.[65]

NORTH INDIANS

While the majority of North Indians who were recruited for police and security work consisted of Sikhs, other North Indians, and in particular Punjabi Muslims, also found employment in the police and army during the colonial period.[66]

The British Army also brought large numbers of North Indians to Malaya and Singapore. However, this did little to directly add to the permanent North Indian population of Malaya. Units were stationed on a rotational basis, and the overwhelming majority of service personnel did not remain in Malaya beyond the duration of their postings.[67] The stationing of army units encouraged the migration of camp followers, who occupied a range of positions associated with provisioning and servicing the armed forces. Most camp followers were Bengali, and many elected to remain permanently in Malaya.[68]

TRADERS AND RELATED MIGRATION

Various categories of independent traders sought to exploit the business opportunities created by the British colonization of the Straits Settlements and the extension of control over the Malay Peninsula. Most of these were North Indian merchants, mainly wholesalers and retailers of Indian produce. They included Parsees, Sindhis, Marathis, Bengalis and Gujaratis (of both Hindu and Muslim background).[69]

Trade also attracted South Indian Muslim merchants, including Coromandel Coast Muslims (known as *Marakkayars* and originating from Tanjore and Ramnad) and Malabar Muslims (also known as *Moplahs*). South Indian Muslims had a long history of trade with the Malay Peninsula, and communities of Indian Muslims were well established in Kedah and Malacca long prior to the British arrival in Malaya.[70] In the main, these traders clustered within the Straits Settlements, most particularly in Singapore and Penang.[71]

Indian immigration also produced a constant stream of minor figures — salesmen, petty entrepreneurs, moneylenders, street-side vendors, shopkeepers, and stall holders — as well as accompanying support staff. Most of these were North Indians. There were influxes of petty traders in 1947–48, 1951 and 1953 (prior to the imposition of immigration controls).[72]

CONCLUSIONS

By the 1930s the heterogeneous Indian community in Malaya comprised a mosaic of ethnic, language, caste and religious groups, reflecting the diversity of the subcontinent from which they had originated. It was regarded as the most comprehensively fragmented and factionalized community in Malaya. Indeed, writing in 1937 the journalist M.N. Nair lamented that the Indian population was rent with "Petty jealousies and dissensions" and concluded that "There is no Indian public opinion in Malaya."[73] Of the entire Indian population, only the South Indian Chettiars, traders, other merchants and professionals had any real freedom to comment or organize against the political structures imposed by colonial rule. Thus, it was from these groups that we might expect to anticipate the nationalist impulses which would produce an overarching political, social and cultural leadership.

Notes

1. Kernial Singh Sandhu, *Indians in Malaya: Some Aspects of their Immigration and Settlement* (Cambridge: Cambridge University Press, 1969), p. 67.
2. *Annual Report of the Agent of the Government of India in British Malaya for the*

Year 1927 (Calcutta: Government of India Press, 1928).

3. Samuel S. Dhoraisingam, *Peranakan Indians in Singapore and Melaka: Indian Babas and Nonyas — Chitty Melaka* (Singapore: Institute of Southeast Asian Studies, 2006), p. 2.

4. Rajesh Rai, "Positioning the Indian Diaspora: The Southeast Asian Experience", in *Tracing an Indian Diaspora: Contexts, Memories, Representations*, edited by Parvati Raghuram, Ajaya Kumar Sahoo, Brij Maharaj and Dave Sangha (New Delhi: Sage, 2008), p. 32.

5. Dhoraisingham, *Peranakan Indians*, p. 4.

6. Ibid.

7. Ibid., p. 11.

8. Ibid., p. 4.

9. Collin Abraham, *The Naked Social Order: The Roots of Racial Polarisation in Malaysia* (Subang Jaya: Pelanduk, 2007), pp. 303–4.

10. Sinnappah Arasaratnam, *Indians in Malaysia and Singapore* (London: Oxford University Press, 1970), p. 33; Amarjit Kaur, "Working on the Railway: Indian Workers in Malaya 1880–1957", in *The Underside of Malaysian History: Pullers, Prostitutes, Plantation Workers*, edited by Peter J. Rimmer and Lisa M. Allen (Singapore: Singapore University Press, 1990), p. 106.

11. R. Rajakrishnan, "Social Change and Group Identity among the Sri Lankan Tamils", in *Indian Communities in Southeast Asia*, edited by K.S. Sandhu and A. Mani (Singapore: Institute of Southeast Asian Studies, 1993), p. 543.

12. Ibid., p. 544.

13. Mavis Puthucheary, "Indians in the Public Sector in Malaysia", in *Indian Communities in Southeast Asia*, edited by K.S. Sandhu and A. Mani (Singapore: Institute of Southeast Asian Studies, 1993), p. 351.

14. Arasaratnam, *Indians in Malaysia and Singapore*, p. 33.

15. Rajakrishnan, "Social Change and Group Identity", p. 543.

16. Usha Mahajani, *The Role of Indian Minorities in Burma and Malaya* (Bombay: Vora, 1960), p. 102.

17. Rajakrishnan, "Social Change and Group Identity", p. 548.

18. Rajakrishnan Ramasamy, "Indo-Ceylonese Relations in Malaysia", *Jurnal Pengajian India* 4 (1986): 89.

19. Ibid., p. 98; Abraham, *The Naked Social Order*, p. 307.

20. Rajakrishnan, "Social Change and Group Identity", p. 545.

21. Rajakrishnan, "Indo-Ceylonese Relations", p. 98.

22. Rajakrishnan, "Social Change and Group Identity", p. 555.

23. Rajakrishnan, "Indo-Ceylonese Relations", p. 98.

24. Abraham, *The Naked Social Order*, p. 307.

25. Michael R. Stenson, *Class, Race and Colonialism in West Malaysia: The Indian Case* (St. Lucia, University of Queensland Press, 1980), p. 64.

26. Rajakrishnan, "Social Change and Group Identity", p. 542.

27. Sir Girja Shankar Bajpai, Secretary to the Government of India, *Memorandum to the Honourable Colonial Secretary, Singapore, 1938* (Memorandum f-44/38-L&O, Oriental and India Office Collection, London).

28. Sandhu, *Indians in Malaya*, p. 291.

29. Ibid.; Hans-Dieter Evers and Jayarani Pavadarayan, "Religious Fervour and Economic Success: The Chettiars of Singapore", in *Indian Communities in Southeast Asia*, edited by K.S. Sandhu and A. Mani (Singapore: Institute of Southeast Asian Studies, 1993), p. 848.

30. Arasaratnam, *Indians in Malaysia and Singapore*, p. 37.

31. Nalini Ranjan Chakravarti, *The Indian Minority in Burma: The Rise and Decline of an Indian Community* (London: Oxford University Press, 1971), p. 56.

32. Ibid.

33. M. Nadarajan, "The Nattukottai Chettiar Community and Southeast Asia", in *International Conference Seminar of Tamil Studies* (Kuala Lumpur: 1966), p. 256; Sandhu, *Indians in Malaya*, p. 117.

34. Mahajani, *The Role of Indian Minorities*, pp. 16–19; Chakravarti, *The Indian Minority in Burma*, p. 68.

35. Evers and Jayarani, "Religious Fervour and Economic Success", pp. 850–52.

36. Arasaratnam, *Indians in Malaysia and Singapore*, pp. 36–37.

37. Ibid., p. 37.

38. Ibid.

39. *Annual Report of the Agent of the Government of India in British Malaya, 1933* (Calcutta: Government of India Press, 1934).

40. Arasaratnam, *Indians in Malaysia and Singapore*, p. 37.

41. Ibid., pp. 92–94.

42. Ibid., pp. 92–95.

43. Ibid., p. 95.

44. Stenson, *Class, Race and Colonialism*, pp. 43–44.

45. Rajeswary Amplavanar, *The Indian Minority and Political Change in Malaya 1945–1957* (Kuala Lumpur: Oxford University Press, 1981), p. 6.

46. Stenson, *Class, Race and Colonialism*, p. 96.

47. Nadarajan, "The Nattukottai Chettiar Community", p. 256.

48. Sandhu, *Indians in Malaya*, pp. 69–71.

49. Tan Sri Dato Seri Darshan Singh Gill, *Sikh Community in Malaysia* (Petaling Jaya: MPH, 2009), pp. 42–45.

50. Ibid., p. 45.

51. Ibid., pp. 46–47.

52. Ibid., p. 47.

53. Arasaratnam, *Indians in Malaysia and Singapore*, p. 35.

54. Kaur, *Working on the Railway*, p. 106.

55. Gill, *Sikh Community in Malaysia*, pp. 56–57.

56. Ibid., p. 41.
57. Ibid., p. 152.
58. Ibid., p. 178.
59. Ibid., p. 55.
60. Ibid., p. 205.
61. Arasaratnam, *Indians in Malaysia and Singapore*, p. 34.
62. Sandhu, *Indians in Malaya*, p. 122.
63. Ibid., p. 67; Arasaratnam, *Indians in Malaysia and Singapore*, pp. 33–34.
64. Arasaratnam, *Indians in Malaysia and Singapore*, p. 34.
65. Ibid.
66. Ibid., p. 35.
67. Sandhu, *Indians in Malaya*, p. 122.
68. Ibid., p. 129.
69. Ibid., p. 119.
70. Arasaratnam, *Indians in Malaysia and Singapore*, p. 36; Judith Nagata, "Religion and Ethnicity Among the Indian Muslims of Malaysia", in *Indian Communities in Southeast Asia*, edited by K.S. Sandhu and A. Mani (Singapore: Institute of Southeast Asian Studies, 1993), p. 515. The Indian Muslim population of Malaya/Malaysia has never constituted a monolithic bloc but has traditionally comprised several distinct communities. Islam was introduced to South India in the seventh and eighth centuries by Middle Eastern traders, many of whom settled in South Indian ports around the Gulf of Manaar and the southern Coromandel Coast. They intermarried with local women and became a recognized and readily accepted presence within South Indian kingdoms. A further group of Muslims arrived with the invasion forces which overthrew the Pandyan kingdom in Madurai in the fourteenth century and subsequently established the short-lived Madurai Sultanate. These were mainly Urdu speakers who maintained a distinct Indo-Persian culture. By 1901 Muslims comprised four per cent of the total population of the Madras Presidency. Tamil-speaking Muslims fell into four major groups: (1) Marakkayars: These were originally merchants who were involved in royal finances and Hindu temple markets. They also maintained trading ties with the Arab world and with Southeast Asia. Following the Portuguese conquest of Melaka, the Marakkayars established trading links with Kedah and East Sumatra. The Marakkayars claimed Arabic descent and followed the Shafi'i *madhab* (school of Quranic law); (2) Labbai: The Labbai were mainly descended from Tamil converts and displayed Sufist influences. They embraced a wider range of occupations; (3) Ravuttan (also known as Rowther): These were descended from former cavalrymen who had once served Hindu rulers. Many later became merchants and traders; (4) Kayalar: These were a subset of the Marakkayar who during the British colonial era established themselves in the skin and hide

trade and owned most of the tanneries of South India. The Labbai, Ravuttan, and Kayalar all paid allegiance to the Hanafi'i *madhab*. Tamil-speaking Muslims identified with Tamil culture and adopted patterns of worship centred on networks of pilgrimage and devotional cults. Urdu Muslims retained their own distinct culture and maintained strong cultural, economic and religious links with North Indian Muslims (Kenneth McPherson, *"How do we Survive": A Modern Political History of the Tamil Muslims* [New Delhi: Routledge, 2010], pp. 1–33). While members of all of these communities established themselves in Malaya, the most influential were the Marakkayars.

71. Arasaratnam, *Indians in Malaysia and Singapore*, p. 35.
72. Sandhu, *Indians in Malaya*, pp. 73, 119–21.
73. Stenson, *Class, Race and Colonialism*, p. 27.

9

INDIAN POLITICAL DEVELOPMENT TO 1941

Until the period immediately preceding the Japanese invasion of December 1941, the Indian population of Malaya showed no real awareness of a common identity; the cleavages of class, caste and ethnicity militated against the development of any expressive communal solidarity.[1] The greatest of these divisions was class. By 1939 there were approximately 700,000 Indians resident in Malaya comprising fifteen per cent of the total population.[2] Of these, only four per cent were occupied in trade, business, or the professions, while approximately ten per cent were employed in skilled and semi-skilled occupations. The remainder were absorbed in unskilled or menial work.[3]

The large working class existed in a continuous state of abject poverty. As we have seen, plantation employers viewed the Indian labourer as a simple being, who had been conditioned by his experiences in India to a desperately low standard of living. By emigrating to Malaya, he had supposedly been rescued from a life of semi-starvation and chronic indigence, and introduced to an environment where his minimal wants and basic needs were more than adequately met by the low wages the industry was prepared to pay.[4]

The contempt felt by European administrators and planters for Indian labourers was echoed by the Indian professional and middle classes. In general, members of these classes spared no attempt to distance themselves from the Indian workforce, and to demonstrate to other Malayan communities their inherent difference from the "illiterate" Indian labouring classes. In asserting their putative superiority, middle-class Indians were just as prepared as Europeans to categorize all Indian labourers with the pejorative label "coolie"; lowly beings unworthy of consideration.[5] These strata of Indian society could not be expected to understand, let alone empathize with the problems faced by Indian labour.

As we have seen in the previous chapters, on plantations and in urban workplaces, workers were directly managed by administrative and field staff consisting mainly of Malayalees and Jaffna Tamils. "Coolie" labour and administrators were thus unable to forge bonds based on common identity, and indeed relations were often riven by mutual distrust and suspicion.[6]

The debasement of "coolie" labour, by both the European community and their own middle class and professional compatriots, effectively isolated the Indian labouring classes and emphasized their social and political impotence. This weakness was further compounded by the chronic, crippling and self-perpetuating segmentation among the labourers themselves. Throughout the 1920s, and in many instances well beyond, Indian workers tended to primarily identify themselves in terms of narrow personal allegiances such as village of origin, caste or sub-ethnicity.[7] Under these circumstances, Indian labourers lacked any understanding of wider class interests, and on the rare occasions when a workforce proved troublesome, employers found it a simple matter to manipulate one sub-group against another.[8]

The comprehensive disunity of the Indian population, coupled with the lack of any fundamental sense of common identity, seriously retarded the development of pan-Indian social and political organizations. The inability of Indians to make common cause or even conceive of a collective communal identity was a recurring theme in the reports of the Agents of the Government of India. Writing in 1936, K.A. Mukundan lamented that:

> One great impediment to the progress of Indians as a whole in this country is the lack of unity among them.... It is high time that the Indians in the country made an earnest attempt to forget their communal jealousies, to sink their differences ... and organize themselves into a common body

which on account of its strength will command the respect and regard of other nationalities and the authorities. I need scarcely emphasize that unless they do this and are able to show a united front, it will be their own fault if their legitimate rights and privileges are denied to them.[9]

Mukundan was especially critical of the Nattukottai Chettiars and the Indian merchants who refused to combine or even interact with other classes of Indians or to recognize that their long-term interests were closely intertwined with those of the wider Indian community.[10]

ASSOCIATIONS

The earliest bodies were friendly societies, often consisting of professional groups, which were arranged upon a caste or territorial basis and which steadfastly maintained their distance from Indian labour.[11] The first association was formed in Taiping, Perak in 1906,[12] and others followed across the Peninsula and in Singapore. Generally these associations were middle class in membership, avowedly loyal to the British, and consumed by factionalism.[13] They were also inefficient. Writing in 1933, the Agent of the Government of India upbraided the associations for their "False notions of independence, mutual jealousies, want of *esprit de corps*, inability to accept leadership ... lack of cooperation and internal dissensions",[14] while in 1936, K.A. Mukundan condemned the "plethora" of associations founded upon the basis of narrow sectarianism.[15]

The major political thrust of the associations was to ensure that Indians were represented on the various Legislative Councils established in the Straits Settlements and the FMS. The first such nominee was Mr P.K. Nambyar, a Penang barrister, who was appointed to the Straits Settlements Legislative Council in 1923.[16] In the same year, the Selangor Indian Association called a meeting of all associations within the FMS, and subsequently petitioned the Governor, Sir Lawrence Guillemard, for the selection of a member to represent Indians on the FMS Council. In 1928, the High Commissioner appointed Mr S.N. Veerasamy, a practising lawyer from Kuala Lumpur, to the Council. However, he was officially regarded as a representative of FMS Hindus rather than the Indian community *in toto*. This move alarmed Indian associations, which generally contained multi-religious memberships and which had scrupulously eschewed the politics of religious communalism.[17]

The practice of appointing Ceylonese members to legislative councils, with the stated assumption that these nominees would articulate the major concerns of the Indian population, created much dissatisfaction among Indian associations. The associations were outraged that these nominees, drawn from a community known for its studied parochialism, its vigorous rejection of the appellation "Indian", and insistent denial of any cultural or political commonality with the Indian community, should be selected to fill seats which the associations believed should be reserved for Indians. This issue, among others, created tensions between the Ceylonese and Indians in Malaya. Writing in 1938, Sir Girja Shankar Bajpai, Secretary to the Government of India, was moved to advise the Colonial Secretary for Singapore that:

> Jaffna Tamils should not be held in any sense to represent Indian opinion ... [The Government of India has] ... pointed out that though there was a historical and racial connection between Indians from Madras and the Jaffna Tamils, the latter in Ceylon were inclined to look upon themselves as distinct from Indians, and had in fact in many matters been in direct opposition to them.[18]

However, even when Indians were nominated to councils, they did not prove particularly effective. We have already noted that the Indian middle class made no real effort to understand or voice issues of concern to the Indian labouring classes. Indeed, the conservative and wealthy educated professionals — the Ceylon Tamils, Bengalis, and Malayalees whom the British had selected as council nominees — proved acquiescent and determined at all costs to avoid controversy, or even to debate contentious issues.[19] In Chapter 8 we noted that Chettiar moneylenders were compelled to contest the passages of the Small Holdings (Restrictions of Sale) Bill of 1931 and the Malay Reservations Act of 1933 through the agency of non-Indian representatives, rather than via the two Indian nominees, both of whom declined to press their case.[20]

SELF-RESPECT

Until the growth of labour militancy in the late 1930s, the political movement which had the greatest impact upon the Tamil labouring classes was the so-called "Dravidian" ideology promulgated by the Self-Respect Movement headed by E.V. Ramasami Naicker. This ideology combined the assertion of Tamil exclusivity with a raft of left-wing influences.

To fully understand the rise of the Self Respect Movement and the emergence of the anti-Brahman ideology, it is necessary to briefly examine the politics of the Madras Presidency.

The South India over which the British East India Company (EIC) was to assume authority consisted of a society of breathtaking diversity, an agglomeration of regional, occupational, caste, *jati*, and religious formations. The great dynasties of South India — the Pallava, Chola, Pandya and Vijayanagara dynasties — had ruled over fluid states through established networks of reciprocity and ritual modes of incorporation.[21] Following the eclipse of Vijayanagara — defeated in 1565 by a coalition of five Deccani Sultanates[22] — power was assumed by a series of "little kings" (*pailayakkars*) whose rule persisted into and occasionally beyond the eighteenth century.[23]

The EIC and later the British Raj increasingly viewed India as an "Orientalism despotism" — a timeless, rigid and hierarchical society.[24] Caste was viewed as the basic building block of India's unyielding institutional and social pyramid, and thus integral to any understanding of India's "difference".[25] British decipherment of caste formations was based on theoretical taxonomies described in classical Hindu texts. These were later to be solidified into contemporary reality by a combination of colonial anthropology and British census operations.[26]

British valorization of textual notions of caste promoted, expanded and institutionalized Brahman power.[27] The colonial authorities accepted without reservation the classical description of the *varna* system, which firmly installed the Brahmans at the apex and as custodians of caste hierarchies. The Brahmans had always furnished the majority of literate functionaries in most Indian polities, and it seemed obvious for the British to employ them as civil servants.[28] However, the power at their disposal under colonialism greatly exceeded that they had exercised in the pre-colonial era.[29]

Although comprising only 3 per cent of the population of the Madras Presidency, between 1870 and 1918 Brahmans had taken 70 per cent of student places at Madras University, and by 1912 occupied over 70 per cent of civil service jobs, 83 per cent of sub-judgeships and 55 per cent of deputy collector posts.[30] In the early twentieth century this resulted in the emergence of a Brahman group known as the Mylapore set, which was pre-eminent in business, professional and civil service circles and which had developed a significant presence in local government. In 1916–17 the Mylaporeans overplayed their hand. Allied with Mrs Annie Besant and the Home Rule League, they embarked upon a bold attempt to translate their considerable influence into more formal networks of power.[31]

Anxious for loyal collaborators, the British seized upon the new movements gathering round the emerging politics of Dravidianism.[32] This as yet inchoate ideology had its origins in the dubious claims of European Sanskrit scholars and missionaries. The influential scholar Max Muller had employed a Biblical framework ("Mosaic Ethnology"[33]) to advance the notion of an invading light-skinned Japthetic "Aryan" race that had vanquished the dark-skinned indigenous Hamitic race. Muller claimed that in South India, the Brahmans ("upon who the noble stamp of the Caucasian race can be seen") had not displaced the "aboriginal" peoples but rather had colonized them.[34]

These theories were consolidated by Bishop Robert Caldwell, who in 1856 had produced his *magnum opus*, *Comparative Grammar of the Dravidian Language*. Caldwell had long been intent upon evangelizing South Indians, and one way he believed he could accomplish this was to detach the South from the "Sankscritic" and Vedic traditions of North India.[35] To this end he proposed an elaborate theory which insisted, against all evidence, that the Tamil Brahmans were "Aryan invaders" who had used the Hindu religion to bamboozle, subjugate and enslave the indigenous inhabitants of the Dravidian regions.[36] Secretly Caldwell regarded South Indians as inferior to the Aryans of the north.[37]

The British now believed that they could exploit the movements fuelled by Caldwell's theories to counter the impetus of the Brahman-dominated Congress. In 1912, colonial authorities encouraged the formation of the Madras Dravidian Association which immediately lobbied for a greater share of government posts.[38] In 1916, again with British support, a rather unwieldy body of non-Brahmans, mainly drawn from the educated and mercantile classes, coalesced into a new political party known as the Justice Party.[39] The Justice Party, consisting of various strands of political opinion and devoid of any coherent ideology or programme, was united only by a rather confused Dravidianism moulded almost wholly by fierce anti-Mylapore resentment.[40] Their political rhetoric denounced the Brahmans as foreign and destructive Aryan interlopers.[41]

After the Montagu-Chelmsford reforms of 1919, the Mylapore/Justice contestation found expression within the political arena. The reforms ushered in a period of dyarchy which divided the conduct of politics between New Delhi and the provinces, and which for the first time created limited legislative assemblies within the presidencies.[42] However, these elected assemblies were granted meagre powers; most of the important portfolios such as local government, education, health, commerce and industry, finance and legal matters remained firmly within the ambit of the colonial bureaucracy.[43] Moreover, the restriction of the franchise to owners of property meant that assemblies were dominated by moneyed elites.[44] Indeed, within the Madras Presidency, only 1.25 million people had the right to vote. Given the low voter turnout, a seat could be won (or in many cases bought) with as little as 3,000–4,000 votes.[45] In 1920, aided by Congress' policy of non-cooperation, the Justice Party was able to claim victory in the elections held that year in the Madras Presidency. The passage of the Hindu Religious Endowments Bill provided the party with an extensive network of patronage which extended its reach throughout the entire Presidency.[46]

The Self-Respect Movement, initially one of several factions within the Justice Party, built on the concept and vocabulary of communal division, and largely driven by the rhetoric of S. Raghavayya Chowdary in Telegu and E.V. Ramasami Naicker in Tamil, developed non-Brahmanism from political invective into a social theory and subsequently an ideology.[47] Ramasami, who is more pertinent to our discussion than Raghavayya, was originally a Congress activist who abandoned the party in the mid-1920s following Congress's refusal to endorse caste quotas in elections. In 1925 he formed the Self Respect Movement and founded its associated publication *Kudi Arasu*. Having lost his religious faith, he became a militant atheist.[48] The ideology of Dravidianism, which as we have seen, had its origins in a colonial shibboleth based upon tenuous racial theorizing, now took on a life of its own in a form that could scarcely have been imagined by its colonial sponsors. Ramasami accused Brahmans of being "northern Aryan invaders", who had somehow assumed control of Dravidian society and who had imposed their caste rules and ritual practices on the indigenous population of South India. Ramasami's increasingly intemperate invective conveniently overlooked the fact that while many Brahmans did occupy positions of power, the overwhelming majority were in occupations that could be described as menial (e.g., scribes, cooks and ritual servants) and that it was generally impossible to make any sweeping assertion regarding the relationship between Brahmans and non-Brahmans that would obtain throughout the Presidency.[49]

Self-Respect promoted a fervent enthusiasm for an imagined Tamil culture, the putative polity which had allegedly existed prior to the advent of northern "Aryan" domination (often portrayed as the result of military invasions), which had supposedly been followed by the manipulation and suppression of autochthonous Tamil society and belief systems. The movement was insistent that Tamils had suffered grave injustices at the hands of "northern" Brahmans, and contended that South Indians continued to be subject to the far-reaching machinations of Northern Indian and Brahman conspirators. Indeed, arguing against all available historical evidence, Self-Respect asserted that Tamil "untouchable" castes were the original Dravidians (Adi Dravida) who had been ensnared by the wiles and deceptive reasoning of the Brahmans.[50] Self-Respect aimed at the elimination of all traces of Brahman intrusion into South Indian culture, as well as campaigning against contemporary manifestations of North Indian/Brahman "chauvinism" such as the promotion of Hindi as the national language, and the emergence of pan-Indian political movements (such as Congress) which supposedly sought to impose (or reinforce) "northern" hegemony over Indian politics and culture.[51] From 1938 onwards, Self-Respect demanded ultimate independence for a separate Dravidian nation. Dravidan identity became defined in terms of a distinct civilization, and arguing after tendentious colonialist discourses, apologists asserted that Dravidian society consisted of a single casteless *jati* from which the "alien" Brahmans were excluded.[52]

Apart from its visceral anti-Brahmanism, the Self-Respect political agenda incorporated sweeping reforms to alleviate the ills which afflicted Indian society. These included the eradication of the evils of caste, especially the disabilities of untouchability, the enforcement of temperance, reforms in education and health, the emancipation of women, the elimination of "superstition", and the registration of monogamous Hindu marriages.[53]

The main support of Self-Respect was derived from lower caste and working class Tamils, but Ramasami also forged links with Christians and Muslims — indeed, with any group which believed it had a need for special political rights which would offer protection from the putative hegemony of the Brahmans.[54]

Self-Respect gained momentum in both Singapore and Malaya following Ramasami's visit in 1929. His tour coincided with the onset of the Depression and the concomitant social and economic dislocation within the Indian workforce. These circumstances produced a more receptive arena for Ramasami's theories of Tamil victimization and his call for radical social renewal.[55]

Ramasami's credibility, never especially high among educated sectors of Malayan Indian society, suffered a major setback in the mid-1930s. In

1932, at the height of the Ukraine famine and associated terror, Ramasami visited the USSR and returned to India full of praise for the Stalinist Bolshevik regime which ruled the Soviet Union. In 1934, following his advocacy of armed revolution, he was arrested for sedition, and in 1935 forced into an embarrassing recantation of his newly acquired political radicalism.[56]

Within Malaya, Self-Respect's shrill suspicion of North Indian and "Sanskrit" influences, its strident adherence to the ideal of a distinct and "purified" Tamil identity, unravelled from its "sinister" Brahmanic accretions, tended to drive the politics of Indian labouring classes into the narrow and introverted cul-de-sac of sub-communalism. Later Self-Respect was to promote an active distrust of the perceived non-Dravidian and North Indian leadership of the emerging Central Indian Association of Malaya (CIAM).[57]

CENTRAL INDIAN ASSOCIATION OF MALAYA

During the 1920s, Malayan Indians remained in a state of political quiescence. Throughout this period the colonial authorities kept a close watch for signs of political activism within the Indian community and maintained a list of potential local agitators. A Special Branch was created in 1919, and two officers were seconded from the Indian police to report upon local political activism and, where necessary, to conduct "black" operations against those designated as militants.[58] Metropolitan Indians suspected of radicalism were either denied entry or allowed only short-term visas. Politically questionable visitors were subject to close observation. Publications from India were filtered to prevent the circulation of subversive materials, and correspondence emanating from influential Indian politicians was intercepted.[59]

In 1928 the Selangor Indian Association organized a pan-Malayan Conference of Indian Associations.[60] This was a forerunner of a series of annual conferences convened to discuss issues affecting Indians domiciled in Malaya. Two major concerns emerged:

1. The need to improve the lot of Indian labourers, including where necessary the provision of land for independent agriculture, and
2. The demand that Indians be granted equal rights with other communities, including the right of permanent residence in Malaya.[61]

Educated Indians stressed the need to establish links with Indian labour and to foster Indian unity.[62]

The fourth annual conference held in Ipoh in 1931 foreshadowed a more radical and activist approach to the conduct of Indian affairs. Indian opinion had been keenly affected by the impact of the Depression, which had starkly demonstrated the powerlessness of the Indian community, and in particular the lack of effective political representation. Throughout the period 1930–33 over 180,000 labourers had been repatriated to India, wages had been cut, and living standards, already basic, had been further eroded.[63] The cavalier colonial disregard for the welfare of Indian workers conjured forth anti-British sentiments which many educated Indians recognized as incipient Indian nationalism. Dr N.K. Menon, a leading Indian intellectual, used the conference forum to make a stirring and far-reaching speech in which he condemned the brutal exploitation of Indian labour at the hands of British capitalism. The speech alarmed conservative Indians, who fearing a vengeful official backlash, withheld their support from future conferences.[64]

The 1931 conference also floated the concept of a Federation of Indian Associations which would act as a forum for the articulation of Malayan Indian public opinion.[65] The call for an overarching organization which would promote Indian unity was repeated at subsequent conferences. In September 1936 these finally resulted in the formation of the CIAM, an organization which incorporated a rather uncertain grouping of politically aware professional men and merchant interests.[66] Although the CIAM was open to all Indians, irrespective of ethnic origin, language, or religious affiliation, the leadership was firmly captured by middle-class, English-educated North Indians and Malayalees.[67] Many Tamil-educated Indians tended to be distrustful, if not actively hostile, to the CIAM.[68]

From its very inception, the CIAM made the promotion of labour rights of Tamil and Telegu estate workers a major priority. Parmer argues that the CIAM was motivated by "a combination of shame for the labourer's ignorance and lack of self-reliance, and of disgust for and opposition to the planting employers' intention, with the aid of the government, of keeping the labourer in this condition".[69] While contacts between the CIAM and the Indian workforce were slow in developing, plantation labourers, lacking any grass-roots organization of their own, were receptive to CIAM attention, and many welcomed the fact that an influential group was willing to speak on their behalf.[70]

The CIAM's political outlook was deeply influenced by the rapid transformation of metropolitan Indian politics, especially the increasing prestige of Congress and its leaders, in particular Gandhi and Nehru, and their growing ability to wring concessions from a reluctant Raj. The new confidence of the Indian nationalists was accompanied by their readiness, often supported by the Government of India, to intervene on behalf of Indians living and working in other parts of the British Empire. Through frequent visits to the subcontinent and exchanges with visiting nationalists, educated Malayan Indians had been able to keep abreast of the changing political dynamics of the subcontinent. The CIAM leadership was thus not only steeped in the ideology of Indian nationalism, but also realized that metropolitan support was a vital and potent force that could be deployed in confronting the colonial Malayan administration and the plantation industry. Although the CIAM emphasized Malayan issues, it never hesitated in using the power of the Indian National Congress and the Government of India to bolster and, to a considerable extent, protect, its own position in Malaya.[71]

In Chapter 7 we discussed the inspectorial tour of the Honourable V.S. Srinivasa Sastri and the reaction of critics in Malaya to his 1937 report. The CIAM had welcomed the concept of a government inquiry into the conditions of Indian labour in Malaya and had applauded Sastri's appointment.[72] However, criticisms of the report were both trenchant and sustained. The report was viewed as apologist in its approach towards the plantation industry and superficial in its apprehension of the extent of civil, political, and economic subjugation of Indian labour.[73] N. Raghavan, a CIAM leader, dismissed the report "as a study of our situation, shallow beyond compare".[74]

The CIAM sponsored the visits of leading nationalists, including Pandit Nehru (1937), Pandit Kunzru (1938) and A.K. Gopalan (1939).[75] Pandit Nehru's tour in May–June 1937 was regarded as a resounding success. Nehru, doyen of Indian politicians, openly supported the CIAM and endorsed the political agenda it had promoted in its dealings with the colonial administration, in particular the need for trade unions to advance the welfare of Indian workers,[76] the payment of wages to the Indian workforce equal to those paid to Chinese labourers, the provision of better education, and the severe restriction of the supply of toddy to Indian workers.[77]

Nehru also urged Indians resident in Malaya to contribute to the Indian fight for independence.[78] His tour not only ignited nationalist awareness among Malayan Indians, but also cultivated the idea of a common Indian identity which embraced all sectors of the community. Nehru's speeches marked the genesis of sustained attempts to foster unity and the commencement of the prolonged (and continuing) process of dismantling the social and psychological barriers, and the petty jealousies and mutual suspicions that had effectively isolated various sub-groups from one another.[79] The greatest impact of Nehru's visit fell upon the labouring classes. His speeches reinforced nationalist impulses, especially the ideals of Mahatma Gandhi which had begun to circulate among plantation workers in the early 1930s.[80]

The Nehru visit led to the establishment of firm and enduring links between the respective leaderships of the CIAM and the Indian National Congress, which promoted a reciprocal flow of information between the two organizations. Members of the CIAM Executive were invited to travel to India to participate in the annual sessions of Congress. As we have noted, the Malayan leadership was thoroughly attuned to the broader currents of Indian nationalist ideology. This had the effect of to some extent subordinating the purely Malayan objectives initially enunciated by the CIAM to the wider nationalist cause of Indian independence.[81]

The tendency to concentrate upon Indian affairs at the expense of domestic political issues produced tensions within the CIAM leadership. Dr A.M. Soosay, inaugural CIAM President, encouraged members to focus upon conditions in Malaya rather than import the politics of the subcontinent.[82] A minority of senior association members continued to argue that immersion in the wider stream of Indian nationalist politics ran the risk of obscuring and undermining the CIAM's local objectives.[83]

However, the partnership with Congress provided the CIAM with tangible benefits. For a start, it furnished the association with a powerful ally which could impart a wealth of tactical and logistical experience in the formulation of policy and the conduct of political and social campaigns. Moreover, Congress proved an invaluable conduit in ensuring that matters affecting the welfare of Indians resident in Malaya were raised with the Government of India. The Sastri visit of December 1936 and the banning of assisted immigration in 1938 were two measures which were both initiated and fully supported by Congress.[84]

The links with Congress also boosted the CIAM's stocks in the sight of the Malayan colonial administration. The possibility that unresolved issues affecting Malayan Indians could be raised, through Congress, with the Indian government, was now a factor that the colonial authorities had to consider in the management of Indian affairs. Moreover, the CIAM was fully aware that communalism lay at the very heart of colonial policy in Malaya. In embracing Indian nationalism, an overarching ideology supposedly sufficiently broad and flexible to appeal to all of the diverse segments of the Indian population, the association could credibly position itself as a mouthpiece for Indian opinion, a properly constituted organization which was authorized to negotiate on behalf of all Malayan Indians.[85]

The CIAM was deeply concerned by the low standing of the Indian community in Malaya, and the condescension, amounting to "slightly veiled contempt" with which labouring classes were viewed by other communities.[86] The association believed that this disdain sprang from deep inequalities imposed upon Indian immigrants, including the lack of citizenship rights. This view was supported, at least in part, by the Government of India. Writing in 1938 to the Colonial Secretary of Singapore, Sir Girja Shankar Bajpai, Secretary to the Government of India, commented that:

> public opinion is already deeply concerned at what appears to be the inferior status usually attributed to the Indian partly because the great majority of Indian settlers in Malaya are of the labouring class. While it may be the statuary restrictions on the Indians as such are few, the fact remains that the Malays, *and even the Chinese* (emphasis added) are inclined to regard the Indians as of lower status. It was not possible to dissociate this position among public opinion and from the actual bar against citizenship which exists in the Malay states.[87]

The issue of citizenship and the immigrant communities was not resolved until well after World War II. While Indians and Chinese domiciled in the Straits Settlements were regarded as British subjects, the colonial authorities were not prepared to contemplate the bestowal of citizenship rights upon non-Malays resident in Malay states.[88] The British continued to believe that the immigrant communities were bound by primordial allegiance to the countries of origin, to which they would ultimately return, and thus could have no genuine interest in the future or destiny of Malaya.[89] Yet throughout the 1920s and 1930s, the proportion of locally born Chinese and Indians had steadily risen, and an increasing number of Indians, especially educated Indians, were committed to remaining in Malaya.[90]

In 1938, under the aegis of its activist Secretary, K.A. Neelakanda Aiyer, the CIAM mounted a widespread "uplift" campaign intended to promote greater social awareness among the Indian population. Although the association leadership was largely dominated by Hindus, the CIAM adopted a secular approach which emphasized the common interests shared by all Malayan Indians,[91] thus seeking to transcend or bypass the discordances of caste and religious affiliation, factors which contributed to the "weak, divided and resigned" standing of the Indian community.[92] The campaign was largely conducted by teachers and kanganies who had hitherto tended to hold themselves aloof from the labouring classes.[93] The CIAM programme of uplift and the championing of working-class grievances also acted as a spur to the growing labour militancy of the late 1930s and early 1940s.[94]

INDUSTRIAL UNREST AND THE KLANG STRIKES

Although Indian workers had mounted occasional industrial actions in the 1920s,[95] prior to the Depression industrial activism was an isolated phenomenon. However, the grievous and unsettling experiences of the Depression years had sown the seeds of discontent and resentment among Indian labourers. This generalized disquiet was accompanied by a growing awareness of employee rights and employer obligations. The 1930s witnessed a gradual but inexorable decline (but by no means a complete disappearance) of inter-caste disputes within workplaces, and a concomitant readiness to cooperate across caste and other primal loyalty boundaries in the pursuit of common objectives.[96]

Throughout the 1930s Indian workers appeared far more prepared to take industrial action in support of their claims. In 1934 there were eleven strikes — eight in the FMS, two in Johor and a strike among railway employees — while in 1936, there were three strikes, all in Perak.[97]

As noted, the formation of the CIAM in 1936 was followed by the cautious initiation and gradual cultivation of contacts between the CIAM and the labouring classes. The consequent dialogue assisted the association to develop policies specifically tailored towards advancing the interests and welfare of the Indian workforce. The CIAM Executive was anxious to identify workers who could be assisted to form and administer trade unions. This development met with sustained employer animosity and the deployment of legal and other measures aimed at crushing the movement in its nascency.[98]

A major factor which contributed to the incremental emergence of Indian working class consciousness was the exposure, especially in urban and industrial settings, to the methods and organization of Chinese workers. Throughout the 1930s there was an increase in the general mobilization of Chinese labour, which was countered with heavy-handed colonial repression. The government introduced an armoury of authoritative legislation, including the Banishment Ordinance, the Aliens Ordinances, and the Registration of Schools Ordinance to attempt to curb Chinese activism.[99] Chinese assertiveness and defiance of colonial intimidation struck a responsive chord with Indian workers, and whenever Indians were employed with Chinese labour, the former acquired some of the industrial militancy of the latter.[100] This development was noted by the Malayan authorities, and by 1939, Mr C.E. Wilson, Controller of Labour, was able to report, "It was evident ... that the modern Indian labourer knows his rights and how to set about getting them just as well as the Chinese."[101]

The CIAM was deeply impressed by the success of the industrial campaign waged in 1937 by Chinese estate workers and the range of concessions they had won. This had a marked influence on the strategies adopted by the association. By 1940, the Selangor Branch of the CIAM had organized Indian labour in many estates.[102]

The late 1930s saw a dramatic upsurge in Indian industrial unrest. Throughout 1939–40 there was continual ferment among stevedore and godown workers employed in Penang harbour.[103] In 1939 Indian workers employed at Sentul railway yards in Kuala Lumpur struck for better wages and conditions.[104] On 28 June 1939, in response to these developments, the Malayan government introduced the Trade Union Ordinance. Although the colonial documents claim that the enactment was modelled on the 1919 Trade Union Acts,[105] historians have noted far greater similarities between the Malayan legislation and the British Trade Union Act of 1927. This act had been passed in the wake of the defeat of the British labour movement in the 1926 General Strike, and was thus conservative in temper and legalistic in application.[106] The enactment stipulated that a Registrar of Trade Unions would be appointed; that trade unions would acquire legal recognition only after a process of registration; and that all union activity was to be conducted in accordance with "lawful purposes".[107] These "purposes" were carefully prescribed by the colonial administration, which sought to impose strict limits on all union activities.[108] Any union action which fell outside these narrowly defined limits was to be deemed "unlawful".

Although the Indian government objected to the use and scope of the term "unlawful" and requested that rights of appeal be incorporated into the legislation, the Trades Union Enactment was gazetted, unaltered, on 17 January 1940.[109] The government also introduced legislation to establish industrial courts. This legislation took effect in June 1941.[110]

Growing labour discontent led to the outbreak of a series of strikes in the Klang district of Selangor in 1941. Although the plantation workforce had traditionally been law abiding and quiescent, the sequence of events between 1939 and 1941, aggravated by colonial mismanagement, created an upsurge of frustration and resentment which pushed labourers beyond their collective endurance.[111] The advent of war in Europe in 1939 had resulted in a boom in the commodity market, particularly in the previously depressed exports of rubber and tin. This was accompanied by heavy demands on the labour force which included augmented workloads and long additional hours of "voluntary" unpaid labour on estates.[112] Although in October 1939 wages had been increased to fifty cents per day for males and forty-five cents for females,[113] this was not sufficient to accommodate the spiralling increase in the cost of living. As a consequence the wages of Indian labour declined in purchasing power, leading to general hardship among the plantation workforce. This had already produced intermittent industrial unrest throughout 1940.[114] The ban on assisted migration in 1938 had provided Indian labour with greater leverage in disputes with employers, and they were both aware of and emboldened by recent victories won by Chinese workers.[115] In the absence of institutionalized grievance procedures and recognized trade unions for plantation workers, industrial campaigns were organized, led, and supported by the CIAM.[116]

In January 1941, in response to worker representations, the UPAM made an offer of five cents per diem increase for rubber tappers. This was rejected by the CIAM-guided Klang District Union, headed by prominent Tamil journalist R.H. Nathan.[117] The first wave of the Klang strikes took place between February and April 1941, initially centred on pay issues rather than the need to overhaul working conditions. When employers refused to consider further wage claims, more than 3,000 workers went out on strike.[118] In response, the UPAM demanded that the government ban the Klang District Union. In some estates, planters withheld food rations in an attempt to force employee acquiescence.[119] A settlement brokered by the Indian Agent, which fell well short of worker expectations, was dismissed by both strikers and the CIAM as a "sell-out" and merely served to fuel Indian anger.[120] The strikers countered employer intransigence with a full schedule of demands, mainly consisting of long-held workplace grievances. These were equal pay for Indian and Chinese plantation workers; removal of supervisory staff known to have abused workers; provision of proper education facilities for children; an end to sexual molestation of female workers; provision of adequate health and medical facilities; prohibition of all toddy outlets within estates; free access to the estates for workers' relatives and friends; freedom of speech and assembly for workers in estates; abolition of the rule requiring workers to dismount from bicycles upon passing European and Asian managers; reduction of excessive working days of ten to twelve hours' duration; non-victimization of workers presenting petitions; and freedom to organize trade unions of plantation workers.[121] Most workers showed their active support for the cause of Indian independence by wearing "Gandhi" caps and by flourishing the Indian nationalist tri-colour flags; both measures openly breached colonial regulations.[122]

Up until this time, colonial attitudes towards the Klang strikes and the CIAM more generally had been divided between the more conciliatory approach taken by the Labour Department, which advocated consultation with the CIAM on labour-related issues, and the more implacable line held by the police. The latter regarded the entire association leadership as inveterate troublemakers indoctrinated with the seditious ideologies of Indian nationalism.[123] It might be speculated that police attitudes had been at least partially shaped by the knowledge that by 1938 at least 200 "educated" Indians had become members of the Malayan Communist Party; the rather simplistic viewpoint held by colonial intelligence erroneously conflated the subversive ideology with the more generic currents of Indian nationalism.[124] However, once it became obvious that the police perspective was shared by Governor Sir Shenton Thomas, the die was cast for an uncompromising confrontation with the strikers.[125]

In April 1941 the strike entered a new phase. A UPAM announcement that wages would be increased to sixty cents per day for males and fifty cents for females did not bring parity with Chinese workers and was seen as inadequate. The offer heralded a new round of strikes.[126] On 6 May the government arrested R.H. Nathan who had publicized and promoted the labourers' cause. Nathan's arrest led to a rapid escalation of strikes and riots in a number of districts.[127] On 7 May strikers held a large demonstration outside the Kuala Lumpur Labour Office calling for Nathan's release. This was followed by a gathering on 10 May outside the

Klang District Police Station, during which a number of protestors were arrested for carrying sticks.[128]

From the very outset of the dispute, UPAM had repeatedly pressured the government to use whatever force was necessary to crush the disturbances.[129] In his report on 10 May to the Colonial Office, Sir Shenton Thomas claimed that the trouble had been wholly fermented by the adherents of the CIAM, acting under the inspiration of Congress propaganda. He imputed special responsibility to journalist and President of the Klang District Union Nathan and to CIAM leaders Dr N.K. Menon and N. Raghavan. The response of the Undersecretary of State for the Colonial Office cleared the way for the use of force with the admonition to embark upon "firm handling of the subversive elements".[130] An initial attempt to use Australian troops to crush the unrest having been rebuffed by the Australian Command,[131] the colonial authorities turned to Indian troops. The strikes were quelled by 10 May, and the troops were withdrawn on 26 May.[132] During the military action, 5 labourers were killed, 60 more severely injured, 404 warrants for arrest were issued (of which 393 were fulfilled), and 220 Indians were scheduled for deportation (including Nathan, who was deported on 19 May 1941).[133] In a cable of 6 August 1941 to the Secretary of State for the Colonies, Thomas advised that of those arrested, 12 were released unconditionally, 186 were released on the condition that they did not return to the district where they had been employed at the time of the strike, 21 had been deported while a further 95 "accepted repatriation", and 49 locally born remained under detention.[134] Following a government review of the strikes, Thomas recommended that C.E. Wilson, Controller of Labour, who had advocated negotiating with the CIAM, be retired and that Major G.M. Kidd, British Resident in Selangor, who had allegedly failed to foresee or suppress strike action, be moved elsewhere.[135]

The heavy handedness of the Malayan government's response aroused the ire of Congress and the indignation of the Government of India, which called for a "searching inquiry".[136] In a private letter to Mr Leo Amery, Secretary of State for India and Burma, Lord Linlithgow, Viceroy of India, expressed his concern that the Malayan government's intolerance of Indian political organizations, even those which had the avowed backing of the Government of India, was needlessly hampering efforts to promote Indian unity and to effect general improvements in the overall standing of the Malayan Indian community. Linlithgow wrote:

Whatever the intentions and goodwill of the Malayan governments, the fact ... [is] ... that in the public life of the country the Indian community is not as a rule regarded as of equal status with the other communities. A good example of that was afforded by the suspicions aroused in the minds of CID in Singapore at the formation of an authoritative Central Indian Association. One of our harder tasks in dealing with Indians overseas is to overcome personal animosities and to develop a unity of purpose and action, and these difficulties are aggravated still further if unions ... despite their purpose and official backing, arouse official suspicion. I quite realize the difficulties regarding citizenship in the Malay States, but at any rate for the present all that is required is the public recognition that an Indian who makes his home in Malaya, has the same claim on the government or governments concerned, over a whole field of citizenship rights whether social, political or economic, as a British subject from any part of the Commonwealth.[137]

On 20 August 1941, Mr S. Dutt, Agent of the Government of India, discussed the strikes with Sir Shenton Thomas. Dutt commented on the indefinite detention of the strikers and the hardship this measure had created among labourers and their families. He also remarked on the unjust actions of estate managers in evicting supposed strike leaders from plantations without regard for their welfare or that of their families. Dutt also complained about the general attitude of Malayan officialdom towards the Indian government. In this regard he instanced the blackballing of the application for membership of the Selangor Golf Club of Mr C.S. Venkatachar, former Agent of the Government of India.[138]

Following the strikes, the Government of India refused a request made by the Malayan government for permission to recruit 500 labourers to work on the docks of Penang Harbour.[139] This action helped confirm the colonial authorities in their view that industrial disruption among the Indian workforce did not reflect genuine grievances, but was rather attributable to the external manipulations of Indian nationalists and especially Congress. In an internal memorandum of 20 September 1941, a colonial official expressed the British outlook in the following terms:

although Indian communities overseas are largely drawn from the poorest classes in India and enjoy in the colonies general conditions much superior to those which they enjoyed in India, they are usually looked down upon socially as a cheap labour class. From the fact that they are outside India, these communities become to Indian politicians a symbol of India's status

in the Empire, and there is a tendency to make claims on their behalf as
a method of asserting India's imperial status.[140]

In his report of 1944, a report which *inter alia* illustrates just how out of
touch colonial officials had become in connection with the surge of Indian
nationalism, Robert Niven Gilchrist made the extraordinary claim that
the Government of India was "developing a kind of Brahmanical Nazism
in relation to other Empire countries in which Indians have settled". He
further opined that:

> The standing Emigration Committee, the two houses of the Indian
> legislature, and many leading Government men, not excluding
> departmental heads in the Government of India, have vied with each
> other in expressing extreme ideas on the rights of Indians overseas,
> without mentioning their duties. The disease has also infected local Indian
> representative associations ....[141]

The inability of the colonial government to assess the legitimacy of the
claims of the Indian workforce, or to view the strikers in terms other than as
dupes of subversive Indian nationalists, blinded the authorities to growing
Indian resentment. In fact, the Malayan government's violent suppression
of the Klang strikes and the vengeful measures which followed antagonized
much of the Indian community and created widespread disillusionment
with British colonialism.[142] As we will see, enduring Indian resentment
was to be skilfuly exploited by the invading Japanese.

CONCLUSIONS

In the period leading to World War II, Indians made their first steps
towards unified political and industrial organization. However, this was
greatly impeded by the determination of many professional and middle-
class Indians to isolate themselves from the great mass of the Indian
"coolie" workforce. Early political movements took the form of Indian
associations which were largely moulded by considerations of class and
sub-ethnicity. These associations generally aimed at little more than securing
the appointment of Indians to legislative councils. Those thus nominated,
invariably wealthy and well connected (and often Ceylonese), proved
ineffective, and did little to articulate the concerns of the broader Indian
community or to advance their interests.

One of the earliest political reform movements was that of Dravidianism,
an ideology largely created as a result of the tendentious racial theorizing of

British colonialist anthropology. Inspired by political developments within the Madras Presidency, the rather confused polemics of the Justice Party, and fierce rhetoric of Ramasami Naicker and the Self-Respect Movement, Dravidianism was informed by nebulous notions of the imagined and wholly illusory autochthonous Tamil society which existed prior to the mythical "invasion" of "Aryan Brahmans". Self-Respect promoted a ferocious distrust of Brahmans and North Indians.

The first genuinely effective Indian political organization in Malaya was the CIAM, founded and led by Indian professionals, and determined to work to improve outcomes for labouring classes and for the granting of citizenship rights for Indians in Malaya. The CIAM enjoyed close relations with the Indian National Congress and sponsored tours of Congress leaders, including Nehru.

The seeds of industrial activism among Indian workers germinated during the Depression, in particular in reaction to the extensive repatriation of Indian labour. Labour unrest became more common throughout the 1930s, especially in urban workplaces, resulting in colonial legislation designed to regulate and quell industrial unrest. Worker dissatisfaction erupted in the widespread 1941 strikes among Klang Valley workers, which gained both the logistical and the moral support of the CIAM. These strikes were ultimately crushed by units of the British Indian Army, an action which was followed by a wave of arrests and deportations. The Klang strikes and the ham-fisted colonial response were to create the ideal political backdrop for the Japanese sponsorship of Indian nationalist organizations dedicated to the overthrow of British colonialism.

Notes

1. Rajeswary Amplavanar, *The Indian Minority and Political Change in Malaya 1945–1957* (Kuala Lumpur: Oxford University Press, 1981), pp. 2–3.
2. Khong Kim Hoong, *Merdeka! British Rule and the Struggle for Independence 1945–1957* (Kuala Lumpur: Insan, 1984), p. 13.
3. Usha Mahajani, *The Role of Indian Minorities in Burma and Malaya* (Bombay: Vora, 1960), p. 5; S. Dutt, *Report of the Agent of the Government of India in British Malaya, 1940* (Calcutta: Government of India Press, 1941).
4. J. Norman Parmer, *Colonial Labor Policy and Administration: A History of Labor in the Rubber Plantation Industry in Malaya 1910–1941* (New York: Augustin, 1960), p. 258.
5. Mahajani, *The Role of Indian Minorities*, p. 95; Sinnappah Arasaratnam, *Indians in Malaysia and Singapore* (London: Oxford University Press, 1970), p. 88.

6. Collin Abraham, *The Naked Social Order: The Roots of Racial Polarisation in Malaysia* (Subang Jaya: Pelanduk, 2004), pp. 291–92. The depths of this distrust and the forms in which it sometimes manifested is illustrated by this 1936 example: "A labour stoppage occurred on the Melentang Coconut Estate involving about 70 labourers. The cause of the stoppage was a rumour that witchcraft was practiced by certain [Malayalee] members of the estate staff" (C.E. Wilson, Controller of Labour, Malaya, *Annual Report of the Labour Department, Malaya, 1936* [Kuala Lumpur: Government Press, 1937]).

7. Chandra Muzaffar, "Political Marginalization in Malaysia", in *Indian Communities in Southeast Asia*, edited by K.S. Sandhu and A. Mani (Singapore: Institute of Southeast Asian Studies, 1993), p. 215.

8. In 1995, when undertaking research for my doctorate, I was informed by employees in coconut and rubber estates in upper Perak that, during the 1920s and 1930s, incipient militancy among Tamil workers was easily forestalled by threatening the use of Telegu labourers; on neighbouring estates, Telegu workers were similarly warned that their jobs would be lost to Tamil workers.

9. K.A. Mukundan, *Report of the Agent of the Government of India in British Malaya, 1936* (Calcutta: Government of India Press, 1937).

10. K.A. Mukundan, *Report of the Agent of the Government of India in British Malaya, 1934* (Calcutta: Government of India Press, 1935).

11. Sinnappah Arasaratnam, "Malaysian Indians: The Formation of an Incipient Society", in *Indian Communities in Southeast Asia*, edited by K.S. Sandhu and A. Mani (Singapore: Institute of Southeast Asian Studies, 1993), p. 197.

12. Arasaratnam, *Indians in Malaysia and Singapore*, p. 83.

13. Michael R. Stenson, *Class, Race and Colonialism in West Malaysia: The Indian Case* (St. Lucia: University of Queensland Press, 1980), p. 27; George Bilainkin, *Hail Penang! A Narrative of Comedies and Tragedies in a Tropical Outpost among Europeans, Chinese, Malays and Indians* (Penang: Areca Books, 2010), pp. 229–30.

14. Mukandan, *Annual Report*, 1934.

15. Mukundan, *Annual Report*, 1936.

16. Arasaratnam, *Indians in Malaysia and Singapore*, p. 85.

17. Mahajani, *The Role of Indian Minorities*, p. 95.

18. Sir Girja Shankar Bajpai, Secretary to the Government of India, *Memorandum to the Honourable Colonial Secretary, Singapore, 1938* (Memorandum No. f-44/38-L&0, Oriental and India Office Collection, London).

19. Rajeswary, *The Indian Minority*, p. 6.

20. Arasaratnam, *Indians in Malaysia and Singapore*, p. 95.

21. Nicholas Dirks, *The Hollow Crown: Ethno History of an Indian Kingdom*, 2nd ed. (Ann Arbor: University of Michigan Press, 1993), p. 19.

22. Burton Stein, *A History of India* (London: Blackwell, 1988), p. 55.
23. Dirks, *The Hollow Crown*, p. 19.
24. David Cannadine, *Ornamentalism: How the British Saw their Empire* (London: Penguin, 2001), p. 41.
25. David Washbrook, "The Development of Caste Organisation in South India 1880–1925", in *South Indian Political Institutions and Political Change*, edited by C.J. Baker and D.A. Washbrook (Delhi: MacMillan, 1975), p. 180.
26. Peter Van der Veer, *Religious Nationalisms: Hindus and Muslims in India* (Berkeley: University of California Press, 1994), p. 19.
27. Maria Misra, *Vishnu's Crowded Temple: India since the Great Rebellion* (London: Allen Lane, 2007), p. 15.
28. Declan Quigley, *The Interpretation of Caste* (Oxford: Clarendon Press, 1993), pp. 124–25.
29. Ibid.
30. Misra, *Vishnu's Crowded Temple*, p. 84.
31. Christopher John Baker, *The Politics of South India 1920–1937* (Cambridge: Cambridge University Press, 1976), pp. 23–24.
32. Misra, *Vishnu's Crowded Temple*, p. 137.
33. Thomas R. Trautmann, *Aryans and British India* (Berkeley: Yale University Press, 1997), pp. 8–9.
34. Ibid., pp. 172–75. These events are described in Genesis, the first book of the Bible. This describes how a Great Flood, unleashed by God, was survived by Noah, his three sons and their families. Furious at the insulting behaviour of his son Ham, Noah cursed Ham's descendents to eternal servitude to the descendents of the other two sons, Shem and Japheth. According to this interpretation, Hamitic people are held to possess dark skins. (Rajiv Malhotra and Aravindan Neelakandan, *Breaking India: Western Interventions in Dravidian and Dalit Faultlines* (New Delhi: Amaryllis, 2011), p. 39).
35. Malhotra and Neelakandan, *Breaking India*, p. 91.
36. Ibid.
37. Nicholas Dirks, *Castes of Mind: Colonialism and the Making of Modern India* (Princeton, NJ: Princeton University Press, 2001), p. 64.
38. Misra, *Vishnu's Crowded Temple*, p. 137.
39. Malhotra and Aravindan, *Breaking India*, p. 91.
40. Misra, *Vishnu's Crowded Temple*, p. 136.
41. Malhotra and Aravindan, *Breaking India*. The Brahman alliance with Mrs Annie Besant served to reinforce the claims made by the Justiceites. The Theosophical Society and in particular Annie Besant herself had assiduously propagated the myth of Brahmans as Aryans. Besant considered that the Aryans were a noble race of great antiquity, who given the right circumstances would "humanize [non-Brahmans] … here, as in Britain they [the 'lower classes'] are a menace to

civilization and undermine the fine fabric of society." (Misra, *Vishnu's Crowded Temple*, pp. 84–85).

42. Mytheli Sreenivas, *Wives, Widows and Concubines: The Conjugal Family Ideal in Colonial India* (Bloomington: Indiana University Press, 2008), p. 55.

43. Misra, *Vishnu's Crowded Temple*, pp. 126–27.

44. Sreenivas, *Wives, Widows and Concubines*, p. 55.

45. Misra, *Vishnu's Crowded Temple*, p. 137.

46. Baker, *The Politics of South India*, pp. 57–63.

47. Ibid., pp. 83–85.

48. Misra, *Vishnu's Crowded Temple*, p. 181.

49. Christopher Baker, "Figures and Facts: Madras Government Statistics 1880–1940", in *South India: Political Institutions and Political Change 1880–1940*, edited by C.J. Baker and D.A. Washbrook (Delhi: MacMillan, 1975), p. 36.

50. Misra, *Vishnu's Crowded Temple*, p. 94.

51. Arasaratnam, *Indians in Malaysia and Singapore*, p. 127.

52. Sreenivas, *Wives, Widows and Concubines*, p. 88.

53. Stenson, *Class, Race and Colonialism*, p. 78.

54. Sreenivas, *Wives, Widows and Concubines*, p. 84; Misra, *Vishnu's Crowded Temple*, p. 182.

55. Arasaratnam, *Indians in Malaysia and Singapore*, pp. 126–27.

56. Baker, *The Politics of South India*, pp. 192–93.

57. Stenson, *Class, Race and Colonialism*, pp. 78–79.

58. Kernial Singh Sandhu, *Indians in Malaya: Some Aspects of their Immigration and Settlement* (Cambridge: Cambridge University Press, 1969), p. 45.

59. Parmer, *Colonial Labor Policy*, p. 66.

60. Arasaratnam, *Indians in Malaysia and Singapore*, p. 96.

61. Stenson, *Class, Race and Colonialism*, p. 43.

62. Arasaratnam, *Indians in Malaysia and Singapore*, p. 96.

63. Stenson, *Class, Race and Colonialism*, p. 44; Parmer, *Colonial Labor Policy*, p. 200.

64. Arasaratnam, *Indians in Malaysia and Singapore*, p. 98.

65. Ibid.

66. Stenson, *Class, Race and Colonialism*, p. 45.

67. Selvakumaran Ramachandran, *Indian Plantation Labour in Malaysia* (Kuala Lumpur: S. Abdul Majeed, 1994), p. 227.

68. Stenson, *Class, Race and Colonialism*, p. 45.

69. Parmer, *Colonial Labor Policy*, p. 259.

70. Selvakumaran, *Indian Plantation Labour*, p. 227.

71. Stenson, *Class, Race and Colonialism*, pp. 47–51.

72. Ibid., pp. 46–47.

73. Selvakumaran, *Indian Plantation Labour*, p. 228.

74. P. Ramasamy, *Plantation Labour, Unions, Capital and the State in Peninsular Malaysia* (New York: Oxford University Press, 1994), p. 48.
75. Selvakumaran, *Indian Plantation Labour*, p. 229.
76. Parmer, *Colonial Labor Policy*, p. 259.
77. Selvakumaran, *Indian Plantation Labour*, p. 229.
78. Stenson, *Class, Race and Colonialism*, p. 47.
79. Ibid.
80. Ravindra K. Jain, *South Indians on the Plantation Frontier in Malaya* (New Haven: Yale University Press, 1970), p. 232.
81. Stenson, *Class, Race and Colonialism*, pp. 47–51.
82. Arasaratnam, *Indians in Malaysia and Singapore*, p. 99.
83. Ibid., p. 101.
84. Stenson, *Class, Race and Colonialism*, p. 48.
85. Arasaratnam, *Indians in Malaysia and Singapore*, p. 101.
86. Virginia Thompson, *Post-Mortem on Malaya* (New York: Macmillan, 1943), p. 133.
87. Bajpai, *Memorandum to the Honourable Colonial Secretary*.
88. Arasaratnam, *Indians in Malaysia and Singapore*, p. 90.
89. Mahajani, *The Role of Indian Minorities*, p. 134.
90. Arasaratnam, "Malaysian Indians", p. 193.
91. Selvakumaran, *Indian Plantation Labour*, p. 229.
92. Thompson, *Post-Mortem on Malaya*, p. 134.
93. Selvakumaran, *Indian Plantation Labour*, p. 229.
94. Ibid.
95. Amarjit Kaur, "Working on the Railway: Indian Workers in Malaya 1880–1957", in *The Underside of Malaysian History: Pullers, Prostitutes, Plantation Workers*, edited by Peter J. Rimmer and Lisa M. Allen (Singapore: Singapore University Press, 1990), p. 120.
96. Wilson, *Annual Report, 1936*.
97. Ramasamy, *Plantation Labour*, p. 47.
98. Parmer, *Colonial Labor Policy*, pp. 258–59; Charles Gamba, *The Origins of Trade Unionism in Malaya: A Case Study in Colonial Labour Unrest* (Singapore: Eastern Universities Press, 1962), p. 4.
99. Gamba, *The Origins of Trade Unionism*, p. 5.
100. Kaur, "Working on the Railway", pp. 119–20.
101. C.E. Wilson, Controller of Labour, Malaya, *Annual Report of the Labour Department, Malaya, 1939* (Kuala Lumpur: Government Press, 1940).
102. Ramasamy, *Plantation Labour*, p. 49.
103. Arasaratnam, *Indians in Malaysia and Singapore*, p. 80.
104. C.E. Wilson, Controller of Labour, Malaya, *Annual Report of the Labour Department, Malaya, 1940* (Kuala Lumpur: Government Press, 1941).

105. *Malaya: Registration and Control of Trade Unions. May–August 1940* (File L/P&J/8/263, Collection 108/21/F, Oriental and India Office Collection, London).

106. A.N. Wilson observes that the 1927 Trade Union Act materially widened the categories of strikes which might be regarded as "illegal" to those which were "designed or calculated to coerce the government either directly, or by inflicting hardship on the community", and which were henceforth banned. The ambiguous wording could be stretched to counter almost any strike. In addition the act also prohibited peaceful picketing at sites of industrial disputation and held that workers who refused to accept changes in their working conditions were deemed to be on strike (A.N. Wilson, *After the Victorians: The World Our Parents Knew* (London: Arrow Books, 2006), pp. 258–59).

107. *Malaya: Registration and Control of Trade Unions.*

108. Gamba, *The Origins of Trade Unionism*, p. 158.

109. *Malaya: Registration and Control of Trade Unions.*

110. Ramasamy, *Plantation Labour*, p. 42.

111. Wilson, *Annual Report, 1941.*

112. Stenson, *Class, Race and Colonialism*, p. 60.

113. Ramasamy, *Plantation Labour*, p. 36.

114. Wilson, *Annual Report, 1941.*

115. Selvakumaran, *Indian Plantation Labour*, pp. 228–29.

116. Ibid., p. 230.

117. Ramasamy, *Plantation Labour*, p. 49.

118. Selvakumaran, *Indian Plantation Labour*, p. 231.

119. Janakey Raman Manickam, *The Malaysian Indian Dilemma: The Struggles and the Agony of the Indian Community in Malaysia*, 2nd ed. (Klang: Janakey Raman Manickam, 2010), p. 87.

120. Selvakumaran, *Indian Plantation Labour*, p. 231.

121. Ibid.

122. Ibid.

123. Ramasamy, *Plantation Labour*, p. 162.

124. C.C. Chin and Karl Hack, "Early History of the Malayan Communist Party", in *Dialogues with Chin Peng: New Light on the Malayan Communist Party*, edited by C.C. Chin and Karl Hack (Singapore: Singapore University Press, 2004), p. 68.

125. Ramasamy, *Indian Plantation Labour*, p. 162; Janakey, *The Malaysian Indian Dilemma*, p. 88.

126. Ramasamy, *Plantation Labour*, p. 50.

127. Selvakumaran, *Indian Plantation Labour*, pp. 231–32.

128. Janakey Raman, *The Malaysian Indian Dilemma*, p. 89.

129. Selvakumaran, *Indian Plantation Labour*, pp. 231–32.

130. Undersecretary of State, Colonial Office, Cable of 14 May 1941, *Indians Overseas:*

Malaya: Strikes by Indian Labourers (File L/PJ/8/264, Collection 108-21-G, Oriental and India Office Collection, London).

131. Philippa Poole, *Of Love and War: The Letters and Diaries of Captain Adrian Curlewis and His Family* (Sydney: Landsdowne Press, 1982), p. 56.

132. Unsigned note for file, Malaya, 27 May 1941, *Indians Overseas: Malaya: Strikes by Indian Labourers* (File L/P&J/8/264, Collection 108-21-G, Oriental and India Office Collection, London).

133. Speech by the Hon. Pandit Hiray Nath Kunzru, 20 November 1941 (Council of State Debates), *Indians Overseas: Malaya: Negotiations between Indian and Malayan Governments 1939–1942* (File L/P&J/8/260, Collection 108-21-C, Oriental and India Office Collection, London); Selvakumaran, *Indian Plantation Labour*, p. 232.

134. Sir Shenton Thomas, Cable of 6 August 1941 to Secretary of State for the Colonies, *Indians Overseas: Malaya: Strikes by Indian Labourers*.

135. Report on File, *Indians Overseas: Malaya: Strikes by Indian Labourers*; Janakey, *The Malaysian Indian Dilemma*, p. 90.

136. *Indians Overseas: Malaya: Negotiations between and Indian and Malayan Governments, 1939–1942*.

137. Extract of Private Letter from Lord Linlithgow, Viceroy of India, to Mr Amery, Secretary of State for the Colonies, 18 April 1941, *Indians Overseas: Malaya: Negotiations between Indian and Malayan Governments 1939–1942*.

138. Report of Conversation between S. Dutt, Agent for the Government of India in British Malaya, and Sir Shenton Thomas, 20 August 1941, *Indians Overseas: Malaya: Strikes by Indian Labourers*.

139. *Indians Overseas: Malaya: Strikes by Indian Labourers*.

140. Minute for file, 20 September 1941, *Indians Overseas: Malaya: Strikes by Indian Labourers*.

141. Robert Niven Gilchrist, Political Department, India Office, *Political and Social Problems of Indians in inter alia Malaya up until 22 April 1944* (Mss Eur D. 819, Oriental and India Office Collection, London).

142. Nadyan Raghavan, *India and Malaya: A Study* (Bombay: Indian Council of World Affairs/Orient Longman, 1954), p. 69.

10

THE JAPANESE INVASION, SUBHAS CHANDRA BOSE AND INDIAN WARTIME NATIONALISM[1]

THE BACKGROUND: JAPANESE WAR AIMS

Throughout the 1930s the idea of creating an economic zone, later to be termed a Greater East Asian Co-Prosperity Sphere, based on the pan-Asian ideal of universal brotherhood (*hakko ichi'u* — the eight corners of the world under one roof), gained wide currency in Japanese academic and political circles. Japan saw itself as the natural leader, indeed the dominant power, in any such regional grouping.[2] This concept was more fully developed by the Japanese government and adopted as policy on 1 August 1940.[3] The new order was to consist of a core economic unit centred on Japan, China and Manchukuo (Manchuria), and to include the mandated islands, French Indo-China, Thailand, Malaya, Borneo, and the Netherlands East Indies, and possibly Australia, New Zealand, and India.[4] While the Japanese were prepared to grant nationhood to the Buddhist countries of the mainland, they intended to hold the "undeveloped" Islamic lands of the Malay Archipelago as permanent colonies.[5] With regard to the Malay Peninsula, Singapore and the other Straits Settlements were to be placed under direct rule, the four northern states (Kelantan, Perlis, Kedah, and Terengganu) were to be ceded to Thailand, while the remaining states were to be maintained under the existing structure but subject to the close guidance of Japanese advisors.[6]

On 7 December 1941, Japanese forces attacked Pearl Harbor in Hawaii, U.S. military installations in the Philippines, Guam, Midway and Wake, and British airfields in Hong Kong. On 8 December the Japanese landed forces in Singora (in Southern Thailand) and Kota Bharu in Kelantan. The Japanese fleet, carrying 24,000 combat troops,[7] effected a landing at Kelantan within two hours, despite heavy seas. The town was fully occupied by 9 December. Another Japanese force made a virtually unopposed landing at a number of strategic points in the Kra Isthmus.[8]

BRITISH SOCIETY ON THE EVE OF THE INVASION

The Japanese invasion met a British administration and society both psychologically and militarily unprepared for war. Undoubtedly the major factor underlying the British sense of security was the massive Singapore naval base, the so-called arsenal of democracy.[9] The base, a vast annexe covering twenty-one square miles, was widely viewed as impregnable, a bastion of the British Empire in the East, a guarantee of protection for both India and Australia, as well as the future site of the Royal Air Force headquarters in the East.[10]

But Singapore was more than just a strategic defence facility. It was a crucial hub in the overall commercial life of the British Empire. By 1930 nearly one-quarter of Empire trade passed through Singapore; for Australia the figure was sixty per cent.[11] At the outbreak of the Pacific War, Malaya exported two-thirds of the world's tin and accounted for about half the world's production of rubber. Most of these exports were handled through the port of Singapore. The Malayan colonies and Singapore made significant contributions to the cumulative wealth of the sterling zone — rubber exports to the United States were worth $118 million per annum, with tin contributing an additional $55 million.[12]

British military strategists had long insisted that any attack on Singapore would necessarily consist of a seaborne assault.[13] As a result, Peninsula defences were generally neglected, and Singapore itself was fortified by large seaward pointing guns.[14] This strategy was based on the conviction that no military force could breach the "impenetrable" jungle which lay to the north of Singapore and that no attack could or would be made down the length of the Peninsula.[15]

Responding to military exercises which exposed the limitations of this approach, and which demonstrated Singapore's vulnerability to a landward attack,[16] the General Commanding Officer, Major-General (Sir) William Dobbie decided to construct a series of defence installations in Southern Johor and across the north coast of Singapore.[17] In addition, he proposed to revise military policy to accommodate a whole of Malaya defence strategy. These measures were opposed and ultimately scuttled by the unyielding opposition of Governor Shenton Thomas. In early 1940, Thomas, supported by the Foreign Office, decided that since it was obvious that Japan was not strong enough to go to war with the British Empire, the Malayan economy would take precedence over defence considerations.[18]

Neither the British civilians nor the military took seriously the prospect of a Japanese military threat. On 4 September 1939, commenting on the outbreak of war in Europe, the *Straits Times* in Singapore advised its readers: "At this distance from the scene of battle, with our defences perfected and Japanese participation in the struggle on the side of Germany a remote possibility, Malaya has little to fear."[19] The widely held expatriate belief that Japan lacked the capacity to launch an assault on Malaya and Singapore,[20] was shared by the British military. As late as 6 December 1941, a mere two days prior to the commencement of the invasion, Sir Robert Brooke-Popham, Commander-in-Chief, dismissed reports of Japanese convoys in Thai waters as "alarmist", while Sir Shenton Thomas privately assured his cipher clerk, "You can take it from me there will never be a Japanese bomb dropped in Singapore, there will never be a Japanese set foot in Malaya."[21]

British complacency was informed by a Social Darwinist perspective that embraced the crudest forms of racial stereotyping. Brooke-Popham regarded the Japanese as "sub-human" specimens,[22] while the upper echelons of the RAF doubted that any "coloured" people would ever make good pilots or operate efficient air forces.[23] British military intelligence provided a picture of an enemy so feeble and disorganized as to be beneath contempt.[24] This view of the Japanese as a woefully inadequate foe persisted until the actual invasion.[25]

So sanguine were the colonial authorities, that few preparations had been made to meet a possible Japanese assault. No evacuation strategies had been devised for the 31,000-strong European population in Malaya and Singapore and, indeed, even discussion of this subject was regarded as "defeatist".[26] The authorities refused to countenance the construction of civilian defence facilities,[27] and actively discouraged the employment of Asians within the defence forces.[28] Those who did succeed in gaining entry met with resentment and open discrimination, especially in matters of pay and conditions of service.[29] A later attempt to create "stay-behind" parties of guerrillas was disallowed "on the grounds that such a scheme which admitted the possibility of enemy penetration would have a disastrous psychological effect on the Oriental mind".[30]

The European society which administered Singapore was politically insulated, socially hidebound and completely out of touch with rapidly changing political realities.[31] Ian Morrison of the London *Times* reported that in European circles "the social round proceeded at the level of the least intelligent .... This state of affairs was symptomatic of the deadness of thought".[32] Indeed, right up until the final surrender, British civilians continued to observe all the petty snobberies and to insist upon official hierarchies of social life.[33] This society was obsessed with distinctions of class and race and openly discriminated against the soldiers sent to protect them.[34] Indian troops were subject to rampant racial prejudice. Officers were denied entry to local clubs and were even instructed not to ride in the same railway carriages as Europeans.[35] However, this bigotry also extended to the "proletarian" white dominion troops, especially Australians.[36]

THE MILITARY CAMPAIGN

The Japanese campaign consisted of a series of rapid and decisive successes. It was aided by indifferent Allied resistance, constant retreats,[37] and uninspired generalship.[38] From the outset, hesitation and indecision cast the British campaign into a defensive posture and had a deleterious psychological impact upon British and Indian troops.[39] On 10 December 1941, Japanese warplanes sank the British battleships *Prince of Wales* and *Repulse*, the so-called Force Z, off the east coast, thus leaving Malaya barren of naval support.[40] With the destruction of Force Z, the Japanese enjoyed total and unchallenged sea and air supremacy for the remainder of the campaign.[41] On 9 December, Duff Cooper, a senior British Cabinet Minister, was appointed Resident Minister for Far Eastern Affairs, but had no clear commission to assume overall control. He was repeatedly frustrated by Brooke-Popham and Shenton Thomas, especially the latter, who viewed his primary role as upholding the prestige of the Raj, and thus who wanted no disturbance to the normal routines of colonial life.[42]

On 12 December a force of 500 Japanese troops broke through the British defences at Jitra in northern Kedah, routing 8,000 British and Indian troops,[43] destroying in fifteen hours a line that their own military planners had calculated would hold for three months.[44] The Japanese advanced swiftly, taking Penang on 19 December and Ipoh on 28 December. The continual British retreats created chaos and often resulted in the abandonment of vast quantities of military stores.[45] On Boxing Day 1941, General Percival's Chief Engineer, Brigadier Simson, submitted a detailed proposal for the construction of fixed defences in Johor and on the northern coastline of Singapore, but Percival rejected this, claiming that "Defences are bad for morale — for both troops and civilians."[46] On 11 January 1941, Japanese forces took a hastily abandoned Kuala Lumpur, in the process acquiring detailed survey maps.[47] The Japanese subsequently occupied Malacca on 16 January, and after crossing the Singapore Strait, Churchill's "splendid moat", in a mere six minutes,[48] Singapore on 15 February. The final capitulation, "a gigantic and wholly successful piece of bluff" on the part of the Japanese,[49] who were not only defending overextended lines of communication but were also critically short of men and ammunition,[50] was in keeping with the inept British conduct of the entire campaign. As a consequence, a defending garrison of over 85,000 surrendered to an assault force of around 30,000 Japanese troops.[51]

The invasion shattered the myth of British invincibility, the prestige or izzat upon which the British Empire was largely based. Lee Kuan Yew states that "In 70 days of surprises, upsets and stupidities, British colonial society was shattered, and with it the assumption of the Englishman's superiority."[52] The precipitate collapse, the feeble and confused British resistance, had a profound impact upon local opinion.[53]

The loss of British prestige was magnified by several notorious incidents which occurred during the course of the invasion. These included the failure of the British authorities to highlight the contributions made by Asian troops and civilians to the defence of Malaya and Singapore;[54] brawls among European civilians over the distribution of cigarettes and other commodities;[55] and squalid scenes of drunkenness, desertion and cowardice among demoralized European troops at the time of the final surrender.[56]

However, the episode which most profoundly damaged British prestige and which most clearly revealed the stark racial ideologies which underpinned the dynamics of British Malaya was the clandestine evacuation of the European population of Penang. Following the decision not to defend Penang, the British administration secretly ordered all Europeans to leave the island.[57] While Europeans made good their escape, Asian volunteers remained on duty and the news of the surrender of the island was delivered to the Japanese by a Eurasian.[58] The betrayal of the Malayan population was compounded by a subsequent broadcast in which Duff Cooper, Churchill's special advisor in Singapore, stated, "It has been necessary to evacuate many of the civilian population. We can only be thankful so many people have been safely removed."[59] His listeners were aware that this did not refer to the Asian population, which had been deserted by the British.[60]

The Allied collapse also demolished the myth of the British as "protectors" of the Malays.[61] As noted in the previous chapters, the British had consistently portrayed their presence in Malaya as necessary to guard the welfare of the Malays from the supposedly avaricious and naked commercial ambitions of the immigrant races. The bitterness felt at the British "desertion" continued to rankle with many Malays for years after the event.[62]

The loss of prestige struck a terminal blow at the European empires of the East. Peter Elphick sets the defeat in a wider context:

> When the Japanese took control of Indo-China from the French in July 1941, captured Malaya and Singapore from the British and drove the Dutch from Indonesia in February and March 1942, they shattered the myth of white superiority. Their victories were the death knell of the European empires in the East. They removed from the Asian mind for ever notions of white supremacy and European hegemony.[63]

THE JAPANESE OCCUPATION

Apart from the Chinese, many Malayans were not initially antagonistic to the invading Japanese, seeing in them a successful Asian power which would respect local aspirations.[64] However, Japanese promises of partnership within the Greater East Asian Co-Prosperity Sphere were quickly replaced with the reality of the ruthless exploitation of occupation — an occupation which was characterized by harshness, arrogance and incompetence. The Japanese administration showed little understanding of the ambitions or cultural sensitivities of the constituent groups of the colonial society they had acquired, and their regime of casual brutality and insistence on inherent Japanese superiority rapidly alienated those they now ruled.[65]

Subjected to months of colonial propaganda which had caricatured the Japanese in terms of crude racial stereotypes, Malayans were left unprepared for the full ferocity which accompanied the initial entry of battle-hardened troops conditioned by a training regime which could only be described as barbarous.[66] From the outset, the undisciplined and savage behaviour of the Japanese troops alienated many of the civilian population.[67] Their arrival often heralded an orgy of rape, looting and theft, sometimes accompanied by murder and sadistic cruelties.[68]

The Japanese military administration was governed by three fundamental objectives, namely the restoration of public order, the production of resources needed for national defence, and self sufficiency for the military.[69] These objectives were designed to consolidate Japanese control of Malaya and Singapore, and in particular to extract from these territories the materials needed to promote the war effort.[70]

Japanese educational and cultural policies for the indigenous peoples of the southern region aimed at rapid Nipponization of the population. These consisted of fostering *Nippon-Go* (the Japanese language as the lingua franca of East Asia); the inculcation of *Nippon Seishen* (the Japanese spirit), comprising an amalgam of rigid discipline, unquestioning compliance with Japanese direction, and unconditional loyalty to *Tenno Heika* (the Emperor); and the mental and physical drilling of younger Malayans who would be thus prepared to serve the Japanese Empire in any capacity — military or civil — as required by the occupying authorities.[71]

Economically, the Japanese had to contend with the dislocation created by the scorched earth policy undertaken by the retreating British who destroyed many key installations and facilities. Early economic measures included the gradual withdrawal of the Straits dollar and its replacement with Japanese military scrip, and the creation of an opium monopoly. The War Ministry transferred large sectors of the economy, including the rubber estates, to largely inefficient public corporations, often directly run by the *Gunseibu* (Military Administration).[72] The Japanese policies not only resulted in the creation of monopolies, but also resulted in widespread corruption and a series of flourishing black markets.[73] The Japanese lacked the expertise required to run a modern economy and proved maladroit as managers and technicians.[74] The Malayan economy's buoyancy was heavily dependent upon its exports of rubber and tin, especially to the United States, a market which was lost in the wake of the Japanese occupation.[75]

Malaya was reliant upon imports of a range of raw materials, especially rice which was traditionally supplied by Thailand and Burma.[76] In 1939 Malaya had imported 983,000 tons of rice, and at the time of the Japanese invasion had stockpiled sufficient rice to provision the country for six months.[77] In late 1942 rice imports fell well below actual needs and continued to decline precipitously throughout the remainder of the occupation.[78] From 1943 onwards Malaya faced calamitous food shortages. In response the military authorities urged people to grow their own food. Tapioca became a widely consumed rice supplement, but it was deficient as a source of nourishment and inadequate to meet dietary requirements. Food shortfalls created widespread malnutrition and resulted in increased levels of morbidity and death.[79]

Japanese economic policies resulted in high inflation, and an ultimately worthless military scrip.[80] By the end of the war the economies of Singapore and Malaya were in a parlous state. There were widespread shortages of food, clothing, medicine and other daily necessities, while the major industries — rubber and tin — lay in ruins.[81] Indeed, rubber production, which had totalled 500,000 tons in 1940, had shrunk to a mere 100,000 tons in 1945.[82]

Japanese Polices on Ethnicity

The most far-reaching changes produced by the Japanese occupying forces involved the politics of ethnicity. In general the Japanese attempted to reach accommodation with the Malays, encourage the growth of nationalism among the Indians, while actively discriminating against the Chinese as despised and reviled enemies.[83] The Japanese ultimately failed to capture the allegiance of any local nationalist movements. Their relations with all ethnic groups were studded with incidents of casual violence and permeated with incessant insistence upon inherent Japanese superiority, and the need for Japanese tutelage of "lesser" Asian races. Japanese anti-Westernism, its most effective mode of propaganda, was undermined by the clumsiness of Japanese political practices, and although used endlessly during the war, brought ever-diminishing returns.[84]

Japanese policies towards the Chinese were charged from the beginning with barbed hostility. Throughout the late 1930s the Nanyang communities had formed a National Salvation movement which had mobilized support for the regime of Chiang Kai Shek in its fight against the invading Japanese.[85] Japanese failure to cultivate Chinese opinion provoked extreme distrust of the Chinese en bloc. As a result the Japanese made no attempt in their dealings with the overseas Chinese now entrapped in the occupied territories to distinguish between those who had actively campaigned against them and those who had remained apolitical.[86]

Retaliatory measures against the Chinese were planned well before the Japanese forces took Singapore. The most infamous of these were the organized massacres collectively known as the "Purge through Purification" (*Kakyo Shukusei* or *Dai Kensho*; in Chinese, *Sook Ching*).[87] The death toll was estimated at between 50,000 and 100,000.[88] Similar operations, often accompanied by the most heinous outrages and cruelties, were repeated against other Chinese communities elsewhere in Malaya.[89]

The series of retaliatory measures also included the imposition of a collective levy of fifty million yen upon the entire Chinese community of Malaya and Singapore. This was viewed as a form of communal punishment on the Nanyang Chinese for their support of those taking up arms against Imperial Japan, and according to the *Gunseibu* provided the Chinese with opportunity to "atone" for their past mistakes.[90]

The policy of violent discrimination, savage reprisals and the displacement of the traditional Chinese leadership, based on age and wealth, especially the obliteration of the local Kuomintang (KMT), greatly increased Chinese support for the MCP, which was viewed as the only organization capable of offering armed resistance to the Japanese.[91] In response to Japanese repression, young Chinese leftists infiltrated the jungle to establish the Malayan Peoples' Anti-Japanese Army (MPAJA).[92] The so-called "hill people" rapidly gained the allegiance of the thousands of Chinese squatters who had been forced by the impact of Japanese economic mismanagement to migrate towards the jungle fringes and Malay Reservation areas to grow food necessary for their survival.[93] Throughout the war, the Chinese developed immense respect for the ideological and organizational skills of the MCP, and for the courage their cadres displayed in the face of overwhelming adversity.[94] The MPAJA created networks among the squatter population; networks which generated a continuous flow of food and intelligence.[95] The bonds forged during these years between the MCP and the Chinese squatters were to survive well beyond the war.[96]

Despite early betrayals which resulted in the elimination of much of its top leadership,[97] after 1943 the MPAJA consistently had a fighting force of between 4,000 and 5,000 men and women.[98] On 26 December 1943, at

Blantan, the British Force 136, representing South East Asian Command (SEAC), signed an alliance with the MPAJA pledging mutual cooperation in the liberation of Malaya.[99]

In general, the Japanese were more accommodating towards the Malays. While prior to the war, the Japanese had issued leaflets assuring the Malays of Japanese friendship, and that their intentions were to expel the Europeans and to "kill off the Chinese who have taken the wealth of your country",[100] the Japanese generally regarded the Malays as lazy and timorous.[101] Because of their perception of Malay economic and cultural backwardness, the Japanese never intended to grant independence to the Malays. This decision was reiterated as late as June 1945.[102]

The Japanese played upon Malay fears of Chinese domination by highlighting the dangers of the Chinese guerrilla movement. They also took steps to involve Malays in the administration of occupied Malaya, thus clearly distinguishing between Malays and non-Malays. Malays were given preference in appointment to the Civil Service and were recruited into the military police (*Kempeitai*), auxiliary troops (*heiho*), peace preservation corps (*jikeiden*), volunteer army (*giyugan*), and the Japanese Special Branch (*toko*).[103]

However, Japanese attempts to create mass collaborative movements among Malays met with failure. Initially the administration fostered the Marxist influenced *Kesatuan Melayu Muda* (KMM, or League of Malay Youth), which had been formed by a group of Malay intellectuals in 1937. Its leader, Ibrahim Yaacob, had run an underground intelligence network on behalf of the Japanese.[104] In December 1941 the leaders of the KMM were arrested by the British but were subsequently released by the Japanese.[105] However, the KMM also largely distrusted the Japanese, and the organization was banned in June 1942 after military intelligence uncovered secret contacts between the KMM and MCP.[106] Japanese attempts to cultivate the Islamic hierarchy met some successes with the convening of conferences in 1943 and 1944 in which the Japanese leadership convinced the Malay elite that they (the Japanese) were the protectors of Islam and that the war against the European colonial powers was a form of jihad.[107] While the Japanese leadership won early plaudits from pan-Malay nationalists by the temporary linking of Peninsula Malaya, Singapore and Sumatra into a single political unit, emphasizing the historic, anthropological and linguistic ties between the two entities, and (for Sumatrans), the freedom from Javanese control,[108] any goodwill won by this measure was lost by the cession of the four northern states to Thailand in August 1943, and by repeated acts of senseless brutality.[109]

The generally favourable treatment shown towards Malays did not exclude their recruitment to Japanese forced labour schemes, both within the Peninsula and on the Burma Railway project. Usually those who were coerced into participating in these schemes were selected by village heads acting under Japanese compulsion and were subject to the callous, arbitrary and savage discipline which marked all Japanese conscripted labour projects.[110]

During the later years of the occupation, anti-Japanese groups were formed in several states. In Perak resistance fighters were known as *Askar Melayu Setia* (Loyal Malay Soldier), while in Pahang, Malay resisters were grouped in *Wataniah* (For the Homeland).[111] One of the most prominent *Wataniah* recruits was a member of the royal house of Pahang, and future Prime Minister, Tun Abdul Razak.[112] As the fortunes of war turned against the Japanese, these groups received the unofficial support of the royal courts.[113] Malays also joined the MCP-sponsored MPAJA and the British run Force 136, though Malay enlistment in the latter was generally drawn from students studying abroad.[114]

Japanese racial policies created a widening gulf between communities now increasingly identified as "Chinese" and "Malay". Pro-Malay measures implemented under Japanese administration created resentment among the Chinese.[115] In turn the Japanese played upon Malay fears of Chinese domination by highlighting the putative dangers of the Chinese guerrilla movement. The MPAJA seemed to underscore Japanese propaganda by conducting indiscriminate reprisals against local informers and collaborators. Since most of the alleged fifth columnists appeared to be Malay, MPAJA retaliation assumed the outward appearance of interethnic score settling.[116] Japanese enlistment of Malays in local military and police forces set the scene for repeated racial clashes, and for inter-racial conflict and distrust which was to last well beyond the Japanese occupation.[117]

THE ESTABLISHMENT OF THE INDIAN INDEPENDENCE LEAGUE AND THE INDIAN NATIONAL ARMY

The rapid collapse of British and Commonwealth forces left the Japanese in control of 65,000 British Indian Army (BIA) prisoners of war (POWs), as well as over 700,000 Indians domiciled in Malaya.[118] Approximately

1,000 BIA officers were captured during the Malayan campaign, of whom approximately 25 per cent were Indian.[119]

The Japanese had long been aware of the instrumental potential of both Indian nationalism and the BIA to further their war aims. Prior to the invasion the Japanese had set up an intelligence unit to investigate ways of fomenting anti-British sentiment within the BIA and among Indian émigré communities in Southeast Asia. As the confrontation between Japan and the Anglo-US-Dutch coalition intensified, Thailand became the main stage of conflict, and a battleground of diplomatic, intelligence, and espionage operations between the rival powers.[120]

Japanese intelligence was aware of the existence of a shadowy organization known as the Indian Independence League (IIL), a secret society of revolutionary Sikhs working for the liberation of India with branches in Hong Kong, Shanghai, Tokyo, San Francisco and Berlin.[121] The Japanese moved quickly to establish links with the IIL. In Thailand, Major Fujiwara, assigned to lead the Malayan *Kikan* (agency), conferred with Pritam Singh, head of a group of disaffected Sikhs.[122] Negotiating as an emissary of the Japanese government, Fujiwara agreed that as the Japanese Army progressed through Malaya, the IIL would be authorized to absorb all Indians who wished to engage in the fight against the British. The IIL would also be charged with the task of organizing a volunteer army which would consist of officers recruited from the BIA as well as the Indian population resident in Malaya and Singapore.[123] As a first step, the Japanese would establish an intelligence operation (or *Kosuku*) in Southern Thailand and Malaya.[124] The IIL would be used as a vehicle for the dissemination of nationalist propaganda to be aimed at both the BIA soldiery and the general Indian population.[125]

Fujiwara also assured the ILL that in conducting military operations the Japanese Army would strive to consider the Indian nationalist cause. The military would be instructed to promote the welfare of Indians and not to treat Indian soldiers and civilians as nationals of an enemy country.[126] Troops would be ordered not to confiscate the property of Indian nationals and not to molest Indian women. In general these instructions were followed by the advancing Japanese Army.[127] The first Malayan headquarters of the IIL were established at Kota Bharu, capital of the northern state of Kelantan, shortly after the successful Japanese landings of 8 December 1941.[128]

The Indian National Army (INA) was established during the Japanese campaign. One of the earliest recruits was Captain Mohan Singh, aged thirty-three, second in command of the 15th Brigade 1 / 14th Punjabis, which had been captured by Japanese forces after the fall of Jitra.[129] Mohan Singh had already decided that he could no longer support the British, having been enraged by the actions of Lord Linlithgow, the Viceroy of India, who, without consultation with the Indian government, had plunged India into World War II.[130] On 20 December 1941, in Alor Setar, Pritam Singh and Mohan Singh were taken by Fujiwara to meet Lt. General Yamashita, who confirmed the Japanese military's full support for the Indian independence movement.[131] Subsequent discussions concluded on 31 December 1941 in Taiping, Perak, with in-principle agreement to the formation of an INA with Mohan Singh as provisional commander.[132] The INA was to be accorded the status of an allied army.[133]

Recruitment to the INA from among the membership of the BIA was stimulated by a sequence of developments which loosened and then overrode the obligatory ties which had mutually bound Indian troops and the British officer cadre. Indian soldiers stationed in Singapore and Malaya had been subject to a series of unsettling experiences before the trauma of the British surrender. Many Indian officers posted to Malaya after 1939 were appalled at the harsh conditions endured by Indian labourers and at their lesser rates of pay relative to Chinese workers.[134] As noted in the previous chapter, Indian troops had been used to quell the disturbances attending the Klang strikes, during which they had been called upon to fire on their own countrymen. Moreover, Indian troops and the officer cadre had been repeatedly insulted and discriminated against in the months leading up to the campaign by the unyielding racial hierarchy of British colonial society. In May 1941, the 4/19th Hyderabad Regiment rebelled when an Indian officer was sent home, reputedly for a liaison with a white woman.[135] Indian soldiers were dismayed by racial incidents which occurred throughout the campaign, in particular the evacuation of the European community of Penang in mid-December 1941 and the abandonment of the Asian population. The British behaviour could be interpreted as discrimination, betrayal, or even cowardice.[136] To many Indians it was a clear demonstration that the British intended to look after their own at all costs; if necessary at the expense of their Asian allies.[137]

The morale of Indian troops in Malaya was gravely affected by the rapid collapse of the British and Allied forces and the dramatic surrender of the supposedly unconquerable fortress of Singapore.[138] Many within the Indian officer cadre were less than impressed with the conduct of the campaign against the Japanese. A.C. Chatterji, Senior Medical Officer within the BIA in Malaya, believed that the campaign amounted to little more than "a case of continuous running away of the British troops, and the Japanese running hard to overtake them. Australian and Indians fought in a far better manner than the British troops".[139] Chatterji's sentiments were shared by a sizeable percentage of BIA officers.[140]

But perhaps the most stunning act of treachery, at least as far as the BIA officer cadre was concerned, was the cavalier manner in which they were treated after the British surrender. Firstly, the British officers were separated, apparently without protest, from the Indian officers and troops that they had commanded.[141] All BIA troops were then ordered to gather in Farrer Park in Singapore on 17 February 1942. The assembled troops were addressed by Lt-Colonel Hunt of the Malayan Command who told his stunned audience that "From today we are all prisoners of war. I now, on behalf of the British Government, hand you over to the Japanese Government, whose orders you will obey as you have been doing ours." For many soldiers this was "the symbolic act by which the bond binding Percival's Indians to the King-Emperor's service was ended."[142] For the BIA officers gathered at Farrer Park, Hunt's words signified nothing less than "the deliberate, formal, one might say almost ceremonial abdication of responsibility towards Indian troops", a calculated renunciation of the traditional allegiances which had bound British and Indians together as a "matter of honour".[143] This perceived betrayal was later seen as a pivotal factor in persuading many Indian officers that their future belonged with the INA.[144]

Following Hunt's address, the nominal rolls were handed to Major Fujiwara. He assured his audience that "Japan is fighting for the liberation of Asiatic nations which have been so long trodden under the cruel heel of British imperialism. Japan is the liberator and friend of the Asiatics."[145] Fujiwara then outlined the Japanese position with regard to India and the future of captured BIA personnel. Britain had been defeated in Malaya. Japan wanted an independent India. To this end, Japan was cooperating in the establishment of an Indian army which would be deployed towards achieving this objective.[146] Having completed this address, Fujiwara now declared, "On behalf of the Japanese Government, I now hand you over to the General Commanding Officer, Mohan Singh, who shall have the power of life and death over you."[147] The speakers had thus consecutively delivered control of the troops, one to another, "not as one speaker making way for another, but as one command surrendering men to another command".[148] Mohan Singh now announced the formation of an Indian National Army, and invited those present to join.[149] To many officers this held little appeal. Most were not attracted by the prospect of fighting their fellow countrymen, while others were astonished that the Japanese had entrusted the command of the INA to Mohan Singh, whom they regarded as a "very average officer".[150]

Several additional factors worked to overcome the reservations felt by large numbers of Indian officers towards joining a Japanese-sponsored INA. The first was the need to consider the long-term welfare of the BIA personnel who were now prisoners of war, in particular to ensure that incarcerated soldiers were not deployed as a source of forced labour. This line of thinking suggested that a properly officered INA might create structures which could, where necessary, resist the Japanese, and thus guarantee the safety of the rank and file. The officer cadre were also anxious to take every action possible to ensure the welfare of the Indian émigré populations now dependent upon Japanese goodwill. They were aware of the appalling crimes the Japanese were committing against the Chinese population. To date the Japanese had shown comparative restraint in their treatment of Indian civilians. But would this restraint evaporate if Indian POWs as a body refused to join the INA? This consideration became more urgent with the Japanese occupation of Burma. Here the position was complicated by the existence of a vigorous nationalist movement which was stridently and potentially violently anti-Indian.[151] Many BIA officers believed that the INA could act as de facto guardians of the Indian civilian population resident within the conquered territories.[152] The most senior BIA Indian officer, Lt-Colonel Naranjan Singh Gill, "reluctantly" agreed to join with Fujiwara and Mohan Singh and to solicit recruitment among captured personnel.[153]

The conduct of the Burma campaign appeared to further expose the weakness of the British Empire, as well as revealing once again the racial hierarchy and moral hollowness which lay at the very heart of British colonial rule. As in Malaya, the Japanese Imperial Army had defeated the British with contemptuous ease. The British had simply withdrawn in the face of the Japanese onslaught and retreated into India. Following the initial Japanese air strikes in Burma in December 1941, there was a mass departure of the Indian, Anglo-Indian and Anglo-Burmese populations and, by autumn 1942, approximately 600,000 people had fled to India.[154] The British had long sought to keep Burma at arm's length from India and had thus consistently refused to construct any overland links between the two countries.[155] This meant that all organized departures had to be by sea. In an attempt to slow the flight of labour, the colonial regime had issued regulations forbidding Indians to travel as deck passengers on ships sailing to Indian ports. As the average labourer could not afford the expense of a cabin, this measure effectively prevented most Indians from evacuating to India by sea and thus compelled thousands to risk the hazardous land crossing.[156] Withdrawing Indians were harassed by the Burmese police, and as many as 80,000 people perished of disease, exhaustion or malnutrition.[157] As with the evacuation of Penang, there was a sense of British perfidy and betrayal, and of the flagrant dereliction of responsibility, on purely racial grounds, to those most in need of protection.[158]

Moreover, the Burma campaign highlighted the geopolitical implications of the Japanese victories in Southeast Asia. The Japanese now stood on the very borders of India. With British defences apparently weak and in disarray, and its forces seemingly incapable of serious resistance, the prospect of a Japanese advance in India now looked very real indeed.[159] The total collapse of the British eastern Empire reverberated among the civilian population of India. The ineffectual British response to the Japanese advances seemed to underscore Japanese claims that the Asian future would be entirely determined by Asians themselves, free of outside interference.[160]

But the crucial and deciding point for many captured Indian troops was the Quit India campaign, launched by the All-Indian Congress Committee on 8 August 1942 following the failure of the Cripps' mission to India.[161] The background to this campaign was as follows. On 3 September 1939, Lord Linlithgow, Viceroy of India, advised on the radio that he had issued an Indian declaration of war on Germany. This declaration had been issued without any pretence of consultation with Indian political opinion.[162] Linlithgow's high handedness outraged Congress, which issued a demand for total and immediate independence, a claim which drew no response from Linlithgow. A month later the Viceroy made the Indian leadership a vague offer of dominion status to be negotiated sometime after the war. In response the Congress ministers resigned en masse on 10 November.[163] Within a month of the fall of Singapore, Churchill sent senior Labour MP Sir Stafford Cripps to India with an offer of dominion status for India when the war was concluded. However, this settlement would be dependent upon the main Indian parties offering total support to the Allied war effort. Moreover, the offer would include major concessions to India's princely states, and electoral representation heavily weighted by considerations of caste and religion.[164] Congress rejected the Cripps' proposal, and Gandhi's subsequent advocacy of massive civil disobedience quickly gained widespread support.[165]

The Quit India campaign aimed to make India ungovernable and was accompanied by an escalating tide of unrest and violence, riots, arson, and acts of sabotage. The British authorities reacted with widespread arrests (including the entire Congress leadership and thousands of local activists) and with armed repression, including police shootings, mass whippings, the burning of villages and the periodic torture of dissenters.[166] More than 30,000 Congressmen and other political activists were detained.[167] Within Malaya, the Congress campaign, the large-scale disorders and the British countermeasures were all the subjects of skilful Japanese, INA and IIL propaganda.[168] For many Indian soldiers this was a crucial turning point. The INA had stipulated that it would not intervene in India until prevailed upon to do so by Congress and the Indian people. The Quit India uprising seemed as clear a request as was likely to be offered.[169]

In 1943 the Bengal famine became a further rallying point for INA activists. The disaster had its origins in a massive cyclone of October 1942 which was followed by three tsunamis. The poor rice harvest of 1942–43 produced panic buying in the open market leading to spiralling prices of all food grains. At the same time Britain shipped both grain and railway stock out of India, not only reducing food supplies but also weakening the internal distributional network.[170] The problem was aggravated by Japan's capture of Burma, thus cutting off its usual source of imported rice.[171] The British response was one of irresolution, indeed seeming indifference to the plight of those affected by food shortages.[172] Between one and two million people died, either of hunger or of the cholera epidemic which followed the famine.[173]

The Indian Independence League

In the months following the fall of Singapore, the IIL appeared to have achieved major success in capturing the public support of the Indian communities of Malaya and Singapore. There was an immediate and genuine response to the IIL among the Indian population of Malaya. Former members of the CIAM were the first to join the IIL and were prominent among the league's Malayan Executive. They also provided the league with high-level organizational skills, political experience, and intellectual leadership.[174] In March 1942, at a conference held in Tokyo, Indian delegates from China and Japan installed Rash Behari Bose, a veteran revolutionary of the Indian independence struggle, and a favourite of the Japanese, as President of a newly formed IIL of East Asia.[175] A conference held in Bangkok in June 1942 brought together representatives of Indian communities from all countries under Japanese control, and formally established the IIL as the overarching vehicle for attaining Indian independence with the INA as its military wing.[176] The IIL quickly established a network of state branches, which arranged a series of public meetings. By August 1942 the membership of the IIL stood at over 200,000.[177]

However, the early triumphs masked growing tensions within and between the IIL and INA. Many of these could be traced to the leadership of Rash Behari Bose. Bose, a one-time Bengali terrorist, had not lived in India since he fled the country following a failed assassination attempt against Lord Hardinge in 1912.[178] Bose had subsequently made his way to Tokyo via Shanghai. Since that date he had remained in Japan, taken a Japanese wife, and fathered a son who was now serving in the Japanese Army. His long residence in Japan and his isolation from mainstream developments in Indian political life were to prove handicaps in his dealings with Indian nationalists. Moreover, he was unable to speak in the name of Congress to which the majority of Indians in Southeast Asia looked for leadership.[179] Many who joined the IIL and INA believed that Bose was directing the movement in accordance with an agenda wholly dictated by the Japanese Army. This conviction, which had earlier surfaced at the IIL conference in Tokyo in March 1942, took firm root among the majority of the Malayan IIL executive, as well as within the INA leadership.[180]

The political impasse was not aided by the Japanese who had neither clearly defined their war aims with regard to India nor discussed the relationship between an independent India and a post-war Southeast Asia. While India had only remotely entered Japanese calculations for the overall design of the Greater East Asia Co-Prosperity Sphere, the fact remained that Japan was at war with the colonial power occupying India. Japan was thus required to develop a policy upon India which would further its own strategic interests and continue to strike blows at the British. While the Japanese were not especially concerned with the aspirations of the IIL/INA (and indeed the Japanese military had little respect for the INA which they considered untrustworthy, secretly pro-British, inexperienced and unreliable), they believed that managed correctly, these were organizations which could be sponsored to the mutual advantage of both Japan and the émigré Indian nationalists.[181]

Moreover, conditions in the subcontinent suggested that the INA/IIL could well prove useful allies. Wartime developments in India, including the civil disobedience campaign, agitation and widespread and continuing unrest, appeared to point to a country in hopeless turmoil, and perhaps on the verge of revolution.[182] The mere existence of the IIL/INA might well contribute to the general confusion, thus further stretching limited British resources. The IIL could be used to ferment anti-British sentiment, possibly within India, but most certainly within Southeast Asia. As a military organization, the INA's very presence would exert psychological if not actual pressure on the eastern borders of the Raj.[183] Finally, the INA would prove a constructive vehicle for Japanese propaganda, which would portray an anti-colonial and sympathetic Japan actively cooperating with Indian nationalists to rid Asia of its European oppressors.[184]

At the same time, the IIL was attempting to clarify the terms of its political and military relationship with the Japanese. At the June 1942 conference, the league executive, the ruling Council of Action, made it clear that further collaboration was dependent upon the Japanese committing themselves "clearly and unequivocally" to the cause of independence.[185] This would entail Japanese respect for Indian sovereignty and territorial integrity, and recognition of the IIL as the Indian government in exile. In addition the Council of Action demanded the release of all Indian POWs and the elevation of the INA to the status of an allied army. Moreover, the Japanese should extend loans to the INA and should clearly recognize that the army's sole function was to fight for the liberation of India. The Bangkok resolutions were passed on to Tokyo by Colonel Iwakuro Hideo, Fujiwara's successor as *Kikan* OIC (and an officer who had little sympathy for the cause of Indian independence), but he did not press the Japanese government for a response. Nor was one ever received.[186]

Throughout the later months of 1942, the strains between the IIL and INA, and both organizations and the Japanese, deepened and intensified. The military leadership increasingly viewed Rash Behari Bose as a Japanese puppet.[187] The Malayan leadership also distrusted the depth of the Japanese commitment to the IIL/INA, and to the cause of Indian independence.[188] Within both the IIL and the INA, there were severe doubts about the military capabilities of Mohan Singh,[189] and there had been considerable disquiet when Fujiwara had promoted him to the rank of general.[190]

Several incidents, clumsily handled by the Japanese, sharpened IIL–Japanese antagonism. The deterioration in relations became acute when the Japanese moved the first batch of INA troops to Burma without any preliminary consultation with the IIL.[191] In November, the Council of Action, deeply concerned, presented a memorandum to Iwakuro, "whose softness of tone did not conceal the fact that a real crisis was at hand".[192]

The Japanese response to this growing discontent was peremptory, ill-considered and maladroit. On 8 December 1942, Colonel N.S. Gill of the INA was arrested as a "spy". In reaction, every member of the Council of Action with the exception of Bose himself submitted his resignation.[193] On 29 December, Bose dismissed Mohan Singh as commander of the INA.[194] The Japanese subsequently arrested a number of recalcitrant officers, including Mohan Singh.[195] Thousands of volunteers reverted to their previous status as prisoners of war.[196]

Despite this grave setback, the loss of so many high-profile leaders and so many military personnel, the IIL and INA slowly recovered. Rash Behari Bose circulated the camps, appealing and persuading, and gradually won back a large measure of support. However, there was an obvious need to find a fresh and dynamic leader, rather than an ageing, terminally ill ex-terrorist who had lost touch with the realities of metropolitan politics.[197] This leadership was to be found in the person of Subhas Chandra Bose, a seasoned campaigner of the Indian nationalist movement.

SUBHAS CHANDRA BOSE

Subhas Chandra Bose had a long and active background in the politics of revolutionary independence. Outside India he was outranked only by Gandhi and Nehru as an Indian nationalist politician of note.[198] Born in 1897 into a well-to-do and high-caste Indian family,[199] Bose was educated in Calcutta and Cambridge[200] and prepared for a career in the Indian Civil Service.[201] However, the 1919 massacre at Jallianwala Bagh, Amritsar, shocked and outraged Bose, and he subsequently dedicated himself to the cause of Indian independence.[202] Bose advanced rapidly through Congress ranks, in 1938 defeating Pattabhi Sitaramayya for the Congress presidency. However, in 1939 his re-election was opposed by Gandhi and others, and he resigned as president in May 1940.[203] Bose subsequently formed the

Forward Bloc within Congress. Following the outbreak of war, the Forward Bloc strenuously opposed cooperation with the British.[204]

Detained by the British authorities after leading a demonstration in Calcutta on 2 July 1940, Bose was transferred to house arrest following a hunger strike.[205] He organized a carefully planned escape and, assuming a false identity as "Muhammad Ziauddin", a Pathan travelling inspector of the Emperor of India Life Insurance Company, made his way to Peshawar. He crossed into Afghanistan on 22 January 1941 and arrived in Kabul on 27 January.[206] There the Italian diplomat Pietro Quaroni issued Bose with a passport under the name of Signor Orlando Mazzotta and arranged for him to travel to Berlin via Moscow.[207] While in Moscow he made a series of unsuccessful attempts to meet the Soviet leadership. Bose departed from Moscow by rail on 31 March 1941, arriving in Berlin on 2 April.[208]

Bose believed that the swift defeat of the Allied forces in France foreshadowed a peace conference at which Germany would dictate the outcomes.[209] He met most of the Nazi leadership which provided him with a generous allowance and encouraged him to open a Free India Centre. In addition he was furnished with facilities to broadcast to India. More importantly, he was allowed access to Indian troops captured in North Africa. By April 1941 some 15,000 Indian men and officers had been taken prisoner by the Axis forces. Preliminary briefings suggested that many were seriously disillusioned with their British officers.[210] Bose persuaded a number of them to join a Free India Legion to be used as a spearhead for the liberation of India.[211] Added inducements to enlist included promises of special treatment, including food, money and access to women.[212] The legion reached its maximum strength of 2,593 in early 1943.[213]

Despite these early successes, Bose quickly became convinced that the main hope for Indian independence lay in active cooperation with the Japanese government.[214] On 29 May 1942, Bose met Nazi leader, Adolf Hitler; a meeting that proved a major disappointment.[215] Bose wanted the Axis powers to commit to the independence of India. Hitler was not interested in this proposal, nor would he agree to remove any disparaging references to Indians in his book *Mein Kampf*.[216] However, he did agree to assist Bose's travel to Japan by submarine. Bose duly left Kiel on 8 February 1943 under the assumed name "Matsuda". He was transferred to a Japanese submarine off the east coast of Madagascar on 28 April, which transported him to Sabang in Sumatra. He finally reached Tokyo on 16 May 1943.[217]

Following his arrival in Japan, Bose met Prime Minister Tojo Hideki upon whom he made a deep impression. On 16 June 1943, Tojo took Bose to the House of Representatives (The Diet) in Tokyo, and in his presence declared Japan's eagerness to support the cause of Indian independence. This declaration had two major outcomes. Firstly, it replaced the ambivalence which had characterized Japanese policy towards India with a clear statement of intent. Secondly, the Japanese imprimatur gave Bose, and under his direction, the IIL and INA, a firm measure of autonomy.[218] Bose could thus proceed to Singapore, not only confident of Japanese cooperation and support, but, what was of equal importance, with the relative freedom to reorganize the IIL and INA according to his own precepts.

On 27 June 1943, Bose left Tokyo, arriving in Singapore on 2 July. Thousands of people turned out to greet him. On 4 July the General Assembly of the IIL confirmed Bose's appointment as President of the league, thus succeeding the ailing Rash Behari Bose.[219] At this meeting, Bose read a message from Tojo which stated, *inter alia*:

> I trust the Indians, with firm faith in the victory of Japan, Germany and Italy, will fight for justice and righteousness shoulder to shoulder with us. I firmly believe that this is the only way the Indians can hasten the glorious day of their freedom and I sincerely wish them every success in their brave fight.[220]

In the period between his resignation as Congress President and his arrival in Singapore, Bose had rejected much of the Congress platform, especially the Gandhian philosophy of *ahimsa* (non-violence).[221] He was a militant activist, tending to authoritarianism, who believed that India required forceful, even dictatorial, leadership.[222] At the same time, he had strong spiritual leanings and was deeply influenced by the teachings of Swami Vivekananda.[223] Bose was an uncompromising advocate of total and immediate independence. He rejected dominion status within the British Empire, because he believed it would perpetuate British capitalist interests in India. He dreamed of an India freed of the hierarchies imposed by wealth, class, and caste, a nation where women had equal status with men, and where there would be no distinction between Hindu and Muslim at election time.[224]

Bose had long subordinated his earlier distaste at the excesses of Axis fascism, in particular the barbarism of Japanese imperialism in China, to the long-term goal of Indian freedom.[225] Indeed, he considered that the Axis successes heralded a new direction in world affairs and that the dynamic fascist dictatorships were destined to sweep away the decadent and directionless democracies. During his time in Berlin, the followers of Bose had bestowed the title "Netaji"(leader) upon him, which some observers mistakenly interprested as evidence of his fascist leanings.[226] Bose believed that both political and military tides were now running with the Japanese and that as a consequence the time was ripe to secure Indian independence by force of arms. Bose was convinced that a combined Japanese and INA invasion of India would lead to insurrection and rebellion throughout India, which would destroy the foundations of British rule.[227]

Bose made an immediate impact upon the Indian population of Southeast Asia and breathed new life into the IIL. Apart from the fact that he was a veteran revolutionary whose credentials were widely recognized,[228] Bose was an outstanding and a charismatic speaker whose speeches and rallies drew enormous crowds, often including Chinese and Malays as well as Indians.[229] Indeed, so completely did Bose dominate the ILL that he became the subject of an intense personality cult. His birthday became a special celebration, and a Netaji Week, which included rallies, processions, and prayers for Bose's health in Hindu temples, mosques and churches, was held from 4 to 10 July 1944. In a re-enactment of a Mughal ceremony, Bose was weighed in gold, the contribution of Indian merchants. This was donated to the IIL after weighing.[230]

Upon assuming the IIL leadership, Bose foreshadowed the total mobilization of Indian manpower and resources. On 5 July 1943, he announced the reform of the INA which was now to be officially renamed Azad Hind Fauj (Free Indian Army).[231] Bose aimed to expand the INA from its enlistment of 13,000 to a targeted strength of 50,000 and ultimately to 3 million soldiers.[232] The revived INA involved local Indians resident in Southeast Asia in a way the earlier INA had not. Bose especially appealed to working class Tamils of Malaya to work for the cause of Indian liberation. In a gesture designed to placate Indian Muslims, Bose replaced the wheel of the Indian National Congress with the symbol of a springing tiger, thus evoking memories of Tipu Sultan, the eighteenth century Muslim ruler of Mysore who had resisted British domination of South India. Bose also stated that Ceylon was a "pendant in the Indian chain" and established a Ceylonese Unit within the INA.[233]

Bose also completely reorganized the governance of the IIL and appointed a supporting administrative apparatus of thirteen departments.[234]

He founded a national bank and issued currency, adopted the tricolour as the national flag, decreed that Hindustani was to be the national language, and proclaimed *Subh Sukh Chain Ki Varsha Barshe* as the national anthem. *Jai Hind* ("Victory to India") was made a common greeting, while *Chalo Delhi* ("On to Delhi"), the rallying cry of the Great Rebellion of 1857, became the war cry.[235] On 21 October 1943, Bose proclaimed the formation of the Provisional Government of Free India (FIPG). This was recognized by the Japanese on 23 October.[236] By 19 November 1943, seven other countries — Germany, Italy, the Japanese regime in China, Manchukuo, Burma, Thailand and Croatia — had extended recognition, while Eamon de Valera, President of Eire, had sent a congratulatory message.[237] Shortly afterwards, Tojo notionally transferred the Andaman and Nicobar Islands to FIPG control which allowed Bose to symbolically raise the Indian flag at Port Blair, on "free" Indian soil.[238]

Bose revolutionized women's participation in the independence struggle, at least within the Malayan context. While women had long been prominent in Indian nationalist politics, and indeed Nehru had successfully pressed for the abolition of social, economic and political discrimination against women,[239] this was not the case among Indians in Malaya. On 9 July 1943, Bose appealed for women volunteers, citing the example of the Rani of Jhansi, a heroine of the Great Rebellion of 1857 who had campaigned actively against the British. On 12 July, a special women's day, forty recruits presented themselves for service.[240] The Rani of Jhansi Regiment was headed by Dr Laksmi Swaminathan, a recent immigrant from India who had set up a medical clinic in Singapore, and who was now accorded the rank of captain and entered Bose's Cabinet as Secretary of the Women's Department.[241] The first central camp for the regiment (popularly known as the Ranees) was opened on 22 October 1943, the anniversary of the Rani's birthday.[242] The first contingent of female soldiers left for Burma in late 1943 where they were trained in jungle warfare and nursing.[243]

Bose's dynamic leadership spurred a continuous flow of recruits to both the INA and the IIL. There was mass recruiting among working-class Indians both within the urban and the estate workforces. By July 1944, over fifty per cent of the Indian population belonged to the IIL.[244] IIL membership peaked at 350,000, and over 100,000 local Indians volunteered to join the INA. This reached a total strength of 50,000, of whom approximately 20,000 were ex-BIA soldiers, and at least 20,000 were recruited from among Indians resident in Malaya.[245]

However, INA ranks included a number of reluctant enlistees. While many ex-BIA soldiers had willingly thrown their lot in with the INA, others had done so under threat of forced labour elsewhere in Japanese-occupied Asia.[246] Similarly, many estate workers joined the INA solely to avoid conscription to forced labour camps, while others saw military service as a means of obtaining work and food. INA membership provided a temporary escape from continual semi-starvation on the estates and furnished a barrier against the tyranny of Japanese rule.[247]

Similarly, the rapid increase in the IIL membership disguised the fact that many who joined did so out of fear or perceived compulsion. Others hoped to use their association with the IIL for personal advantage.[248] The backbone of the IIL was made up of those who were generally enthusiastic about the league's aims and objectives — political intellectuals who had previously been associated with the CIAM, and who now provided overall leadership, and the estate workers and labourers who comprised the rank and file.[249] Extreme pressure was exerted both by the IIL leadership and more openly by the Japanese administration upon those who hesitated to declare their support for Bose and the independence movement. Bose made it clear that it was the "duty" of every adult male to enrol in the local branch of the IIL.[250] The Japanese were far blunter — those who remained outside the league would be regarded as enemies.[251] Furthermore, the Japanese military advised that it would not tolerate adherence to or perpetuation of sub-ethnic divisions (such as Ceylonese, Malayalees, and Muslims) among the Malayan Indian population.[252] The combined IIL/Japanese coercion induced large numbers of the Indian middle classes, often members of the Indian minority ethnic groups, into joining the movement. When Indian Muslims, who at first held aloof from the IIL/INA were informed that internal travel was dependent upon special passes issued by IIL officers, they had little choice but to become members.[253]

As head of the provisional government, Bose decided that the considerable funds needed for the civilian administration and for the equipment required by the army would be procured through taxation of the Indian population. On 25 October 1943, Bose foreshadowed that the provisional government would levy a tax of ten per cent of all assets on all members of the Indian community. All Indians were required to provide details of their personal assets to specially constituted Boards of Management. Those who tried to evade the tax regime were liable to arrest by the Kempeitai and could be subject to severe torture. However, the monies raised were insufficient to cover INA/IIL expenditure, and Bose appealed for financial sacrifices from the community. While voluntary donations were often generous, Bose never hesitated to persuade, cajole and even threaten Indians for a greater flow of capital for the cause. Much of this fund raising was undertaken at public meetings, where Bose's oratory would often rouse the crowd to fever pitch.[254] By the end of 1943, the IIL was raising a total of almost two million dollars each month from its Malayan network of approximately seventy branches.[255]

Imphal and Beyond

However, despite Bose's success in reorganizing the IIL and INA, the league's effectiveness continued to be hampered by chronic doubts about the genuineness and extent of Japanese support for the league as an agent for attaining Indian independence, and by continuous distrust of the actions and goodwill of the Japanese authorities.[256] From June 1944 to August 1945, these forebodings were augmented by growing Indian disillusionment within the IIL itself, and to a lesser extent with the leadership of Subhas Chandra Bose.[257] Much of this resulted from the failure of the Imphal campaign, and the growing realization that the Allies were by no means a spent force.

The Japanese planned a major offensive in eastern India for March to April 1944. The intention was to knock British India out of the Pacific War. They were encouraged by Bose who informed them that once their troops reached the Bengal plains, the entire country would rise in revolt.[258] However, influential elements within the Japanese military opposed the campaign. They argued that the operation would be hazardous, and even a successful invasion would prove problematic.[259]

In November 1943 the main body of the INA had left for Rangoon preparatory to the planned India campaign. Bose had followed, moving his headquarters to Rangoon on 4 January 1944.[260] A total of 40,000 INA men were deployed alongside the Japanese Army for the offensive. But when the INA reached the front line, they were assigned a series of subordinate and even menial non-combatant tasks which ranged from basic maintenance and repair work down to conveying rations for Japanese troops. Moreover, they had been informed that BIA troops would desert in large numbers when they encountered a genuinely independent Indian Army.[261] The predicted defections did not materialize. Instead, the INA had to contend with a BIA resolute in its opposition. Some INA soldiers, unnerved and demoralized by the unexpected hostility, surrendered to the BIA.[262] The Imphal campaign left 65,000 Japanese and 2,000 INA soldiers dead, and paved the way for the Allied advance into Burma.[263]

The failure of the Imphal campaign was a shattering blow to both INA and IIL morale. Bose had placed great store upon the outcome of the campaign, believing that success would provoke revolution in India.[264] Indians throughout Malaya had been advised to prepare for a "momentous event", and plans were devised for elaborate celebrations to mark the fall of Imphal.[265] News eventually leaked out through returning Indian soldiers that the Imphal campaign had been a comprehensive defeat.[266] They revealed that the INA had been denied any major combat role, had been poorly supplied, and in the opening stages of the campaign had been wasted on security duties or labour battalions.[267] Casualty rates, not least from disease and desertion, had been enormous.[268] News of the Imphal catastrophe spread rapidly throughout the Indian community in Malaya, resulting in a rash of desertions and general loss of morale within the INA and IIL.[269] The Allied bombing of Penang, Kuala Lumpur, and Singapore was a further tangible demonstration that military ascendency had passed to Britain and the Allies,[270] and undermined Bose's repeated insistence that the war would be won by the Axis powers.[271]

After Imphal, relations between the Japanese and INA began to deteriorate.[272] Morale declined even further when Bose placed the 3rd Division of the INA — consisting entirely of recruits from Malaya — under the control of the Japanese, to be used in defence of Malaya in the event of a British invasion. The INA had been created and staffed by Indians with the express intention of fighting, under Indian direction, for the liberation of India. Thus, Bose's action, which anticipated that the Army would join battle in defence of Japanese rule, represented a fundamental breach of the underlying assumptions and the specific nature of the agreement which had governed the formation of the INA. This move created profound disenchantment and led to a further flood of desertions.[273]

Political developments within India gravely weakened the appeal of the IIL and threatened to undermine its very *raison d'être*. The Quit India campaign had, according to Congressional sources, been a disappointing failure.[274] The new Viceroy, Wavell, made conciliatory gestures towards the Indian leadership, and in May 1944, he ordered Gandhi's release from prison.[275] On 14 June 1945, Wavell announced the convening of a conference to consider the formation of a new Viceroy's Executive Council which would move India closer to full self-government.[276] The foreshadowing of self-government destroyed the moral and political premises upon which the IIL/INA had been structured, and led many Indians to question their continuing involvement in an organization which appeared to have been superseded.[277] For if the British were prepared to negotiate independence, and those negotiations involved Nehru and Gandhi, the giants of Congress, what point was there to the INA?[278] To the horror of his publicity officer, Bose attacked the "compromise mongers" within India,[279] and threatened to prosecute for high treason those who temporized with the British.[280] The vehemence of his denunciations appeared to put him on a collision course with Congress, and thus lessened his standing among many Malayan Indians.[281]

Towards the end of 1944 and throughout 1945, there was growing uneasiness within the ranks of the IIL/INA. The gathering realization that Japan had lost the war served to reinforce habitual Indian suspicion of Japanese attitudes, motives, and actions.[282] Indeed, some locally raised units and estate workers cooperated with and provided intelligence to MPAJA guerrillas, though Bose took steps to counter such activities.[283] Moreover, many Indians were weary of Bose's ever-expanding tax regime, and his unremitting calls for voluntary contributions.[284] While, during an earlier phase of the war, these demands had been met on the understanding that they constituted the sacrifices that were necessary to fund the independence struggle, this was manifestly no longer the case. Now the taxes were experienced as a crushing imposition upon an already impoverished Indian community, largely reduced to grinding privation and a grim daily battle for survival.[285] Lowered morale within the IIL was reflected in the monthly recruitment figures, down from 10,000 throughout the month of April 1944, to 500 in November, and in plummeting returns from taxation which had dipped to $600,000 by November. Desertions from the INA multiplied in the face of the relentless British advance.[286]

Although Bose's position appeared to be increasingly untenable, he refused to countenance defeat. As late as November 1944, Bose was insisting that the war would be won by Germany and Japan.[287] As the British neared Rangoon, the Japanese prevailed upon Bose to leave the city. He was reluctant to depart. For him the city had a highly symbolic significance both as a staging post for the march on Delhi and as the site of the internment of the last Mughal Emperor.[288] He left with the retreating

INA on 24 April 1945, leading the Rani of Jhansi Regiment. After his car was strafed, and despite suffering severe pain, he led the Ranees on foot on what might be considered an epic retreat to safety in Thailand.[289] His mission complete, Bose travelled on to Singapore by air.[290]

In August 1945, learning of the imminent surrender of the Japanese, Bose called for a meeting of his Cabinet to discuss the implications for the INA. There was unanimous agreement that the INA would surrender where it stood and that its records and documents would be destroyed. Bose himself was prepared to stay and surrender with his men. But his Cabinet and advisors believed that he should continue his struggle elsewhere.[291] On 15 August 1945, when the Japanese announced their surrender to the Allies, Bose indicated that Indian nationalists would continue to wage their armed resistance to the British.[292]

Bose was severely injured in a plane crash in Taipei, Formosa, on 18 August 1945, and died the same day in a Japanese military hospital.[293] He was en route to Darien and Manchuria,[294] purportedly to negotiate with USSR officials about the possibility of continuing the independence struggle from that country.[295] His death, although reported, was widely disbelieved, and he became the object of a continuing cult.[296]

After news of Bose's death reached Malaya, the INA command ordered that all records be destroyed for fear of reprisals by returning British troops.[297] In the weeks of anarchy which followed the Japanese surrender, and prior to the arrival of Allied troops, locally enlisted INA members quietly dispersed.[298]

Even before his death, Bose had achieved the stature of a national hero. His death traumatized many Indian civilians in Malaya and Singapore who viewed him as a martyr to the cause of Indian independence.[299] News of Bose's death had an immediate impact in India. Both Gandhi and Nehru, as well as other Congress leaders (so recently attacked as "Gandhi flunkeys" by Bose in his Singapore broadcasts) paid tribute to Bose and his achievements.[300]

WARTIME CONDITIONS WITHIN MALAYA: THE INDIAN EXPERIENCE

To date, we have concentrated upon the growth of Indian nationalism in response to the collapse of British colonial power and the appeal of Indian independence. But there was another and much darker side to the Japanese occupation; namely the plight and indeed the survival of the average Indian civilian in the face of the intransigent harshness of an incompetent and uncaring Japanese regime.

The immediate impact of the Japanese occupation upon the bulk of the Indian workforce was widespread economic dislocation and hardship. The community, especially the large working class, had been overwhelmingly dependent upon the paid employment provided within the economic framework generated by British colonialism. The network of waged labour collapsed under the inept Japanese administration and was not replaced with any alternative forms of regular or guaranteed income. Workers and their families were thus denied any obvious means of subsistence.[301] On the plantations, rubber production was all but paralysed, and unemployment and underemployment were widespread. Most of the labour force was left destitute.[302]

The Japanese military assumed responsibility for the importation and distribution of food, but had neither the requisite experience nor the expertise to fulfil this role.[303] By the end of 1942 grain prices in the Straits Settlements were on average twelve to fifteen times their 1940 level.[304] An already chronic food shortage was exacerbated by the Japanese cession in October 1943 of the four northern rice-producing states — Kelantan, Terengganu, Kedah and Perlis — to Thailand.[305] While later in the war the Japanese promoted a "grow more food" campaign, the entire period of occupation was marked by prolonged food shortages, the periodic and sustained unavailability of crucial medicines and medical supplies, and the breakdown of health and sanitation services.[306]

Most Indian labourers experienced an acute struggle for survival. Because they had little money, very basic items were placed beyond their reach.[307] Workers were required to garden and scavenge to stay alive. Many Indian women sold their jewellery to purchase food. Nearly all workers grew crops such as tapioca (which for the duration of the war replaced rice as a food staple) to provide basic nourishment.[308] Despite sustained efforts to ward off starvation, malnutrition-related deaths, which were especially prevalent among children, became a common experience on the estates.[309] Towards the end of the war, the appalling hardships endured by the Indian labour force were aggravated by the systematic and punitive taxation regime introduced by the administration of Subhas Chandra Bose.[310]

The Japanese military administration imposed a regime of ruthless management and a relentless and brutal system of justice upon the workforce (e.g., the penalty of beheading was often exacted for thievery).[311] Throughout the period of the Japanese occupation, the British estate and public utility managers were replaced by the second-tier Asian clerical staff, the *kirani*, most of whom, as we have seen, were either Malayalees or Ceylonese Tamils, and hence of different ethnic background to their overwhelmingly Tamil workforces.[312] While the *kirani* were thus elevated to new levels of responsibility, they were now immediately answerable to the Japanese authorities who insisted upon total and unquestioning compliance with their demands. The *kirani* also bore the full harshness of Japanese rule; they were frequently humiliated, abused and physically assaulted for failure to meet Japanese expectations, often in the presence of their workers.[313]

One of the most serious abuses perpetrated by the Japanese against Indians as a community was the conscription or kidnapping of personnel to work upon Japanese forced-labour schemes.[314] While there were a number of such projects within Malaya and other countries under Japanese control, the most notorious was the Burma Railway (the so-called Death Railway).

The construction of this railway, traversing 445 kilometres of mountainous jungle and malarial swamps, was ordered in 1942 by Imperial General Headquarters. By this stage of the war, the Japanese Southern Army was rapidly losing both air and naval supremacy. It was thus increasingly dependent on land transport within occupied Southeast Asia.[315] The railway would shorten communication lines and allow the rapid transfer of personnel and supplies to support the Japanese Army in Burma.[316] Although Japanese engineers estimated that under normal circumstances the project would take between five and six years, they were ordered to complete the railway within eighteen months.[317] Work commenced in November 1942. A huge labour force, consisting of 250,000 personnel, mainly recruited from Malaya and Burma, together with 61,000 Allied POWs, was assembled to construct the line.[318]

Up to 120,000 Malayan Indian workers were coerced or persuaded to work on the Railway.[319] While some were enticed by Japanese-placed advertisements which promised good wages and work conditions,[320] and even the prospect of being sent to India,[321] most were forcibly enlisted. Many of these were estate workers who were nominated for labour service by the *kirani*, often acting under Japanese pressure. However, after the war, there were allegations that some *kirani* were only too willing to connive with the Japanese to conscript supposed troublemakers or certain labourers they wanted off the estate.[322] Other personnel were kidnapped and abducted by Japanese troops as they emerged from public places such as temples and mosques. This practice was ended at the insistence of Subhas Chandra Bose.[323] Work on the railway was undertaken under primitive and unhygienic conditions, and the labourers were poorly fed and at all times subject to the savage discipline and repeated cruelties of the Japanese and Korean guards. Most workers died of poor nutrition, diseases and the effects of physical abuse.[324] Responding to reports of mass deaths, Bose sent an IIL observer, Amar Singh, who duly reported on the abominable circumstances endured by Tamil labourers. Bose subsequently complained to the Japanese, who promised to improve conditions.[325] However, the Japanese considered Tamils "highly expendable",[326] and less than 12,000 workers (40,000 according to Japanese estimates) managed to find their way back to Malaya upon completion of the railway. Those who survived were often severely traumatized and broken in health.[327]

The Japanese occupation proved devastating to the Malayan Indian community. Disease, more easily spread and contracted as a result of chronic malnutrition and the breakdown of sanitation and health services; starvation, especially of the very young, sick and other vulnerable members within the community; and Japanese labour schemes took a very heavy toll of Indian life. Throughout these years, the Indian population fell by over 100,000, or approximately fourteen per cent, from 700,000 in 1939 to 599,000 in 1947,[328] and the Indian component of the overall Malayan population declined from fourteen per cent in 1940 to ten per cent in 1947.[329]

CONCLUSIONS

The INA/IIL movements profoundly affected the Indian population of Malaya. Under Bose's leadership, Malayan and Singaporean Indians felt that they had been propelled from the periphery of metropolitan affairs to the very heart of Indian nationalist politics and could justifiably claim to have served in the front rank of those who had worked directly against the might of the British Empire for the liberation of the Motherland. Indian nationalist ideology had emphasized pan-Indian identification and the need for every Indian to contribute to the anti-colonial struggle regardless of his or her caste, ethnicity, language, or religious affiliation.[330] The inclusive nationalist discourses which stated unequivocally that *all* Indians were descended from one of the world's great and most enduring civilizations, one which had bequeathed incomparable gifts to humanity in terms of religion, philosophy, statecraft and artistic expression, was repeated in countless speeches, was absorbed by significant numbers of Indians, and affected all sectors within the community. The idea that the community had a role to play in the establishment of a free India had captured the imagination of Indians of all classes and backgrounds.[331] The experiences during the war years were to engender a renewed and enduring interest among Malayan Indians in their cultural heritage and their links to the metropolitan civilization, which was to inform all aspects of Indian political and social life in the post-war era.[332]

The INA/IIL background had also impressed upon Malayan Indians the value of political organization and activism as a vehicle for mobilization of community resources and as an agent of change. Membership in the IIL and INA had promoted a sense of communal solidarity which united Indians under the aegis of an overarching organization.[333] Meetings and training sessions conducted by the IIL and INA not only inculcated nationalist and anti-imperialist sentiments, but also exposed members to a wide range of political and social potentialities.[334] Though the CIAM, albeit animated by a sense of Indian nationalism, had principally focused upon investigating the socio-economic problems of Malayan Indians, its post-war successor, the Malayan Indian Congress, was to adopt a broader political programme.[335] In this respect, the Congress was the direct intellectual and ideological heir to the IIL, which had been "the catalyst that cemented Malayan Indians of different creeds, castes and languages".[336]

A corollary of working-class experience of participation in the IIL and INA was the inexorable Tamilization of post-war Indian Malayan political organizations. Prior to the war, the principle political body, the CIAM, had consisted of a largely professional leadership, many of whom did not speak Tamil.[337] However, the IIL had taken politics and political organizations into the plantations where kanganies and school teachers had assumed leadership roles.[338] Those who trained in the INA were exposed to military discipline, which inculcated organizational skills and instilled a sense of self-worth.[339] Given the fact that working-class Tamils comprised an overwhelming majority of Malaya's Indian population,[340] it was only a matter of time before this newly politicized group dominated the course of post-war Malayan Indian affairs.

The traditional apathy which had prevailed among many educated Indians in Malaya had also been irrevocably shattered by political developments throughout the period of Japanese occupation.[341] Involvement in the IIL and INA not only stimulated a sense of obligation among educated Indians towards the remainder of the community, but also elevated many intellectuals, merchants and professionals into prominent leadership and organizational roles which were to equip them for similar duties within Indian and social bodies in post-war Malaya.[342]

The confidence garnered by Indians through IIL/INA negotiations with the Japanese, now extended to dealings with other political organizations in post-war Malaya.[343] This new self-assurance was perhaps at its most obvious in the Indian relationship with the returning British. The contemptuous ease with which the Japanese had defeated the Allied forces throughout the opening phases of the Pacific War had destroyed forever the belief in British invincibility, and thus as a concomitant the inevitability of British rule in both India and Malaya. Among other things, the Tamils who had been recruited to the INA had shown that they could adjust to military life, and their performance as soldiers had discredited the previously accepted British nostrums as to which groups constituted martial and non-martial "races".[344] The experiences of the Japanese occupation had also exploded the model of paternalism propounded by British colonialism — that is, of dependence upon the British for welfare and succour. For several years the Indians had been forced to get by on their own resources, and had survived the ordeals of harsh repression and chronic shortages, albeit often under appalling circumstances. However, the culture of survival engendered throughout these years was also one of implied resistance. It was a culture in which constant deprivation and tyranny created a need for subterfuge, ingenuity and innovation.[345] The Indian workforce thus no longer viewed the British managers as an indispensible component of the future. Labourers were no longer prepared to accord to British expectations of servility and quiescence. This new attitude surprised colonial officials, especially those who had held managerial positions prior to the war.[346]

This transformation in collective attitudes and outlook among Malayan Indians was observed by Nehru in March 1946. At a meeting in Ipoh, he commented upon "the tremendous change that he saw in the Indians since his last visit in 1937 in which he had referred to Malayan Indians as the 'backwater' of Indian nationalism".[347] This upsurge of collective awareness and pride which had invigorated the Indian community was to spill over into the turbulent years which followed the return of the British, and was to prove fundamental in reshaping Indian society.

But the Japanese invasion did more than promote Indian nationalism and reshape Indian perceptions. The former commanding role of the British in Malaya had been recast. The humiliations of defeat had exposed the brittleness of colonial rule, and meant that the earlier mystique of British supremacy, the prestige and unquestioned authority they had hitherto enjoyed, had been forever destroyed.[348] Moreover, the boundaries of ethnicity and ethnic relations had been comprehensively redrawn. The ethnic compartmentalization which had served the British so well, had, under the impetus of Japanese administration, precipitated into three main ethnic communities, animated by a fierce Sino-Malay rivalry.[349] Communalism, structured on primary and exclusive concepts of racial identity, was to increasingly define the social and economic landscape of post-war Malaya.[350] In writing of post-war Singapore, Asad-ul Iqbal Latif has made the profound but often overlooked point that the war created a sense of localized belonging, but this was a belonging which largely responded to the disparate pulls of diasporic nationalism — the KMT and MCP among the Chinese, the IIL among the Indians, and Indonesian Raya and KMM among the Malays.[351] While Latif is writing of Singapore, this observation is equally applicable to Malaya. These disparate pulls, with all their potential for misunderstanding and conflict, were to manifest in various ways in the immediate period following the British return.

Notes

1. This chapter was enriched by the many interviews I conducted with IIL/INA veterans. I am particularly indebted to the late Puan Sri Janaki Athi Nahappan, who as a young woman joined the Rani of Jhansi Regiment, and who was kind enough to share her recollections with me.
2. Haruko Taya Cook and Theodore F. Cook, *Japan at War: A New Oral History* (New York: The New Press, 1992), p. 50; Peter Thompson, *The Battle for Singapore: The True Story of the Greatest Catastrophe of World War II* (London: Portrait, 2005), p. 51.
3. Willard H. Elsbree, *Japan's Role in Southeast Asia: Nationalist Movements 1940–1945* (Harvard University Press, 1953), p. 9; Thompson, *The Battle for Singapore*, p. 63.
4. Elsbree, *Japan's Role*, p. 18; Louis Allen, *Singapore, 1941–1942* (Singapore, MPH, 1977), p. 12.
5. Christopher Bayly and Tim Harper, *Forgotten Armies: The Fall of British Asia*

(Cambridge, MA: The Belknap Press of Harvard University Press, 2004), p. 129.

6. Elsbree, *Japan's Role*, p. 18.

7. Martin Gilbert, *A History of the Twentieth Century, Volume Two 1933–1953* (London: Harper-Collins, 1998), p. 408.

8. Allen, *Singapore 1941–1942*, pp. 116–20.

9. Noel Barber, *A Sinister Twilight: The Fall of Singapore, 1942* (Boston: Houghton Miflin, 1968), p. 8.

10. Virginia Thompson, *Post-Mortem on Malaya* (New York: Macmillan, 1943), pp. 245–47.

11. Bayly and Harper, *Forgotten Armies*, p. 106.

12. Christopher Bayly and Tim Harper, *Forgotten Wars: The End of Britain's Asian Empire* (London: Penguin Books, 2008), pp. 10–12.

13. Sir John Smyth, *Percival and the Tragedy of Singapore* (London: McDonald, 1971), p. 47.

14. Barber, *A Sinister Twilight*, p. 8.

15. Peter Elphick, *Singapore: The Pregnable Fortress* (London: Coronet Books, 1995), p. 37.

16. Thompson, *The Battle for Singapore*, pp. 27–29, 31–33.

17. Ibid., pp. 27–29.

18. Margaret Shennan, *Out in the Midday Sun: The British in Malaya 1880–1960* (London: John Murray, 2009), p. 213.

19. Thompson, *The Battle for Singapore*, p. 16.

20. Kent Fedorowich, "The Evacuation of Civilians from Hong Kong and Malaya/ Singapore", in *A Great Betrayal? The Fall of Singapore Revisited*, edited by Brian Farrell and Sandy Hunter (Singapore: Marshall Cavendish Editions, 2010), p. 109.

21. Shennan, *Out in the Midday Sun*, p. 229.

22. Thompson, *The Battle for Singapore*, p. 43.

23. John R. Ferris, "Student and Master: The United Kingdom, Japan, Airpower and the Fall of Singapore", in *A Great Betrayal? The Fall of Singapore Revisited*, edited by Brian Farrell and Sandy Hunter (Singapore: Marshall Cavendish Editions, 2010), p. 85.

24. Kate Caffrey, *Out in the Midday Sun* (London: Andre Deutsch, 1974), p. 52.

25. Thompson, *The Battle for Singapore*, p. 249.

26. Fedorowich, "The Evacuation of Civilians", p. 108.

27. Caffrey, *Out in the Midday Sun*, p. 95.

28. Thompson, *Post-Mortem on Malaya*, p. 249.

29. Ibid., pp. 249–50.

30. E. Spencer Chapman, *The Jungle is Neutral* (London: Corgi Books, 1957), p. 17.

31. Caffrey, *Out in the Midday Sun*, p. 29; Phillipa Poole, *Of Love and War: The Letters and Diaries of Captain Adrian Curlewis and His Family* (Sydney: Landsdowne, 1982), p. 47.

32. Shennan, *Out in the Midday Sun*, p. 228.

33. Caffrey, *Out in the Midday Sun*, p. 142.

34. Bayly and Harper, *Forgotten Armies*, pp. 63–65.

35. Ibid., pp. 65–66; Allen, *Singapore 1941–1942*, p. 250.

36. Bayly and Harper, *Forgotten Armies*, p. 63; Russell Braddon, *The Naked Island* (Hawthorn: Lloyd O'Neill, 1975), pp. 32–33.

37. Smyth, *Percival and the Tragedy*, p. 76.

38. Shennan, *Out in the Midday Sun*, p, 261.

39. Akashi Yoji, "General Yamashita Tomoyuki: Commander of the Twenty-Fifth Army", in *A Great Betrayal? The Fall of Singapore Revisited*, edited by Brian Farrell and Sandy Hunter (Singapore: Marshall Cavendish Editions, 2010), pp. 152–53.

40. Smyth, *Percival and the Tragedy*, p. 133; Malcolm H. Murfett, "An Enduring Theme: The Singapore Strategy", in *A Great Betrayal? The Fall of Singapore Revisited*, edited by Brian Farrell and Sandy Hunter (Singapore: Marshall Cavendish Editions, 2010), p. 14.

41. Alan Warren, "The Indian Army and the Fall of Singapore Revisited", in *A Great Betrayal? The Fall of Singapore Revisited*, edited by Brian Farrell and Sandy Hunter (Singapore: Marshall Cavendish Editions, 2010), p. 225.

42. Thompson, *The Battle for Singapore*, p. 140.

43. Gilbert, *A History of the Twentieth Century*, pp. 411–12.

44. Bayly and Harper, *Forgotten Armies*, p. 118.

45. Ibid.

46. Thompson, *The Battle for Singapore*, p. 182; Clifford Kinvig, "General Percival and the Fall of Singapore", in *A Great Betrayal? The Fall of Singapore Revisited*, edited by Brian Farrell and Sandy Hunter (Singapore: Marshall Cavendish Editions, 2010), p. 201.

47. Thompson, *The Battle for Singapore*, p. 208.

48. Ibid., p. 289.

49. Bayly and Harper, *Forgotten Armies*, p. 143.

50. Thompson, *The Battle for Singapore*, p. 289; Elphick, *The Pregnable Fortress*, pp. 164, 529–30; Akashi, *General Yamashita Tomoyuki*, p. 158.

51. Bayly and Harper, *Forgotten Armies*, p. 146.

52. Lee Kuan Yew, *The Singapore Story: Memoirs of Lee Kuan Yew* (Singapore: Prentice Hall, 1998), p. 52.

53. Khong Kim Hoong, *Merdeka! British Rule and the Struggle for Independence in Malaya 1945–1957* (Kuala Lumpur: Insan, 1984), p. 30.

54. William Shaw, *Tun Razak: His Life and Times* (Kuala Lumpur: Longman Malaysia, 1976), p. 41; Patricia Lim Pui Huen, "War and Ambivalence: Monuments and

Memorials in Johor", in *War and Memory in Malaysia and Singapore*, edited by Patricia Lim Pui Huen and Diana Wong (Singapore: Institute of Southeast Asian Studies, 2000), p. 151.

55. Barber, *A Sinister Twilight*, p. 250.

56. Ibid., pp. 142–43, 238–39.

57. Bayly and Harper, *Forgotten Armies*, pp. 119–20.

58. Ibid., p. 120; Shaw, *Tun Razak*, p. 41.

59. Thompson, *The Battle for Singapore*, p. 72.

60. Caffrey, *Out in the Midday Sun*, p. 84; Shennan, *Out in the Midday Sun*, pp. 236–37.

61. Lee Kuan Yew, *The Singapore Story*, p. 51.

62. Daud Latiff, "Japanese Invasion and Occupation", in *Malaya: The Making of a Neo-Colony*, edited by Mohamed Amin and Malcolm Caldwell (Nottingham: Spokesman, 1977), p. 87; Said Zahari, *Dark Clouds at Dawn: A Political Memoir* (Kuala Lumpur: Insan, 2001), p. 17; Rehman Rashid, *A Malaysian Journey* (Petaling Jaya: Rehman Rashid, 1993), p. 25.

63. Elphick, *The Pregnable Fortress*, p. 3.

64. Elsbree, *Japan's Role*, pp. 162–63.

65. Ibid.

66. Bayly and Harper, *Forgotten Armies*, p. 46; Tominaga Shozo, "Qualifying as a Leader", in *Japan at War: An Oral History*, edited by Haruko Taya Cook and Theodore F. Cook (New York: The New Press, 1992), pp. 41–42.

67. Sybil Kathigasu, *No Dram of Mercy* (London: Neville Spearman, 1954), p. 39.

68. Ibid; Agnes Khoo, *Life as the River Flows: Women in the Malayan Anti-Colonial Struggle* (Petaling Jaya: Strategic Information Research Development, 2004), pp. 185, 229; Abu Talib Ahmad, *The Malay Muslims, Islam and the Rising Sun* (Kuala Lumpur: MBRAS, 2003), p. 39.

69. Akashi Yoji, "Colonel Watanabe Wataru: The Architect of the Military Administration, December 1941–March 1943", in *New Perspectives on the Japanese Occupation in Malaya and Singapore 1941–1945*, edited by Akashi Yoji and Yoshimura Mako (Singapore: NUS Press, 2008), p. 35.

70. Yoshimura Mako, "Japan's Economic Policy for Malaya/Singapore 1941–45", in *New Perspectives on the Japanese Occupation in Malaya and Singapore*, edited by Akashi Yoji and Yoshimura Mako (Singapore: NUS Press, 2008), p. 118.

71. Kathigasu, *No Dram of Mercy*, pp. 44–45.

72. Akashi, "Colonel Watanabe", pp. 51–53.

73. Cheah Boon Kheng, "Memory as History and Moral Judgement: Oral and Written Accounts of the Japanese Occupation of Malaya", in *War and Memory in Malaysia and Singapore*, edited by Patricia Lim Pui Huen and Diana Wong (Singapore: Institute of Southeast Asian Studies, 2000), p. 29.

74. Chin Kee Ong, *Malaya Upside Down*, 3rd ed. (Kuala Lumpur: Federal Publications, 1976), pp. 82–87.

75. Yoshimura, "Japan's Economic Policy", pp. 116–18.
76. Ibid.
77. Akashi, "Colonel Watanabe", p. 54.
78. Yoshimura, "Japan's Economic Policy", p. 118.
79. Akashi, "Colonel Watanabe", pp. 54–55; Bayly and Harper, *Forgotten Wars*, p. 11.
80. Chin, *Malaya Upside Down*, pp, 38–45; 192–95.
81. Bayly and Harper, *Forgotten Wars*, p. 11.
82. Yoshimura, "Japan's Economic Policy", p. 125.
83. Cheah Boon Kheng, *Red Star Over Malaya: Resistance and Social Conflict During and After the Japanese Occupation of Malaya 1941–1946*, 2nd ed. (Singapore, Singapore University Press, 1987), pp. 294–95.
84. Elsbree, *Japan's Role*, pp. 162–63.
85. Bayly and Harper, *Forgotten Wars*, p. 24.
86. Wang Gungwu, "Memories of War", *in War and Memory in Malaysia and Singapore*, edited by Patricia Lim Pui Huen and Diana Wong (Singapore: Institute of Southeast Asian Studies, 2000), pp. 16–17.
87. Hayashi Hirofumi, "Massacres of Chinese in Singapore and Its Coverage in Post-War Japan", in *New Perspectives on the Japanese Occupation in Malaya and Singapore 1941–1945*, edited by Akashi Yoji and Yoshimura Mako (Singapore: NUS Press, 2008), pp. 235–36.
88. Lee, *The Singapore Story*, p. 58.
89. Chapman, *The Jungle is Neutral*, pp. 125, 282; Shan Ru-Long, *The War in the South: The Story of Negri Sembilan's Guerillas* (Bangkok: Mental Health Pubishing, 2003), p. 60; Lim, *War and Ambivalence*, pp. 144–45.
90. Akashi, "Colonel Watanabe", p. 40.
91. Cheah, *Red Star Over Malaya*, p. 54.
92. Bayly and Harper, *Forgotten Wars*, p. 30.
93. Cheah, "Memory as History", pp. 28–29.
94. Khong, *Merdeka!*, p. 32.
95. Bayly and Harper, *Forgotten Wars*, p. 31.
96. Cheah, *Red Star Over Malaya*, p. 55.
97. Shan, *The War in the South*, pp. 81–84; Bayly and Harper, *Forgotten Wars*, p. 34.
98. Bayly and Harper, *Forgotten Wars*, p. 32.
99. Chin Peng, *My Side of History* (Singapore: Media Masters, 2003), p. 26; Bayly and Harper, *Forgotten Wars*, pp. 31–32.
100. Lawrence James, *Raj: The Making and Unmaking of British India* (London: Little, Brown, 1997), p. 547.
101. Akashi Yoji, "Introduction", in *New Perspectives on the Japanese Occupation in Malaya and Singapore, 1941–1945*, edited by Akashi Yoji and Yoshimura Mako (Singapore: NUS Press, 2008), p. 5.

102. Ibid., p. 18.
103. Wan Hashim, *Race Relations in Malaysia* (Kuala Lumpur: Heinemann Educational Books (Asia), 1983), p. 39.
104. Bayly and Harper, *Forgotten Wars*, pp. 17–18.
105. Abu Talib, *The Malay Muslims*, p. 92.
106. Wan Hashim, *Race Relations*, p. 40; Abu Talib, *The Malay Muslims*, p. 98.
107. Abu Talib, *The Malay Muslims*, pp. 212–40.
108. Elsbree, *Japan's Role*, pp. 112–13; Cheah Boon Kheng, "The 'Blackout Syndrome' and the Ghosts of World War II; The War as a 'Divisive Issue' in Malaysia", in *Legacies of World War II in South and East Asia*, edited by David Koh Wee Hock (Singapore: Institute of Southeast Asian Studies, 2007), p. 52.
109. Elsbree, *Japan's Role*, p. 164.
110. Abu Talib, *The Malay Muslims*, pp. 212–40.
111. Bayly and Harper, *Forgotten Wars*, p. 46.
112. Shaw, *Tun Razak*, p. 47.
113. Bayly and Harper, *Forgotten Wars*, p. 46.
114. Abu Talib, *The Malay Muslims*, pp. 124–27.
115. Cheah, "Memory as History", p. 28.
116. Cheah, *Red Star over Malaya*, p. 55.
117. Cheah, "The 'Blackout' Syndrome", p. 51.
118. Allan, *Singapore 1941–1942*, p. 261.
119. Warren, *The Indian Army*, p. 234.
120. Fujiwara Iwaichi (trans. Akashi Yoji), *F. Kikan: Japanese Army Intelligence Operations and Southeast Asia during World War II* (Hong Kong: Heinemann Asia, 1983), p. 21.
121. Ibid.
122. Allen, *Singapore 1941–1942*, p. 260.
123. Gerard R. Corr, *The War of the Springing Tigers* (London: Osprey, 1975), p. 64.
124. Ibid., p. 54.
125. Fujiwara, *F. Kikan*, p. 40.
126. Corr, *The War of the Springing Tigers*, p. 64.
127. Chin, *Malaya Upside Down*, p. 122; Joginder Singh Jessy, "The Indian Army of Independence", (BA [Hons] Thesis, University of Singapore, 1957–58).
128. Joyce Lebra, *Jungle Alliance: Japan and the Indian National Army* (Singapore: Asia Pacific Press, 1971), p. 14.
129. Corr, *The War of the Springing Tigers*, p. 73.
130. Sunanda K. Datta-Ray, "World War II Legacies for India", in *Legacies of World War II in South and East Asia*, edited by David Koh Wee Hock (Singapore: Institute of Southeast Asian Studies, 2007), p. 185.
131. Fujiwara, *F. Kikan*, p. 90.

132. Ibid., pp. 105–6.
133. Corr, *The War of the Springing Tigers*, p. 93.
134. Bayly and Harper, *Forgotten Armies*, p. 43.
135. Ibid., p. 66.
136. A.C. Chatterjee, *India's Struggle for Freedom* (Calcutta: Chuckervatty, Chatterjee, 1947), p. 4.
137. Corr, *The War of the Springing Tigers*, pp. 93–94.
138. Jessy, *The Indian Army of Independence*.
139. Chatterjee, *India's Struggle for Freedom*, p. 5.
140. Maria Misra, *Vishnu's Crowded Temple: India since the Great Rebellion* (London: Allen Lane, 2007), pp. 228–29.
141. Peter Ward Fay, *The Forgotten Army: India's Armed Struggle for Independence, 1942–1945* (Ann Arbor: University of Michigan Press, 1995), p. 83.
142. Allen, *Singapore 1941–1942*, p. 260.
143. Fay, *The Forgotten Army*, p. 83.
144. Bayly and Harper, *Forgotten Wars*, p. 89.
145. Louis Allen, *Burma: The Longest War 1941–45* (London: Dent, 1984), p. 605.
146. Fay, *The Forgotten Army*, p. 83.
147. Allen, *Singapore 1941–1942*, p. 260.
148. Fay, *The Forgotten Army*, p. 83.
149. Ibid.
150. Allen, *Singapore 1941–1942*, p. 261.
151. Bayly and Harper, *Forgotten Armies*, pp. 90–93; Nalini Ranjan Chakravarti, *The Indian Minority in Burma: The Rise and Decline of an Indian Community* (London: Oxford University Press, 1971), p. 112.
152. These lines of thought are comprehensively summed up by Captain P.K. Saghal who stated: "After protracted negotiations the only solution we could think of was the formation of a strong and well-disciplined armed body which should fight for the liberation of India from the existing alien rule, [and which] should be able and ready to provide protection to their countrymen against any possible molestation by the Japanese and to resist any attempt by the latter to establish themselves as rulers of the country in place of the British." (Warren, *The Indian Army*, p. 234).
153. Ibid.
154. Bayly and Harper, *Forgotten Armies*, p. 167.
155. Chakravarti, *The Indian Minority in Burma*, pp. 106–7.
156. Allen, *Burma: The Longest War*, p. 81.
157. Bayly and Harper, *Forgotten Armies*, p. 167; Allen, *Burma: The Longest War*, p. 81.
158. Fay, *The Forgotten Army*, p. 96.
159. Ibid., pp. 98–100.

160. C.P. Ramachandra, "The Indian Independence Movement in Malaya 1942–45", (M.A. Thesis, Universiti Malaya, 1970).

161. James, *Raj*, p. 564; Alex Von Tunzelmann, *Indian Summer: The Secret History of the End of an Empire* (London: Simon and Schuster, 2007), pp. 121–22.

162. Datta-Ray, "World War II Legacies", p. 185.

163. Von Tunzelmann, *Indian Summer*, p. 109.

164. Ibid., p. 121.

165. Bayly and Harper, *Forgotten Armies*, p. 147.

166. James, *Raj*, pp. 565–66; Bayly and Harper, *Forgotten Armies*, p. 248.

167. Bayly and Harper, *Forgotten Armies*, p. 277.

168. Elsbree, *Japan's Role*, pp. 150–52.

169. Fay, *The Forgotten Army*, p. 134.

170. Von Tunzelmann, *Indian Summer*, p. 138.

171. Bayly and Harper, *Forgotten Armies*, p. 284.

172. Ibid., p. 286.

173. Von Tunzelmann, *Indian Summer*, p. 138; Bayly and Harper, *Forgotten Armies*, p. 287.

174. Ramachandra, *The Indian Independence Movement*.

175. Lebra, *Jungle Alliance*, pp. 45-46; Usha Mahajani, *The Role of Indian Minorities in Burma and Malaya* (Bombay: Vora, 1960), p. 146.

176. Lebra, *Jungle Alliance*, p. 77.

177. Ramachandra, *The Indian Independence Movement*.

178. James, *Raj*, p. 550.

179. Elsbree, *Japan's Role*, p. 33.

180. Lebra, *Jungle Alliance*, pp. 45–46.

181. Jessy, *The Indian Army of Independence*.

182. Elsbree, *Japan's Role*, p. 150.

183. Lebra, *Jungle Alliance*, pp. 60–67.

184. Elsbree, *Japan's Role*, p. 150.

185. Fay, *The Forgotten Army*, p. 144.

186. Bayly and Harper, *Forgotten Armies*, p. 257.

187. Lebra, *Jungle Alliance*, p. 84.

188. Ramachandra, *The Indian Independence Movement*.

189. Lebra, *Jungle Alliance*, p. 84.

190. Bayly and Harper, *Forgotten Armies*, p. 256.

191. Fay, *The Forgotten Army*, pp. 148–49.

192. Ibid., p. 148.

193. Ibid., p. 149.

194. Lebra, *Jungle Alliance*, pp. 95–96.

195. Jessy, *The Indian Army of Independence*.

196. Fay, *The Forgotten Army*, pp. 150–51.

197. Ibid., p. 152.

198. Hugh Toye, *The Springing Tiger: A Study of a Revolutionary* (London: Cassell, 1959), p. 42.

199. Fay, *The Forgotten Army*, p. 133.

200. Ibid., pp. 154–55.

201. K.C. Yadav and Akiko Saki, *Subhas Chandra Bose: The Last Days* (Gurgaon: Hope India, 2003), p. 14.

202. *Netaji Subhas Bose — A Malaysian Perspective* (Kuala Lumpur: Netaji Centre, 1992), p. 151. For a detailed study of the Jallianwala Bagh incident and its aftermath, see Nigel Collet's *The Butcher of Amritsar: General Reginald Dyer* (London: Hambledon & London, 2005).

203. Toye, *The Springing Tiger*, pp. 52–53.

204. Yadav and Akiko, *Subhas Chandra Bose*, pp. 16–17.

205. *Netaji Subhas Bose*, p. 166.

206. Mihir Bose, *Raj, Secrets, Revolution: A Life of Subhas Chandra Bose* (London: Grice Chapman, 2004), pp. 182–83; Sugata Bose, *His Majesty's Opponent: Subhas Chandra Bose and India's Struggle against Empire* (Cambridge, MA: The Belknap Press of Harvard University Press, 2001), p. 188.

207. Yadav and Akiko, *Subhas Chandra Bose*, p. 23.

208. Bose, *Raj, Secrets, Revolution*, p. 188.

209. Yadav and Akiko, *Subhas Chandra Bose*, p. 23.

210. Subodh Markendeya, *Subhas Chandra Bose: Netaji's Passage to Immortality* (New Delhi: Arnold, 1990), p. 158.

211. Fay, *The Forgotten Army*, p. 199.

212. Bose, *Raj, Secrets, Revolution*, p. 211.

213. Markendeya, *Netaji's Passage to Immortality*, p. 173.

214. Toye, *The Springing Tiger*, p. 77.

215. Lebra, *Jungle Alliance*, p. 110. While Sugata Bose claims that the meeting took place on 29 May at the Reich Chancellory, Mihir Bose has shown that it was held on 27 May at the Wolf's Lair, Hitler's East Prussian redoubt (Bose, *Raj, Secrets, Revolution*, pp. 221–23; Bose, *His Majesty's Opponent*, p. 219).

216. Bayly and Harper, *Forgotten Armies*, p. 278; Yadav and Akiko, *Subhas Chandra Bose*, p. 24.

217. Yadav and Akiko, *Subhas Chandra Bose*, pp. 25–26.

218. Fujiwara, *F. Kikan*, pp. 248–49.

219. Markendeya, *Netaji's Passage to Immortality*, pp. 194–95.

220. *Netaji Subhas Bose*, p. 189.

221. Jessy, *The Indian Army of Independence*.

222. Toye, *The Springing Tiger*, p. 60.

223. During interviews, I was advised that whenever possible, Bose would visit the prayer shrines in the homes of his confidants, where attired in the traditional

dress of the *sannyasin* he would spend hours in meditation. Bose also expressed a deep interest in the writings of Sri Aurobindo Ghose.

224. Toye, *The Springing Tiger*, p. 89; Fay, *The Forgotten Army*, pp. 234–36. In taking this approach, Bose was completely rejecting British proposals of an electoral system weighted by considerations of religion or caste.

225. Bayly and Harper, *Forgotten Armies*, p. 279; Markendeya, *Netaji's Passage to Immortality*, p. 165.

226. Lebra, *Jungle Alliance*, p. 107; Bose, *Raj, Secrets, Revolution*, p. 209. Sugata Bose states that the term "was a very Indian form of expressing affection mingled with honour" (Bose, *His Majesty's Opponent*, p. 209).

227. Allan, *Burma: The Longest War*, p. 169.

228. Fay, *The Forgotten Army*, p. 212.

229. Bayly and Harper, *Forgotten Armies*, p. 332.

230. Ramachandra, *The Indian Independence Movement*.

231. Jessy, *The Indian Army of Independence*.

232. Bose, *Raj, Secrets, Revolution*, p. 251.

233. Bayly and Harper, *Forgotten Armies*, pp. 324–26.

234. Jessy, *The Indian Army of Independence*; *Netaji Subhas Bose*, p. 193.

235. Yadav and Akiko, *Subhas Chandra Bose*, p. 32; Bayly and Harper, *Forgotten Armies*, p. 32.

236. Lebra, *Jungle Alliance*, p. 129.

237. Bose, *Raj, Secrets, Revolution*, p. 253.

238. Lebra, *Jungle Alliance*, p. 133.

239. Von Tunzelmann, *Indian Summer*, p, 70.

240. Fay, *The Forgotten Army*, pp. 215–20. The Rani of Jhansi's unique contribution to resistance against the British during the Great Rebellion was the formation and training of a women's corps who were to fight as regular soldiers alongside the men (Michael Edwardes, *Red Year: The Indian Rebellion of 1857* (London: Cardinal, 1975), p. 119).

241. Chatterjee, *India's Struggle for Freedom*, p. 85.

242. Fay, *The Forgotten Army*, p. 221; *Netaji Chandra Bose*, p. 43.

243. Bayly and Harper, *Forgotten Armies*, pp. 326–27.

244. Rajeswary Amplavanar, *The Indian Minority and Political Change in Malaya 1945–1957* (Kuala Lumpur: Oxford University Press, 1981), p. 8.

245. Ramachandra, "The Indian Independence Movement"; Warren, *The Indian Army*, p. 237.

246. Bayly and Harper, *Forgotten Armies*, pp. 324–26; Mahajani, *The Role of Indian Minorities*, p. 148.

247. Ramachandra, "The Indian Independence Movement".

248. Tan Sri S. Chelvasingam-MacIntyre, *Through Memory Lane* (Singapore: Education Press, 1973), p. 120; Chin Kee Onn, *Malaya Upside Down*, p. 130.

249. Chelvasingam-MacIntyre, *Through Memory Lane*, p. 127.

250. Fay, *The Forgotten Army*, p. 214.

251. Chelvasingam-MacIntyre, *Through Memory Lane*, p. 284.

252. Ramachandra, "The Indian Independence Movement".

253. P. Ramasamy, "Indian War Memory in Malaysia", in *War and Memory in Malaysia and Singapore*, edited by Patricia Lim Pui Huen and Diana Wong (Singapore: Institute of Southeast Asian Studies, 2000), p. 96. Several Indian Muslim scholars whom I interviewed disputed this account and pointed out that Indian Muslims in Malaysia had played pivotal roles in the leadership and organisation of both the IIL and the INA. A number of Indian Muslim women also joined the Rani of Jhansi Regiment. Scholars also highlighted the role played by Muslims in the British Indian Army mutiny in Singapore in February 1915. This incident unfolded as follows. Members of the Indian 5th Light Infantry, mainly consisting of Punjabi Muslims, were incensed that Britain was at war with Muslim Turkey. They had discussed their anti-British sentiments with one Kassim Mansoor, a Gujarati Muslim activist who owned a coffee shop near the Alexandria Barracks, and had also been subject to the propaganda of German Prisoners of War whom they were guarding. Members of the 5th Light had secretly joined the mainly Punjabi Ghadar movement which aimed at expelling the British from India. (This movement was also supported by members of the Sikh diaspora, and indeed in December 1914, one Jegat Singh of Singapore had been instrumental in persuading Sikh Malay Guards not to embark for active service in Europe.) The spark which appears to have ignited the revolt was the rumour that the Infantry was being sent, not to Hong Kong, but rather to fight in Turkey. Troops murdered their officers, set free German POWs, and in a series of random attacks killed forty-four Europeans. The mutiny was ultimately quelled by a British naval detachment which also exacted retribution on "all kinds of dark skinned but quite innocent people" (Shennan, *Out in the Midday Sun*, p. 96). Thirty-seven mutineers were subsequently executed, others were transported, and Kassim Mansoor was hung (see Asad-ul Iqbal Latif, "From Mandalas to Microchips: The Indian Imprint on the Construction of Singapore", in *Rising India and Indian Communities in East Asia*, edited by K. Kesavapany, A. Mani, and P. Ramasamy (Singapore: Institute of Southeast Asian Studies, 2008), pp. 554–55; Shennan *Out in the Midday Sun*, pp. 88–99).

254. Fay, *The Forgotten Army*, pp. 214–15. Attendees interviewed by the author attested to the immense power of his oratory, and the mesmerism he seemed to exercise over his audiences.

255. Ibid., p. 215.

256. Ibid.

257. Michael R. Stenson, *Class, Race and Colonialism in West Malaysia: The Indian Case* (St. Lucia: University of Queensland Press, 1980), p. 98.

258. Bayly and Harper, *Forgotten Armies*, pp. 370–71.
259. Hata Shoryu, "A War Correspondent", in *Japan at War: An Oral History*, edited by Haruko Taya Cook and Theodore F. Cook (New York: The New Press, 1992), p. 210.
260. Jessy, *The Indian Army of Independence*.
261. Bayly and Harper, *Forgotten Armies*, pp. 373–74; Allen, *Burma: The Longest War*, p. 169.
262. Bayly and Harper, *Forgotten Armies*, p. 248.
263. Ramachandra, "The Indian Independence Movement".
264. Lebra, *Jungle Alliance*, pp. 175–76.
265. Chin, *Malaya Upside Down*, pp. 129–31.
266. Ibid., p. 133.
267. Corr, *The War of the Springing Tigers*, p. 163.
268. James, *Raj*, pp. 571–72.
269. Ramachandra, "The Indian Independence Movement"; Selvakumaran Ramachandran, *Indian Plantation Labour in Malaysia* (Kuala Lumpur: S. Abdul Majeed, 1994), p. 235.
270. Chin, *Malaya Upside Down*, p. 133.
271. Lebra, *Jungle Alliance*, p. 197.
272. Bayly and Harper, *Forgotten Armies*, p. 401.
273. Ramachandra, "The Indian Independence Movement"; Fay, *The Forgotten Army*, p. 379.
274. James, *Raj*, p. 571.
275. Fay, *The Forgotten Army*, p. 377.
276. Ibid., pp. 377–78.
277. Ramachandra, "The Indian Independence Movement".
278. Ibid.
279. Fay, *The Forgotten Army*, p. 379.
280. Chin, *Malaya Upside Down*, p. 133.
281. Ramachandra, "The Indian Independence Movement".
282. Chelvasingam-McIntyre, *Through Memory Lane*, p. 123.
283. Ravindra K. Jain, *South Indians on the Plantation Frontier in Malaya* (New Haven: Yale University Press, 1970), p. 304; P. Ramasamy, *Plantation Labour, Unions, Capital and the State in Peninsular Malaysia* (New York: Oxford University Press, 1994), p. 59.
284. Stenson, *Class, Race and Colonialism*, pp. 98–100.
285. Selvakumaran, *Indian Plantation Labour*, p. 236.
286. Bose, *Raj, Secrets, Revolution*, pp. 271–73.
287. Lebra, *Jungle Alliance*, p. 191.
288. Bayly and Harper, *Forgotten Armies*, pp. 435–36.
289. Allen, *Burma: The Longest War*, p. 485.

290. Yadav and Akiko, *Subhas Chandra Bose*, p. 41.
291. *Netaji Subhas Bose*, p. 213.
292. Toye, *The Springing Tiger*, pp. 163–65.
293. Yadav and Akiko, *Subhas Chandra Bose*, p. 43.
294. *Netaji Subhas Bose*, p. 214.
295. Toye, *The Springing Tiger*, p. 165.
296. Lebra, *Jungle Alliance*, pp. 197–98; James, *Raj*, p. 575.
297. Jessy, *The Indian Army of Independence*.
298. *Netaji Subhas Bose*, p. 216.
299. Bayly and Harper, *Forgotten Wars*, pp. 22–23.
300. Fay, *The Forgotten Army*, pp. 433–34.
301. Ramasamy, *Indian War Memory*, p. 92.
302. Selvakumaran, *Indian Plantation Labour*, p. 236; Paul W. Wiebe and S. Mariappen, *Indian Malaysians: The View from the Plantation* (Delhi: Manohar, 1978), p. 27.
303. Jain, *South Indians on the Plantation Frontier*, p. 299.
304. Bayly and Harper, *Forgotten Armies*, p. 328.
305. Ibid., p. 327.
306. Selvakumaran, *Indian Plantation Labour*, p. 233.
307. Ramasamy, *Indian War Memory*, p. 92.
308. Sinnappah Arasaratnam, *Indians in Malaysia and Singapore* (London: Oxford University Press, 1970), pp. 102–3.
309. Jain, *South Indians on the Plantation Frontier*, p. 299; Selvakumaran, *Indian Plantation Labour*, p. 236.
310. Selvakumaran, *Indian Plantation Labour*, p. 236.
311. Jain, *South Indians on the Plantation Frontier*, p. 298.
312. Ramasamy, "Indian War Memory", pp. 96–97.
313. Ibid.
314. Selvakumaran, *Indian Plantation Labour*, p. 233.
315. Ota Koki, "Railway Operations In Japanese-Occupied Malaya", in *New Perspectives on the Japanese Occupation in Malaya and Singapore 1941–1945*, edited by Akashi Yoji and Yoshimura Mako (Singapore: NUS Press, 2008), p. 155.
316. Cook and Cook, *Japan at War*, p. 99.
317. Lord Russell, *The Knights of Bushido: A Short History of Japanese War Crimes* (London: Corgi, 1967), p. 74.
318. Cook and Cook, *Japan at War*, p. 99.
319. The actual figures for Tamils and other Indians who worked on the railway are the subject of some dispute, and at this distance are perhaps impossible to assess with any precise degree of accuracy. However, Mihir Bose indicates that Subhas Chandra Bose sent Brahmachariar Kailasan of the Singapore Ramakrishna Mission to report on the conditions under which Indians were

required to work on this project. Bose read his report in June 1945. Bose and N. Raghavan then discussed this report with the Japanese who admitted that 120,000 Tamils had been taken from Malaya, of whom one-third had survived. Raghavan estimated that 60,000 additional Indians had been recruited from Burma, of whom a mere 20,000 had returned (Bose, *Raj, Secrets, Revolution*, pp. 275–76).

320. Bayly and Harper, *Forgotten Armies*, p. 406.

321. Andrew C. Wilford, *Cage of Freedom: Tamil Identity and the Ethnic Fetish in Malaysia* (Ann Arbor: University of Michigan Press, 2006), p. 23.

322. Charles Gamba, *The Origins of Trade Unionism in Malaya: A Study in Colonial Labour Unrest* (Singapore: Eastern Universities Press, 1962), p. 253.

323. Ramachandra, "The Indian Independence Movement".

324. Russell, *The Knights of Bushido*, pp. 80–84.

325. Bayly and Harper, *Forgotten Armies*, pp. 407–8.

326. Ibid., p. 406.

327. Selvakumaran, *Indian Plantation Labour*, p. 236. For Japanese figures, see note 319.

328. Arasaratnam, *Indians in Malaysia and Singapore*, p. 31; Stenson, *Class, Race and Colonialism*, p. 90.

329. Ramachandra, "The Indian Independence Movement".

330. Arasaratnam, *Indians in Malaysia and Singapore*, p. 109.

331. Ramasamy, "Indian War Memory", p. 98; Kernial Singh Sandhu, "The Coming of Indians to Malaysia", in *Indian Communities in Southeast Asia*, edited by Kernial Singh Sandhu and A. Mani (Singapore: Institute of Southeast Asian Studies, 1993), p. 183.

332. Ramachandra, "The Indian Independence Movement".

333. Arasaratnam, *Indians in Malaysia and Singapore*, p. 109.

334. Ramasamy, *Plantation Labour*, p. 59.

335. Ramachandra, "The Indian Independence Movement".

336. *Netaji Subhas Bose*, p. 231.

337. Ramachandra, "The Indian Independence Movement".

338. Arasaratnam, *Indians in Malaysia and Singapore*, p. 109.

339. Ramasamy, "Indian War Memory", p. 99.

340. Sinnappah Arasaratnam, "Malaysian Indians: The Formation of an Incipient Society", in *Indian Communities in Southeast Asia*, edited by Kernial Singh Sandhu and A. Mani (Singapore: Institute of Southeast Asian Studies, 1993), p. 193.

341. Sinnappah Arasaratnam, "Political Attitudes and Political Organization among Malayan Indians 1945–1955", *Jernal Sejarah* 10 (1971/72): 1.

342. Ramasamy, "Indian War Memory", p. 99.

343. Rajeswary, *The Indian Minority*, p. 48.

344. Chatterjee, *India's Struggle for Freedom*, p. 188.
345. Bayly and Harper, *Forgotten Armies*, p. 322.
346. Selvakumaran, *Indian Plantation Labour*, p. 239.
347. Jessy, *The Indian Army of Independence*.
348. Allen, *Singapore*, p. 187.
349. Mahajani, *The Role of Indian Minorities*, p. 163; Chin, *Malaya Upside Down*, p. 187.
350. Arasaratnam, "Malaysian Indians: The Formation of an Indian Society", p. 210.
351. Asad-ul Iqbal Latif, "Singapore's Missing War", in *Legacies of World War II in Southeast Asia*, edited by David Wee Hock (Singapore: Institute of Southeast Asian Studies, 2007), p. 95.

11

THE POST-WAR PERIOD
Reform and Repression: 1945–48

Although the Japanese surrender in Malaya came into effect on 19 August, it was not until 4 September that the main Allied landings were made in Singapore. On 9 September, Louis Mountbatten, Supreme Commander, South East Asian Command (SEAC), accepted the final surrender of 70,000 Japanese troops.[1] The Japanese used the intervening period to burn archives, to murder witnesses to their atrocities, and to falsify documents.[2]

THE MPAJA AND SINO–MALAY RACIAL CLASHES

In Chapter 10 we noted that Japanese policies on ethnicity served to solidify incipient "racial" identities and exacerbated Sino-Malay rivalry and distrust. Japanese propaganda had highlighted Chinese "exploitation" of impoverished Malays and Japanese championship of Malay interests.[3] Post-war violence was to deepen and indeed entrench inter-ethnic cleavage.

The unexpected swiftness of the Japanese capitulation left an interregnum of several weeks — months in some districts — in which there was a complete absence of government control. In many areas law and order collapsed, and diverse groups throughout the country took matters into their own hands.[4] Mobs exacted revenge against those who had collaborated, or were rumoured to have collaborated, with the Japanese, and there was a spate of lynching, murder, torture and other acts of violence.[5]

Under the agreement signed at Blantan in December 1943, the MPAJA had allied with the British and agreed to accept SEAC direction. With the Japanese surrender, the MPAJA, hailed as heroes among the squatter population (and generally admired by many urban Chinese as well), and numbering between 5,000 and 7,000 armed members,[6] now emerged from the jungle and signalled their intention of maintaining order within Malaya until the arrival of British and Allied forces.[7] Ultimately approximately seventy per cent of small towns and villages throughout Malaya came under MPAJA control.[8]

The MPAJA instigated a regime of savage and arbitrary reprisals against known as well as putative collaborators. Many of those dealt with by MPAJA tribunals were arraigned as a result of unfounded and trumped-up charges (often provoked by the personal grievances of informers and agents), and were convicted on the basis of uncorroborated and even contrived evidence.[9] Most of the accused were Malays, who, as noted in Chapter 10, had been actively recruited by the Japanese.[10] Those convicted of serious offences, the "so-called traitors and running dogs" were summarily executed. The lynch law mentality of the MPAJA, their far-reaching pursuit of "enemies of the people", together with their brutalities, alienated Malays en masse, and shocked moderates of all communities.[11]

However, the extent of the post-war violence attributed to the MPAJA, as serious as it was, is frequently overstated. Many of the outrages imputed to the MPAJA were often the work of criminal and other elements which took advantage of the general confusion and lawlessness to pursue their own activities. Gangs, supposedly operating under the auspices of the MPAJA, made various demands on Malay kampung dwellers, frequently abducting villagers and molesting women.[12] These transgressors desecrated mosques, and committed other acts offensive to Muslims, including the mutilation of corpses.[13]

Upon surrender, the Japanese military, fearing complications, had withdrawn from the rural districts, and had concentrated its forces in large towns and cities. On 22 August, faced with rapidly deteriorating conditions in the countryside, the Supreme Commander of the Nippon Army in Malaya issued a proclamation taking responsibility for public order.[14]

To many Malays, the generic wave of lawlessness, whether MPAJA or otherwise, appeared to specifically target Malays and was viewed as the first stage of a determined Chinese attempt to assert control over the entire Malay Peninsula. Initial resistance to the MPAJA was mounted by the Malay organizations often working in conjunction with KMT Chinese,[15] but as the incidents became more common and more widespread, a range of Malay millenarian cults, which did not distinguish between the MPAJA and the general Chinese population, began to exact a grisly and bloody revenge. One of these groups was the viscerally anti-Chinese *Sabillah* (Path of God) movement, headed by *Kyai* Salleh bin Abdullah (*Kyai*: religious leader of a Sufi order). Sabillah, which was supported by the Japanese, was an invulnerability cult, which used ritual magic, charms and talismans, and met its victims with paroxysms of violence.[16] Racial incidents and clashes, sometimes resulting in the massacres of entire villages, were reported in Johor, Negeri Sembilan, Perak and Pahang, as well as other locations.[17] The racial violence, which threatened to become general, was resolved through the intervention of Onn bin Jaafar, *Menteri Besar* (Chief Minister) of Johor who brokered negotiations between the MPAJA and Sabillah.[18]

The racial atrocities left a deep wound in Sino–Malay relations.[19] The crudity of MPAJA actions provided Malays with an imagined foretaste of the imperiousness of rule and the scale of repression that would accompany a Chinese takeover in Malaya, and the general humiliations to which Malays would be subject if they were to lose control of their own country to "outsiders". The MPAJA interregnum left an ineradicable imprint upon Malay consciousness, instilling a deep and enduring suspicion not only of the MCP, but in more general terms the scope of Chinese political intentions in Malaya. It also inculcated a determination to prevent Chinese ascendency.[20]

Many Chinese drew different conclusions from the racial carnage. They noted the rapidity with which a campaign initially aimed at checking MPAJA excesses had escalated into a violent racial vendetta against accessible and defenceless Chinese targets, as well as blanket condemnations of the entire Chinese community. They feared that this reaction portended a possible pattern of Malay response to perceived challenges to its political and cultural pre-eminence, and that Malayan political processes might always be subject to Malay passions. They concluded that there was thus an urgent need to develop strategies to protect and advance Chinese interests.[21]

The British Military Administration

From the period between the arrival of the British forces in Singapore, to the full restoration of civilian government on 1 April 1946, Malaya and Singapore came under the transitional rule of a body known as the British Military Administration (BMA). The BMA assumed control at a time when the fabric of governmental authority and public order had all but disintegrated, and had been replaced with racial volatility, general lawlessness and complete economic dislocation. The administration was charged with restoring British rule and authority, boosting public confidence, reinvigorating industry, and importing sufficient food to meet basic needs. It was faced with major social and economic problems, including widespread unemployment, chronic food shortages and the total collapse of basic health and other social amenities.[22]

The BMA, generally known as the "Black Market Administration", was both corrupt and inefficient.[23] One of its earliest actions was its refusal to recognize Japanese currency still circulating in Malaya. This not only occasioned extreme hardship to those who had no access to Straits dollars, including the vast majority of the labour force, but resulted in spiralling inflation which drove the price of rice up to between thirty to forty times pre-war levels. To counter the hunger resulting from rice shortages, the administration imported fifty million grams of opium to distribute within the workforce. Many essential commodities were traded within the black economy.[24] The BMA alienated locally employed civil servants by payment of the back salaries of European civil servants interned during the Japanese occupation, without making a countervailing offer to Asian civil servants, many of whom had suffered severe reductions in pay under the Japanese as well as enduring persecution by the Kempeitai.[25]

The period of BMA rule coincided with widespread industrial unrest. This resulted from a combination of factors, including unstable economic and political conditions within Malaya, high unemployment, inadequate wages, rapid inflation and food shortages.[26] Union resentment was stimulated by the heavy-handedness of the BMA, and later by that of the colonial administration, which tended rather simplistically to view all industrial action, more particularly strikes, as examples of communist subversion.[27]

CONSTITUTIONAL REFORM

The Malayan Union

During the later years of the war, British officials had made plans for the future administration of Malaya. It was decided to retain Singapore as a base for projection of British imperial power, but to overhaul the cumbersome administrative apparatus of colonial Malaya.[28] In October 1945, details of the proposed settlement, to be known as the Malayan Union, were made public.[29] These were formalized in a white paper released on 22 January 1946. The paper set forth two main objectives. These were:

1. To create an effective and centralized government. This was to be achieved by bringing the Straits Settlements of Penang and Malacca together with the nine Malay states under a single administration. Sovereignty was to be transferred from the nine Malay rulers to the British Crown. Under this arrangement the sultans would cease to head their respective states but would continue to exercise responsibility for control and interpretation of Islam.[30]
2. To make citizenship available to non-Malays, thus promoting a sense of unity and belonging. Non-Malays claiming Malaya as their home (based on birth or domicile) were to be made eligible for equal citizenship rights to those enjoyed by Malays.[31] Citizenship provisions under the Malayan Union were intended to ensure that every person, regardless of racial origin or creed, could substantiate claim to citizenship "by reason of birth or suitable period of residence to belong to the country".[32] This would render eighty-three per cent of the Chinese and seventy-five per cent of the Indians resident in Malaya immediately eligible for citizenship.[33]

The Malayan Union proposal negated the basic principles which had undergirded the British settlement with the Malay states, namely that of recognition of the sovereign independence of the Malay Rulers, and the special position accorded to the Malays.[34] The proposal came as a "great shock" to the Malay elites. First, it was in stark contrast to the pro-Malay policy the British had pursued prior to World War II, when the colonial authorities had anointed themselves "protectors" of the Malays. Second, according to the perspective of the Malay elites, the proposal denied the special status of Malays as a "nation", the Peninsula's indigenous people, and reduced them to a mere community, one of several. Third, in removing the traditional rulers and abolishing the nine territorial entities previously recognized as state/sultanates by the British, the reforms would not only revoke the formal agreements which defined the terms under which authority had been ceded to the British government, but more fundamentally would destroy a key political institution around which, it was asserted, Malay identity was constructed, and upon which all cultural and social organization was ultimately predicated. Finally, the citizenship provisions of the Malayan Union would encourage non-Malays to share in the conduct of public affairs in Malaya, and would open all branches of government service to non-Malays.[35]

Among these concerns, the primary focus of Malay anxieties was the imagined impact of the extension of citizenship laws to non-Malays. Malays believed that these laws would not only lead to the loss of control of their own country, thus denying them of the right to chart their own destiny, but would also, at worst, extinguish Malay cultural identity or at least substantially modify that identity to accord with the dictates of other communities.[36] Many Malays believed that they had already lived through a determined Chinese attempt, via the MPAJA, to impose non-Malay rule upon the country.[37]

Malay political mobilization was immediate. A group of radical journalists, largely under the direction of Ahmad Boestaman (a nom de plume for Abdullah Seni bin Raja Kechil) formed the *Partai Kebangsaan Melayu* (Malay Nationalist Party or MNP), which aimed to unite the peoples of the Malay Archipelago within the inclusive folds of a free and independent Indonesia.[38] Conservative repudiation of the Union was mounted by groups based around Onn bin Jaafar, who was considered the defender of the Malays.[39] Between 1 and 4 March 1946, forty-one Malay associations from both Malaya and Singapore gathered at the Selangor Club in Kuala Lumpur to articulate their opposition to the constitutional provisions of the Malayan Union.[40] The meeting also marked the genesis of the *Pertubuhan Kebangsaan Melayu Bersatu* (United Malays National Organization or UMNO), which was formally constituted on 11 May 1946 with Onn elected as the first President, and a leadership largely drawn from the traditional Malay aristocracy.[41]

Surprisingly, the Malayan Union proposal engendered little support among the Chinese and Indian communities. The immigrant communities continued to direct their primary loyalties to their countries of origin, and as a consequence most were unenthusiastic about the possibility of obtaining citizenship in Malaya.[42] Many non-Malays were both astonished and dismayed by the exclusion of Singapore, which was seen as having indivisible historical, political, economic, social and military ties to the mainland.[43]

In view of continued Malay opposition, George Hall, Secretary of State, sent two British parliamentarians to gauge public reaction to the Malayan

Union proposals. The duo found little support for the Union. The British were made fully aware of the importance that UMNO and the general Malayan leadership imputed to the formal authority of the sultans and their centrality to Malay notions of culture and statecraft, and the need to guarantee the special position of the Malays in any political settlement.[44] In May 1946, the newly appointed Governor-General of British Southeast Asia, Malcolm McDonald, concluded that the Malayan Union should be jettisoned lest it provoke an Indonesian-style reaction within Malaya.[45] The Union was formally abandoned in July 1947.[46]

The Malayan Union campaign stimulated pan-Malay awareness and political activism. Agitation against the proposals had percolated throughout the entire Malay population and had involved ordinary people along with the traditional ruling elites. It fostered Malay awareness of the common interests which transcended the boundaries of the sultanates in which they were resident. It also revealed the extent of the broader social, cultural and religious heritage shared by Malays across the Peninsula.[47]

However, the supposed Malay unity could not disguise the deep divisions between UMNO and the MNP. The MNP strongly rejected Onn's reiterated contention that Malaya as a society was insufficiently mature to manage the transition to independence. Many Malay radicals had fought in the Indonesian revolution, and remained committed to Malayan incorporation within Indonesia. The MNP leadership believed that UMNO was an elite organization which had donned the garb of Malay nationalism in order to contain the challenges posed by the aspirations of the Malay masses. During a Malay congress convened in June 1946, the MNP and its youth wing, *Angkatan Pemuda Insaf* (API or Generation of Aware Youth), staged a walkout following a congress refusal to adopt the Indonesian flag.[48]

Federation

Following the collapse of the Malayan Union proposal, the traditionally close relationship between the British colonial administration and the Malay elite was revived. The British were aware that their long-term political and economic interests in Malaya would be best served through the assiduous cultivation of the elites which would eventually rule an independent Malaya — elites that were moulded in their own image; that is, English educated, preferably in schools and universities that had inculcated the values of the British ruling class, that were pro-British and determined to maintain strong and enduring links with the Commonwealth. The colonial-UMNO nexus appeared to offer the greatest prospect of delivering this outcome.[49] In July 1946 the rulers and UMNO met with both Governor Gent and Governor-General McDonald to set forth their proposals for a new constitutional framework. No Chinese or Indian representatives were invited to participate in these discussions.[50] The subsequent consultations emphasized the distinctiveness of each of the Malay states as well as the entrenched and alienable rights of the Malay people as central to any final constitutional settlement. In-principle agreement to these terms was finalized by November 1946.[51] The polity was to be known as the *Persekutuan Tanah Melayu* (Federation of Malay Lands).[52]

In October 1946 the prominent and highly respected Straits Chinese identity Tan Cheng Lock castigated the colonial authorities for their refusal to involve non-Malays in constitutional talks.[53] Gathering opposition to the Federation resulted in the formation of the Pan-Malayan Council for Joint Action, later to be renamed as the All-Malaya Council for Joint Action (AMCJA). The council was a loose coalition of parties representing a spectrum of opinion ranging from nationalists through to more radical elements, and given mass support by the MCP.[54] The council held its initial meeting on 19 November 1946. It was joined by members of the MNP, which considered that in limiting their consultations to representatives of UMNO, the colonial authorities were ignoring the divergent views of the wider Malay community.[55] Facing predictable charges that it had betrayed the Malay people, the MNP withdrew from the AMCJA to form its own broad association, *Pusat Tenaga Rakyat* (Centre of People's Power) or PUTERA. AMCJA-PUTERA was chaired by Tan Cheng Lock, whom the British promptly depicted as a "dupe" of the communists.[56] The AMCJA-PUTERA negotiations represented a genuine attempt at nation building, and resulted in the formulation of a People's Constitution, a radical alternative to the Federation proposal. The Constitution held out the promise of a more inclusive Malaya, and incorporated the concept of a single nationality to be known as *Melayu* (as opposed to the UMNO position in which this term was reserved solely for Malays). The colonial administration, firmly allied to UMNO and thus resolutely opposed to AMCJA-PUTERA, barely acknowledged the People's Constitution.[57] Faced with British-UMNO indifference, AMCJA-PUTERA embarked upon a course of direct action and declared a hartal on 20 October 1947. In the resultant backlash, the influential newspaper, the *Straits Times*, portrayed the entire coalition as communists, and Tan Cheng Lock came under virulent criticism from more conservative elements of the Chinese community.[58] Ultimately the AMCJA-PUTERA was to be overtaken by the Emergency and was ensnared, fatally, in the British-MCP hostilities.[59]

On 21 January 1948, the rulers of the nine Malay states met in Kuala Lumpur and signed a treaty with the British government. The Federation of Malaya was proclaimed on 1 February 1948.[60] The Federation vested special rights in the High Commissioner, who was to be supported by a nominated legislative council including representatives from all communities. More importantly, from the Malay perspective it guaranteed the special position of the Malays,[61] and restored the sultans as the traditional and spiritual leaders of their respective states.[62]

The Federation agreement considerably tightened the criteria by which non-Malays might attain Malayan citizenship. While all Malays were automatically citizens, non-Malays were automatically citizens if they were permanently resident in Malaya having been born of a parent born there, or if their families were federal citizens at the time of their birth. Others could apply to become citizens if they had been born in the Federation and had lived there for eight of the twelve years prior to application or, alternatively, had lived in Malaya for fifteen of the twenty years prior to application. Candidates for citizenship were required to fulfil two further qualifications, namely (1) to show proficiency in both Malay and English, and (2) to undertake to settle permanently in the country.[63]

Moreover the Federation Agreement clearly stipulated who could be considered a Malay. Henceforth a Malay was to be defined culturally rather than in terms of "racial" or political attributes and would possess three distinct behavioural attributes, namely:

1. He/she habitually spoke the Malay language,
2. He/she professed the Muslim religion, and
3. He/she conformed to Malay custom (*adat*).[64]

Thus, as Maznah Mohamad pungently observes, the generic descriptor "Malay" which had been first used as a census classifier had now been legally transformed into a clearly defined racial entity.[65] By re-inscribing the concept of "Malayness" in broad assimilationist terms it became possible to make citizenship available to Indonesians resident in Malaya, thus increasing the Malay percentage of the citizenry while continuing to exclude the majority of Chinese and Indians.[66] The inclusion of "Indonesian Malaysians" allowed the Malays to numerically emerge from the 1947 census as comprising fifty per cent of the population, whereas Chinese and Indians totalled thirty-eight per cent and eleven per cent respectively.[67] Colonial discourse glossed over the fact that a sizeable percentage of those now defined as "Malays" had in fact originated from other parts of the Archipelago, and could scarcely be regarded as indigenous to the Peninsula. The fiction of a homogenous indigenous group was henceforth employed to privilege one ethnic group over the others, and increasingly to define the politics and society of Malaya/Malaysia in terms of communal allegiance. The Colonial Office's disingenuous declaration that "The Malays ... are peculiarly the people of this country. They have no other country. They have no other homeland, no other loyalty" was to become inscribed in the foundational ideology of Malaya.[68]

However, while claims that the Federation of Malaya Agreement had left the overwhelming majority of the Chinese and Indian population as "aliens" are undoubtedly valid,[69] the agreement did endow non-Malays with the eventual possibility of citizenship, and stipulated the rights and responsibilities which would flow from possession of that citizenship. By noting that non-Malays had "legitimate interests" in Malaya, the Federation Agreement suggested new lines of thought about "immigrant" communities, one which recognized, however tenuously, that non-Malays had a permanent political stake in the future of Malaya.[70]

THE BRITISH RETURN TO MALAYA AND THE INDIAN COMMUNITY

The IIL/INA leaders were aware that a Japanese loss would herald the return of the victorious British, and would be followed by the inevitable initiation of legal and other reprisals against those who had agitated, organized, or taken up arms against the British Empire. The IIL/INA had adopted measures designed to reduce the volume of evidence which could be used against them. Following the death of Subhas Chandra Bose, the INA command had directed that all official records be destroyed. The Japanese surrender led to the disbandment of the army, and the dispersal of locally enlisted members.[71]

The BMA proved extremely hostile to those who had participated in the Indian nationalist movement. One of the first British actions upon their return to Singapore was the destruction of the memorial dedicated to the INA dead. This had been erected on the Singapore waterfront and consecrated by Bose in July 1945.[72] The memorial was immediately noticed upon British disembarkation on 5 September 1945, and was blown up by sappers three days later.[73] Many Indians were appalled by this deed, which they considered wilful desecration.[74]

But more stringent measures were soon to follow. The British had taken 23,268 INA soldiers as prisoners. They had been recruited from the ranks of BIA POWs who had been captured by the Japanese during their successful campaign in Malaya and Singapore. INA soldiers were categorized into three groups — whites, greys and blacks — according to the alleged seriousness of their transgressions against the British crown.[75] Of the total now held by the British, 3,880 were classified as "white" (meaning that they had joined the INA in order to desert or infiltrate the organization), 13,211 were regarded as "grey", while 6,177 fell into the most serious category of "black".[76] Some personnel were sent to India for further investigation, and there were a number of courts martial of former BIA/INA officers.[77] On reoccupying Singapore, Penang and Kuala Lumpur, the British interred most of the IIL leadership, especially journalists.[78] While the total membership of the IIL/INA was too great for the British to seriously contemplate mass retaliatory legal action,[79] the authorities ordered the arrest of twenty-four Malayan leaders of the former IIL.[80] The British were also determined to bring INA personnel to trial and made their first arrests in Singapore and Malaya where the INA had consisted mainly of civilian volunteers. These included leading figures within the Indian community. Ultimately 114 locally based members of the IIL and INA were detained.[81]

Following the Japanese surrender the Government of India appointed a new agent, Mr S.K. Chettur, to Malaya and Singapore. Chettur arrived in November 1945, and immediately drew Indian attention to the continuing incarceration of the former IIL/INA leaders in Kuala Lumpur. The detainees were being held in solitary confinement and at the time of Chettur's arrival only three of the 114 had been formally accused of treason. By December the issue had so outraged Indian opinion that Viceroy Wavell pleaded with Lord Louis Mountbatten, Supreme Commander, South-East Asia to either arrange for the trial of those arrested or to release them.[82] The British imprisonment of twenty-four former IIL leaders provoked anger and concern among the leadership of the Indian National Congress, which protested against the arrests, and nominated Pandit Nehru to proceed to Burma and Malaya to organize local defence and relief for those detained.[83]

Nehru arrived at Kallang Airport, Singapore, on 18 March 1946, and was greeted by 200,000 people. Prior to his arrival, Viceroy Wavell had indicated to Mountbatten that Nehru was to be received as the future Prime Minister of an independent India.[84] Mountbatten took this instruction so seriously that when the BMA was unable to offer Nehru any assistance with transport, Mountbatten furnished his own vehicle and travelled with him. The appearance of Mountbatten by Nehru's side was regarded as a "political sensation".[85]

One of Nehru's first acts was to demonstrate Congress solidarity with those who had worked for the nationalist cause by laying a wreath on the site of the demolished war memorial. He addressed huge crowds in several Malayan centres, and at Alor Setar inspected a guard of honour presented by ex-INA personnel, including women of the Rani of Jhansi Regiment, most of whom were clad in their respective uniforms.[86] Nehru's visit led, *inter alia*, to the widespread wearing of Gandhi caps by Malayan Indians, a practice regarded as "subversive" by colonial planters.[87] Nehru repeatedly praised Netaji for the great contribution he had made to the nationalist movement, but emphasized that the fighting spirit Bose had displayed was no longer relevant to the Indian cause.[88] A medical mission, sent by Congress to Malaya to coincide with Nehru's visit, and under the direction of an ex-INA officer, treated some 17,000 labourers over a ten week period.[89]

Nehru also visited the twenty-four imprisoned ex-IIL leaders. Two days prior to Nehru's departure on 27 March 1946, SEAC announced the release of the detainees, as well the government's decision not to proceed with any further INA prosecutions.[90]

Indians Politics and Society 1945–48

The 1947 census revealed an Indian population of 599,000. The overwhelming majority of the population were Tamils, who comprised seventy-seven per cent of the total. Other main groups were Malayalees (seven per cent of the total); Telugu (seven per cent); and North Indians (nine per cent).[91] The largest and most marginalized component of the Indian community was the plantation workforce, which was spread throughout the rubber, tea and oil palm estates, and was principally located within the Federated Malay States. A lesser number of labourers worked in the cities and major towns, and were employed mainly within public utilities such as the railways, waterworks and electricity authority. There was a small English-educated class of clerical and technical workers who were employed within government offices, mercantile firms and commercial enterprises. A tiny minority of Indians occupied elite positions within both the public and private sectors or in professions. Indian participation in the business sector was spread between a small upper class of capitalist entrepreneurs, a rather larger group of medium-sized business owner-operators, and a substantial base of street vendors, hawkers, and peddlers whose earnings were barely above those received by the labouring classes.[92] The classification of the Indian population in terms of occupation was overlaid by deep divisions created by differences in and between regional and linguistic cultures and issues surrounding religious affiliation. However, even though the Indian population was riven by a complex of competing allegiances and loyalties, it found itself increasingly subject to powerful centripetal impulses. As we have noted, the politics of communalism, incipient and inchoate throughout the long period of pre-war British rule, had been activated and given substance by the Japanese occupation and reinforced by the events which followed the Japanese surrender. Communalism, structured on primary and inclusive concepts of racial identity, was increasingly to define the social and economic landscape of post-war Malaya, a country which many Indians had now begun to view as their homeland.[93]

After their dramatic and catalytic wartime experiences with the IIL and INA, Malayan Indians were not prepared to revert to the compliant servility of the pre-war years. Their new-found assertiveness set them at odds with the returning British, whose agenda was primarily economic and who had little understanding or tolerance for the aspirations of a newly politicized Indian community. The colonial administration's most urgent priority was the immediate restoration of the profitability of the Malayan economy, especially the rehabilitation of British companies and agencies.[94]

The re-establishment of British rule elicited a marked response among the Indian population generally, and more particularly among the younger generation of Tamil workers.[95] Indian activism found expression within four generic and often overlapping sociopolitical streams; namely the formation of the Malayan Indian Congress political party, the short-lived

Thondar Padai movement, the emerging arena of trade unionism, and Dravidianism. These latter movements often found their most vigorous adherents within the previously marginalized plantation sector.

The Formation of the Malayan Indian Congress

We have noted that at the end of the Pacific War Malayan Indians were more politically conscious and more generically united than ever before. Educated Indians were more aware of their corporate responsibilities to the community as a whole, and more willing to assert their leadership.[96] In theory, therefore, the community should have been well placed to respond to the immediate political challenges of the post-war era. However, the British imprisonment of the local leadership of the IIL/INA for well over six months in the period following the Japanese surrender was to deprive the Indian community of its most senior and politically prominent leaders at a time when their expertise was most urgently required.

The Malayan Union proposal, initially unveiled on 10 October 1945, was released at a time when much of the Indian intellectual leadership languished in jail. Indian reaction was at first muted, but by early 1946 representatives of the various communities began voicing an array of anxieties. Minority ethnic groups — the Ceylonese, Indian Muslims, Punjabis, and Malayalees — expressed concern that they would lose their sub-communal identities within a Malayan Union. The Indian press objected to the detachment of Singapore, which was regarded as integral to the overall political and economic viability of any Malayan state. However, apart from Indian Muslims who were firmly opposed to the Union proposal, most Indian organizations remained ambivalent.[97]

The most contentious issue for most Indians was that of citizenship. As we have noted, the Malayan Union incorporated a broad and inclusive concept of citizenship. However, those obtaining citizenship were expected to forsake allegiance to their countries of origin, and eschew looking to them for "political leadership and guidance".[98] The Malayan Union thus placed many of those classified as Indians in a quandary. They were required to make a definite choice between citizenship of either one of the emerging countries of the subcontinent — India, Pakistan and Ceylon — still regarded by many as "home" and which in the case of India had so recently through the agencies of the IIL and INA mobilized the active loyalties of perhaps a majority of the community, or the uncertain benefits of full citizenship of a newly defined entity to be known as Malaya, the latter option entailing legal and public renunciation of primary political allegiance to the country of origin.[99]

The arrest of the INA/IIL leadership had left the Indian community bereft of prominent political figures who might have fashioned a coherent and broader Indian response to the Malayan Union proposal. Indeed, it was only after the formation of the Malayan Indian Congress (MIC) in August 1946 that Indians became aware of the deeper implications of the Malayan Union proposals, especially the inclusive citizenship provisions, and what these might have portended for their future as a community.[100]

The moving influence behind the formation of the Congress was J.A. Thivy, a locally born Christian and a former member of the Central Indian Association of Malaya (CIAM) who had been appointed a Minister in Subhas Chandra Bose's FIPG Cabinet.[101] Promptly imprisoned by the BMA, Thivy was finally released following Nehru's visit to Malaya in March 1946.[102] He immediately set about the task of rebuilding Indian organizations within Malaya and devoted himself to the construction of an Indian nationalist movement. He was greatly assisted by Indian community leaders and by the Devasthanam (Board) of the Sri Maha Mariamman Temple of Kuala Lumpur. The Devasthanam provided financial backing, accommodation (Thivy lived in temple premises for sixteen months), and logistical help to Thivy throughout this crucial period.[103]

The MIC was launched in August 1946 with Thivy as its Foundation President. Thivy's leadership drew the strong endorsement of those middle-class elements which had been prominent in the pre-war CIAM.[104] The discussions and negotiations resulting in the creation of the MIC were permeated with the ideologies and sentiments which informed pan-Indian nationalism, especially the political and philosophical approaches of Gandhi, Nehru and the Indian National Congress, and for several years the party was to bear their impress.[105] Indeed, Thivy regarded the Indians of East Asia as "Ambassadors of India" and promoted Hindi as an Indian lingua franca even though there were few Hindi speakers in Malaya. In addition Thivy opposed the provisions of Malayan Union citizenship lest it deny Indians of dual citizenship rights.[106] The MIC leadership attempted to closely model the party upon the Indian National Congress, and as far as possible replicated Congress's ideology and organizational structure within Malaya.[107] The party's constitution was drafted with the assistance of veteran Indian Congressman Dr Bhattacharya.[108] The first two presidents of the MIC were to retain close and enduring links with Nehru and Congress,[109] and until 1950 members of the MIC attended annual meetings of Congress.[110]

The MIC was founded during a period of intra-communal dissension and flux. In its early years the MIC was largely a party of urban clerks and commercial elements who had been vitally involved in the politics of the IIL.[111] Party members, especially the upper echelons, tended to be middle class, English educated, and Westernized in their habits and attitudes, and most typically subscribed to Indian nationalist ideologies.[112] In 1947 Thivy was advised by the Indian National Congress that Malayan Indians should recognize that their future belonged to that country and that as a consequence the policies of the party should embrace specifically Malayan issues, in particular that of citizenship rights. Given the prevailing ethos of the party, few MIC rank and file were prepared to heed Thivy's call.[113]

The MIC aimed to become a focal point for the Indian community in Malaya, and adopted a comprehensive and far-reaching programme which incorporated support for the independence of India as well as demands for major political reforms in Malaya.[114] However, the fixation upon Indian nationalist ideologies, infused with a broad and often nebulous radicalism, often obstructed deeper consideration of the political realities of colonial Malaya.[115] The MIC leadership attempted to emulate the inclusive political formula which had proved effective in India, and was thus prepared to commit the party to broad and multi-ethnic anti-colonial fronts. Indian newspapers and journals were vociferously anti-colonial, and their repeated and scathing denunciations of the British Empire helped mould nationalist opinion and the alignments of opposition forces within Malaya.[116] As a result the MIC seemed tardy in shaping policies which responded to the political, social and economic realities of a nascent polity which was inexorably inching towards independence.[117]

Throughout the first decade of its existence the MIC presidency was held by representatives of minority sub-communal groups. When Thivy resigned in 1947 to take up an Indian government diplomatic appointment, he was replaced by a Sikh, Budh Singh (1947–50). Subsequent leaders were a Chettiar, K. Ramanathan Chettiar (1950–51), and a Punjabi Hindu, K.L. Devasar (1951–55).[118] This diversity was reflected throughout the entire party; office holders at all levels of the MIC were drawn from the complete regional and linguistic spectrum of the Malayan Indian community. This variegated membership manifested as a series of inter-communal cleavages — ethnic, regional, political, foreign born/local born — which had lain dormant throughout the war years but which now re-emerged to complicate policymaking within the MIC.[119] Organization within the MIC was further handicapped by a lack of coordination between its leadership and regional and local branches, so that an autocratic centre was often in open conflict with its constituent organs. In addition the party was plagued by a series of sharp personality clashes, the legacy of political divisions bequeathed from the days of the IIL/INA.[120]

The party's middle-class membership made it all but inevitable that leading MIC operatives would largely overlook or at least underplay the political and economic imperatives of the Tamil working class, which comprised the vast majority of the Indian population of Malaya.[121] The MIC proved largely unsuccessful in its attempts to co-opt labour into its ranks. As we will see in succeeding sections, in the years of hardship following the war, labour was more immediately impelled by left-wing political ideologies than by Indian nationalism, and sought an identity which accommodated the twin imperatives of community and class. This dilemma was partially resolved by the formation of unions such as those which represented estate labour, which were largely communal in character. The relationship between the union movement and the MIC was always uneasy and frequently tense. Whereas the party attempted to articulate a political agenda which purported to meet the needs of the community as a whole, the outlook of the unions was sharply focused on the push for tangible economic and social benefits for its membership.[122] This dichotomy tended to drive a wedge between the MIC and the unions; on the one hand the MIC feared union radicalism and the disruption which might result from the pursuit of purely economic goals, while the unions worried that their industrial claims, and indeed their very legitimacy, would be challenged, bypassed or even dismissed by a pusillanimous party intent on meeting short-term political objectives.[123] This mutual suspicion persisted throughout the years and continues to operate within the broader sphere of Indian politics in contemporary Malaysia.

Nor, despite the MIC's broad membership, did the party succeed in ameliorating separatist political tendencies among the general Indian population. After the Pacific War, Sikhs re-formed their own organizations, many Indian Muslims joined local branches of the pro-Pakistani Muslim League, while Jawi Peranakan Muslims tended to broadly identify with the Malay Muslim community. The murderous communal clashes which accompanied Indian–Pakistani Partition resulted in tensions between Hindus and Muslims in Penang. Indian independence, attained on

14 August 1947, was not an occasion of widespread celebration among Malayan Indians.[124]

Although the MIC did not press the claims or hold the allegiance of the Indian community, the party quickly gained official recognition as the mouthpiece of the entire Indian population. In this regard MIC stocks were greatly boosted by British policy on communal matters. According to this viewpoint, Malaya was composed of three major "races", each represented by an "authorized" communal structure which bore responsibility for negotiating on the full gamut of issues which were of concern to the community. This policy implicitly discouraged the formation of sub-communal groups and associations. Indeed, the British refused to entertain approaches from minority parties, including those of the Muslim League whose adherents argued that developments on the subcontinent entitled them to establish their own lines of political representation in Malaya. The government's stance preserved the MIC's privileged standing as the "official" purveyor of Indian interests, and thus sidelined separatist political movements.[125]

In January 1947 the MIC joined the AMCJA, which as we have noted, was opposed to the draft constitution of the Federation of Malaya. In concert with the AMCJA-PUTERA, the MIC boycotted discussions relating to the overall shape of the constitution of the Federation. The party argued that Malaya was a multiracial entity and there should be a common citizenship for all regardless of ethnicity.[126] The outbreak of the Emergency put an end to the united front, and the AMCJA-PUTERA, caught in the British–MCP conflict, fragmented in disarray.[127]

The Thondar Padai Movement

Thondar Padai, variously translated as "Volunteer Corps",[128] or "Youth Corps",[129] was a militant movement which aimed at the "socio-economic, cultural and moral uplift of estate labourers".[130] The movement strove to secure better conditions for estate workers and to generally improve the position and the overall standing of the Indian community in Malaya. Thondar Padai was founded in 1945 by A.M. Samy, a driver/shopkeeper on the Harvard Estate in Kedah.[131]

Thondar Padai drew inspiration from two main sources, namely the intensifying independence movement on the subcontinent, as well as the Tamil radicalism of the *Dravidar Kazagham* of Madras.[132] The reform agenda adopted by the movement incorporated a self-renewal programme which had as its centrepiece the eradication of toddy consumption, which was seen as a major cause of poverty among the Indian workforce[133] and responsible for much of the putative servility evinced among Indian labourers in the pre-war period.[134] But the movement also drew upon Gandhian principles of social reform, especially as these related to issues of caste and personal discipline.[135]

Upon Harvard Estate the Thondar Padai developed a comprehensive programme of reform. This concentrated upon enforcement of temperance, especially among the older workers, but also included discourses on reform, education and the protection and uplift of women. Thondar Padai also planned to establish a mutual benefit fund for workers, and members provided assistance and protection to workers during religious festivals, including Thaipusam in nearby Sungai Petani.[136] Occasionally Thondar Padai members resorted to violence in support of their objectives, and there were reports of beatings and finings of habitual drunkards, and the tying of offenders to trees.[137]

Thondar Padai rapidly evolved into a quasi-military organization. Although there was no official uniform, most members dressed in khaki shorts and drill caps (many wore INA caps), each carried a stick, and groups of volunteers exercised and drilled regularly and in military formation.[138] The movement spread to other estates in Kedah, and to Kluang and adjacent districts in Southern Johor. The emergence of unions and union activism was firmly supported by Thondar Padai which was detailed to carry out strong-arm tactics, especially the intimidation of non-strikers on behalf of the unions. Thus, in Kluang, Thondar Padai worked very closely with the Paloh Rubber Workers Association, punishing strike breakers and those who had ignored an order not to consume toddy.[139]

The growing combativeness of Thondar Padai, its general acceptance on other estates, and its involvement with militant unions, aroused the suspicions of British authorities, and provoked claims that it was communist inspired. The showdown with the British occurred during a wave of unrest in Kedah, involving a series of strikes and demonstrations. On 28 February 1947, security forces broke up a peaceful picket comprised of women and children outside a toddy shop on Bedong Estate. In the ensuing fracas one worker was killed after being struck on the head with a baton, and nine were injured. A coroner later recorded the death as a case of "justifiable homicide".[140] There were further incidents on Bukit Sembilan Estate

(3 March 1947) and Dublin Estate (28 April 1947), the latter incident involving loss of life.[141] At Bukit Sembilan Estate, strike action followed the dismissal of union activists. A total of sixty-six people were arrested, of whom sixty-one were imprisoned after a trial which lasted less than a day. An investigation conducted by the MIC revealed premeditated action coordinated between planters and police. Indian government agent S.K. Chettur alleged that women were beaten by authorities, and there were claims that two young women were raped while being held in custody. On Dublin Estate the estate manager invited police to break up proposed May Day celebrations, and a worker was shot dead.[142]

The British authorities proved completely unsympathetic. Mr S.T. Rea, Deputy Controller of Labour, stated that the issue "was really labour trouble. He said that the labourers were well paid and that there was no evidence of shortage and want among them."[143] The colonial authorities refused to hold any inquiry into the abuse of police power on the estates.[144] The police action was followed by a wave of arrests, dismissals, and banishments.[145] Thondar Padai was subsequently banned in March 1948.[146] A.M. Samy was among those arrested, and he was ultimately banished to India in 1949.[147]

Indian Unionism

The years leading to World War II had witnessed growing uneasiness within the colonial workforce, especially among organized Chinese labour. This militancy had begun to spread to Indian labour. The cumulative effects of the Depression and the war, especially the history of grass-roots involvement with the INA and IIL, had produced a profound transformation in the fundamental psychology of Indian labour, which had now discarded its former compliant acquiescence, and was prepared to embrace militancy in pursuit of its aims and objectives. Among Indians, unionism tended to be both nationalist and anti-colonial.[148] Because Tamil labour was concentrated upon the docks and within the railways, as well as dominating the plantation sector, union activity among Indians had the potential to cause serious disruption to the colonial economy.[149]

The returning British believed that they could rapidly regain the absolute control over estates which had characterized their pre-war relationship with the labour force. However, managements were now confronted with a more volatile workforce, one which appeared to respect neither their elders, nor the estate *dorai* (master).[150] To the plantation labourers, the British appeared as remote and as indifferent as they had been in the pre-war years. There were no reforms which might have improved the socio-economic or working conditions of the Indian labouring classes, nor indeed any recognition that such reforms were necessary. The British alienated many workers by the immediate and unconditional reincorporation into the estate management structures of the *kirani*, many of whom had collaborated (albeit often under extreme duress), with the Japanese, despite widespread allegations that estate clerks and conductors had proven more diligent in safeguarding their own interests than in promoting or protecting the welfare of their labourers and their families.[151] British indulgence over the wartime behaviour of the *kirani* appeared to contrast with their vindictiveness towards those who had joined the INA/IIL, or those who now supported the cause of Indian independence. To many Indians it seemed that the British were applying a double standard, one which favoured chosen minority groups over the broader Indian community.[152]

Conditions on the estates after World War II were often dire. Wartime casualties had left 5,591 widows employed within the rubber industry, nearly 7,000 children with one parent, and over 2,300 orphans. Women and children aged seven and above comprised forty per cent of the total estate workforce of 354,694, of whom 221,240 were Indians.[153] During the BMA period, at a time of rapidly escalating food prices, Indian labourers were paid at the 1941 wage rates, with women receiving a much lower rate of pay than males.[154] Inadequacy of diet was reported by nutritionists, who advised of the high incidence of beri-beri and tropical sores among the Indian workforce.[155]

As we have noted, the period of BMA rule coincided with industrial unrest created by unstable economic and political conditions, including high unemployment, rapid inflation and food shortages.[156] During this period a number of General Labour Unions (GLUs) were formed, most of which had strong links to the MCP. In February 1946, the GLUs were grouped into the Pan-Malayan General Labour Union (PMGLU).[157] The PMGLU proved an effective coordinating body for Malayan labour. By putting forward "basic" universal demands for all workers, the PMGLU aimed to break the classic "divide and rule" tactics which had been hitherto used to great effect by the colonial administration.[158]

The PMGLU made every effort to accommodate Indian communalism. The Union encouraged the creation of small trade unions on individual estates or in specific workplaces, as well as state unions which looked after a largely Indian workforce. Larger rubber estate workers' unions provided for workers of all ethnic backgrounds, while the MCP-influenced GLUs operated at state level.[159] In an attempt to break down communal boundaries, the PMGLU appointed Indian leaders to various national and state-level positions. Accordingly, S. Mohan was made Vice Chairman of the Selangor Federation of Trade Unions, while S.A. Ganapathy, who had served in both the INA and the MPAJA, became President of the PMGLU. A large number of Indian workers joined the PMGLU-sponsored unions.[160] In 1947 the PMGLU was able to claim the affiliation of about eighty per cent of all trade unionists in Malaya, and boasted a total membership of 263,598.[161]

The MCP made early attempts to capture control of the Indian labour movement and to direct its activities.[162] While several leading Indian intellectuals were sympathetic to the MCP,[163] the MCP never won the confidence of the Indian workforce. Indian labourers were prepared to support the MCP campaign to rebuild working conditions which had collapsed throughout the war years, and they were in fundamental agreement with communist sentiments regarding anti-imperialism.[164] But in general the MCP was perceived and distrusted as a Chinese-dominated party by the vast bulk of the Indian workforce, and seen as a movement which was largely manipulated in the interests of Chinese workers (whose wages, on average, were three times those paid to Indian workers[165]), and hence of little relevance to the deeper needs of Indian labour. Moreover, in general, Indian workers subscribed to the traditions established by Indian nationalism, especially the Gandhian principles of *ahimsa* (non-violence).[166]

Industrial unrest among Indians commenced shortly after the return of European planters to the Malayan estates in 1946. Early strikes in April 1946 were the result of workers' resentment against the unconditional reincorporation of the *kirani*, against many of whom the labour force held grievances. Strikes between April and June 1946 were directed towards obtaining increases in wages and rice rations, and against the United Planters Association of Malaya's (UPAM) policy of wage restraint.[167] During the immediate post-war period, Indian labourers were paid at 1941 rates. In 1946, wage rates were raised to sixty-five cents per diem for male workers, and fifty-five cents for females, and in April the male wage rate was increased by five cents a day.[168] However, this was insufficient to keep pace with the cost of living. Between April and December 1946, basic household costs increased by 352 per cent; thus, for example, during this period the price of an eight-pound bag of rice rose from $1.80 to $5.20.[169] The UPAM claimed that the strikes were politically motivated, the result of subversive and inflammatory agitation, and denied that they were based upon genuine grievances.[170]

The wave of strikes continued in 1947. In April the UPAM suggested that wages be reviewed in the light of falling rubber prices. In May the association subsequently recommended that all planting employers reduce the tapping rates of contract workers by twenty per cent.[171] In response, the PMGLU established the All-Malayan Rubber Workers' Council (AMRWC). This body, headed by S.V. K. Moorthi, the President of the Selangor Estate Workers' Trade Union (SETWU), pushed for a reversal of UPAM policy, but both the government and the UPAM refused to negotiate with the council. When it became obvious that the UPAM had no intention of raising wages, the AMRWC called for a nationwide strike on 25 August. However, both the UPAM and the government contended that the workers were being "manipulated" by radical forces and refused to concede the validity of the strike. No wage concessions were granted.[172]

In 1946–47 the UPAM and employers launched action to neutralize Indian militancy within the estate sector. This included evicting labourers identified, however dubiously, as "troublemakers" or "agitators", together with their families, from their estate homes, sometimes from locations where they had lived for many years.[173] In 1947 planters' groups formed a new peak body, the Malayan Planting Industry Employers' Association (MPIEA), and appointed C.D. Ahearne, who, during the early 1930s, had held the position of Controller of Labour. Ahearne enjoyed privileged access to key officials within the colonial government, and his appointment strengthened planter resolve to crush the militancy of organized labour.[174]

Despite the severe neglect of plantations throughout the war, and the fact that the British were reliant on a workforce which was reduced in numbers and which was impoverished, under nourished, ill clothed and poorly housed, the rubber industry managed to produce a record output in 1947, thus earning Britain US$200 million.[175]

In July 1946, the government had decided that all "legitimate" unions should be registered. In February 1948 the Registrar of Trade Unions denied registration to the AMRWC. No reasons were provided. The decision left many Indian workers without union representation. Moreover, the UPAM declined to negotiate with the state-based Federations of Trade Unions, and generally ignored the designated bodies of organized Indian labour.[176] In June 1948, unions and other supposed sites of left-wing activity found themselves overtaken by events associated with the armed confrontation between the government and the MCP known as the Emergency. This was to have dramatic implications for the future of unionism within Malaya, and was to permanently weaken the standing and effectiveness of organized labour within Malaya.

Tamil Revivalism

As we have seen in Chapter 10, throughout the war years Indian political activity was concentrated in the IIL/INA and thus devoted to the Indian struggle for independence. Under the leadership of Subhas Chandra Bose, separatist claims, including those of the Dravidian movement, were temporarily quelled.

Within India, Self-Respect had closely allied itself with Mohammad Ali Jinnah's Muslim League. Following the league's 1940 resolution demanding the creation of a separate Muslim state, Ramasami had advanced claims for an independent South Indian state to be known as Dravidistan.[177] In 1941 Ramasami shared the main dais with Jinnah at the Twenty-eighth Annual Session of the Muslim League. He used this platform to launch prolonged attacks on Hinduism.[178] In 1942 Self-Respect merged with what remained of the Justice Party to form the *Dravidar Kazhagam* (Dravidian Association).[179] This entity subsequently aligned itself with Jinnah's Muslim League. *Dravidar Kazhagam's* failure to support the 1942 Quit India campaign resulted in falling membership and a loss of public support.[180]

After 1946, with the independence of India imminent, movements emphasizing the distinct cultural, linguistic and religious traditions of Tamil society began to gain momentum within the Madras Presidency. Its most extreme manifestation, the *Dravidar Kazhagam*, disavowed any linkage between an imagined autochthonic Tamil society and the broader patterns of Indian culture. The ideas and concepts which animated these movements began to circulate among Tamils in Malaya and were widely reported in the local press.[181] However, the Tamil revival was not a unitary phenomenon and flowed into several often overlapping streams.

Dravida Kalagam

The Pan-Malayan Dravidian Federation (PMDF) had been established in 1932. While the Federation had remained dormant throughout the war years, it resumed its activities following the return of the British. As a left-leaning body the PDMF closely associated itself with the PMGLU. Its express aim was to undermine the leadership of the MIC, thereby disentangling Tamil involvement with other Indian communities. This replicated the strategy employed by the Dravidian movement in Madras, where similar tactics had been utilized in an attempt to discredit the political authority of Congress.[182]

A related body was the Tamil Reform Association (TRA), which although established in Singapore as early as 1932,[183] did not have formal Peninsular presence until the foundation of a Kuala Lumpur branch after World War II.[184] The TRA adopted policies designed to effect social and economic uplift of Tamil society, as well as setting forth a programme of moderate social reform. The association was increasingly opposed to the MIC, which it saw as linking the future political fortunes of the Tamil population to those of other Indian communities. It advocated that Tamils should create their own political machinery and agitate for separate electoral representation. However, the Tamil movement was restricted by the fact that it had only a small educated elite, and was thus not equipped to sustain the intense campaigns that political representation would have required.[185]

Dravida Kalagams were formed in Singapore and Ipoh in 1946, and in several other towns throughout 1947. They were later brought together under the umbrella of the peak body, the All-Malaya Central Dravida Kalagam, which published a monthly journal called *Dravida Murasu*.[186] E.V. Ramasami visited Malaya in February 1948 and again in December 1954, and advised his adherents to follow the direction of local *Dravida Kalagams* which would enable them to maintain links with the parent body in Madras.[187]

Tamil Cultural Heritage

The Tamil movement spawned a number of organizations concerned with the identification, exploration and fostering of Tamil culture, and the renewal of Tamil society in Malaya. The cultural renaissance revolved about the promotion of Tamil literature and drama, performances of Tamil classical music of the Carnatic school and of *Bharatanatyam* dance, and a broad revival of Hindu traditions and observances.[188]

The major bodies responsible for this cultural revitalization were the Malayan Tamil Pannai, formed in Kuala Lumpur after the war, the

Tamil Education Society, founded in Singapore in 1948, and the Tamil Representative Council, which came into existence in 1951.[189] This council selected Thaipongal as the festival of special relevance to the Tamil population of Malaya. Not only would it supposedly replace the Hindu festival of Deepavali, perceived as a "northern" Hindu observance, but it would also serve as a "secular festival of the arts to symbolize the unity of Tamil-speaking people of all religions, castes and classes".[190]

TOWARDS THE BRINK: THE MCP AND
THE DECLARATION OF THE EMERGENCY

In accepting the return of the British and Allied military forces after the Japanese surrender, the MCP signalled an outward programme of cooperation with the BMA. However, the party secretly harboured plans to implement the full political and economic agenda which had been articulated and accepted as policy throughout the war years. This included an independent Malaya free of colonial control. The BMA soon made it clear that it had no intention of cooperating with its erstwhile allies. In October 1945 the administration closed two Chinese newspapers and jailed two editors for sedition. This action heralded the introduction of wider measures against the MCP.[191] However, the BMA did manage to negotiate a form of settlement with the MPAJA, which handed over its weapons at a special passing out ceremony on 1 December 1945 (though the bulk of its weaponry was retained by the party and stored in secret caches).[192]

The MCP strove to extend its influence within civil society. It founded a number of "front" organizations, and set out to recruit cadres in Chinese-medium schools, which were now re-establishing themselves after the years of closure throughout the Japanese occupation, and which were, as a consequence, enrolling many young adult students.[193] The MCP also began to infiltrate cadres into the trade unions, and within a year of the Japanese surrender dominated most of the trade unions in Singapore and Malaya. The party set out to establish links with non-Chinese labour with the aim of radicalizing the entire workforce.[194]

The colonial government made use of three basic tactics to attempt to counter nascent union power:

1.   The strict enforcement of the registration provisions of the Trade Union Ordinance. As we have observed, the years leading into the Pacific War had witnessed growing unrest within the colonial workforce, especially

among Chinese labour. In response, the Administration had introduced the Trade Union Ordinance and the Industrial Courts Ordinance.[195] The ordinances imposed severe restrictions on the operations of the unions, which included their compulsory registration,[196] and the insistence that unions confine their role to stipulated social and welfare activities, a measure clearly designed to curb the incidence of political and industrial strikes. In 1946 the registration provisions of the Trade Union Ordinance were strictly enforced, especially Article 10 which decreed that the Registrar was authorized to extend registration to a union only if it was not likely to be used for unlawful purposes inconsistent with its objectives and rules.[197]

2. The Administration combined with employers to crush trade unions wherever and whenever they proved inconveniently assertive. The British responded to the general labour unrest, strikes and hartals with the use of troops, and until early 1948 consistently deployed Japanese Surrendered Personnel as strike-breaking labour.[198] Demonstrations were met with force, occasionally entailing loss of life.[199] The Administration also rigidly enforced the laws of trespass on estates, mines and other industrial sites, which denied access to union organizers and officials and allowed managements to immediately evict dismissed workers from employer-supplied accommodation.[200]

3. In December 1945 the British government despatched an expert union advisor, who was charged with the task of constructing a "moderate", "responsible" and non-communist trade union movement. The Advisor, John Brazier, was given the title of Pan-Malayan Trade Union Advisor (TUAM).[201] His attempts to create an "independent" trade union movement brought him into conflict with the MCP on one hand and the colonial administration on the other,[202] as well as much of the colonial employer class, which he found hopelessly out of touch with developments in labour relations.[203]

Throughout 1946 and 1947 Malaya was hit by an unparalleled wave of strikes. Much of the industrial unrest arose as a reaction to a concerted and coordinated state-employer offensive to break labour militancy and to channel workers into "responsible" unions.[204] This included evictions from workplaces and estates, and dismissals of workers seen as agitators.[205] As the strike action continued, the government revived pre-war measures to try to re-establish control over the workforce. In March 1947 the Malayan government cautioned all new trade unions that 1 April 1947 was the deadline for registration, and that action would be taken against those who refused to comply. This measure not only significantly increased the power of the Registrar of Trade Unions, but also implied that henceforth the colonial authorities intended to closely supervise the operations of trade unions.[206] Moreover, the Administration also moved against Chinese squatters by enforcing forestry regulations, often ruthlessly, against those who had taken refuge on the fringes of society during the Japanese occupation.[207]

In March 1947, Lai Teck, Secretary-General of the MCP, who was on the verge of exposure as a British "plant", absconded with party funds.[208] Lai was replaced as Secretary-General by Chin Peng, aged twenty-three, who was to prove far more militant and more revolutionary in outlook. The MCP boasted a membership of about 11,800, which included 760 Indians and 40 Malays.[209]

The decision to embrace the revolutionary path was taken at the Fourth Plenum of the MCP held between 17 and 21 March 1948.[210] In April–May 1948 there was a further surge of labour militancy in Malaya.[211] On 15 May the MCP Central Committee met to discuss practical measures in connection with instigating the revolution. The Party decided that a "plan of struggle" be implemented immediately. Between 17 May and 7 June, twelve workplace managers and a foreman were assassinated, and on 3 June three KMT leaders were murdered in their homes.[212] The Federal Legislative Council signalled a renewed determination to crush union activities when on 31 May 1948 it activated revisions to the Trade Union Ordinance, which in effect proscribed the Pan-Malayan Federation of Trade Unions (PMFTU), the Singapore Federation of Trade Unions, and all state federations, as well as imposing other restrictions.[213] This was followed in June by police action against strikers on the Chan Keng Swee estate at Segamat, Johor, in which seven workers were beaten to death and ten more were injured.[214] On 16 June 1948 a major strike among dockworkers at Port Swettenham spread to rubber workers in Johor and Perak.[215] This was accompanied by rioting and violent clashes with police and troops.[216] On the same day, three European managers and three Chinese employees were murdered on estates in Sungei Siput in Perak. The British reacted by declaring a state of emergency in several districts in Perak and Johor. This was extended to the remainder of both these states on 17 June, and on 18 June to the whole of Malaya.[217] The Emergency, as the insurgency was to be known, was to stay in force until 1960.

THE AFTERMATH: COLONIAL REPRESSION

The declaration of Emergency furnished the colonial authorities with unrestricted powers. The government moved to suppress all organizations with suspected communist affiliations and to confine individuals known or thought to have links with the MCP. Although the colonial administration claimed that the anti-MCP measures adopted following the declaration of Emergency were highly selective, and that it aimed to suppress only those organizations with actual communist affiliations, in practice the arrests extended well beyond the MCP and MCP bodies to embrace many figures on the moderate left, and most particularly radical Malays, especially those associated with the MNP. Throughout the Emergency the British myth of a united communist front was used to justify the detention of many moderate socialists, and to isolate radical nationalist bodies.[218] Thousands of activists, many of them possessing no obvious links to the MCP, were arrested under Emergency laws.[219] Over 600 people were detained on 20 June 1948 alone.[220] By September 1948 some 185 trade unionists had been incarcerated.[221] Of those interred, approximately 800 were Indians, most of whom were not released until September 1949.[222] However, as we shall see, only a handful of Indians followed the MCP into the jungle.[223]

Following the declaration of the Emergency, the colonial government banned the PMFTU, leaving the majority of workers unorganized.[224] Strikes were declared illegal, and severe penalties were imposed on those who instigated industrial action.[225] The colonial government, supported by UMNO, redoubled its efforts to quell union radicalism, especially in the plantation and tin mining sectors, and to promote "moderate" unionism.[226] This was to be achieved through the dismantling of the GLUs and reconstitution of the entire apparatus of Malayan trade unionism. Accordingly, the Registrar of Trade Unions made it clear that he would register only small unions staffed by "responsible" officials.[227] Further measures included restricting leadership positions to those involved in crafts and who possessed a minimum of three years' experience, and limiting union federations to specific occupational or industrial categories.[228] Many employers used the cover provided by the Emergency to suppress legitimate union activity, to sack or intimidate union branch officers, and to quash any attempt to form unions.[229] Emergency regulations provided employers with the power to evict workers from estates should they be shown or even suspected of being communist sympathizers.[230] In February 1949, against a backdrop of strong protests from the Government of India,

S.A. Ganapathy, former President of the PMGLU was hanged after he was found in possession of a revolver, while in May 1949, P. Veerasenam, Vice President of the PMFTU, was shot dead during a raid conducted by security forces.[231]

The British actions effectively removed an entire generation of potential political and social activists from the Malayan public arena, thus depriving Malaya of some of its most outstanding political talent.[232] The destruction of the moderate left, especially Malay radicalism, as well as trade unionism, formed part of a wider strategy devised by the colonial government in concert with the Malay elite leadership of UMNO, and was designed to fortify British interests in Malaya and to ensure the ascendency of communal rather than class-based parties. This communalism would naturally be dominated by the reliable, conservative and pro-British leadership of UMNO.[233] As Chandra Muzaffar has observed, economic conservatism was part and parcel of the communal agenda. Communalism would submerge "internal class dichotomies" within the inscribed boundaries of the politics of ethnicity.[234] The inculcation of communalism was to have profound implications for the future direction of Malayan political and social structures, and far-reaching ramifications for Indians as the smallest and least powerful ethnic community.

CONCLUSIONS

MPAJA attempts to assume control in the wake of the Japanese surrender, coupled with reprisals against suspected collaborators, resulted in serious Sino-Malay racial clashes and atrocities, leaving a legacy of profound inter-ethnic distrust, as well as an enduring Malay suspicion of Chinese political intentions in Malaya.

Malay wariness was further fuelled by the Malaysian Union proposal which provoked all but universal Malay opposition without attracting non-Malay support. The Union was foisted upon a Malaya deeply sundered between competing nationalisms which directed localized loyalties to regions — Indonesia, China, India — which fell beyond the Peninsula. Faced with implacable Malay hostility, the British abandoned the Union and reverted to the traditional colonial partnership with English-educated Malay elites, a relationship, they believed, would prove more reliable in protecting Britain's long-term economic and geopolitical interests. The resultant Federation agreement of 1948 was negotiated between the colonial administration and UMNO. The broader Malay community and non-Malays were not consulted. A People's Constitution, submitted by the mutliracial AMCJA-PUTERA coalition, was largely ignored by the British. In the course of UMNO negotiations with the British, the definition of what constituted a Malay moved from the status of a mere census classification to that of a legally defined entity. "Malays" now included all migrants from Indonesia.

Throughout the immediate post-war period the colonial administration manoeuvred to neutralize and isolate the MCP. The MCP decision to launch revolution provided the colonial-UMNO partnership with the opportunity and putative justification to crush all sites of perceived radical or left-wing opposition. Many targets of this action, in particular Malay nationalist groups and trade unions, were both moderate and avowedly democratic in orientation.

The British return to Malaya was accompanied by a rigorous determination to exact reprisals against those who had participated in the IIL and INA. The subsequent detentions sidelined Indian leadership throughout the crucial period of the Malayan Union. The British action against Indian nationalism was ultimately abandoned in the face of Indian government pressure, the intervention of Viceroy Wavell, and the subsequent visit to Malaya of Indian leader Pandit Nehru.

The post-war colonial administration directed its energies towards the immediate restoration of the Malaysia economy, which was regarded as essential to British economic recovery. Colonial officials paid little regard to the welfare of the Indian workforce, or the hardships they had endured throughout the Japanese occupation.

Indian political activism flowed into four main groupings, namely the MIC, Thondar Padai, trade unionism, and a rather ill-defined Dravidianism.

The MIC, formed in August 1946, reflected the ideologies which had guided the Indian National Congress. Eschewing the politics of communalism, it aimed at forging multi-ethnic anti-colonial coalitions to agitate for Malayan independence. The MIC, containing a largely middle-class and English-educated membership, was riven by factionalism and was all but ignored by the British.

Thondar Padai was a short-lived grass-roots reform movement which incorporated an amalgam of Gandhian nationalist and Dravidian impulses. Its tendency to militancy and its alliance with other activist bodies led to colonial repression and, in March 1948, proscription.

Indians were largely involved in trade unionism. Worker distress following the British return was aggravated by sharp increases in the cost of living and severe and sustained food shortages. Despite their rejection of communism, numbers of Indian unionists were detained at the outbreak of the Emergency. Indian politics were also influenced by Dravidian ideologies, though in Malaya these were expressed by the diverse channels into which they flowed. These ranged from the militant, which proposed establishing distinct lines of political representation for those of Dravidian background, to cultural and religious movements which sought to explore the literary, artistic and philosophical heritage bequeathed by the Tamil homeland.

Notes

1. Christopher Bayly and Tim Harper, *Forgotten Wars: The End of Britain's Asian Empire* (London: Penguin Books, 2008), pp. 48–57.
2. Peter Thompson, *The Battle for Singapore: The True Story of the Greatest Catastrophe of World War II* (London: Portrait, 2005), pp. 416–17; Christopher Bayly and Tim Harper, *Forgotten Armies: The Fall of British Asia 1941–1945* (Cambridge, MA: The Belknap Press of Harvard University Press, 2004), p. 459.
3. Kah Seng Loh et al., *The University Socialist Club and the Contest for Malaya: Tangled Strands of Modernity* (Amsterdam: Amsterdam University Press, 2012), p. 51.
4. Cheah Boon Kheng, *Red Star Over Malaya: Resistance and Social Conflict During and After the Japanese Occupation of Malaya 1941–1946*, 2nd ed. (Singapore: Singapore University Press, 1987), p. 127.
5. Lee Kuan Yew, *The Singapore Story: Memoirs of Lee Kuan Yew* (Singapore: Prentice Hall, 1998), p. 78.
6. Bayly and Harper, *Forgotten Wars*, p. 32; Cheah, *Red Star Over Malaya*, p. 149.
7. Cheah, *Red Star Over Malaya*, p. 149.
8. Chin Kee Onn, *Malaya Upside Down*, 3rd ed. (Kuala Lumpur: Federal, 1976), p. 183.
9. Ibid., pp. 183–84.
10. Wan Hashim, *Race Relations in Malaysia* (Kuala Lumpur: Heinemann Educational Books (Asia), 1983), p. 42; Abu Talib Ahmad, "The Malay Community and Memory of the Japanese Occupation", in *War and Memory in Malaysia and Singapore*, edited by Patricia Lim Pui Huen and Diana Wong (Singapore: Institute of Southeast Asian Studies, 2000), pp. 46–47.
11. Chin, *Malaya Upside Down*, pp. 183–84.

12. Bayly and Harper, *Forgotten Wars*, pp. 43–45.
13. Cheah, *Red Star Over Malaya*, p. 197.
14. Chin, *Malaya Upside Down*, pp. 183–84.
15. Cheah, *Red Star Over Malaya*, p. 170.
16. Bayly and Harper, *Forgotten Wars*, pp. 43–44.
17. Wan Hashim, *Race Relations in Malaysia*, p. 42.
18. Bayly and Harper, *Forgotten Wars*, p. 47.
19. Heng Pek Koon, *Chinese Politics in Malaysia: A History of the Malaysian Chinese Association* (Singapore: Oxford University Press, 1988), p. 42.
20. Wan Hashim, *Race Relations in Malaysia*, p. 42.
21. Cheah, *Red Star Over Malaya*, p. 298.
22. Khong Kim Hoong, *Merdeka! British Rule and the Struggle for Independence in Malaya 1945–1967* (Kuala Lumpur: Insan, 1984), p. 42; Bayly and Harper, *Forgotten Wars*, pp. 100–4.
23. Khong, *Merdeka!*, pp. 42–43.
24. Bayly and Harper, *Forgotten Wars*, pp. 105–7; Chin Peng, *My Side of History* (Singapore: Media Masters, 2003), p. 135.
25. Bayly and Harper, *Forgotten Wars*, p. 199.
26. Rajeswary Amplavanar, *The Indian Minority and Political Change in Malaya 1945–1957* (Kuala Lumpur: Oxford University Press, 1981), p. 46.
27. Charles Gamba, *The Origins of Trade Unionism in Malaya: A Case Study in Colonial Unrest* (Singapore: Eastern Universities Press, 1962), p. 100.
28. Geoff Wade, "The Origins and Evolution of Ethnocracy in Malaysia", Working Paper Series no. 112 (Singapore: Asia Research Institute, National University of Singapore, April 2009), pp. 3–5.
29. Bayly and Harper, *Forgotten Wars*, p. 130.
30. Ariffin Omar, "The Struggle for Ethnic Unity of Malaya after the Second World War", in *Multiethnic Malaysia: Past, Present and Future*, edited by Lim Teck Ghee, Alberto Gomes, and Azly Rahman (Petaling Jaya: Strategic Information and Research Development Centre, 2009), p. 46.
31. Heng, *Chinese Politics in Malaysia*, p. 46.
32. William Shaw, *Tun Razak: His Life and Times* (Kuala Lumpur: Longman Malaysia, 1976), p. 60.
33. Ariffin, "The Struggle for Ethnic Unity", p. 46.
34. Bayly and Harper, *Forgotten Wars*, p. 99.
35. R.S. Milne and Diane K. Mauzy, *Politics and Government in Malaysia* (Singapore: Federal, 1976), pp. 27–29; Mahathir Mohamad, *A Doctor in the House: The Memoirs of Tun Dr Mahathir Mohamad* (Petaling Jaya: MPH, 2011), pp. 85–91.
36. Mahathir, *A Doctor in the House*, pp. 85–91.
37. Khong, *Merdeka!*, p. 85.
38. Ibid., pp. 87–88.

39. Bayly and Harper, *Forgotten Wars*, p. 195.

40. Wan Hashim, *Race Relations in Malaysia*, p. 46.

41. Ibid., p. 47; Shamsul A.B. *From British to Bumiputera Rule: Local Politics and Rural Development in Peninsular Malaysia* (Singapore: Institute of Southeast Asian Studies, 2004), p. 237.

42. Cheah, *Red Star Over Malaya*, p. 293.

43. Khong, *Merdeka!*, pp. 48–49.

44. Ibid.

45. Bayly and Harper, *Forgotten Wars*, p. 216.

46. Shaw, *Tun Razak*, p. 64.

47. Khong, *Merdeka!*, p. 84.

48. Bayly and Harper, *Forgotten Wars*, pp. 216–17.

49. Kah et al., *The University Socialist Club*, pp. 52–53; Bayly and Harper, *Forgotten Wars*, p. 437.

50. Wade, *The Origins and Evolution of Ethnocracy*, p. 9.

51. Bayly and Harper, *Forgotten Wars*, p. 227.

52. Ibid., p. 362.

53. Lee Kim Hing, "Forging Interethnic Cooperation: The Political and Constitutional Process towards Independence 1951–1957", in *Multiethnic Malaysia: Past, Present and Future*, edited by Lim Teck Ghee, Alberto Gomes, and Azly Rahman (Petaling Jaya: Strategic Information and Research Development Centre, 2009), p. 63.

54. Sinnappah Arasaratnam, "Political Attitudes and Political Organization among Malayan Indians 1945–1955", *Jernal Sejarah* 10 (1971/72): 4.

55. Lee, "Forging Interethnic Cooperation", p. 63.

56. Bayly and Harper, *Forgotten Wars*, pp. 363–65.

57. Ariffin, "The Struggle for Ethnic Unity", pp. 51–52, 56. Major constitutional proposals included: (1) A united Malaya including Singapore; (2) Elected central, state and Settlement legislatures; (3) Equal rights for all who made Malaya their home; (4) Constitutional sultans who governed through democratic state councils; and (5) Special measures for the uplift and advancement of the Malay people (Wade, "The Origins and Evolution of Ethnocracy", p. 11).

58. Bayly and Harper, *Forgotten Wars*, pp. 366–68.

59. Ibid., p. 370.

60. Shaw, *Tun Razak*, p. 64.

61. Raj K. Vasil, *Tan Chee Khoon: An Elder Statesman* (Petaling Jaya: Pelanduk, 1987), p. 60.

62. K.J. Ratnam, *Communalism and the Political Process in Malaya* (Kuala Lumpur and Singapore: University of Malaya Press, 1965), p. 118.

63. Richard Allen, *Malaysia: Prospect and Retrospect* (London: Oxford University Press, 1968), p. 85.

64. Ratnam, *Communalism and the Political Process*, pp. 78–79.

65. Maznah Mohamad, "Politics of the NEP and Ethnic Relations in Malaysia", in *Multiethnic Malaysia: Past, Present and Future*, edited by Lim Teck Ghee, Alberto Gomes, and Azly Rahman (Petaling Jaya: Strategic Information and Research Development Centre, 2009), p. 122.
66. Ratnam, *Communalism and the Political Process*, pp. 78–79.
67. Bayly and Harper, *Forgotten Wars*, p. 332.
68. Wade, "The Origins and Evolution of Ethnocracy", p. 12.
69. Michael R. Stenson, *Repression and Revolt: The Origins of the 1948 Communist Insurrection in Malaya and Singapore* (Athens: Ohio University Press, 1969), p. 9.
70. Ratnam, *Communalism and the Political Process*, pp. 104–5.
71. Joginder Singh Jessy, "The Indian Army of Independence", B.A. (Hons) Thesis, University of Singapore, 1957–58; *Netaji Subhas Bose — A Malaysian Perspective* (Kuala Lumpur: Netaji Centre, 1992), p. 212.
72. *Netaji Subhas Bose*, p. 212.
73. Peter Ward Fay, *The Forgotten Army: India's Armed Struggle for Independence 1942–1945* (Ann Arbor: University of Michigan Press, 1995), p. 385.
74. *Netaji Subhas Bose*, p. 212. The Singapore government later rebuilt this monument, though because of land reclamation it is now some distance from the waterfront.
75. Bayly and Harper, *Forgotten Wars*, p. 19.
76. Alan Warren, "The Indian Army and the Fall of Singapore Revisited", in *A Great Betrayal? The Fall of Singapore*, edited by Brian Farell and Sandy Hunter (Singapore: Marshall Cavendish Editions, 2010), p. 237.
77. Sinnappah Arasaratnam, *Indians in Malaysia and Singapore* (London: Oxford University Press, 1970), p. 112.
78. Bayly and Harper, *Forgotten Wars*, p. 87.
79. Selvakumaran Ramachandran, *Indian Plantation Labour in Malaysia* (Kuala Lumpur: S. Abdul Majeed, 1994), p. 239.
80. Jessy, "The Indian Army".
81. Bayly and Harper, *Forgotten Wars*, pp. 86–87.
82. Ibid., p. 91.
83. Arasaratnam, *Indians in Malaysia and Singapore*, p. 112.
84. Alex Von Tunzelmann, *Indian Summer: The Secret History of the End of an Empire* (London: Simon and Schuster, 2007), p. 140.
85. Bayly and Harper, *Forgotten Wars*, p. 226.
86. Jessy, "The Indian Army".
87. Rajeswary, *The Indian Minority*, p. 22.
88. Bayly and Harper, *Forgotten Wars*, p. 226.
89. Ibid.
90. Arasaratnam, *Indians in Malaysia and Singapore*, p. 112.
91. Sinnappah Arasaratnam, "Malaysian Indians: The Formation of an Incipient

Society", in *Indian Communities in Southeast Asia*, edited by K.S. Sandhu and A. Mani (Singapore: Institute of Southeast Asian Studies, 1993), pp. 190–91.

92. Ibid.

93. Ibid.

94. Selvakumaran, *Indian Plantation Labour*, pp. 238–39.

95. K. Nadaraja, "The *Thondar Padai* Movement of Kedah 1945–1947", in *Malaysia in History* 24, n.d.

96. Arasaratnam, *Indians in Malaysia and Singapore*, p. 122.

97. Rajeswary, *The Indian Minority*, pp. 78–79.

98. *Representations of the Government of India in Malaya and Certain other Colonial Territories in the Far East, October 1938–January 1950* (File L/P&J/8/261 Collection 108-D, Oriental and India Collection, London).

99. Ibid.

100. Rajeswary, *The Indian Minority*, pp. 78–79.

101. G.P. Ramachandra, "The Indian Independence Movement in Malaya 1942–1945", M.A. Thesis, Universiti Malaya, 1970.

102. Bayly and Harper, *Forgotten Wars*, p. 330.

103. Ramachandra, *The Indian Independence Movement; Netaji Subhas Bose*, pp. 227–28.

104. Ramachandra, *The Indian Independence Movement*.

105. Rajeswary, *The Indian Minority*, pp. 25–27.

106. Bayly and Harper, *Forgotten Wars*, p. 330.

107. Arasaratnam, "Political Attitudes", p. 2.

108. *Netaji Subhas Bose*, p. 230.

109. Rajeswary, *The Indian Minority*, pp. 25–26.

110. Bayly and Harper, *Forgotten Wars*, p. 330.

111. Michael R. Stenson, *Class, Race and Colonialism in West Malaysia: The Indian Case* (St. Lucia: University of Queensland Press, 1980), p. 149.

112. Arasaratnam, *Indians in Malaysia and Singapore*, p. 124.

113. Bayly and Harper, *Forgotten Wars*, p. 330.

114. Ramachandra, *The Indian Independence Movement*.

115. Bayly and Harper, *Forgotten Wars*, p. 330.

116. Arasaratnam, "Political Attitudes", p. 4.

117. Stenson, *Class, Race and Colonialism*, p. 156.

118. Rajeswary, *The Indian Minority*, pp. 168–72.

119. Ibid., pp. 154–56.

120. Ibid.

121. Arasaratnam, "Political Attitudes", pp. 2–3.

122. Ibid., pp. 5–6.

123. Ibid., p. 3.

124. Bayly and Harper, *Forgotten Wars*, pp. 330–31.

125. Arasaratnam, "Political Attitudes", p. 4.

126. Rajeswary, *The Indian Minority*, p. 84.

127. Arasaratnam, "Political Attitudes", p. 4.

128. Nadaraja, "The *Thondar Padai* Movement", p. 95.

129. Selvakumaran, *Indian Plantation Labour*, p. 239.

130. Nadaraja, "The *Thondar Padai* Movement", p. 95.

131. Ibid., p. 96.

132. Rajeswary, *The Indian Minority*, pp. 49–50.

133. Selvakumaran, *Indian Plantation Labour*, p. 242.

134. Michael Morgan, "The Rise and Fall of Malayan Trade Unionism 1945–1950", in *Malaysia: The Making of a New-Colony*, edited by Mohamed Amin and Malcolm Caldwell (Nottingham: Spokesman, 1977), p. 169.

135. Rajeswary, *The Indian Minority*, p. 50.

136. Nadaraja, "The *Thondar Padai* Movement", p. 98.

137. Ibid.

138. Ibid., p. 97.

139. P. Ramasamy, *Plantation Labour, Unions, Capital and the State in Peninsular Malaysia* (New York: Oxford University Press, 1994), p. 73.

140. Bayly and Harper, *Forgotten Wars*, p. 338.

141. Selvakumaran, *Indian Plantation Labour*, pp. 242–44.

142. Ramasamy, *Plantation Labour*, p. 70.

143. Nadaraja, "The *Thondar Padai* Movement", p. 107.

144. Selvakumaran, *Indian Plantation Labour*, p. 244.

145. Nadaraja, "The *Thondar Padai* Movement", p. 102.

146. Selvakumaran, *Indian Plantation Labour*, p. 244.

147. Nadaraja, "The *Thondar Padai* Movement", p. 102.

148. Arasaratnam, *Indians in Malaysia and Singapore*, pp. 136–37.

149. Rajeswary, *The Indian Minority*, p. 46.

150. Selvakumaran, *Indian Plantation Labour*, p. 239.

151. Ravindra K. Jain, *Indians on the Plantation Frontier in Malaya* (New Haven: Yale University Press, 1970), p. 358; Nadaraja, "The *Thondar Padai* Movement", p. 96; Gamba, *The Origins of Trade Unionism*, pp. 252–53.

152. These sentiments were forcefully expressed by plantation workers interviewed on estates in Perak, Selangor and Negri Sembilan in 1995.

153. Bayly and Harper, *Forgotten Wars*, pp. 224–25. The minimum working age remained seven years until the passage of the Children and Young Person's Ordinance No. 33 of 1947 which raised the minimum age to eight years. The Ordinance also stipulated that children aged between eight and twelve years were restricted to employment in "light" agricultural or horticultural work (Gamba, *The Origins of Trade Unionism*, p. 259).

154. Ramasamy, *Plantation Labour*, p. 65.

155. Bayly and Harper, *Forgotten Wars*, p. 105.

156. Rajeswary, *The Indian Minority*, p. 46.

157. Morgan, "The Rise and Fall", p. 165.

158. Selvakumaran, *Indian Plantation Labour*, p. 240.

159. Ramasamy, *Plantation Labour*, p. 187.

160. Selvakumaran, *Indian Plantation Labour*, p. 240.

161. Ibid., p. 239.

162. Arasaratnam, *Indians in Malaysia and Singapore*, p. 137.

163. Rajeswary, *The Indian Minority*, pp. 46–49, 218.

164. Arasaratnam, *Indians in Malaysia and Singapore*, p. 138.

165. Ramasamy, *Plantation Labour*, pp. 65–66.

166. Ibid., p. 139.

167. Ibid., pp. 67–69.

168. Ibid., p. 65.

169. Amarjit Kaur notes that the overall cost of living index escalated from 100 in 1939 to 340 for Malays and 328 for non-Malays in 1948, while wages declined from 100 to 71 between 1939 and 1949 (Amarjit Kaur, "Tappers and Weeders: South Indian Plantation Workers in Peninsular Malaysia, 1880–1970", *Journal of South Asian Studies* 21, Special Issue, 1998, p. 98).

170. Ramasamy, *Plantation Labour*, p. 69.

171. Ibid., pp. 75–76.

172. Ibid., pp. 76–80.

173. Bayly and Harper, *Forgotten Wars*, p. 339.

174. Ramasamy, *Plantation Labour*, p. 83.

175. Selvakumaran, *Indian Plantation Labour*, p. 239.

176. Ramasamy, *Plantation Labour*, pp. 83–84.

177. Rajiv Malhotra and Aravindan Neelakandan, *Breaking India: Western Interventions in Dravidian and Dalit Faultlines* (New Delhi: Amaryllis, 2011), pp. 394–95.

178. Ibid.

179. Christopher John Baker, *The Politics of South India 1920–1937* (Cambridge: Cambridge University Press, 1976), p. 318.

180. Mytheli Sreenivas, *Wives, Widows and Concubines: The Conjugal Family Ideal in Colonial India* (Bloomington: Indiana University Press, 2008), p. 90.

181. Arasaratnam, *Indians in Malaysia and Singapore*, pp. 127–28.

182. Jain, *Indians on the Plantation Frontier*, p. 383.

183. Vineeta Sinha, "Hinduism in Contemporary Singapore", in *Indian Communities in Southeast Asia*, edited by K.S. Sandhu and A. Mani (Singapore: Institute of Southeast Asian Studies, 1993), p. 829.

184. Arasaratnam, *Indians in Malaysia and Singapore*, pp. 128–29.

185. Ibid.

186. Ibid.

187. Ibid.

188. Ibid.

189. Ibid.; Sinha, "Hinduism in Contemporary Singapore", p. 829.

190. Arasaratnam, *Indians in Malaysia and Singapore*, pp. 128–29.

191. Bayly and Harper, *Forgotten Wars*, p. 128; Khong, *Merdeka!*, pp. 51–52.

192. Richard Clutterbuck, *Riot and Revolution in Singapore and Malaya 1955–1963* (London: Faber and Faber, 1973), p. 40; Chin Peng, *My Side of History*, p. 138.

193. Bayly and Harper, *Forgotten Wars*, pp. 117–18.

194. Heng, *Chinese Politics in Malaysia*, p. 40.

195. Gamba, *The Origins of Trade Unionism*, p. 4.

196. Stenson, *Class, Race and Colonialism*, pp. 126–27.

197. Morgan, "The Rise and Fall", pp. 174–75.

198. Ibid.

199. Gamba, *The Origins of Trade Unionism*, pp. 200–1.

200. Morgan, "The Rise and Fall", pp. 174–75.

201. Gamba, *The Origins of Trade Unionism*, p. 100.

202. Ibid., p. 102.

203. Ibid., p. 110.

204. Ramasamy, *Plantation Labour*, p. 80.

205. Bayly and Harper, *Forgotten Wars*, p. 424.

206. Gamba, *The Origins of Trade Unionism*, p. 148.

207. Bayly and Harper, *Forgotten Wars*, p. 421.

208. Clutterbuck, *Riot and Revolution*, p. 37; Aloysius Chin, *The Communist Party of Malaya: The Inside Story* (Kuala Lumpur: Vinpress, 1995), pp. 26–27; Bayly and Harper, *Forgotten Wars*, pp. 344–45.

209. Chin, *The Communist Party of Malaya*, p. 42.

210. Bayly and Harper, *Forgotten Wars*, p. 415.; Khong, *Merdeka!*, p. 137.

211. Morgan, "The Rise and Fall", p. 184.

212. Bayly and Harper, *Forgotten Wars*, p. 426.

213. Morgan, "The Rise and Fall", pp. 185–86. Following the passage of the Trade Union Ordinance on 1 July 1946, the Singapore General Labour Union and the PMGLU changed their statuses to that of peak coordinating bodies, becoming the Singapore Federation of Trade Unions and the PMFTU respectively. The latter change was made on the advice of Brazier himself (Ramasamy, *Plantation Labour*, p. 63).

214. Morgan, "The Rise and Fall", p. 184.

215. Khong, *Merdeka!*, p. 146.

216. Anthony Short, *The Communist Insurrection in Malaya 1948–1960* (London: Frederick Muller, 1975), p. 93.

217. Ibid., pp. 93–94.

218. Kah et al., *The University Socialist Club*, pp. 23, 30.

219. Said Zahari, *Dark Clouds at Dawn: A Political Memoir* (Kuala Lumpur: Insan, 2001), pp. 2, 280.
220. Morgan, "The Rise and Fall", p. 187.
221. Ramasamy, *Plantation Labour*, p. 86.
222. Usha Mahajani, *The Role of Indian Minorities in Burma and Malaya* (Bombay: Vora, 1960), p. 203.
223. Chin, *The Communist Party of Malaya*, p. 32.
224. Morgan, "The Rise and Fall", p. 188.
225. Ramasamy, *Plantation Labour*, p. 86.
226. Chandra Muzaffar, "Political Marginalization in Malaysia", in *Indian Communities in Southeast Asia*, edited by K.S. Sandhu and A. Mani (Singapore: Institute of Southeast Asian Studies, 1993), p. 219.
227. Selvakumaran, *Indian Plantation Labour*, p. 244.
228. Kaur, "Tappers and Weeders", p. 98.
229. Gamba, *The Origins of Trade Unionism*, pp. 354–55.
230. Ramasamy, *Plantation Labour*, p. 86.
231. Ibid. At the time of writing, relevant colonial documents dealing with the deaths of Ganapathy and Veerasenam remained unavailable to scholars.
232. Bayly and Harper, *Forgotten Wars*, pp. 433–34; Ahmad Fauzi Abdul Hamid, *Islamic Education in Malaysia*, Monograph No. 18 (Singapore: S. Rajaratnam School of International Studies, 2010), pp. 19–20.
233. Morgan, "The Rise and Fall", p. 192: Gamba, *The Origins of Trade Unionism*, p. 38.
234. Muzaffar, "Political Marginalization in Malaysia", p. 219.

12

FROM FEDERATION TO MERDEKA

THE EMERGENCY

The war against the Chinese-dominated MCP, known as the Emergency, endured for twelve years — from 1948 to 1960. The insurgency claimed the lives of 6,697 members of the Malayan National Liberation Army (MNLA), while a further 3,000 surrendered and 1,286 were captured by security forces. On the government side, 1,865 members of the security forces, mainly Malays, were killed, and a further 2,560 wounded. A total of 2,473 civilians, mainly Chinese, died in the insurgency. Over 12,000 personnel passed through the ranks of the MNLA.[1] Despite the high financial and human toll the British had no intention of withdrawing from their most valuable colony. In 1948 rubber brought $120 million into the sterling zone, and by 1952–53, following the Korean War boom, Malayan exports were providing 35.26 per cent of Britain's balance of payments within the dollar area. Moreover, the retention of the Singapore naval base was regarded as essential in projecting Britain's military posture as a great power within Southeast Asia.[2]

In launching the insurrection, the MCP adopted the essential principles of Leninist theory, namely creating a revolutionary situation, vitiating the machinery of government and exsanguinating its military power, and assuming party control of all state functions both during and after the revolution. The military campaign was planned around the theories of protracted revolutionary war developed by Mao Tse-tung and based on his experiences in China.[3] The MCP programme failed dismally. The MNLA's actions were often poorly coordinated and frequently concentrated upon immediate military outcomes rather than the political agitation and education necessary to create a climate of widespread popular support.[4] The MNLA never seriously threatened British rule.[5]

A unified strategy for defeating the MCP was developed by a retired general, Sir Harold Briggs, who was appointed Director of Operations on 21 March 1950. Briggs realized that the early failures of the British counter-insurgency could be largely attributed to a dearth of reliable intelligence and the fact that the British neither understood the Chinese community, nor acknowledged their permanency within the Malayan political landscape.[6] He also drew attention to the existence of the two complementary strands of the MCP, namely the MNLA and the *Min Yuen* (Mass Organisation, which worked among the civilian population[7]), and the role ascribed to each. He argued that the *Min Yuen* could operate freely among the large Chinese squatter population because the people had no confidence in the ability of the government to protect them from "communist extortion and terrorism".[8] Until they were offered reliable military protection, the squatters would have no choice but to continue to comply with MCP demands.

The Federation Plan for the Elimination of the Communist Organization and Armed Forces in Malaya, more commonly known as the Briggs Plan, was presented on 24 May 1950, and set out a strategy for the containment and defeat of the MNLA. This would require British military and political "domination" of the populated areas, which would be, where necessary, brought under British purview by means of an ambitious programme of forced resettlement, and the concomitant destruction of MCP sources of intelligence and supply, finally compelling the MNLA to combat British and allied forces on their own ground.[9] Briggs highlighted the importance of maintaining a full framework of civilian government. He argued that military operations should be conducted against the backdrop of recognized political authority. He emphasized that all action in the field should be firmly subordinated to the dictates of intelligence.[10]

Briggs' proposal for resettlement of squatters was implemented with considerable speed.[11] Over the first eighteen months, from June 1950 until late 1951, over 400,000 people, mainly landless Chinese, who were in general sympathetic to the guerrillas, and who had little reason to trust any central government, whatever its hue, were moved away from the squatters' settlements and the soil they had tilled, in many cases for upwards of ten years, and concentrated in new quarters known as Resettlement Centres. A further 600,000 people, many of them estate workers, were later resettled.[12] Despite the many problems associated with the implementation of the resettlement policy, the political and military objectives which undergirded the programme were successful. The British authorities managed to severely disrupt the links between the squatter-based *Min Yuen* and the jungle forces of the MNLA, and in particular the supply of food and information. Chin Peng was to later identify the resettlement programme, and in particular the privations created by the reduction of food supplies, as decisive in isolating and hence defeating the MNLA.[13]

In February 1952, General Sir Gerald Templer was appointed to the specially tailored executive "supremo" position which combined the functions of High Commissioner, Commander in Chief of the Security Forces, and Director of Operations. His role was to direct a coordinated approach to both military strategy and civil administration in Malaya.[14] Templer adopted a new strategy which was focused upon winning the "hearts and minds" of the Malayan peoples.[15] He created an efficient command structure with a fully integrated intelligence network.[16] He directed that the Home Guard receive better training. The Resettlement Centres were renamed New Villages and were furnished with improved services and facilities.[17] The incremental provision of basic infrastructure coupled with the cultivation of local participation in the administration of the New Villages eventually re-aligned many Chinese within the broader spectrum of mainstream Malayan political life.[18]

But Templer also used the cover of the Emergency to effect wide ranging reforms. He was able to argue that by providing "alien" Chinese with a stake in the future of Malaya, the Malay leadership was not only shortening the period of the Emergency, but also providing a long-term and necessary antidote to communism. He negotiated with community leaders and the sultans to introduce more liberal citizenship laws. Accordingly, as of midnight, 14 September 1952, 1,200,000 Chinese, 60 per cent of the Chinese in Malaya, and 180,000 Indians, were entitled to Malayan citizenship.[19]

In 1955, faced with the realization that the Federation of Malaya was achieving independence through a process of negotiation, and that the MCP would thus be permanently excluded from the political scenery of postcolonial Malaya, Chin Peng responded to peace feelers offered by the

Malayan leadership. His aim was to gain political legitimacy for the MCP on the basis that the MNLA had been fighting against British imperialism rather than waging war on the elected peoples of Malaya.[20] The resultant talks of 28–29 December 1955, held in Baling, Kedah, their relationship to the attainment of Merdeka, and the nature of the independence settlement will be discussed more fully in the following section.

In 1959, in recognition of its own dwindling stocks and the futility of its continuing campaign, the MCP issued a new policy directive entitled "Lower the Banners and Muffle the Drums", which in effect suspended all guerrilla activities and made provision for the surrender of any member of the MNLA who chose to do so.[21]

The MCP lost the campaign because, among other factors, they failed to recognize that independence could not be attained and subsequently held by a single community within a multi-ethnic state such as Malaya.[22] Although the party made fitful attempts to recruit Malays and Indians, these never formed more than a small minority of the MNLA forces. MCP propaganda neither exploited the grievances of the Malay peasantry and fisherfolk, nor the hardships experienced by the Indian estate workers and urban labourers. Indeed there is little evidence to suggest that the party ever seriously contemplated establishing a broad base of support among all ethnic groups.[23]

The most prominent Malay MNLA cadres were Abdullah C.D. (Cik Dat Anjang Abdullah) and Rashid Maidin, both holding high office within the MCP/MNLA. With the outbreak of the Emergency, the MCP made a determined effort to recruit Malays from around Temerloh in Pahang, the site of a previous Malay anti-British revolt.[24] The MCP managed to persuade about 500 Malays to enlist, thus enabling the formation of the Malay majority 10th Regiment of the MNLA, which was placed under the command of Abdullah C.D.[25] However, this initial recruitment marked the fullest extent of Malay participation, and thereafter the number of Malays within the 10th Regiment rapidly dwindled to approximately 160. The total number of Malays in all other units was placed at about 140.[26]

Because of the lack of detailed documentation it is difficult to assess the extent of Indian participation in the MNLA. However, the most prominent Indian member of the MCP was R.G. Balan, who had worked as a publicist with the MPAJA. Based in the Kampar-Tapah region, south of Ipoh, Balan was responsible for producing and circulating Tamil-medium anti-Japanese propaganda. He was arrested by the colonial authorities on

30 May 1948 prior to the outbreak of the Emergency and detained until 1961. In 1955 he was elected *in absentia* to the position of Vice Chairman of the MCP Central Committee.[27]

British military observers commented on the presence of Tamil cadres within the ranks of the MNLA. Thus an MNLA unit which "skilfully" attacked a British force near Kuala Selangor, contained a "number" of Tamils,[28] while other reports indicate that communist guerrillas received food and general support from "sympathetic" rubber tappers.[29] While these accounts would tend to substantiate Stewart's claims that the MNLA contained a "significant Indian element" which enjoyed "solid support" among Indian workers,[30] it is doubtful that Indian enlistment within the MNLA ever exceeded several hundred. An MCP plan, conceived at the outbreak of the Emergency, to form an all-Indian regiment had to be abandoned in the light of the tepid response from the wider Indian community,[31] while Special Branch estimated that Indians never at any stage comprised more than five per cent of the total MNLA strength.[32] At the time of the final peace agreement between the Malaysian government and the MCP, signed in Haad Yai, Thailand, on 8 December 1989, MNLA membership totalled 1188, of whom a mere 2 were ethnic Indians.[33]

The rather ambiguous status of the Indian community in Malaya was highlighted by an action taken by the colonial government during the Emergency. Angered at the behaviour of the Chinese commercial class, which it suspected of financing the MNLA's campaign through the payment of protection money, the administration decided to send a warning by targeting Indian business interests. A number of Chettiar financiers, many of whom were absentee plantation owners, were arrested and charged with making payments to the MNLA. Their reaction was both immediate and understandable. Having been singled out as scapegoats, most sold off their assets and took themselves and their capital back to India.[34]

The Emergency once again highlighted the extent of racial cleavage in Malaya. Essentially the war was a Chinese-dominated insurrection which was resisted by Malays. The heaviest civilian casualties were among the Chinese, while those within the security forces were Malay.[35] The Emergency left a legacy of ethnic distrust. The fact that the MCP's ranks were predominantly composed of Chinese further fuelled Malay suspicions that the Chinese aimed at nothing less than long-term economic and political hegemony over Malaya.[36]

POLITICS AND THE ALLIANCE FORMULA

British reliance on UMNO increased in the years following the declaration of the Emergency. However, the Malay leadership demanded an ever-increasing array of concessions in return for their support. As we noted in Chapter 11, principal among these was the destruction or marginalization of the sites of potential or actual opposition, and in particular those which were held to be left-wing and/or Islamic/Malay nationalist.[37] To the British this was a price well worth paying.[38]

The Emergency forced consideration of the Chinese issue to the centre stage of Malayan politics. The formation of the Malayan Chinese Association (MCA) on 27 February 1947 consolidated Chinese conservative groups into a body which could negotiate on behalf of the entire Chinese community.[39]

In late 1948 the British arranged a carefully controlled meeting between elite Malays and Chinese at the home of senior Malay statesman Dato Onn bin Jaafar.[40] In January 1949 the members of this meeting were grouped into the Sino-Malay Goodwill Committee. This body represented a British attempt to promote and foster a group of potential national leaders with whom the colonial authorities could work.[41] The committee's formation was also an implicit recognition that inter-ethnic cooperation was essential if Malaya was to have any future as an independent nation. The Malays recognized that while they commanded political power, some form of agreement with the non-Malay communities was essential if progress towards genuine independence was to be achieved. For their own part the Chinese realized that while they enjoyed considerable economic power, their ultimate position in Malaya would be dependent upon the concessions that they were able to negotiate with the Malays.[42]

The Goodwill Committee was replaced later in the year by the Communities Liaison Committee (CLC), which became a forum for discussion of ethnic issues. Meetings of the CLC continued throughout 1949 and 1950. The CLC was a British attempt to devise a communal framework for consociational democracy whereby complex matters would be brokered behind closed doors by the elites of different communities. Although the CLC membership was later broadened to include the appointment of a Ceylonese lawyer, E.E.C. Thuraisingham,[43] the bulk of its membership was drawn from the elite ranks of UMNO and the MCA. The committee proved to be a major success. The Malay aristocracy which comprised the UMNO leadership and their wealthy MCA *towkay* (merchant) counterparts forged an easy relationship largely based on shared conservative, political, social and economic ideologies.[44]

UMNO used the CLC as a forum to establish the essential conditions under which Malays would agree to share power with other communities. "Immigrant" communities would be required to unequivocally accept that:

1. Malays (including recent migrants from Indonesia), were the true indigenous people of Malaya,
2. The British authority in Malaya derived from treaties signed with the sultans. These acknowledged the sultans as the locus of authority within each territory. In signing the treaties at the inception of colonial rule, the British had demonstrated their recognition of Malaya as a Malay country,
3. While acknowledging that members of other "races" had made Malaya their home, Malaya would concede their status as political participants in the affairs of the country only if special provisions were made to provide Malays with a just share of the wealth of the motherland.[45]

Both the colonial authorities and UMNO made it abundantly clear that the politics of Malaya would be conducted along communal lines — albeit under Malay-dictated terms — and that attempts to reorganize Malayan politics around class-based parties would be firmly resisted. The key issue in achieving political independence was thus the attainment of a binding "racial" settlement which simultaneously fulfilled Malay demands as well as meeting the primary aspirations of other ethnic communities. Two alternative modes of political organization by which this objective might be achieved were offered; the first a multiracial forum institutionalized as a political party, the second a brokered agreement between communally based political parties representing ethnic blocs.[46]

Between 1950 and 1953 the former approach was pursued under the leadership of Dato Onn Jaafar. Onn had argued that UMNO should be open to non-Malays and that inclusive citizenship should be offered to those who were genuinely prepared to embrace Malaya as their home. He also advocated stalling the quest for independence until the putative political immaturity of the Malays had been overcome, and they no longer required colonial protection.[47] When these ideas were rejected by the UMNO membership, Onn resigned from the party he had helped found, and formed the Independence of Malaya Party (IMP). IMP membership was open to people of all ethnic backgrounds. The IMP generated wide support among Malayan political organizations and attracted some members of the MCA and several labour and trade union bodies. Dato Onn and the IMP enjoyed good relations with the colonial administration.[48]

Onn's resignation from the leadership of UMNO resulted in the election of a new leader. This was Tunku Abdul Rahman, a flamboyant and emollient man, British educated, a devout Muslim, but regarded as "progressive" and eclectic — sometimes controversially so — in his interpretation of Islam. The Tunku believed that inter-ethnic cooperation and a formalized partnership between the major communities would be integral to an independent settlement and in ensuring the subsequent successful management of the political affairs of post-Merdeka Malaya. He considered that any system based on political inclusiveness along the lines advocated by Dato Onn would prove unworkable in a country like Malaya, with its background of ethnic remoteness, suspicion, and hostility.[49]

UMNO attempted to accommodate Muslim perspectives and held two conferences of the *ulama* (religious leaders) in February 1950 and August 1951. The latter conference expressed dissatisfaction with the UMNO leadership, and the supposed failure of mainstream political parties to defend Muslim interests. The *Persatuan Islam Se-Tanah Melayu* (Pan-Malayan Islamic Party or PMIP) was founded on 24 November 1951.[50] The newly formed PMIP was deeply critical of the policies adopted by UMNO on a number of issues, including the future administration of Islam in the Malay states, and the supposed generosity of UMNO concessions to non-Malays.[51] It aimed to establish an Islamic state based on the model of Pakistan.[52] The PMIP split from UMNO and became a fully independent political party in 1955.[53]

In 1952, under the respective leaderships of Tunku Abdul Rahman and Tan Cheng Lock, UMNO and MCA formed an ad hoc Alliance to conduct local government elections. The Alliance, aided by the personal friendship of the two party leaders, and a genuine desire for cooperation, proved an effective framework for communal brokerage. The fact that the leaderships of both parties were English-educated and were familiar with British political institutions provided a shared background which promoted a constructive and productive relationship between the executives of UMNO and MCA.[54]

Throughout 1952–53, the Alliance won a series of crushing victories in all elections it contested, routing all competitors, including the multi-ethnic

IMP headed by Dato Onn. In February 1952, encouraged by the scale of their success, the Alliance negotiated a pan-Malayan partnership.[55] Alliance triumphs reflected the complementary strengths of both parties. UMNO's broad membership base and ability to attract the vote of rural Malay communities throughout the Peninsula were sustained and underwritten by the substantial financial resources of the MCA.[56]

Stunned by the reverses sustained by the IMP, Dato Onn abandoned the policies of inter-ethnic cooperation and organization, and retreated into the politics of communal exclusivity. He now formed the short-lived and ill-fated Malay-based Party Negara, which promoted a policy of uncompromising Malay supremacy, including an Islamic state, severe immigration restrictions and rigorous citizenship requirements.[57] Neither Dato Onn nor Party Negara were able to make other than a transient and superficial impression on the conduct of Malayan politics, and both were ultimately consigned to political irrelevancy.[58]

In the first general elections held in July 1955, the Alliance, now augmented by the addition of the MIC (to be discussed in the next section), won fifty-one out of a possible fifty-two seats, and eighty per cent of the votes cast.[59] Tunku Abdul Rahman was appointed Chief Minister and formed his first cabinet.[60] The massive majorities accrued by the Alliance enabled it to claim in its dealings with the colonial authorities that it spoke on behalf of the overwhelming mass of Malayans.[61]

In May 1955, during the election campaign, the Alliance, led by Tunku Abdul Rahman, suggested direct talks with the MCP, and that as a means of ending the Emergency, a general amnesty be offered to the communists.[62] The MCP responded positively. It believed that its actions had helped win British concessions which were inexorably propelling Malaya towards self-government.[63] The MCP was also aware that because of the revised political boundaries, political discourse, especially the politics of anti-colonialism, was being expressed through legitimate forums and recognized political parties, and it wished to join the resultant debate.[64] Following the Alliance victory, the Tunku, as Chief Minister, was adamant that he should be permitted to talk to Chin Peng. The British had no option but to grant the Tunku his wish. They were dependent upon UMNO cooperation, and could not manage Malaya without Malay support. However, they did make it plain that they would not tolerate recognition of the MCP as a legitimate political party, a position which was reiterated throughout the Baling talks.[65] The major concession won by the

Tunku was a promise from the MCP leadership to end hostilities should independence be attained. This was a "trump card" which he could play in his discussions with the British.[66]

The Baling talks of 28–29 December were followed by a constitutional conference early in 1956 in London. This was attended by representatives of the rulers and the Alliance. This conference reached the decision that Malaya should become an independent member within the Commonwealth by August 1957, and that a Constitutional Commission should be appointed to prepare a draft constitution.[67]

In August 1956, an Alliance compromise was reached on the issue of citizenship. This was based on the principle of *jus soli*. Under this agreement any person born in the Federation on or after independence, could become a citizen by application. Residency qualifications for citizenship were reduced to a period of five years from the previous seven.[68] It was decided that these changes would be implemented immediately after the attainment of independence.[69] Under Malayan law there would be no allowance for dual citizenship, nor was there to be any category of Commonwealth citizenship.[70]

A Constitutional Commission, chaired by Lord Reid, an English judge, and containing members from Britain, Australia, India and Pakistan, toured Malaya between March and May 1956 to seek public submissions. The Reid Commission's report was published in February 1957. The commission took special account of Alliance perspectives. It proposed that Malaya should enjoy a parliamentary system of government, with a non-political head of state (the *Yang di-Pertuan Agong*, or King), a legislature of two houses, one of which would be directly elected, a neutral civil service, and an independent judiciary which would safeguard the constitution.[71] Malaya would be a federation with each state electing its own legislature. The latter provision reflected the British desire to accommodate the rulers and to respect the integrities of their traditional territories and thus avoid any repetition of the protests similar to those voiced against the Malayan Union proposals of 1946.[72]

The Alliance did not accept the Reid Commission's proposals in their entirety. Between March and July 1957, the government parties embarked on a series of internal negotiations with the aim of modifying certain aspects of the constitutional proposals, largely to accord with UMNO priorities. The main MCA objective was the establishment of *jus soli* as a principle of citizenship, and the Association was prepared to sacrifice much to obtain this.[73] UMNO was prepared to cede the principle of *jus soli* on the proviso that the non-Malays accepted the special positions of the Malays and the enshrinement of Malay privileges,[74] which the Reid Commission had recommended be reviewed after fifteen years.[75] The UMNO–MCA compact, an inter-ethnic "bargain", rather than the Reid proposals, was ultimately accepted by Whitehall as the basis for the Malayan constitution.[76] The Constitution of independent Malaya thus incorporated the dominant Alliance perspectives, reflecting UMNO's views on national policy, state religion, culture and state education, and addressing MCA's concerns on the codification of citizenship rights for non-Malays.[77]

The main features of the Constitution were as follows:

1. Malays were to be defined as those who habitually spoke the Malay language, practiced Islam and followed *adat*.
2. Islam was to be the sole official religion of Malaya.[78]
3. Malay was to become the sole official language.
4. The *Yang di-Pertuan* and the Malay rulers were to be accorded roles that extended beyond the ceremonial. A Conference of Rulers was to meet each five years to elect the *Yang di-Pertuan* from among their ranks, and to discuss, as necessary, issues relating to Malay rights and culture and interpretation of Islam.
5. The claims relating to Malay special rights were to be made permanent rather than temporary.[79]
6. The Constitution guaranteed the rights of non-Malays to practice and propagate their religions and languages.[80]

Independence was proclaimed on 31 August 1957. The Malayan constitutional settlement had been brokered by an Alliance which claimed to fully represent the major communities of Malaya.[81] The settlement consisted of a contractual "bargain" reached on Malay terms and which enshrined Malay political primacy expressed in the four fundamental pillars of Malay identity, namely "Malayness", the Malay language, Islam and royalty. These were viewed by the Malay elite as the fundamental and non-negotiable template of the Malayan nation. The political elites who fashioned the Alliance compact considered the constitutional outcome as a binding "bargain" between the "races" — the price to be paid by non-Malays for admission to full political participation in the Federation.[82] Sino-Malay claims would be resolved within the framework delineated by the "bargain"; Chinese economic power would be balanced by the undisputed acknowledgement of Malay political ascendency in a state structured around Malay symbols and guided by Malay tutelage and statecraft.[83] The Alliance leadership considered that the compromises embodied in the constitutional settlement would prove sufficient to mould a new and distinctly Malayan political community.[84] Close ethnic cooperation, coupled with the promotion of national policies on language, education and culture would result in the formulation of a recognizable and widely accepted Malayan identity.[85]

However, the Alliance formula was founded on assumptions which would not long survive the political and social pressures of an independent Malaya. It did not recognize the true nature of Malayan pluralism; that is, that Malayan communities did not consist of neat vertical divisions into discrete and homogenous entities whose legitimate aspirations could be fully articulated by the elites who dominated the Alliance structure.[86] The Alliance formula had skated over a fundamental schism between Malay and non-Malay political aspirations. In essence, while the Malays regarded their community as the "natural" political society within the Malayan state, embodying the organizational principles to which the immigrant communities should incline,[87] the non-Malays aimed for a truly inclusive nation-state based upon social equality and full democracy.[88] Many non-Malays were chary of the permanent constitutional establishment of Malay special privileges as the normative basis for Malayan political and cultural life, which they believed militated from the very outset against a genuine multiracial partnership built upon the principles of equal citizenship and equal opportunity.[89] Nor was it recognized that the politics of communalism would impel political parties to direct their energies into the inscription of ethnicity, thus safeguarding the cultural boundaries of their "racial" constituencies; a process that would necessarily consolidate and perpetuate internal divisions within the wider body politic.[90]

Malaya entered independence as a country rent by suspicion, and with a plethora of unresolved and contentious issues, including language, citizenship, education, culture and religion. Moreover, the Malayan economy remained largely under the control of British interests. Not only were Malayan sterling reserves held in London,[91] but 75 per cent of all rubber acreage, 61 per cent of tin production, 75 per cent of all services and trade, and almost the entire palm oil output were owned by British enterprises.[92] Deep fissures had been papered over and forgotten in the goodwill and enthusiasm which had greeted Merdeka. These fissures were to be revealed in all their starkness in the years which followed.

THE MIC AND MERDEKA

In general, the MIC was treated as an adjunct to the processes leading to Merdeka. Pointedly ignored by the colonial regime, it was only after the intervention of Tunku Abdul Rahman that the MIC and the wider Indian community were invited to join the Alliance, and thus participate in the final deliberations which were to result in independence. Even then, the MIC was viewed as marginal to the UMNO–MCA compact which formed the basis of the constitutional settlement.

In the years following the declaration of the Emergency, the colonial authorities were determined to isolate the MIC. The regime had viewed the party's radicalism, its involvement in the AMCJA and the boycott of the Federation agreement, with extreme disfavour. The MIC was regarded as both compromised and unreliable.[93] In what was intended as an explicit rebuke, the MIC was not invited to nominate a representative to the Communities Liaison Committee, although, as we have noted, the British appointed Ceylonese lawyer E.E.C. Thuraisingham.[94]

In July 1950, in a direct challenge to the MIC, an unlikely grouping of professionals, businessmen and trade unionists tried to form a successor party to the CIAM. Against MIC protests, this party, the Federation of Indian Organizations (FIO), was registered, but attracted very little support.[95]

Stung by colonial accusations that it was controlled by foreign-born Indians, the MIC introduced a number of changes aimed at clearly demonstrating its Malayan orientation. The party made attempts to attract "Pakistani" (Indian Muslims) and Ceylonese members, even though the party had little appeal to either community. A new party constitution, the subject of much vociferous debate, resulted in increased Tamil influence within the MIC. The replacement of Budh Singh as President by K. Ramanathan Chettiar in 1950 heralded the abandonment of the constitutional boycott.[96] However, these changes were insufficient to engender British confidence in the party.[97] In April 1951 the party failed to secure any appointment when Sir Henry Gurney, the High Commissioner, introduced a "member" system which provided for selected members of the Federal Legislative Council to head various departments, in the process gaining political and administrative experience.[98]

Dato Onn bin Jaafar's formation of the IMP seemed to provide an opening for the MIC to re-engage with the political mainstream. As we have noted, from the time of the party's inception, the MIC leadership had always favoured the formation of broad nationalist fronts which would produce inter-ethnic cooperation and agitate for independence. The party thus viewed the IMP's ideals and objectives, in particular the design to create nationalist parties which spanned the communities, as consistent with its own policies and political agenda.[99] Dato Onn's political manoeuvring seriously wrong-footed the MIC. In deference to its links with the IMP and the policy of ethnic cooperation the IMP purported to represent, the party had declined an invitation to attend the 1953 Alliance National Convention. The hitching of MIC fortunes to those of the IMP left the party increasingly isolated, and thus unable to influence the constitutional reforms introduced by the colonial government in the early 1950s. In addition, the MIC remained out of favour with the Malayan government, and in 1953 the party was once again overlooked when local appointments to the Cabinet were announced.[100] The party subsequently found itself increasingly alienated from the uncompromising pro-Malay stance and the hard-line policies now enunciated by Dato Onn and Party Negara. The MIC decided to chart an independent course free from any entanglements with other parties. In August 1954, the vulnerability of the MIC's "stand-alone" position was fully revealed when it was humiliated in the elections for the Ipoh Town Council.[101]

In December 1953 the MIC was approached by the colonial government to furnish the names of prospective nominees to the Legislative Council. In 1954 President K. Ramanathan was selected to represent the MIC.[102] On 27 July 1954, a senior MIC official, V.T. Sambanthan, became the first party member to be appointed to Cabinet. These developments, together with the Ipoh defeat, impelled a comprehensive reassessment of MIC policies. By this time it had become plain, at least for the time being, that Malayan politics would be organized along communal lines, and that the MIC strategy of attempting to forge inter-communal and nationalist fronts that would collectively secure concessions from the British had been a failure. Many MIC members were apprehensive that as matters stood the party was of little consequence within the Malayan political arena, and were dismayed by the obvious disdain with which the party was viewed by the British. These considerations led to an intense debate within the Congress, and resulted in the formulation of a suite of revised and markedly less radical policies.[103]

Until 1954 the MIC maintained its distance from the UMNO–MCA Alliance and instead agitated for communally reserved seats in all governing bodies. However, in late 1954 Tunku Abdul Rahman hinted that the MIC would be admitted to the Alliance provided that it could demonstrate that it had the confidence of the Indian electorate.[104] By this time, the MIC Executive no longer contained any member who had participated in the politics of the IIL / INA and thus had no real commitment to the cause of Indian nationalism. Reflecting this change, MIC President Devasar contended that the Indian community could no longer remain sidelined from crucial constitutional discussions, and must be an active participant if it wished to contribute to the overall political landscape of an independent Malaya.[105] The leadership believed that the MIC faced political extinction unless it sought patronage through partnership — albeit subordinate partnership — within the Alliance.[106] In December 1954, the MIC joined the Alliance, thus linking all major communities in a single dominant multiracial coalition.[107]

Subsequent to joining the Alliance the MIC initiated reforms designed to assure its new political allies that it commanded the support of the majority of the Indian community, and that it could be relied upon to deliver the Indian vote. In May 1955, V.T. Sambanthan, a businessman and estate owner, replaced Davasar as MIC President. His deputy was another businessman, V. Manickavasagam. Their accession to the top leadership positions was a belated acknowledgement that the Tamil labouring class constituted the overwhelming majority of the Indian population in Malaya. Prior to Sambanthan, the MIC had been an urban-based, professional and middle-class party, whose upper ranks had consisted largely of English-educated Indians, mainly of northern origin.[108] Meetings had been conducted in English. This had militated against the participation of Tamil speakers, and left the Tamil labouring majority under-represented in higher level appointments.[109]

With the increased Tamil membership, the fulcrum of party support moved from Kuala Lumpur to the smaller regional towns and plantations. This resulted in the domination of the MIC by the Tamil working classes, and the gradual transformation of the ethos of the party to reflect the impress of the Indian "plantation-oriented culture",[110] a world view which had evolved out of Tamil labouring experiences on the estates and which was emphatically Dravidian, Hindu and often viscerally anti-Brahman in outlook.

With the "Tamilization" of the MIC, the party and the National Union of Plantation Workers (NUPW) (see next section) stood as the political and industrial guardians of the Indian workforce respectively. However, undercurrents of suspicion and jealousy between the two organizations, especially in claiming the allegiance of plantation labour, were to produce continual tensions and intermittent disputes between the rival leaderships.[111]

The radical Dravidianism which had had such a profound impact upon sections of Tamil society in Malaya and Singapore in the 1930s and 1940s was to gradually moderate throughout the 1950s. Although the 1949 anti-Hindu agitation in Madras had attracted considerable attention among Tamils in Malaya, in many respects this action marked the final high-water mark of Ramasami's influence. In 1949 Ramasami's marriage to a much younger woman, whom he immediately named as heir to his presidency, precipitated a schism within the metropolitan Dravidian movement and the establishment of the *Dravida Munnetra Kazhagam* (DMK), led by the more youthful leader C.N. Annadurai.[112] Although the DMK embodied the principal constructs of Dravidian ideologies, the new party took steps to distance itself from Ramasami's iconoclasm.[113] The DMK's more inclusive Dravidianism encouraged a broader and more flexible cultural policy which permitted the exploration of Tamil religiosity centring on the worship of the deity Murugan.[114] This less abrasive approach was to have an impact upon Dravidian groups within Malaya.[115]

With its admission to the Alliance, the MIC was compelled to revise its overall political agenda, and to divest itself of much of the radical and inclusive programme which had guided the party's fortunes in the years since its foundation. It now articulated a range of conservative policies consistent with those espoused by its larger and more powerful Alliance partners. These policies, which endorsed the continuation of the liberal capitalist regime which had developed under British colonialism, gave primacy to the preservation of inter-ethnic harmony.[116] The laissez-faire economic approach and the emphasis on communalism meant that class-related issues were largely neglected, and the pressing reforms needed on the estates, especially those pertaining to living conditions and the terms of employment, and thus of immediate relevance to a large section of its constituency, were largely overlooked.[117]

The ideological repositioning of the MIC estranged the English-educated classes, numbers of whom withdrew their support from the party.[118] Many of those who were unable to accept the MIC policy of accommodation within the Alliance framework transferred their support to non-communal parties. Indians were prominent within the Pan-Malayan Labour Party which was formed in June 1952. In May 1954 this party was renamed the Labour Party.[119] Adopting a moderate social democratic platform, the Labour Party won considerable support throughout the period 1954–59, but became increasingly irrelevant to the Indian community after 1958 when control of the party was captured by left-wing Chinese and the party was transformed into a vehicle for Chinese chauvinism.[120] Indians were also involved in the Perak People's Party founded in Ipoh in January 1953 by two Ceylonese-Tamil brothers, D.R. and S.P. Sreenivasagam. The party, renamed as the People's Progressive Party (PPP) in 1956, stood for the rights of non-Malays. Support for the PPP was largely confined to Ipoh and the adjacent Kinta Valley.[121] Indians also joined the left-wing multiracial but Malay-dominated *Partai Rakyat* (later known as the *Partai Sosiaslis Rakyat Malaysia*), founded by ex-MNP leader Ahmad Boestemam.[122] Indian participation in Labour and other opposition parties created a non-communal Indian leadership, an alternative to the power brokers of the MIC.[123] This also meant that some of the pre-eminent intellectuals within the Indian community were offered no role within the emerging governing and administrative apparatus of a soon-to-be independent Malaya.[124]

The membership drain, especially the loss of accomplished figures that might have provided the party with intellectual depth and stimulus, provoked popular charges that the MIC was the weak and exploited party within the Alliance.[125] Feuding within the party led to further attrition of membership and deprived the party of some of its leading talent. Sambanthan's leadership and his standing within the overall community were undermined by repeated and sustained criticism, and continued ructions within the party.[126] Endemic factional fighting, sporadically erupting into physical violence, was to become an unwelcome feature of internal MIC politicking, and on two occasions (1957 and 1972) sustained intra-party feuding was to force the executive into the humiliating position of having to request UMNO adjudication upon otherwise insoluble disputes.[127]

Membership of the Alliance brought mixed benefits to the Indian community. On the whole, however, the plusses would seem to outweigh the minuses. Throughout the 1950s, the Alliance negotiated with the British to achieve a progressive and peaceful transfer of power leading to independence. As a member of the Alliance, the MIC was now able to participate, however fitfully, in this process. MIC members were nominated as Alliance candidates; this arrested the inexorable drift towards the electoral oblivion that would have occurred had the party remained outside the Alliance.[128] With the onset of self-government in April 1957, Sambanthan was appointed to the Cabinet as Minister of Postal Services and Telecommunications.[129] However, as we have seen, membership of the Alliance structure resulted in MIC sacrifices and compromises. In particular it meant compliance with the conservative agenda set by the two larger and more powerful parties, and the jettisoning of most of the intellectual and ideological ideals which had underscored the party's formation in 1946.[130]

Issues of Concern

The MIC raised several major concerns in the period leading to Merdeka. These included the likely impact and extent of Malay privileges, especially their effects upon appointment to the government service, a traditional source of employment for the Indian middle class, as well as a large-scale hirer of Indian labour (which formed the majority of the workforce in several key government utilities),[131] the constitutional enshrinement of Islam as the official religion, and the UMNO insistence that Malay would ultimately become the sole official language. While the MIC extensively canvassed these issues with their Alliance partners, few concessions were gained by the party. Apart from the fact that the MIC was the smallest and most junior party in the Alliance, it was additionally handicapped by UMNO–MCA awareness that it did not command the full support of the Indian community, especially of the intellectual and professional classes.[132]

Citizenship

Immediately after World War II, many Indians were to advocate a form of dual citizenship which would have allowed them to claim citizenship in one of the emerging nations of the subcontinent while retaining a stake in Malaya. However, Indian opinion was not unanimous, nor was the issue considered one of overriding concern.[133] With the abandonment of the

Malayan Union and its generous citizenship provisions, citizenship was awarded by application. The criteria for eligibility consisted of a minimum of fifteen years' residence over the previous twenty years, providing that (1) applicants possessed knowledge of English or Malay, and (2) made a declaration of permanent settlement in Malaya (thus automatically renouncing any claim to dual citizenship).[134] These provisions altered with the Federation of Malaya agreement, which allowed citizenship to be awarded to those who had resided in Malaya for eight of the previous twelve years. However, the language requirements and the declaration of permanent settlement were retained. These stipulations cumulatively barred or deterred many Indians from seeking citizenship.[135]

As we have seen, the ordinance of 1952, the outcome of General Templer's persistent negotiations with the Malay leadership, further liberalized citizenship provisions. Citizenship could now be claimed by those who had resided for at least ten years in the Federation, but was also awarded to those born in the Straits Settlements. The ordinance extended the right of citizenship to those born in the Federation who also had one locally born parent. The reforms fell short of the principle of *jus soli*.[136] Under these laws 220,000 Indians became citizens and a further 186,000 possessed the necessary birth qualifications to qualify. Over sixty per cent of the Indian population could thus enter the political community.[137]

The ordinance was followed by two acts of 1953 which cumulatively checked the immigration of Indians to the Federation of Malaya. The right of entry was restricted to British subjects born or naturalized in Malaya; the subjects of the ruler of a Malay state; Federal citizens, British subjects normally resident in Malaya; aliens who held Resident's Certificates; and the dependents (wives and children under eighteen years of age) of all eligible persons.[138] The option of immigration was restricted to those with professional or specialist skills (whose entry would not prejudice the interests of a person born in Malaya); the owner of an established firm; and the employer of a private firm, provided he/she was in receipt of a minimum remuneration of M$500 per month (in 1959 this was raised to $1200 per month).[139] Indians were deeply concerned about these developments and protested vigorously, albeit without any great effect.[140]

The principle of *jus soli*, which was to offer citizenship to the vast majority of "immigrant" communities, was formally conceded as part of the Merdeka racial "bargain" following vigorous negotiations between the MCA and UMNO. MIC representations played little, if any, part in determining the final outcome.[141]

Language and Education

The preservation of community languages and the right for communities to be educated in their own languages and cultural traditions were highly emotive issues. The 1951 Report of the Committee on Malay Education (the Barnes Report) advocated a system of National Schools in which children of all communities would be taught only in English and Malay.[142] The 1952 ordinance amended this report with the provision that facilities be furnished for instruction in Chinese or Tamil when fifteen or more students requested this. In 1955 the Alliance reached a compromise on this issue. The Razak Report recommended the preservation of both Chinese and Tamil schools, but contended that English and Malay should be the main media of instruction in secondary schools. These recommendations were incorporated into the Education Ordinance of 1957.[143] However, while Chinese medium schools were to offer both primary and secondary education, Tamil schools were restricted to primary education.[144]

INDIANS, THE NATIONAL UNION OF PLANTATION WORKERS AND UNIONISM

Following the declaration of the Emergency, the colonial government proscribed the MCP-led PMFTU, leaving the majority of workers unorganized.[145] Numbers of leading trade unionists were detained under Emergency regulations, often following denunciation by paid informers or anonymous opportunists.[146] A number of employers had already made it known that they would use the Emergency as a cover to destroy trade unions considered troublesome, and to limit the activities of others. Branch officials and activists were threatened with indictment as suspected communists, while others were dismissed. The sustained intimidation and official harassment made it largely impossible for unions to conduct legitimate business.[147]

The colonial government, supported by UMNO, now redoubled its efforts to quash union radicalism, especially in the strategically important plantation and tin mining sectors, and to promote "moderate" unionism.[148] This was to be achieved through the enforced dismantling of the GLUs and the reconstruction of the entire apparatus of Malayan trade unionism along colonially vetted lines. As discussed in Chapter 11, the Registrar of Trade Unions made it clear that he would only register small unions staffed by "responsible" officials.[149] The result was a number of "new" unions, inconsequential in size, and limited in their capacity to bargain with employers.[150] Many of the new unions, robbed of their experienced leadership and unsure of their rights and power, became increasingly dependent upon the guidance of the TUAM.[151]

Until the declaration of the Emergency, the TUAM had experienced little success in influencing the shape or direction of unionism in Malaya. The dismantling of the GLUs now provided Brazier with his opportunity to restructure the trade unions in a manner more amenable to colonial control.[152] The plantation unions were the obvious sites for Brazier to begin. Rubber (and thus by extension the largely Indian labour force which produced this commodity) was of critical importance to the struggling British economy. Indeed, the Chairman of the RGA commented that "The rubber industry was the mainstay of British finance and but for the contributions it made to Britain's trade balance, every man, woman and child in the United Kingdom would suffer a serious reduction in their standard of living."[153]

Brazier was especially interested in several small rubber unions which had remained outside the ambit of the MCP-influenced Federation of Trade Unions. These unions were the Negri Sembilan Indian Labour Union (NSILU), Perak Estate Employees Union (PEEU), North Johor Indian Labour Union (NJILU), Malacca Estates Employees Union (McEEU), and the Alor Gajah Labour Union.[154] These unions were communal in nature, and all possessed an Indian leadership that was both middle class and English speaking.[155] The key union was the NSILU led by P.P. Narayanan and N.K. Choudry. This union was to later change its name to the Negri Sembilan Plantation Workers Union (NSPWU), not only to evade charges that it was a narrowly based ethnic organization, but also to attract workers from other ethnic backgrounds.[156] Later still this union was to be reborn as the Plantation Workers Union of Malaya (PWUM).[157]

In June 1949 the first tentative steps were taken towards the concept of collective bargaining. With Brazier's support six "responsible" unions acting under the aegis of the PWUM met with the MPIEA to discuss wages. These negotiations failed to produce any agreement and the unions subsequently approached the government to set up arbitration machinery. This resulted in the Rubber Industry Arbitration Board (RIAB I). While the board made some recommendations and offered rubber industry workers a small increase in pay, it also linked wages to rubber prices, thus intimating that wages could be reduced when returns fell.[158]

During 1950 there were further moves towards establishing a united employee front to negotiate with the MPIEA. Acting on Brazier's advice, some twenty-six unions agreed to elect a peak committee, known as the Pan-Malayan Rubber Workers Union (PMRWU) to negotiate with the MPIEA.[159] In December 1950 a strike by the North Johor Indian Labour Union on Labis estate, which was crushed by a combined military and police operation, highlighted the risks attendant upon a small union launching industrial action on its own.[160]

The same year witnessed the formation, under the patronage of the colonial government, of the Malayan Trade Union Council (MTUC), with P.P. Narayanan of the PWUM elected president.[161] However, the council was regarded as timid and hesitant in its approach to labour issues, and the leadership was viewed as complacent and remote from the rank and file.[162] The MTUC was responsible for a membership that was almost entirely Indian.[163]

The outbreak of the Korean War (1950–53) resulted in a major boom in the rubber industry and huge profits for producers.[164] Despite the Emergency and MNLA disruption, estate workers maintained a steady work regime, and output remained stable throughout these years.[165] However, the boom conditions were not matched by commensurate increases in wages or conditions. When, in 1951, negotiations with the MPIEA failed, the PMWRU once again requested government intervention. The government-appointed arbitration board, RIAB II, handed down a liberal award, and the union and the MPIEA subsequently signed a collective agreement on 19 June 1951. However, a number of MPIEA's members refused to honour RIAB II's decision, and declined to pass on wage increases.[166]

Moreover, although RIAB II's ruling had explicitly revoked the rubber price/wages linkage set forth by RIAB I, this was not accepted by the industry. In 1952 the MPIEA advised that it would cut workers' pay due to falls in the price of rubber. In 1953 RIAB III approved an increase in wages, a decision instantly rejected by MPIAE and only grudgingly accepted in June. However, several months later, citing a further decline in rubber prices, MPIEA unilaterally rescinded the pay increase arbitrated by RIAB III. The MPIEA's disregard for the processes of arbitration and its seeming indifference to the PMWRU as a peak negotiating body highlighted the weaknesses of the unions and their relative inability to influence outcomes.[167]

Worse was to follow. In July 1954, RIAB IV, headed by Justice Taylor, cut the daily wages of tappers by 25 cents and those of field workers by

15 cents.[168] In accepting MPIEA's submission for the need for a reduction in wage levels, Taylor offered trenchant criticism of the PMRWU's lack of professionalism, in particular the absence of an efficient union secretariat and the ad hoc preparation and presentation of PMRWU's case. This led him to query whether the PMRWU could be regarded as truly representative of the entire estate workforce.[169]

Following RIAB IV's arbitration, the PMRWU conducted a secret ballot among rubber workers. The response was overwhelming; ninety-eight per cent of the labour force rejected the new award and invested the PMRWU with the authority to launch whatever action was necessary to oppose the wage reduction. The MPIEA, facing the prospect of a nationwide strike, agreed to negotiate a new wage structure, and increases were duly announced on 11 June 1954.[170]

Taylor's remarks had emphasized the need for estate unions to adopt a more professional and coordinated approach. The threat of a nationwide strike had demonstrated that even the MPIEA could be pressured into granting concessions by the threat of unified action. Leading Indian unionists, most notably P.P. Narayanan, now pushed for a single union to represent all estate workers. In June 1954, the five major plantation unions, namely the PWUM, the PEEU, the NJILU, the McEEU, and the Alor Gajah Rubber Workers Union, agreed to amalgamate.[171] On 29 September 1954, the National Council of the PMRWU circularized all union officials to advise that a meeting would be held on 1 November to elect a pro-tempore committee for the new NUPW.[172]

The inaugural meeting was opened by the High Commissioner and was attended by a number of dignitaries, including Brazier.[173] The Foundation President of the NUPW was P.P. Narayanan, a former member of the INA.[174] He was supported by an Executive of thirty members.[175] At its inception the NUPW claimed a membership of 46,835, but this was to rise to 82,300 in 1955 representing 26.6 per cent of the total estate workforce. The union was largely communal in character, with an overwhelming Indian membership and Executive.[176]

The NUPW was to extend its activities beyond rubber workers and sought to unionize labour in all commercial agricultural enterprises, including oil palm, coconut and pineapple estates.[177] Although the NUPW admitted an increasing number of Malay and Chinese plantation workers, the NUPW's membership was to remain mainly Indian, and the union continued to be directed by a largely Indian leadership.[178] The NUPW became Malaya/Malaysia's largest trade union, and as such was to exercise a disproportionate influence on the Malayan Trade Union Congress (which was to later succeed the Malayan Trade Union Council; P.P. Narayanan was to become the congress's first leader).[179]

Concerned about the potential power that might be wielded by a large and united union that commanded the support of a critical mass of workers within an industry which underpinned the colonial economy, and the new resolve evinced by estate workers, the colonial government now suggested that a Joint Consultative Committee be established to discuss, and where necessary reach agreement on, issues of mutual interest to both the MPIEA and the NUPW. Under considerable pressure from the government the NUPW reluctantly acquiesced.[180]

Following the formation of the NUPW, the union struck a collective agreement with the MPIEA on 27 November 1954. This awarded field workers rates of pay of $2.40 and $2.05 respectively, inclusive of a cost of living allowance at the 65–70 cents price zone. The agreement removed pay differentials based on sex, and provided three days' paid holiday per annum.[181]

However, the main objective of the NUPW was to establish a wage-fixing mechanism independent of the tie between wages and rubber prices. In early 1956 the union was provided with an opportunity to challenge this nexus. On 27 March 1956, the MPIEA, citing reduced returns for rubber, advised that as from 1 April wage levels for field workers would be cut by 20–40 cents.[182] In response, the NUPW called for a go-slow among its members, a move which prompted concern within the government, and led to a call by the Chief Minister, Tunku Abdul Rahman, for NUPW rank and file to avoid violence and for the union leadership to retain control over its membership.[183] On 22 May, once again adducing falling rubber prices, the MPIEA announced a further decrease in wages. At the end of the month, its objectives unfulfilled, the NUPW tacitly admitted defeat, and abandoned the go-slow.[184]

A new agreement between the NUPW and the MPIEA resulted in a partial restoration of lost wages; tappers were granted an increase of 20 cents while field workers received 55 cents. However, while the MPIEA conceded the principle of a six-day working week, the NUPW failed to either gain a guaranteed minimum wage for its labour force, or to successfully challenge the linkage between rubber prices and wage structures.[185]

The NUPW's emphasis on Indian estate labour aroused concern among the Chinese membership. Early in 1956, with the support of the Labour

Party, attempts were made to establish a breakaway union which would be known as the Pan-Malayan Chinese Rubber Workers Union. However, the incipient union's application for registration was rejected by the Registrar of Trade Unions on the grounds that a Chinese-managed union would be used for "unlawful purposes".[186]

Given the restrictive conditions which prevailed during this period, it is unsurprising that the NUPW was to repeatedly restate its credentials as a "moderate" union. The union expressed its determination to cooperate and cultivate close relations with both the government and employers, including its readiness to contain labour discontent.[187] To have behaved otherwise while under the rule of a colonial regime and during a proclaimed Emergency, might well have risked official proscription. However, in discussing these years, informants advised this writer that even at this early stage of its history, the NUPW leadership had become supine and remote from its membership, and its overt eagerness to collaborate with the MPIEA rendered it both increasingly out of touch and ineffective.

Indians continued to dominate Malayan unionism well into the early years of independence. In 1961, Indians totalled 63 per cent of the membership of Malayan trade unions, with Malays making up 21 per cent and Chinese 16 per cent. Many trade unions were led by Indians, and Indians were also strongly represented within the ranks of union executive appointments.[188]

CONCLUSIONS

The outbreak of the Emergency caught the colonial administration militarily unprepared and its initial responses were clumsy, heavy-handed, and often brutal. The Brigg's Plan produced a comprehensive and imaginative strategy to contain and combat the insurgency. Military operations were conducted against a backdrop of civilian authority, and a major programme to forcibly resettle Chinese squatters cut links and sources of supply between the broader Chinese community and the MCP. Under the leadership of General Sir Gerald Templer, wide-ranging political reforms, including more liberal citizenship provisions, were enacted. Essentially the Emergency consisted of a Chinese-led insurgency which was resisted by Malay security forces. This reinforced Malay suspicions of Chinese political intentions and Malay determination to retain absolute political power. However, the Emergency and MCP resistance to British colonialism was decisive in expediting the attainment of Malayan independence.

The fostering of the British–UMNO axis was regarded by the colonial administration as fundamental in the protection of long-term British interests in Malaya. Nevertheless, it was obvious that if Malaya was to become an independent nation, some degree of power sharing between Malays and non-Malays would have to be negotiated. Under British sponsorship, lines of dialogue were cultivated between Malay and Chinese conservative elites. During these discussions UMNO made it clear that power sharing would be on Malay terms, based upon a normative template of a Malay polity and structured according to the politics of communalism. An attempt to establish a multi-ethnic political party, the IMP, foundered against an UMNO–MCA Alliance which enjoyed a succession of electoral triumphs.

Peace talks with the MCP greatly strengthened the Alliance's bargaining power vis-à-vis the British in independence negotiations. While the constitutional talks between UMNO and the MCA might have led to the agreement of *jus soli* as the basis for citizenship, thus granting many hitherto excluded Chinese and Indians the right to apply for citizenship, it also established a Malay-centric polity built around principles of Malay statecraft, which established Islam as the official religion and enshrined Malay special privileges. The settlement also provided a constitutional definition of a Malay as a person who habitually spoke Malay, who practised Islam, and who followed *adat*. The constitutional agreement was regarded as an inter-ethnic "bargain" which clearly established Malay political dominance in return for Malay agreement to the right of other "races" to make Malaya their home. The politics of communalism inscribed racial boundaries which were to persist and become entrenched, while the Merdeka agreement papered over deep and enduring divisions.

Between the Emergency and Merdeka the MIC moved from its existence on the fringe of Malayan politics into the formal structures of the Alliance government. The MIC had been left isolated following the declaration of the Emergency and the breakup of AMCJA-PUTERA. The failure both of the MIC's association with the multi-ethnic IMP and of the party's subsequent "stand-alone" position left the Congress facing the stark possibility of electoral oblivion. Following a comprehensive re-evaluation of its policies, the MIC was admitted to the Alliance in December 1954. The abandonment of its radical and more inclusive programme to accord with the far more conservative posture of its new political allies not only alienated many Indian intellectuals, but also hamstrung the party in advocating reforms needed to alleviate poverty among the Indian working classes. The accession of V.T. Sambanthan to the leadership foreshadowed the Tamilization of the MIC and the more active involvement of the Tamil working classes in the affairs of the party.

Following the outbreak of the Emergency the entire structure of organized trade unionism in Malaya was dismantled and reconstituted under the restrictive guidelines laid down by the colonial administration. The post-1948 unions were weak and ineffective and easily held in check by employers. In the early 1950s a number of smaller unions combined to form the PWUM, which in late 1954 incorporated several other unions to become the NUPW. The NUPW, largely Indian controlled, was at all times required to display its credentials as a "moderate" union. Although there were some improvements in the working conditions of estate labour throughout this period, these were minor and wages remained depressed.

Notes

1. Christoper Bayly and Tim Harper, *Forgotten Wars: The End of Britain's Asian Empire* (London: Penguin Books, 2008), p. 521; Brian Stewart, *Smashing Terrorism in the Malayan Emergency: The Vital Contribution of the Police* (Subang Jaya: Pelanduk, 2004), p. 340.

2. Bayly and Harper, *Forgotten Wars*, pp. 408–9.

3. Richard Clutterbuck, *Riot and Revolution in Singapore and Malaya 1945–1963* (London: Faber and Faber, 1973), p. 25.

4. Michael R. Stenson, *Repression and Revolt: The Origins of the 1948 Communist Insurrection in Malaya and Singapore* (Athens: Ohio University Press, 1969), p. 21.

5. C.C. Chin, "In Search of the Revolution: A Brief Biography of Chin Peng", in *Dialogues with Chin Peng: New Light on the Malayan Communist Party*, edited by C.C. Chin and Karl Hack (Singapore: Singapore University Press, 2004), p. 359.

6. Anthony Short, *The Communist Insurrection in Malaya, 1948–1960* (London: Frederick Muller, 1975), pp. 93–94; Chin Peng, *My Side of History* (Singapore: Media Masters, 2003), p. 268.

7. Leon Comber, *Malaya's Secret Police 1945–1969: The Role of the Special Branch in the Malayan Emergency* (Singapore: Institute of Southeast Asian Studies, 2008), p. 17; Bayly and Harper, *Forgotten Wars*, p. 480.

8. Francis Loh Kok Wah, *Beyond the Tin Mines: Coolies, Squatters and New Villagers in the Kinta Valley, Malaysia c1880–1980* (Singapore: Oxford University Press, 1988), pp. 122–23.

9. Noel Barber, *The War of the Running Dogs* (London: Fontana, 1971), p. 90.

10. Ibid., pp. 89–91.

11. Ibid., pp. 92–93.

12. Karl Hack and C.C. Chin, "The Malayan Emergency", in *Dialogues with Chin Peng: New Light on the Malayan Communist Party*, edited by C.C. Chin and Karl Hack (Singapore: Singapore University Press, 2004), p. 15.

13. Chin Peng, in Chin and Hack, *Dialogues with Chin Peng*, pp. 159–60.

14. Comber, *Malaysia's Secret Police*, p. 121; Barber, *War of the Running Dogs*, p. 40.

15. Richard Stubbs, "Guerilla Strategies and British Counterinsurgency Strategies of the 1950s and 1960s: Why was the War Lost?" in *Dialogues with Chin Peng: New Light on the Malayan Communist Party*, edited by C.C. Chin and Karl Hack (Singapore: Singapore University Press, 2004), p. 302.

16. Bayly and Harper, *Forgotten Wars*, p. 524.

17. Stubbs, *Guerrilla Strategies*, pp. 302–3.

18. Clutterbuck, *Riot and Revolution*, p. 190.

19. Barber, *War of the Running Dogs*, pp. 162–63; Khong Kim Hoong, *Merdeka! British Rule and the Struggle for Independence in Malaya 1945–1957* (Kuala Lumpur: Insan, 1984), p. 166.

20. Aloysius Chin, *The Communist Party of Malaya: The Inside Story* (Kuala Lumpur: Vinpress, 1995), p. 45.

21. Chin, "In Search of the Revolution", p. 366.

22. Chin, *The Communist Party of Malaya*, p. 112.

23. Wang Gungwu, in *Dialogues with Chin Peng*, p. 229.

24. Chin Peng, *My Side of History*, p. 263.

25. James Wong Wing On, *From the Pacific War to Merdeka: Reminiscences of Abdullah C.D., Rashid Maidin, Suriani Abdullah and Abu Samah* (Petaling Jaya: Strategic Information Research Development Centre, 2005), p. 54.

26. Comber, *Malaysia's Secret Police*, pp. 93–94.

27. Wong, *From Pacific War to Merdeka*, p. 20.

28. Stewart, *Smashing Terrorism*, p. 62.

29. Ibid., p. 168.

30. Ibid.

31. Comber, *Malaysia's Secret Police*, p. 90.

32. Ibid., p. 81.

33. Chin, *The Communist Party of Malaya*, p. 246.

34. Bayly and Harper, *Forgotten Wars*, p. 486.

35. Short, *The Communist Insurrection in Malaya*, p. 504.

36. Rehman Rashid, *A Malaysian Journey* (Petaling Jaya: Rehman Rashid, 1993), p. 57.

37. Bayly and Harper, *Forgotten Wars*, p. 504; Ahmad Fauzi Abdul Hamid, *Islamic*

Education in Malaysia, Monograph Number 18 (Singapore: S. Rajaratnam School of International Studies, 2010), p. 19; Kah Seng Loh et al., *The University Socialist Club and the Contest for Malaya: Tangled Strands of Modernity* (Amsterdam: Amsterdam University Press, 2012), p. 155.

38. Bayly and Harper, *Forgotten Wars*, p. 504.
39. Heng Pek Koon, *Chinese Politics in Malaysia: A History of the Malaysian Chinese Association* (Singapore: Oxford University Press, 1988), p. 54.
40. Nicholas Tarling, *Southeast Asia: Past and Present* (Melbourne: F.W. Cheshire, 1966), p. 298.
41. R.S. Milne and Diane K. Mauzy, *Politics and Government in Malaysia* (Singapore: Federal, 1978), pp. 125–26; Heng, *Chinese Politics*, p. 147.
42. Tarling, *Southeast Asia*, p. 298.
43. Bayly and Harper, *Forgotten Wars*, p. 500.
44. Heng, *Chinese Politics*, p. 147.
45. Ibid., p. 151.
46. John Funston, *Malay Politics in Malaysia: A Study of UMNO and PAS* (Kuala Lumpur: Heinemann Educational Books (Asia), 1980), pp. 80–83.
47. Ibid., pp. 82–83.
48. Milne and Mauzy, *Politics and Government in Malaysia*, pp. 34–35; Cheah Boon Kheng, *Malaysia: The Making of a Nation* (Singapore: Institute of Southeast Asian Studies, 2002), p. 26.
49. Richard Allen, *Malaysia: Prospect and Retrospect* (London: Oxford University Press, 1968), pp. 104–5; Tunku Abdul Rahman Putra Al-Haj, *Looking Back: The Historic Years of Malaya and Malaysia* (Kuala Lumpur: Pustaka Antara, 1977), p. 44.
50. Liew Chin Tong, *Speaking for the Reformasi Generation* (Kuala Lumpur: Research for Social Advancement, 2007), p. 107.
51. Bayly and Harper, *Forgotten Wars*, p. 531; K.J. Ratnam, *Communalism and the Political Process in Malaya* (Kuala Lumpur and Singapore: University of Malaya Press, 1965), p. 165.
52. Syed Muhammad Khairudin, "Rethinking Riots in Colonial Southeast Asia: The Case of the Maria Hertogh Controversy in Singapore, 1950–1954", in *Southeast Asia Research* 18, no. 1 (2010): 114.
53. Liew, *Speaking for the Reformasi Generation*, p. 108.
54. Heng, *Chinese Politics*, p. 136.
55. Ibid., p. 169.
56. Ibid. See also Ooi Kee Beng, *The Reluctant Politician: Tun Dr Ismail and His Time* (Singapore: Institute of Southeast Asian Studies, 2006), p. 53.
57. Rajeswary Amplavanar, *The Indian Minority and Political Change in Malaya 1945–1957* (Kuala Lumpur: Oxford University Press, 1981), p. 189.
58. Funston, *Malay Politics*, p. 42.

59. Khong, *Merdeka!*, pp. 196–97; Ratnam, *Communalism and the Political Process*, p. 196.

60. Milne and Mauzy, *Politics and Government in Malaysia*, pp. 35–36.

61. Tunku Abdul Rahman Putra Al-Haj, *Looking Back*, pp. 50–51.

62. Karl Hack, "From Baling to Merdeka 1955–1960", in *Dialogues with Chin Peng: New Light on the Malayan Communist Party*, edited by C.C. Chin and Karl Hack (Singapore: Singapore University Press, 2004), p. 310.

63. Ibid.

64. Stubbs, "Guerrilla Strategies", p. 304.

65. Hack, "From Baling to Merdeka", p. 310.

66. Cheah, *Malaysia*, p. 32.

67. Ibid., pp. 32–33. However, the British were also prepared to speed up the processes of constitutional change in order to counter MCP charges of continuing colonial control (Kah et al., *The University Socialist Club*, p. 23).

68. Sinnappah Arasaratnam, *Indians in Malaysia and Singapore* (London: Oxford University Press, 1970), p. 122.

69. Rajeswary, *The Indian Minority*, p. 128.

70. Ibid., pp. 197–98.

71. Milne and Mauzy, *Politics and Government in Malaysia*, p. 36.

72. Ibid.

73. Heng, *Chinese Politics*, p. 234.

74. Lee Kim Hing, "Forging Inter-Ethnic Cooperation: The Political and Constitutional Process towards Independence 1951–1957", in *Multiethnic Malaysia: Past, Present and Future*, edited by Lim Teck Ghee, Alberto Gomes, and Azly Rahman (Petaling Jaya: Strategic Information and Research Development Centre, 2009), p. 70.

75. Geoff Wade, *The Origins and Evolution of Ethnocracy in Malaysia*, Working Paper Series No. 112 (Singapore: Asia Research Institute, National University of Singapore, April, 2009), p. 23.

76. Heng, *Chinese Politics*, p. 232.

77. Ibid., p. 230.

78. This provision had not been included in the Alliance memorandum to the Reid Commission, nor was it to be found in the Draft Constitution. The incorporation of Islam as an official religion was suggested by the Pakistani representative on the Reid Commission (Wade, *The Origins and Evolution of Ethnocracy*, p. 25). Tunku Abdul Rahman subsequently argued that this was of psychological importance to the Malay community, but assured both the MCA and the MIC that the measure was largely symbolic and would in no way affect the rights of non-Malays (Lee, *Forging Inter-ethnic Cooperation*, p. 71).

79. Milne and Mauzy, *Politics and Government in Malaysia*, pp. 40–42. The provisions

of Article 153 were viewed as of crucial importance in terms of the psychological and symbolic reassurance they conveyed to the Malay community, and were regarded as a central component of the UMNO-MCA "bargain" (Milne and Mauzy, *Politics and Government in Malaysia*, p. 41).

80. Heng, *Chinese Politics*, p. 231.

81. Sheila Nair, "Constructing Civil Society in Malaysia: Nationalism, Hegemony and Resistance", in *Rethinking Malaysia*, edited by Jomo K.S. (Kuala Lumpur: Malaysian Social Science Association, 1999), p. 92.

82. Milne and Mauzy, *Politics and Government in Malaysia*, pp. 38–39.

83. Cheah, *Malaysia*, p. 54; Nair, "Constructing Civil Society", p. 92.

84. Nair, *Constructing Civil Society*, p. 92.

85. Joel Kahn and Francis Loh Kok Wah, "Introduction" in *Fragmented Vision: Culture and Politics in Contemporary Malaysia*, edited by Joel Kahn and Francis Loh Kok Wah (Sydney: Asian Studies Association of Australia/Allen and Unwin, 1992), p. 9.

86. Ibid., p. 10.

87. Ratnam, *Communalism and the Political Process*, p. 29; Clive Kessler, "Archaism and Modernity: Contemporary Malay Political Culture", in *Fragmented Vision: Culture and Politics in Contemporary Malaysia*, edited by Joel Kahn and Francis Loh Kok Wah (Sydney: Asian Studies Association of Australia/Allen and Unwin, 1992), pp. 136–38.

88. Muhammad Ikbal Said, "Ethnic Perspectives of the Left in Malaysia", in *Fragmented Vision: Culture and Politics in Contemporary Malaysia*, edited by Joel Kahn and Francis Loh Kok Wah (Sydney: Asian Studies Association of Australia/Allen and Unwin, 1992), p. 275.

89. Ibid., pp. 262, 272; Milne and Mauzy, *Politics and Government in Malaysia*, pp. 38–42; Ratnam, *Communalism and the Political Process*, p. 132.

90. Sheila Nair, "Colonialism, Nationalism, Ethnicity: Constructing Identity and Difference", in *Multiethnic Malaysia: Past, Present and Future*, edited by Lim Teck Ghee, Alberto Gomes, and Azly Rahman (Petaling Jaya: Strategic Information and Research Development Centre, 2009), p. 88.

91. Malcolm Caldwell, "From 'Emergency' to 'Independence'", in *Malaya: The Making of a Neo-Colony*, edited by Mohamed Amin and Malcolm Caldwell (Nottingham: Spokesman, 1977), p. 244.

92. Ibid., p. 251.

93. Michael R. Stenson, *Class, Race and Colonialism in Malaysia: The Indian Case* (St. Lucia: University of Queensland Press, 1980), p. 142.

94. Bayly and Harper, *Forgotten Wars*, p. 500.

95. Janakey Raman Manickam, *The Malaysian Indian Dilemma: The Struggles and Agony of the Indian Community in Malaysia*, 2nd ed. (Klang: Janakey Raman Manickam, 2010), p. 114.

96. Stenson, *Class, Race and Colonialism*, p. 174.
97. Arasaratnam, *Indians in Malaysia and Singapore*, p. 119.
98. Ooi, *The Reluctant Politician*, p. 56.
99. Sinnappah Arasaratnam, "Political Attitudes and Political Organization among Malayan Indians 1945–1955", *Jernal Sejarah* 10 (1971/72): 4.
100. Arasaratnam, *Indians in Malaysia and Singapore*, pp. 119–20.
101. Rajeswary, *The Indian Minority*, p. 191.
102. Janakey, *The Malaysian Indian Dilemma*, p. 114.
103. Arasaratnam, "Political Attitudes", p. 5.
104. Rajeswary, *The Indian Minority*, p. 192.
105. Ibid., pp. 191–92.
106. Arasaratnam, "Political Attitudes", p. 5.
107. Shamsul A.B. *From British to Bumiputera Rule: Local Politics and Rural Development in Peninsular Malaysia* (Singapore: Institute of Southeast Asian Studies, 2004), p. 185.
108. Selvakumaran Ramachandran, *Indian Plantation Labour in Malaysia* (Kuala Lumpur: S. Abdul Majeed, 1994), p. 302.
109. Arasaratnam, *Indians in Malaysia and Singapore*, pp. 124–25.
110. Sinnappah Arasaratnam, "Malaysian Indians: The Formation of an Incipient Society", in *Indian Communities in Southeast Asia*, edited by K.S. Sandhu and A. Mani (Singapore: Institute of Southeast Asian Studies, 1993), p. 193.
111. Arasaratnam, "Political Attitudes", p. 5.
112. Mytheli Sreenivas, *Wives, Widows and Concubines: The Conjugal Family Ideal in Colonial India* (Bloomington: Indiana University Press, 2008), p. 146.
113. Sumathi Ramaswamy, *Passions of the Tongue: Language Devotion in Tamil India 1891–1970* (New Delhi: Munshiram Manoharlal, p. 199), pp. 64–70; Maria Misra, *Vishnu's Crowded Temple: India Since the Great Rebellion* (London: Allen Lane, 2007), p. 293.
114. Ramaswamy, *Passions of the Tongue*, p. 70.
115. An observation based upon interviews with officials of the Malaysian Indian Congress.
116. Arasaratnam, "Political Attitudes", p. 5; Chandra Muzaffar, "Political Marginalization in Malaysia", in *Indian Communities in Southeast Asia*, edited by K.S. Sandhu and A. Mani (Singapore: Institute of Southeast Asian Studies, 1993), pp. 219–20.
117. Muzaffar, "Political Marginalization", p. 219.
118. Arasaratnam, "Political Attitudes", p. 5.
119. Usha Mahajani, *The Role of Indian Minorities in Burma and Malaya* (Bombay: Vora, 1960), pp. 214–15.
120. Stenson, *Class, Race and Colonialism*, p. 186.
121. Milne and Mauzy, *Politics and Government in Malaysia*, p. 148.
122. Ibid., p. 146.

123. Rajeswary, *The Indian Minority*, p. 212.
124. Arasaratnam, "Political Attitudes", p. 5; Rajeswary, *The Indian Minority*, pp. 172–75, 212; Muzaffar, "Political Marginalization", p. 219; Mahajani, *The Role of Indian Minorities*, pp. 214–15.
125. Rajeswary, *The Indian Minority*, pp. 174–75.
126. Ibid., p. 175.
127. Milne and Mauzy, *Politics and Government in Malaysia*, p. 135.
128. Arasaratnam, "Political Attitudes", p. 6.
129. Ooi, *The Reluctant Politician*, p. 78.
130. Arasaratnam, "Political Attitudes", p. 6.
131. Rajeswary, *The Indian Minority*, p. 199; Mavis Puthucheary, "Indians in the Public Sector", in *Indian Communities in Southeast Asia*, edited by K.S. Sandhu and A. Mani (Singapore: Institute of Southeast Asian Studies, 1993), pp. 355–36.
132. Rajeswary Amplavanar-Brown, "The Political Contemporary Elite in Malaysia", in *Indian Communities in Southeast Asia*, edited by K.S. Sandhu and A. Mani (Singapore: Institute of Southeast Asian Studies, 1993), p. 238; Muzaffar, "Political Marginalization", p. 220.
133. Arasaratnam, *Indians in Malaysia and Singapore*, pp. 39–40.
134. Ibid., p. 115.
135. Ibid., p. 118.
136. Rajeswary, *The Indian Minority*, p. 127.
137. Arasaratnam, *Indians in Malaysia and Singapore*, p. 122.
138. Kernial Singh Sandhu, *Indians in Malaya: Some Aspects of their Immigration and Settlement 1786–1957* (Cambridge: Cambridge University Press, 1969), p. 150.
139. Arasaratnam, *Indians in Malaysia and Singapore*, pp. 40–41.
140. Ibid., p. 122.
141. Rajeswary, *The Indian Minority*, pp. 237–39.
142. Arasaratnam, *Indians in Malaysia and Singapore*, p. 187.
143. Muzafar Desmond Tate, *The Malaysian Indians: History, Problems and Future* (Petaling Jaya: Strategic Information Research Centre, 2008), pp. 165–66.
144. Funston, *Malay Politics*, pp. 49–50.
145. Selvakumaran, *Indian Plantation Labour*, p. 245.
146. Charles Gamba, *The Origins of Trade Unionism in Malaya: A Case Study in Colonial Labour Unrest* (Singapore: Eastern Universities Press, 1962), p. 353.
147. Ibid., pp. 354–61.
148. Muzaffar, "Political Marginalization", p. 219.
149. Selvakumaran, *Indian Plantation Labour*, pp. 244–45.
150. Ibid., p. 246.
151. Gamba, *The Origins of Trade Unionism*, p. 113.
152. P. Ramasamy, *Plantation Labour, Unions, Capital and the State in Peninsular Malaysia* (New York: Oxford University Press, 1994), p. 92.

153. Gamba, *The Origins of Trade Unionism*, p. 379.
154. Ramasamy, *Plantation Labour*, p. 87.
155. Ibid., pp. 87–89.
156. Selvakumaran, *Indian Plantation Labour*, p. 249.
157. Ramasamy, *Plantation Labour*, p. 87.
158. Ibid., p. 97.
159. Ibid, p. 93.
160. Ibid., p. 90.
161. Gamba, *The Origins of Trade Unionism*, p. 404.
162. Ibid., p. 407.
163. Ibid., pp. 414–15.
164. Selvakumaran, *Indian Plantation Labour*, p. 249.
165. Gamba, *The Origins of Trade Unionism*, p. 379.
166. Ramasamy, *Plantation Labour*, p. 97.
167. Ibid., pp. 97–98.
168. Ibid., p. 98.
169. Selvakumaran, *Indian Plantation Labour*, p. 250.
170. Ramasamy, *Plantation Labour*, pp. 97–98.
171. Ibid., p. 95.
172. Ibid., pp. 95–96.
173. Ibid., p. 96.
174. C.P. Ramachandra, "The Indian Independence Movement in Malaya 1942–1945", M.A. Thesis, Universiti Malaya, 1970.
175. Ramasamy, *Plantation Labour*, p. 95.
176. Selvakumaran, *Indian Plantation Labour*, pp. 252–53.
177. Ibid., p. 250.
178. Arasaratnam, *Indians in Malaysia and Singapore*, p. 140.
179. Ramachandra, "The Indian Independence Movement".
180. Ramasamy, *Plantation Labour*, p. 99.
181. Ibid.
182. Ibid., p. 100.
183. Ibid., p. 101.
184. Ibid.
185. Ibid.
186. Ibid., p. 133.
187. Ibid.
188. Arasaratnam, *Indians in Malaysia and Singapore*, p. 153.

13

FROM MALAYA TO MALAYSIA
Singapore, 13 May and the
New Economic Policy

In general the post-Merdeka Alliance government continued those economic and social policies that had been formulated prior to the attainment of Merdeka. While Malaya experienced steady economic expansion, industrialization was sluggish, and export earnings continued to be overreliant on the three staples of the colonial era — tin, rubber, and timber. Foreign economic domination continued and in 1970, 70.8 per cent of the nation's wealth remained in the hands of non-Malaysians.[1]

During his years in office the Tunku adopted a policy of gradualism towards nation building. His efforts were directed towards developing a pluralistic society based on multiracial cooperation and goodwill out of which would naturally evolve loyalty to Malaya as a nation. While the Tunku advanced Malay symbols of nationhood — the King, the national language — he also encouraged the promotion of ethnic cultures and languages. The Tunku believed that the routine interactions of quotidian life, as well as national activities including sport, festivals, and cultural events would foster an identifiable and definitive Malayan nationalism.[2]

Support for the Alliance declined significantly in the 1959 elections. The Alliance vote fell from 79.6 per cent of the electorate in 1955 to 51.5 per cent in 1959. The PMIP's vote increased from 3.9 per cent to 21.2 per cent, while Chinese support drifted from the Alliance to opposition parties, so that the MCA won only 19 of the 31 seats it contested.[3] The results hinted at growing ethnic polarization in Malaya.

THE FORMATION OF MALAYSIA

Schemes to form a Malaysian Federation, comprising Malaya, Singapore, and the British colonies of Sarawak, North Borneo (later known as Sabah), and the British Protectorate of Brunei, had been repeatedly mooted by the British authorities throughout the 1950s.[4] For some years the Malayan government evinced little enthusiasm for the proposal.[5] The Malayan leadership feared that such a union would infuse an unacceptably large number of Chinese voters into Malaya, thus destroying the delicate racial balance and threatening the precarious Malay control of the politics of the Peninsula. Moreover, the firmly anti-communist Alliance government viewed Singapore with its supposedly inherent left-wing politics and its non-communal policies as a potential source of political instability.[6]

It is thus ironic that the potential volatility of Singapore's internal politics proved the decisive factor in inducing Alliance agreement to the Malaysia proposal. In 1959 the People's Action Party (PAP) under the leadership of Lee Kuan Yew won a commanding election victory in Singapore. However, the PAP was divided between the "moderate" English-educated leadership and a far more radical Chinese-educated rank and file.[7] Lee believed that a merger with Malaya was the only guarantee of a long-term non-communist Singapore. This view was supported by the British, who had indicated that independence could not be contemplated without some form of wider political association.[8] On 27 May 1961, worried that the PAP moderates were in danger of being displaced by the radicals, the Tunku finally gave the proposal his formal imprimatur.[9]

The British government now undertook to broker a binding agreement between the two entities — Malaya and Singapore — seen as crucial to any "Greater Malaysia" settlement. British decolonization aimed at fulfilling two main (and mutually reinforcing) objectives, namely, continued Malay ascendency within the Federation, and the suppression of communist impulses within Singapore.[10]

While the incorporation of the Borneo territories proceeded relatively smoothly, negotiations between Singapore and Malaya proved difficult, and bargaining, often conducted at the highest level, continued up until the very inauguration of the Federation.[11] The most contentious issue in the discussions between Malaya and Singapore was that of citizenship. The Tunku refused to compromise on this issue. He and UMNO generally were adamant that the Chinese role in the Federation should be curbed. Provisions for obtaining citizenship in Singapore had been much more relaxed than those in Malaya, and the Tunku now insisted that the 327,000 Singaporeans born in China, India and Malaya would need to pass a Malay language test before they could qualify for Federal citizenship.[12] While it was formally agreed that all Singapore citizens would be granted parity with those of Malaya, those without Federal citizenship would be ineligible to stand for office or vote in Federal elections.[13] Moreover, Singapore would be underrepresented in the Federal Parliament proportionate to its population, but by way of compensation would retain substantial autonomy including full control over labour and education.[14] The final allocation of parliamentary seats reflected UMNO's determination to quarantine the impact of the Chinese majority in Singapore:

Malaya: Population 7.9 million: 104 seats
Sabah: Population less than 0.5 million: 16 seats
Sarawak: Population less than 0.8 million: 24 seats
Singapore: Population 1.8 million: 15 seats.[15]

An agreement for the establishment of Malaysia was co-signed on 9 July 1963 by Great Britain, Malaya, North Borneo and Singapore.[16] However, following Indonesian objections to the incorporation of the North Borneo territories, the inauguration date was deferred from 31 August 1963 to 16 September 1963,[17] and came into existence only after a United Nations Malaysia mission had determined that participation in the Federation was supported by a substantial majority of the North Borneo electorate.[18] Indonesian President Sukarno subsequently insisted that Malaysia was a neo-colonial project designed to deny North Borneo its rightful place in *Indonesia Raya* (Greater Indonesia), and in early 1963 embarked upon the prolonged quasi-military anti-Malaysia operation known as *Konfrontasi*.[19]

The consummation of the Malaysian Federation fulfilled two key and interlinked objectives of the Malayan leadership. First, by classifying all of the indigenous peoples as bumiputeras or "sons of the soil",[20] and hence as ethnic "brothers" of the Malays (the putative indigenes of the Malay Peninsula — not all bumiputeras relished this new familial relationship[21])

— the awkward racial equilibrium which had dominated the politics of Malaya was to be superseded by a society which would be under the assured and indefinite political control of the Archipelago's indigenous peoples. This could be manipulated to defuse the perceived threat posed by the large Chinese majority in Singapore. Second, by enmeshing the putative loose cannon of Singapore within the political structures of the Federation, UMNO had assuaged a long-term strategic worry. Left-wing Singapore had been viewed as a potential Cuba, an island which left to its own devices could well develop its own uncontrolled momentum which might destabilize the entire region.[22]

The Expulsion of Singapore

From the earliest days of the Federation there were serious frictions between Tunku Abdul Rahman's Alliance and the People's Action Party (PAP) of Singapore, headed by Lee Kuan Yew. These difficulties involved a potent amalgam of constitutional, ethnic, political, and personal factors, and were ultimately to lead to Singapore's expulsion from the Federation.

Most of these battles took place within the sensitive arena of communalism. The respective political forces within the Federation adopted approaches in considering and resolving ethnic issues which were diametrically opposed. While the Alliance eschewed transparent discussion of communalism on the grounds that public ventilation of ethnic grievances was fraught with risk, the PAP, a party with a non-communal structure and open to Singaporeans of any ethnic background, encouraged candid and vigorous debate and the forthright settlement of all communal matters. The Alliance found the PAP approach both disruptive and unnecessarily acerbic.[23] Moreover, the Malayan leadership, whose monopoly on power had hitherto remained largely uncontested, found it difficult to tolerate or even acknowledge the legitimacy of any political discourse which fell beyond its control.[24] Given this backdrop, the political ructions created by an energetic and assertive PAP, and the incisive pungent oratory of its leader Lee Kuan Yew, could hardly be viewed by the Alliance leadership as anything other than destabilizing, threatening, and even subversive.[25]

Early in the life of the Federation, conflict developed over the political representation of the nation's Malay electorate. As a communal party formed by Malays, UMNO claimed the exclusive right to speak on behalf of all Malays, and disputed the need, if not the actual permissibility, for other groups to trespass on its constituency or to debate or articulate policy on Malay issues. In the September 1963 elections, the UMNO-sponsored Singapore Alliance Party failed to win any of the three Malay-majority seats on the island, all returning PAP candidates.[26] The day after the election the Tunku made a speech in which he expressed his shock that Malays would vote for Lee Kuan Yew's PAP.[27] His comments foreshadowed the commencement of an anti-PAP campaign, sustained by known UMNO "ultras", and allegedly covertly supported by the UMNO leadership, which was designed to discredit and destabilize the PAP.[28]

Aware that UMNO intended to involve itself in the Singapore political arena, Lee felt obliged to reciprocate at the Federal level.[29] In the April 1964 elections the PAP fielded eleven candidates in Peninsular electorates, all of which were held by the MCA,[30] an action viewed by the Tunku as a direct challenge to the Alliance Formula and thus the established framework of inter-communal cooperation developed by its constituent parties.[31] The Alliance scored a convincing electoral victory, winning 89 of 104 seats, and attracting 51.8 per cent of the vote.[32]

On 21 July 1964, the date celebrating the Prophet Mohammad's Birthday, riots broke out in Singapore, leaving 23 people dead and 465 injured.[33] Although some commentators later attributed the riots to the actions of Indonesian agents provocateur and local sympathizers,[34] Lee Kuan Yew lays the blame squarely upon UMNO incitement and negligence, and the inability to control the "ultras" within UMNO.[35] He contends that the riots were instigated with the joint aim of establishing UMNO political influence among Singapore Malays, but more crucially of using the issue of Singapore Malays to fortify UMNO support among Peninsular Malays.[36] A further, albeit less serious, outbreak of violence occurred in September 1964.[37]

While Lee and the PAP were still subject to the overheated (and often risible) invective of the UMNO ultras,[38] the party was devising a new strategy to combat the divisive politicking of Malay extremists and to promote a national identity that would reach beyond communalism.[39] The PAP joined with four political parties — two in Peninsular Malaysia (the United Democratic Party and the People's Progressive Party), and two in Sarawak (the Sarawak United People's Party [SUPP] and MACHINDA) — to form the Malaysian Solidarity Convention. On 8 May 1965 the convention unveiled its new national programme, to be known as "Malaysian Malaysia",[40] with the following declaration:

A Malaysian Malaysia means that the state is not identified with the supremacy, well-being and interests of any one community or race. A Malaysian Malaysia is the antithesis of a Malay Malaysia, a Chinese Malaysia, a Dayak Malaysia, an Indian Malaysia, and so on. The special and legitimate interests of different communities must be secured and promoted within the framework of the collective rights, interest and responsibilities of all races.[41]

The "Malaysian Malaysia" concept was diametrically opposed to the Alliance formula and the mechanics of inter-ethnic brokerage agreed upon at the time of Malayan independence, and appeared to issue a serious challenge to UMNO/Malay hegemony.[42] Indeed the Tunku states that Lee's perceived opposition to the constitutionally guaranteed rights of Malays aroused the omnipresent fears of Chinese domination, and an undermining of the "bargain" which had underscored the constitutional settlement of 1957.[43]

The Malaysian Malaysia concept aroused instinctive fears within the Tunku, who foresaw a Federation beset with racial strife and serious civil discord.[44] On 7 August 1965, the Tunku advised Lee that racial discord had reached a "flashpoint" and that a crisis would now only be averted by a formal separation.[45] Once the decision to exclude Singapore had been reached, secret consultations were held between the Alliance and the PAP to formalize the terms of disassociation. These negotiations were kept secret from both the Sabah and Sarawak leaderships, and from the British government.[46] On 9 August 1965, Singapore ceased to be a constituent state within the Federation of Malaysia, and declared itself an independent nation.[47]

THE 13 MAY INCIDENT

Throughout the 1960s, the UMNO/MCA relationship was one of agreed reciprocity. In return for UMNO moderation on the issue of Malay rights, the MCA deliberately softened Chinese cultural and political demands.[48] Singapore's inclusion within the Federation had greatly increased the agreed boundaries of political debate. The "Malaysian Malaysia" ideology had questioned both the rationale and the modus operandi of Alliance political structures, and indeed had suggested that the inter-ethnic compact reached among UMNO, MCA, and MIC at the time of Merdeka was no longer binding, and might be superseded or at the very least re-negotiated. At the grass-roots level there was increasing ethnic polarization, a sharpening divide which went largely unnoticed by the Alliance leadership.[49]

Chinese and Indian concerns were largely aroused by the educational and language policies implemented by the Alliance, which were perceived as threatening the viability of the Chinese- and Tamil-medium schools, and ultimately the very survival of minority community languages. Alliance educational policies were geared towards replacing the British school system with a national education system incorporating Malay as a compulsory subject.[50] On 31 August 1967 Malay became the Federation's national and sole official language,[51] a measure which greatly eroded Chinese confidence in and support for the MCA.[52]

Malay support for the Alliance also languished throughout the late 1960s. This was largely due to the failure of the government to alleviate harsh and widespread rural poverty, or to remedy the continuing dearth of educational opportunities for Malays. Shortly after independence the average annual income for adult males had been assessed at $3,223 for Chinese, $2,130 for Indians, and $1,463 for Malays.[53] Despite consistent economic growth, and the introduction of (largely ineffective[54]) programmes designed to benefit rural Malays, the agricultural sector remained stagnant, and the incomes of rural Malays actually declined in the period 1957–69.[55] The 1970 census revealed that 64.8 per cent of the Malay population was living below the poverty line.[56]

The period 1964–69 was marked by a number of portentous inter-racial incidents, which to astute observers might have warned of the potential for major communal disturbances. These included clashes in Bukit Mertajam (July 1964); as we have noted, serious riots in Singapore on the occasion of the Prophet Mohammad's birthday (July 1964); skirmishes between Chinese supporters of the Socialist Front protesting against compulsory national military service and the Malay-dominated security forces leading to a wave of arrests under the Internal Security Act (ISA) (early 1965); Malay–Chinese rioting in Penang and Butterworth in the wake of a strike protesting against the devaluation of the Malaysian dollar, and less serious clashes in Kuala Lumpur and Johor (November 1967); and an MCP ambush on a police convoy which killed fifteen Malay officers (June 1968).[57]

Throughout the 1960s a succession of contentious issues served to heighten ethnic tensions. These included pockets of Malay support, especially within the PMIP, for Sukarno's vision of a Greater Indonesia, and for the more nebulous concept of Malphilindo (in which President

Sukarno called for the unification of the Malay "race"[58]); the introduction of conscription in 1964, and subsequent rumours that "disloyal" Indian and Chinese youths were leaving the country to avoid the call-up; Lee Kuan Yew's campaign for a "Malaysian Malaysia"; and the subsequent expulsion of Singapore from the Federation.[59] In the late 1960s the emotive issues of language and education became the subjects of fervent and often acrimonious debate. The public forum was increasingly commandeered by ethnic extremists of all communities, and considered discussion was largely replaced with heated polemics and the politics of accusation and disdain.[60]

The ill-will generated by these disputes flowed into the 1969 election campaign. Sensitive matters such as non-Malay rights, education, the status of Malay as the official language, were all the subject of sustained, bitter, and intemperate invective among non-Malays. Malays counter attacked with charges of racism and disloyalty.[61] Tensions were further aggravated with the murder of an UMNO election worker on 24 April 1969 in the Jelutong area (in Penang), and the death, in early May 1969, of a Chinese youth, killed in a clash between security forces and members of the Peking-oriented Labour Party. On 9 May 1969, the day before the election, the Labour Party, in breach of police regulations, staged a huge funeral procession through the streets of Kuala Lumpur.[62] The National Operations Council (NOC) later claimed that the Labour Party had:

> ...defied police instructions and organised a large parade in which an estimated number of ten thousand persons took part.... They chanted Maoist slogans, sang 'The East is Red', and displayed portraits of Mao Tse-Tung and the Red Flag. The Parade ... provoked Malay bystanders with shouts of 'Malai si' (Death to the Malays!) and 'Hutang darah di bayar darah' (Blood will be repaid with blood!)[63]

Witnesses to this event advised the writer that the apparent open Chinese pledges of allegiance to the ruler of a foreign power and the advocacy of an alien ideology were not lost upon Malay observers.

The elections, held on 10 May 1969, resulted in significant Alliance losses. The Alliance share of the vote plummeted to 48.1 per cent, and although the Alliance won 66 of the 104 West Malaysian seats, it lost its crucial two-thirds majority.[64] A large number of MCA-held seats swung to the opposition Gerakan Ra'ayat Malaysia Party (Malaysian People's

Party), and the Democratic Action Party (DAP). The Gerakan won the state of Penang, the PMIP retained control of Kelantan, and Alliance majorities were lost in Perak and Selangor.[65]

Large-scale "victory" parades, organized by the opposition parties, were staged in Kuala Lumpur. These were both ill-disciplined and provocative.[66] Youthful supporters of the DAP and Gerakan booed and jeered at Malays they encountered, especially police and members of the security forces, and shouted insults.[67]

We have previously noted that the "Malaysian Malaysia" concept had been interpreted by UMNO, and disseminated to its supporters, as a direct threat to Malay primacy, and hence as a prelude to a collective Chinese takeover of the politics of Malaysia.[68] The Report of the National Operations Council (NOC), set up in the wake of the 1969 riots, later suggested that opposition ridicule had rekindled memories among Malays of the kangaroo courts and summary executions of the MPAJA era.[69] In reaction, a Malay group calling itself "Rugged Youth" (*Pemuda Tahan Lasak*), a specially trained division of UMNO Youth,[70] applied for permission to hold a demonstration on 13 May. This was approved by the Selangor Chief Minister, Datuk Harun, who agreed to lead the march.[71]

On the afternoon of 13 May 1969, the MCA leader, Tun Tan Siew Sin, announced that as the MCA no longer commanded the support of a majority of Chinese voters, the party felt disqualified from serving in any official capacity within the government, though it would continue to support the Alliance.[72] Thus for the first time since independence the Chinese community would be unrepresented in government. The precipitate MCA action, was, in effect, responsible for terminating the Alliance formula, thus seemingly abandoning the established pattern of inter-ethnic brokerage which dated back to the UMNO–MCA compact negotiated prior to Merdeka.[73]

The crowd that gathered at Datuk Harun's residence on the evening of 13 May was tense and prepared for trouble,[74] and contained known agitators.[75] Ahmad Mustapha Hassan, an UMNO official who was present that evening, suggests that the sudden appearance of weaponry and the initial killing of a Chinese coffee shop boy indicates that mob violence had been premeditated.[76] While accounts differ as to the actual causative spark,[77] what is clear is that all semblance of order rapidly vanished, and Malay mobs rampaged through the streets. In some places they were confronted by armed Chinese and Indian mobs.[78] Government figures to the end of May listed fatalities as 196,[79] with 180 wounded by firearms, and 259 injured by other weapons, and 6,000 people left homeless. Damage to property was assessed as 211 destroyed vehicles with 753 buildings damaged or destroyed by fire. In addition, 9,143 persons were arrested of whom 5,561 were formally arraigned.[80] The outbreaks were met by the largely Malay police and security forces. While the police were held to have conducted themselves with professional impartiality, there was documented evidence of anti-Chinese bias among military forces.[81]

On 15 May the government proclaimed a state of emergency and devolved total political power to a special eight-man National Operations Council (NOC) under the direction of Tunku Abdul Rahman's anointed successor, Tun Abdul Razak. The only non-Malay members of the NOC were MCA leader Tun Tan Siew Sin and MIC leader Tun V.T. Sambanthan.[82] In the weeks following 13 May, responsibility for the riots was repeatedly laid at the feet of elements within the Chinese community.[83]

On 28 June 1969 the Indian community was the target of mob violence when Sentul, in those days a largely Indian working class suburb, was attacked. Officially six people were killed and seventeen injured.[84] However, witnesses to this attack and its aftermath, including police officers, advised the author that in fact there were seventeen fatalities — fifteen Indians and two Chinese. This figure is supported by the report filed by Bob Reece, correspondent for the *Far Eastern Economic Review*.[85] According to my informants the attackers were alleged to have accompanied the attack with the shouted injunction, "We have killed the pig, let us now kill the goat."

THE NEW ECONOMIC POLICY

Shortly after the riots Tun Abdul Razak met with a small group of advisors to consider the implications of the collapse of the Alliance formula and to chart an agreed framework for the future conduct of Malaysian politics. They realized that Malaysia could afford no repeat of 13 May, and that further clashes of this magnitude would spell disaster for the nation.[86] They believed that they could identify two underlying causes which had led to the riots, namely (1) the wide and deepening distrust and suspicion between the ethnic communities, and (2) the extreme and widening imbalances between the communities, in particular putative Chinese wealth as opposed to Malay privation.[87]

In meeting these objectives the government adopted a far-reaching two-pronged approach which was to fundamentally restructure Malaysian political, economic, and social culture.

Malay political primacy would be enshrined by enforcing the provisions of the constitutional "bargain" of 1957, and prohibiting public discussion of a range of selected issues relating to this settlement. These would include querying the status of the Malay language, the role and standing of the sultans, the position of Islam as the state religion, and the citizenship rights enjoyed by "immigrant peoples", including their legitimate claims to participate in the administrative and economic structures of the country. Non-Malays would no longer be permitted to question the constitutional contract.

The economy would be re-engineered to encourage full Malay participation within all sectors, including the most advanced and modern economic sectors. A suite of economic and educational policies would be introduced with the long-term aim of alleviating Malay poverty and integrating Malays into the full structure of Malaysian economic, social and cultural life.[88]

In July 1969, the NOC launched two major initiatives. The first was the promulgation of a package of Essential Goodwill Regulations. These allowed for the establishment of a hierarchy of district and state Goodwill Committees, conducted under the umbrella of a National Goodwill Committee (NGC) chaired by Tunku Abdul Rahman. A Department of National Unity was created the same month.[89] The second initiative was the unveiling of a programme of economic development, a five-point policy designed to eliminate poverty and unemployment.[90]

In July 1969 the NOC established a National Consultative Council (NCC) to establish formal lines of dialogue between ethnic communities, to lay the foundations of inter-ethnic cooperation, and to create a harmonious and agreed context for the resumption of parliamentary democracy.[91] In August 1970 the NOC announced two important initiatives, namely the introduction of Emergency Ordinance No. 45 which strengthened the Sedition Act,[92] and on National Day the release of the National Ideology, known as the Rukunegara. This "ideology" — more a statement of intent — was based on five general principles, in essence (1) belief in God, (2) loyalty to King and country, (3) upholding the Constitution, (4) the rule of law, and (5) good behaviour and morality.[93]

However, the centrepiece of the "new realism" was the New Economic Policy (NEP). The NEP, enunciated within the context of the Second Malaysia Plan of 1971–75, was structured on the premise that the economics of private enterprise and open competition had disadvantaged the Malays (as well as other sectors of the community), and that equitable sharing of the benefits of economic expansion could only be fully ensured by direct government intervention.[94] In essence, the NEP sought, through a process of vigorous affirmation, to attain for Malays and other indigenous groups, a thirty per cent share of corporate assets by 1990. This objective was to be subsumed within a policy structure which promoted the dual objectives of the eradication of poverty regardless of race, and the elimination of the identification of race with economic function.[95]

The government moved to create state enterprises which would provide employment and training opportunities for Malays, reorienting the major thrust of development from agriculture to rapid industrialization.[96] In the field of education, the government amended the constitution with the direction that more places in higher education, especially within universities, be reserved for Malays, and that additional resources be devoted to teaching Malay students in schools and in reducing the high "drop-out" rate among Malay secondary school students.[97]

It is now often overlooked that the UMNO leadership envisaged the NEP as a necessary but strictly temporary measure which would be rescinded once its main objectives had been achieved. The new Deputy Prime Minister, Tun Dr Ismail, stated that "The Malays should not think of these privileges as permanent, for then they will not put their efforts to the tasks. In fact, it is an insult for the Malays to be getting these privileges." Indeed, Ismail had attempted to impose a twenty-year time limit on the NEP.[98]

Parliamentary rule was restored on 23 February 1971. However, the first issue facing the newly convened assembly was the controversial Constitutional (Amendment) Bill which extended to Parliament itself as well as to the State Assemblies the already announced revisions to Article 10 (freedom of speech), Article 152 (the national language), Article 153 (the special position of the Malays and the legitimate interests of other communities), and Article 181 (the supremacy of the Rulers). Razak advised the House that unless these amendments were approved with the requisite two-thirds majority, Parliament itself would be disbanded. Although these measures were opposed by the DAP and the PPP, the measures were ultimately passed with a 126 to 17 majority.[99]

In August 1971, a Congress of National Culture, made up almost entirely of Malay cultural groups,[100] enunciated the following three principles on which an integrated Malaysian culture would be founded:

1. It would be based on the indigenous culture of the region,
2. Suitable elements from other cultures would be accepted and incorporated within the National Culture, and
3. Islam would be an important component of the National Culture.[101]

The Congress made it explicitly clear that as Malays constituted the foundational "race" of Malaysia, the national culture would be constructed around an irreducible core of Malay culture.[102] These principles, which engendered alarm, resentment, and ultimately resistance among non-Malay communities,[103] were later endorsed as policy by the Ministry of Culture, Youth and Sports. This policy categorically distinguished a Malay-based society from the "immigrant" races who were regarded as "splinters" from their home ethnic societies.[104]

The major change in the Malaysian political structure was the augmentation of the Alliance with the negotiated addition of a number of former opposition or unaligned parties in an expanded coalition. Razak aimed to create a "government of national unity".[105] UMNO considered that the Alliance formula had outlived its usefulness. The formula had been predicated upon the assumption that the component parties represented the majority of their respective ethnic communities.[106] This was demonstrably not true in the case of the MCA,[107], and may have been doubtful in regard to the MIC. Between 1970 and 1973 the coalition was widened to include Partai Islam Se Malaysia (PAS),[108] thus achieving a dubious Malay unity,[109] the Gerakan, the PPP, Sarawak United People's Party (SUPP), Parti Pesaka Bumiputera Bersatu (PSB), and Sabah Alliance Party (SAP). The coalition, now known as Barisan Nasional (BN), was formally inaugurated on 19 June 1974.[110] UMNO also augmented its own base with the rehabilitation of a number of dissidents, including influential figures Musa Hitam and Dr Mahathir Mohamad.[111]

The formation of the coalition reflected UMNO's desire to incorporate the broadest possible political representation within the ranks of government, and in particular to enlarge the context in which ethnic issues and national policy were negotiated. By providing a wide and diverse communal forum for the aggregation of political interests and the articulation of policy, the government now believed that its component parties covered the spectrum of legitimate public opinion and that it could thus claim to speak for the entire nation. As a consequence the BN made it increasingly clear that it doubted the motives, aspirations and the very loyalty of the opposition parties.[112]

The post 1969 settlement profoundly reshaped the contours of Malaysian political processes and discourse, and became the established foundation for the nation's subsequent domestic policy. UMNO hegemony was now firmly entrenched and Malay ascendency was guaranteed by the revised constitutional framework which had placed the issue beyond legal challenge and even beyond the scope of public debate.[113] At the same time the expanded coalition had gravely diminished the standing of MCA and MIC as advocates for their communities. The inevitable result was the downgrading and even marginalization of Chinese and Indian concerns.[114]

INDIANS IN MALAYA/MALAYSIA: 1957 TO THE NEP

The Indian population entered Merdeka as a minor community sandwiched between Malay political dominance and Chinese economic strength. From Merdeka its trajectory has been one of increasing political, economic and social marginalization. From the outset, the Indian community lacked the economic foundation necessary to develop capital-intensive enterprises, or to provide the level of entrepreneurial opportunities which would have assisted in alleviating widespread Indian poverty.[115]

Following the Pacific War there was a consistent drift of Indian labour from the plantations to the urban centres. Whereas in 1947 some 61 per cent of the population had been rurally based, by the time of Merdeka, this figure had shrunk to 53 per cent.[116] Most of the urban immigrants had moved into low-paid and unskilled work. Throughout these years unemployment among Indians consistently exceeded that of other communities. In 1967/68, a full decade after independence, Indian unemployment stood at 12.32 per cent, compared to 8.77 per cent for Malays, and 7.98 per cent for Chinese. Educationally, levels of enrolments were consistently lower at all levels of post-primary education than those among other communities.[117] The 1970 census revealed that 39.2 per cent of Indians were living below the poverty line.[118] Politically the community remained profoundly divided, its support fragmented between the MIC, a series of opposition parties, and the trade union movement.

The Malayan Indian Congress

The MIC representing a minority community comprising approximately one-tenth of the population could never hope to be other than a small and junior party. Its total dependency upon UMNO patronage for allocation of seats and its very existence within the Alliance mean that it necessarily operated from a position of weakness and marginality.[119] Although the leadership of the party held Cabinet portfolios, the Congress had limited influence in determining policies likely to deliver outcomes favourable to Indian voters.[120] From the outset of his tenure as party President, V.T. Sambanthan made it clear that while the MIC was a political party formed to represent Indians, sectional interests would always be subjugated to national priorities.[121] Although the trade union movement was largely dominated by its Indian membership, the MIC complied with the Alliance perspective that in order to encourage foreign investment, the claims and role of organized labour should be severely circumscribed.[122]

In general, the MIC's base of support was built around plantation labour, the business sector and the Chettiar community.[123] In effect, the party was viewed by the small Indian professional and mercantile classes as a vehicle for delivery of economic opportunities, in particular contracts, licences, employment and other forms of government patronage. It was not seen, nor did it function, as a party of reform.[124]

The limited authority of the MIC and its apparent failure to defend or promote wider Indian interests led to middle-class resentment and the party was largely shunned by non-Tamils, intellectuals and trade unionists. As we have seen, the perennial distrust of Indian intellectuals deprived the party of valuable expertise, in particular the skills needed for effective organization, in-depth analysis and policy research and formulation, as well as the political adroitness needed to respond to the demands of working within a multi-party coalition. Much of the talented leadership within the community was concentrated in opposition parties such as the People's Progressive Party (PPP), the Socialist Front, and, after 1965, the Democratic Action Party (DAP).[125]

The Fragmentation of Estates

The MIC's first major political test revolved around the issue of subdivision or "fragmentation" of estates. The so-called fragmentation of estates began during the 1950s when several sterling companies, alarmed by the uncertain prospects and possible instability of an independent Malaya, decided to sell their properties and repatriate their capital. The process of divestment triggered a chain of speculation involving real estate agents and investors. Typically, the estates were subdivided into small lots of four to five acres, which were then resold at vastly inflated prices to absentee landlords.[126] Between 1950 and 1967, 324,931 acres (133,551 hectares or eighteen per cent of the total estate land area), was thus subdivided.[127] Thousands of employees were thrown out of work, and they and their dependents were left without any means of support. In addition, vital amenities, won over years of protracted negotiation, were irretrievably lost.[128] The hardships endured by those forced out of plantations, many of whom had lived and worked on the estates since childhood, were often extreme. In interviews with former estate employees, social workers and political officials, I was informed that "fortunate" dispossessed labourers and their families found temporary accommodation with urban-based relatives while they sought employment (invariably low waged and unskilled), but many workers were rendered homeless, sometimes for months at a time, and in many instances their children were taken into welfare.

The NUPW and MIC, observing the loss of employment of plantation workers in estates, and the dismal conditions endured by the few former estate workers engaged by the new ownership of subdivided properties, repeatedly urged the government to intervene to halt or at least regulate this process.[129] However, the ensuing 1957 *Report on the Subdivision and Fragmentation of Estates* reflected the government's preoccupation with creating a class of small-scale indigenous peasant proprietors rather than maintaining the more efficient and productive estate sector. Against all evidence the report concluded that the overall impact of fragmentation was socially and economically beneficial to Malays in that it was creating a new class of landed smallholders.[130]

Subdivision gained momentum in the early 1960s, and a further committee headed by Professor Ungku Aziz, Chair of the Department of Economics, University of Malaya, was appointed in 1963 to report on the phenomenon. Professor Ungku Aziz's report unequivocally condemned fragmentation. The report demonstrated that subdivision was driven by speculation rather than a demand for land, and rather than creating a class of peasant proprietors, the process benefitted absentee landlords and urban investors.[131] It also revealed that many displaced estate workers were being rendered destitute.[132] The Aziz Report concluded that "there is absolutely no doubt that subdivision has a deleterious effect upon the Malayan economy.... subdivision is an 'anti-development' process. It increases the inequality of incomes in rural areas and promotes increased ownership of farm land by urban people."[133]

The report also noted the serious impact that fragmentation had upon Indian labour, especially older workers. Because labour on smaller units was casual rather than permanent, wages were invariably reduced, and working conditions were inferior to those on established plantations. The Labour Code required that a range of amenities be established and maintained on all estates greater than one thousand acres in area. Fragmentation adversely affected a wide range of social and institutional facilities, including workers' quarters, roads, bridges, hospitals, dispensaries, schools and even water supplies.[134]

The Aziz Report recommended the introduction of legislation which would prevent further subdivision, and oblige all estate owners to maintain all amenities, and where these had been run down preparatory to sale, to adopt a programme of rehabilitation.[135] However, the government was quick to set aside the cogent evidence provided by the committee, and to seize upon a minority report which stated that fragmentation represented the operations of the forces of private enterprise, and should be permitted to continue without government interference.[136]

Although over these years both the MIC and NUPW made numerous entreaties to the government to halt fragmentation, it was not until 1969 that the government heeded these appeals.[137] In the interim it is estimated that more than 50,000, mainly Tamil, workers were affected by the subdivision of estates.[138] The hereditary occupations of many were lost, and those who managed to secure employment in the fragmented properties endured substandard working and living conditions.[139] Profits were maximized at the expense of the basic requirements of the workforce, recreational facilities were non-existent, and labour laws were poorly enforced.[140] The inability of the MIC to effect changes on the policy of fragmentation — an issue which reflected the most basic interests of its core constituency — exposed the weakness of the party within the overall Alliance structure.[141]

National Land and Finance Cooperative Society

Frustrated by the government's refusal to look beyond the interests of capital to the plight of dispossessed workers, the MIC, under the leadership of President V.T. Sambanthan, responded to the fragmentation by forming the cooperative movement. The National Land Finance Cooperative Society Ltd. (NLFCS) was founded in May 1960.[142] The cooperative aimed to contribute to the alleviation of the problems of landlessness and unemployment among plantation workers. This would be achieved by using the funds generated by those subscribing to the cooperative movement to purchase rubber estates which would be then run by the NLFCS.[143] Plantation workers were exhorted to join and purchase shares in the cooperative.[144] Shares were priced at $100 which workers could pay off at $10 per month. The immediate appeal of the NLFCS was obvious, and by August 1961, the cooperative boasted a membership of 15,000 and had raised over $1 million capital. The NLFCS purchased its first estate the same month. Although the NUPW viewed Sambanthan, and the cooperative more generally, as a threat to its own control of the plantation workforce, and poured scorn on both, the expansion of the NLFCS appeared unstoppable. By 1967 membership stood at 54,000 and the NLFCS controlled twelve estates totalling more than 30,000 acres.[145] By 1980 the cooperative owned 12,400 hectares of land and membership had reached 60,000.[146] Its assets in 1985 were estimated at close to RM350 million. The NLFCS remains the largest enterprise owned by Malaysian Indians.[147]

The Citizenship Crisis

In 1969, following the racial riots of 13 May, and the imposition of emergency rule, the NOC announced that all employment, whether in the public or private sectors, would be restricted to Malaysian citizens.[148] Many Indians, including about twenty per cent of the plantation workforce, were affected by this measure. Up to 10,000 Indian labourers (and their dependents) made application to the Indian Labour Fund, which had been directed by the government to offer cash inducements and a free passage to those prepared to accept "repatriation" to India. By December 1969, shipping agents had reported the receipt of 60,000 one-way bookings to Madras. However, this mass exit was forestalled by a combination of a severe labour shortfall within the plantation sector, and the Malaysian Agricultural Producer's Association (MAPA)[149] threat to shut down the entire estate sector if the government did not rescind the measure.[150] This resulted in a government agreement to the granting of temporary employment permits.[151] The rubber industry was a vital sector of the

Malaysian economy and the government was unable to ignore the demands of the MAPA.[152] Of the 140,000 applicants for special work permits, 59,000 were from Indian plantation workers.[153]

The citizenship crisis of 1969 was a largely avoidable development which represented the manifest failure of both Indian political and industrial leadership. Upon independence in 1957, the Malayan Constitution offered citizenship on three bases, namely (1) citizenship by operation of law, or the principle of *jus soli*, (2) citizenship by registration, and (3) citizenship by naturalization.[154] Most Indian plantation workers who faced problems in acquiring citizenship were those who had applied through the processes of naturalization and registration. While the vast majority of these workers were eligible to obtain citizenship, many remained ignorant of the relevant legislation, especially of the rights and privileges bestowed upon the holders of Malaysian citizenship. The procedures in acquiring citizenship were unnecessarily cumbersome, convoluted, time consuming and confusing, especially to those such as estate workers who were often illiterate or poorly educated. Moreover, the processes often involved several visits to relevant government offices over a period of months or even years. Each day spent in an office, rather than at work, entailed a loss of income. As a result many labourers did not bother to apply for citizenship. Selvakumaran Ramachandran contends that the MIC should have pursued the matter much more vigorously, especially among the workers themselves. He claims that "The leaders did not effectively take up the issue in Parliament, encourage the workers to take up citizenship, nor use the party machinery to help poor workers or warn them that fence-sitting could be a dangerous practice in determining their status in the country."[155] As a result by 1969, while about eighty per cent of the Indians in Malaysia had taken up citizenship, the remaining twenty per cent (largely from the plantations), effectively remained "non-citizens" despite the fact that all of them had the residential qualifications necessary to become citizens.[156]

The NUPW had also seriously failed its members on the issue of citizenship. The union had not conducted campaigns to highlight the importance of securing Malaysian citizenship, nor had it assisted individual members with claims. As a result NUPW members who were designated non-citizens were obliged to secure employment permits, and were relegated to the most menial and casual jobs within the labour market.[157]

The citizenship crisis erupted at the very point when the MIC was least capable of offering a decisive response. Between 1969 and 1973 the party was increasingly paralyzed by a prolonged and increasingly personalized leadership crisis. From 1969 onwards opposition to the leadership of V.T. Sambanthan increased, and centred upon the English-educated professional wing of the party, led by Datuk Athi Nahappan, a Cabinet Minister in the administrations of both Tunku Abdul Rahman and Tun Abdul Razak.[158] The MIC was plunged into a bitter and intemperate internecine conflict which revolved around well-defined factions led by Sambanthan and his deputy, Tan Sri V. Manickavasagam. Party meetings became heated affairs, with invective sometimes exploding into violence. Large numbers of party members were expelled, and no new members were recruited.[159] These developments were noted within UMNO and in January 1971 Tun (Dr) Ismail suggested that UMNO should sever its links with both the MIC and MCA should these parties continue to be "neither dead nor alive".[160] The stasis within the party was finally broken in March 1972 with the personal intervention of Tun Abdul Razak, an embarrassing development which suggested that the MIC, and by implication the wider Indian community which it represented, was incapable of managing its own affairs. In the compromise negotiated by Razak, Sambanthan agreed to retain the leadership no longer than the MIC General Assembly scheduled for 30 June 1973.[161] He was duly succeeded by Manickavasagam who made attempts to end the ructions within the MIC.[162] The party had sufficiently revived by 1974 to deliver the Indian vote to the BN in the election held that year.[163]

The National Union of Plantation Workers 1957–69

Throughout the period 1957–69 most plantation workers continued to be represented by the NUPW. Although the union won some pay increases and other concessions throughout this period, these were barely sufficient to keep pace with rises in the basic cost of living. In 1969 estate labour remained among the most exploited and underpaid sectors of the economy.[164]

In November 1957, in the wake of increasing tension upon estates, overtly manifested in an escalating incidence of unauthorized strikes, the NUPW requested consultations with the MPIEA to resolve anomalies in wages paid to rubber tappers and field workers. A formal memorandum was submitted to the MPIEA on 13 January 1958. After more than a year of inconclusive discussions and MPIEA procrastination, the NUPW sought the intervention of the Minister of Labour. On 7 February 1959, a new agreement provided a guaranteed daily wage for rubber tappers, but this was not extended to field workers.[165] In 1962 a further settlement offered slightly increased wages, with sixteen days of holiday leave. However, important concessions were delivered on conditions of service. Hospital benefits were increased and sick leave was extended. In 1964 further wage increases were delivered and annual leave was increased to nineteen days per year.[166]

During this period the NUPW's monopoly on representational rights over plantation workers was challenged by the formation of two rival unions, both of which were ultimately deregistered by the government.

Malayan Estate Workers Union

This union had its genesis in disputes within the Sungei Gadut division of the Seremban Estate. On 16 March 1960, disputes on the estate led to dismissals among the workforce and the deployment of blackleg labour. A violent clash between the regular workforce and imported strike-breakers provoked police intervention as well as further dismissals and evictions. The NUPW's attempts at mediation were ineffective and its intervention was ultimately limited to publicity and the provision of financial assistance. The union's seemingly flaccid, and in the eyes of the workers, disappointing response to the management actions led to the creation in 1961 of the Malayan Estate Workers' Union (MEWU). The union aimed not only to represent the workers at Sungei Gadut, but to expand to agricultural workers in other estates and to cover labour other than those involved in rubber plantations. The MEWU was formally registered on 6 January with its headquarters in Seremban. The union was subsequently deregistered later that year.[167]

United Malayan Estate Workers' Union

Following the MEWU's deregistration, members approached the recently appointed Minister of Labour, V.T. Sambanthan, with the aim of forming a new union. The United Malayan Estate Workers Union (UMEWU) was registered on 19 April 1961. However, the union faced a number of major hurdles including lack of recognition by the peak plantation owners' associations, especially the powerful MPIEA which preferred to deal with the NUPW. In addition it lacked the funds necessary to employ fulltime field workers. As a consequence of these setbacks the union requested V. David, a member of the left-wing Labour Party and General Secretary of the Transport Workers' Union to direct UMEWU affairs. However, the union increasingly fell under the control of left-wing elements and met with a marked lack of cooperation from both employers and government officials.[168]

The Bukit Asahan Incident

NUPW inaction in the face of retrenchment at Bukit Asahan Estate, Melaka, in 1965, led to UMEWU involvement. The union gained the confidence of the estate workers, including the Chinese and Malays, and by 1966 represented eighty per cent of the Estate workforce. However, the management refused to negotiate with the union, claiming that in Malaysia-wide terms the UMEWU did not represent the majority of Guthrie employees.[169] After political intervention failed to resolve the impasse, the union began a general strike on 25 February 1967. The involvement of left-wing political figures in the dispute alarmed the government. On 26 March 1967 the Federal Reserve Unit (FRU) was deployed, and twenty-eight workers were subsequently arrested. On 8 April 1967 the union was deregistered.[170] In response the union planned a protest march to Kuala Lumpur, which would proceed via Malacca, Tampin, Seremban and Kajang. The march commenced on 14 April, and after an incident-packed journey, during which the protestors were assaulted with tear gas, and fourteen of their members were arrested, the unionists reached Kuala Lumpur on 20 April. On 24 April, after protests in the capital, during which they were joined by members of the Labour Party and Partai Raayat, Tunku Abdul Rahman agreed to meet the workers' representatives. The matter was subsequently referred to Manickavasagam, the Minister for Labour who subsequently met with Guthries' management on 5 May 1967. The ultimate outcome of this rather epic action was that Guthries agreed to re-employ all of the workers the company had originally retrenched.[171]

The UMEWU action was to result in the detention under the ISA of a considerable number of Labour Party and union activists. The union's deregistration had also left the more pliant NUPW as the sole union representing plantation labour.[172] In 1967 the Alliance government, which was noticeably unsympathetic to the claims of organized labour, introduced the Industrial Relations Act, which aimed to regulate the relationship between employers and unions. Under the provisions of this act, unresolved claims would be settled by compulsory arbitration within the newly formed Industrial Court.[173] Additional revisions in 1967 and 1969 to the Trade Union Ordinance further restricted the scope of legitimate union activism.[174]

CONCLUSIONS

Following Merdeka the government continued the economic and social policies of the colonial era. Malaya remained dependent upon a commodity-based economy which was largely British owned and managed.

The formation of Malaysia was undertaken with the primary objective of containing and neutralizing the potentially destabilising influence of Singapore. UMNO aimed to nullify the political impact of the large Chinese population in Singapore. This was achieved, *inter alia*, by under-representing the island state in the Federal Parliament, while attaining an indigenous majority for the nation by granting the "natives" of Sabah and Sarawak the status of bumiputeras.

From the outset the relationship between Singapore and Peninsular Malaysia was fraught. Singapore's robust non-communalism conflicted with UMNO's attempts to secure the allegiance of Singapore's Malay community and a concomitant campaign to destabilise the government of Lee Kuan Yew. Following an outbreak of racial riots in Singapore in July 1964, Lee launched his proposal for a "Malaysian Malaysia", an approach to the resolution of the structural and societal problems which eschewed the primal politics of communalism. This raised omnipresent Malay fears of Chinese domination and ultimately led to the expulsion of Singapore.

The detachment of Singapore on 9 August 1965 did little to halt escalating ethnic tensions within Peninsular Malaysia. During the period leading to the 1969 elections, the Alliance lost considerable support. The ethnic divide was starkly illustrated throughout an election campaign noted for its bitterness and the fierce and intemperate racial polemics. The election resulted in significant Alliance losses and was followed by the staging of ill-advised opposition victory parades and unwise racial taunts. A counter-demonstration, organized by UMNO Youth, and containing known agitators intent on instigating inter-ethnic violence, resulted in major riots targeting both the Chinese and Indian communities.

The rising UMNO leadership deployed the 13 May incident to profoundly reshape Malaysian political discourse and to enshrine Malay political primacy, which was now placed beyond challenge or even debate. Constitutional changes were underpinned by a raft of political and economic reforms, the most crucial of which was the NEP. This was originally viewed as a strictly temporary measure which would fulfil two objectives, namely the elimination of identification of occupational function with ethnicity, and the eradication of poverty, regardless of "race". The NEP was complemented by a Malay-centric national cultural policy which privileged "indigenous" culture and Islam as the fundamental cornerstones of a future unified Malaysian culture. Politically the Alliance was replaced with an expanded coalition which incorporated several former opposition parties, and thus, in theory, broadened the context in which government policy was formulated. The new coalition, Barisan Nasional, was dominated by UMNO and became increasingly authoritarian and intolerant of opposition.

Indians entered Merdeka as the smallest ethnic community, over-represented in unemployment, under-represented at all levels of educational attainment, and overshadowed respectively by Malay political dominance and Chinese economic power.

Throughout the years leading to the 1969 elections, both the MIC and the NUPW achieved little for the Indian community. Because the MIC was dependent upon UMNO patronage, it was unable to advance the measures that would have been necessary to uplift either the Indian estate sector or the Indian urban working classes. Similarly, the NUPW's rather circumspect leadership failed to gain significant wage increases or improved working conditions for its membership. The potential muscle of Indian labour had been largely truncated by the stumbling hesitancy of its own leadership, together with the repressive anti-union legislation enacted by the colonial administration and later reinforced by the Malaysian government.

Both political and industrial wings were to fail Indian workers in the two greatest crises in this period; namely, fragmentation of estates and the post 13 May citizenship issue. The MIC's inability to influence its coalition partners to halt fragmentation, a matter vital to its own constituency, revealed its general weakness within the overall Alliance structure. Fragmentation proceeded unimpeded until 1969 despite the findings of the government-commissioned 1963 Aziz Report which unequivocally condemned the practice.

The post 13 May citizenship crisis reflected badly upon both the MIC and NUPW, neither of which had been sufficiently diligent in assisting eligible workers to take out citizenship or warning them of the risks inherent in failure to do so. At the time the government announced measures to "repatriate" Indians, the MIC was convulsed by a bitter leadership dispute and was hamstrung in its ability to respond. Ultimately it was left to the estate management rather than any Indian agency to defuse the threat of mass deportations.

However, throughout this rather bleak period there was one encouraging development. In responding to the gathering pace of fragmentation, MIC President, V.T. Sambanthan, formed the National Land and Finance Cooperative Society which purchased estates on behalf of its membership. Overcoming determined NUPW opposition, the NLFCS's continuing success serves as a pointer to the Indian community of what might be achieved for its membership by a well-managed cooperative.

Notes

1. Sheila Nair, "Colonialism, Nationalism, Ethnicity: Constructing Identity and Difference", in *Multiethnic Malaysia: Past, Present and Future*, edited by Lim Teck Ghee, Alberto Gomes, and Azly Rahman (Petaling Jaya: Strategic Information Research Centre, 2009), p. 89.
2. Cheah Boon Kheng, *Malaysia: The Making of a Nation* (Singapore: Institute of Southeast Asian Studies, 2002), p. 111.
3. Cheah, *Malaysia*, p. 90; Ooi Kee Beng, *The Reluctant Politician: Dr Ismail and His Time* (Singapore: Institute of Southeast Asian Studies, 2006), p. 127.
4. R.S. Milne and Diane K. Mauzy, *Politics and Government in Malaysia* (Singapore: Federal, 1978), p. 54.
5. Tan Tai Yong, *Creating "Greater Malaysia": Decolonization and The Politics of Merger* (Singapore: Institute of Southeast Asian Studies, 2008), pp. 23–24.
6. Patrick Keith, *Ousted!* (Singapore: Media Masters, 2005), p. 20; Kah Seng Loh et al., *The University Socialist Club and the Contest for Malaya: Tangled Strands of Modernity* (Amsterdam: Amsterdam University Press, 2012), p. 168.
7. James Mackie, "The Formation of Malaysia (1961–63) and 'Konfrontasi' (1963–66): The Role of the Malaysian Communist Party and other Leftist Forces", in *Dialogues with Chin Peng: New Light on the Malayan Communist Party*, edited by C.C. Chin and Karl Hack (Singapore: Singapore University Press, 2004), p. 318.
8. Tan, *Creating "Greater Malaysia"*, pp. 23–24.
9. Kah et al., *The University Socialist Club*, p. 162; Milne and Mauzy, *Politics and Government in Malaysia*, p. 54.
10. Kah et al., *The University Socialist Club*, pp. 260–61.

11. Tan, *Creating "Greater Malaysia"*, p. 83.
12. Lee Kuan Yew, *The Singapore Story: Memoirs of Lee Kuan Yew* (Singapore: Prentice Hall, 1998), p. 407.
13. Milne and Mauzy, *Politics and Government in Malaysia*, pp. 64–65.
14. Lee, *The Singapore Story*, pp. 406–7.
15. Wong Chin-Huat, James Chin and Noraini Othman, "Malaysia: Towards a Topology of an Electoral One-Party State", *Democratization* 17, no. 5 (2010): 931.
16. Tan, *Creating "Greater Malaysia"*, p. 142.
17. Ibid., p. 189.
18. Ooi, *The Reluctant Politician*, p. 142.
19. Ibid.; Milne and Mauzy, *Politics and Government in Malaysia*, p. 298.
20. Maznah Mohamad, "Politics of the NEP and Ethnic Relations in Malaysia", in *Multiethnic Malaysia: Past, Present and Future*, edited by Lim Teck Ghee, Alberto Gomes, and Azly Rahman (Petaling Jaya: Strategic Information and Research Development Centre, 2009), pp. 123–24.
21. Milne and Mauzy, *Politics and Government in Malaysia*, p. 61.
22. Mackie, *The Formation of Malaysia*, p. 318.
23. Kah et al., *The University Socialist Club*, p. 38; Milne and Mauzy, *Politics and Government in Malaysia*, p. 71.
24. Felix V. Gagliano, *Communal Violence in Malaysia 1969: The Political Aftermath* (Ohio: Ohio University Center for International Studies, Southeast Asia Project, 1970), p. 16.
25. John Funston, *Malay Politics in Malaysia: A Study of UMNO and PAS* (Kuala Lumpur: Heinemann Educational Books (Asia), 1980), pp. 67–68.
26. Ooi, *The Reluctant Politician*, p. 144.
27. Lee, *The Singapore Story*, p. 508.
28. Ibid., pp. 551–57.
29. Tan, *Creating "Greater Malaysia"*, p. 195.
30. Cheah, *Malaysia*, p. 99.
31. Keith, *Ousted!*, p. 92.
32. Cheah, *Malaysia*, p. 99.
33. Keith, *Ousted!*, p. 103.
34. Ibid., p. 58.
35. Lee, *The Singapore Story*, p. 562.
36. Ibid.
37. Cheah, *Malaysia*, p. 101.
38. Lee, *The Singapore Story*, p. 606.
39. Tan, *Creating "Greater Malaysia"*, p. 195.
40. Ibid.; Milne and Mauzy, *Politics and Government in Malaysia*, p. 72.
41. Cheah, *Malaysia*, p. 101.

42. Tan, *Creating "Greater Malaysia"*, p. 196.
43. Tunku Abdul Rahman Putra Al-Haj, *Looking Back: The Historic Years of Malaya and Malaysia* (Kuala Lumpur: Pustaka Antara, 1977), p. 120.
44. Keith, *Ousted!*, p. 187.
45. Ibid.
46. Milne and Mauzy, *Politics and Government in Malaysia*, p. 75; Keith, *Ousted!*, pp. 190–92.
47. Tunku Abdul Rahman, *Looking Back*, p. 80.
48. Heng Pek Koon, *Chinese Politics in Malaysia: A History of the Malaysian Chinese Association* (Singapore: Oxford University Press, 1988), p. 259.
49. R.K. Vasil, *Ethnic Politics in Malaysia* (New Delhi: Radiant, 1980), pp. 210–12.
50. Cheah, *Malaysia*, p. 87.
51. Kua Kia Soong, *May 13: Declassified Documents on the Malayan Riots in 1969* (Petaling Jaya: Suaram Komunikasi, 2007), p. 28.
52. Geoff Wade, *The Origins and Evolution of Ethnocracy in Malaysia*, Working Paper Series No. 12 (Singapore: Asia Research Institute, National University of Singapore) p. 19.
53. Funston, *Malay Politics*, pp. 2–3.
54. Milne and Mauzy, *Politics and Government in Malaysia*, p. 323.
55. Funston, *Malay Politics*, pp. 62–63. Professor Shamsul A.B. points out that the failure of UMNO's rural development policy was largely due to the continuation of colonial policies designed to encourage Malay landholders to grow food crops and to eschew cash crops. According to this perspective rubber was viewed as an "alien and capitalistic venture", and the government aimed to wean Malay smallholders off their "dependency" on rubber. This reflected the government's commitment to achieve self-sufficiency in food. This colonialist approach was reinforced by the class bias of the UMNO elite, which viewed rice cultivation as representing the "true" Malay traditional Kampung life (Shamsul A.B., *From British to Bumiputera Rule: Local Politics and Rural Development in Peninsular Malaysia* (Singapore: Institute of Southeast Asian Studies, 2004), pp. 85–86).
56. Ragayah Haji Mat Zin, "Affirmative Action and Poverty Eradication in Malaysia", in *The New Economic Policy in Malaysia: Affirmative Action, Ethnic Inequalities and Social Justice*, edited by Edmund Terence Gomez and Johan Saravanamuttu (Singapore and Kuala Lumpur: NUS Press, Institute of Southeast Asian Studies and Strategic Information and Research Development Centre, 2013), p. 39.
57. Gagliano, *Communal Violence in Malaysia*, pp. 7–8.
58. Kua, *May 13*, p. 27.
59. Gagliano, *Communal Violence in Malaysia*, p. 12.

60. Raj K. Vasil, *Tan Chee Khoon: An Elder Statesman* (Petaling Jaya: Pelanduk, 1987), p. 110.

61. Gagliano, *Communal Violence in Malaysia*, p. 12.

62. Ibid., p. 14; Bob Reece, "Requiem for a Democracy?", *Far Eastern Economic Review* 64, no. 21 (22 May 1969): 438.

63. Funston, *Malay Politics*, pp. 208–9. However, *Far Eastern Economic Review* journalist Bob Reece claims that while there were "occasional" Chinese flags in the 14,000 strong procession, the demonstration was disciplined and showed restraint ("Requiem for a Democracy?", p. 438).

64. Cheah, *Malaysia*, p. 105; Ahmad Mustapha Hassan, *The Unmaking of Malaysia: Insider's Reminscences of UMNO, Razak and Mahathir* (Petaling Jaya: Strategic Information and Research Development Centre, 2007), p. 24.

65. Gagliano, *Communal Violence in Malaysia*, p. 12.

66. Ahmad Mustapha, *The Unmaking of Malaysia*, p. 27.

67. Goh Cheng Tiek, *The May 13th Incident and Democracy in Malaysia* (Kuala Lumpur: Oxford University Press, 1971), pp. 20–24.

68. Ibid., p. 24.

69. Gagliano, *Communal Violence in Malaysia*, p. 15.

70. William Shaw, *Tun Abdul Razak: His Life and Times* (Kuala Lumpur: Longman Malaysia, 1976), p. 207.

71. Goh, *The May 13th Incident*, p. 22.

72. Gagliano, *Communal Violence in Malaysia*, p. 15.

73. Cheah, *Malaysia*, p. 106.

74. Gagliano, *Communal Violence in Malaysia*, p. 15.

75. Shaw, *Tun Razak*, pp. 206–7.

76. Ahmad Mustapha, *The Unmaking of Malaysia*, p. 31. During the course of my duties with the Australian High Commission (1976–1979), a number of non-Malays advised me that during the day preceding the riots they were warned by Malay friends, neighbours, associates and students that certain groups had planned violent racial confrontation, and that the major thoroughfares of central Kuala Lumpur should be avoided.

77. Goh, *The May 13th Incident*, p. 22; Gagliano, *Communal Violence in Malaysia*, p. 16; Ooi, *The Reluctant Politician*, pp. 189–90.

78. Gagliano, *Communal Violence in Malaysia*, p. 16.

79. The number of fatalities is certainly a gross underestimate. During the course of my duties in Malaysia between 1976 and 1979 I was informed by authoritative figures that the number killed throughout the riots was approximately one thousand people, many of whom were later interred in unmarked mass graves.

80. Kua, *May 13*, p. 9.

81. Ibid., pp. 45, 53, 64; Ooi, *The Reluctant Politician*, p. 198.

82. Gagliano, *Communal Violence in Malaysia*, p. 19.

83. Ooi, *The Reluctant Politician*, p. 202.

84. Ibid., p. 204.

85. Bob Reece, "Pigs and Goats", *Far Eastern Economic Review* 65, no. 28 (10 July 1969): 116.

86. Senior Malaysian officials, discussing this incident with the writer in 1977–78, suggested that Malaysia would not survive another 13 May, at least not as a functioning multi-ethnic democracy.

87. Milne and Mauzy, *Politics and Government in Malaysia*, p. 81. Scholars have pointed out that while the control (and wealth) of the Malaysian economy largely lay in foreign (primarily British) hands, at a localized market level, transactions within Malaysia were often interpreted in terms of Chinese exploitation of poorer Malays. Thus James Puthucheary observed "about 70 per cent of Malays are engaged in subsistence activities, and are brought into the ambit of the market economies by the activities … of the Chinese traders. To the two or three million [Malay] people involved, British capital does not constitute the exploiting group. To them, the Chinese are the exploiters." (Kah et al., *The University Socialist Club*, p. 181).

88. Cheah, *Malaysia*, pp. 126–27; Ooi, *The Reluctant Politician*, p. 200; Milne and Mauzy, *Politics and Government in Malaysia*, pp. 81–82.

89. Ooi, *The Reluctant Politician*, p. 205.

90. Gagliano, *Communal Violence in Malaysia*, pp. 23–24.

91. Cheah, *Malaysia*, p. 138; Shaw, *Tun Razak*, p. 216.

92. Francis Loh Kok Wah, *Beyond the Tin Mines: Coolies, Squatters and New Villagers in the Kinta Valley, Malaysia c.1880–1980* (Singapore: Oxford University Press, 1988), p. 237; Maznah, *Politics of the NEP*, p. 115.

93. Milne and Mauzy, *Politics and Government in Malaysia*, p. 93.

94. Shaw, *Tun Razak*, pp. 220–21.

95. Rehman Rashid, *A Malaysian Journey* (Petaling Jaya: Rehman Rashid, 1993), p. 97.

96. Milne and Mauzy, *Politics and Government in Malaysia*, p. 322.

97. Ibid., pp. 339–40.

98. Ooi, *The Reluctant Politician*, pp. 215–17.

99. Milne and Mauzy, *Politics and Government in Malaysia*, pp. 95–97.

100. Lim Teck Ghee and Alberto Gomes, "Culture and Development in Malaysia", in *Multiethnic Malaysia: Past Present and Future*, edited by Lim Teck Ghee, Alberto Gomes, and Azly Rahman (Petaling Jaya: Strategic Information and Research Development Centre, 2009), pp. 233–34.

101. Joel S. Kahn and Francis Loh Kok Wah, "Introduction", in *Fragmented Vision: Culture and Politics in Contemporary Malaysia*, edited by Joel S. Kahn and Francis Loh Kok Wah (Sydney: Asian Studies Association of Australia/ Allen and Unwin, 1992), p. 13.

102. Funston, *Malay Politics*, p. 238.

103. Alberto Gomes, "Superlative Syndrome, Cultural Politics and Neoliberalism in Malaysia", in *Multiethnic Malaysia: Past, Present and Future*, edited by Lim Teck Ghee, Alberto Gomes, and Azly Rahman (Petaling Jaya: Strategic Information and Research Development Centre, 2009), p. 192.

104. Cheah, *Malaysia*, p. 13.

105. Ibid., p. 123.

106. Gagliano, *Communal Violence in Malaysia*, p. 29.

107. Heng, *Chinese Politics*, pp. 225–28.

108. On 27 June 1971 PMIP had changed its name from Persatuan Islam Se-Tanah Melayu to Partai Islam Se Malaysia (PAS).

109. Ahmad Mustapha, *The Unmaking of Malaysia*, p. 40.

110. Cheah, *Malaysia*, p. 147.

111. Ibid., p. 138.

112. Vasil, *Tan Chee Khoon*, p. 167.

113. Loh, *Beyond the Tin Mines*, p. 237.

114. Heng, *Chinese Politics*, p. 261.

115. Chandra Muzaffar, "Political Marginalization in Malaysia", in *Indian Communities in Southeast Asia*, edited by K.S. Sandhu and A. Mani (Singapore: Institute of Southeast Asian Studies, 1993), p. 212.

116. Sinnappah Arasaratnam, *Indians in Malaysia and Singapore* (London: Oxford University Press, 1970), p. 42.

117. Funston, *Malay Politics*, p. 22.

118. Ragayan, "The New Economic Policy", p. 39.

119. Rajeswary Amplavanar-Brown, "The Contemporary Indian Political Elite in Malaysia", in *Indian Communities in Southeast Asia*, edited by K.S. Sandhu and A. Mani (Singapore: Institute of Southeast Asian Studies, 1993), p. 239; Janakey Raman Manickam, *The Malaysian Indian Dilemma: The Struggle and Agony of the Indian Community in Malaysia*, 2nd ed. (Klang: Janakey Raman Manickam, 2010), p. 132.

120. Selvakumaran Ramachandran, *Indian Plantation Labour in Malaysia* (Kuala Lumpur: S. Abdul Majeed, 1994), pp. 322–23.

121. Muzafar Desmond Tate, *The Malaysian Indians: History, Problems and Future* (Petaling Jaya: Strategic Information Research Centre, 2008), p. 114.

122. Michael R. Stenson, *Class, Race and Colonialism in West Malaysia: The Indian Case* (St. Lucia: University of Queensland Press, 1980), pp. 199–202.

123. Rajeswary, "The Contemporary Indian Political Elite", p. 237.

124. Janakey, *The Malaysian Indian Dilemma*, p. 183.

125. Rajeswary, "The Contemporary Indian Political Elite", p. 237; Tate, *The Malaysian Indians*, pp. 111–12.

126. P. Ramasamy, *Plantation Labour: Unions, Capital and the State in Peninsular Malaysia* (New York: Oxford University Press, 1994), p. 107.

127. Stenson, *Class, Race and Colonialism*, p. 203.
128. Ramasamy, *Plantation Labour*, p. 107.
129. Paul W. Wiebe and S. Mariappen, *Indian Malaysians: The View from the Plantation* (Delhi: Manohar, 1978), p. 38. This information was supplemented by sometimes graphic evidence gleaned from interviews with former estate workers and (now retired) Malaysian social workers.
130. Arasaratnam, *Indians in Malaysia and Singapore*, p. 154.
131. Selvakumaran, *Indian Plantation Labour*, p. 305.
132. Tate, *The Malaysian Indians*, p. 119.
133. Selvakumaran, *Indian Plantation Labour*, p. 305.
134. Ramasamy, *Plantation Labour*, p. 107.
135. Arasaratnam, *Indians in Malaysia and Singapore*, p. 155.
136. Ibid., p. 157.
137. Ramasamy, *Plantation Labour*, p. 107.
138. Stenson, *Class, Race and Colonialism*, p. 197.
139. Wiebe and Mariappen, *Indian Malaysians*, p. 38.
140. Ibid.
141. Muzaffar, *Political Marginalization*, p. 222.
142. Arasaratnam, *Indians in Malaysia and Singapore*, p. 158.
143. Ibid., p. 158.
144. Selvakumaran, *Indian Plantation Labour*, p. 306.
145. Ramasamy, *Plantation Labour*, p. 108.
146. Rajeswary, "The Contemporary Indian Political Elite", p. 240.
147. Information gathered from interviews conducted in 2010 and 2011.
148. Selvakumaran, *Indian Plantation Labour*, p. 274.
149. The MPIEA was restructured as the Malaysian Agricultural Producer's Association (MAPA) in 1966 (Selvakumaran, *Indian Plantation Labour*, p. 272).
150. Tate, *The Malaysian Indians*, p. 128.
151. Ibid.
152. Ibid., p. 304.
153. Estimates of the number of Indians who were actually "repatriated" remain vague. However, Stenson asserts that 60,000 Indians journeyed to India in a state of "fear and uncertainty" (Stenson, *Class, Race and Colonialism*, p. 206).
154. Selvakumaran, *Indian Plantation Labour*, p. 302.
155. Ibid., p. 303.
156. Ibid., p. 303–4.
157. Ibid., p. 274.
158. Rajeswary, "The Contemporary Indian Political Elite", p. 243.
159. Funston, *Malay Politics*, p. 243.
160. Milne and Mauzy, *Politics and Government in Malaysia*, p. 175.

161. Rajeswary, "The Contemporary Indian Political Elite", p. 243.
162. Milne and Mauzy, *Politics and Government in Malaysia*, p. 194.
163. Funston, *Malay Politics*, p. 274.
164. Ramasamy, *Plantation Labour*, p. 138.
165. Ibid., p. 103.
166. Ibid., pp. 103–5.
167. Ibid., pp. 110–16.
168. Ibid., pp. 116–23.
169. Ibid., pp. 124–25.
170. Ibid., p. 129.
171. Ibid., pp. 129–33.
172. Ibid. p. 135.
173. Ibid., p. 166.
174. Stenson, *Class, Race and Colonialism*, pp. 199–202.

14

THE MAHATHIR YEARS
A Changing Malaysian Landscape

In 1976 Tun Abdul Razak, the architect and overseer of much of the NEP, died in office. He was succeeded by Datuk Hussein Onn who had entered Tun Abdul Razak's first Cabinet as Minister of Education in September 1970.[1] Datuk Hussein Onn's premiership was seen as an interregnum, a stewardship. In general, Hussein continued Razak's policies.[2] Although PAS left the BN coalition in 1977, Hussein led BN to a comprehensive victory in the 1978 elections.[3]

On his accession to the premiership, Hussein appointed Dr Mahathir Mohamad as his Deputy. Given Mahathir's chequered background, the appointment was considered controversial.[4] Following the release of his infamous "open letter" to the Tunku in 1969, which explicitly imputed responsibility for the deaths of those slain in the mob violence of 13 May to the Tunku's leadership,[5] Mahathir had been expelled from UMNO. He had subsequently returned to his medical practice in Alor Setar, where he wrote the book *The Malay Dilemma*, a work regarded as so contentious that it remained banned in Malaysia until after Mahathir's accession to the Prime Ministership.[6] Mahathir was re-admitted to UMNO in 1972, and was allocated the Education portfolio under Tun Abdul Razak.[7] Upon Hussein's retirement on 16 July 1981, Mahathir assumed the Prime Ministership.[8]

Mahathir came to office with a mission to transform Malaysia into a sophisticated, developed and respected nation, with Malays playing a dominant role.[9] His earliest political manifesto and guiding template for political action is established within *The Malay Dilemma*. This insists, *inter alia*, that the Malays comprise the founding and definitive "race" within Malaysia, and thus form the normative basis for Malaysian culture to which other "races" must acculturate themselves.[10] Mahathir's analysis of the Malay character and capabilities consist of a series of broad, superficial and occasionally contradictory generalizations which collectively place Malays at an intrinsic disadvantage in their quest to achieve economic and intellectual parity with other "races".[11]

These views consolidated a nationalist narrative which had been bequeathed by, and had continued unbroken from, the racial ideologies of British colonialism, and which had been largely accepted by the UMNO leadership.[12] In 1971, UMNO had published *Revolusi Mental* (Mental Revolution), which portrayed Malays in a completely negative light; as people who lacked the courage to face the truth, and as a "race" weakened by the qualities of fatalism and irrationality.[13] *The Malay Dilemma* inculcated this Social Darwinist narrative, a discourse which identified Malays as a race of ancient kampung dwellers, and small farmers; rather timid and unsophisticated rustics, circumscribed by their history, environment and genetics, and rendered incapable of resisting, let alone competing with the more vigorous and predatory Chinese.[14]

Dr Mahathir remained in office for more than twenty-two years, making him the longest serving Malaysian Prime Minister. He was also the most provocative and controversial. As both a Malay and, more generally, a Malaysian nationalist, Mahathir's strategies were directed towards crafting a "carefully managed revolution",[15] which would transform the Malay *Weltanschauung*, resulting in the production of the *Melayu Baru* (new Malay), confident, vigorous and assertive, and capable of competing and indeed thriving in the new world. The arrival of the *Melayu Baru* would herald a harmonious and innovative Malaysia which had outgrown memories of its colonial origins and the racial tensions and divided loyalties which had blighted its history.[16] All Mahathir's policies — the "Look East" policy launched in 1981, the programme of heavy industry and privatization (both initiated in 1983), the Wawasan 2020 (Vision 2020) policy enunciated in 1991, the *Malaysia Boleh!* (Malaysia Can Do It!) exhortations — represented far-reaching attempts to construct the foundations of a truly postcolonial, modernist, and unified Malaysian nation, one in which Malay achievement and inter-ethnic cooperation would be accepted facts of life.[17] Mahathir also embarked upon a series of prestigious mega-projects — for example, the Formula One Racing Circuit, the KLCC Twin Towers, the ambitious new capital Putra Jaya — not only to engender a sense of national consciousness and pride in Malaysian achievement, but also to instil Malay confidence, and as an expression of a new counter-colonial ideology, the overcoming of the residual interiority of colonialism.[18]

While Mahathir oversighted years of extensive structural and social change, and initiated sweeping proposals for reform and nation building, in many respects the net effect of his rule was the entrenchment of trends and tendencies which had had their origins in colonial Malaya and which were greatly accelerated following the adoption of the NEP. These trends included increasing authoritarianism, justified by a discourse emphasizing the very survival of the Malay people and by extension the Malaysian nation, and the growth of officially tolerated corruption, especially money politics, patronage, and cronyism. The post-NEP years also witnessed a stasis, even deterioration in ethnic relations. In the following paragraphs I will touch upon each of these topics.

Authoritarianism

Mahathir was the most single-minded of Malaysia's Prime Ministers. He demonstrated little respect for the basic institutions of a democratic society, and demanded total and unconditional loyalty from his parliamentary colleagues and from the bureaucracy.[19] Mahathir's style was often dogmatic and combative, and brooked no criticism or contradiction. Aided by a complaisant media, almost wholly affiliated to the ruling coalition,[20] an expanded state regulatory apparatus created to enforce the implementation of the NEP,[21] and an armoury of repressive legislation, Mahathir took steps to silence critics and to steadily concentrate power in the Executive. In the process he confronted and curbed alternative sites of authority — the bureaucracy, legislature, judiciary and monarchy.[22] He also revealed his capacity to ruthlessly crush opposition within his own party, defeating a 1987 challenge to his leadership and subsequently purging the party of dissidents,[23] thus greatly weakening the overall intellectual calibre of the higher echelons of UMNO.[24] In 1998 he was to dismiss his designated heir Anwar Ibrahim who was later to be arrested, calumniated and humiliated.[25] Mahathir's rule moved Malaysia from what observer Harold Crouch has termed a "modified democratic system" to a more restrictive "modified authoritarian system".[26]

The NEP, Money Politics, Corruption, Cronyism

Financial scandals, which were to cost the Malaysian government billions of dollars, attended the Mahathir government from its earliest years. These included the 1981–82 attempt, via a shelf company, to corner the international tin market;[27] the so-called Carrian Affair (1981–83) which involved profligate Bank Bumiputra Finance lending to Hong Kong investors (and which sustained losses greater than two-thirds of its entire loan portfolio[28]); the Forex scandal (1992) in which Bank Negara speculated billions of dollars on the assumption that Britain would continue with the European Exchange Rate Mechanism;[29] and the Perwaja Terengganu scheme, in which billions of dollars were lost in devious business transactions and associated financial rackets.[30] The government refused to take responsibility for these or for other financial irregularities, and the reaction to each of these scandals was to eschew disclosure or open investigation, and to curb information flows beyond the innermost government circles.[31]

Since independence, political office in Malaysia has been regarded as a sinecure which, *inter alia*, allowed for the creation of personal wealth and the cultivation of networks of patronage to be mobilized as and when required.[32] The introduction of the NEP and the concomitant expansion of the public sector, and later privatization programme (inaugurated by Mahathir in 1983), placed considerable power within the grasp of all ruling UMNO politicians and the bureaucracy, and provided many opportunities for the allocation of economic resources.[33] The abolition of tender processes meant that many, often huge, contracts were awarded without open and transparent competition, nor were they subject to official regulation or scrutiny.[34] In many cases, profitable public enterprises were handed directly to UMNO affiliates.[35] Moreover, in many cases the government often guaranteed certain levels of returns upon contracts so that in effect profits but not losses were privatized.[36] The practice of dispensing contracts to those close to UMNO was justified on the grounds that it would create Malay businessmen and was thus consistent with the NEP's objective of achieving targeted levels of bumiputera participation in the Malaysian economy.[37] This accorded with Mahathir's belief in "trickle down" economics; that is, that the creation of a core group of

Malay millionaires would ultimately reward the entire Malay community as money percolated from the top to the lower reaches of society.[38] In practice the preferential distribution of lucrative contracts — known as "cronyism" or "money politics" — enabled a selected few, those who enjoyed favoured access to UMNO, to appropriate much of the wealth which had been originally intended to benefit the mass of "ordinary" bumiputeras.[39] By 2009 concentration of bumiputera wealth had become seriously skewed; seventy-five per cent of bumiputera equity was in the hands of a mere 1.3 per cent of the community.[40] Control of wealth produced networks of nepotism and patronage, and by 2005 Malaysia could claim a total of 42,313 contractors, of whom 35,000 were small licence holders dependent upon government contracts worth $100,000 or less.[41]

Ethnic Relations

The 1969 riots and its aftermath demonstrated to non-Malays the hazards of attempting to wrest political power from the Malays.[42] The subsequent constitutional amendments, initiated by the UMNO leadership, and the adumbration and implementation of the post-1969 suite of affirmative action policies, ensured that henceforth political accommodation would be on Malay, and more specifically, UMNO terms, and clearly signalled that Malay power brokers would not tolerate any challenge to their authority.[43]

In the processes of inculcating the objectives of *Ketuanan Melayu* (Malay supremacy) as the pivotal ideology, the ruling elite successfully marginalized all competing currents of political thought (though, as we shall observe, this was challenged by *Reformasi* in 1999 and by the elections of 8 March 2008). Indeed, this elite has firmly identified all alternative ideologies with an inadmissible "Other", which if allowed to flourish, would threaten the very survival of the nation.[44] However, the state has been unable to replicate this outcome either in creating or imposing a widely accepted national culture.

Sheila Nair has argued that nationalism relies upon a complex amalgam of cultural, social and political processes, a dynamic interplay between elites and subaltern cultures that establishes a definitive portrayal of a nation that "transcends class, caste and ethnic differences".[45] The politicization of the cultural arena, and privileging of selected aspects of neo-traditionalism and a disputed Malay culture have produced both widespread alienation[46] and multiple sites of particularistic resistance.[47] This has been compounded by deep and seemingly irreconcilable ambiguities within the main body of Malaysian official nationalist ideology. Thus, the promotion of a nationalist cultural project structured upon Malay symbols and sustained by Malay political dominance has to coexist with an exclusionary state project based upon "race" and "ethnicity".[48] The resultant incompleteness and contradictions inherent within the construction of the nationalist project have exposed continuing uncertainties surrounding the articulation of self and other, thus opening space for alternative applications and ideological discourses.[49] While this ideological space has been exploited by a number of overtly political organizations, generically known as New Social Movements (NSM), and generally formed to resist specific aspects of public policy,[50] on the cultural level the nationalistic project has been countered by a myriad of particularistic ethnic and religious sites collectively representing the "fragmented vision" of the complex heterogeneous society which exists below the level of official nationalist ideology.[51]

Given this backdrop, the achievement of national unity, especially when defined in terms of inter-ethnic harmony and social cohesion, has proven highly problematic. Indeed, it has been suggested that in the forty years since the introduction of the NEP, communal relations have become increasingly fraught.[52] Many scholars have argued that in defining an increasingly wide range of issues in purely ethnic terms, the NEP has reinforced ethnicity in Malaysia.[53] Moreover, the NEP's perceived emphatic benevolence to Malays, and the concomitant and sometimes stringent restriction of educational, training and public sector employment places allocated to other communities, left many non-bumiputeras with the impression that their needs were considered of little moment, and that they had been relegated to the status of second-class citizenry.[54] Continued racial polarization manifested in the spiralling 1987 Sino-Malay tensions which were finally quelled by the police action known as "Operation *Lalang*";[55] the categorical non-Malay voter rejection of the perceived Malay-Islamic chauvinism of the *Reformasi* platform offered by the opposition Barisan Alternatif in the 1999 elections;[56] the 2001 outbreak of Indian-Malay racial violence in the environs of the impoverished squatter settlement Kampong Medan, Kuala Lumpur;[57] and more recently the rise of the opposition Malay supremacist body Perkasa, seemingly formed with the specific objective of checking Prime Minister Najib Razak's more concessionary and inclusive "1Malaysia" policy.[58]

Operation Lalang

In late 1987 a series of inter-communal incidents inflamed ethnic tensions which were finally quashed by a sweeping government crackdown. Communal passions came to a head over the seemingly innocuous decision of the Ministry of Education to appoint English-educated Chinese school teachers to various Chinese-medium schools in Melaka, Penang, Selangor, and Kuala Lumpur.[59] This action provoked the vociferous opposition of the entire Chinese community, and threats of student boycotts.[60] Instead of simply defusing the issue, UMNO organizers responded to Chinese "disloyalty" with a huge rally at Kelab Sultan Suleiman which "featured fiercely anti-Chinese speakers and banners", some of which called for the Malay kris to be soaked in Chinese blood.[61] UMNO announced a further rally on 1 November with an anticipated attendance of 500,000 Malays.[62] Some immediate observers believe that this crisis was artificially manufactured by prominent UMNO leaders who "played the race card" in order to promote dangerous levels of racial tension which would warrant an authoritarian response.[63] On 24 October the Malaysian police launched Operation *Lalang* which ultimately resulted in the detention of 119 people under the ISA. None of the leading organizers or provocateurs associated with the UMNO rallies were arrested.[64] Those detained included some members of the opposition, some minor government figures, and Chinese educationists. However, the wave of arrests also encompassed other targets, many of whom had not been immediately involved in the communal crisis. The government action had thus moved well beyond the diffusion of inter-communal tensions and could be interpreted as attempted intimidation of a wide range of oppositional groups and as a warning to Chinese groups not to push the tolerated boundaries of political debate.[65] In addition three newspapers, the English medium *Star*, the Malay-medium *Watan*, and the Chinese-medium *Sin Chew Jit Poh*, were suspended indefinitely.[66] In December 1987 Mahathir introduced legislation which placed further restrictions on the printed media, and which furnished the police with even greater powers in the management of public gatherings.[67]

The Anwar Incident

Anwar Ibrahim originally gained prominence in Malaysian political life as the charismatic leader of the Islamic reform movement *Angkatan Belia Islam*

(ABIM — Islamic Youth Force Malaysia), and had played a prominent role in the 1974 Baling poverty demonstrations.[68] Prior to the 1982 elections Mahathir invited Anwar to join UMNO. He was appointed Deputy Minister and achieved full ministerial status the following year. In 1982 Anwar was elected head of UMNO Youth.[69] In 1993, Anwar replaced Ghafar Baba as Deputy Prime Minister, thus becoming Mahathir's heir-apparent.[70]

The 1997–98 financial crisis had a severe impact upon the Malaysian economy and exposed major policy and personality differences between Mahathir and Anwar. Many of the larger Malaysian conglomerates, especially those created as a result of UMNO patronage, had been poorly managed and proved unable to weather the recession.[71] While Mahathir railed against Western interests which he believed lay behind the crisis, Anwar assigned blame for the failure of the conglomerates to "corruption, cronyism and nepotism".[72] Anwar's dismissal was spurred by Mahathir's fear that should Anwar succeed him he might well adopt the measures proposed by the International Monetary Fund. These would have precluded the financial rescue of enterprises associated with the government, and that as a consequence Mahathir could not rely upon Anwar to protect the interests of Mahathir, his family and colleagues once he, Mahathir, had retired.[73] Amidst charges of homosexual conduct, Anwar was dismissed as Deputy Prime Minister on 2 September 1998 and was expelled from UMNO two days later.[74] He was arrested under the Internal Security Act on 20 September, several hours after addressing a gathering of 200,000 people at the *Masjid Negara* (National Mosque) in Kuala Lumpur.[75]

Prior to his arrest, Anwar's rallies had drawn large, mainly but not exclusively, Malay crowds, and had instigated a broad popular movement united by the desire for *Reformasi* (Reform). His ill-treatment — the bashing in the cells at the hands of no less a personage than the Inspector-General of Police, Mahathir's suggestion that the injuries sustained were self-inflicted and a ruse designed to garner public sympathy, and the lurid and detailed sexual allegations made against him — breached all Malay cultural norms and were greeted with widespread revulsion.[76] Outrage deepened as Anwar was charged with five counts of corruption and five counts of sodomy, and was indicted after two trials which independent observers believed failed to meet the most basic standards of justice.[77] Anwar was jailed for fifteen years and was banned from holding political office and from sitting in Parliament until April 2008.[78]

Throughout these trials *Reformasi* continued to generate support among Malays. The 1999 elections were dominated by the Anwar issue. BN was opposed by the so-called *Barisan Alternatif*, a coalition of PAS, DAP, Parti Rakyat Sosialis Malaysia, and *Parti Keadilan Nasional* (National Justice Party), the latter is a new political movement formed by Anwar's wife, Wan Azizah Ismail.[79] BN was returned on the back of the non-Malay vote. Seventy per cent of the Malay electorate voted for opposition parties while non-Malays, worried about the possibility of a PAS-imposed theocracy, swung heavily behind BN.[80] The voting revealed continued ethnic distrust, but it also hinted at a new fluidity within the electorate which under the right conditions could well foreshadow fresh political alignments.

MAHATHIR'S LEGACY

Mahathir was to remain in office until 30 October 2003. Despite the many billions of ringgit lost in the numerous scandals and ill-conceived projects associated with Mahathir's rule, Malaysia's economy largely prospered during these years. Driven by a dynamic and foreign capitalized manufacturing sector, the Malaysian economy was transformed from its dependency upon the export of primary products to that of manufactured goods.[81] While in 1970 rubber and tin had accounted for 54.3 per cent of Malaysia's exports, by 1990 this comprised a mere 4.9 per cent of total exports.[82] This had been accompanied by the growth of a substantial and expanding Malay middle class which was employed in all sectors of the economy and was well represented within the professions and among the managerial class.[83] Under the NEP, the Malay share of corporate wealth had increased from an insignificant two per cent in 1969 to approximately twenty per cent in 1990.[84] This was supplemented by a considerable body of assets held in trust for bumiputeras by state-owned enterprises.[85] Moreover, in launching the Wawasan 2020 policy, Mahathir had stimulated an incipient nationalism, one which held the prospect of moving beyond a Malay-centric ideology to foster a more general and inclusive Malaysian unity.[86]

However, Mahathir's achievements were counterbalanced and perhaps outweighed by the authoritarianism and self-interest which had circumvented and often etiolated many of Malaysia's core institutions. Barry Wain comments:

> Apart from turning UMNO into a powerful patronage machine that eventually slipped from his grasp, and leaving the party singularly

ill-equipped to face a globalizing future, Dr Mahathir cut Malaysia adrift institutionally. Similar to the way he personalized control of the Party, he emasculated almost all institutions so that he would meet no obstruction. He handed them to loyalists, shrank their authority or by-passed them altogether. While that left the police, the courts and other agencies unable to discharge their public obligations professionally, his attacks on the doctrines of the separation of powers struck at 'the very soul of principled, democratic governance'... unchecked, Dr Mahathir created a culture that rewarded obedience and short changed integrity, allowing Malaysia to drift into a period appropriately described as 'the lost ethical years.'[87]

Mahathir's role in promoting a destabilizing process of Islamization will be examined in Chapter 15.

INDIANS AND THE MALAYSIAN ECONOMIC "MIRACLE"

NEP and the Indian Community

The NEP, while creating a Malay middle class, had also produced a number of negative outcomes. First, its benefits were delivered unequally. As we have seen, the politics of patronage and nepotism ensured that rents were captured by well-connected Malays, while many poorer Malays, especially those in rural areas, received few or no benefits at all. Second, the NEP, originally designed to last for no longer than twenty years, was transformed into a continuous policy which became regarded as an entitlement and created a culture of dependency.[88] Finally, the NEP promoted inequality within Malaysia, sidelining a number of groups, including poor Malays, the Orang Asli and the bulk of the Indian community.[89] In the rest of the chapter I will examine the post-NEP fortunes of Indians and their history throughout the years of economic growth often described as the "Malaysian miracle".

The implementation of the NEP resulted in the further marginalization of the Indian community. From 1969 onwards, Indians have recorded in relative terms higher unemployment rates, and lower levels of educational attainment, than either Malays or Chinese. Moreover, Indian participation in the corporate sector has been inconsequential. While in 1969 the Indian share of corporate capital stood at 0.9 per cent, in 2008, nearly forty years later, it had expanded to a mere 1.6 per cent.[90] In this period Malays have been the subject of intense government patronage, while the Chinese have been able to draw upon a wealthy and influential business sector.[91] With the introduction of the NEP and the abandonment of the Alliance formula in favour of the BN coalition, the MIC, already a minor component of the wider ruling structure, further declined in significance. The influence the party has been able to bear upon the formulation of policy, has, in general, been minimal.[92]

We have noted that the NEP aimed at rapid growth of the Malaysian economy to provide increased opportunities for all segments of society and in particular a sharp reduction in poverty, especially that among Malays, together with a programme of industrialization which would reduce overall economic reliance upon the export of commodities. In the years subsequent to the introduction of the NEP, the Malaysian economy has been radically transformed from dependence upon agriculture and mining to a more mature and diversified economy based upon manufacturing and services. The tables that follow,[93] reveal the extent of this transformation:

At the time of the inauguration of the NEP, the bulk of the Indian working population was employed within the low-waged and largely semi- and unskilled agricultural and service sectors.[94] While the 1970 Third Malaysia Plan identified Indian estate workers as among those affected by hard-core poverty and thus as a target for assistance,[95] the NEP functioned on the assumption that as a composite ethnic group Indians were on average better off than Malays, and that as a consequence resources would be largely directed towards alleviating Malay poverty.[96] Moreover, Malaysian authorities claimed that estate workers, as employees of financially buoyant private limited companies which actually owned the properties upon which the labour force resided, fell beyond the parameters

TABLE 14.1
Growth and Sectional Composition of GDP 1970 and 2005
Share to GDP (per cent)

	1970	2005
Agriculture	29.0	8.2
Manufacturing	13.9	31.4
Services	36.2	58.1
Construction	3.8	2.7
Mining	13.7	6.7

TABLE 14.2
Employment by Occupations 1970 and 2000
Workforce (per cent)

	1970	2000
Agriculture	44.9	18.1*
Sales	9.1	11.0
Production	27.3	32.8
Professional/Technical	4.8	11.0
Administrative/Managerial	1.1	4.2
Services	7.9	11.8

*By 2005, the agricultural workforce had further declined and employed a mere eleven per cent of the workforce.[97]

of NEP guidelines. By this act of sophistry, governmental agencies absolved themselves of all responsibility for the uplift of an entire impoverished sector of the workforce.[98]

Over the years assistance provided to the Indian community has been minimal and local authorities (invariably bumiputera dominated), have frequently overlooked or ignored the delivery of basic services to the Indian poor.[99] As will be detailed in the following section, the decline in prices of rubber and the overall profitability of the estate sector generally stimulated a major rural–urban migration among Indian labourers, forcing many unskilled Indians in to the squalor and intractable poverty of Malaysia's urban squatter settlements.

Civil Service

The introduction of stringent and inflexible employment policies within the Malaysian Civil Service had a dramatic impact upon Indians who had since colonial times traditionally found employment with the industrial-manual sector of the service, and in particular utilities such as the railways, posts, telegraphs, and the Public Works Department.[100] Under the NEP, the government civil sector became a major employer of Malays/bumiputeras as the service expanded to foster the extensive range of programmes tailored to train and advance bumiputeras. Thus, while Malays held only 37 per cent of all civil service positions in 1969,[101] by 1971 this figure had already risen to 60.8 per cent, and by 2005 stood at 77 per cent. In addition, Malays occupied 84 per cent of top management positions.[102] Between 1970 and 1981, the percentage of Indians employed within the Civil Service declined from 26.2 per cent to 14.4 per cent, and by 2005 this figure had plummeted to 5.12 per cent. Indians held 5.1 per cent of top management positions.[103] But advancement within the ranks was no longer a realistic possibility for ambitious or qualified Indians; under the NEP, senior positions were almost invariably offered to Malays.[104]

Plantation Workers

As we have noted, with the launch of the NEP, Indian plantation workers were formally identified as one sector suffering from chronic hard-core poverty. As we also observed, plantations were classified as private property and thus considered to fall beyond the ambit of rural development programmes.[105] It is now generally agreed that in many respects plantation workers are now worse off than they were at the time of independence, and that conditions of service in the first decade of the twenty-first century compare unfavourably to those provided during the 1950s.[106] Moreover, wages paid to plantation workers have declined in real terms as demonstrated in Table 14.3:[107]

The situation of estate workers will be more fully examined later in this chapter.

Middle Class Indians

The NEP also had a profound impact upon the hitherto buoyant Indian middle class. Within the private sector government contracts for which Indian business might have hitherto tendered were now routinely awarded to bumiputera firms, and professional appointments within the public sector were all but entirely the preserve of Malays.[108] The NEP also had an adverse effect upon those business sectors which had previously

TABLE 14.3
Plantation Wages, 1975, 1990, 2003

	Average monthly wage	Real monthly wage in 1967 prices
1975	RM189	RM131
1990	RM336	RM134
2003	RM350	RM117

been dominated by Indians, including textiles, pharmaceuticals, and the book trade.[109]

As a consequence there was a continuous post-NEP decline in rates of Indian participation in white-collar employment. Between 1970 and 1988 the Indian share of administrative and managerial positions fell from 7.8 per cent to 4.6 per cent, while the percentages of clerical and sales positions held by Indians contracted from 17.2 and 11.1 per cent to 8.8 and 5.0 per cent, respectively.[110]

The Indian decline in the percentile share of professional employment was just as sharp as Table 14.4[111] reveals.

The difficulties faced by middle-class Indians have been aggravated by the diminution of tertiary places now available to them. The affirmative action policies of the NEP mandates that admission to universities is no longer decided upon merit but rather by ethnicity. Thus many highly talented Chinese and Indian high school graduates have been denied places in public universities to facilitate the enrolment of sometimes very mediocre Malay students. Gordon Means has pointed out that "To avoid the appearance of discrimination ... universities established a grade review process that equalized grade averages between Malay students and non-Malay students"; a review process that was subsequently extended to postgraduate outcomes.[112] During numerous interviews, I have been made aware that under this formula many Indian students, who achieve grades that would (and often do) secure them places in prestigious foreign universities, are rejected for admission to local public universities. Currently the intake of Indian students into public universities (excluding the Universiti Teknologi Mara) is estimated at about 6.8 per cent of total admissions.[113]

Quotas have also been extended to academic and administrative appointments within public universities, with the result that many highly

TABLE 14.4
Indian Share of Professional Employment (%), 1980 and 2007

	1980	2007
Doctors	41.7	20.2
Lawyers	35.4	23.5
Veterinary surgeons	46.5	22.5
Dentists	21.3	16.9

qualified staff have sought appointments in foreign universities. This has resulted in a precipitous decline in the quality and academic standing of Malaysian public universities.[114] Indeed a World Bank comparative study of the National University of Singapore and the Universiti Malay found that the "implementation of affirmative action policies in Malaysia has hurt the higher education system, sapping Malaysia's economic competitiveness and driving some (mainly Chinese and Indians) to more meritocratic countries."[115]

Rural–Urban Migration

The increasing marginalization of the Indian population coincided with the large-scale rural/urban migration of Indian labour, which was to result in the transformation of a workforce largely engaged in the rural plantation sector to one which is predominantly urban based and employed in manufacturing and other low-skilled occupations. Whereas in 1957 some 70.4 per cent of Indians were engaged within the plantation sector or in mining, by 2000 only 15.1 per cent remained in these occupations. In the same period the proportion engaged in manufacturing and service sectors rose from 1.8 to 62 per cent of the Indian population.[116] While this rural–urban migration began after World War II among younger Tamils, and increased throughout the period of fragmentation of the estates and the resultant displacement of Tamil labourers and their families,[117] the migration intensified with the economic changes of the late 1960s.

Throughout the 1960s the profitability of rubber and its importance as an export commodity began a prolonged decline. In many instances, rubber plantations were replaced with oil palm. By the mid-1960s Malaysia had become the world's largest exporter of palm oil.[118] Oil palm provided planters with better and more consistent economic returns, and more crucially could be managed with a smaller and lower-paid workforce. Surplus workers were made redundant and forced to seek alternate employment.[119] In other instances, plantations, especially those bordering towns, were converted into industrial estates, townships, golf courses, or other developments, and the labourers were simply evicted.[120] Between 1980 and 2000 more than 300,000 Indians, workers and their families, were evicted from the plantations.[121]

In leaving the estates in which labouring families had lived, sometimes for several generations, workers were not only relinquishing well-established networks of community support, but were also losing vital facilities, however rudimentary, such as housing, crèches, material and recreational amenities, centres of religion, and access to land for vegetable farming and the grazing of cattle.[122] Thus many of those departing the estates suffered not only the trauma and grief of dispossession, but also the abrupt termination of their employment and an inculcated way of life.[123]

Most migrating workers received no formal assistance of any kind in terms of retraining or resettlement. Few possessed any savings or access to financial resources which might have offered a chance to procure or commence a small business.[124] Despite the enormous profits realized by companies in the sale of their estates, workers' entitlements were often miniscule, and in most cases were barely sufficient to cover the costs associated with relocation.[125] Many of those forcibly removed from the estates could not rely upon the support of kinship networks in adjusting to urban life, and thus experienced major social problems throughout the years of transition.[126] A substantial minority of Indians leaving the estates became squatters living on the urban fringes of the cities. In research conducted in 1986, K.S. Susan Oorjitham found that while a majority of recent arrivals shared overcrowded quarters (rooms and houses), thirty per cent were compelled to inhabit squatter areas.[127] Moreover, there was no quick escape from these substandard living conditions. Indians were obliged to live with the reality that in allocating available public low-cost accommodation (flats or housing), precedence is nearly always given to Malays.[128] Recent observations made by scholars and social workers suggest that living conditions of urban Indians have further deteriorated over the past twenty years.

This internal migration coincided with the rise in the late 1960s of export-oriented industrialization and the availability of low-skilled employment.[129] Most of the Tamil workers were poorly educated; indeed 73 per cent of estate labourers had received no education above the primary school level.[130] A workforce habituated to the routines of estate life, possessed of rudimentary education, had limited options within the urban environment. Most were thus condemned to unskilled and low-waged employment, repetitive work which provided no scope for vocational or social mobility.[131] Often incomes were insufficient to meet basic needs, and habitual indebtedness often forced workers to take up secondary employment.[132]

On the basis of his research, S. Nagarajan has concluded that most working-class households "comprised hard working and religious people, intent on educating children for a better future".[133] However, these families seemed condemned to a repetitive cycle of inter-generational poverty, the result of low-wage structures, the high cost of urban living (especially land prices), poor educational opportunities, and political powerlessness.[134] In recent years their problems have been aggravated by the importation of unskilled or foreign labour which has depressed wage structures and against whom Indian workers must now often compete for low-skilled positions.[135]

In total, the rural/urban migration neither resulted in any improvement in the economic standing of the Indian working class, nor did it promote inter-generational social mobility. Indeed, some observers believe that since the introduction of the NEP the overall plight of the Indian indigent actually deteriorated.[136] The internal migration created a large pool of Tamil labour, minimally educated and low skilled, which was compelled to occupy positions that were basic, repetitive and poorly paid, and which offered little or nothing in the way of vocational advancement. Indian workers generally found that their wages were insufficient to maintain a family, and in most cases did not keep pace with inflation. Financial pressures forced most to rent shoddy housing, often slum and squatter dwellings.[137]

Thus the essential problems confronting the Indian labouring classes remained unchanged and unresolved. The plantation culture of chronic underachievement and social stasis, forged over the years and generations of subjugation to the rigid and unyielding controls of physical and psychological oppression and demoralization, which robbed the Indian worker of the qualities of initiative and independence, has merely been transferred to and reproduced within an urban setting.[138] As D. Jeyakumar remarks: "The values and attitudes which have been etched upon the consciousness of a people by generations of dehumanizing experiences do not fade away easily. Values and attitudes, once inculcated, have a momentum of their own."[139] Indian labourers, possessing limited financial and social resources, have accomplished next to nothing in the way of inter-generational vocational and economic mobility.[140]

THE MALAYSIAN INDIAN CONGRESS

As noted, following the 1969 elections the Alliance formula was abandoned in favour of the augmented coalition known as Barisan Nasional. In the years following the introduction of the NEP this was increasingly dominated by a hegemonic UMNO which placed the interests of Malays ahead of other ethnic groups and generally minimized the participation of non-Malays in Malaysian political affairs.[141] Throughout these years the MIC remained the sole officially recognized "Indian" party. The party, diminished by its poor performance in 1969, remained utterly dependent upon UMNO goodwill, and the party hierarchy adopted the tactic of cultivating close and personal relationships with UMNO leaders in the hope of winning concessions for the Indian community.[142] The MIC leadership throughout this period has largely been controlled by an urban-based business and professional class which has tended to look after its own interests at the expense of its working-class constituency.[143] The MIC is generally perceived as a weak and ineffectual party, unable to mitigate the serious problems facing the Indian community, or even influence the course of political debate.[144]

Following the accession of Tun Abdul Razak to the Prime Ministership, MIC representation within the Cabinet was halved from two appointees to one. V.T. Sambanthan was relieved of the important portfolio of Works, Posts, and Telecommunications and was granted the compensatory post of Ministry of National Unity. This was largely a token appointment; most of the policy development within his department was aggregated and formulated by Malay civil servants.[145]

As noted in Chapter 13, in 1973, in an UMNO-negotiated succession, V. Manickavasagam replaced V.T. Sambanthan as MIC President. Manickavasagam attempted to revitalize the party and to broaden the scope of its appeal and to nurture talent within the MIC. He encouraged intellectuals to become involved in the party and appealed for the participation of the minority Indian communities.[146] His efforts did little to lift the party's fortunes. The MIC remained a largely Tamil body, concerned with the Tamil language, culture and traditions.[147] Resurgent Dravidian impulses invigorated the politics of caste within the MIC and complicated the already-intense factionalism with which the party was plagued.[148]

In 1979 Manickavasagam died in office and was replaced as party leader by S. Samy Vellu. Samy Vellu had entered Parliament in 1974, having won retiring member V.T. Sambanthan's seat of Sungai Siput. A member of the Thevar caste, Samy Vellu had built support through caste networks as well as via his involvement in Tamil drama societies.[149] In 1975 he became one of the three Vice-Presidents within the MIC and in 1977 was elected to the Deputy Presidency. In 1978 he was appointed Deputy Minister of Housing and Local Government. Following Manickavasagam's death Samy Vellu was appointed to Cabinet.[150] Samy Vellu was to become the longest-serving President of the MIC, retaining his hold on the party even after the loss of his parliamentary seat in March 2008. Regarded as vigorous, deft, and capable in the early period of his leadership, as the years passed his style became formulaic, stale, autocratic and increasingly out of touch with the wider Indian community. He was held to be high-handed, bombastic, dictatorial and with a marked proclivity to make decisions affecting policy or projects without reference to colleagues or party. He was subject to accusations of nepotism and patronage in managing party affairs. During his tenure the power of the Presidency was greatly enhanced, and decision-making was increasingly concentrated in the Executive at the expense of the party's grass roots.[151]

The waning influence of the MIC is best illustrated by Mahathir's decision to halve the party's allocation of portfolios from two to a single position.[152] The party's external decline was paralleled by the confused state of its internal structures. Party branches are often poorly organized and a lack of internal training or professional development has meant that many office holders are inadequately equipped to perform their duties. The nepotism and patronage which is rampant within the party has often led to the selection of mediocre candidates who are neither intellectually nor strategically placed to match their coalition counterparts.[153] The Executive's increasing remoteness from its grass roots has meant that the concerns of the rank and file were rarely taken up within the upper echelons of the party.[154] The party was largely ineffectual in addressing the major issues of ameliorating Indian poverty and marginalization, or improving the socio-economic or educational outcomes for the community.[155] Indeed, throughout the lengthy period of Samy Vellu's presidency the difficulties faced by the Indian poor appeared to become increasingly intractable.[156]

The MIC and the NEP

Throughout these years the MIC made a number of attempts to persuade the government to take remedial action on the problems facing the Indian poor. These efforts had little success, and UMNO's response rarely rose above the tokenistic.

In 1974, the MIC convened an economic seminar with the theme "NEP and the Malaysian Indians" which, *inter alia*, produced a paper which was promoted as a blueprint for improving the overall standing of the Indian community. The paper highlighted major issues that were of concern to the party, namely unemployment, which was higher among Indians than among other ethnic groups, and the need for Indians to participate in land settlement schemes.[157] Specific recommendations included the oversight of the estate sector by the Ministry of Rural Development, and the establishment of quotas for Indian participation in the mining, quarrying, logging, construction and transport sectors.[158] The overall blueprint, considered vague and ineffectual by some observers, failed to impress Prime Minister Razak who remained disinclined to consider the problems of the Indian community as a national priority.[159]

However, MIC recommendations were incorporated in the Third Malaysia Plan of 1976–80. The plan identified Indian plantation workers as a target group and specified a number of measures which would help break the cycle of long-term poverty. These included (1) relocation of unemployed Indians and impoverished families to new government land schemes, (2) provision of vocational training to young Indians selected from among the hard-core poor which would equip them to work in the agricultural and industrial sectors, (3) the establishment of cooperative societies, and (4) insistence that estates supply all workers with basic services such as electricity and running water.[160] Follow-up action never translated into anything more than a few perfunctory measures, and both Indian plantation labourers and the urban working classes remained largely isolated from Malaysian policy planning.[161]

In 1980 the MIC organized the Second Economic Seminar with the aim of attempting to promote a series of recommendations for incorporation into the Fourth Malaysia Plan which was to be introduced the following year.[162] The seminar concluded that the implementation of the NEP had not resulted in any economic advancement of the overall Indian community.[163] The government remained unmoved by MIC submissions and made it clear that the Indian community could expect little in the way of targeted assistance. It contended that the NEP was designed to promote the social and economic welfare of the "indigenous" rather than "immigrant" communities. It could also claim that per capita income within the Indian community en bloc remained higher than that received by Malays.[164]

The government exculpated itself from responsibility for the welfare of plantation workers by employing the rationale that estates were private property and it was therefore the responsibility of owners to improve facilities and to increase wage levels.[165] Thus in 1977 when the government conducted a socio-economic survey of agricultural households it pointedly overlooked estate workers. However, in 1981 the high-powered Economic Planning Unit, located within the Prime Minister's Department, conducted a major survey of rubber plantation workers. This was followed by a 1983 survey of oil palm estate labourers.[166] These surveys provided a bleak portrayal of life on the estates. They revealed that 24.4 per cent of estate workers occupied dwellings that lacked basic amenities. Those residing in non-MAPA estates were significantly worse off. A mere 29.8 per cent of non-MAPA dwellings were connected to electricity, and only 70.5 per cent were equipped with running water. Wages were barely adequate to meet day-to-day needs; an average of 72 per cent of income was expended on food while a further 25 per cent was spent on essential goods and services. The surveys ascertained that 20 per cent of the workforce was illiterate.[167] There is evidence that throughout the life of the Third Malaysia Plan (1981–95) conditions on estates continued to deteriorate and real poverty among estate labourers actually worsened.[168]

The Third Malaysian Indian Economic Congress in 1990 deliberated upon the government categorization of plantations as private property and hence falling beyond the scope of targeted government programmes. The Congress recommended that economic planners designate all workers within the agricultural sector as belonging to "rural areas". However, the generally weak position of the MIC within BN meant that this issue was not followed up. Although the Sixth Malaysia Plan (1991–95) made some reference to the gravity of the problems affecting the Indian community, little assistance was actually provided.[169]

In 2005 the report submitted to the government in respect of the Ninth Malaysia Plan detailed the problems faced by low-income Indians, including the fact that many of these difficulties could be traced to their displacement from the plantation sector, and that previous government programmes had proven ineffective in reaching the Indian community.[170] The Ninth Malaysia Plan (2006–10) specified several measures designed to improve the overall economic standing of the Indian community. These included programmes to expand Indian participation within the economy with the aim of increasing Indian equity to three per cent by 2020, to furnish opportunities for Indians to participate in nominated trust schemes, and of providing monetary assistance and relevant training to selected budding business people and potential entrepreneurs.[171]

NUPW AND ESTATE LABOUR

Throughout the period under review, ownership of the large rubber and oil palm estates was largely transferred to Malaysian hands. Mahathir was determined to ensure that the foreign and mainly British-dominated plantation sector was owned and managed by Malaysians. His campaign to this effect was inaugurated with the so-called Dawn Raid of 7 September 1981 which resulted in *Permodalan Nasional Berhad* (National Equity Corporation) purchasing 50.41 per cent of the ordinary share capital of the British flagship estate company Guthries. Other acquisitions followed.[172] Plantations were increasingly managed by Malaysian boards of directors, and the majority of administrative positions were held by Malays. However, the autocratic style of management inherited from colonialism remained unchanged, with an inflexible managerial hierarchy oversighting a pliant labour force. Nor did Malaysian ownership result in better wages and conditions.[173] On the contrary, some informants advised the writer that general conditions on the estates were now in many respects worse under Malaysian control than they had been during the colonial era. That this outlook was obviously shared by the workforce was demonstrated in a managerial survey of management-labour relations conducted at the end of the 1980s. In a telling and rather depressing commentary upon the new breed of managers, a large number of Tamil estate workers opined that "the European planter of yesteryear had been more humane in his dealings with them than the average Malaysian manager who had replaced him".[174]

In the years since 1969 the NUPW has done little to improve wages or conditions of Indian estate labour. Indeed, Milne and Mauzy's 1977 description of the NUPW as "decidedly responsible" and "non-revolutionary" continues to apply.[175] The NUPW is viewed by the government as an invaluable ally in restraining wages and in ensuring stability upon estates, so much so that estate workers continue to receive low wages and on many plantations remain bereft of such basic amenities as running water, electricity and primary health care.[176]

As a union bound to defend and extend planation workers' interests the NUPW has failed its members on nearly every front. P. Ramasamy has pointed out that between 1960 and 1980 the productivity of tappers increased by a significant 126 per cent (thus rising from an average output of 2,247 kilograms per month in 1960 to 5,083 kilograms per month in 1980). Remuneration to workers did not reflect this increased output.

Rises in wage levels over this period do not disguise the fact that, in real terms, wages as measured by purchasing power declined from RM3.40 per diem in 1960 to RM3.07 in 1981.[177] Thus despite increases in both productivity and the overall profitability of the plantation sector, estate workers failed to maintain incomes commensurate with rises in the general cost of living.[178] The NUPW's attempt to institute a basic monthly wage was finally dismissed by the Industrial Court in 1985.[179]

Although quality and availability of housing was a fundamental issue for all plantation workers, it was not a matter that the NUPW pursued with any great vigour. In 1973, at the prompting of Prime Minister Razak, the government established a task force to examine the provision of housing on estates. The task force recommended a scheme of house ownership, and gained the support of fifty-one plantation companies. However, by 1989 the scheme had been implemented on only three estates. While there were a number of factors which led to the scheme's failure, a key determinant was the lack of NUPW interest or resolution in promoting the scheme either with the government or within the industrial sphere.[180]

The NUPW has not taken responsibility for representing or protecting the interests of estate workers who reside on plantations which are not managed by members of the Malayan Agricultural Planters' Association (MAPA). Thus some forty per cent of workers employed on smaller estates remain without union cover, and often under significantly worse conditions and receive less pay than those employed in MAPA plantations.[181]

The NUPW failures may be attributed to a number of factors. Perhaps the most obvious is that many leading officials have come to regard their positions as sinecures, appointments which are vital to accumulating power and establishing networks of patronage. By the early 1990s many NUPW officials had occupied their positions for upwards of forty years, and had never once been subject to any serious challenge.[182] It might reasonably be anticipated that uninterrupted tenure would breed both complacency and staleness, and indeed informants suggested that the upper echelons of the NUPW are unresponsive to grass-roots concerns, and enjoy over-familiar and cosy relationships with government officials. It is also alleged that in mounting cases the NUPW neglects the detailed research and level of preparation that might reasonably be expected of a well-managed union.[183]

From the 1970s onwards the wages and conditions of Tamil and other Malaysian estate workers were affected by the competition provided by large numbers of illegal Indonesian entrants who were willing to work for below NUPW-negotiated wage rates. As illegals, these labourers were exempt from the recognized legal obligations which bound employer–employee relations and were prepared to accept the most rudimentary living conditions and terms of employment.[184] In addition from the 1980s onward the government allowed large numbers of other foreign labourers into Malaysia. These largely unskilled workers laboured under contract at costs that were significantly less than those which pertained to Indian labour, and had the overall effect of reducing wages and established conditions of employment for local workers.[185]

During the 1970s a system of contract labour was introduced into the estates. Under this system the planter abrogates control of his labour force to a nominated contractor. This is achieved through a signed agreement between the estate management and the contractor, the latter agreeing to fulfil an allotted workload in return for a negotiated payment. He, rather than the estate, employs the labour and is responsible for supervision, payment of wages, and other benefits. The contract system thus relieves the estate of responsibility for the management and welfare of labour, thus cutting overall labour costs.[186] By 1984 some twelve per cent of estate workers were hired under the contract system.[187]

Selanchar Empat

The contract system was responsible for one of the ugliest labour scandals involving Indian workers in Malaysia in recent years. This occurred on a Federal Land Development Authority (FELDA) site, a plantation at Selanchar Empat in Kedah. This development had been awarded to a contractor. In 1983 it was revealed that the contractor had treated his Indian workforce as virtual slave labour. The workers had not been paid for years, and they and their families had been fed on minimum rations. The workforce was kept under guard twenty-four hours per day, and neither they nor their families were permitted to leave the site. Women were subjected to sexual abuse and children were ill-treated. Labourers were "disciplined" by being incarcerated in a chicken coop without food for days on end.[188] When the scandal broke, the government promised swift punishment for transgressors and appointed Samy Vellu as Works Minister to lead an investigation. However, before this could commence the ramshackle sheds in which the workers had been accommodated were burned down, and it was subsequently decided that all indictable evidence had vanished in the flames. Although the subcontractors were fined for failure to abide by the relevant legislation no serious charges were ever laid.[189]

COOPERATIVE AND SELF-HELP PROJECTS

Over the past fifty-sixty years the Indian community has experimented with a number of self-help projects, including cooperatives, all of which have been designed to uplift the Indian community as a whole. Apart from the National Land Finance Cooperative Society founded in 1960 by MIC President V.T. Sambanthan (described in Chapter 13), most other self-help schemes have proven failures, often dismally so. In most cases the factors which contributed to the collapse of these ventures — nepotism, patronage, self-interest, poor management — might have easily been avoided. Thus enterprises which might have produced beneficial results for the wider Indian community were often sidetracked by the very people who claimed to be the champions of the impoverished. The liquidation of these projects often left poorer sections of the Indian community — estate and working class Indians — significantly worse off.

NUPW Projects

Land Settlement

One of the first major NUPW-initiated projects was the Land Settlement scheme advanced by President P. Narayanan in 1955. Under this scheme it was proposed that labourers' accommodation as well as the roads leading to the workers' lines would be declared public property, and each labourer would be allocated a plot of land to which he would be given title. The NUPW contended that this would resolve the problem of the welfare of retired labourers as well as reducing plantation expenditure on housing. However, the plan was defeated by the combined opposition of the MPIEA and the colonial government. Off estate housing would have entailed planters relinquishing absolute control of their labour force, and in particular foregoing the application of the Trespass Law which gave them power to evict individuals deemed undesirable. The government, while seeing the merit of the scheme, was not prepared to enter into a dispute with the MPIEA, especially during the Emergency.[190]

Old Age Benefits

Although the NUPW had raised the issue of provision of old age pensions in discussions with the MPIEA, the latter regarded this as a state responsibility. In 1958 the NUPW negotiated an insurance scheme with Great Eastern Life Assurance. This arrangement not only provided endowment policies which matured upon retirement, but also incorporated accident benefits and medical coverage. Unfortunately these premiums were set too high for the low-waged estate workforce to meet monthly repayments, and the scheme ultimately fell into abeyance.[191]

GATCO and Multipurpose Cooperative Society

The Great Alonioners Trading Corporation (GATCO) was established in January 1967 and its partner body, the Multipurpose Cooperative Society, in 1968. While the NUPW had been shrilly critical of V.T. Sambanthan's NLFCS and had discouraged plantation workers from subscribing, it now maintained that Indian labour should raise their collective sights beyond routine pay claims and invest in business enterprises which would encourage productivity and self-reliance.[192] GATCO was established with an authorized capital of RM30 million. Earlier attempts to raise RM1 million from the NUPW membership had yielded a mere RM150,000 and the remainder had been accumulated from union and bank loans.[193] Directorships in GATCO and its subsidiaries were monopolized by leading members of the NUPW who received handsome remunerations for their services.[194]

GATCO moved into an array of enterprises, including textiles, confectionary, vehicle assembly, investments and essential oils.[195] None of these enterprises performed to expectations and indeed all operations were curtailed within a few years with accumulated losses running into the millions.[196] Its most cherished project was the Chempaka Negri Lakshmi Textiles Sdn Bhd. In order to ensure the overall success of the venture it was necessary to send a group of workers to India for advanced training in the textile industry. This training was funded by the NUPW. However, the candidates selected did not comprise any of the needy workers GATCO had been established to assist. Rather they consisted of the children and relatives of leading union officials.[197] Unsurprisingly, the company was poorly run and in 1988 GATCO sold its shares in Chempaka at a loss of RM3.45 million.[198]

In the late 1970s, GATCO embarked upon a project designed to promote entrepreneurial skills among agricultural workers. GATCO leased over 4,000 hectares of land in Bahau, Negeri Sembilan. It was envisaged that this would be converted into a flourishing cooperative growing sugar cane, and refining and retailing sugar. Participants were to be allocated one acre of land for housing and general agriculture with a further ten acres for sugar cultivation.[199] It was planned that a total of 540 families would ultimately work the estate. However, shortly after the first group of settlers had taken up residence, the nearby sugar mill, upon which the success of the entire scheme was dependent, ceased operations.[200] GATCO later converted the scheme into a rubber estate, but the project was never developed, and settlers were left heavily indebted, and without regular employment.[201] None of the workers who had invested in GATCO received any returns.[202]

GATCO's partner company, the National Multipurpose Cooperative Society, was established in 1968. The Society purchased two rubber estates, both of which were poorly managed.[203] The fact that the estates were owned by a cooperative under the control of the NUPW appeared to make no difference to wages and conditions upon these estates. Workers' wages were set no higher than the award rates struck between the union and the MAPA, and labourers and their families were accommodated in substandard housing, in many instances lacking access to such basic amenities as reticulated water, electricity and sanitation.[204]

Other NUPW Projects

The NUPW was also involved in investment schemes. Drawing on funds garnered from its members, the NUPW invested in two banks, Bank Buruh and the United Asian Bank. However, the promised returns failed to materialize, and the members' contributions were lost. As Janakey Raman Manickam cynically remarks, "The leaders of the NUPW and their cronies were the only ones to benefit under these economic plans."[205]

MIC Projects and Cooperatives

In finally acknowledging that the primary target of the NEP was the socio-economic transformation of the bumiputera population, and that the government was therefore unlikely to deliver other than basic resources to the Indian community, the MIC decided to embark upon a series of self-help projects. In pursuing this approach the party could point to the successful precedent of the NLFCS, launched under the leadership of V.T. Sambanthan.[206]

Two major self-help cooperative businesses were inaugurated in the mid-1970s under the leadership of MIC President V. Manickavasagam. These ventures were the *Syarikat Kerjasama Nesa Pelbagai* (NESA) and the MIC Unit Trust. Because these enterprises were established under the regulatory umbrella of the Cooperative Societies Act, their operations were subject to the close supervision and concomitant controls imposed by the Malaysian Director of Cooperatives and his senior officers. In founding and managing these undertakings the MIC did not draw upon available business expertise and, rather than concentrating upon long-term commercial outcomes, focused upon meeting immediate political demands and expectations. Given this backdrop it is not surprising that these enterprises struggled to survive and did not deliver the anticipated returns.[207]

NESA

This was a multipurpose cooperative formed under Manickavasagam's direction in 1974 with the aim of assisting Indians to acquire land for farming, housing, and business.[208] Following Manickavasagam's death in 1979, S. Subramaniam, Deputy President of the MIC, assumed control.[209] Throughout its early years NESA appeared to be flourishing and by the 1980s membership had risen to 38,000. However, while NESA continued to experience modest growth, the economic recession of the mid 1980s created cash flow problems, and the cooperative was placed in receivership in 1989.[210] A subsequent audit by Bank Negara disclosed financial mismanagement.[211] In 1997 NESA was once again allowed to function, but only under the stringent supervision of the relevant authorities.[212]

MIC Unit Trust

This scheme, launched in 1977 by V. Manickavasagam, was designed to boost Indian involvement in the share market with an ultimate aim of capturing ten per cent of the nation's wealth. However, from its inception the trust was stymied by internal politicking. Senior MIC members rather than qualified experts were appointed to the Board of Directors. Under their lacklustre leadership returns were mediocre and the trust did little to enhance overall Indian wealth.[213]

MAJU

Although the *Koperasi Belia Majujaya* (MAJU) was not established under the aegis of the MIC, it later fell within the party's power to retrieve its fortunes. MAJU was founded by the Tamil Youth Bell Club in April 1977 with the combined aim of assisting young Tamils to set up businesses and providing existing businesses with the help they needed for expansion. However, like NESA, MAJU experienced leadership issues and cash flow problems during the 1980s recession and passed into receivership in 1989.[214]

The difficulties experienced by NESA and MAJU were exacerbated by deep factional divisions within the MIC. Following Manickavasagam's death in 1979, both NESA and MAJU became associated with a faction opposed to the leadership of S. Samy Vellu, and were thus the subjects of internal MIC politicking. It was perceived that both NESA and MAJU were abandoned by the MIC leadership, not so much because of their financial difficulties, but rather because their revival might have reflected positively upon Samy Vellu's rivals within the party.[215]

Maika Holdings

Despite the chequered history of the MIC involvement in financial undertakings, the party leadership continued to assert that economic opportunities for Indians could only be furnished through MIC-sponsored projects designed to increase the Indian community's equity participation in commerce and business. Maika Holdings was a favoured project of MIC leader S. Samy Vellu, who contended that Indian prosperity would be best boosted through the agency of an investment company.[216] The MIC's insistence on creating a business ethos among Indians was driven by the "obsession" of its leadership that the wealth created by a new entrepreneurial class of Indians would ultimately lift the entire community out of poverty.[217]

Maika Holdings was established as a limited company on 13 September 1982.[218] The company was fully inaugurated in 1984 with a public subscription of RM106 million, contributed by 60,000 mainly working-class families, some of whom had pooled savings, borrowed money and pawned jewellery in order to acquire shares.[219] The MIC aimed to purchase equity in leading Malaysian firms and to promote its own business ventures. The company's immediate objective was to increase the Indian share of corporate wealth from its modest base of one per cent to a level of seven per cent by the end of the decade.[220]

Maika Holdings never delivered the anticipated returns. There were two fundamental factors which militated against success. First, the government extended little in the way of support. The imperatives of the NEP closed large sections of the economy to Indian participation. Samy Vellu commented, "We could not go into banking, finance, insurance, transportation, or even distribution sectors. Could not even get an agency. Wherever you look the word no, no, no was there. All we need was a small lift in life and the rest will be done by us."[221] But many of Maika's failings could be located within the company itself. Maika suffered from uninspired and underprepared leadership, limited vision and an ill-conceived investment strategy. Most of its investments were in faltering companies, including soft drink operations, book stores, a construction company, as well as manufacturing and trading ventures, all of which recorded heavy losses. Maika's poor performance never delivered the promised returns to the Indian community, and indeed left many worse off.[222] By 2000 Maika's net assets had dwindled to between RM30 and 40 million and the cooperative teetered on the verge of bankruptcy.[223]

However, Samy Vellu's claim that the government offered *no* support is incorrect. In a well-publicized scandal it was revealed that in September 1990 the government offered ten million shares of the newly privatized Telekom to Maika. Following the disclosure of this offer Samy Vellu initially responded that Maika could not afford to purchase the shares, but he later claimed that the shares would not be allocated to Maika because of its poor investment strategies.[224] Samy Vellu instructed the Finance Ministry to allocate a mere one million shares to Maika, and three million to each of three nominated companies, namely Advance Personnel Computers, SB Management, and Clearway Sdn Bhd. These transactions were highly controversial. The companies were all recently established, and were regarded as fronts to obfuscate dubious financial dealings. While Advance Personnel Computers had a paid-up capital of RM250,000, both SB Management and Clearway were RM2 shell companies.[225] Maika also received allocated shares from a number of other publicly listed companies, including MAS, TV3, MISC, EON, as well as others. However, Maika sold many of these shares in 1992 to enable the issue of a dividend to its members.[226] Thus, even when government support, however limited, was offered, the MIC failed to capitalize upon it for the greater good of the community.[227]

Educational Projects

Other MIC-initiated projects designed to benefit the wider Indian community have included the Maju Institute for Educational Development (MIED), the Vanto Academy and the *Institute Teknologi Negera* (ITN), all purchased in the 1980s. In 2001 the MIED established a medical college.[228] This was a contentious project which was viewed by opponents as an expensive "prestige" enterprise which did little to address the educational needs of Indian youths. Most MIC-related educational undertakings have been accessed by better-off elements within the Indian community, and have done little to assist poor or working class Indians.[229]

Throughout recent years, groups of concerned and well-educated Indians have established outreach educational bodies. The best known of these are the Education Welfare and Research Foundation (EWRF) which was founded in 1978 by a group of academics based at Universiti Malaya; the Sri Murugan Centre (1982); CHILD (1984);[230] and the Tamil Foundation, which, in addition to conducting research, provides a range of educational and cultural programmes, and in conjunction with EWRF helps Tamil schools with appropriate educational methodologies and in the establishment of interactive administrative structures.

EDUCATION

The broad parameters of the contemporary Malaysian education system were established by a committee, chaired by Tun Abdul Razak, and appointed in the wake of the Alliance victory of 1955.[231] The Razak Report of May 1956 recommended that all four language streams — Malay, English, Chinese, and Tamil — be maintained at primary school level, but that only three media — Malay, English, and Chinese — be retained at Secondary level.[232] This decision — not to provide Tamil secondary education — prevented an orderly transition between Tamil primary education and national secondary schools and has created major problems for countless Tamil students. Under the Razak proposals, all higher education was to be conducted in English.[233] The main recommendations of the Razak Report were subsequently incorporated into the Education Ordinance of 1957.[234]

But while the Razak Report allowed for Chinese and Tamil medium schools, the ultimate goal was to focus upon the establishment of Malay as the main medium of instruction within the national education system. The Education Act of 1961, which provoked prolonged criticism within the Chinese community, ruled that public examinations at secondary level were to be conducted in the two official languages of the Federation, namely English and Malay.[235]

Tamil Schools

Tamil schools are the neglected component of the Malaysian education system. They are regarded as poorly resourced, inadequately staffed and lacking community support structures. Many are dilapidated and neglected, and lack basic facilities such as electricity, running water, and sanitation. The majority have nothing that resembles a library.[236] In justifying the perennial underfunding of estate-based Tamil schools, the Ministry of Education fell back upon arguments that had persisted from the colonial era; namely that because the majority of schools are on private lands, it is the responsibility of estate owners rather than the government to maintain school buildings and to provide appropriate facilities.[237] Indeed, of 524 Tamil schools currently operating in Peninsular Malaysia, only 148 are fully funded by the government, while the remainder are partially funded.[238]

Many observers have highlighted the inadequacy of staffing within Tamil schools. Teachers are held to be poorly trained and underqualified and see their role as "custodians and gatekeepers" rather than as providers of quality education which will equip their charges to compete on equal terms with students from national or Chinese schools.[239] Following the introduction of Malay as the national educational medium, there was a pronounced shortage of Malay-language teachers throughout the Tamil school system which persisted well into the 1980s.[240] The most obvious solution would seem to be to extend the Tamil-medium schools to embrace secondary education, but this has been resisted by the government, and by some educators within the Indian community.[241]

Tamil schools labour under a number of handicaps. The most obvious problem for Tamil-educated primary students is the requirement to transfer into Malay-medium national-type secondary schools.[242] While Tamil students may achieve average scores at primary level, they often fail Bahasa Malaysia in large numbers.[243]

One of the major and seemingly insuperable problems is the low socio-economic environment in which Tamil schools are implicated and the lack of social and cultural capital which are invested within schools. As Rabindra Daniel has pointed out, many students come from homes which lack a tradition of learning and in which they may not be exposed to a single new idea, and in which culture is both enclosed and self-referential.[244] In such a milieu even parents who want their children to achieve a good education have no concept of how to facilitate this process.[245] Without some form of external stimulus to act as a circuit breaker, it is all but inevitable that the mutually reinforcing cycle of poverty, cultural deprivation, and educational underachievement becomes an inter-generational phenomenon.

As a result the qualifications and participation rates of Indian students fall well below those of students educated in Malay or Chinese medium schools. The drop-out rates at primary and lower secondary levels are estimated at 30 per cent; indeed a high proportion of estate children leave school at the end of Standard Six, in many cases to supplement family incomes.[246]

In the years since independence the number of Tamil schools and the percentage of Indians educated within them have both fallen dramatically. While at Merdeka there were 888 Tamil schools, by 1969 the figure stood at 662, whereas in 2009 the number had fallen to 524.[247] The percentage of Indian students studying at Tamil-medium schools has correspondingly reduced. By 2005 Tamil schools were educating approximately 100,000 children consisting of about 53 per cent of the Indian school-age cohort. While some 75 per cent of working class Indian families continue to enrol their children in Tamil-medium schools, most middle class Indians now send their children to Malay-medium schools.[248]

In 2000 the National Economic Consultative Council (NECC) discussed the plight of the Tamil school system and noted, *inter alia*, the poor quality of the teaching cadre, the inadequacy of staff to pupil ratios, and the paucity of funding. The NECC's deliberations did not translate into action,[249] and Tamil education remains the poor cousin of Malay education. In general the qualifications obtained by and the actual participation rates of Indian students fall below national averages. Approximately 30 per cent of Tamil students are estimated to drop out before completing their lower-secondary years. Moreover, some 20,000 Malaysian Indians miss out on pre-school each year, and the participation rate of 2.4 per cent falls substantially below the national figure of 3.2 per cent. More tragically, because they do not possess requisite official documentation (birth certificates, identity cards) an estimated 15,000 Indian children are each year excluded from the education system altogether.[250]

Muzafar Desmond Tate has pointed out that "For any community language and culture give it its identity and education provides the medium by which identity is transmitted to members. The issues associated with the education system that a given community adopts are as crucial as they are sensitive, particularly in a multiracial society such as Malaysia."[251] International comparative studies show conclusively that optimal educational outcomes among primary and secondary students are attained by students educated in their mother tongues. Unless addressed, the under-resourcing of Tamil schools, both in terms of human capital and physical infrastructure, will continue to impose a huge handicap upon the working-class Tamil community.

THE KAMPUNG MEDAN INCIDENT

In March 2001 violence broke out following two minor incidents within Kampong Medan, a squatter settlement where Indians and Malays had lived together peacefully for a number of years. On the night of 8 March gangs of Malays were observed attacking Indians along the roads leading through housing estates in the neighbouring suburbs of southern Petaling Jaya.[252] By 12 March six people had been killed in these attacks (five Indians and one Indonesian), and thirty-seven injured (thirty-four Indians and three Malays).[253] The first deployment of 400 police did not immediately stabilize the situation, and the attacks continued for a further three days, by which time fifty people had been injured, many seriously.[254] Casualties were overwhelmingly Indian.[255] While these disturbances are commonly referred to as the Kampung Medan incident and the victims were largely from the squatter settlement, in point of fact most of the actual violence occurred within the adjacent housing estates.[256]

Authorities were quick to cast this incident in terms of Malay reaction to Indian provocation. The setting lent itself to stereotyped judgements — a densely populated and impoverished suburb afflicted with crime, particularly Indian "gangsterism". Those accounts which highlighted the economic and social frustrations associated with a deprived squatter area conveniently glossed over the fact that the violence did not take place within Kampong Medan itself.[257] Although the vast majority of those killed and injured were Indian, the media portrayed the incident as Malays preyed upon by Indian gangs. Media reports suggested that there had been a recent "influx of Tamil gangs" which had created problems between the two communities.[258] Mainstream press accounts showed no photographs depicting Tamil victims.[259] Although the racial "clashes" had consisted of a series of organized attacks on Indians, UMNO politicians suggested that the violence had been a gang fight with Indians as the aggressors. Thus Taman Medan assemblywoman and Selangor Executive Councillor Norkhala Jamaluddin (UMNO) claimed that resident Malays had "long been patient although the Indians have attacked us again and again. Every three or four months we hear of incidents such as these. We [the Malays] have long been patient and many have been *terbokin*"(i.e., ending up as victims).[260] This theme was continued by Selangor Menteri Besar (Chief Minister) Mohamad Khir Toyo (UMNO) who informed a large (and indignant) Indian audience that the incident should be regarded as a "lesson".[261]

Indian victims maintain that their attackers were not local Malays, but rather unknown outsiders whose motives remain unclear. Indeed, Indian families informed the writer and other researchers of the kindness and consideration shown to them by their Malay neighbours who assisted them throughout this traumatic period.[262] Claims of outside intervention were supported by police investigations which revealed the participation of an organized militant Malay group.[263] More disturbingly, observers believe the police were both slow and reluctant to respond to the outbreak of violence, and in many cases showed unmistakable bias in fulfilling their duties.[264] Indeed, one injured victim claimed that the police refused to tender assistance, instead offering the comment that "it is better if you die".[265] Despite the presence of numerous eye witnesses prepared to testify, the police made few arrests and there were no convictions.[266]

Nor was there any official follow-up on the Kampung Medan incident. In the immediate wake of the violence, both the Home Minister and the Inspector-General of Police issued assurances that investigations would be both thorough and transparent.[267] However, although various groups — the victims themselves, the Bar Council of Malaysia, Indian human rights groups, and opposition political parties — pressed for an independent enquiry, no official action was taken.[268] Attempts to submit a memorandum to the Prime Minister and to launch an appeal through Malaysia's Human Rights Commission (*Suhukam*), proved fruitless.[269] Neither the police findings nor the official report of the National Unity and Social Development Ministry were made public.[270] The lack of official response gave rise to disconcerting rumours about the identity of the instigators of the violence and the consequent need of the government to hold silence on the incident. Nor did victims receive any official redress. Allegations were made that affected residents were bullied into silence by the MIC and in particular by its leader Samy Vellu, who was not prepared to imperil MIC's standing within the BN by pursuing the range of the troubling issues that the racial attacks had raised.[271] Thus victims were trebly punished. Not only had they been subjected to racial attacks, and denied the official protection of the law, but they were also vilified for supposedly causing the violence and finally they were refused either redress or assistance from the authorities and in particular from the very people who had been elected to represent them and to advance their interests.

SOCIAL PROBLEMS

The migration of former Indian estate labourers and their families to urban areas has been accompanied by a sharp rise in social problems. These include family breakdown and a concomitant rise in divorce, child abuse and suicide; the growth of gangs and an associated gang culture; drug and alcohol addiction; crime and prostitution. However, while these problems are acknowledged by all social commentators and scholars working within the community, conflicting statistics and social comparisons make it difficult to map the actual incidence of these phenomena. As M. Nadarajah points out, the extent of Tamil social ills has been the subject of ill-informed speculation and is easily overstated. He remarks:

> Many years ago, the Indians of the lower classes were labelled 'drunkards' and 'wife beaters' and later still they were known as 'child abusers'. While the multi-racial nature of these social ills was established, it was either ascribed to 'biology' or to the 'backward culture' of the Indians (Tamils).[272]

In discussing the extent of social problems among recently urbanized Indians, most scholars have emphasized the substandard living conditions endured by displaced plantation labourers. Left without social assistance, most Indians have ended up in squatter areas or in cheap and invariably overcrowded government flats, the latter often regarded as little more than "high rise slums".[273] Relocation to urban areas results in the break-up of the close-knit extended family structures and wider social communities which offered support and stability upon the estates.[274] The new living arrangements are devoid of social and community leadership as well as recognized community touchstones such as temples, Tamil schools and recreational outlets. They result in social isolation and alienation producing a sense of profound deprivation often amounting to a sense of crisis and despair.[275]

Youth gangs

Within Malaysia discussion of Indian social problems invariably returns to the vexed issue of youth gangs and the linkages between these gangs and organized crime. In their 1978 study Wiebe and Mariappen noted the arrival of gang chapters on the estates in the 1960s, and their putative function as a supposed self-defence force against outsiders.[276] My own research, based on extensive interviews with social and youth workers, academics and religious leaders, reveals that these estate-based gangs largely modelled themselves upon celluloid and musical heroes, and in the main avoided overtly antisocial behaviour. With the Tamils exodus from estates to urban centres the gang culture assumed an entirely different complexion. Gangs form around local associative hubs — neighbourhoods, schools, complexes. Many of these gangs associate themselves with a style which is highly particularistic and adopt the characteristics — mode of dress, patois, choice of music — emulated from specified elements of Tamil popular culture (especially films), and engage in behaviour which signifies resistance to dominant cultural norms. Those recruited into hard-core gangs originate from readily identifiable strata of society; they are generally from socially deprived families, are poor academic achievers, possess low self-esteem, and have few if any life goals. Generally recruits are initiated into the world of criminality with the performance of a nominated indictable action (often chosen under the specific instructions of the gang leader). Once this threshold has been crossed, the initiate finds it difficult to move back into the world he has left. Gangs will search out the recalcitrant among their number, and the fact that he has broken the law makes the reluctant member subject to blackmail and other pressures.

The extent of the gang problems is difficult to ascertain with any degree of accuracy. In 2001 A. Letchumanan estimated that there were thirty-eight known crime gangs in Peninsular Malaysia, with a total membership of approximately 1,500.[277] A 2010 study claims that 60 per cent of gang-related crime is committed by Indians, and that imprisoned gang members account for 63 per cent of all detainees under the Emergency Ordinance and 14 per cent of all incarcerated juveniles.[278] Nearly all social commentators interviewed by the writer stated that while detailed studies have identified an array of causative factors — alienation, poverty, social deprivation, and lack of inclusive government programmes — many BN politicians are content to attribute all Tamil youth problems to the supposed malign influences of violent Tamil cinema. Indian social commentators allege that police routinely profile Tamil youth for crimes and for antisocial behaviour,[279] and often make little distinction between those who are guilty of little more than exuberance and outward defiance and those who commit more serious transgressions.

While the influence of cinema upon Tamil youth may be over-emphasized, and has long been used as a convenient simplistic explanation for violent crime, antisocial behaviour and suicide within the Indian community, there is no doubt that films do have an impressionistic impact upon Indian audiences.[280] Indeed prominent film stars frequently become the subjects of almost cultic adulation, and posters and cut-outs are often venerated by fans through acts of idolatrous reverence more generally associated with religious observance.[281] Janakey Raman Manickam has pointed out that poorer Indians are habitual cinema attendees, and that young men often adopt the crude and uncouth mannerisms of film characters. In 2007 when tickets were sold out for premier screenings of a popular film entitled *Sivaji*, enraged patrons rioted and damaged the theatres and other property.[282] While I could locate no detailed research which traces the impact of cinema upon underprivileged Tamil youth, extensive anecdotal evidence suggests that antisocial influences are marked. This is a field which requires more extensive study.[283]

Stateless Indians

The issue of stateless Indians, in many cases an enduring legacy of the citizenship crisis of 1969–70, is a difficult issue to fully research or even quantify. Official statistics are unavailable, and there is an almost total absence of accessible documentation. However, I was informed by social workers that the number of stateless Indians, some of whom are fourth- or fifth-generation residents of Malaysia, could be as many as 100,000 people. Those without identity documents are ineligible to work within the civil service or even to obtain formal employment, are unable to obtain pensions or other benefits, cannot secure driving licences or trading permits, and are unable to open bank accounts or engage in any legal transactions. The children of the stateless, estimated to number between 30,000 and 40,000, are denied access to formal education. The extraordinary delays in securing citizenship, sometimes extending over decades, and the array of often pettifogging bureaucratic obstacles placed in the path of intending citizens, have discouraged many stateless Indians from pursuing their initial citizenship applications. Indian observers contrast the difficulties placed in the path of prospective ethnic Indian citizens with the comparative ease with which recent Indonesian migrants acquire citizenship.[284]

THE VIEW FROM ABOVE: UPPER CLASS INDIANS AND THE INDIAN DILEMMA

The political and social powerlessness of labouring Indians is aggravated by the continued studied indifference of many middle- and upper-class Indians towards their working-class counterparts. Indeed, many better-off Indians continue to feel shame and disgust at the plight of the Indian underclass and "often feel impatient and angry with the poor caught within the subculture of poverty".[285] In undertaking fieldwork for this volume, the author was informed on a number of occasions, often vociferously, that poor Indians only had themselves to blame for their predicament, and that any sympathy for their wretched condition was misplaced.

In his finely argued work, *Cage of Freedom: Tamil Identity and the Ethnic Fetish in Malaysia*, Andrew Wilford has commented upon the small but influential minority of those upper class "westernized" Indians who are seemingly ashamed of their own Indian heritage, and who are deeply critical of Indian culture, especially as it is manifested in working-class Tamils.[286] I have encountered this phenomenon frequently enough in my own research to confirm Wilford's observation that this assumed behaviour amounts to little more than a "gross caricature of Western decadence",[287] and would be regarded as such in most Western societies.

In Chapter 8, we noted that the varying streams of immigration to Malaya produced a minority Indian professional and mercantile class, and a small Indian middle class. Throughout the colonial period, with rare exceptions, these classes studiously maintained their social distance from the mass of labouring Indians who were characterized as lowly coolies. One could argue that the social gulf within Indian society remains as entrenched now as at any time throughout the entire history of the modern Indian presence in Malaya/Malaysia. Speaking at a conference convened in 2002 to explore ways of uniting the Indian community, Datuk Professor Ramachandran outlined the implications of this class divide in the following terms:

> K.S. Sandhu in his seminal work on Indian migration to Malaysia … describes the genesis of the middle class–working class chasm: 'Once this movement of literate Indians to Malaya began, many more emigrated from the same localities, and found employment on plantations and in other private enterprises where the employers found them invaluable assistants in dealing with Indian labour'. 'Invaluable assistants in dealing with Indian labour' is the operative phrase. Herein lay the mindset of the middle class Indian of today. A mindset steeped in sublime ignorance and blind arrogance, even to the point of denying the very roots of our common genetic heritage. A mindset that readily identified with the ruling class to subjugate and lord-over our downtrodden brethren. The same mindset persists today in the way we view ourselves. The microcosmic minority that has achieved the riches desired by all and sundry remains miniscule and withdrawn from the mainstream of daily problems faced by the toiling underclass majority. In between we have the not so significant middle class that wallows in its illusions of grandeur and is equally divorced from the problems of the vast majority. And all this is rooted in history.[288]

CONCLUSIONS

Mahathir's political outlook was shaped by Social Darwinist perspectives derived from colonial racial discourse which juxtaposed intrinsic Chinese "superiority" against inherent Malay "inferiority". Mahathir proposed nothing less than a revolution from above which would result in a modern and unified state that had outgrown the mental constraints of its colonial past, and in which Malay accomplishment would be an accepted fact of life.

The Mahathir years brought not only transformation, but also political tumult. The Malaysian economy was restructured from its dependence upon agriculture and extraction and became highly industrialized. But this was achieved against a backdrop of repeated financial scandals, growing authoritarianism, and deepening ethnic division. The overall failure of the Mahathir project to create a Malay class of entrepreneurs was starkly revealed during the 1997–98 financial crisis when many of the UMNO-sponsored conglomerates were rendered insolvent.

While Mahathir inspired genuine non-Malay enthusiasm for his Wawasan 2020 policy with its vision of a post-communal Bangsa Malaysia, Mahathir left Malaysia a deeply sundered nation. Throughout his tenure the ideology of race and inherent racial difference increasingly permeated both official and popular discourse, and a growing number of issues were defined solely in terms of race. His authoritarianism vitiated and politicized those institutions upon which the emergence of a national civic life ultimately depended, and concentrated power within the Executive, and increasingly within the office of Prime Minister. His sacking and humiliation of Anwar created deep rifts within the Malay community. Moreover his reliance upon the process of trickle-down economics while entrenching cronyism, patronage, and money politics within BN (and more particularly within UMNO), brought few benefits to those afflicted by hard-core poverty (including significant segments of the Malay community).

The initial promise that the NEP would eradicate hard-core poverty regardless of race did not translate into practice. The imperatives generated by communally based political structures meant that the principles of social justice were subordinated to those of ethnicity. Obligations to the indigent within non-bumiputera communities were easily evaded. The aggregation of "races" as composite wholes meant that average incomes could be used as a template to gauge the relative fortunes of entire "races", thus avoiding a more nuanced approach in identifying overall levels of poverty within the broader Malaysian community.

The implementation of the NEP coupled with a programme of rapid industrialization resulted in increasing marginalization of large sections of the Indian community. Positions within the civil service, traditionally a major employer of Indian labour, became increasingly scarce, and those that were offered were invariably at the lowest levels. At the same time educational policies mandated that preference should be given to Malays seeking enrolment in tertiary and technical institutions.

The central development affecting the Indian community throughout these years was the rural-urban migration of Indian labour, accelerated by the mass evictions of hundreds of thousands of Indian workers from rubber and other agricultural estates. These workers not only lost hereditary occupations and established vocational and social facilities, but received no assistance in relocating to the cities. Many struggled to find accommodation and were forced into squatter quarters. Unskilled and poorly educated, most Indian workers found employment in repetitive and poorly paid jobs which offered little in the way of training or vocational mobility. The poor living conditions spawned a range of attendant social problems, including alcoholism, drug abuse, marital breakdown, the growth of gang culture and alienation.

Throughout this period both Indian political and industrial wings proved generally ineffective. MIC attempts to secure BN support for redress of the problems facing the Indian community were largely unsuccessful, the UMNO leadership making it abundantly clear that Indian issues were not a government priority. Similarly the NUPW did little for its membership or to lift remuneration for plantation workers; indeed in comparative terms the conditions under which Indian estate employees laboured actually deteriorated and compared unfavourably to those of the colonial era. A series of self-help projects launched by the MIC and NUPW, each of which might have generated opportunities — both financial and vocational — for indigent Indians were all failures; the collective result of self-interest, incompetent leadership, poor investment strategies, political intrigue, corruption and nepotism.

Throughout the Mahathir period Tamil schools remained the poor cousin of Malay education. Tamil schools were under-resourced, poorly equipped, badly maintained and generally neglected, and classes were conducted by teachers, who, in the main, were inadequately trained and underqualified. Moreover, the failure of Tamil-medium education to offer secondary education continued to act as a major handicap to Tamil students proceeding beyond the primary level.

The Kampung Medan incident encapsulated the totality of the marginalization of the Indian working classes. A systematic series of attacks upon Indians which left six people dead and scores injured was not subject to any rigorous investigation, nor did it lead to a single prosecution. Indeed Indians gained the impression that they were officially held to be the instigators rather than victims of the violence, and that the established political and legal processes offered no points of redress or even explanation. For many Indians the Kampung Medan incident seemed not only to reveal the increasing political and social disregard for the Indian community as a whole, but also provided an alarming snapshot of how they were viewed by political elites.

Notes

1. J. Victor Morais, *Hussein Onn: A Tryst with Destiny* (Singapore: Times Books International, 1981), p. 32.
2. Cheah Boon Keng, *Malaysia: The Making of a Nation* (Singapore: Institute of Southeast Asian Studies, 2002), pp. 159–60.
3. Geoff Wade, *The Origins and Evolution of Ethnocracy in Malaysia*, Working Paper Series No. 12 (Singapore: Asia Research Institute, National University of Singapore, 2009), p. 21.
4. Rehman Rashid, *A Malaysian Journey* (Petaling Jaya: Rehman Rashid, 1993), p. 168.
5. Wade, *The Origins and Evolution of Ethnocracy*, p. 20.
6. Khoo Boo Tiek, *Paradoxes of Mahathirism: An Intellectual Biography* (Kuala Lumpur: Oxford University Press, 1995), p. 25.
7. Barry Wain, *Malaysian Maverick: Mahathir Mohamad in Turbulent Times* (Basingstoke: Palgrave MacMillan, 2009), p. 31.
8. Ibid., p. 40.
9. Ibid., p. 54.
10. John Funston, *Malay Politics in Malaysia: A Study of UMNO and PAS* (Kuala Lumpur: Heinemann Educational Books (Asia), 1980), pp. 181–82. Note that Mahathir specifically excludes religion from this process of acculturation (Ibid.).
11. Khoo, *Paradoxes of Mahathirism*, pp. 30–32; Gordon Means, *Political Islam in Southeast Asia* (Boulder, CO: Rienner, 2009), p. 121; Mahathir Mohamad, *A Doctor in the House: The Memoirs of Tun Dr Mahathir Mohamad* (Petaling Jaya: MPH Group Publishing, 2011), p. 91.
12. Syed Hussein Alatas, *The Myth of the Lazy Native* (London: Frank Cass, 1977), p. 154.
13. Ibid., p. 147.
14. Joel S. Kahn, *Other Malays: Nationalism and Cosmopolitanism in the Modern Malay World* (Singapore: Asian Studies Association of Australia in association with Singapore Press and NIAS Press, 2006), pp. 109–11.
15. Khoo Jay Jin, "The Grand Vision: Mahathir and Modernization", in *Fragmented Vision: Culture and Politics in Contemporary Malaysia*, edited by Joel S. Kahn and Frances Loh Kok Wah (Sydney: Asian Studies Association of Australia/ Allen and Unwin, 1992), pp. 58–60; Rehman, *A Malaysian Journey*, p. 166.
16. Khoo, *Paradoxes of Mahathirism*, pp. 74, 327–36.

17. Ibid., pp. 65–74; Edmund Terence Gomez and Jomo K.S., *Malaysia's Political Economy: Politics, Patronage and Profits* (Cambridge: Cambridge University Press, 1997), p. 169.

18. Cheah, *Malaysia*, p. 193; Alberto Gomes, "Superlative Syndrome: Cultural Politics and Neoliberalism in Malaysia", in *Multiethnic Malaysia: Past, Present and Future*, edited by Lim Teck Ghee, Alberto Gomes and Azly Rahman (Petaling Jaya: Strategic Information and Research Development Centre, 2009), p. 188; Khoo Boo Tiek, *Beyond Mahathir: Malaysian Politics and its Discontents* (London and New York: Zed Books, 2003), pp. 30–32.

19. James Chin and Wong Chin-Huat, "Malaysia's Electoral Upheaval", *Journal of Democracy* 20, no. 3 (July 2009): 73: Ahmad Mustapha Hassan, *The Unmaking of Malaysia: Insider's Reminiscences of UMNO, Razak and Mahathir* (Petaling Jaya: Strategic Information and Research Development Centre, 2007), p. 63.

20. Harold Crouch, "Authoritarian Trends, the UMNO Split and Limits to State Power", in *Fragmented Vision: Culture and Politics in Contemporary Malaysia*, edited by Joel S. Kahn and Francis Loh Kok Wah (Sydney: Asian Studies Association of Australia/Allen and Unwin, 1992), p. 25.

21. Sheila Nair, "Constructing Civil Society in Malaysia: Nationalism, Hegemony and Resistance", in *Rethinking Malaysia*, edited by Jomo K.S. (Kuala Lumpur: Malaysia Social Science Association, 1999), p. 92.

22. Crouch, *Authoritarian Trends*, pp. 23–27; Cheah, *Malaysia*, pp. 216–22.

23. Wain, *Malaysian Maverick*, pp. 64–65.

24. Ismail Kassim, *A Reporter's Memoir: No Hard Feelings* (Singapore: Ismail Kassim, 2008), p. 134.

25. Hwang In-Won, *Personalised Politics: The Malaysian State under Mahathir* (Singapore: Institute of Southeast Asian Studies, 2003), p. 293; Sabri Zain, *Face-Off: A Reformasi Diary (1998–99)* (Singapore: Big O Books, 2000), pp. 3–4; Cheah, *Malaysia*, p. 226.

26. Crouch, *Authoritarian Trends*, pp. 21–22.

27. Rehman, *A Malaysian Journey*, p. 186.

28. Ibid., pp. 186–88.

29. Wain, *Malaysian Maverick*, p. 166.

30. Ibid., pp. 172–73.

31. Rehman, *A Malaysian Journey*, p. 206.

32. Ibid., pp. 212–13; Hwang, *Personalised Politics*, p. 133.

33. Gomes and Jomo, *Malaysia's Political Economy*, p. 94.

34. Cheah, *Malaysia*, p. 190; Khoo, *Beyond Mahathir*, p. 143.

35. Maznah Mohamad, "Politics of the NEP and Ethnic Relations in Malaysia", in *Multiethnic Malaysia: Past, Present and Future*, edited by Lim Teck Ghee, Alberto Gomes and Azly Rahman (Petaling Jaya: Strategic Information and Research Development Centre, 2009), p. 133.

36. Wain, *Malaysian Maverick*, p. 102.

37. Gomes and Jomo, *Malaysia's Political Economy*, p. 27.

38. Ahmad Mustapha, *The Unmaking of Malaysia*, p. 270.

39. Gomes and Jomo, *Malaysia's Political Economy*, p. 238; Karim Raslan, *Ceritalah: Malaysia in Transition* (Singapore and Kuala Lumpur: Times Books International 1996), p. 69: Zawawi Ibrahim, "The New Economic Policy and the Identity Question of the Indigenous Peoples of Sabah and Sarawak", in *The New Economic Policy in Malaysia: Affirmative Action, Ethnic Equalities and Social Justice*, edited by Edmund Terence Gomez and Johan Saravanamuttu (Singapore: NUS/Institute of Southeast Asian Studies, 2013), p. 297.

40. Edmund Terence Gomez, Johan Saravanamuttu and Maznah Mohammad, "Introduction: Malaysia's New Economic Policy: Resolving Horizontal Inequalities, Creating Inequities", in *The New Economic Policy in Malaysia: Affirmative Action, Ethnic Inequalities and Social Justice*, edited by Edmund Terence Gomez and Johan Saravanamuttu (Singapore: NUS/Institute of Southeast Asian Studies, 2013), p. 17.

41. Ooi Kee Beng, *Arrested Reform: The Unmaking of Abdullah Badawi* (Kuala Lumpur: Research for Social Advancement, 2009), pp. 172–73.

42. Raymond L.M. Lee, "Symbols of Separatism: Ethnicity and Status Politics in Contemporary Malaysia", in *Ethnicity and Ethnic Relations in Malaysia*, edited by Raymond L.M. Lee (Northern Illinois University: Center for Southeast Asian Studies, 1986), p. 34; Maznah, "Politics of NEP and Ethnic Relations", p. 115.

43. Gomez and Jomo, *Malaysia's Political Economy*, pp. 22–23.

44. Nair, "Constructing Civil Society", p. 92; Karim, *Ceritalah*, pp. 164–65.

45. Sheila Nair, "Colonialism, Nationalism, Ethnicity: Constructing Identity and Difference", in *Multiethnic Malaysia: Past, Present and Future*, edited by Lim Teck Ghee, Alberto Gomes and Azly Rahman (Petaling Jaya: Strategic Information and Research Development Centre, 2009), p. 85.

46. Cheah, *Malaysia*, p. 144; Nair, "Constructing Civil Society", p. 93.

47. Joel S. Khan and Francis Loh Kok Wah, "Introduction", in *Fragmented Vision: Culture and Politics in Contemporary Malaysia*, edited by Joel S. Kahn and Francis Loh Kok Wah (Sydney: Asian Studies Association of Australia/Allen and Unwin, 1992), pp. 3–4.

48. Nair, "Constructing Civil Society", pp. 92–94.

49. Ibid., p. 94.

50. Ibid., pp. 95–96.

51. Kahn and Loh, "Introduction", pp. 3–4.

52. Gomez and Jomo, *Malaysia's Political Economy*, p. 168; Crouch, *Authoritarian Trends*, pp. 40–41. My own fieldwork supports this contention.

53. Cheah, *Malaysia*, p. 67.

54. Gomez and Jomo, *Malaysia's Political Economy*, pp. 39–40; Cheah, *Malaysia*, p. 144.

55. Hwang, *Personalised Politics*, pp. 149–54; Rehman, *A Malaysian Journey*, pp. 229–30.

56. Cheah, *Malaysia*, p. 67.

57. Ibid., p. 266.

58. In early 2010, when discussing political issues with members of BN component parties, I was informed that Malay "ultras" with strong links to retired leader Tun Dr Mahathir and certain cliques within UMNO were in fundamental opposition to the Prime Minister Najib Tun Razak's "1Malaysia" concept and the potential for reforms that would create a more inclusive Malaysia. These "ultras" intended to form a pressure group to check reforms which were perceived as detrimental to the philosophy of *Ketuanan Melayu* (Malay Supremacy). The group would articulate a range of extreme postures and make "ambit claims" on behalf of an imagined Malay constituency, thus in theory minimizing the manoeuvrability of the UMNO leadership. Several months after this conversation Perkasa made its appearance upon the political scene. The pressure group would appear to match the criteria adumbrated by my informants.

59. Heng Pek Koon, *Chinese Politics in Malaysia: A History of the Malaysian Chinese Association* (Singapore: Oxford University Press, 1988), p. 275.

60. Khoo, *Paradoxes of Mahathirism*, p. 282.

61. Kua Kai Soong, *May 13: Declassified Documents on the Riots of 1969* (Petaling Jaya: Suaram Komunikasi, 2007), p. 7.

62. Khoo, *Paradoxes of Mahathirism*, pp. 283–84.

63. Ismail, *A Reporter's Memoir*, p. 145.

64. Wain, *Malaysian Maverick*, p. 66.

65. Deborah Johnson, "Intellectual Statesmanship in the Mahathir Era", in *Malaysia: Public Policy and Marginalized Groups*, edited by Phua Kai Lit (Kajang: Persatuan Sains Sosial Malaysia, 2007), p. 152.

66. Heng, *Chinese Politics*, p. 275.

67. Wain, *Malaysian Maverick*, p. 69.

68. Ahmad Mustapha, *The Unmaking of Malaysia*, p. 48; R.S. Milne and Diane K. Mauzy, *Politics and Government in Malaysia* (Singapore: Federal, 1978), p. 226.

69. Wain, *Malaysian Maverick*, pp. 60–61.

70. M.C. Ricklefs et al., *A New History of Southeast Asia* (London: Palgrave Macmillan, 2010), p. 439.

71. Khoo, *Beyond Mahathir*, p. 65; Terence Edmund Gomez, "Ethnicity, Equity and Politics in Multiethnic Malaysia", in *Multiethnic Malaysia: Past, Present and Future*, edited by Lim Teck Ghee, Alberto Gomes, and Azly Rahman (Petaling Jaya: Strategic Information and Research Development Centre, 2009), p. 170.

72. Chin and Wong, "Malaysia's Electoral Upheaval", p. 74.

73. Cheah, *Malaysia*, p. 226; Liew Chin Tong, *Speaking of the Reformasi Generation* (Kuala Lumpur: Research for Social Advancement, 2009), pp. 62–63.

74. Wain, *Malaysian Maverick*, p. 79.

75. Wong and Chin, "Malaysia's Electoral Upheaval", p. 75.

76. Wain, *Malaysian Maverick*, pp. 231, 292–93; Cheah, *Malaysia*, p. 186; Sabri, *Face Off*, p. 30.

77. Wain, *Malaysian Maverick*, pp. 277, 299–300.

78. Ibid., p. 30.

79. Ibid., p. 75; Means, *Political Islam*, p. 140.

80. Cheah, *Malaysia*, pp. 67, 195: Liew, *Speaking for the Reformasi Generation*, p. 28.

81. Wain, *Malaysian Maverick*, p. 103.

82. Ricklefs et al., *A New History of Southeast Asia*, p. 396.

83. Johan Saravanamuttu, "The Great Middleclass Debate: Ethnicity, Politics or Lifestyle", in *Multiethnic Malaysia: Past, Present and Future*, edited by Lim Teck Ghee, Alberto Gomes, and Azly Rahman (Petaling Jaya: Strategic Information and Research Centre, 2009), p. 142.

84. The NEP was replaced by the National Development Policy (NDP: 1991–2000). This ran until 2000 when it was replaced with the National Vision Policy (NVP: 2001–10). While both the NDP and NVP introduced some modifications to overall government policy, in essence both maintained the main thrust of the NEP (Gordon Means, *Political Islam in Southeast Asia* [Boulder, CO: Rienner, 2009], pp. 351–52). The New Economic Model (NEM) which was proposed in 2010 continues to be structured around the concept of affirmative action (Gomez, Saravanamuttu, and Maznah, "Introduction", p. 1).

85. Khoo, *Beyond Mahathir*, p. 19.

86. Ahmad Fauzi Abdul Hamid, "Politically Engaged Muslims in Malaysia in the Era of Abdullah Badawi (2003–2009)", *Asian Journal of Political Science* 18, no. 2 (August 2010): 164.

87. Wain, *Malaysian Maverick*, p. 347.

88. Ibid., pp. 86, 113; Zaid Ibrahim, *In Good Faith: Articles, Essays and Interviews* (Kuala Lumpur: Zaid Ibrahim Publications, 2007), p. 280.

89. A major new study of the NEP (Edmund Terence Gomez and Johan Saravanamuttu [Editors], *The New Economic Policy in Malaysia: Affirmative Action, Ethnic Inequalities and Social Justice* [Singapore: NUS/Institute of Southeast Asian Studies, 2013]) and its successors suggests that the Policy was most effective throughout the socially redistributive phase of its existence (1970–90), when it significantly reduced poverty and created a large Malay middle class. Since then, the study suggests, the impacts have been largely negative. Apart from its failure to reach groups which might be regarded as

underprivileged (including substantial numbers of Malays), its deleterious outcomes include massive patronage and corruption, ethnic alienation, intra-group contestation and elite rent capture, institutional decline and poor delivery of services, deterioration in the quality of public education (especially at the tertiary level), underqualified and underperforming graduates, serious skills shortages, lack of entrepreneurship, low investment in research and development, reluctance to participate in new forms of economic enterprise, and serious brain drain especially, but not exclusively, among non-Malays to more meritocratic countries. Moreover, a policy designed to promote national unity has perpetuated and perhaps exacerbated ethnic polarization.

90. The comparative figures for Malays are 1.5 per cent and 21.9 per cent, and for Chinese 22.8 per cent and 34.9 per cent. (Edmund Terence Gomez, "Nurturing Bumiputera Capital: SMEs, Entrepreneurship and the New Economic Policy", in *The New Economic Policy in Malaysia: Affirmative Action, Ethnic Inequalities and Social Justice*, edited by Edmund Terence Gomez and Johan Saravanamuttu [Singapore: NUS/Institute of Southeast Asian Studies, 2013], p. 89).

91. Selvakumaran Ramachandran, *Indian Plantation Labour in Malaysia* (Kuala Lumpur: S. Abdul Majeed, 1994), pp. 306–7.

92. Ibid., pp. 222–323.

93. R. Thillainathan, "A Critical Review of Indian Economic Performance and Priorities for Action", in *Rising India and Indian Communities in East Asia*, edited by K. Kesavapany A. Mani, and P. Ramasamy (Singapore: Institute of Southeast Asian Studies, 2008), p. 322.

94. K. Anbalakan, "Socio-Economic Self-Help among Indians in Malaysia", in *Rising India and Indian Communities in East Asia*, edited by K. Kesavapany, A. Mani, and P. Ramasamy (Singapore: Institute of Southeast Asian Studies, 2008), pp. 422–23.

95. Janakey Raman Manickam, *The Malaysian Indian Dilemma: The Struggles and Agony of the Indian Community in Malaysia*, 2nd ed. (Klang: Janakey Raman Manickam, 2010), p. 232.

96. S. Nagarajan, "Marginalisation and Ethnic Relations: The Indian Malaysian Experience", in *Multiethnic Malaysia: Past, Present and Future*, edited by Lim Teck Ghee, Alberto Gomes, and Azly Rahman (Petaling Jaya: Strategic Information and Research Development Centre, 2009), p. 372.

97. Johan Saravanamuttu, "The Great Middle Class Debate", p. 142.

98. Muzafar Desmond Tate, *The Malaysian Indians: History, Problems and Future* (Petaling Jaya: Strategic Information Research Development Centre, 2008), p. 134.

99. Anbalakan, "Socio-Economic Self-Help", p. 422; S. Nagarajan, "Indians in Malaysia: Towards 2020", in *Rising India and Indian Communities in East Asia*, edited by K. Kesavapany, A. Mani, and P. Ramasamy (Singapore: Institute of Southeast Asian Studies, 2008), p. 112.

100. Nagarajan, "Marginalisation and Ethnic Relations", p. 372; Mavis Puthucheary, "Indians in the Public Sector in Malaysia", p. 337; Rajeswary Amplavanar-Brown, "The Contemporary Political Elite in Malaysia", p, 250, both in *Indian Communities in Southeast Asia*, edited by K. S. Sandhu and A. Mani (Singapore: Institute of Southeast Asian Studies, 1993).

101. These figures are exclusive of the police and army, both of which are bumiputera dominated.

102. Nagarajan, "Indians in Malaysia", pp. 382–83; Janakey Raman, *The Malaysian Indian Dilemma*, p. 312; Lim Hong Hai, "The Public Service and Ethnic Restructuring under the New Economic Policy: The New Challenges of Correcting Selectivity and Excess", in *The New Economic Policy in Malaysia: Affirmative Action, Ethnic Inequalities and Social Justice*, edited by Edmund Terence Gomez and Johan Saravanamuttu (Singapore: NUS/Institute of Southeast Asian Studies, 2013), pp. 178–82.

103. Puthucheary, "Indians in the Public Sector", p. 349; Janakey Raman, *The Malaysian Indian Dilemma*, p. 312; Lim, "The Public Service and Ethnic Restructuring", pp. 178–82.

104. Puthucheary, "Indians in the Public Sector", p. 349.

105. Nagarajan, "Indians in Malaysia", p. 381.

106. Nagarajan, "Marginalisation and Ethnic Relations", p. 373.

107. Ibid.

108. Andrew Wilford, *Cage of Freedom: Tamil Identity and the Ethnic Fetish in Malaysia* (Ann Arbor: The University of Michigan Press, 2006), p. 36.

109. Nagarajan, "Indians in Malaysia", p. 383.

110. However, these figures must be viewed in the context of the general expansion and transformation of the Malaysian economy and the rapid growth of middle class Malaysia.

111. Nagarajan, "Marginalisation and Ethnic Relations", p. 372.

112. Means, *Political Islam*, p. 350.

113. Lee Hock Guan, "Racial Citizenship and Higher Education in Malaysia", in *The New Economic Policy in Malaysia: Affirmative Action, Ethnic Inequalities and Social Justice*, edited by Edmund Terence Gomez and Johan Saravanamuttu (Singapore: NUS/Institute of Southeast Asian Studies, 2013), pp. 243–44.

114. Means, *Political Islam*, p. 351; P. Ramasamy, "Politics of Indian Representation in Malaysia", in *Rising India and Indian Communities in East Asia*, edited by K. Kesavapany, A. Mani, and P. Ramasamy (Singapore: Institute of Southeast Asian Studies, 2008), p. 364; Lee, "Racial Citizenship", pp. 247–49.

115. Lee, "Racial Citizenship", p. 249. However, it would seem that undertaking study in a meritocratic university is no guarantee of fair treatment. Claims of institutionalized discrimination against the Indian community surfaced during the so-called Ukrainian medical degree crisis. In 2001 the Malaysian Medical Council recognized the medical degree offered by the Crimea State

Medical University of the Ukraine. In August 2003 Prime Minister Mahathir, accompanied by the Minister of Education Tan Sri Musa Mohamad, met with students studying at the university. Popular discourse opined that Mahathir was shocked by the number of Malaysian Indians studying at the University. Shortly after his visit, the Malaysian Medical Council withdrew recognition of the medical degree, a degree which had received wide international acknowledgement. At the time, an estimated 581 Indian Malaysians, 220 Chinese and 231 Malays were studying at the University. Whether there was an actual linkage between Mahathir's visit and the subsequent Malaysian Medical Council's withdrawal of recognition is to some extent beside the point; the fact remains that many Indians believed that the withdrawal was the result of a direction issued by Mahathir. (Personal communications; see also Lim Kit Siang, *Emergency Motion-Call for Suspension of MMC's Derecognition of Ukraine's Crimea Medical University Medical Degree*, 21 June 2005 <http://www.dapmalaysia.org/all-archive/English/2005/jun05/lks/lks3525.htm> [accessed 12 February 2010]).

116. C.P. Ramachandran, "The Malaysian Indian in the New Millennium"; Keynote Address, The Malaysian Indian in the New Millennium Conference, Kuala Lumpur, May 2002.

117. K.S. Susan Oorjitham, "Economic Profile of the Tamil Working Class in Peninsular Malaysia", *Jurnal Pengajian India* 5, 1993, p. 102.

118. Tate, *The Malaysian Indians*, p. 129.

119. Nagarajan, "Indians in Malaysia", p. 377.

120. An example of this process may be seen with the establishment of the capital Putrajaya. This resulted in the resumption of four estates comprising 4,580 hectares and the eviction of 875 families or about 2,000 people. Although the workers were promised low-cost houses, a temple, a Tamil school and shops, in fact they were relocated to 400 substandard flats which lacked most social and recreational facilities (Liew, *Speaking for the Reformasi Generation*, p. 159; Janakey Raman, *The Malaysian Indian Dilemma*, pp. 212–15).

121. Nagarajan, "Indians in Malaysia", p. 374; Lim Teck Ghee, "Malaysia's Prospects: Rising to or in Denial of Challenges?" in *Multiethnic Malaysia: Past, Present and Future*, edited by Lim Teck Ghee, Alberto Gomes, and Azly Rahman (Petaling Jaya: Strategic Information and Research Development Centre, 2009), p. 485.

122. Lim, "Malaysia's Prospects", p. 485; Oorjitham, "Economic Profile", p. 105; Sivachandralingam Sundara Raj, "The London Dawn Raid and its Effect on Malaysian Plantation Workers", *Indonesia and the Malay World* 40, no. 116 (2012): 89.

123. Nagarajan, "Marginalisation and Ethnic Relations", p. 374.

124. Nagarajan, "Indians in Malaysia", p. 378.

125. Sivachandralingam cites the instance of the Tanjong Malim estate which was acquired by the government in 1997 at a price of RM321 million. The profit realized by the vendor, Kuala Lumpur Kepong, totalled RM301.7 million. The 137 workers received legally entitled benefits which totalled RM900,000, each worker being awarded RM6,600. Sivachandralingam notes that termination benefits paid to workers comprised a mere 0.28 per cent of the selling price of the estate (Sivachandralingam, "The London Dawn Raid", p. 89).

126. Nagarajan, "Marginalisation and Ethnic Relations", p. 377.

127. K. S. Susan Oorjitham, "Urban Indian Working Class Households", *Jurnal Pengajian India* IV (1986): 76.

128. Nagarajan, "Marginalisation and Ethnic Relations", p. 385.

129. Oorjitham, "Economic Profile", p. 101.

130. Ibid., p. 102.

131. Ibid.

132. Oorjitham, "Urban Indian Working Class Households", pp. 76–77.

133. Nagarajan, "Marginalisation and Ethnic Relations", p. 376.

134. D. Jeyakumar, "The Indian Poor of Malaysia: Problems and Solutions", p. 414; K.S. Susan Oorjitham, "Urban Working Class Indians in Malaysia", both in *Indian Communities in Southeast Asia*, edited by K.S. Sandhu and A. Mani (Singapore: Institute of Southeast Asian Studies, 1993), p. 508.

135. Thillainathan, "A Critical Review", p. 336.

136. Chandra Muzaffar, "Political Marginalization in Malaysia", in *Indian Communities in Southeast Asia*, edited by K.S. Sandhu and A. Mani (Singapore: Institute of Southeast Asian Studies, 1993), pp. 227–28; Thillainathan, "A Critical Review", p. 324.

137. Oorjitham, "Economic Profile", p. 102; R. Rajoo, "Indian Squatter Settlers: Rural-Urban Migration in West Malaysia", in *Indian Communities in Southeast Asia*, edited by K.S. Sandhu and A. Mani (Singapore: Institute of Southeast Asian Studies, 1993), p. 485.

138. Oorjitham, "Economic Profile", pp. 104–5; Oorjitham, "Working Class Indians in Malaysia", p. 507; Jeyakumar, "The Indian Poor of Malaysia", pp. 419–20.

139. Jeyakumar, "The Indian Poor of Malaysia", p. 421.

140. Oorjitham, "Urban Working Class Indians in Malaysia", p. 506.

141. Ramasamy, "Politics of Indian Representation", p. 355.

142. Ibid., pp. 361–62.

143. Selvakumaran, *Indian Plantation Labour*, pp. 318–22.

144. Ibid., p. 323; Wilford, *Cage of Freedom*, p. 45.

145. Janakey Raman, *The Malaysian Indian Dilemma*, p. 130; Tate, *The Malaysian Indians*, p. 131.

146. Rajeswary, "The Contemporary Indian Political Elite", p. 239.

147. Ramasamy, "Politics of Indian Representation", p. 364.

148. Rajeswary, "The Contemporary Indian Political Elite", pp. 242–45.
149. Ibid., p. 247. Indeed, it is popularly averred that his thespian talents served him well throughout his political career.
150. Tate, *The Malaysian Indians*, p. 133.
151. Janakey Raman, *The Malaysian Indian Dilemma*, pp. 351–53.
152. Ibid.
153. Rajeswary, "The Contemporary Indian Political Elite", p. 253.
154. Selvakumaran, *Indian Plantation Labour*, p. 319; Ramasamy, "Politics of Indian Representation", p. 361.
155. Selvakumaran, *Indian Plantation Labour*, p. 319; Janakey, *The Malaysian Indian Dilemma*, p. 244.
156. Tate, *The Malaysian Indians*, p. 148.
157. Milne and Mauzy, *Politics and Government in Malaysia*, p. 347.
158. Sivachandralingam, "The London Dawn Raid", p. 79.
159. Selvakumaran, *Indian Plantation Labour*, p. 307.
160. Janakey Raman, *The Malaysian Indian Dilemma*, p. 138.
161. Ibid.
162. Selvakumaran, *Indian Plantation Labour*, pp. 307–8.
163. Sivachandralingam, "The London Dawn Raid", p. 80.
164. Selvakumaran, *Indian Plantation Labour*, p. 310.
165. Ibid., p. 309.
166. Janakey Raman, *The Malaysian Indian Dilemma*, p. 164.
167. In 1980 a study conducted by J. Rabindra Daniel revealed that "materially speaking, the majority of the estate workers had a bare minimum of everything". Daniel found that seventy-two per cent of all labourers' income was expended on food; that the typical diet was of low nutritional value; that there was a high incidence of anaemia as well as deficiencies in iron and vitamin C; that family outlays often exceeded income; that the labourer and his family received poor medical care; and that the children of labourers were not only inadequately educated, but were not exposed to new ideas or concepts. (Rabinda. J. Daniel, "Poverty among the Indian Plantation Community", *Jurnal Pengajian India* I (1983): 126–33.
168. Selvakumaran, *Indian Plantation Labour*, p. 308; Janakey Raman, *The Malaysian Indian Dilemma*, p. 176.
169. Selvakumaran, *Indian Plantation Labour*, p. 309.
170. Lim, "Malaysia's Prospects", pp. 484–85.
171. Nagarajan, "Indians in Malaysia", p. 387.
172. Sivachandralingam, *The London Dawn Raid*, pp. 75–76, 80.
173. Tate, *The Malaysian Indians*, p. 147.
174. Ibid.
175. Milne and Mauzy, *Politics and Government in Malaysia*, p. 223.

176. Janakey Raman, *The Malaysian Indian Dilemma*, p. 232.
177. P. Ramasamy, *Plantation Labour, Unions, Capital and the State in Peninsular Malaysia* (New York: Oxford University Press, 1994), p. 138.
178. Tate, *The Malaysian Indians*, p. 145.
179. Ramasamy, *Plantation Labour*, pp. 139–40.
180. Ibid., pp. 145–46.
181. Ibid., pp. 141–42.
182. Ibid., p. 166.
183. Ibid., pp. 139–40.
184. Tate, *The Malaysian Indians*, p. 130.
185. Thillainathan, "A Critical Review", p. 337; Sivachandralingam, "The Dawn Raid", p. 80.
186. Ramasamy, *Plantation Labour*, pp. 148–49.
187. Ibid., p. 151.
188. Janakey Raman, *The Malaysian Indian Dilemma*, pp. 160–61; Ramasamy, *Plantation Labour*, p. 151.
189. Janakey Raman, *The Malaysian Indian Dilemma*, p. 162.
190. Ramasamy, *Plantation Labour*, p. 106.
191. Ibid., p. 106.
192. Selvakumaran, *Indian Plantation Labour*, p. 253.
193. Ibid., p. 286.
194. Janakey Raman, *The Malaysian Indian Dilemma*, pp. 316–18.
195. Selvakumaran, *Indian Plantation Labour*, p. 287.
196. Anbalakan, "Socio-Economic Self Help", p. 425; Selvakumaran, *Indian Plantation Labour*, p. 288.
197. Janakey Raman, *The Malaysian Indian Dilemma*, p. 319.
198. Selvakumaran, *Indian Plantation Labour*, p. 288.
199. Ibid., pp. 289–90.
200. Ibid.
201. Ramasamy, *Plantation Labour*, pp. 152–53.
202. Janakey Raman, *The Malaysian Indian Dilemma*, p. 318.
203. Selvakumaran, *Indian Plantation Labour*, p. 287.
204. Ibid.; Ramasamy, *Plantation Labour*, p. 152.
205. Janakey Raman, *The Malaysian Indian Dilemma*, p. 321.
206. Anbalakan, "Socio-Economic Self Help", p. 425.
207. Selvakumaran, *Indian Plantation Labour*, p. 311.
208. Anbalakan, "Socio-Economic Self Help", p. 426.
209. Janakey Raman, *The Malaysian Indian Dilemma*, p. 322.
210. Anbalakan, "Socio-Economic Self Help", pp. 426–27.
211. Janakey Raman, *The Malaysian Indian Dilemma*, p. 322.
212. Ibid.

213. Ibid.
214. Anbalakan, "Socio-Economic Self Help", pp. 426–27.
215. Ibid., p. 430.
216. Selvakumaran, *Indian Plantation Labour*, p. 312.
217. Tate, *The Malaysian Indians*, p. 229.
218. Janakey Raman, *The Malaysian Indian Dilemma*, p. 325.
219. Selvakumaran, *Indian Plantation Labour*, p. 311; Anbalakan, "Socio-economic Self Help", p. 427.
220. Janakey Raman, *The Malaysian Indian Dilemma*, p. 324.
221. Selvakumaran, *Indian Plantation Labour*, p. 312.
222. Ibid.
223. Tate, *The Malaysian Indians*, p. 154; Anbalakan, "Socio-Economic Self Help", p. 427.
224. Selvakumaran, *Indian Plantation Labour*, p. 312.
225. Janakey Raman, *The Malaysian Indian Dilemma*, pp. 328–29.
226. Anbalakan, "Socio-Economic Self Help", pp. 431–32.
227. Selvakumaran, *Indian Plantation Labour*, p. 312.
228. Anbalakan, "Socio-Economic Self Help", p. 429.
229. Ibid.
230. Ibid.
231. Ooi Kee Beng, *The Reluctant Politician: Tun Dr Ismail and His Time* (Singapore: Institute of Southeast Asian Studies, 2006), p. 79; T. Marimuthu, "The Plantation School as an Agent of Social Reproduction", in *Indian Communities in Southeast Asia*, edited by K.S. Sandhu and A. Mani (Singapore: Institute of Southeast Asian Studies, 1993), p. 470.
232. Tate, *The Malaysian Indians*, p. 165.
233. Ibid., p. 166.
234. Ooi, *Reluctant Politician*, pp. 79–80.
235. Tate, *The Malaysian Indians*, p. 166.
236. Daniel, "Poverty among the Indian Community", p. 131; Wilford, *Cage of Freedom*, p. 45.
237. Tate, *The Malaysian Indians*, p. 173; Janakey Raman, *The Malaysian Indian Dilemma*, p. 295.
238. Janakey Raman, *The Malaysian Indian Dilemma*, p. 294.
239. Marimuthu, "The Plantation School", p. 480; K. Arumugan, "Tamil School Education in Malaysia: Challenges and Prospects in the New Millennium", in *Rising India and Indian Communities in Malaysia*, edited by K. Kesavapany, A. Mani, and P. Ramasamy (Singapore: Institute of Southeast Asian Studies, 2008), p. 401.
240. Tate, *The Malaysian Indians*, p. 171.
241. Ibid., pp. 174–75.

242. Ibid., p. 17.

243. Thillainathan, "A Critical Review", p. 345.

244. Daniel, "Poverty among the Indian Community", p. 131.

245. Arumugan, "Tamil School Education", p. 404; Marimuthu, "The Plantation School", p. 480.

246. Janakey Raman, *The Malaysian Indian Dilemma*, p. 359; Daniel, "Poverty among the Indian Community", p. 131.

247. Janakey Raman, *The Malaysian Indian Dilemma*, p. 294.

248. Arumugan, "Tamil School Education", pp. 401–4.

249. Janakey Raman, *The Malaysian Indian Dilemma*, p. 287.

250. Ibid., p. 359.

251. Tate, *The Malaysian Indians*, p. 159.

252. Nagarajan, "Marginalisation and Ethnic Relations", p. 379.

253. Andrew C. Wilford, "Ethnic Clashes, Squatters and Historicity in Malaysia", in *Rising India and Indian Communities in Malaysia*, edited by K. Kesavapany, A. Mani, and P. Ramasamy (Singapore: Institute of Southeast Asian Studies, 2009), p. 440.

254. Nagarajan, "Marginalisation and Ethnic Relations", p. 379.

255. Ibid. The final injury toll was seventy people. The ethnic breakdown comprised fifty-six Indians, eight Malays, three Indonesians, one Chinese, one Bangladeshi, and one Sahaban (S. Nagarajan and K. Arumugam, *Violence against an Ethnic Minority in Malaysia: Kampung Medan, 2001* [Petaling Jaya: Suaram, 2012], p. 45).

256. Nagarajan, "Marginalisation and Ethnic Relations", pp. 390–92.

257. Wilford, "Ethnic Clashes", p. 441.

258. Nagarajan and Arumugam, *Violence against an Ethnic Minority*, p. 31.

259. Nagarajan, "Marginalisation and Ethnic Relations", p. 380; Wilford, "Ethnic Clashes", p. 440.

260. Nagarajan, "Marginalisation and Ethnic Relations", p. 382.

261. Wilford, "Ethnic Clashes", p. 443.

262. See, for example, Nagarajan and Arumugam, *Violence against an Ethnic Minority*, p. 92.

263. Nagarajan, "Marginalisation and Ethnic Relations", p. 387. Witnesses noted that the attackers were "uniformly dressed", spoke with a non-familiar accent, and chanted Islamic slogans throughout the assaults (Nagarajan and Arumugam, *Violence against an Ethnic Minority*, p. 96).

264. The Malaysian Police force is now overwhelmingly Malay in composition. In 2010 80 per cent of the police force were Malay (14 per cent other bumiputeras) while Indians constituted a mere 4 per cent and Chinese only 2 per cent (Lim, *Public Service and Ethnic Restructuring*, p. 182).

265. Wilford, "Ethnic Clashes", p. 443.

266. Ibid., p. 444.
267. Nagarajan and Arumugam, *Violence against an Ethnic Minority*, p. 77.
268. Nagarajan, "Marginalisation and Ethnic Relations", p. 380.
269. Lim, "Malaysia's Prospects", p. 486.
270. Nagarajan, "Marginalisation and Ethnic Relations", p. 380.
271. Ibid., p. 382.
272. M. Nadarajah, "The Indian Community and Minority Status", in *Another Malaysia is Possible and Other Essays*, edited by M. Nadarajah (Kuala Lumpur: Nohd, 2004), p. 215.
273. Nagarajan, "Marginalisation and Ethnic Relations", p. 386; Wilford, *Cage of Freedom*, p. 290.
274. A. Letchumanan, "Nagging Pains of Local Indians", in *Another Malaysia is Possible and Other Essays*, edited by M. Nadarajah (Kuala Lumpur: Nohd, 2004), p. 173.
275. Nagarajan, "Marginalisation and Ethnic Relations", p. 386; Wilford, *Cage of Freedom*, p. 290.
276. Paul W. Wiebe and S. Mariappen, *Indian Malaysians: The View from the Plantations* (Delhi: Manohar, 1978), pp. 87–88.
277. Letchumanan, "Nagging Pains of Local Indians", p. 169.
278. Haris Ibrahim, *Gangsterism in the Indian Community*, 7 June 2010 <http//www.harismibrahim/wordpress/com/2010/06/07/gangsterism-in-the-Indian-community> (accessed 10 June 2010).
279. Wilford, *Cage of Freedom*, p. 31.
280. Ibid, p. 213; Janakey Raman, *The Malaysian Indian Dilemma*, p. 383.
281. "Malay Indians urged not to 'over-idolise' Tamil actors", *Malaysian Sun*, 4 March 2013 <http://www.malaysia.com/index.php/sid/212965/sat/48cbc686fe041718/nt/e/Malay-Indians-urged-not-to-over-idolise-Tamil-actors> (accessed 5 May 2013).
282. Janakey Raman, *The Malaysian Indian Dilemma*, p. 383.
283. Many Tamil movies are highly stylised and tend to follow a predictable formula which incorporates dancing, fantasy, and escapism. Increasingly Tamil movies contain scenes of gratuitous and often graphic violence. Social activists who work with disadvantaged Tamil youth have informed me that when gangs assemble and fight they often employ salutes, tactics, slogans, and verbiage learned from the latest movies. The influence of Tamil cinema upon Tamil society appears to be deeper than some commentators will allow. Maria Misra points out that when the famous Tamil actor M.G. Ramachandran (popularly known as MGR) suffered a stroke during a tour of the United States, dozens of his fans hacked off their own limbs in acts of self-identification, and following his death in 1982, thirty-three fans committed suicide (Maria Misra, *Vishnu's Crowded Temple: India Since the Great Rebellion* [London: Allen Lane, 2007], p. 293).

284. Personal field research; P. Uthayakumar, *Marginalization of the Indians* (copy emailed to author on 6 April 2010).
285. Jeyakumar, *The Indian Poor of Malaysia*, p. 419.
286. Wilford, *Cage of Freedom*, p. 210.
287. Ibid.
288. Ramachandran, *The Malaysian Indian in the New Millennium*.

15

ABDULLAH BADAWI, ISLAMIZATION, AND THE RISE OF HINDRAF

Dato Seri Abdullah Ahmad Badawi succeeded Dr Mahathir as Prime Minister on 31 October 2003, having served as his loyal Deputy in the period which followed the sacking of Anwar Ibrahim. Abdullah was a well-credentialed Islamic scholar who brought a mild and mannered approach to the conduct of public affairs.[1] Initially Abdullah won wide support. He discarded some of Mahathir's more extravagant projects, offered no opposition to the Supreme Court ruling which quashed Anwar's sodomy conviction, and abandoned Mahathir's plans for a population of seventy million.[2] He enunciated plans for tackling poverty and reinvigorating agriculture and rural development. His liberal approach foreshadowed greater freedom of expression.[3] Following several high-profile arrests for corruption, Abdullah promised to curb abuses of power and to reform a police force notorious for its corruption and brutality.[4] He introduced a programme of *Islam Hadhari* (Civilizational Islam), which appeared to be tolerant and moderate and which he proclaimed as the guiding lodestar of his administration.[5] Asking Malaysians to "work with me, not for me", Abdullah won a sweeping election victory on 21 March 2004 with BN claiming 199 of 219 seats. Abdullah was aided by an astonishingly inept campaign by PAS which openly supported Osama Bin Laden and Afghanistan's Taliban.[6]

The 2004 election marked the apogee of Abdullah's leadership. Early in the second term the seeming reformist zeal which had led to his electoral triumph petered out and was replaced with hesitancy and indecision. Muhammad Takiyuddin Ismail and Ahmad Fauzi Abdul Hamid contend that from the very outset Abdullah faced near impossible obstacles. He lacked an established power base within UMNO and many of his Malay Cabinet colleagues were hard-line Malay nationalists. He was unable to develop patronage networks or deliver economic rewards to supporters within the party, and key reforms were opposed by influential elements within UMNO and the police.[7] Abdullah was accused of protecting the business interests of his son, Kamaluddin, and son-in-law Khairy Jamaluddin,[8] and of shrouding government decisions, especially the awarding of contracts, cumulatively worth billions of dollars, in secrecy.[9] Moreover, Abdullah's *Islam Hadhari* did not translate to moderation at the grass-roots level, and he appeared to be both incapable and unwilling to impose any curbs on the more obvious excesses of Islamic bureaucrats.[10] His jettisoning of some of Mahathir's most prized projects resulted in his former leader launching a series of vitriolic denunciations which were to continue throughout the remainder of his Prime Ministership.[11] More crucially, Mahathir was able to activate opposition among his loyalists within UMNO and the media.[12]

Abdullah's Prime Ministership was marked by increasing public disquiet about the culture of Malaysian political life, worries about racial and religious polarization, and concerns about the independence and integrity of the nation's public institutions.

The Lingam Tape

In September 2007 Anwar Ibrahim released a video clip which showed a prominent lawyer, V.K. Lingam, in a telephone conversation with a major judge of the Mahathir period, apparently engaged in fixing appointments to the Supreme Court.[13] The government's initially tepid response provoked the Malaysian Bar Council to organize a protest and on 26 September 2000 lawyers and their supporters marched through the capital Putrajaya demanding a proper investigation into the issues raised by the tape.[14] The Royal Commission subsequently appointed by Abdullah and convened in early 2008 summonsed a number of very senior witnesses, including Dr Mahathir, his associate Vincent Tan, two retired judges, and a former minister.[15] The commission's report, released after the election of 8 March 2008, found that Mahathir and others had been involved in fixing the appointments of judges, thus casting severe doubts on the propriety and fairness of judicial hearings over the previous twenty years.[16]

Bersih

In early 2007 a number of concerned NGOs and opposition parties formed a committee to demand electoral reforms. This new organization, known as *Bersih* (Clean), appeared to gain significant public support.[17] On 10 November 2007 Bersih staged a major public demonstration. Between 30,000 and 50,000 people, mainly Malays, but including members of other ethnicities, marched to the Istana (royal palace) to present the Agong with a memorandum requesting electoral reforms.[18] The Malaysian press, downplaying the extent of public support, reported that the demonstration had attracted a mere 4,000 participants.[19]

Ketuanan Melayu

Abdullah also proved ineffective in controlling the extreme elements in his party, especially those attempting to impose an extremist Malay–Muslim agenda. This phenomenon, known as *Ketuanan Melayu* (perhaps best translated as Malay mastery or supremacy) manifested not only in political culture but also that of public institutions.

Many scholars noted the emergence of a culture of complacency and indeed arrogance among certain sections of the Malay elite, coupled with deliberate efforts to downplay, belittle, obfuscate or even deny the contributions of non-Malays.[20] In November 2005 delegates to the UMNO General Assembly made disparaging remarks about non-Malays who were referred to as *pendatang* (recent arrivals).[21] No less a personage than the Education Minister, Hishammuddin Hussein, brandished a kris, a threatening and offensive gesture repeated at the 2006 conference, while other speakers warned that any challenge to Malay dominance would lead to bloodshed. The UMNO General Assembly of November 2006 was also replete with racial posturing, and jibes and insults directed at non-Malays.[22] Public concern, especially among non-Malays, deepened when it was later revealed that civic courses mounted by the *Biro Tata Negara*

(National Civics Bureau) habitually lauded the superiority of the Malay "race" while downplaying the contributions of non-Malays, who were referred to as "temporary residents".[23]

Although undergoing modifications, the NEP, initially introduced for a period of twenty years, appeared to have become firmly entrenched as a permanent feature of the Malaysian political and social landscape; indeed, many commentators (both Malay and non-Malay) consulted by this writer habitually refer to the NEP as "the never ending policy". The NEP (and its successors the NDP and the NVP) has become a formidable weapon within the UMNO armoury, not only in terms of generating Malay support, but also to reward politicians and their supporters and to distribute favours to vested interests.[24] A 2004 study which indicated that the bumiputera corporate share of national wealth had reached 45 per cent (15 per cent greater than the 30 per cent target and more than double the "official" figure of 18.7 per cent), created a furore.[25] A further study in August 2005 contended that 36 per cent of total market capitalization was under the control of corporations associated with UMNO.[26]

By late 2007 disillusionment with the Abdullah regime was widespread. While it was recognized that he had succeeded to the Prime Ministership of a country governed by a culture of entrenched patronage and in which all public institutions had been comprehensively politicized, his early promises of reforms had excited hopes of fresh approaches to public policy. However, it had become obvious that Abdullah had promised more than he could deliver, and that he was unwilling and perhaps unable to confront a political culture that was deeply embedded within UMNO. The ethos of urgency which appeared to mark the opening stages of his leadership was replaced with a sense of drift and indecision, and inability to engage with pressing issues. Among the most compelling of these were the tensions engendered by what appeared to be the inexorable Islamization of Malaysian public life.

ISLAM AND ISLAMIZATION IN MALAYSIA

In the years since the 1969 racial riots and the introduction of the NEP, Malaysia has witnessed a powerful Islamic resurgence which has led to an exhaustive and often contentious debate about the role of Islam within the state. This has been accompanied by a comprehensive re-evaluation of religious structures and practices. These processes have revealed deep and often bitter fissures within the Malay community. This section will provide an overview of the processes of Islamization and their impact both upon Malay and non-Malay communities.

As we have noted, the definition of Malay ethnicity contained within the Malayan Constitutional Settlement of 1957 incorporated both Islam and *adat*, and enshrined Islam as the official religion of Malaya.[27] However, the Alliance stressed that while no person would be permitted to proselytize "among persons professing the Muslim religion", the Malayan state would be secular and would guarantee freedom of religious belief. In practice, the Alliance assurance that Islam would not widely impinge on public and political life was essentially compromised from the time of the declaration of Merdeka. The constitutional definition of a Malay as both a person who professed the Muslim faith and as one who because of his/her "race" enjoyed a suite of special privileges in perpetuity, conflated ethnicity and religion, thus creating from the outset a fundamental split in the Malayan population between Malay/Muslim and non-Malay/non-Muslim. The various measures taken by Islamic authorities to protect the religion from the perceived encroachments of other civilizational or religious impulses, and to prevent its own adherents from lapsing into secularism, ensured that this division, would, over time, become both immutable and impermeable.[28]

Most scholars date the genesis of the contemporary Islamic revival from the period immediately following the 1969 racial riots.[29] While Islamization has led to a heightening of religious consciousness, especially among the Malay middle class,[30] and among many of the thousands of young Malays who have migrated from rural areas to work in the newly established trade zones,[31] in the main the activists have been young, tertiary educated, and often influenced by pan-Islamic ideologies.[32] Islamic revivalism has fragmented into a wide array of groups encompassing a diversity of stances ranging from moderate to radical.[33] Indeed, specific groups find it largely impossible to develop claims or speak on behalf of the wider Muslim community.[34] The spread of Islamic movements has been accompanied by deepening divisions within the Malay community, especially between the radical *dakwah* (missionary) groups which advocate the imposition of a theocratic state, and the more moderate "secular" Malays.[35]

The processes of Islamization have been given considerable impetus by developments of recent years. Many Malays genuinely believe that the Islamic world is the target of a major US-led Western-Christian conspiracy to infiltrate and thus destroy their religion.[36] The impression of an Islam besieged by a relentlessly Christianizing West gained wide currency during the years of the presidency of George W. Bush. While many countries were initially sympathetic to the United States in the wake of the attacks on the World Trade Center in New York on 11 September 2001, and subsequently supported the American-led invasion of Afghanistan,[37] Muslim concern was aroused by the events that followed. These included neo-conservative depictions of a monolithic and inherently violent Islam;[38] the establishment of a concentration camp at Guantanamo Bay; the invasion of Iraq in March 2003 and the subsequent detention and torture of Muslim prisoners (many of whom were compelled to eat pork and consume alcohol).[39] The perceived demonization of Islam by US commentators and agencies, and the anti-Muslim and pro-Zionist posture of US Christian fundamentalists,[40] coupled with the continuing encroachments of a globalizing Western culture, viewed as nihilist, decadent and corrosive,[41] has strengthened the determination of many Muslims to take whatever steps are necessary to buttress Islam as a cardinal pillar of Malay culture.

However, one of the most potent impulses which has underscored Islamic resurgence in Malaysia has been that of religion as a signifier of Malay identity. While Malays have generally regarded Islam as coterminous with "Malayness",[42] until 1969 religion was merely one of several obvious components of Malay ethnic identity. The constitutional amendments of 1971 and the cultural policies of the same year clearly established aspects of Malay ethnicity other than religion — language, the sultanates, Malay culture — as the fundamental organizational principles around which the modern Malaysian nation was to be constructed. In an ethnically charged environment in which notions of Malayness and Malay statecraft were to be regarded as normative, Islam could be viewed as the final bulwark of Malay exclusivity and thus as a potential or actual basis for political mobilization.[43] Within Malaysia the universalism of Islam has thus assumed a particularistic form, which integrates Islam under the rubric of Malay ethnicity and may be employed as a means to both define and insulate Malayness. This particularism may also be called upon to demarcate Malay Islam from that of other communities, for example Indian Muslims, and the smaller community of Chinese Muslims and recent converts.[44] In relation to non-Muslims, Islam is a potent ethnic marker, and Islamic symbols, rituals and practices become means of emphasizing and reinforcing Malay distinctiveness.[45] In more extreme instances Islam may be erected as a barrier to interaction and as an expression of superiority to other communities.[46]

A spate of violent incidents since the mid-1970s heightened public unease, and led to the introduction of measures to curb the activities of radical Islamic groups. These episodes included the following:

1. Between December 1977 and August 1978, a band of young men, university lecturers and students, clad in Arab attire, and calling themselves "The Army of Allah" conducted a series of nocturnal assaults on Hindu temples in various parts of the country, resulting in the destruction of statuary including dedicated *murthis*.[47] These raids ceased following an armed clash with Hindu temple guards in the Subramaniar Temple at the Southern Perak town of Kerling on 19 August 1978. Four young Malays were killed in this exchange.[48]
2. In October 1980, a group of entranced Muslim radicals, believing themselves invulnerable to bullets, and acting under the tutelage of a Cambodian visionary — himself a recent convert and claiming to be the Mahdi — launched a frenzied attack on a police station in Batu Pahat, Johor. Eight people were killed, including a pregnant Muslim woman who was slashed to death by the attackers, and twenty-three people were injured.[49]
3. In 1985, police attempts to arrest an Islamic leader, Ibrahim Mahmud, known as Ibrahim Libya, who had established a commune in Kampong Memali in the Baling area of Kedah, resulted in armed confrontation in which eighteen people were killed. The police subsequently arrested 159 villagers, including women and children.[50]
4. In 2001, the government took measures to destroy *Al Ma'unah*, an alleged Islamic terrorist organization, whose leader had reportedly led an armed body in a raid aimed at stealing weaponry and ammunition from an army camp in Perak; an action which was seen as a prelude to an attempted coup.[51]

The government is thus aware that, if left unchecked, Islamic radicalism has the potential to foment political instability and to ignite both inter-ethnic and intra-Malay violence.[52]

Islamization: The Government's Response

As we have seen, the constitutional settlement bestowed upon Malays, by definition Muslims, a suite of special privileges. It was thus perhaps inevitable that Islam should become a key symbol and factor in both the enhancement of Malay rights and the enforcement of Malay political dominance.[53] As Ahmad Fauzi Abdul Hamid comments: "Given the legally coterminous position between Islam and Malayness in Malaysia, it is hardly surprising that politicians of all divides have manipulated Islam as a political tool to realize their racial agendas".[54]

The struggle to define and control Malay Islamic identity has been fiercely and occasionally violently contested between the two Malay-based political parties, the ruling UMNO and the opposition party PAS, both of which view Malay-Muslims as their natural constituency.[55] The ideological conflict between the two parties has often been couched in misleadingly reductive terminology, namely UMNO "modernism" as opposed to the "traditionalism" of PAS. In fact, the debate largely reflects Malay ambivalence to the impact of "modernization" and the massive social pressures unleashed by rapid economic growth and sweeping structural changes.[56] Thus the ideology enunciated by each party represents a critique of contemporary Malaysian society, "a political vision grounded in modern realities."[57] In fashioning narrative structures which clearly locate Malaysia within mainstream Islam, Malay Muslims have turned to the broader intellectual currents of an imagined Islamic *ummah* (Islamic community), in particular those which emphasize the histories and traditions of classical Islamic triumphalism focussing especially upon the glories of the seventh century Caliphate.[58] However, competing ideologies interpret this history and extrapolate central themes in radically different ways.[59] In general, while UMNO has propounded the benefits of a fully developed state, informed by a moderate, revitalized and pragmatic Islam, PAS has cultivated a programme rooted in the history of an imagined classicist *ummah*, and defined in terms of the enduring framework of *fiqh* (or Islamic jurisprudence).[60] PAS thus transcends issues relating to Malay ethnic specificity in search of a perceived Islamic universalism; that is, the establishment of an Islamic, rather than a Malay state.[61] It is important to note, however, that all narratives posit Islam as a religion able to negotiate and accommodate the processes of modernization according to its own history and traditions, and in terms of its own belief structures.

Apart from the attempt to portray PAS as an extreme and dangerous force, the government has responded with what has been basically a three-pronged policy; namely (1) reassurance of non-Muslim communities, including a series of speeches by high-profile leaders and the sultans in which it has been repeatedly emphasized that it is an Islamic duty to display tolerance towards those of other religious persuasions; (2) the pursuit of legal and extra-judicial measures to curb the growth of Muslim radicalism and to check the activities and organization of student *dakwah* movements; and (3) the adoption of a policy of Islamization. The latter measure was viewed as a strategy which would both counter and outflank the growing pressures by Islamic reform groups, as well as nullifying accusations that UMNO was doing little to advance the cause of Islam.[62] However, UMNO is aware that this policy must be carefully calibrated to avoid alienating the powerful Chinese business sector or deterring foreign investment.[63]

In 1982, UMNO proclaimed itself the largest Islamic party in the world, and adumbrated a policy of official Islamization.[64] The Malaysian government's programme resulted in the establishment of an International Islamic University (*Universiti Islam Antarabangsa Malaysia* or UIAM), the founding of an Islamic banking system, the setting up of an Institute for Islamic Research, and the introduction of measures to assist poorer Muslims to undertake the Haj.[65] At the same time the programme of Islamization was initially both measured and cautious, and Mahathir, as Prime Minister, assured both coalition partners and foreign investors that Malaysia would remain a moderate and stable regime, and that Islamization would complement rather than retard modernization.[66]

In 1988 Mahathir and UMNO approved a constitution amendment to Article 121(A) which stipulated that the High Court or judiciary "shall have no jurisdiction in respect of any matter within the jurisdiction of the *syariah* courts" (i.e., the courts administering Islamic law).[67] Non-Malay parties within BN were persuaded to vote for the measure after receiving UMNO assurances that the amendment would in no way infringe upon the rights of non-Muslims.[68] In effect the amendment meant that any decision reached by the *syariah* courts was beyond the review or appeal of the civil courts.[69] As we shall see this was to have far-reaching implications.

In September 2001 Mahathir created pandemonium when he declared that Malaysia was an "Islamic state". A subsequent booklet, issued by the government and intended to clarify the statement, but which, in the process, clearly relegated non-Muslims to a secondary position, only succeeded in deepening non-Muslim alarm. Mahathir's comment was made following the introduction of a welter of measures designed to shore up UMNO's "Islamic" credentials vis-à-vis PAS.[70] Mahathir's deliberate use of loaded but ambiguous religious terminology (for example, "Muslim nation", "Muslim state", "Islamic State", "Muslim fundamentalism") was clearly an exercise in multi-vocality aimed at sending coded messages to a varied Muslim audience.[71] In 2007 Deputy Prime Minister Najib Razak reiterated Mahathir's claim that Malaysia was an Islamic state with the added comment that Malaysia had never been secular.[72]

During Abdullah's tenure it appeared that the Prime Minister had scant commitment to the defence of religious freedom, or to the rights of minority religions. Abdullah abrogated control of the direction of *Islam Hadhari*, entrusting its administration to an ever expanding and conservative Islamic bureaucracy which launched "a definite push ... to recognize Islam as the core central and overriding feature of the constitution".[73] This agenda consisted of the inculcation of a statist Islam that is "performative in nature, not because it is not substantive, but part of the process of making Islam obvious and overwhelming through the process of reification, reiteration, repetition and citation in public life". Under bureaucratic guidance, a homogenous Islam would be enforced through *syariah*, in the process rendering it beyond contestation of even the formal processes of scholarly inquiry.[74] Zaid Ibrahim has portrayed this version of Islam as:

> strongly pedagogical with an emphasis on rites and rituals, and what is *haram* (forbidden) and *halal* (possible), rather than on the principles of Islam. The Islam in Malaysia is more concerned with the appearance of piety — through dress, prayers, recitations, observations of appropriate dates — than the religion's emphasis on strength of character, spiritual faith and making use of one's talents and abilities to advance human civilization.... Many *ulamas* have rarely demonstrated any intellectual rigour in finding meaningful solutions to real problems confronted by Malays in their daily lives.[75]

The unease felt by many non-Muslims escalated throughout the years of Abdullah's rule. While there were a number of incidents involving religion throughout this period, two issues, namely the fate of the organization known as Article 11 and the Azlina Jalim/Lina Joy controversy, served as sharp focal points for crystallization of both Muslim and non-Muslim concerns.

Article 11

In 2005 a group of concerned citizens — both Muslims and non-Muslims — formed an Interfaith Council to discuss religious issues. Following the organized opposition of vocal Muslim groups, the government ordered the council to disband. However, a new multi-faith group, named Article 11 (after the article in the Constitution guaranteeing religious freedom), was subsequently formed. This was subject to the active opposition of a body known as the Allied Coordinating Council of Islamic NGOs (ACCIN).[76] Claiming that Article 11 was "anti-Islamic", ACCIN-organized mobs disrupting Article 11 meetings in Kuala Lumpur and Johor Bahru.[77] Following an ACCIN-inspired demonstration in Kuala Lumpur, the government banned Article 11 and ordered an immediate cessation of the discussion of interfaith issues. However, this ban was not extended to public meetings held by Muslims to discuss the issue of apostasy.[78]

Lina Joy

Azlina Jalim declared herself a Christian in 1990, and subsequently took the name Lina Joy. Advised by the National Registration Department that she was not permitted to alter her legally registered religious status without a certificate of apostasy from the Syariah Court, Ms Joy appealed to the Federal Court on 30 May 2007. In a majority two-to-one judgement, the Federal Court declined her application, commenting, *inter alia*, that: "A person who wants to renounce his/her religion must do so according to existing laws or practices of the particular religion ... *a person cannot, at one's whims and fancies, renounce or embrace a religion*" (emphasis added).[79]

In 2007 public disquiet increased after outgoing Chief Justice Ahmad Faruz Sheik Abdul Halim suggested that Malaysia dispense with English common law.[80] His remarks were subsequently endorsed by Dr Abdullah Zin, a Minister in the Prime Minister's Department, and won the approval of Attorney-General Gani Patail.[81] In 2008 a further outgoing Chief Justice suggested that Malaysia should consider an amalgam of *syariah* and common law.[82]

The increasing imposition of an imagined Islamic orthodoxy upon the Malay community, and the greater prominence bestowed upon Islam as a fundamental marker of ethnic identity, not only allows the deployment of Islam in terms of ethnic privileging, but also reflects continuing displacement of *adat* in the social construction of "Malayness".[83] In this regard the seeming obsession of the Islamic hierarchy with the issue of apostasy is instructive. A recurring motif of Malay discourse is a fear than Malays might "disappear from the world".[84] Commenting upon the Lina Joy decision Azza Basarudin makes the profound point that the case casts attention on the Malay-Muslim fixation with demarcation of ethnic boundaries, that is of "insiders" as opposed to "outsiders". She states that "Individuals, particularly women ... who transgress the pre-set borders of racial and/or ethnic purity are ... [conceived of as] ... deviant communal actors with blatant disregard for the survival of the Muslim *ummah*, thus the act of transgressing these borders allows for racial and/or ethnic superiority to be normalized, reproduced and reinforced".[85] Apostasy, or *takut aqidah rosak* (fear of faith being undermined[86]), has in recent years been viewed as a potential "floodgate", which if permitted would open the way for wide-scale Malay conversion and undermine or even destroy the Malay "race". Thus, commenting on the Lina Joy case, Islamic clerics opined that if apostasy was allowed it would signal a mass exodus of Muslims which "would be the end of the Malay race".[87] Another cleric, the Mufti of Perak, announced, without any supporting evidence, that 100,000 Muslims had left Islam and that a further 250,000 were waiting to leave.[88] This fear is sometimes expressed in terms that appear to verge on the apocalyptic. Thus in late 2006 a widely circulated SMS text message foretold of a supposed large-scale conversion of Malays to Catholicism. Those arriving at the scene, presumably to defend Islam, discovered nothing more portentous than a number of non-Malays taking their first communion.[89] In 2007, writing on the Joy judgement, Noor Yahayah Hamzah, in a statement that appears to reflect animist rather than Islamic beliefs, reported: "There is a rumour going round in Malay circles that Christian churches, give out 'Holy Water' and that if a Malay drinks it, he/she will be possessed and become Christian."[90]

The emphasis upon Islam tends to obscure the general moderation of the Malay community and their wide acceptance of the multi-ethnic and multi-religious nation in which they form the undisputed majority.[91] This contention is supported by an analysis of Malay voting patterns; Maznah Mohamad has clearly demonstrated that Islamization has no great electoral appeal, and indeed PAS suffered its worst results when "it was strident with its Islamization agenda".[92]

Islamic Revivalism and Inter-Ethnic Relations

In general the rise of Islam and the process of Islamization have been viewed with alarm, occasionally approaching panic, by non-Muslims. Most non-Muslims believe that Islamization poses a severe threat to both ethnic and religious integrity, and perceived the official emphasis upon Islam as further confirmation of their second-class status. Many feel intimidated by the intolerance and incipient authoritarianism of radical *dakwah* groups, and by the continual intermittent calls issued by PAS and other Islamic bodies for the development of an Islamic state and the full implementation of Islamic law for citizens whether Muslim or non-Muslim.[93] The passage of the Islamic Administration Bill of 1989, which *inter alia* allows non-Muslim minors to convert to Islam upon reaching the age of puberty (*balign*) according to the *syariah*, was seen by many non-Muslims as a prelude to an Islamic campaign of mass conversion of the children of non-Muslims thus denying other religions of future generations of adherents.[94] There has been growing non-Muslim suspicion that UMNO's attempts to counter PAS radicalism through a process of Islamization represent a continual and incremental form of appeasement, and will ultimately result in the adoption of extreme measures which will gravely diminish the rights of non-Muslims.[95]

THE RISE OF HINDRAF

Ultimately it was the perceived excesses of the Islamic authorities and the general disrespect shown towards the major Hindu symbols which were to serve as the catalyst for translating simmering Indian frustrations into action. Chapter 14 outlined events surrounding the introduction of the NEP and the growing marginalization of the working-class Tamil population which constitutes the overwhelming majority of the Indian community. These included their displacement from the estates, and the seeming systemic denial of education, vocational, and economic opportunities. Throughout these years one might have formed the impression that influential elements of BN, together with the leadership of the MIC, had taken the Indian vote for granted and had assumed that Indians would remain content with a regime of benign neglect. However, my own long-term observations — confirmed in discussions with other scholars, and by widespread consultations within the broader Indian community — revealed mounting alienation, despair and anger, and rapidly escalating resentment at the official dismissal of social, economic, and vocational needs. Following the Maika scandal (outlined in Chapter 14), there appeared to be a sharp decline in public confidence in the MIC, the leadership of which was portrayed as being out of touch with its constituency, corrupt, self-interested, and powerless. During the period 2002–5 one gained the impression that Indian tensions were close to breaking point. The rise of Hindraf followed a series of well-publicized incidents which included the seizure by Islamic officials of the remains of individuals whose families identified them as Hindus; forced conversions and attempted forced conversions of people who identified themselves as practicing Hindus; the tearing asunder of established families; and the destruction of temples, several of which had served Hindu communities for more than a century. The following paragraphs will outline some of these developments.

"Body Snatching"

Although there have been several incidents in which Islamic authorities seized the bodies of individuals whose families identified them as practising Hindus, the most prominent of these was that of mountaineering hero Maniam "Everest" Moorthy who died on 20 December 2005. The Islamic authorities alleged that Moorthy had secretly converted to Islam and that he should therefore be buried according to Islamic rights. As a Hindu, his widow, Kaliammal Sinnasamy, who had not been notified of her husband's alleged conversion, was locked out of the Syariah Court which determined the validity of his religious standing. The court ruled that Moorthy had died a Muslim despite Ms Kaliammal and other witnesses arguing within the public sphere that Moorthy had lived as Hindu, had eaten pork, drunk beer, attended Hindu festivals and practised Hindu rituals until his death. When Ms Kaliammal took the matter to the High Court, the judge invoked Article 121(A), thus ruling that the civil court was not empowered to review the judgement passed by the Syariah Court. The Islamic authorities subsequently buried the body according to Islamic rites.[96]

The Moorthy incident was one of a number of similar such bizarre instances. In several cases Islamic authorities accompanied by riot police, forcibly removed the bodies of others — Buddhists, Hindus, Sikhs, and Christians, all of whom had been deemed Muslims by *Jabatan Kemajuan Islam Malaysia* (Malaysian Department of Islamic Development or JAKIM) — from the homes of grieving relatives. In certain cases relatives were forbidden to pray for the deceased.[97]

In October 2006 Fauzi Mustaffar, Director of the Islamic Law Department within the insurance company Takaful Malaysia circulated an email forbidding Muslim employees from extending Deepavali greetings to Hindus. Fauzi claimed that because the festival involved the worship of Hindu deities, wishing people well was endorsing if not actually practising polytheism and was thus contrary to the tenets of Islam. In the ensuing uproar, government spokesmen stated that Fauzi's approach did not reflect official policy and Fauzi later issued a retraction. However, in the interim the declaration was seen by many Hindus as a gratuitous insult and confirmation of their second-rate status.[98]

Conversions

Revathi

While Revathi Masoosai was born to parents who had converted to Islam, she was raised by her grandmother as a Hindu and given a Hindu name. As an adult she married V. Suresh according to Hindu rites. She was advised by the Melaka Islamic Religious Department to apply to the Melaka Syariah High Court to resolve her religious status. She was immediately charged with apostasy and forcibly separated from her sixteen month old baby which was handed to her Muslim mother.[99] Revathi was confined in prison-like conditions within an Islamic "rehabilitation" centre in Ulu Yam, Selangor, for six months. There attempts were made to force her to pray, to wear a head scarf, and to eat beef.[100] At the end of this period, when Ms Revathi continued to prove resistant to conversion, the court ruled that she had to live with her parents.[101]

While the Revathi controversy was creating discontent and resentment among Malaysian Hindus, comments made in March 2007 by Muhammad Burok of the Syariah Lawyers Association created further unease. Exhorting non-Muslims to accept the reality of the jurisdiction of the Syariah Court, and not to fear its fairness, he stated "*Syariah* law is not a written law as it is based on Allah's revelation. Obviously it did not come after independence.... But in Malaysia it becomes a problem because *Syariah* law is written." When it was suggested that a system of law framed specifically for Muslims might not be acceptable to those of other religions, Muhammad responded, "They will have to learn to accept it."[102]

P. Marimuthu

P. Marimuthu and his wife of twenty-one years had been wed according to Hindu rites. His spouse, known to the authorities by the Muslim name

Ramiah Bibi Nordin, was an ethnic Indian adopted by Muslim parents, but her status as a Muslim was discovered only when she applied for a new identity card.[103] The couple's children were detained after a raid by religious officials who told Marimuthu that as Ramiah remained a Muslim (despite practising Hinduism for over two decades), their marriage was invalid.[104] Indeed, at one point Marimuthu was warned by an *ustaz* (religious scholar) that unless he converted to Islam he would be charged with *khalwat* (close proximity).[105] In May 2007, Marimuthu was awarded custody of his children, but his wife was ordered to live separately.[106]

Temple demolitions

However, the issue which provoked the greatest Hindu outrage was that of a wave of temple demolitions. These commenced in the early 2000s and created profound hurt, grief and distress among Hindu Malaysians, as well as sense of profound misgiving among other non-Muslim communities. In earlier days when there was a need to demolish temples the authorities had taken a conciliatory approach which respected the sensitivities of the communities affected. Time was allowed for the de-sanctification of the temple, including the performance of necessary rites, and the orderly removal of the *murthis* and other sacred objects. Alternative sites were offered for the relocation of temples.

No such considerations attended the demolitions in the period from 2004 onwards. A precedent had occurred in the 1990s in Perak when some seventy temples had been demolished on a week's notice to make way for a road development.[107] After 2004 temples were demolished with patent disregard for the feelings or beliefs of Hindus. Often occupying gangs operating under the protection of police quite wilfully destroyed temple statuary and sacred objects. Communities were rarely given the opportunity to retrieve temple effects or to conduct appropriate de-sanctification rituals. In the few cases where alternative sites were made available for the relocation of temples, the plots of land were too small or completely unsuitable (for example in one instance adjacent to a sewage pond, and in another a site that had recently been used as an abattoir).[108]

Most of the temples thus destroyed were "plantation" temples: that is, temples that had originally been constructed on estates which had subsequently been sold or broken up for housing or industrial development. Many of these temples had been in use for over a hundred years and had a deep significance for the devotees who frequented them. Because these temples had no formal title to the land which they occupied they were regarded as "illegal" structures. However, the circumstances of their construction coupled with the length of prior occupation and the fact of community ownership would seem to make such claims both legally and morally tenuous.[109]

S. Nagarajan has argued that the haste with which these demolitions were carried out and the failure to negotiate with the relevant communities could be attributed to two factors, namely:

1. The high price of land. Many of the plantations had been acquired at considerable cost and the companies involved wanted to obtain returns on their investments as soon as possible. The formal and potentially tedious process of consultation with temple committees was viewed as a time consuming and unnecessary encumbrance standing in the path of rapid development and subsequent financial returns.
2. Companies reached agreement with state and local authorities to conduct demolitions with the understanding that efficient action would be rewarded with certain favours (for example, the granting of contracts, business concessions, etc.). These authorities were not inclined to delay demolition to accord with the sensitivities of the communities involved.[110]

In video footage shown to the author, and in interviews, informants reported that in many cases the prelude to the actual demolition followed a predictable format. A group of people would appear, claim to be devout Hindus, dispute the legitimacy or control of the temple within the community, and spark some sort of physical confrontation with devotees. In most cases these people were unknown to the community. In the ensuing fracas security personnel would move in, ostensibly to control the crowd, but in fact to occupy the temple. Video coverage showed that several readily identifiable provocateurs were present at a number of these incidents lending weight to devotee claims that these individuals had been hired as professional troublemakers.

As the temple demolitions became more frequent, Hindu communities noted a decreasing lack of concern, often amounting to a patronising dismissiveness, among the relevant sections of the bureaucracy. Thus attempts to present a petition to the Kuala Lumpur City Hall regarding the projected destruction of the sixty-year-old Aum Sri Siva Balakrishnan Muniswarar temple in Setapak proved fruitless; the nominated official, Mohammad Amin Nordin Abdul Aziz, Deputy Director of Services, refused to meet with petitioners.[111] Interviewees reported a new sense of arrogance and condescension among civil servants regarding the representations of affected Hindu communities, having little regard for their distress and generally responding as though their religion had little claim upon the officials' time and was in any case unworthy of respect or consideration. As the demolitions continued, dangerous confrontations occurred with increasing regularity between the largely Muslim demolition crews and police on the one hand, and Hindu devotees on the other.[112]

Matters reached a crisis point with the demolition of a century old temple in Shah Alam on 30 October 2007, a week prior to the major Hindu festival of Deepavali. The demolition crew was accompanied by a large contingent of regular and riot police.[113] A group of Hindu devotees had gathered to protect the temple. In the clash that followed fourteen devotees were arrested, temple statuary was vandalized, and the temple priest, Siva Ramalinga Gurukkal, was assaulted by police while he attempted to carry sanctified temple *murthis* from the temple. The security personnel were alleged to have resorted to unnecessary violence, and photographic evidence clearly spotlighted police carrying weapons including *parangs* and pieces of wood, and throwing stones at devotees.[114] Several arrests were made. This incident sparked local outrage and was covered in news services around the world.

Hindraf

In 1993 S. Arasaratnam pointed to the growth of an Indian working-class consciousness with a class culture of its own which has developed within the specific circumstances faced by the estate labour force. He described this as "plantation-oriented culture". Arasaratnam suggested that this class, comprising between seventy and eighty per cent of the Indian population of Malaysia, had been "buffeted by authoritarianism and paternalism ... [at]... every turn".[115] In Chapter 14 we noted the displacement of plantation workers, their drift into urban poverty, and the daunting array of social and economic problems which had resulted from this transition. Most scholars agree that the perceived attacks on the beliefs of Hindus — the forced conversions, and the concomitant break-up of established families;

the seizure of bodies of alleged converts to Hinduism thus entailing the committal of the remains of loved ones by strangers rather than by families and friends; the insensitive demolition of temples which lay at the very heart of enduring Hindu communities, and the deliberate, often provocative destruction of sacred items, usually without a pretence of negotiation — struck at the very essence of Hindu identity and integrity within Malaysia, and pushed many Indians beyond their limits of endurance.[116] The MIC was increasingly viewed as incapable of dealing with this issue; it was seen as corrupt and ineffective;[117] "a toothless and hopelessly compromised coterie of moribund elitists concerned solely with advancing matters of pecuniary interest to the party leadership".[118]

The activists who were to form the Hindu Rights Action Force (Hindraf) arose from the ranks of the Tamil "plantation culture". In the period 2003–4 a number of Indian NGOs were formed to monitor developments within the broader Indian community, such as the alarming number of Indian deaths in police custody, and Tamil education.[119] In January 2006 in the wake of the "Everest" Moorthy case, representatives of forty-eight Indian NGOs formed Hindraf to examine the perceived oppression of Hindus within the wider context of the generalized marginalization of the Indian community as a whole.[120]

During the twelve months following Hindraf's formation, some of the more conservative and pro-MIC elements left Hindraf which increasingly fell under the influence of two brothers, Wayamoorthy and Uthayakumar Ponnusamy. Both were energetic activists who believed that the path of direct action was the only way of forcing the government to take note of Indian concerns. Both were criticized within the broader Indian community for being "too extreme", for the use of over-emphatic language, and for being unwilling to compromise.[121]

In an interview conducted on 14 May 2010, P. Uthayakumar explained the philosophy which underlay Hindraf's approach. He stated that he first became aware of the possibilities for the Indian community during his studies in the United Kingdom. He had observed that within the mature western democracies the rights of minorities were enshrined in law, and that racism in these countries was not an institutionalized phenomenon. By way of contrast Malaysia had been founded on racial ideologies and that as a consequence racism permeated society from the top down. These racial attitudes were now institutionalized, so that, for example, the death of an Indian in custody was regarded as a routine occurrence and rarely worthy of investigation. The main issues facing the Indian community were:

1. The lack of opportunities, whether educational, social or economic.
2. The growing social dislocation and cynicism among younger Indians which manifested as a sense of hopelessness and a lack of direction.
3. The lack of resources devoted to Tamil schools, and the generally poor training accorded to staff.
4. A deeply entrenched culture of poverty which had to be broken.

Hindraf's main goal therefore had to be empowerment of the Indian community. Uthayakumar emphasized that Hindraf knew that in launching its campaign it would struggle against an engrained regime resistant to change, and against an "implacably hostile government controlled media".

On 12 August 2007, having addressed a rally of about 2,000 supporters in the administrative capital Putrajaya, the Hindraf leadership submitted a list of demands to the office of Prime Minister Abdullah Badawi. This petition set forth eighteen basic points which covered the full gamut of Indian grievances, calling for an end to discrimination, improvements in Tamil education, respect for the religious and cultural integrity of the community, and a range of interventionist programmes which provided employment and educational opportunities.[122] The government offered no response to the Hindraf submission.[123]

On 31 August 2007 (Merdeka Day), Hindraf took the extraordinary step of filing a suit in the British courts against the British Secretary of State for Foreign and Commonwealth Affairs. The suit sought compensation of US$4 trillion for the putative "pain, suffering, humiliation, discrimination and continuous colonialism" endured by the Indian community, alleging that the British government had failed to guarantee the protection of the Indian community during the negotiations leading to the granting of independence to Malaya.[124] On 15 November 2007, following the controversial destruction of the temple in Shah Alam on the eve of Deepavali, Hindraf faxed a submission to Gordon Brown, British Prime Minister, which compared the Malaysian government actions to "ethnic cleansing" and which rather unwisely suggested that continued repression might force Tamils into "terrorism".[125] As the Malaysian government had still not responded to the petition of 12 August 2007, and the media had studiously ignored Hindraf, the leadership vowed to proceed with a major demonstration planned for 25 November 2007.[126]

The rally, organized for a non-working day, planned to present a memorandum to Queen Elizabeth via the British High Commission in Kuala Lumpur, highlighting the plight of the Indian community in Malaysia. While this gesture was the subject of considerable criticism, the tactic drew international attention to the protest and to Indian grievances, and clearly embarrassed the Malaysian government.[127] The Malaysian authorities moved to counter the gathering, and denied the organizers a police permit on the grounds that the demonstration would not only disrupt traffic, but would constitute a threat to law and order.[128] The Cheras police chief, Ahmad Amir Mohammad Hashim, sought and obtained an "unprecedented" court order to prohibit the rally and road blocks were placed outside Kuala Lumpur to prevent the ingress of potential rally participants.[129]

A crowd estimated by diplomats at 40,000 people, but by independent scholars at up to 50,000, attended the rally.[130] But for police checks and roadblocks this figure would have been significantly higher. The organizers were not permitted to hand the petition to representatives of the British High Commission, despite the expressed preparedness of the British authorities to receive it. The demonstrators, many of whom were clad in saffron and carrying pictures of Gandhi, thus emphasizing the non-violent civil disobedience which had characterized his campaigns, were met with tear gas, water cannon firing chemically laced water and police baton charges. Ninety-four people were arrested for attending an illegal rally and many demonstrators, including children, were beaten by police.[131] Chin and Wong commented that "The use by police of tear gas and water cannon against ordinary marchers carrying nothing more than pictures of Gandhi and a petition addressed to the Queen of England shocked the country and electrified the entire Indo-Malaysian community. On that day BN lost ethnic-Indian voters — its most loyal constituency for half a century."[132] The Hindraf rally revealed the extent of the loss of Indian trust in the MIC, and informants reported that there was loud jeering from the crowd each time Samy Vellu's name was mentioned.

A further incident related to the Hindraf rally, which also met with police violence, created outrage among Hindu Malaysians and generated significant media coverage in the wider Indic-Hindu world. This occurred at the famous Batu Caves complex, regarded as one of Malaysia's most sacred Hindu sites. Some 2000 people gathered at Batu Caves prior to their planned attendance at the Hindraf demonstration.[133] The police, allegedly acting in concert with the President of the Batu Caves Devasthanam,[134] locked the gate at 4.30 a.m., and then proceeded to fire tear gas and chemical-laced water at the crowd. The Federal Reserve Unit later entered the compound and assaulted a number of people, many of whom had no connection with the Hindraf gathering and were at the Caves to offer prayers for the festival of Skanda Shasti.[135] This action incensed the Hindus involved, some of who had hitherto been unsympathetic to Hindraf and its objectives.[136] Thirty-one people were arrested for allegedly attempting to murder a policeman, supposedly by hurling a brick at him.[137]

Throughout this period the Malaysian government appeared consistently clumsy, wrong-footed and unnecessarily vindictive in their handling of the Hindraf phenomenon. The government-dominated media attacked the credibility of the movement and attempted to tarnish the leadership by linking them to the Liberation Tigers of Tamil Eelam (LTTE).[138] The most puerile and fatuous response was the repeated comment that Indians should respect the "sacrifices" made by Malays in granting Indians Malaysian citizenship, and that suggestion that Indians should be grateful for being allowed to live in Malaysia, and that if they were not happy they should return to India.[139] That this reaction was strikingly reminiscent of colonial dismissals of Indian concerns some seventy to eighty years earlier did not go unnoticed by many Indian intellectuals. Responding to the demonstration, Law Minister Nazri Aziz described the protestors as "20,000 Indian gangsters",[140] a reaction which was received as a smear upon the Indian community and which combined both stereotyping and racial vilification. Other UMNO members suggested that Indian demonstrations faced potential violence from Malays resident in Kampong Baru,[141] though in fact many Indians spoke of the kindness and consideration they received from the Kampong Baru Malay community throughout the rally.[142] More unwisely, UMNO members stated that they did not care about the Indian vote which was not decisive in winning elections.[143] At no point did the mainstream media attempt to analyse or discuss the issues raised by Hindraf.[144] Nor did the UMNO leadership appear to recognize that Hindraf had mobilized wide support by tapping into deeply held grievances and that repression merely increased Hindraf's popular appeal.[145]

On 13 December 2007, five leading Hindraf legal advisors and speakers — P. Uthayakumar, P. Kengadharu, V. Ganibatirau, M. Manoharan, and K. Vasantha Kumar — were detained under the ISA. Inspector Musa Hassan claimed that all had links with international terrorism and were guilty of spreading hatred.[146] In the interim the government had belatedly, if tacitly, acknowledged a breakdown in its relationship with the Indian community. On 30 November 2007, Prime Minister Abdullah Badawi called upon the MIC to form a special committee to examine problems faced by Indian Malaysians.[147] On 14 December 2007, the day after the Hindraf detentions, Abdullah met with a number of Indian NGOs to discuss issues of concern; this was his first meeting with the Indian community in the four years of his Prime Ministership. However, in keeping with rigidly communal conceptions of governance, Abdullah insisted that all Indian grievances should be raised with BN through the agency of the MIC.[148]

In December Abdullah called upon Samy Vellu and the MIC to comment upon the status of disputed temples.[149] In response, the Batu Caves Devasthanam, closely allied to the MIC, formed a new Hindu peak body known as the Malaysian Hindu Council, chaired by Devasthanam President, R. Nadarajah. Significantly this new body excluded the highly influential Malaysian Hindu Sangam which had hitherto taken responsibility for voicing the Hindu community's protests on the issue of temple demolitions and which constituted the official Hindu representation on the Malaysian Council of Buddhism, Christianity, Hinduism, Sikhism, and Taoism.[150] Many Hindus regarded the new Council as little more than a MIC front.

In December 2007, due to the perceived unrest among Indian Malaysians, the Cabinet took the extraordinary step of suspending the recruitment of Indian workers to fill temporary vacancies within the Malaysian workforce. As an additional measure it was agreed that Indian workers who were currently employed within Malaysia would not have their work visas renewed. Although this decision was reached on 18 December, the announcement was delayed until 31 December, immediately following the departure of India's Defence Minister, A.K. Antony, who had conducted talks with members of Malaysia's Cabinet over a three-day visit.[151]

On 20 January 2008 the MIC sponsored a rally at which Prime Minister Abdullah was the principal guest. During the gathering Abdullah announced that as from 2008 the major Hindu festival of Thaipusam would become a public holiday in both the Federal Territory and Putra Jaya, thus fulfilling an MIC request of many years' standing.[152] Samy Vellu later claimed that attendance at the rally had topped 20,000, but most informants regard this figure as a gross overestimate.[153]

In the interim a group called Makkal Sakthi (People's Power) had arisen from Hindraf, and in January called for a boycott of the major Hindu festival of Thaipusam at Batu Caves. In its communications, mainly circulated by mobile phone messages and via the Internet, Makkal Sakthi highlighted the Devasthanam's collaboration with the police throughout the Batu Caves incident of 25 November, and the closeness of the committee to the MIC and in particular to its leader, Samy Vellu. The campaign requested devotees to eschew Batu Caves and to conduct their prayers and fulfil their vows at other temples.[154] The boycott was a resounding success with crowds estimated at below 400,000 as opposed to attendance of over a million the previous year.[155] Indeed traders who had catered for the anticipated crowd found themselves with unprecedented quantities of unsold food.[156] Major temples around Kuala Lumpur and in Kuala Selangor, Penang and Ipoh were inundated with those devotees who normally would have attended Thaipusam at Batu Caves.[157]

Samy Vellu's appearance at the festival was somewhat less than auspicious. Upon arrival he was guarded by a phalanx of riot police,[158] and his customary speech from the podium was greeted with "a smattering of applause".[159] Speaking to reporters Samy Vellu denied that there was any decline in crowd numbers at Batu Caves,[160] and predicted the usual vote for the MIC in the forthcoming general election scheduled for 8 March, stating that the idea that Indians would vote for parties other than those within BN was a "pipe dream of the opposition".[161]

On Valentine's Day 2008 Hindraf organized a further rally in which they planned to present roses to Prime Minister Abdullah. Once again the protest was declared illegal and the police met the demonstrators with undue violence. Two hundred arrests were made, ten of whom were detained while seeking shelter in a temple.[162]

On 20 February 2008, Makkal Sakthi issued a statement entitled "What Must We Do?" which outlined the history of Hindraf. The statement, circulated by email and by other media, emphasized the government's repeated rejection of Hindraf's claims, and its refusal to negotiate. It also described how peaceful demonstrations had been quelled by police violence, and, referring to the accusations of attempted murder made against those arrested at Batu Caves, how protestors had been arrested on trumped-up charges. Makkal Sakthi pointed to the successful boycott of Thaipusam at Batu Caves as an example of what Indians could achieve if they remained united. Finally, the statement provided a list of the federal electorates where Indians comprised more than ten per cent of the enrolled voters with the injunction that Indians should cast their vote for the opposition coalition.[163]

8 MARCH 2008

The government dissolved parliament in mid-February 2008 in readiness for elections in March. It entered the campaign confident, perhaps over-confident, that it would easily retain its two-thirds majority.[164] However, perhaps sensing a potentially eroding support base, it took the extraordinary step of warning non-Malays of the inevitability of violence should UMNO, the party of Malays, lose power.[165] On the opposition side, PAS, strengthened by the inclusion of an increasing number of middle-class Malays, adopted a moderate stance, most notably abandoning its call for the establishment of an Islamic state.[166] PAS joined forces with Parti Keadilan Rakyat and the DAP to form the opposition coalition *Pakatan Rakyat*.[167]

The election of 8 March delivered a massive jolt to the governing coalition and transformed the Malaysian political landscape. BN lost fifty-nine seats, thirty-one of which had been held by UMNO, and was only kept in power by the continuing support it received in East Malaysia.[168] Pakatan Rakyat won eighty-two seats, and swept into office in four states — Penang, Kedah, Perak, and Selangor — as well as retaining power in Kelantan.[169] The MIC vote virtually collapsed. The party lost six of its nine seats, and in a personal rebuff party leader Samy Vellu suffered a resounding defeat.[170] The PPP and its Indian member lost the sole seat held by the party.[171] While Malay support for the BN had declined, and a significant proportion of the Chinese electorate shifted to the opposition, the most dramatic voter movement was that of the Indian community, which largely abandoned BN.[172]

Indeed, the Indian swing against BN was estimated at thirty-five per cent. The Hindraf demonstration, the violent and heavy-handed response of security personnel, the police intrusion at the sacred site of Batu Caves, and the facile and dismissive jibes directed at the protestors, collectively seemed to confirm to many Hindus the lack of regard in which the community was held, and the low priority accorded to their needs. It seemed to be a poor reward for the loyalty the Indian community had consistently shown over many years, firstly to the Alliance and subsequently to BN, and it clearly demonstrated that their allegiance could no longer be taken for granted.

The Immediate Aftermath

The initial UMNO reactions to the election appeared to be general confusion which on occasion appeared to hint at panic within the ranks. A number of

UMNO rank and file condemned the Indian community for their supposed "disloyalty" while others asserted that Indians had proven "unworthy" of the citizenship awarded to them.[173]

Following the elections UMNO called for talks with PAS to promote "Malay unity", upon which it was contended that Malay survival was dependent, and which could only be guaranteed by UMNO. UMNO's statements seemed to ignore the fact that the allegiance of the Malay electorate was now divided between three political parties — UMNO, PAS and Keadilan — and that UMNO had managed to attract only forty-nine per cent of the Malay vote.[174] A number of prominent UMNO figures, joined by Dr Mahathir, called for Abdullah's immediate retirement.[175]

Hindraf: Post 8 March

Following the election, far from consolidating its position and influence vis-à-vis the Indian electorate, Hindraf appeared to be both leaderless and without direction. Many scholars and political observers interviewed by the author believe that Hindraf made a number of tactical blunders in this period. These included launching sustained attacks on UMNO, rather than highlighting the grievances of the community and, more importantly, alienating a number of potential allies, such as Pakatan Rakyat, which might have otherwise proven sympathetic to its cause. Hindraf's public statements became more emotional and uncompromising and its general intransigence proved counterproductive. Moreover Hindraf appeared blind to the likely official reaction (and that of the broader Muslim community), to its choice of terminology, in particular its insensitive use of the phrase "ethnic cleansing", which to many Muslims referred specifically to the atrocities committed against Bosnian Muslims in the wake of the break-up of the former state of Yugoslavia. This phrase probably unnecessarily lost Hindraf a great deal of political support.[176]

It seemed that it would only be a matter of time before BN took concerted action against Hindraf. In August 2008 the government issued a statement alleging that Hindraf had well-established links with the LTTE of Tamil Eelam in Sri Lanka.[177] In September Hindraf organized an anti-ISA rally which attracted about 2,000 supporters, but alarmingly from the government perspective included both Chinese and Malay participants.[178] On 1 October 2008 a number of members of Hindraf were alleged to behaved in an unruly manner at Prime Minister Abdullah's open house celebrations for the major Muslim festival of Hari Raya. There, according to media reports, the Hindraf contingent unsuccessfully attempted to present the Prime Minister with a greeting card and a teddy bear. When these were declined "the activists voiced their demands without shaking hands with Cabinet Ministers who were playing host along with Abdullah". (However, it should be noted that participants who were present throughout this incident informed me that media reports were greatly exaggerated and that at no time did Hindraf activist behave with the rudeness attributed to them.) However, reports of indecorous and ill-mannered conduct and the rejection of Malay-Muslim hospitality created a most unfavourable public image of Hindraf and its leadership.[179]

On 15 October 2008, a mere two weeks after the Hari Raya contretemps, the government banned Hindraf. In claiming that the organization was in breach of the 1966 Societies Act, Home Minister Datuk Seri Syed Hamid Albar asserted that "Hindraf members had consistently carried out extreme activities and were clearly using religion as a tool to create disharmony." He further contended that Hindraf posed a threat to "public order, peace, security, and morality" in Malaysia, and went so far as to conclude that Hindraf's continued existence would threaten the very sovereignty of the nation.[180]

On 23 October 2008, in a rearguard action, Hindraf activists gathered outside Prime Minister Abdullah's office and made unsuccessful attempts to present him with a memorandum. Eleven members were arrested including K. Shanti, wife of self-exiled Hindraf leader, P. Wayamoorthy, and her six year old daughter. In a truly petty and Orwellian twist, the police announced that Ms Shanti would be investigated for possible child abuse, presumably for bringing her daughter to a public demonstration.[181]

Largely under the direction of P. Uthayakumar, released from ISA detention, the former Hindraf adopted a new strategy. This was to found a new political party, the Human Rights Party (HRP), which would adopt a "stand alone" stance. The party would aim to enrol enough Indian voters in a handful of electorates to guarantee success in two or three seats and thus a continuing voice in Parliament.[182] This approach appeared to overlook or ignore the tactical lessons of the 8 March election in which Indian votes were decisive in delivering a number of seats to the opposition, or the need to build political alliances to produce outcomes for constituents. However, the strategy proved largely theoretical as the HRP was denied registration as an official political party. The movement maintains an official and active website which monitors issues affecting the Indian community, but its self-imposed alienation from the political mainstream rendered it largely irrelevant to the practical needs of the Indian community, and much of the influence and respect it once commanded has been squandered.

MIC

The extent of the decline in respect for the leadership of Samy Vellu was demonstrated in two well-publicized incidents, the latter perhaps apocryphal, which occurred during the election campaign. At the commencement of the campaign a group of students conducted funeral prayers for Samy Vellu claiming that the leader was about to meet his political demise. Later in the campaign, in a gesture intended to reinforce this message, a coffin was sent to his home.[183] These two actions portended the MIC's electoral fortunes. As we have seen MIC's electoral support all but evaporated, and Samy Vellu suffered a humiliating loss in his once impregnable seat of Sungei Siput.

Despite the fact that he had been decisively rejected by Indian voters, Samy Vellu was determined to retain the MIC presidency and remained adamant that he was the only person who could restore the party's fortunes.[184] Samy's unquestioned control of the party saw him re-elected unopposed to the leadership of the MIC.[185] Despite obvious UMNO exasperation, Samy retained power until 6 December 2010 when he finally resigned to be replaced by Datuk G. Palanivel.[186]

The failure of the MIC executive to generate leadership renewal or to develop fresh policies forced UMNO to look elsewhere to re-establish lines of communication with the broader Indian community. While this process commenced during the latter portions of Abdullah's tenure, these initiatives were to gain impetus following Najib Razak's appointment as Prime Minister.[187]

CONCLUSIONS

The accession of Abdullah to the Prime Ministership on 31 October 2003 seemed to hold out the promise of reforms, a curbing of corruption, and a restoration of the integrity of Malaysia's institutional structures. However, Abdullah's tenure petered out into a morass of indecision. Abdullah did little to check crude racial chauvinism within UMNO, to contain blatant corruption within Malaysian public life, or to control what was publicly perceived as an increasingly rampant Islamism.

The period since the 13 May incident has been accompanied by an upsurge of Islam which has become the major defining feature of Malay cultural life. The impulses which have generated Islamization are many and varied; however, a major factor appears to the foregrounding of Islam as the ultimate bulwark of Malayness and its concomitant deployment as a trope of political and cultural authority. The state-sponsored project of Islamization took on a new and more intrusive dimension with the 1988 constitutional amendment which placed *syariah* courts beyond the overall jurisdiction of civil courts. This was followed by the contentious 2001 declaration that Malaysia was an "Islamic State". While Abdullah enunciated a programme of *Islam Hadhari*, at the grass-roots level this failed to translate into moderation or respect for the rights of non-Muslims.

Throughout the latter years of the Mahathir era and the early years of the Abdullah Prime Ministership there was increasing resentment and frustration among Indian Malaysians. Indians were aware that the Malaysian "economic miracle" was passing them by and that their needs barely registered with the ruling coalition. However, it was the processes associated with Islamization and the high-handed actions of the Islamic bureaucracy which finally provoked an Indian reaction. Hindraf's creation followed a series of insensitive and well-publicized incidents. However, the final goad was the demolition of a number of Hindu temples, many of them long established, often accompanied by violence, and without even the pretence of consultation with affected communities.

Hindraf was formed from a loose coalition of Hindu NGOs which had united to trace developments within the broader Indian community, but came increasingly under the control of the militant and energetic Ponnusamy brothers. The initial action, the filing of a suit against the British government for neglect of the welfare or long-term interests of the Indian community during negotiations leading to Merdeka, drew immediate attention to the Hindraf cause. However, it was the official reactions to the Hindraf rally on 25 November 2007 which boosted Hindraf's profile and which adumbrated loss of support for BN. At Batu Caves, riot police invaded Malaysian Hinduism's most sacred site and assaulted worshippers along with those who had intended to attend the rally. During the subsequent elections of 8 March 2008 the Indian community expressed its anger, largely deserting BN, thereby breaking a voting nexus which dated back to Merdeka.

Notes

1. Deborah Johnson, "Intellectual Statesmanship in the Mahathir Era", in *Malaysia: Public Policy and Marginalized Groups*, edited by Phua Kai Lit (Kajang: Persatuan Sains Sosial Malaysia, 2007), p. 157; James Chin and Chin-Huat Wong, "Malaysia's Electoral Upheaval", in *Journal of Democracy* 20, no. 3 (July 2009): 76.

2. Barry Wain, *Malaysian Maverick: Mahathir Mohamad in Turbulent Times* (Basingstoke: Palgrave Macmillan, 2009), pp. 313–14; Ooi Kee Beng, *Arrested Reform: The Unmaking of Abdullah Badawi* (Kuala Lumpur: Research for Social Advancement, 2009), p. 14; Liew Chin Tong, *Speaking for the Reformasi Generation* (Kuala Lumpur: Research for Social Advancement, 2009), p. 189.

3. Muhammad Takiyuddin Ismail and Ahmad Fauzi Abdul Hamid, "Abdullah Ahmad Badawi and Malaysia's Neo-Conservative Intellectuals", *Pacific Affairs* 86, no. 1 (March 2013): 79.

4. Ooi, *Arrested Reform*, p. 14; Chin and Wong, "Malaysia's Electoral Upheaval", p. 77.

5. The main tenets of *Islam Hadhari* were: (1) faith and piety in God, (2) a just and trustworthy government, (3) free and independent people, (4) a vigorous mastery of knowledge, (5) balanced and comprehensive development, (6) a good quality of life, (7) protection of rights of minority groups and women, (8) cultural and moral integrity, (9) conservation of the environment and (10) strong defence capabilities (Ahmad Fauzi Abdul Hamid, *Islamic Education in Malaysia*, Monograph No. 18 (Singapore: S. Rajaratnam School of International Studies, 2010), p. 30; M.C. Ricklefs et al., *A New History of Southeast Asia* (London: Palgrave Macmillan, 2010), pp. 453–54).

6. Chin and Wong, "Malaysia's Electoral Upheaval", p. 77; Ahmad Fauzi Abdul Hamid, "Politically Engaged Muslims in Malaysia in the Era of Abdullah Ahmad Badawi", in *Asian Journal of Political Science* 18, no. 2 (August 2010): 159; Wain, *Malaysian Maverick*, pp. 317–18.

7. Muhammad Takiyuddin and Ahmad Fauzi, "Abdullah Ahmad Badawi", pp. 80–82, 85, 91.

8. Ooi, *Arrested Reform*, p. 70; Chin and Wong, "Malaysia's Electoral Upheaval", p. 77.

9. Lim Teck Ghee, "Malaysia's Prospects: Rising to or in Denial of Challenges?", in *Multiethnic Malaysia: Past, Present and Future*, edited by Lim Teck Ghee, Alberto Gomes, and Azly Rahman (Petaling Jaya: Strategic Information and Research Development Centre, 2009), p. 492; Zaid Ibrahim, *In Good Faith: Articles, Essays and Interviews* (Kuala Lumpur: Zaid Ibrahim, 2007), p. 197.

10. Ahmad Fauzi, "Politically Engaged Muslims", p. 166.

11. Wain, *Malaysian Maverick*, p. 319; Chin and Wong, "Malaysia's Electoral Upheaval", p. 77.

12. Muhammad Takiyuddin and Ahmad Fauzi, "Abdullah Ahmad Badawi", p. 89.
13. Ibid.; Chin and Wong, "Malaysia's Electoral Upheaval", p. 78.
14. Ooi, *Arrested Reform*, p. 19.
15. Wain, *Malaysian Maverick*, p. 328.
16. Ibid., p. 330; Lim, *Malaysia's Prospects*, p. 492.
17. Gordon P. Means, *Political Islam in Southeast Asia* (Boulder, CO: Rienner, 2009), p. 354.
18. Chin and Wong, "Malaysia's Electoral Upheaval", p. 78; Ooi, *Arrested Reform*, p. 10.
19. Means, *Political Islam*, p. 354. This information was also conveyed to me by participants and observers.
20. Zaid, *In Good Faith*, pp. 247–48.
21. Chin and Wong, "Malaysia's Electoral Upheaval", p. 78.
22. Ibid; Ooi, *Arrested Reform*, pp. 2, 9.
23. Ooi Kee Beng, *Between UMNO and a Hard Place: The Najib Era Begins* (Kuala Lumpur and Singapore: Research for Social Advancement/Institute of Southeast Asian Studies, 2010), p. 99.
24. Edmund Terence Gomez, "Ethnicity, Equity and Politics in Multiethnic Malaysia", in *Multiethnic Malaysia: Past, Present and Future*, edited by Lim Teck Ghee, Alberto Gomes, and Azly Rahman (Petaling Jaya: Strategic Information and Research Development Centre, 2009), p. 170.
25. Wain, *Malaysian Maverick*, p. 110.
26. Means, *Political Islam*, p. 341.
27. Mohamed Abu Bakar, "Islam, Civil Society and Ethnic Relations in Malaysia", in *Islam and Civil Society in Southeast Asia*, edited by Nakamura Mitsuo, Sharon Siddique, and Omar Farouk Bajunid (Singapore: Institute of Southeast Asian Studies, 2001), p. 61.
28. Susan E. Ackerman and Raymond L.M. Lee, *Heaven in Transition: Innovation and Ethnic Identity in Malaysia* (Honolulu: University of Hawai'i Press, 1988), p. 40.
29. Zainah Anwar, *Islamic Revivalism in Malaysia: Dakwah among the Students* (Petaling Jaya: Pelanduk, 1987), p. 10; Judith Nagata, *The Reflowering of Malaysian Islam: Modern Religious Radicals and their Roots* (Vancouver: University of British Columbia Press, 1984), p. 55; Means, *Political Islam*, p. 85.
30. Sharifah Zaleha Syed Hassan, "Islamization and Emerging Civil Society: A Case Study", in *Islam and Civil Society in Southeast Asia*, edited by Nakamura Mitsuo, Sharon Siddique, and Omar Farouk Bajunid (Singapore: Institute of Southeast Asian Studies, 2001), p. 77.
31. Virginia Hooker, "Still 'Islam and Politics' But Now Enmeshed in a Global Web", in *Malaysia: Islam, Society and Politics*, edited by Virginia Hooker and

Norani Othman (Singapore: Institute of Southeast Asian Studies, 2003), p. 20.

32. Zainah, *Islamic Revivalism*, p. 24; Nagata, *The Reflowering of Malaysian Islam*, p. 77.

33. Zainah, *Islamic Revivalism*, p. 2; Sharifah Zaleha, "Islamization and Emerging Civil Society", p. 79.

34. Jomo K.S. and Ahmad Shabery Cheek, "Malaysia's Islamic Movements", in *Fragmented Vision: Culture and Politics in Contemporary Malaysia*, edited by Joel S. Kahn and Francis Loh Kok Wah (Sydney: Asian Studies Association of Australia/Allen and Unwin, 1992), pp. 79–80; Maznah Mohamad, "Politics of the NEP and Ethnic Relations in Malaysia", in *Multiethnic Malaysia: Past, Present and Future*, edited by Lim Teck Ghee, Alberto Gomes, and Azly Rahman (Petaling Jaya: Strategic Information and Research Development Centre, 2009), p. 132.

35. Zainah, *Islamic Revivalism*, pp. 88–89.

36. Their concerns are given substance by the insensitive behaviour of some Christian missionaries. In 1997 a US evangelical, obviously mistaking me for another individual, accosted me in Penang Airport, and in a stentorian voice, seeming oblivious to the mainly Malay airport staff standing nearby, told me that it was a "strategic priority" to convert all Chinese and Indian "children" in preparation for the forthcoming war between Christianity and Islam. In subsequent conversations with Malaysian colleagues I was informed that these intentions were (and remain) well known among the Malay Muslim leadership.

37. Ricklefs et al., *A New History*, p. 447.

38. Talmiz Ahmad, *Children of Abraham at War: The Clash of Messianic Militarisms* (Delhi: Aakar Books, 2010), p. 206.

39. Ibid., pp. 372–74.

40. Barbara Victor, *The Last Crusade: Religion and the Politics of Misdirection*, (London: Constable, 2005), pp. 3–4, 23–26, 28–32, 89–90, 150; Reza Aslan, *No God but God: The Origins, Evolution and Future of Islam* (London: Heinemann, 2005), pp. xv–xvi.

41. Joel S. Kahn, "Islam, Modernity and the Popular in Malaysia", in *Malaysia: Islam, Society and Politics*, edited by Virginia Hooker and Norani Othman (Singapore: Institute of Southeast Asian Studies, 2003), pp. 148, 152–53; Abdul Rashid Moten, "Modernization and the Process of Globalization: The Muslim Experience and Response", in *Islam in Southeast Asia: Political, Social and Strategic Challenges for the 21st Century*, edited by K.S. Nathan and Mohammad Hashim Kamali (Singapore: Institute of Southeast Asian Studies, 2005), pp. 240–45.

42. Mohamed Abu Bakar, *Islam, Civil Society and Ethnic Relations*, p. 6.

43. Zainah, *Islamic Revivalism*, pp. 80–81.

44. Nagata, *The Reflowering of Malaysian Islam*, pp. 187–88.

45. Zainah, *Islamic Revivalism*, pp. 80–81.

46. Chandra Muzaffar, *Islamic Resurgence in Malaysia* (Petaling Jaya: Penerbity Fajar Bakti, 1987), p. 30.

47. Nagata, *The Reflowering of Malaysian Islam*, p. 217.

48. The sole survivor was a medical student studying under a Colombo Plan scholarship at the Flinders University of South Australia for whom I exercised administrative responsibility. My extended discussions with this student and with the Malaysian authorities provided me with insights into the world of *dakwah* student radicalism.

49. Nagata, *The Reflowering of Malaysian Islam*, p. 127; Cheah, *Malaysia*, p. 167.

50. Cheah, *Malaysia*, p. 212.

51. Ibid., p. 215.

52. This observation is based on discussions with Malaysian officials.

53. Means, *Political Islam*, p. 365.

54. Ahmad Fauzi, *Islamic Education in Malaysia*, p. 76.

55. Farish A. Noor, "The Localization of Islamist Discourse in the *Tasfir* of Tuan Guru Nik Aziz Mat Mushid'ul Am of PAS", in *Malaysia: Islam, Society and Politics*, edited by Virginia Hooker and Norani Othman (Singapore: Institute of Southeast Asian Studies, 2003), p. 323.

56. Kahn, "Islam, Modernity and the Popular", pp. 149–53.

57. Amrita Mahli, "The PAS-BN Conflict in the 1990s: Islamism and Modernity", in *Malaysia: Islam, Society and Politics*, edited by Virginia Hooker and Norani Othman (Singapore: Institute of Southeast Asian Studies, 2003), p. 239.

58. Personal field research.

59. Mahli, "The PAS-BN Conflict", p. 258.

60. Ibid., p. 254; Anwar Ibrahim, *The Asian Renaissance* (Singapore and Kuala Lumpur: Times Books International, 1996), pp. 116–21.

61. Cheah, *Malaysia*, p. 234.

62. Mahli, "The PAS-BN Conflict", p. 245.

63. Kikue Hamatyotsu, "The Politics of *Syariah* Reform: The Making of the State Religio-Legal Apparatus", in *Malaysia: Islam, Society and Politics*, edited by Virginia Hooker and Norani Othman (Singapore: Institute of Southeast Asian Studies, 2003), pp. 67–68.

64. Zainah, *Islamic Revivalism*, pp. 90–91.

65. Cheah, *Malaysia*, p. 213; Wain, *Malaysian Maverick*, pp. 222–23.

66. Hwang In-Won, *Personalised Politics: The Malaysian State under Mahathir* (Singapore: Institute of Southeast Asian Studies, 2003), pp. 245–46.

67. Means, *Political Islam*, pp. 345–56.

68. Interview with Datuk A. Vaithalingam, former President, Malaysian Hindu Sangam, 13 February 2013.

69. Wain, *Malaysian Maverick*, p. 225.
70. Ibid., pp. 228–34; Ahmad Mustapha Hassan, *The Unmaking of Malaysia: Insider's Reminiscences of UMNO, Razak and Mahathir* (Petaling Jaya: Strategic Information and Research Development Centre, 2007), p. 220.
71. Khoo Boo Tiek, *Beyond Mahathir: Malaysian Politics and Its Discontents* (London: Zed Books, 2003), p. 185; Wain, *Malaysian Maverick*, p. 235.
72. Wain, *Malaysian Maverick*, p. 237.
73. Ahmad Fauzi, "Politically Engaged Muslims in Malaysia", p. 166.
74. Maznah Mohamad, "Paradoxes of State Islamization in Malaysia: Routinization of Religious Charisma and the Secularization of the *Syariah*", Working Paper Series No. 129 (Singapore: Asian Research Institute, 2009), p. 21; Ahmad Fauzi, "Politically Engaged Muslims in Malaysia", p. 170; Zaid, *In Good Faith*, p. 217.
75. Zaid, *In Good Faith*, pp. 215–16.
76. Means, *Political Islam*, p. 347.
77. Ooi, *Arrested Reform*, pp. 8–9.
78. Means, *Political Islam*, pp. 347–48.
79. Nathaniel Tan and John Lee, "Introduction", in *Religion under Siege? Lina Joy, The Islamic State and Freedom of Speech*, edited by Nathaniel Tan and John Lee (Kuala Lumpur: Kini Books, 2008), p. 12.
80. Ahmad Fauzi, "Politically Engaged Muslims in Malaysia", p. 166.
81. S Nagarajan, "Indians in Malaysia: Towards 2020", in *Rising India and Indian Communities in East Asia*, edited by K. Kesavapany, A. Mani, and P. Ramasamy (Singapore: Institute of Southeast Asian Studies, 2008), p. 390.
82. Ahmad Fauzi, "Politically Engaged Muslims in Malaysia", p. 166.
83. Maznah, "Paradoxes of State Islamization", p. 19; Ahmad Fauzi, *Islamic Education in Malaysia*, p. 76.
84. Anthony Milner, *The Malays* (Chichester: Wiley Blackwell, 2011), p. 16.
85. Azza Basarudin, "Gatekeeping Will Not Stop Apostasy", in *Religion under Siege? Lina Joy, the Islamic State and Freedom of Faith*, edited by Nathaniel Tan and John Lee (Kuala Lumpur: Kini Books, 2008), p. 63.
86. Ismail Kassim, *A Reporter's Memoir: No Hard Feelings* (Singapore: Ismail Kassim, 2008) p. 174.
87. Baradan Kuppusamy, "Body Blow to Tolerance", in *Religion under Siege? Lina Joy, the Islamic State and Freedom of Faith*, edited by Nathaniel Tan and John Lee (Kuala Lumpur: Kini Books, 2008), p. 203.
88. Zainah Anwar, "State Intervention in Personal Faith: The Case of Malaysia", in *Multiethnic Malaysia: Past, Present and Future*, edited by Lim Teck Ghee, Alberto Gomes, and Azly Rahman (Petaling Jaya: Strategic Information and Research Development Centre, 2009), p. 255.
89. Personal correspondence.
90. Noor Yahaya Hamzah, "Anything to do with Islam, Hands-off Please", in

Religion under Siege? Lina Joy, the Islamic State and Freedom of Faith, edited by Nathaniel Tan and John Lee (Kuala Lumpur: Kini Books, 2008), p. 208.

91. Patricia Martinez, "Malaysian Muslims: Living with Diversity", *Malaysiakini,* 25 August 2006 <http://www.malaysiakini.com/opinionfeatures/558997> (accessed 31 August 2006).

92. Maznah, "Paradoxes of State Islamization", p. 11.

93. Mohamed Abu Bakar, "Islam, Civil Society and Ethnic Relations", p. 70.

94. Ibid., p. 69. This observation was confirmed during numerous interviews.

95. Kikue, *The Politics of Syariah Reform,* p. 68.

96. Lim Teck Ghee, "Malaysia's Prospects", pp. 483–84.

97. Nagarajan, "Indians in Malaysia", p. 390.

98. "Muslims Warned against Deepavali Greetings", *Malaysiakini,* 6 October 2006 <http://www.malaysiakini/com/news/58029> (accessed 8 October 2006).

99. Nagarajan, "Indians in Malaysia", p. 390.

100. Wain, *Malaysian Maverick,* pp. 238–39.

101. Andrew Ong, "Woman Released from Islamic Rehab", *Malaysiakini,* 6 July 2007 <http://www.malaysiakini.com/news/69580> (accessed 25 July 2007). See also Azza Basarudin, "Revathi has made her Choice Crystal Clear", in *Religion under Siege? Lina Joy, the Islamic State and Freedom of Faith,* edited by Nathaniel Tan and John Lee (Kuala Lumpur: Kini Books, 2008), pp. 209–10.

102. "Non-Muslims Urged not to Fear Muslim Courts", *Malaysian Sun,* 23 July 2007.

103. N. Anbalagan, "Hindu Man Gets Custody of Children by Muslim 'wife'", *News Straits Times,* 4 May 2007.

104. Nagarajan, "Indians in Malaysia", p. 390.

105. Keuk Kuang Keng, "Hindu Man Gets Custody of Children", *Malaysiakini,* 3 May 2007 <http://www.malaysiakini.com/news/66742> (accessed 5 May 2007).

106. Nagarajan, "Indians in Malaysia", p. 390.

107. S. Nagarajan, "Marginalisation and Ethnic Relations: The Indian Malaysian Experience", in *Multiethnic Malaysia: Past, Present and Future,* edited by Lim Teck Ghee, Alberto Gomes, and Azly Rahman (Petaling Jaya: Strategic Information and Research Development Centre, 2009), p. 378.

108. Observation based on discussion with various Hindu temple authorities.

109. Lim, "Malaysia's Prospects", p. 488; Nagarajan, "Marginalisation and Ethnic Relations", p. 378.

110. Nagarajan, "Marginalisation and Ethnic Relations", pp. 378–79.

111. Andrew Ong, "Hindus Protest Temple Demolition", *Malaysiakini,* 25 May 2006 <http://www.malaysiakini/com/news/51572> (accessed 28 May 2006).

112. Nagarajan, "Indians in Malaysia", p. 386.

113. Lim, "Malaysia's Prospects", p. 487.

114. Andrew Ong, "Temple Row: 12 Freed by Police", *Malaysiakini,* 3 November

2007 <http://www.malaysiakini.com.news/74341> (accessed 5 November 2007).

115. Sinnappah Arasaratnam, "Malaysian Indians: The Formation of an Incipient Society", in *Indian Communities in Southeast Asia*, edited by K.S. Sandhu and A. Mani (Singapore: Institute of Southeast Asian Studies, 1993), p. 193.

116. Ahmad Fauzi, "Politically Engaged Muslims", p. 166; Ooi, *Arrested Reform*, p. 6.

117. Ooi, *Arrested Reform*, p. 6.

118. Interview, P. Uthayakumar, 14 May 2010.

119. Nagarajan, "Indians in Malaysia", p. 387.

120. A. Letchumanan, "Hindraf Seeks a Fresh Start", *Focus, Sunday Star*, 26 July 2009.

121. Baradan Kuppasamy, "Hindraf: A New Force is Born", *Malaysiakini*, 23 November 2007 <http://www.malaysiakini.com/news/75179> (accessed 27 November 2007).

122. Nagarajan, "Marginalisation and Ethnic Relations", p. 369; Sivachandralingam Sundara Raja, "Hindu Rights Action Force (Hindraf) from the Perspective of *Utusan Malaysia*", unpublished research paper, not dated, p. 3. Copy of paper presented to author by writer during interview at Universiti Malaya, May 2010.

123. Lim, "Malaysia's Prospects", p. 487.

124. Ibid.

125. Sivachandralingam, "Hindu Rights Action Force", p. 23.

126. Letchumanan, "Hindraf Seeks a Fresh Start".

127. Ooi, *Arrested Reform*, p. 7.

128. Lim, "Malaysia's Prospects", p. 458.

129. Soo Li Tan, "Cops Obtain Rare Court Order against Hindraf", *Malaysiakini*, 23 November 2007 <http:www.malaysiakini.com.news/75175> (accessed 27 November 2007).

130. Julia Zappei, "Malaysia to set up Hot Line for Ethnic Indians after Mass Rally", Yahoo News Malaysia, 30 November 2007 <http://Malaysia.news.yahoo.com/ap/20071130tap-as-gen-Malaysian-indian-unrest-63c65> (accessed 6 December 2007).

131. Zappei, "Malaysia to Set up Hot Line"; Andrew Ong, "A Gandhi Inspired Mass Civil Disobedience", Malaysiakini, 30 November 2007 <http://www.malaysiakini.com/news/75259> (accessed 7 December 2007).

132. Chin and Wong, "Malaysia's Electoral Upheaval", p. 79.

133. Nagarajan, "Indians in Malaysia", p. 392.

134. Personal correspondence.

135. Andrew Ong, "Hindu Rally: Police Slammed for 'Racial Stance'", *Malaysiakini*, 30 November 2007 <http://www.malaysiakini.com/news/75519> (accessed 7 December 2007).

136. Personal correspondence.
137. P.S. Suryanarayan, "Political Echo", *Frontline*, 27 November 2007 <http:www. flonnet-com/flo1501/stories/200801/8503605300/htm.worldaffairs>(accessed 30 November 2007).
138. Lim, "Malaysia's Prospects", p. 488.
139. Sivachandralingam, "Hindu Rights Action Force", pp. 5–6.
140. Zappei, "Malaysia to Set Up Hotline".
141. "Makkal Sakthi: What Must We Do?", 20 February, 2008; emailed to author anonymously.
142. Personal correspondence.
143. Janakey Raman Manickam, *The Malaysian Indian Dilemma: The Struggles and Agony of the Indian Community in Malaysia*, 2nd ed. (Klang: Janakey Raman Manickam, 2010), p. 378.
144. Sivachandralingam, "Hindu Rights Action Force", p. 5.
145. Nagarajan, "Marginalisation and Ethnic Relations", p. 387.
146. Nagarajan, "Indians in Malaysia", p. 392; Janakey Raman, *The Malaysian Indian Dilemma*, p. 376.
147. Sivachandralingam, "Hindu Rights Action Force", p. 11.
148. Janakey Raman, *The Malaysian Indian Dilemma*, p. 378.
149. Yoges Paliniappin, "MIC Tampered with Temple Relocations", *Malaysiakini*, 24 December 2007 <http://www.malaysiakini.com/news/76374> (accessed 29 December 2007).
150. K. Kabilan, "Don't Mess with Poseurs, Khir Urged", *Malaysiakini*, 3 January 2008 <http://www.malaysiakini.com/news/76651> (accessed 7 January 2008).
151. "Malaysia Bans Recruitment of Indian Workers", *Dawn.com*, 9 January 2008 <http://www.archives.dawn.com/2008/01/09/int3.htm> (accessed 12 January 2008).
152. Ooi, *Arrested Reform*, p. 27.
153. Personal correspondence.
154. Personal correspondence.
155. Nagarajan, "Indians in Malaysia", p. 392.
156. Personal correspondence.
157. Anil Netto, "A New Movement Springs to Life as Thaipusam Devotees Shun Batu Caves, Throng Temples Elsewhere", *anil.netto.com*, 21 January 2008 <http://www.anil.netto.com/2008/01/21/thaipusam-turn-out-distinctly-smaller-at-Batu-Caves> (accessed 30 January 2008).
158. Personal correspondence.
159. Kimberly Lau, "Samy Vellu Calls for Indian Unity", *Malaysian Sun*, 24 January 2008.
160. Netto, "A New Movement Springs to Life".
161. Lau, "Samy Vellu Calls for Indian Unity".

162. Personal correspondence.
163. "Makkal Sakthi: What is to be Done?"
164. Chin and Wong, "Malaysia's Electoral Upheaval", p. 80.
165. Ooi, *Arrested Reform*, p. 60.
166. Ahmad Fauzi, "Politically Engaged Muslims in Malaysia", pp. 160–61.
167. Chin and Wong, "Malaysia's Electoral Upheaval", p. 73.
168. Ibid.
169. Wain, *Malaysian Maverick*, p. 329.
170. Ooi, *Arrested Reform*, pp. 44–55.
171. Ibid., p. 55.
172. Lim, "Malaysia's Prospects", p. 492.
173. Personal field research.
174. Ooi, *Arrested Reform*, pp. 85–86.
175. Wain, *Malaysian Maverick*, p. 329.
176. Based on conversations with Muslim scholars.
177. "Hindraf Unhappy Over Failure to Win Posts in Malaysian Party", *Malaysian Sun*, 25 August 2008.
178. Personal field research.
179. "Revoke Utusan's Permit, PM Urged", *Malaysiakini*, 3 October 2008 <http: www.malaysiakini.com/news/91031> (accessed 10 October 2008).
180. Janakey Raman, *The Indian Malaysian Dilemma*, p. 377; "Hindraf Pushed the Boundaries Says Home Minister", *New Straits Times*, 17 October 2008 <http:// www.nst.como.my/Friday/National/2371889/Article/ppvii_index> (accessed 20 October 2008).
181. Personal field research.
182. Interview, P. Uthayakumar, 14 May 2010.
183. Personal field research.
184. G. Krishnan, "Samy in MIC Like Bull in a China Shop", *Malaysiakini*, 21 March 2008 <http://www.malaysiakini.com/letters/80211> (accessed 24 March 2008).
185. James Chin, "Malaysia and the Rise of Najib and 1Malaysia", *Southeast Asian Affairs*, 2010, p. 169.
186. Personal field research.
187. Chin, "Malaysia and the Rise of Najib", p. 169.

16

NAJIB AND 1MALAYSIA
A New Deal?

Najib Abdul Razak succeeded Abdullah Badawi as Prime Minister on 3 April 2009. The son of former Prime Minister Tun Abdul Razak, Najib entered politics following his father's demise. Najib ascended to the Prime Ministership with a somewhat mixed reputation; he was perceived in some circles as a womanizer who gave his wife far too much public space and a politician prone to occasional race-baiting.[1] However, he was also known as a highly skilled politician and tactician, a clever and patient negotiator with an ability to strike a compromise, and largely free of undue racial and religious baggage. He was also held to be aware of the problems confronting BN and the urgent need for far-reaching reforms. However, it was recognized that Najib had limited room in which to manoeuvre, and that deeply entrenched and vested interests would oppose any overhaul of a system dominated by networks of patronage and the imperatives of "race". The rise of the Malay chauvinist body Perkasa, with its extremist agenda, and linked to Mahathir and Mahathir loyalists within UMNO, was cited as indicative of the forces arraigned against meaningful reform.[2]

Following his appointment as Prime Minister Najib introduced a new political philosophy known as "1Malaysia". This approach appeared to represent an attempt to rebuild the political and social consensus that had prevailed in pre-Mahathir Malaysia. Najib was aware that certain groups (for example, Indians and the Orang Asli) had been marginalized from the main body politick, that their concerns were not being addressed, and that there was a need for greater inclusivity in formulating public policy. The election of 8 March 2008 had demonstrated the need to address these concerns.[3]

1Malaysia, opposed by large sections of UMNO, suggested a fresh and more dynamic approach to the politics of ethnicity, and as with Mahathir's *Bangsa Malaysia* it generated considerable enthusiasm among those yearning for a Malaysian identity which ranged beyond the primary considerations of race/communalism.[4]

Najib introduced a range of reforms, including further liberalization of the NEP (however without significantly diluting the affirmative action provisions of the policy), and financial reforms designed to attract foreign investment.[5] He oversighted the repeal of the hated Internal Security Act and removed other colonial-era restrictions designed to limit freedom of speech and political association.[6] He also abolished the law which forbade student participation in political movements.[7] However, these reforms were to some extent counterbalanced by the introduction of a Peaceful Assembly Act which banned street protests, which were henceforth to be allowed only in designated enclosed areas.[8] The government also retained the power to detain suspects without trial.[9]

Reforms supposedly delivering greater freedom of expression appear to have been unevenly applied. In October 2012 a report released by the US-based Global Assessment of Internet and Digital Media noted that in this regard Malaysia was only "relatively free", and that bloggers and Internet users critical of the government were subject to various forms of harassment, including arrest and detention.[10] Moreover, restrictions on free speech appear to have been selectively applied. Observers have noted that blatant transgressions of publicly allowed comment on issues considered sensitive (such as race and religion) have been allowed to pass without any form of censure when committed by BN supporters, especially UMNO-affiliated organizations such as the chauvinist Malay rights group Perkasa or individuals like Muslim-convert Datuk Ridhuan Tee.[11]

Most observers believe Najib's greatest weakness has been his failure to curb or even check the established networks of corruption which continue to plague Malaysian public life.[12] In December 2012 Transparency International, "a global graft watchdog", rated Malaysia as the most corrupt country in the world in which to do business, citing, in particular, the high incidence of bribery within the public sector. (However, despite acknowledging officially tolerated corruption, the World Bank's "Doing Business Report" placed Malaysia in the twelfth most favoured position in global rankings.[13])

NAJIB AND THE INDIAN COMMUNITY

Even prior to Najib's accession to the Prime Ministership there were moves within the government to seek rapprochement with the estranged Indian community. As mentioned, BN had long taken the Indian constituency for granted, and during the 2008 election government MPs were shocked by the sight of Indian grass-roots activists campaigning for PAS and Keadilan. In June 2008 the government established a Cabinet committee to investigate problems facing the Indian community. The committee, chaired by then Deputy Prime Minister Najib, reported in early 2009, and introduced several measures, including grants to Tamil schools, vocational training for Indian youth, grants for Indian students undertaking postgraduate studies and micro-credit grants for promoting Indian small businesses.[14] The government also announced that Indian representation in the civil service would be increased from four to seven per cent.[15]

Since his accession to the Prime Ministership Najib has gone to considerable lengths to demonstrate his goodwill towards the Indian community. He has twice attended the major Hindu festival of Thaipusam at Batu Caves as a guest of the MIC-linked Sri Maha Mariamman Devasthanam which manages the complex, the first Prime Minister to do so since Datuk Hussein Onn visited in 1978.[16] During the first of these visits, in 2010, he unveiled plans to upgrade the cave surrounds, and to replace the cable car which had ceased operations thirty years previously.[17] He also promised to revamp the largely Indian Kuala Lumpur suburb of Brickfields and create a "Little India" tourist and trading precinct. One of his most important early initiatives was to strike an agreement with executives of the CIMB group to assume control of the failed Maika Holdings and to repay the investments of 60,000 Indians who had taken out shares in this cooperative, thus neutralizing an issue which had provoked lingering anti-MIC resentment within the Indian community.[18]

But Najib set in motion more far-reaching measures with which to engage the Indian community. He openly acknowledged that for too long BN had taken the support of the Indian community for granted but had failed to listen to or respond to their concerns. He made it clear that he was willing to consult with all segments of the community (including Hindraf), and that he was prepared to discuss all grievances.[19] He announced measures to fund Tamil schools and to resolve the plight of stateless Indians. By the end of 2012 he was able to report that since he had attained office his government had spent RM540 million on Tamil schools and had approved some 4,500 citizenship requests with a further 4,500 pending. Najib once again apologised to the Indian community remarking that for far too long BN had regarded the Indian constituency as a "fixed deposit" but had failed to accord them the "interest rates" which were its due.[20]

Najib's openness and his renewed focus on the Indian community undoubtedly won him a large measure of Indian goodwill, and did much to instil Indian trust in his leadership. But it remained to be seen whether confidence in Najib would translate into renewed support for BN as a whole (many observers noted that Najib's popularity far exceeded that of the government he headed[21]), or more crucially for the MIC, which under its low-profile post–Samy Vellu leadership appeared to have failed to reconnect with the wider Indian community. Many Indian observers commented that Indian voters were fully aware that the measures delivered by the government were not a reward for MIC loyalty, but rather represented a wider BN response to the pressures exerted prior to the 2008 election by extra-parliamentary Indian activism. Moreover, these initiatives were identified wholly with Najib rather than the MIC.

INDIAN GOVERNMENT SCHOLARSHIPS

In October 2010, during an official visit to Malaysia, Indian Prime Minister, Manmohan Singh, announced a major contribution, amounting to approximately one million Malaysian ringgit, to open the scholarship fund, initially established by Nehru in 1946 to assist Malayan Indian students with further studies.[22] While the Malaysian media made no mention of this gesture, the Malaysian government would be aware that the treatment of the Indian minority in Malaysia has in recent years been the subject of critical scrutiny in the Indian media, and that given

India's rising economic, political and military power, Indian perceptions of Malaysia may be increasingly difficult to ignore. A continued range of scholarships have been offered to "children of Indian descent" over subsequent years.[23]

THE FUTURE OF POLITICAL ISLAM

In the period under review a series of incidents appeared to reveal an entrenched and widening intolerance of the part of certain Muslim groups towards other religions as well as a blatant disregard for the rights of non-Muslims. Some commentators have suggested that this phenomenon represents the rise of a Salafist–Wahhabi approach to Islam in contrast to the more flexible and accommodating Shafi'i school which has traditionally prevailed within the Malay Archipelago.[24]

Religious controversies included JAKIM's seizure of the body of one Mohan Singh, who was alleged to have secretly converted to Islam, even though his family contended he had practised Sikhism up until his death;[25] the participation in a Catholic Church service and the taking of Holy Communion by two Muslim journalists acting under the suspicion that Catholics were illicitly converting Muslims to Christianity;[26] a major and very public altercation over Christian usage of the word "Allah" amid claims by the Islamic authorities that non-Muslim usage would "confuse" Muslims (this was despite the fact that "Allah", pre-Islamic in origin,[27] is commonly employed by both Muslims and Christians in the Middle East and in Indonesia); a series of subsequent attacks on Christian churches;[28] and PAS proposals to ban the sale of beer in Muslim-majority areas.[29]

In September 2011, acting on a tip-off that a gathering had been organized to evangelize Muslims, Islamic enforcement officers raided a Methodist Church near Kuala Lumpur.[30] A number of Muslims who had attended the meeting, described as a charity function, were provided with counselling, designed, in the words of religious officials, "to restore their belief and faith."[31] The meeting, and the alleged attempted conversions, provoked a counter-rally organized by a group known as Gathering of One Million Muslims (*Himpun*) with the theme "Save our faith". This was attended by a mere 4,000 people.[32]

In the period leading to the election of May 2013 there were a number of "Islamic" issues which created uncertainty, confusion and controversy. These included PAS leaders' objections to the building of a cinema in Bangi because screening films that were not in accordance with Islamic/Eastern values might contribute to vice;[33] the Kelantan government's insistence that a new Buddhist building should incorporate Islamic motifs to reflect the state's Islamic heritage;[34] a call by a PAS local council for the segregation of unmarried Muslim couples attending films at a Kuala Selangor cinema;[35] a Kelantan government ban on non-Muslim hairdressers cutting the hair of members of the opposite sex; the arrest of non-Muslims in Kota Bharu on charges of *khalwat* (close proximity);[36] and the PAS-led Kedah government's decision to ban Chinese New Year performances by female dancers and singers.[37]

In January 2013 the controversy over the non-Muslim usage of "Allah" resurfaced with a ruling by the Syura Council of Ulama, PAS's highest decision-making body, that "Allah" was exclusive to Islam.[38] In late January Perkasa publicized a demonstration in which members planned to burn copies of the Bible containing the word "Allah" (allegedly to prevent such "contaminated" Bibles from falling into the hands of impressionable Muslim students). The demonstration was later abandoned through lack of public interest.[39]

"Islamic" issues persisted throughout the election campaign. Controversy was stirred by PAS insistence that the election of a Pakatan government would be followed by the full implementation of *hudud* (that is, punishment for crimes according to *syariah* law).[40] In September 2011 Datuk Nik Abdul Aziz Nik Mat, Kelantan Mentri Besar (Chief Minister) insisted that *hudud* was central to PAS policy. The issue provoked a DAP ultimatum in which party officials warned that they would resign from all Pakatan posts should PAS persist with this demand.[41] However, throughout the latter stages of the prolonged election campaign PAS leaders reiterated that *hudud* remained integral to PAS ideology.[42] On 28 April 2013, a week prior to the election, Norman Fernandez, the DAP Deputy Chairman, Johor, issued an extraordinary personal statement in which he warned "DAP must realize that PAS is no longer an honest partner of Pakatan, and must be courageous enough to admit it."[43]

In general UMNO under Najib has maintained a low-key approach to Islamic affairs. He has continued to uphold the Mahathir assertion that Malaysia is an Islamic state, and that UMNO is an Islamic party committed to struggle to defend Malay Muslims from outside threats and from internal deviationist tendencies such as pluralism and liberalism. However, alert to the destructive power of religious extremism and danger of inter-religious conflict, Najib established a body, the Global Movement of Moderates, designed to promote religious understanding, and to enhance inter-faith harmony and acceptance.[44]

The Cow's Head Incident

The "Islamic" episode which had the greatest impact upon the Indian community throughout this period was the so-called cow's head incident. In August 2009 a group of Malays, including members of UMNO, protesting against the proposed relocation of a Hindu temple to the suburb of Shah Alam, a Muslim-majority suburb, carried a cow's head to the gates of the (Pakatan) Selangor Government's State Secretariat.[45] Photos released via the Internet clearly showed demonstrators stamping on the cow's head — a gesture designed to offend Malaysian Hindus. Police took no action throughout the protest.[46] Malaysians were shocked when Hishammuddin Hussein, Minister for Home Affairs, met with the protestors and even defended their actions.[47] One of the protestors later justified his behaviour with the provocative statement, "It's proven historically that this is *Tanah Melayu*. Others are categorized as second class citizens."[48] In subsequent compromise talks convened the following week Muslims shouted down speakers and claimed that the mere presence of a Hindu temple would disturb their prayers.[49] A peaceful protest held by Hindus to condemn racial and religious intolerance resulted in sixteen arrests.[50]

INDIAN ISSUES

The "cow's head" incident was one of a series of developments which attracted the attention of the Indian community in the period leading to the May 2013 elections. Some of these major issues are outlined in the paragraphs that follow.

Interlok

Interlok is a Malay novel written by prominent Malaysian author Abdullah Hussein. The book, which explores themes of Malayan colonial history, was set as a literary text for senior high school students. Indians objected to *Interlok* on the grounds that the book perpetuates gross stereotypes of the Indian community. In particular *Interlok* is held to portray Indian labourers as wretched coolies, as "black people", all members of the *pariah* caste (among Indians the term *pariah* is considered deeply offensive), and fleeing an intractable caste-bound metropolitan society to enjoy the relative freedom of Malaya. Moreover *Interlok* is not only held to be superficial in its understanding of the modern Indian presence in Malaya (Malaysia), but ignores the wider historical context of the Indian association with the Malay Peninsula and the Indic contribution to the culture and political structures of the region. A national *Interlok* Action Team was founded to campaign against the setting of the book within the national curriculum. Responding to Indian criticisms the government appointed a panel of eight experts to investigate the book. In March 2011 the panel reported to Deputy Prime Minister and Minister of Education, Datuk Muhyiddin Yassin, recommending that over 100 alterations be made to the book. Muhyiddin stated that he regarded the number of amendments as excessive, and suggested that the revisions be kept to a minimum. Three of the eight experts subsequently resigned from the panel.[51]

Bersih and Ambiga Sreenevasan

As noted in the previous chapter, Bersih was formed to press for electoral reforms, most specifically for the conduct of elections within Malaysia to be open and transparent. Specific demands included the independence of the Electoral Commission and the elimination of perceived abuses such as malapportionment, gerrymandering, media bias, vote rigging, and vote buying.[52] A major demonstration held in April 2012, and attended by at least 100,000 people, ended in police violence, the use of tear gas, and mass arrests, including several of the leading organizers.[53] The Bersih leadership was later subject to various forms of petty harassment, including a demand submitted by the Kuala Lumpur City Council for additional expenditure incurred in the staging of the rally, including the cost of officers' meals and overtime claims.[54]

As a co-leader of Bersih, Datuk Ambiga Sreenevasan, a former member of the Malaysian Bar Council and a prominent member of the Indian community, became the subject of a concerted BN campaign of harassment and indeed demonization. As the *Economist* reports:

> When it started in May the harassment of Ms Ambiga was almost farcical. A posse of traders turned up outside her door frying burgers to protest about their lost earnings on the day of the [Bersih] rally. Silly stuff, though offensive to a Hindu vegetarian. Sillier still, a group of ex-soldiers marched on her house and shook their buttocks at it, calling her subversive.[55]

However, these rather petty antics were to take a rather more sinister turn. Ambiga was presented with a petition which asserted that she was "anti-Islam" and should quit Malaysia. This was followed on 26 June by UMNO politician Datuk Mohamad Aziz's grotesque query, "Can we not consider Ambiga a traitor ... and sentence her to hang?"[56] Other UMNO figures spoke darkly of revoking Ambiga's citizenship and deporting her. These remarks gained wide coverage in the Tamil press finally eliciting a warning from MIC leader Datuk G. Palanivel that many Indians viewed Ambiga as a heroine, and the continuing harassment would lessen Indian support for BN.[57]

Batu Caves Condominium

In late October 2012 Datuk R. Nadarajah, Chairman of the Sri Maha Mariamman Devasthanam which manages the Batu Caves temple compound, stated that he had been advised that a twenty-nine storey condominium was to be constructed in the immediate vicinity of the Caves. Nadarajah warned that the structure would pose a major threat to the Caves and reminded the public that Batu Caves constituted a national heritage site. His remarks were echoed by the Malaysian Nature Society and by MIC President Palanivel.[58] A subsequent protest held on 26 October was attended by about 600 people (Nadarajah had forecast turnout of 100,000). Nadarajah, closely linked to the MIC, blamed the Selangor state Pakatan government for the decision to construct the condominium and pledged legal action to halt the development.[59]

Dr Xavier Jayakumar, Selangor State Executive Councillor for Indian Affairs, responded that the Selangor government was completely unaware of the project.[60] Within four days of Nadarajah's initial announcement the Selangor government ordered the cessation of the project pending relevant environmental checks.[61] Jayakumar also pointed out that the project had not been authorized by the Pakatan government, but had been approved by the BN government which had ruled the state prior to the 2008 elections.[62] Jayakumar's assertions were supported, perhaps inadvertently, by Liew Choong Kiong, the Managing Director of the developer Dolomite Holdings Sdh Bhd., who indicated that the requisite approvals had been sought in November 2007.[63]

In November 2012 Prime Minister Najib announced that should BN regain power in Selangor it would immediately halt the project and make application for Batu Caves to be listed as a world heritage site.[64]

In December 2012 the Selangor government appointed a committee to examine all aspects of the proposed development.[65]

The Sepang Altar

In November 2012 a crew sent by Sepang Municipal Council demolished a Hindu altar within the gated compound of a private home.[66] The MIC immediately attributed blame to the Pakatan government of Selangor and offered to fund its reconstruction.[67] MIC Youth subsequently organized a protest outside the home where the destruction had occurred. This was attended by several hundred people. In response Dr Xavier Jayakumar stated that Council personnel had acted without the authorization of the Council President. He also intimated that the demolition might well have constituted an "act of sabotage" designed to reflect badly upon the Selangor Pakatan government and to evoke within the Indian community memories of the wave of temple demolitions which had preceded the 2008 elections.[68]

INDIAN POLITICAL MOVEMENTS

Several Indian political groups emerged in the period between the 2008 and 2013 elections. Some like the Indian Progressive Front (IPF) and Hindraf had been formed prior to the 2008 election (in IPF's case some years before), but all attained an evanescent prominence in its wake.

Makkal Sakthi

In May 2009 several erstwhile Hindraf members under the direction of former Hindraf coordinator R.S. Thanenthran formed a new Indian political party named Makkal Sakthi (or "People's Party"; earlier, the rallying cry of Hindraf). On 10 October 2009, Prime Minister Najib launched Makkal Sakthi as a political party, in the process signalling to the MIC that unless they were prepared to embrace genuine reform, UMNO would deal with Indian organizations that were more responsive to and in touch with the broader Indian community.[69] Unfortunately when presented with a real opportunity to articulate Indian needs, Makkal Sakthi suffered an almost immediate leadership split and subsequently descended into a round of damaging internal disputes.[70]

The Indian Progressive Front (IPF)

The IPF was formed in 1990 by former MIC member, Tan Sri G. Pandithan (1940–2008), a man of modest birth. After a major falling out with Datuk Samy Vellu, Pandithan founded the IPF as an alternative party to the MIC. In the 1990 election Pandithan stood unsuccessfully as a candidate for the Federal seat of Teluk Intan. In 1994 he attempted to secure the IPF's admission to BN but was blocked by Samy Vellu and the MIC. In 1995 Mahathir appointed Pandithan to the Senate.[71]

Following Pandithan's death the party suffered internal dissension and factionalism. The IPF's relevance to the political mainstream, never more than marginal, further declined. In July 2012 senior UMNO politicians, including Najib, urged the IPF to resolve its internal problems in order to assist BN throughout the election campaign.[72] While the IPF staged rallies in support of BN, the party's overall impact was negligible.

Hindraf

In Chapter 15 we noted that following the banning of Hindraf and the fracturing of its leadership, a group of former members, led by P. Uthayakumar, attempted to register the Human Rights Party, and had launched a supporting website which contained daily releases of Indian news and exposes of alleged discrimination against the Indian community.

The ban on Hindraf was lifted on 25 January 2013, on the very eve of the major Hindu festival of Thaipusam. P. Uthayakumar's brother Waythamoorthy had returned to Malaysia from his self-imposed British exile in August 2012. He later released a policy document, a "blueprint" regarded as a template for political action. This called for immediate resolution of a number of outstanding problems faced by the community, including displaced workers, the issue of stateless Indians, provision of educational, employment and business opportunities, transparent and fair policing, and recognition of fundamental human rights.[73]

Waythamoorthy initially opened negotiations with Pakatan, ostensibly to explore avenues of possible Hindraf-Pakatan cooperation. A key Hindraf demand was that Pakatan allocate seven Federal and ten state seats to Hindraf, and that Pakatan commit to the establishment of a Ministry for Minority Affairs which would be headed by a Hindraf appointee.[74] Waythamoorthy's approach represented a comprehensive misreading of the policy directions embraced by Pakatan, in particular its rejection of the politics of race and communalism, and its attempts to create a needs-based rather than an ethnic-specific approach to social reform.[75] Reporting that Pakatan had been "stunned" by Hindraf's ultimatum, Terence Netto commented,

> In effect Hindraf is asking Pakatan components, PKR and DAP, to hand them on a silver platter their incumbencies (where relevant) of these seats and (where it applies) cede the groundwork done over the last five years in seats where PKR and DAP have been working to win over from BN.[76]

Faced with Pakatan reluctance Waythamoorthy began a hunger strike with the aim of compelling either Pakatan or BN to endorse Hindraf's blueprint. The fast ended after twenty-one days with Waythamoorthy's physical collapse.[77] He was invited to meet with Najib to discuss possible cooperation with BN.[78] Waythamoorthy later signed a Memorandum of Understanding with BN and called upon Indian voters to return BN to power with a two-thirds majority.[79]

Waythamoorthy's manoeuvring resulted in a split with his brother Uthayakumar. The latter described Waythamoorthy's actions as a betrayal of Hindraf's ideals, claiming that "He has pledged free votes in exchange for empty promises."[80] However, on 8 March 2013 the Registrar of Societies approved Waythamoorthy's application for registration of *Persatuan Hindraf*, meaning that his faction was now entitled to legal ownership of the name.[81] In the interim Uthayakumar had sought PAS endorsement as a parliamentary candidate for the Federal seat of Kota Raya.[82] Denied PAS sponsorship, he unsuccessfully stood for election as an independent in this seat.

Indian Rights Action Force

The Indian Rights Action Force (Indraf) was the creation of an NGO, Malaysian Indian Voice, and is linked to the DAP and thus more generally to Pakatan. It was formed in May 2012 during a rally convened in Brickfields and attended by some hundreds of people. The meeting was addressed by several Pakatan luminaries, including opposition leader Anwar Ibrahim.[83] Several days later two Indraf leaders, V. Ganabatirao (a former Hindraf detainee) and his brother Raidu were hospitalised after an assault by three men. Ganabatirao believed that the attack was linked to the Indraf rally. Little was heard of Indraf in the period leading to the May elections.[84]

SABAH, CITIZENSHIP AND THE ELECTION

Najib dissolved Parliament on 3 April 2013 and called elections for Sunday 5 May. Two incidents, both in Sabah, were to provide an unwelcome distraction to the election campaign.

Citizenship

Following unusual and unexplained increases in Sabah's population over many years, Sahabans pressed for a Royal Commission of Inquiry to investigate the matter. In January 2013 it was revealed that in 1994, during the Mahathir period, citizenship had been extended to up to 800,000 Filipino Muslims with the alleged aim of altering the demographic make-up of Sabah and ensuring that the state had a Muslim majority.[85] The bulk of these citizenships were granted in the period immediately preceding the 1994 election, thus ensuring that their names were entered on the electoral roll prior to voting.[86] It was further alleged that these newly enfranchised citizens were enrolled in seats that were (or might prove) marginal for BN.[87] Many commentators believed that this action promoted fraudulent electoral practices, especially multiple voting, that were later emulated in other parts of Malaysia.[88]

In response to accusations that he had manipulated Sabah's ethnic make-up, Mahathir conceded that the citizenships were granted during his premiership, but contended that he had no control over what was implemented "on the ground" in immigration matters.[89] He also suggested that any Royal Commission of Inquiry into citizenship in Sabah should be extended to cover the granting of citizenship to one million "foreigners" prior to Merdeka. In defending his actions he commented, "One should ... remember that Tunku Abdul Rahman was worse than me, he gave one million citizenships to people who are not qualified and not tested."[90] This observation not only seemed to traduce the pre-Merdeka settlement negotiated between the component parties of the Alliance, the departing British and the sultans, but appeared to question the very legality of the Merdeka "bargain" struck between the Malay and non-Malay communities, a compact which has been a fundamental tenet of UMNO's post-Merdeka political ideology. Mahathir's remarks, not for the first time, created a furore.

Lahad Datu

This extraordinary incident, which some observers have linked to the citizenship issues, erupted in February 2013 when a party of approximately 200 men, supporters of a pretender to the title of Sultan of Sulu, whose predecessors in the southern Philippines had once held sway over Sabah, "invaded" the state, in the process occupying the district of Lahad Datu.[91] Prolonged peaceful negotiation failed to persuade the intruders to depart or surrender. In the resultant violence scores of people were killed, including members of the Malaysian security forces.[92] A subsequent, rather clumsy BN attempt to link Pakatan leader Anwar Ibrahim to the "invasion" provoked a demonstration on 11 March outside PKR's Kuala Lumpur headquarters.[93]

The Election

The election was marred by charges of widespread fraud. These included allegations that large numbers of bogus votes were entered on the electoral roll;[94] that temporary Malaysian identity was provided to large numbers of foreign nationals allowing them to vote;[95] that planes were chartered to fly in large numbers of voters from Sabah and Sarawak (BN contended that this was to "get out the vote" and was funded by — unidentified — "friends of BN");[96] and that votes were "bought" with lavish expenditure on food, drink and other inducements as well as outright cash grants.[97] In addition the international organization Human Rights Watch reported "well-planned attacks" against independent online media at critical moments throughout the campaign.[98]

The election brought mixed fortunes for BN. While it won 133 seats to Pakatan's eighty-nine, BN received a minority of the overall popular vote (46.8 per cent as opposed to Pakatan's 50.3 per cent),[99] and was returned on the basis of heavily weighted seats won in its traditionalist rural heartland and the "fixed deposit" states of East Malaysia.[100] BN's Peninsula-based component Chinese parties suffered devastation, with the MCA winning a mere five seats (as opposed to the fifteen it held after 2008), while the Gerakan was reduced to a solitary seat (compared to two in 2008). Pakatan retained the states of Selangor, Kelantan and Penang, but lost Kedah and narrowly failed to win Perak.[101]

While Chinese voters largely abandoned BN, the ruling coalition also lost votes among urban-based Malays.[102] (Indeed observers had noted that middle-class Malays are often at the forefront of those demanding reform and have been conspicuous in organizations like Bersih.[103]) Despite the plea of Khairy Jamaluddin (head of UMNO's youth wing) that the election results should not be interpreted through a racial lens,[104] some UMNO commentators were quick to accuse the Chinese of "disloyalty" and "ingratitude".[105] Najib claimed the electoral swing against BN was the result of a "Chinese tsunami",[106] while Mahathir, (who appeared throughout the campaign alongside members of the Malay chauvinist body, Perkasa),[107] indicated that the loss of support could be attributed to "ungrateful Chinese" as well as "greedy Malays".[108] Conservative UMNO spokesmen warned of future trouble should Malay rule be challenged, while the UMNO-controlled newspaper *Utusan Malaysia* rhetorically queried *"Api Lagi Cina Mahu?"* ("What more do the Chinese want?").[109] On 8 May the Malaysian Bar Council issued a press release calling for an immediate cessation of "racially charged" comments within the media and among politicians,[110] and moderate UMNO politicians, including Najib, recognized the changing dynamics of Malaysian society and the need for BN to respond accordingly. Indeed, racial obfuscation appeared to overlook what has become increasingly obvious; namely in modern Malaysia raw or emotional appeals to primal communal loyalties are rewarded with ever diminishing returns and that younger Malaysians appear to be developing a national identity which reaches beyond ethnic boundaries and religious adherence.

Indian vote

BN commentators and the mainstream media asserted that Indian support for BN had increased and suggested that the coalition was returned in a number of seats on the basis of a recovery in the Indian vote. However, there appears to be scant evidence to support these claims.[111] The MIC retained four parliamentary seats out of the nine it contested, but at the state level secured a mere five seats (three in Johor, one in Malacca, and one in Negri Sembilan) out of the eighteen it contested.[112] Datuk Denison Jayasooria (Universiti Kebangsaan Malaysia) claimed that the MIC's performance was the worst in its history, and the party now needed to review its relevance. Jayasooria believed that the party required a shakeup of its leadership and the appointment of candidates who were aware of grass-roots needs.[113] Other observers pointed out that Indian sitting members of opposition parties were returned. Many of these were considered high-calibre candidates who were more than a match for their MIC counterparts.[114]

In unveiling his new Cabinet, Najib announced the appointment of six Indians, four of whom were MIC representatives. MIC President Palanivel was appointed Minister of Natural Resources and Environment, while his deputy, S. Subramaniam, was awarded the Health portfolio. M. Saravanan was made Deputy Minister of Youth and Sport, while P. Kamalanathan was appointed Deputy Minister of Education and Higher Learning.[115]

Of the two non-MIC appointments, the more controversial was that of Hindraf representative P. Waythamoorthy as a Deputy Minister within the Prime Minister's Department. This provoked a furious reaction from brother Uthayakumar who insisted that as Waythamoorthy had been sacked from the Hindraf Supreme Council on 25 April, he no longer represented the Hindraf movement.[116] The final Indian appointee, Loga Bala Mohan, of the Penang People's Progressive Party, who was made Deputy Minister of Federal Territories and Urban Wellbeing, aroused little comment.[117]

The non-MIC Indian appointments reflect Najib's long-expressed wish to open up effective new lines of communication with the Indian electorate, and in particular to work with representatives who possess a detailed understanding of grass-roots concerns. Many within UMNO's upper echelons have long believed that Samy Vellu's extended leadership and his total domination of the MIC left the party denuded of political talent, and incapable of articulating Indian needs. While UMNO has maintained traditional links with the MIC, Waythamoorthy's appointment, and to a lesser extent that of Loga Bala Mohan, is viewed as significantly broadening UMNO awareness of Indian opinion, and thus enhancing BN's ability to formulate policies to meet on the ground concerns. This approach accords with the BN/UMNO desire to incorporate the widest range of political opinion possible with the UMNO-dominated communal structures which have governed Malaysia since Merdeka.

Notes

1. Ooi Kee Beng, "Even Political Status Quo Spells Change in Malaysia", *Straits Times*, 22 February 2013.
2. Anil Netto, "Knives Out for Malaysia's Najib", *Asia Times*, 19 August 2011 <http://www.aitimes.com.aitimes/Southeast_Asia/MH19Ae02.html> (accessed 30 December 2011); "A Misconception of Perkasa", *Free Malaysia*

Today, 5 July 2012 <http://www.freemalaysiatoday.com/category/opinion/2012/07/05/a-misconception-of-perkasa> (accessed 8 July 2012).

3. Edmund Terence Gomez, Johan Saravanamuttu and Maznah Mohamad, "Introduction: Malaysia's New Economic Policy: Resolving Horizontal Inequalities; Creating Difficulties", in *The New Economic Policy in Malaysia: Affirmative Action, Ethnic Inequalities and Social Justice* (Singapore: NUS/Institute of Southeast Asian Studies, 2013), edited by Edmund Terence Gomez and Johan Saravanamuttu, p. 16.

4. James Chin, "Malaysia and the Rise of Najib and 1Malaysia", *Southeast Asian Affairs*, 2010, p. 166.

5. Ooi, "Even the Political Status Quo".

6. "Malaysian Bans Street Demonstrations", *United Press International*, 30 November 2011 <http://www.upi.com/Top-News/special/2011/11/30/Malaysia-bans-street-demonstrations> (accessed 2 December 2011).

7. Julia Zappei, "Malaysia Lifts Security Law, Students Politics Ban", *Yahoo News Malaysia*, 25 November 2011 <http://www.news.yahoo.com/Malaysia-lifts-security-law-student-politics-ban-072140324html> (accessed 26 November 2011).

8. "Malaysia Bans Street Demonstrations".

9. "Hisham: New Law Replacing ISA to Include Detention without Trial", *The Star*, 21 November 2011 <http://www.thestar.com.my/services/printerfriendly.asp?file+/2011/11/21/nation/201111211> (accessed 22 November 2011).

10. "Malaysia Slips in Internet Freedom", *Malaysian Insider*, 2 October 2012 <http://www.themalaysianinsider.com/print/malaysia-slips-in-internet-freedom> (accessed 5 October 2012).

11. Datuk Ridhuan Tee is a Chinese convert to Islam known for his polemical newspaper columns and his intemperate criticisms of non-Muslims. It has been suggested that some of Ridhuan's comments breach Article 11 of the Constitution (guaranteeing religious freedom) and are thus actionable by the government ("PKR Decries Tee's 'Racist' Article", *Malaysiakini*, 18 February 2013 <http://www.malaysiakini.com/news/221686> [accessed 20 February 2013]).

12. Ooi, "Even Political Status Quo".

13. Simon Roughneed, "Malaysia Bound for Pivotal Polls", *Asia Times*, 21 December 2012 <http://www.atimes.com/atimes/southeast_Asia/NL.21Ae01.html> (accessed 23 December 2012).

14. Personal field research.

15. Lim Hong Hai, "The Public Service and Ethnic Restructuring under the New Economic Policy: The New Challenge of Correcting Selectivity and Excess", in *The New Economic Policy in Malaysia: Affirmative Action, Ethnic Inequalities and Social Justice*, edited by Edmund Terence Gomez and Johan Saravanamuttu (Singapore: NUS/Institute of Southeast Asian Studies, 2013), p. 197.

16. Neville Spykerman, "PM on Charm Offensive at Batu Caves", *Malaysian Insider*, 29 September 2010 <http://www.themalaysianinsider.com.index. php/malaysia/51348-pm-on-charm-offensive -in-batu-caves> (accessed 1 January 2011); personal field research.

17. Personal field research; I was present when this announcement was made.

18. Observers informed me that this was greeted with widespread relief within the Indian community and gained Najib considerable support. Note that the government has a considerable investment in CIMB (Edmund Terence Gomez, "Nurturing Bumiputera Capital: SMEs, Entrepreneurship and the New Economic Policy", in *The New Economic Policy in Malaysia: Affirmative Action, Ethnic Inequalities and Social Justice*, edited by Edmund Terence Gomez and Johan Saravanamuttu [Singapore: NUS/Institute of Southeast Asian Studies, 2013], p. 107).

19. "Hindraf, Indian Groups Invited for Dialogue with PM", *The Star*, 7 November 2012 <http://www.thestar.com.my/services/printerfriendly. asp?file=/2012/11/7/nation/20121107153> (accessed 10 November 2012).

20. A. Lethchumanan, Martin Carvalho and P. Aruna, "Indian Community Will Be Rewarded for Being a 'Fixed Deposit'", *The Star*, 10 December 2012 <http://www.thestar.com.my/news/story.asp?file=/2012/12/10/nation/ 12438168&sec=nation> (accessed 11 December 2012).

21. Personal correspondence.

22. Personal field research.

23. "Indian Government Offers Scholarships", *The Star Online*, 4 June 2012 (accessed 8 June 2012).

24. For a general discussion on this topic, see Means, Gordon P. *Political Islam in Southeast Asia* (Boulder, CO: Rienner, 2009).

25. "Body Snatching Divides Malaysian Society", *Malaysian Sun*, 24 June 2009.

26. Chin, "Malaysia and the Rise of Najib", p. 170.

27. Reza Aslan, *No God but God: The Origins, Evolution and Future of Islam* (London: Heinemann, 2005), pp. 6–7.

28. M.C. Ricklefs et al., *A New History of Southeast Asia* (Basingstoke: Palgrave Macmillan, 2010), p. 454.

29. Personal correspondence.

30. Razak Ahmad, "Analysis: Religious Tensions Simmer in Malaysia", *Yahoo News Malaysia*, 12 September 2011 <http://www.news.yahoo.com/analysis-religious-tensions-simmer-in-malaysia-02555608.html> (accessed 15 September 2011).

31. "Malaysian Muslims Get Counselling after Church Meet", *Taiwan News*, 10 October 2011 <http://www.taiwannews.com.tw/etn.print.php> (accessed 12 October 2011).

32. "Muslims Hold Anti-conversion Rally", *Daily Express*, 23 October 2011 <http://

www.dailyexpress.com.my/print.cfm?News.ID=79503> (accessed 24 October 2011).

33. "GE 13: PAS Won't Budge on Hudud", *The Star*, 26 April 2013 <http://www.thestar.com.my/news/story.asp?file=/2013/4/26/nation/13025402&sec=nation> (accessed 30 May 2012).

34. Rahimy Rahman, "Malaysian State Kelantan Demands Islamic Designs in Buddhist Building", *Jakarta Post*, 26 May 2012 <http://www.thejakartapost.com/news/2012/05/26/Malaysia-s-Kelantan-demands-Islamic-designs-in-Buddhist-building> (accessed 30 May 2012).

35. "GE 13: PAS won't budge on hudud".

36. Ibid.

37. Ibid. Previous Kelantan measures included the following: that men and women stand in separate lines at supermarket checkouts; that men and women sit separately at cinemas and that the lights be switched on throughout screenings; that no liquor be served in clubs, that men and women be segregated and that women be "properly attired"; and that women entertainers are forbidden from dancing or singing ("Kelantan Plagued by Gender Segregation Controversies", *The Star*, 24 November 2012 <http://www.archives.thestar.com.my/services/printerfriendly.asp?file=/2012/11/24/nation> (accessed 30 November 2012).

38. Jocelene Tan, "At Odds over Sacred Word", *The Star*, 20 January 2013 <http://www.thestar.com.my/news/story.asp?file=/2013/1/20/nation/12581443&see=nation> (accessed 30 January 2013).

39. "Perkasa Defends Ibrahim Ali — Bible Burning Threat was to PREVENT VIOLENCE!", *Malaysian Chronicle*, 24 January 2013 <http://www.malaysianchronicle.com/index.php?option=com_K2&view=item&id=4374> (accessed 30 January 2013).

40. Baradan Kuppusamy, "Pakatan Rakyat in Danger of Breaking Up over Hudud", *The Star*, 27 September 2011 <http://www.thestar.com.my/service/printerfriendly.asp?file/2011/9/27/nation/20110992716> (accessed 28 September 2011).

41. Ibid.

42. Sina Habibu, Ian McIntyre, and Syeda Zhar, "PAS Members Firm on Hudud", *The Star*, 16 November 2012 <http://www.thestar.com.my/news/story.asp?file=/2012/11/16/nation/12326306&sec=nation> (accessed 17 November 2012).

43. Benjamin Nelson. "Don't Vote for PAS Says DAP Man", *The Star*, 28 April 2013 <http://www.thestar.com.my/news/story.asp?file=/2013/4/28/nation/13037605&sec=nation> (accessed 29 April 2013).

44. "Make the Voice of Reason be Heard Louder: PM", *Daily Express*, 19 January 2012 <http://www.dailyexpress.com.my/print.cfm?NewsID=80385> (accessed 10 March 2012).

45. "Malaysian State to Seek New Site for Temple", *Taipei Times*, 7 September 2009 <http://www.taipeitimes.com/news/world/archives/2009/09/07/20003452999> (accessed 9 September 2009).
46. Ibid.
47. John R. Malott "The Price of Malaysia's Racism", *Wall Street Journal*, 8 February 2011 <http://www.on.line.wsj.com/article.SB1000142405274870442204576129 66360557634.html> (accessed 28 February 2011).
48. Chin, "Malaysia and the Rise of Najib", p. 170.
49. "Malaysian State to Seek New Site for Temple".
50. Ibid.
51. Field research and interviews. See also S. Thayapran (Commander, Rtd, Royal Malaysian Navy), "The Issue is Not the 'P' Word", *The Sun*, 1 February 2011.
52. "Spectre of Bias Hovers over Malaysian Vote", *West Australian*, 20 March 2013 <http://www.au.news.yahoo.com/Thewest/a/_/world/16407902/spectre-of-bias-hovers-over-malaysian-vote> (accessed 20 March 2013).
53. "Malaysians Gather in Tens of Thousands Demanding Political Reforms", *Russia Today*, 11 January 2013 <http://www.rt.com/news/malaysia-protest-election-opposition_886/print/> (accessed 15 January 2013).
54. "Politics in Malaysia: The Racial Question: Harassment of Pro-democracy Activists in Malaysia Reveals a Worrying Undercurrent of Racism," *The Economist*, 14 July 2012 <http://www.economist.com/node/21558619> (accessed 16 July 2012).
55. Ibid.
56. Ibid.
57. Clara Chooi, *Malaysian Insider*, 3 July 2012 <http://www.themalaysianinsider.com/Malaysia/article/bans-in-support-at-risk-after-hang-ambiga-calls> (accessed 5 July 2012).
58. "Condos Rock Batu Caves", *The Star Online*, 22 October 2012 (accessed 23 October 2012).
59. Aruna, P. "Batu Caves Temple Serves Stop-Work Notice on Developer", *The Star Online*, 23 October 2012 (accessed 26 October 2012).
60. "Condos Rock Batu Caves".
61. Aruna, "Batu Caves Temple Serves Stop-Work"; Loksana K. Shagar, "Batu Caves at Risk of Caving In", *The Star Online*, 26 October 2012 (accessed 28 October 2012).
62. The Eng Hock and Jonathan Fernandez, "Exco Man Slams Hindraf Leader for Linking Issue to Buah Pala Incident", *The Star Online*, 27 October 2012 (accessed 29 October 2012).
63. Aruna, "Batu Caves Serves Stop-Work". This was also confirmed in interviews with relevant officials.
64. Mazwin Nik Anis, "PM: Selangor BN Will Stop Batu Caves Condo Project",

The Star, 13 November 2012 <http://www.thestar.com.my/news/story. asp?file=/2012/11/13/nation/20121113122955&sec=nation> (accessed 14 November 2012).

65. "Batu Caves Condo Issue: 5 Professionals Appointed to Independent Committee", *The Star*, 19 December 2012 <http://www.thestar.com.my/news/ story.asp?file=/2012/12/19/nation/20121219230237&sec=nation> (accessed 21 December 2012).

66. "Indians Outraged over Demolition of Hindu Altar in House", *The Star*, 30 November 2012 <http://www.thestar.com.my/news/story.asp?file=/2012/ 12/13/nation/12385013&sec=nation> (accessed 1 December 2012).

67. Razak Ahmad, "MIC to Rebuild Altar in House", *The Star*, 13 December 2012 <http://www.thestar.com.my/news/story.asp?file=/2012/12/13/nation/ 12452527&sec=nation> (accessed 15 December 2012).

68. Ibid.

69. "Malaysia's Makkal Sakthi Low on Power", *Malaysian Sun*, 23 January 2010.

70. "Malaysia's Newest Party Plans to Remove Chief", *Malaysian Sun*, 22 December 2009.

71. Interviews with IPF members.

72. "IPF Urged to Resolve Internal Strife to Help BN Win Big in Poll", *The Star Online*, 22 July 2012 (accessed 3 August 2012).

73. N. Ganesan, "Digging Deeper into Hindraf's Blueprint", *Malaysiakini*, 19 February 2013 <http://www.malaysiakini.com/news/221725> (accessed 3 March 2013).

74. P. Waythamoorthy, "Leaking of Hindraf-Pakatan Discussions is Sinister", *Malaysiakini*, 15 February 2013 <http://www.malaysiakini.com/news/221464> (accessed 20 February 2013).

75. V. Ganabatirao and K. Vasantha Kumar, "Hindraf is on the Wrong Track", *Malaysiakini*, 20 February 2013 <http: www.malaysiakini.com/news/221817> (accessed 21 February 2013).

76. Terence Netto, "Seats Demand behind Hindraf-Pakatan Impasse", *Malaysiakini*, 14 February 2013 <http://www.malaysiakini.com/news/221361> (accessed 20 February 2013).

77. Nicholas Cheng, "Hindraf Chief Calls Off 21 Day Hunger Strike after He Collapses", *The Star*, 31 March 2013 <http://www.thestar.com/my/news/ story/asp?/file=/2013/3/31/nation/20130331220826&sec=nation> (accessed 4 April 2013).

78. Wani Muthiah, "GE 13: Hindraf Waits Outcome of Meeting with PM", *The Star*, 25 March 2013 <http://www.thestar.com.my/news/story. asp?file=/2013/3/25/nation/20130325124012&sec=nation> (accessed 28 March 2013).

79. Tamil Mani, "Waytha, Choosing between Ravana and Rama Matters", *Malaysiakini*, 25 April 2013 <http://www.malaysiakini.com/letters/228008>(accessed 26 April 2013).

80. Wani Muthiah, "GE 13: Hindraf Today is Nothing Like It was in 2007 Says Uthayakumar", *The Star*, 27 April 2013 <http://www.thestar.com.my/news/story.asp?file=/2013/4/27/national/20130427170825&sec=nation> (accessed 29 April 2013).

81. Ibid.

82. "GE 13: Hindraf Founder Seeks PAS Polls Ticket", *The Star*, 19 March 2013 <http://www.thestar.com.my/news/story.asp?file=/2013/3/19/nation/12856231&sec=nation> (accessed 21 March 2013). Uthayakumar had sought pre-selection under a PAS scheme that would allow a certain number of non-Muslim candidates to contest seats under the aegis of PAS.

83. "Gathering to Form Indraf 2.0 Attracts Hundreds", *The Star Online*, 28 May 2012 (accessed 31 May 2012).

84. The Eng Hock, "Two Indraf Leaders Hospitalised with Fractures", *The Star Online*, 31 May 2012 (accessed 2 June 2012).

85. Romzi Attiong, "Citizenship for Votes Scandal in Sabah", *New Mandala*, 28 April 2013 <http://www.asiapacific.anu.edu.au/newmandala/2013/04/28/citizenship-for-votes-scandal-in-Sabah> (accessed 4 May 2013).

86. "Dompok: Mahathir Wrong on Who Qualifies for Citizenship", *Daily Express*, 23 January 2013 <http://www.dailyexpress.com.my/print.cfm?NewsID=84099> (accessed 26 January 2013).

87. Patrick Lee, "Dr M says ICs in Sabah Handed Out Legally to Foreigners", *The Star*, 17 January 2013 <http://www.thestar.com.my/news/story.asp?file=/2013/1/17/nation/2013011718530&sec=nation> (accessed 26 January 2013).

88. Romzi, "Citizenship for votes".

89. "Dr M Hints Only Now Aware of Wrong Doings under His Watch", *Daily Express*, 7 February 2013 <http://www.dailyexpress.com.my/print.cfm?NewsID=84240> (accessed 10 February 2013).

90. "Getting Malaysian Citizenship Cheaply", *Malaysian Insider*, 17 January 2013 <http://www.themalaysianinsider.com/print/sideviews/getting-malaysian-citizenship-cheaply> (accessed 20 January 2013).

91. "Malaysia's Looming Election: Video Nasties — A Two Year Election Campaign Nears its Climax", *The Economist*, 23 March 2013 <http://www.economist.com/news/asia/21574013-two-year-election-campaign-nears-its-climax-video-nasties/print> (accessed 25 March 2013).

92. Ibid.

93. "PKR: BN Using Sabah Crisis to Instil Hatred against Anwar", *The Edge Malaysia*, 12 March 2013 <http://www.theedgemalaysia.com/indexphp?option=com_content&task=view&id=23> (accessed 15 March 2013).

94. "Elections in Malaysia: 'Ubah' You Can Believe In?", *The Economist*, 4 May 2013 <http://www.economist.com/news/asia/21577123-malaysia-opposition-optimistic-ahead> (accessed 7 May 2013). *The Economist* records that when in November 2012 the Selangor Pakatan government investigated the electoral register they found that twenty-seven per cent of newly registered votes (numbering more than 134,000) could not be identified.

95. "Malaysia Votes in Closely Contested Elections", *BBC News*, 5 May 2013 <http://www.bbc.co.uk/news/world_asia-22394752?print=true> (accessed 6 May 2013).

96. Andrew Buncombe, "Malaysian PM Accused of 'Importing Voters' by Air," *The Independent*, 2 May 2013 <http://www.independent.co.uk/news/world/asia-malaysian-pm-accused-of-importing-voters-by-air> (accessed 4 May 2013).

97. "Malaysia's Election: A Tawdry Victory", *The Economist*, 6 May 2013 <http://www.economist.com/blogs.banyan/2013/015/malaysia's-elections> (accessed 7 May 2013).

98. "Malaysia Votes in Closely Contested Elections".

99. Ho Wah Foon, "GE 13 Results: Anwar Claims PR Wins Elections with 50.3% of Popular Vote", *The Edge Malaysia*, 7 May 2013 <http://www.theedge.malaysia.com/index.php?option=com_content&task+view&id=238> (accessed 8 May 2013).

100. Stuart Grudgings, "Analysis: Race Politics May Stunt Reforms after Malaysian Election", *The Edge Malaysia*, 9 May 2013 <http://www.theedge.malaysia.com/index.php?option=com-context&task=view&id=23> (accessed 10 May 2013).

101. Stuart Grudgings and Al-Zaquan Amer Hamzah, "Malaysia's Coalition Extends Rule Despite Worst Electoral Showing", *Reuters*, 5 May 2013 <http://www.reuters.com/assets/print?aid=USBRE9430B720130505> (accessed 6 May 2013).

102. "Analysis: Race Politics May Stunt Reforms".

103. For a full discussion of this phenomenon, see Johan Saravanamuttu, "The New Economic Policy, New Malay Middle Class and the Politics of Reform", in the *New Economic Policy in Malaysia; Affirmative Action, Ethnic Inequalities and Social Justice*, edited by Edmund Terence Gomez and Johan Saravanamuttu (Singapore: NUS/Institute of Southeast Asian Studies, 2013).

104. Grudgings and Al-Zaquan, "Malaysia's Coalition Extends Rule Despite Worst Showing".

105. Syed Jaymal Zahiid, "MIC's Saravanan Backs Utusan, Says Chinese Ungrateful", *Malaysian Insider*, 7 May 2013 <http://www.themalaysianinsider.com/print/malaysia/mics-saravanan-backs-utusan-says-chinese-ungrateful> (accessed 8 May 2013).

106. Grudgings, "Analysis: Race Politics May Stunt Reforms".

107. "Elections in Malaysia: 'Ubah' You Can Believe In?"

108. Grudgings, "Analysis: Race Politics May Stunt Reforms".

109. Syed Jaymal, "MIC's Saravanan".

110. Christopher Liong, President, "There Should Be No Space for Racist Rhetoric in Malaysia", *Malaysian Bar Council*, Press release, 8 May 2013.

111. Razak Ahmad and Florence A. Samy, "GE 13: BN Wins with 133, Wrests Back Kedah", *The Star*, 6 May 2013 <http://www.thestar.com.my/news/story.asp?file=2013/5/6/nation/20130506041947&sec=nation> (accessed 7 May 2013).

112. A. Letchumanan, "GE 13: Barisan Had Regained Indian Support Says Assoc Prof Dr. Sivamurugan Pandian", *The Star*, 7 May 2013 <http://www.thestar.com.my/news/story.asp?file=/2013/5/7/nation/13075869&sec+nation> (accessed 8 May 2013).

113. Ibid.

114. Personal correspondence.

115. Ida Lim, "Waythamoorthy Big Winner with Government Appointment", *Malaysian Insider*, 15 May 2013 <http://www.themalaysianinsider.com/malaysia/article/mic-faces-contest-from-hindraf-as-indian-voice-in-cabinet> (accessed 17 May 2013).

116. "Uthaya: Waytha Is the New Samy Vellu", *Malaysiakini*, 15 May 2013 <http://www.malaysiakini.com/news/23061> (accessed 17 May 2013).

117. Lim, "Waythamoorthy big winner".

CONCLUSIONS

The large-scale migration of Indians to Malaya throughout the nineteenth century and the first four decades of the twentieth century led to the creation of a distinct Indian Malaysian society. This community remains divided horizontally between the minority upper classes — the middle, professional and business classes — and a large working class which constitutes over eighty per cent of the population. The schism between the classes — upper and lower — within the community can be generally traced to the differing circumstances of their migration to Malaysia. Thus the descendants of "labour" recruitment — those who were contracted under indenture, kangany, or assisted-labour schemes to work in the plantations and within government utilities — now makes up an underclass which continues to fill labouring and unskilled occupations within modern Malaysia. The middle and upper classes have their origins in "non-labour" migratory streams; that is, their forbears were those Indians who were appointed to clerical and technical positions in colonial Malaya, or who established themselves in professions and businesses. The social gulf between the classes remains an obvious feature of Indian society, and many "non-labour" Indians endeavour to maintain their social distance from "labour" Indians, and in extreme cases many even deny all bonds of common ethnicity.

S. Arasaratnam has argued that the shared experiences of working-class Indians from the time of indenture and kangany recruitment have coalesced into a "plantation-oriented culture" characterized by stasis and underachievement, representing the world view of a neglected and marginalized underclass.[1] It is a culture which is marked by meagre educational attainment, low income, a marked absence of inter-generational vocational and economic mobility, and is plagued by a range of social problems. Moreover this culture has developed its own paradigmatic impulses, which unless broken, threaten to lock Indian labouring classes into a permanent underclass.[2]

The plantation culture had its genesis in the early milieu of Indian labour migration. Workers recruited under both indenture and kangany auspices were subject to repressive regulation, constant invigilation, and harsh discipline. Both systems bore a striking resemblance to slavery in that they established complete legal domination over the labourer and treated him/her as a mere (and dispensable) component in the process of production. The rigidity of contractual obligations and the willingness of employers to enforce them, stripped the worker of all but a bare minimum of personal rights, denied him/her even the most basic occupational mobility, and firmly placed him/her under the control of those who paid his/her wages. The Indian labourer was enclosed in a self-contained and isolated world and subject to a regime of permanent impoverishment and physical and psychological brutalization; a regime which discouraged initiative, independence of thought or any sense of personal integrity.[3] As we have seen, the labourer and his/her family lived in poverty, endured harsh working conditions, dwelt in substandard accommodation, lacked proper medical care, was exposed to the risk of disease, was often malnourished, and was subject to a range of intractable social problems, including poor child care and educational opportunities, and a high incidence of alcoholism, gambling, violence and suicide.

In recent years there has been a continuous migration of labour from rural to urban areas, a movement which accelerated with fragmentation and later with mass evictions from estates. The rural/urban migration did not result in any improvements in the economic standing of the Indian working classes, nor did it promote inter-generational mobility. Indeed, some observers believe that over the past forty years the conditions of the Indian indigent have actually worsened.[4] This internal flow of Indian labour occurred against the backdrop of the NEP, which closed many avenues of traditional employment to urban-based Indians.[5] The migration created a large pool of Indian labour, minimally educated and low-skilled, who were compelled to occupy positions that were basic, repetitive and poorly remunerated, and which offered little or nothing in the way of vocational advancement. Indian workers generally found that their wages were insufficient to maintain a family, and in most instances did not even keep pace with rises in the cost of living. Financial pressures forced most to rent shoddy housing; often slum and squatter dwellings. Thus the plantation culture of chronic underachievement and social stasis, lodged over generations of subjugation, of subordination to rigid and unyielding controls, and physical and psychological oppression which robbed the Indian worker of the qualities of innovation and independence, was replicated within urban Malaysia.

Nor have those trapped within the plantation culture been able to look to their more affluent compatriots for leadership and support. In general the social gulf between lower- and middle/upper-class Indians remains as deep and fixed now as it has throughout the entire history of the modern Indian presence in Malaya/Malaysia.[6] Writing in 1993, D. Jeyakumar observed that the many middle- and upper-class Indians felt disgust and shame at the miserable state of the Indian underclass and "often feel impatient and angry with the Indian poor caught in this subculture of poverty".[7] My own fieldwork suggests that this situation remains largely unchanged (though it would appear that many better-off Indians supported the Hindraf rally and were outraged by police actions at Batu Caves).

The history of the Indian poor in Malaya/Malaysia, now extending over 150 years, and encompassing up to seven generations of Indian working-class families, has been one of continual marginalization and oppression. The occasional impulses towards reform and self-organization, which have aimed at the general uplift of the broader community, have been curbed with swift and comprehensive official retaliation. Thus the CIAM's efforts to promote genuine Indian unity and to advance measures to improve the lot of the labouring classes were countered with the implacable hostility of the colonial administration. The subsequent Klang Valley strikes of 1941 were met not with offers of negotiation, but with the brute force of military suppression coupled with arrests and deportations. While the evanescent wartime unity achieved under Subhas Chandra Bose did not long survive the end of the Pacific War, the veterans of both the INA and IIL were subject to the full vengeful animosity of the returning British. Post-war movements such as Thondar Padai were designated as subversive and subsequently proscribed, while Indian attempts to create a vibrant and effective trade union movement were defeated by a British–UMNO alliance determined to root out and stifle sites of perceived leftist radicalism. In order to gain a representative voice for Indians within the ruling structures of an emerging Malaya, the MIC, the largest Indian political party, was compelled to jettison its policies of inclusive reformism to accord with the ideologies promulgated by the communally structured and conservative UMNO-MCA Alliance. The policies of communalism and the concomitant aggregation of "racial" communities as composite wholes ensured that the problems of the Indian poor would remain submerged and ignored. The implementation of the NEP in 1971, and the consequent contraction of social, vocational, economic, and educational opportunities for non-bumiputeras closed avenues of social and economic advancement for many Indians. Perceived official indifference to the plight of the Indian poor was impressed upon the collective Indian consciousness by the experiences of fragmentations, the post-1969 citizenship crisis and summary mass evictions from estates.

The general position of the Indian community has been complicated by the "neo-colonial"[8] racial ideologies which had become deeply inculcated in the political and cultural life of contemporary Malaysia. As we have seen, these ideologies had their origins in colonialist racial theorising; as Anthony Milner has observed: "a world classified in terms of 'race' was part of the European derived epistemological structure set in place during the early nineteenth century".[9] Colonial discourse posited an indigenous "Self" as backward, tradition bound, engaged in subsistence agriculture, and in need of protection from the more energetic immigrant "Other".[10] This colonialist construct was inscribed after World War II as a defensive ideology of "Malayness",[11] and the concomitant privileging of claims of those officially proclaimed indigenous,[12] a process aided by the British-UMNO suppression of alternative visions of a more inclusive Malaya.[13] The politics of communalism, and reification of indigene/non-indigene rivalry, has had the effect of continually reinscribing ethnic boundaries thereby reinforcing ethnic polarization and distrust. Malaysia remains one of the few countries in the world in which official discourse is primarily, indeed fundamentally, shaped by issues of "race", and the negotiation of daily life is predicated upon notions of inherent racial difference,[14] and in which proposals for greater inclusivity are viewed by political agents as not only subversive of official ideologies, but also as a possible threat to national integrity.[15]

Within the context of a Malaysia dominated by Malay and Islamic power brokers, a society in which both the Indian community and Hindus generally are relegated to the margins, it is perhaps not surprising that religion was the site from which the Indian underclass launched its challenge to Malaysia's political establishment.[16] Given the causative factors which precipitated Indian discontent — the forced conversions, the destroyed families, the seizure of bodies, the destruction of temples — it was perhaps inevitable that Hinduism should become a rallying point for Indian activism.[17]

But while Hindraf activism may have been spurred by religious issues, the movement rapidly embraced a broader platform which included demands for structural and economic reforms, and for thorough investigation of systemic failures (for example, Indian deaths in police custody). The Indian poor — still largely socially defined by their ascribed lowly status within the colonial racial and vocational hierarchy,[18] reduced to irrelevance by Malaysian political processes, neglected by the better-off in their own community, often betrayed by their own political and industrial leadership, and regarded as "forgotten people",[19] second-class citizens in the land of their birth — were making a statement of intent; a determination to escape the shackles of the "plantation culture". In this respect it is significant that Hindraf moved beyond Hinduism and that its calls for social justice attracted the involvement of Indians of other religious beliefs.[20] The subsequent abandonment of BN during the elections of 8 March 2008 was a further gauge of Indian discontent. But it also revealed that the regime of "benign neglect" was no longer to be tolerated, and that future Indian support for BN would be conditional.

An earlier generation of UMNO leaders, including Najib's father, Tun Abdul Razak, recognized the social and political dangers posed by the failure to alleviate Malay poverty. Similarly Najib perceived the need to devise immediate political responses to address Indian alienation. These measures, as yet limited, appear to have won considerable Indian goodwill. Moreover, Najib's 1Malaysia policy appears to recognize the need to build a more inclusive Malaysia; one in which "racial" boundaries are softened and which accepts and indeed celebrates ethnic and religious pluralism. 1Malaysia perhaps adumbrates the realities of a rapidly changing political, cultural and social landscape. A younger generation of urbanized Malaysians — for whom the foundational ideologies of Merdeka, and in particular the racial compact, are increasingly irrelevant — is inexorably reshaping Malaysian political and cultural discourse in ways that will have profound implications for the structures of communalism and the politics of race which have hitherto dominated Malayan/Malaysian life. The May 2013 elections and the continual erosion of support for UMNO's traditional ethnic-based allies, the MCA and MIC, may well foreshadow major challenges to UMNO itself should it remain an ethnic-specific party. It might well be anticipated that the eclipse of communalism and its concomitant — the need for continual re-inscription of ethnic boundaries which define Self and Other — would, over time, produce institutional and social reforms that would have a major, and most probably a positive, impact upon minorities, including Indian Malaysians. But to venture further is to enter the realm of speculation, and that is not the province of the historian.

Notes

1. Sinnappah Arasaratnam, "Malaysian Indians: The Formation of an Incipient Society", in *Indian Communities in Southeast Asia*, edited by K.S. Sandhu and A. Mani (Singapore: Institute of Southeast Asian Studies, 1993), p. 193.
2. M. Nadarajah, *Another Malaysia Is Possible and Other Essays: Writings on Culture and Politics for a Sustainable World* (Kuala Lumpur: Nohd, 2004), p. 142.
3. D. Jeyakumar, "The Indian Poor of Malaysia: Problems and Solutions", in *Indian Communities in Southeast Asia*, edited by K.S. Sandhu and A. Mani (Singapore: Institute of Southeast Asian Studies, 1993), p. 421.
4. Based on interviews conducted in 2010 and 2011. However, it should be noted that in the mid-1990s no less an observer than Samy Vellu commented that "Indians were more marginalised and alienated than ever before" (Edmund Terence Gomez and Jomo K.S., *Malaysia's Political Economy: Politics, Patronage and Profits* [Cambridge: Cambridge University Press, 1997], p. 168).
5. Mavis Puthucheary, "Indians in the Public Sector", in *Indian Communities in Southeast Asia*, edited by K.S. Sandhu and A. Mani (Singapore: Institute of Southeast Asian Studies, 1993), pp. 348–57.
6. G.P Ramachandran, "The Malaysian Indian in the New Millennium", Keynote Address, *The Malaysian Indian in the New Millennium* (Kuala Lumpur: May 2002).
7. Jeyakumar, *The Indian Poor of Malaysia*, p. 419.
8. Azly Rahman, "The 'New *Bumiputarism*' as Pedogogy of Hope and Liberation: Teaching the Alternative Malaysian Ethnic Studies", in *Multiethnic Malaysia: Past, Present and Future*, edited by Lim Teck Ghee, Alberto Gomes, and Azly Rahman (Petaling Jaya: Strategic Information and Research Centre, 2009), p. 454.
9. Anthony Milner, *The Malays* (Chichester: Wiley Blackwell, 2011), p. 154.
10. Sheila Nair, "Colonialism, Nationalism, Ethnicity: Constructing Identity and Difference", in *Multiethnic Malaysia: Past, Present and Future*, edited by Lim Teck

Ghee, Alberto Gomes, and Azly Rahman (Petaling Jaya: Strategic Information and Research Development Centre, 2009), p. 87.

11. Maznah Mohamad, "Politics of the NEP and Ethnic Relations in Malaysia", in *Multiethnic Malaysia: Past, Present and Future*, edited by Lim Teck Ghee, Alberto Gomes, and Azly Rahman (Petaling Jaya: Strategic Information and Research Development Centre, 2009), p. 122.

12. Ong Puay Liu, "Identity Matters: Ethnic Perception and Concerns", in *Multiethnic Malaysia: Past, Present and Future*, edited by Lim Teck Ghee, Alberto Gomes, and Azly Rahman (Petaling Jaya: Strategic Information and Research Development Centre, 2009), p. 466.

13. Ahmad Fauzi Abdul Hamid, *Islamic Education in Malaysia*, Monograph No. 18 (Singapore: S. Rajaratnam School of International Studies, 2010), pp. 13–14.

14. Ooi Kee Beng, "Beyond Ethnocentrism: Malaysia and the Affirmation of Hybridisation", in *Multiethnic Malaysia: Past, Present and Future*, edited by Lim Teck Ghee, Alberto Gomes, and Azly Rahman (Petaling Jaya: Strategic Information and Research Development Centre, 2009), p. 456.

15. Lim Teck Ghee, "Introduction: Historical Roots of Identity in Malaysia", in *Multiethnic Malaysia: Past, Present and Future*, edited by Lim Teck Ghee, Alberto Gomes, and Azly Rahman (Petaling Jaya: Strategic Information and Research Development Centre, 2009), p. 425.

16. In the 2000 Malaysian census, Hindus accounted for 84.1 per cent of the Indian population, while Christians numbered 7.8 per cent, and Muslims 4.1 per cent (Saw Swee-Hock, "Population Trends and Patterns in Multi-Racial Malaysia", in *Malaysia: Recent Trends and Challenges*, edited by Saw Swee-Hock and K. Kesavapany (Singapore: Institute of Southeast Asian Studies, 2006), p. 19).

17. There is perhaps another dimension to the Indic-Hindu issue. In Chapter 1, we noted that the Malay world was deeply influenced by Indic culture, religion, and statecraft, and that the two great earlier states of the Malay Archipelago — Srivijaya and Majapahit — were both Hindu-Buddhist kingdoms. Moreover, the Melaka Kingdom, to which the modern Malaysia pays official homage, was founded by a Hindu prince, and itself derived legitimacy from the kingdom of Srivijaya. Much of this is now openly disavowed by Malay nationalists and has been the subject of considerable revisionism in *Ketuanan Melayu* discourse. For a full discussion of this phenomenon, and in particular the subject of the contemporary presence of Indian/Hindu Malaysians as a reminder of a "surmounted past", see Andrew Wilford's perceptive and subtly argued, *Cage of Freedom: Tamil Identity and the Ethnic Fetish in Malaysia* (Ann Arbor: University of Michigan Press, 2006).

18. Rajesh Rai, "'Positioning' the Indian Diaspora: The Southeast Asian Experience", in *Tracing an Indian Diaspora: Contexts, Memories, Representations*,

edited by Parvati Raghuram, Ajaya Kumar Sahoo, Brij Maharaj, and Dave Sangham (New Delhi: Sage, 2008), p. 48.

19. Chandra Muzaffar, "Political Marginalization in Malaysia", in *Indian Communities in Southeast Asia*, edited by K.S. Sandhu and A. Mani (Singapore: Institute of Southeast Asian Studies, 1993), p. 228.

20. Personal field research.

BIBLIOGRAPHY

Abdul Rahman Putra Al-Haj, Tunku. *Looking Back: The Historic Years of Malaya and Malaysia*. Kuala Lumpur: Pustaka Antara, 1977.

———. *Viewpoints*. Kuala Lumpur: Heinemann Educational Books (Asia), 1978.

Abdul Rashid Moten. "Modernization and the Process of Globalization: The Muslim Experience and Responses". In *Islam in Southeast Asia: Political, Social and Strategic Challenges for the 21ˢᵗ Century*, edited by K.S. Nathan and Mohammad Hashim Kamali. Singapore: Institute for Southeast Asian Studies, 2005.

Abraham, Collin. "Manipulation and Management of Racial and Ethnic Groups in Colonial Malaysia: A Case Study of Ideological Domination and Control". In *Ethnicity and Ethnic Relations in Malaysia*, edited by Raymond L.M. Lee. Illinois: Northern Illinois University, Center for Southeast Asian Studies, 1986.

———. *The Naked Social Order: The Roots of Racial Polarisation in Malaysia*. Subang Jaya: Pelanduk, 2004 (1997).

———. *"The Finest Hour": The Malaysian-MCP Peace Accord in Perspective*. Petaling Jaya: Strategic Information and Research Development Centre, 2006.

Abu Talib Ahmad. "The Malay Community and Memory of the Japanese Occupation". In *War and Memory in Malaysia and Singapore*, edited by Patricia Lim Pui Huen and Diana Wong. Singapore: Institute of Southeast Asian Studies, 2000.

———. *The Malay Muslims, Islam and the Rising Sun: 1941–1945*. Kuala Lumpur: MBRAS, 2003.

Ackerman, Susan E. and Raymond L.M. Lee. *Heaven in Transition: Innovation and Ethnic Identity in Malaysia*. Honolulu: University of Hawai'i Press, 1988.

Aeria, Andrew. "Skewed Economic Development and Inequality: The New Economic Policy in Sarawak". In *The New Economic Policy in Malaysia: Affirmative Action, Ethnic Inequalities and Social Justice*, edited by Edmund Terence Gomez and Johan Saravanamuttu. Singapore: NUS/Institute of Southeast Asian Studies, 2013.

Ahearne, C.D. *Annual Report of the Labour Department, Malaya, 1934*. Kuala Lumpur: Government Press, 1935.

Ahmad Fauzi Abdul Hamid. *Islamic Education in Malaysia*, Monograph No. 18. Singapore: S. Rajaratnam School of International Studies, 2010.

———. "Politically Engaged Muslims in Malaysia in the Era of Abdullah Ahmad Badawi (2003–2009)". *Asian Journal of Political Science* 18, no. 2 (August 2010): 154–76.

Ahmad Mustapha Hassan. *The Unmaking of Malaysia: Insider's Reminiscences of UMNO, Razak and Mahathir*. Petaling Jaya: Strategic Information and Research Development Centre, 2007.

Ahmad, Talmiz. *Children of Abraham at War: The Clash of Messianic Militarisms*. Delhi: Aakar Books, 2010.

Ainsworth, Leopold. *The Confessions of a Planter in Malaya: A Chronicle of Life and Adventure in the Jungle*. London: Witherby, 1933.

Akashi Yoji. "Colonel Watanabe Wataru: The Architect of the Malayan Military Administration, December 1941–March 1943". In *New Perspectives on the Japanese Occupation in Malaya and Singapore, 1941–1945*, edited by Akashi Yoji and Yoshimura Mako. Singapore: NUS Press, 2008.

———. "Introduction". In *New Perspectives on the Japanese Occupation in Malaya and Singapore, 1941–1945*, edited by Akashi Yoji and Yoshimura Mako. Singapore: NUS Press, 2008.

———. "General Yamashita Tomoyuki: Commander of the Twenty-Fifth Army". In *A Great Betrayal? The Fall of Singapore Revisited*, edited by Brian Farrell and Sandy Hunter. Singapore: Marshall Cavendish Editions, 2010.

Akashi Yoji and Yoshimura Mako, eds. *New Perspectives on the Japanese Occupation in Malaya and Singapore, 1941–1945*. Singapore: NUS Press, 2008.

Alatas, Syed Hussein. *The Myth of the Lazy Native*. London: Frank Cass, 1977.

Allen, Louis. *Singapore 1941–1942*. Singapore: MPH Distributors (S), 1977.

———. *Burma: The Longest War 1941–45*. London and Melbourne: Dent, 1984.

Allen, Richard. *Malaysia: Prospect and Retrospect*. London: Oxford University Press, 1968.

Anbalakan, K. "Socio-economic Self-help among Indians in Malaysia". In *Rising India and Indian Communities in East Asia*, edited by K. Kesavapany, A. Mani, and P. Ramasamy. Singapore: Institute of Southeast Asian Studies, 2008.

Andaya, Leonard Y. *Leaves of the Same Tree: Trade and Ethnicity in the Straits of Melaka*. Honolulu: University of Hawai'i Press, 2008.

Annual Report of the Agent of the Government of India in British Malaya for the year 1927. Calcutta: Government of India Press, 1928.

Annual Report of the Agent of the Government of India in British Malaya for the year 1932. Calcutta: Government of India Press, 1933.

Annual Report of the Agent of the Government of India in British Malaya for the year 1933. Calcutta: Government of India Press, 1934.

Annual Report of the Government of India in British Malaya for the year 1926. Calcutta: Government of India Press, 1927.

Annual Report of the Labour Department, Federated Malay States, for the year 1933. Kuala Lumpur: Government Press, 1934.

Anwar Ibrahim. *The Asian Renaissance*. Singapore and Kuala Lumpur: Times Books International, 1996.

Arasaratnam, Sinnappah. *Indians in Malaysia and Singapore*. London: Oxford University Press, 1970.

———. "Political Attitudes and Political Organization among Malayan Indians 1945–1955." *Jernal Sejarah* 10 (1971/72): 1–6.

———. "Malaysian Indians: The Formation of an Incipient Society". In *Indian Communities in Southeast Asia*, edited by K.S. Sandhu and A. Mani. Singapore: Institute of Southeast Asian Studies, 1993.

Ariffin Omar. "The Struggle for Ethnic Unity of Malaya after the Second World War". In *Multiethnic Malaysia: Past, Present and Future*, edited by Lim Teck Ghee, Alberto Gomes, and Azly Rahman. Petaling Jaya: Strategic Information and Research Development Centre, 2009.

Arumugam, K. "Tamil School Education in Malaysia: Challenges and Prospects in the New Millennium". In *Rising India and Indian Communities in East Asia*, edited by K. Kesavapany, A. Mani, and P. Ramasamy. Singapore: Institute for Southeast Asian Studies, 2008.

Aslan, Reza. *No God but God: The Origins, Evolution and Future of Islam*. London: Heinemann, 2005.

Azly Rahman. "The 'New *Bumiputarism*' as Pedagogy of Hope and Liberation: Teaching the Alternative Malaysian Ethnic Studies". In *Multiethnic Malaysia: Past, Present and Future*, edited by Lim Teck Ghee, Alberto Gomes, and Azly Rahman. Petaling Jaya: Strategic Information and Research Centre, 2009.

Azza Basarudin. "Gatekeeping Will Not Stop Apostasy". In *Religion under Siege? Lina Joy, The Islamic State and Freedom of Speech*, edited by Nathaniel Tan and John Lee. Kuala Lumpur: Kinibooks, 2008.

———. "Revathi has Made Her Choice Crystal Clear". In *Religion under Siege? Lina Joy, The Islamic State and Freedom of Speech*, edited by Nathaniel Tan and John Lee. Kuala Lumpur: Kinibooks, 2008.

Bajpai, Sir Girja Shankar (Secretary to the Government of India). *Memorandum to the Honourable Colonial Secretary, Singapore, 1938*. London: Memorandum No f-44/38-L&O, 1938, Oriental and India Office Collection.

Baker, Christopher John. "Figures and Facts: Madras Government Statistics, 1880–1940". In *South India: Political Institutions and Political Change 1880–1940*, edited by C.J. Baker and D.A. Washbrook. Delhi: Macmillan, 1975.

———. *The Politics of South India 1920–1937*. Cambridge: Cambridge University Press, 1976.

Baker, C.J. and D.A. Washbrook, eds. *South India: Political Institutions and Political Change 1880–1940*. Delhi: Macmillan, 1975.

Balaji Sadasivan. *The Dancing Girl: A History of Early India*. Singapore: Institute of Southeast Asian Studies, 2011.

Baradan Kuppusamy. "Body Blow to Tolerance". In *Religion Under Siege? Lina Joy, The Islamic State and Freedom of Speech*, edited by Nathaniel Tan and John Lee. Kuala Lumpur: Kinibooks, 2008.

Barber, Noel. *A Sinister Twilight: The Fall of Singapore 1942*. Boston: Houghton Miflin, 1968.

———. *The War of the Running Dogs*. London: Fontana, 1971.

Barlow, Colin. "Changes in the Economic Position of Workers on Rubber Estates and Small Holdings in Peninsular Malaysia 1910–1985". In *The Underside of Malaysian History: Pullers, Prostitutes, Plantation Workers*, edited by Peter J. Rimmer and Lisa M. Allen. Singapore: Singapore University Press, 1990.

Baron, J.M. *Annual Report of the Labour Department, Malaya, 1935*. Kuala Lumpur: Government Press, 1936.

Bayly, Christopher and Tim Harper. *Forgotten Armies: The Fall of British Asia 1941–1945*. Cambridge, MA: Belknap Press of Harvard University Press, 2004.

———. *Forgotten Wars: The End of Britain's Asian Empire*. London: Penguin Books, 2008.

Belle, Carl Vadivella. "Thaipusam in Malaysia: A Hindu Festival Misunderstood?". PhD dissertation, Deakin University, 2004.

———. "Forgotten Malaysians? Indians and Malaysian Society". In *Tracing an Indian Diaspora: Contexts, Memories, Representations*, edited by Parvati Raghuram, Ajaya Kumar Sahoo, Brij Maharaj, and Dave Sangha. New Delhi: Sage Publications, 2008.

———. "Indian Hindu Resurgence in Malaysia". In *Rising India and Indian Communities in East Asia*, edited by K. Kesavapany, A. Mani, and P. Ramasamy. Singapore: Institute of Southeast Asian Studies, 2008.

———. *The Development of Indian Political Consciousness in Malaysia: Colonialism, Nationalism and Subhas Chandra Bose*, CSID Paper No. 4. Hyderabad: Centre for the Study of the Indian Diaspora, University of Hyderabad, 2009.

Bilainkin, George. *Hail Penang! Being a Narrative of Comedies and Tragedies in a Tropical Outpost, among Europeans, Chinese, Malays and Indians*. Penang: Areca Books, 2010 (1932).

Blackburn, Robin. *The Making of New World Slavery: From the Baroque to the Modern 1492–1800*. London: Verso, 1997.

Bolt, Christine. *Victorian Attitudes to Race*. London: Routledge and Kegan Paul, 1971.

Bose, Mihir. *Raj, Secrets, Revolution: A Life of Subhas Chandra Bose*. London: Grice Chapman, 2004.

Bose, Sugata. *His Majesty's Opponent: Subhas Chandra Bose and India's Struggle against Empire*. Cambridge, MA and London: Belknap Press and Harvard University Press, 2011.

Braddon, Russell. *The Naked Island*. Hawthorn: Lloyd O'Neil, 1975.

Breman, Jan. *Taming the Coolie Beast: Plantation Society and the Colonial Order in Southeast Asia*. Delhi: Oxford University Press, 1989.

Brendon, Vyvyen. *Children of the Raj*. London: Weidenfeld and Nicolson, 2005.

Butcher, John G. *The British in Malaya 1880–1941: The Social History of a European Community in Southeast Asia*. Kuala Lumpur: Oxford University Press, 1979.

Caffrey, Kate. *Out in the Midday Sun: Singapore 1941–45*. London: Andre Deutsch, 1974.

Caldwell, Malcolm. "From 'Emergency' to Independence". In *Malaya: The Making of a Neo-Colony*, edited by Mohamed Amin and Malcolm Caldwell. Nottingham: Spokesman, 1977.

———. "The British 'Forward Movement' 1874–1914". In *Malaya: The Making of a Neo-Colony*, edited by Mohamed Amin and Malcolm Caldwell. Nottingham: Spokesman, 1977.

———. "War, Boom and Depression". In *Malaya: The Making of a Neo-Colony*, edited by Mohamed Amin and Malcolm Caldwell. Nottingham: Spokesman, 1977.

Cannadine, David. *Ornamentalism: How the British Saw Their Empire*. London: Penguin, 2001.

Carter, Marina. "Indians and the Colonial Diaspora". In *Rising India and Indian Communities in East Asia*, edited by K. Kesavapany, A. Mani, and P. Ramasamy. Singapore: Institute of Southeast Asian Studies, 2008.

Carter, Marina and Khal Torabully. *Coolitude: An Anthology of the Indian Labour Diaspora*. London: Anthem Press, 2002.

Chakravarti, Nalini Ranjan. *The Indian Minority in Burma: The Rise and Decline of an Indian Community*. London: Oxford University Press, 1971.

Champakalakshmi, R. *Trade, Ideology and Urbanization: South India 300 BC to AD 1300*. New Delhi: Oxford University Press, 1996.

———. *Religion, Tradition and Ideology: Pre-colonial South India*. New Delhi: Oxford University Press, 2011.

Chapman, E. Spencer. *The Jungle is Neutral*. London: Corgi Books, 1957 (1949).

Chatterjee, A.C. *India's Struggle for Freedom*. Calcutta: Chuckervetty, Chatterjee, 1947.

Cheah Boon Kheng. *Red Star over Malaya: Resistance and Social Conflict during and after the Japanese Occupation of Malaya 1941–1946*, 2nd ed. Singapore: Singapore University Press, 1987.

———. "Memory as History and Moral Judgement: Oral and Written Accounts of the Japanese Occupation of Malaya". In *War and Memory in Malaysia and Singapore*, edited by Patricia Lim Pui Huen and Diana Wong. Singapore: Institute of Southeast Asian Studies, 2000.

―――. *Malaysia: The Making of a Nation*. Singapore: Institute of Southeast Asian Studies, 2002.

―――. "The 'Blackout' Syndrome and the Ghosts of World War II: The War as a 'Divisive Issue' in Malaysia". In *Legacies of World War II in South and East Asia*, edited by David Koh Wee Hock. Singapore: Institute of Southeast Asian Studies, 2007.

―――. "Race and Ethnic Relations in Colonial Malaya during the 1920s and 1930s". In *Multiethnic Malaysia: Past, Present and Future,* edited by Lim Teck Ghee, Alberto Gomes, and Azly Rahman. Petaling Jaya: Strategic Information and Research Development Centre, 2009.

Chelvasingam-MacIntyre, Tan Sri S. *Through Memory Lane*. Singapore: University Education Press, 1973.

Chin, Aloysius. *The Communist Party of Malaya ― The Inside Story*. Kuala Lumpur: Vinpress, 1995.

Chin, C.C. "In Search of the Revolution: A Brief Biography of Chin Peng". In *Dialogues with Chin Peng: New Light on the Malayan Communist Party*, edited by C.C. Chin and Karl Hack. Singapore: Singapore University Press, 2004.

Chin, C.C. and Karl Hack, eds. *Dialogues with Chin Peng: New Light on the Malayan Communist Party*. Singapore: Singapore University Press, 2004.

―――. "Early History of the Malayan Communist Party". In *Dialogues with Chin Peng: New Light on the Malayan Communist Party*, edited by C.C. Chin and Karl Hack. Singapore: Singapore University Press, 2004.

Chin, James. "The Malaysian Chinese Dilemma: The Never Ending Policy (NEP)". *Chinese Southern Diaspora Studies* 3 (2009): 167–82.

―――. "Malaysia: The Rise of Najib and 1Malaysia". *Southeast Asian Affairs, 2010:* 166–79.

Chin, James and Chin-Huat Wong. "Malaysia's Electoral Upheaval". *Journal of Democracy* 20, no. 3 (July 2009): 71–85.

Chin Kee Onn. *Malaya Upside Down*, 3rd ed. Kuala Lumpur: Federal, 1976.

Chin Peng (as told to Ian Ward and Norma Miraflor). *My Side of History*. Singapore: Media Masters, 2003.

Clammer, John R. "Ethnic Processes in Urban Melaka". In *Ethnicity and Ethnic Relations in Malaysia*, edited by Raymond L.M. Lee. Illinois: Northern Illinois University, Center for Southeast Asian Studies, 1986.

Clifford, Sir Hugh. *Malayan Monochromes*. New York: E.P. Dutton, 1913.

Clutterbuck, Richard. *Riot and Revolution in Singapore and Malaya 1945–1963*. London: Faber and Faber, 1973.

Coedes, G. *The Indianized States of Southeast Asia*, 3rd ed., translated by Susan Brown Cowling. Canberra: Australian National University Press, 1975 (1963).

Collett, Nigel. *The Butcher of Amritsar: General Reginald Dyer*. London: Hambledon and London, 2005.

Colley, Linda. *Britons: Forging the Nation 1707–1837*. New Haven: Yale University Press, 1992.

Comber, Leon. "Notes on the Adoption of the Armed Struggle in 1948 and Questions on the First Malayan Emergency in Peninsular Malaysia". In *Dialogues with Chin Peng: New Light on the Malayan Communist Party*, edited by C.C. Chin and Karl Hack. Singapore: Singapore University Press, 2004.

———. *Malaysia's Secret Police 1945–1960: The Role of the Special Branch in the Malayan Emergency*. Singapore: Institute of Southeast Asian Studies, 2008.

Cook, Haruko Taya and Theodore F. Cook. *Japan at War: A New Oral History*. New York: The New Press, 1992.

Corr, Gerard H. *The War of the Springing Tigers*. London: Osprey, 1975.

Crouch, Harold. "Authoritarian Trends, the UMNO Split, and the Limits to State Power". In *Fragmented Vision: Culture and Politics in Contemporary Malaysia*, edited by Joel S. Kahn and Francis Lok Kok Wah. Sydney: Asian Studies Association of Australia/Allen and Unwin, 1992.

Dalrymple, William. *The Last Mughal: The Fall of a Dynasty, Delhi 1857*. London: Bloomsbury, 2006.

Daniel, Rabindra J. "Poverty among the Malaysian Indian Plantation Community". *Jurnal Pengajian India* I (1983): 125–42.

Datta-Ray, Sunanda K. "World War II Legacies for India". In *Legacies of World War II in South and East Asia*, edited by David Koh Wee Hock. Singapore: Institute of Southeast Asian Studies, 2007.

Daud Latiff. "Japanese Invasion and Occupation". In *Malaya: The Making of a Neo Colony*, edited by Mohamed Amin and Malcolm Caldwell. Nottingham: Spokesman, 1977.

———. "The British Military Administration, September 1945 to April 1946". In *Malaya: The Making of a Neo-Colony*, edited by Mohamed Amin and Malcolm Caldwell. Nottingham: Spokesman, 1977.

Davis, Mike. *Late Victorian Holocausts: El Nino Famines and the Making of the Third World*. London: Verso, 2001.

Devare, Hema. "Cultural Implications of the Chola Maritime Fabric Trade with Southeast Asia". In *Nagapattinam to Suvarnadwipa: Reflections on the Chola Naval Expeditions to Southeast Asia*, edited by Hermann Kulke, K. Kesavapany, and Vijay Sakhuja. Singapore: Institute of Southeast Asian Studies, 2009.

Dhoraisingam, Samuel S. *Peranakan Indians of Singapore and Melaka: Indian Babas and Nonyas — Chitty Melaka*. Singapore: Institute of Southeast Asian Studies, 2006.

Dirks, Nicholas B. *The Hollow Crown: Ethnohistory of an Indian Kingdom*, 2nd ed. Ann Arbor: University of Michigan Press, 1993.

————. *Castes of Mind: Colonialism and the Making of Modern India*. Princeton, NJ: Princeton University Press, 2001.

Drabble, John. "Politics of Survival: European Reactions in Malaya to Rubber Smallholders in the Inter-War Years". In *The Underside of Malaysian History: Pullers, Prostitutes, Plantation Workers*, edited by Peter J. Rimmer and Lisa M. Allen. Singapore: Singapore University Press, 1990.

Dutt, S. *Annual Report of the Government of India in British Malaya, 1940*. Calcutta: Government of India Press, 1941.

Dutton, Geoffrey. *Founder of a City: The Life of Colonel William Light*. Adelaide: Rigby, 1984 (1960).

Edwardes, Michael. *Red Year: The Indian Rebellion of 1857*. London: Cardinal, 1975.

Elphick, Peter. *Singapore: The Pregnable Fortress*. London: Coronet Books, 1995.

Elsbree, Willard H. *Japan's Role in Southeast Asian Nationalist Movements 1940–1945*. Harvard University Press, 1953.

Emigration from India to the Crown Colonies and Protectorates (Report of the Sanderson Committee), 1910. London: Parliamentary Paper (HC) XXVIII, Oriental and India Office Library.

Evers, Hans-Deiter and Jayarani Padarayan. "Religious Fervour and Economic Success: The Chettiars of Singapore". In *Indian Communities in Southeast Asia*, edited by K.S. Singh and A. Mani. Singapore: Institute of Southeast Asian Studies, 1993.

Farish A. Noor. "The Localization of Islamist Discourse in the *Tasfir* of Tuan Guru Nik Aziz Mat, *Murshid'ul Am* of PAS". In *Malaysia: Islam, Society and Politics*, edited by Virginia Hooker and Norani Othman. Singapore: Institute of Southeast Asian Studies, Singapore, 2003.

Farrell, Brian and Sandy Hunter, eds.. *A Great Betrayal? The Fall of Singapore Revisited*. Singapore: Marshall Cavendish Editions, 2010.

Fauconnier, Henri. "The Soul of Malaya". In *Where Monsoons Meet: The Story of Malaya in the Form of an Anthology*, edited by Donald Moore. London: Harap, 1956.

Fay, Peter Ward. *The Forgotten Army: India's Armed Struggle for Independence 1942–1945*. Ann Arbor: University of Michigan Press, 1995.

Fedorowich, Kent. "The Evacuation of Civilians from Hong Kong and Malaya/Singapore". In *A Great Betrayal? The Fall of Singapore Revisited*, edited by Brian Farrell and Sandy Hunter. Singapore: Marshall Cavendish Editions, 2010.

Ferris, John R. "Student and Master: The United Kingdom, Japan, Airpower and the Fall of Singapore". In *A Great Betrayal? The Fall of Singapore Revisited*, edited by in Brian Farrell and Sandy Hunter. Singapore: Marshall Cavendish Editions, 2010.

Fujiwara Iwaichi. *F Kikan: Japanese Army Intelligence Operations and Southeast Asia during World War II*, translated by Akashi Yoji. Hong Kong: Heinemann Asia, 1983.

Funston, John. *Malay Politics in Malaysia: A Study of UMNO and PAS*. Kuala Lumpur: Heinemann Educational Books (Asia), 1980.

Gagliano, Felix V. *Communal Violence in Malaysia 1969: The Political Aftermath*. Ohio: Ohio University Center for International Studies, Southeast Asia Program, 1970.

Gamba, Charles. *The Origins of Trade Unionism in Malaya: A Study in Colonial Labour Unrest*. Singapore: Eastern Universities Press, 1962.

Gandhi, Mohandas K. *An Autobiography: The Story of My Experiments with Truth*, translated by Mahadev Desai. London: Penguin, 1983.

Gilbert, Martin. *A History of the Twentieth Century, Volume Two 1933–1951*. London: HarperCollins, 1998.

Gilchrist, Robert Niven. "Political and Social Problems on Indians in *inter alia* Malaya up until 22 April 1944". London: Mss Eur D.819, India and Oriental Office Collection.

Gill, Tan Sri Dato Seri Darshan Singh. *Sikh Community in Malaysia*. Petaling Jaya: MPH Group, 2009.

Gilmour, Robin. *The Idea of the Gentleman in the Victorian Novel*. London: Allen and Unwin, 1981.

Goh Cheng Teik. *The May 13ᵗʰ Incident and Democracy in Malaysia*. Kuala Lumpur: Oxford University Press, 1971.

Gomes, Alberto. "Ethnicisation of the Orang Asli". In *Multiethnic Malaysia: Past, Present and Future*, edited by Lim Teck Ghee, Alberto Gomes, and Azly Rahman. Petaling Jaya: Strategic Information and Research Development Centre, 2009.

———. "Introduction: Marginalised Communities, Marginalised Identities". In *Multiethnic Malaysia: Past, Present and Future*, edited by Lim Teck Ghee, Alberto Gomes, and Azly Rahman. Petaling Jaya: Strategic Information and Research Development Centre, 2009.

———. "Superlative Syndrome, Cultural Politics and Neoliberalism in Malaysia". In *Multiethnic Malaysia: Past, Present and Future*, edited by Lim Teck Ghee, Alberto Gomes, and Azly Rahman. Petaling Jaya: Strategic Information and Research Development Centre, 2009.

Gomez, Edmund Terence. *The State of Malaysia: Ethnicity, Equity and Reform*. London: RoutledgeCurzon, 2004.

———. "The 2004 Malaysian General Elections: Economic Development, Electoral Trends, and the Decline of the Opposition". In *Malaysia: Recent Trends and Challenges*, edited by Saw Swee-Hock and K. Kesavapany. Singapore: Institute of Southeast Asian Studies, 2006.

———. "Ethnicity, Equity and Politics in Multiethnic Malaysia". In *Multiethnic*

Malaysia: Past, Present and Future, edited by Lim Teck Ghee, Alberto Gomes, and Azly Rahman. Petaling Jaya: Strategic Information and Research Development Centre, 2009.

———. "Nurturing Bumiputera Capital: SMEs, Entrepreneurship and the New Economic Policy". In *The New Economic Policy in Malaysia: Affirmative Action, Ethnic Inequalities and Social Justice,* edited by Edmund Terence Gomez and Johan Saravanamuttu. Singapore: NUS/Institute of Southeast Asian Studies, 2013.

Gomez, Edmund Terence, Johan Saravanamuttu, and Maznah Mohamad. "Introduction: Malaysia's New Economic Policy: Resolving Horizontal Inequalities: Creating Inequalities?" In *The New Economic Policy in Malaysia: Affirmative Action, Ethnic Inequalities and Social Injustice,* edited by Edmund Terence Gomez and Johan Saravanamuttu. Singapore: NUS/Institute of Southeast Asian Studies, 2013.

Gomez, Edmund Terence and Johan Saravanamuttu, eds. *The New Economic Policy in Malaysia: Affirmative Action, Ethnic Inequalities and Social Justice.* Singapore: NUS/Institute of Southeast Asian Studies, 2013.

Gomez, Edmund Terence and Jomo K.S. *Malaysia's Political Economy: Politics, Patronage and Profits.* Cambridge: Cambridge University Press, 1997.

Gray, John. *Black Mass: Apocalyptic Religion and the Death of Utopia.* London: Allen Lane, 2007.

Gullick, J.M. *The Story of Kuala Lumpur 1857–1939.* Singapore: Eastern Universities Press, 1983.

Hack, Karl. "Communist Party and Support". In *Dialogues with Chin Peng: New Light on the Malayan Communist Party,* edited by C.C. Chin and Karl Hack. Singapore: Singapore University Press, 2004.

———. "From Baling to Merdeka 1955–60". In *Dialogues with Chin Peng: New Light on the Malayan Communist Party,* edited by C.C. Chin and Karl Hack. Singapore: Singapore University Press, 2004.

Hack, Karl and C.C. Chin. "The Malayan Emergency". In *Dialogues with Chin Peng: New Light on the Malayan Communist Party,* edited by C.C. Chin and Karl Hack. Singapore: Singapore University Press, 2004.

Harper, Tim. "A Long View of the Great Asian War". In *Legacies of World War II in South and East Asia,* edited by David Koh Wee Hock. Singapore: Institute of Southeast Asian Studies, 2007.

Hata Shoriyu. "A War Correspondent". In *Japan at War: An Oral History,* edited by Haruko Taya Cook and Theodore F. Cook. New York: The New Press, 1992.

Hayashi Hirofumi. "Massacre of Chinese in Singapore and Its Coverage in Post-War Japan". In *New Perspectives on the Japanese Occupation in Malaya and Singapore, 1941–1945,* edited by Akashi Yoji and Yoshimura Mako. Singapore: NUS Press, 2008.

Heng Pek Koon. *Chinese Politics in Malaysia: A History of the Malaysian Chinese Association*. Singapore: Oxford University Press, 1988.

Hermann, Arthur. *The Idea of Decline in Western History*. New York: The Free Press, 1997.

Hirschmann, Charles. "The Making of Race in Colonial Malaya: Political Economy and Racial Ideology". *Sociological Forum* 1, no. 2 (Spring 1986): 330–61.

———. "The Meaning and Measurement of Ethnicity in Malaysia: A Study of Census Classifications". *Journal of Asian Studies* 46, no. 3 (August 1987): 566–82.

Ho Engseng. "Before Parochialism: Diasporic Arabs Cast in Creole Waters". In *Arabs, Politics, Trade and Islam in Southeast Asia*, edited by Huub De Jonge and Nico Kaptein. Leiden: KLTLV Press, 2002.

Holmes, Richard. *Sahib: The British Soldier in India*. London: Harper Collins, 2005.

Hooker, Virginia. "Still 'Islam and Politics' But Now Enmeshed in a Global Web". In *Malaysia: Islam and Society and Politics*, edited by Virginia Hooker and Norani Othman. Singapore: Institute of Southeast Asian Studies, 2003.

Hooker, Virginia and Amin Saikal, eds. *Islamic Perspectives on the New Millennium*. Singapore: Institute of Southeast Asian Studies, 2004.

Hooker, Virginia and Norani Othman, eds. *Malaysia: Islam, Society and Politics*. Singapore: Institute of Southeast Asian Studies, 2003.

Huang Jianli. "Remembering World War II: Legacies of the War Fought in China". In *Legacies of World War II in South and Southeast Asia*, edited by David Koh Wee Hock. Singapore: Institute of Southeast Asian Studies, 2007.

Hughes, Tom Eames. *Tangled Worlds: The Story of Maria Hertogh*. Singapore: Institute of Southeast Asian Studies, 1982.

Hwang In-Won. *Personalised Politics: The Malaysian State Under Mahathir*. Singapore: Institute of Southeast Asian Studies, 2003.

Hwok-Aun Lee. "Affirmative Action in Occupational Representation: Policies and Outcomes". In *The New Economic Policy in Malaysia: Affirmative Action, Ethnic Inequalities and Social Justice*, edited by Edmund Terence Gomez and Johan Saravanamuttu. Singapore: NUS/Institute of Southeast Asian Studies, 2013.

Hyam, Ronald. *Empire and Sexuality: The British Experience*. Manchester: Manchester University Press, 1990.

Indian Emigration Rules 1923 and Special Rules Application to Ceylon and Malaya. London: File V/27/826/6, Oriental and India Office Collection.

Indians in Malaya: December 1930–September 1934. London: File L/P&J/8/258, Collection 108/21A, Oriental and India Office Collection.

Indians in Malaya: Appointment of an Agent, November 1934–October 1938. London: File L/P&J/8/259, Collection 108/21B, Oriental and India Office Collection.

Indians in Malaya: Constitutional Reforms and Malayan Union Citizenship, March 1946–February 1948. London: File L/P&/J/8/266, Collection 108/21J, Oriental and India Office Collection.

Indians in Malaya: Status and Duties of Governor-General of Malaya, January 1946–May 1949. London: L/P&J/8/266, Collection 108/21I, Oriental and India Office Collection.

Indians Overseas: Malaya: Negotiations between Indian and Malayan Governments Concerning the Rights of Indians in Malaya, February 1939–June 1942. London: L/P&J/8/260, Collection 108/21C, Oriental and India Office Collection.

Indians Overseas: Malaya: Strikes by Indian Labourers. London: File L/P&J/8/264, Collection 108/21G, Oriental and India Office Collection.

International Labour Office. *Asiatic Labour Enquiry: Report of Malaya, October 1927–November 1928.* London: File 7306A/1925, Oriental and India Office Collection.

Ismail Kassim. *A Reporter's Memoir: No Hard Feelings.* Singapore: Ismail Kassim, 2008.

Jain, Ravindra K. *South Indians on the Plantation Frontier in Malaya.* New Haven: Yale University Press, 1970.

———. "South Indian Labour in Malaya 1840–1920: Asylum, Stability and Involution". In *Indentured Labour in the British Empire 1834–1920*, edited by Kay Saunders. London: Croom Helm, 1984.

James, Lawrence. *Raj: The Making and Unmaking of British India.* London: Little, Brown, 1997.

———. *The Rise and Fall of the British Empire.* London: Abacus, 1998.

Janakey Raman Manickam. *The Malaysian Indian Dilemma: The Struggles and Agony of the Indian Community in Malaysia*, 2nd ed. Klang: Janakey Raman Manickam, 2010.

Jessy, Joginder Singh. "The Indian Army of Independence". BA (Hons) dissertation, University of Singapore, 1957–58.

Jeyakumar, D. "The Indian Poor of Malaysia: Problems and Solutions". In *Indian Communities in Southeast Asia*, edited by K.S. Sandhu and A. Mani. Singapore: Institute of Southeast Asian Studies, 1993.

Johnson, Deborah. "Intellectual Statesmanship in the Mahathir Era". In *Malaysia: Public Policy and Marginalized Groups*, edited by Phua Kai Lit. Kajang: Persatuan Sains Sosial Malaysia, 2007.

Johnson, Eric and Karl-Heinz Rueband. *What We Knew: Terror, Mass Murder and Everyday Life in Nazi Germany.* London: John Murray, 2005.

Jomo, K.S. "Plantation Capital and Indian Labour in Colonial Malaya". In *Indian Communities in Southeast Asia*, edited by K.S. Sandhu and A. Mani. Singapore: Institute of Southeast Asian Studies, Singapore, 1993.

———. "A Malaysian Middle Class". In *Rethinking Malaysia*, edited by K.S. Jomo. Kuala Lumpur: Malaysian Social Science Association, 1999.

———, ed. *Rethinking Malaysia.* Kuala Lumpur: Malaysian Social Science Association, 1999.

Jomo, K.S. and Ahmad Shabery Cheek. "Malaysia's Islamic Movements". In *Fragmented Vision: Culture and Politics in Contemporary Malaysia*, edited by Joel S. Kahn and Francis Loh Kok Wah. Sydney: Asian Studies Association of Australia/Allen and Unwin, 1992.

Kah Seng Loh, Edgar Liao, Cheng Tju Lim, and Gua-Quan Seng. *The University Socialist Club and the Contest for Malaya: Tangled Strands of Modernity*. Amsterdam: Amsterdam University Press, 2012.

Kahn, Joel S. "Islam, Modernity and the Popular in Malaysia". In *Malaysia: Islam, Society and Politics*, edited by Virginia Hooker and Norani Othman. Singapore: Institute of Southeast Asian Studies, 2003.

———. *Other Malays: Nationalism and Cosmopolitanism in the Modern Malay World*. Singapore: Asian Studies Association of Australia in association with Singapore University Press and NIAS Press, 2006.

Kahn Joel S. and Francis Loh Kok Wah, eds. *Fragmented Vision: Culture and Politics in Contemporary Malaysia*. Sydney: Asian Studies Association of Australia/Allen and Unwin, 1992.

———. "Introduction". In *Fragmented Vision: Culture and Politics in Contemporary Malaysia*. Sydney: Asian Studies Association of Australia/Allen and Unwin, 1992.

Kapur, Pradeep K. "India's Engagement with East Asia". In *Rising India and Indian Communities in East Asia*, edited by K. Kesavapany, A. Mani, and P. Ramasamy. Singapore: Institute of Southeast Asian Studies, 2008.

Karim Raslan. *Ceritalah: Malaysia in Transition*. Singapore and Kuala Lumpur: Times Books International, 1996.

Kathigasu, Sybil. *No Dram of Mercy*. London: Neville Spearman, 1954.

Kaur, Amarjit. "Working on the Railway: Indian Workers in Malaya 1880–1957". In *The Underside of Malaysian History: Pullers, Prostitutes, Plantation Workers*, edited by Peter J. Rimmer and Lisa M. Allen. Singapore: Singapore University Press, 1990.

———. "Tapper and Weeders: South Indian Plantation Workers in Peninsular Malaysia, 1880–1970". *Journal of South Asian Studies* 20 (1998): 73–102.

———. "The Movement of Indians in East Asia: Contemporary and Historical Encounters". In *Rising India and Indian Communities in East Asia*, edited by K. Kesavapany, A. Mani, and P. Ramasamy. Singapore: Institute of Southeast Asian Studies, 2008.

Keith, Patrick. *Ousted!* Singapore: Media Masters, 2005.

Kennedy, J. *A History of Malaya*. London: Macmillan, 1970.

Kesavapany, K., A. Mani, and P. Ramasamy, eds. *Rising India and Indian Communities in East Asia*. Singapore: Institute of Southeast Asian Studies, 2008.

Kessler, Clive. "Archaism and Modernity: Contemporary Malay Political Culture". In *Fragmented Vision: Culture and Politics in Contemporary Malaysia*, edited by

Joel S. Kahn and Francis Loh Kok Wah. Sydney: Asian Studies Association of Australia/Allen and Unwin, 1992.

Khong Kim Hoong, *Merdeka! British Rule and the Struggle for Independence in Malaya 1945–1957*. Kuala Lumpur: Insan, 1984.

Khoo, Agnes. *Life as the River Flows: Women in the Malayan Anti-Colonial Struggle*. Petaling Jaya: Strategic Information Research Development, 2004.

Khoo Boo Tiek. *Paradoxes of Mahathirism: An Intellectual Biography*. Kuala Lumpur: Oxford University Press, 1995.

———. *Beyond Mahathir: Malaysian Politics and its Discontents*. London: Zed Books, 2003.

Khoo Jay Jin. "The Grand Vision: Mahathir and Modernization". In *Fragmented Vision: Culture and Politics in Contemporary Malaysia*, edited by Joel S. Kahn and Francis Loh Kok Wah. Sydney: Asian Studies Association of Australia/Allen and Unwin, 1992.

Khoo Kay Kim. "The Emergence of Plural Communities in the Malay Peninsula before 1874". In *Multiethnic Malaysia: Past, Present and Future*, edited by Lim Teck Ghee, Alberto Gomes, and Azly Rahman. Petaling Jaya: Strategic Information and Research Development Centre, 2009.

Kiernan, V.G. *The Lords of Human Kind: European Attitudes towards the Outside World in an Imperial Age*. Harmondsworth: Penguin Books, 1972 (1969).

Kikue Hamatyotsu. "The Politics of Syariah Reform: The Making of the State Religio-Legal Apparatus". In *Malaysia: Islam, Society and Politics*, edited by Virginia Hooker and Norani Othman. Singapore: Institute of Southeast Asian Studies, 2003.

Kinvig, Clifford. "General Percival and the Fall of Singapore". In *A Great Betrayal? The Fall of Singapore Revisited*, edited by Brian Farrell and Sandy Hunter. Singapore: Marshall Cavendish Editions, 2010.

Kloosterboer, W. *Involuntary Labour since the Abolition of Slavery*. Leiden: Brill, 1960.

Koh Wee Hock, David, ed. *Legacies of World War II in South and East Asia*. Singapore: Institute of Southeast Asian Studies, 2007.

Kohn, Marek. *A Reason for Everything: Natural Selection and the English Imagination*. London: Faber and Faber, 2004.

Kua Kai Soong. *May 13: Declassified Documents on the Malaysian Riots of 1969*. Petaling Jaya: Suaram Komunikasi, 2007.

Kulke, Hermann. "The Naval Expeditions of the Cholas in the Context of Asian History". In *Nagapattinam to Suvarnadwipa: Reflections on the Chola Naval Expeditions to Southeast Asia*, edited by Hermann Kulke, K. Kesavapany, and Vijay Sakhuja. Singapore: Institute of Southeast Asian Studies, 2009.

Kumar, Dharma. *Land and Caste in South India: Agricultural Labour in the Madras Presidency during the Nineteenth Century*. London: Cambridge University Press, 1965.

Kunhiram, Rao Sahib M. *Annual Report of the Government of India in British Malaya, 1931*. Calcutta: Government of India Press, 1932.

Lambert, Angela. *Unquiet Souls: The Indian Summer of the British Aristocracy*. London: Papermac, 1985.

Latif, Asad-ul Iqbal. "Singapore's Missing War". In *Legacies of World War II in South and East Asia*, edited by David Koh Wee Hock. Singapore: Institute of Southeast Asian Studies, 2007.

―――. "From *Mandala* to Microchips: The Indian Imprint on the Construction of Singapore". In *Rising India and Indian Communities in East Asia*, edited by K. Kesavapany, A. Mani, and P. Ramasamy. Singapore: Institute of Southeast Asian Studies, 2008.

Lebra, Joyce. *Jungle Alliance: Japan and the Indian National Army*. Singapore: Asia Pacific Press, 1971.

Lee, Raymond L.M., ed. *Ethnicity and Ethnic Relations in Malaysia*. Illinois: Northern Illinois University, Center for Southeast Asian Studies, 1986.

―――. "Symbols of Separatism: Ethnicity and Status Politics in Contemporary Malaysia". In *Ethnicity and Ethnic Relations in Malaysia*, edited by Raymond L.M. Lee. Illinois: Northern Illinois University, Center for Southeast Asian Studies, 1986.

Lee, Risha. "Rethinking Community: The Indic Carvings of Quanzhou". In *Nagapattinam to Suvarnadwipa: Reflections on the Chola Naval Expeditions to Southeast Asia*, edited by Hermann Kulke, K. Kesavapany, and Vijay Sakhuja. Singapore: Institute of Southeast Asian Studies, 2009.

Lee Hock Guan. "Globalization and Ethnic Integration in Malaysian Education". In *Malaysia: Recent Trends and Challenges* edited by Saw Swee-Hock and K. Kesavapany. Singapore: Institute of Southeast Asian Studies, 2006.

―――. "Language, Education and Ethnic Relations". In *Multiethnic Malaysia: Past, Present and Future*, edited by Lim Teck Ghee, Alberto Gomes, and Azly Rahman. Petaling Jaya: Strategic Information and Research Centre, 2009.

―――. "Racial Citizenship and Higher Education in Malaysia". In *The New Economic Policy in Malaysia: Affirmative Action, Ethnic Inequalities and Social Justice*, edited by Edmund Terence Gomez and Johan Saravanamuttu. Singapore: NUS/Institute of Southeast Asian Studies, 2013.

Lee Kam Hing. "Forging Interethnic Cooperation: The Political and Constitutional Process towards Independence, 1951–1957". In *Multiethnic Malaysia: Past, Present and Future*, edited by Lim Teck Ghee, Alberto Gomes, and Azly Rahman. Petaling Jaya: Strategic Information and Research Development Centre, 2009.

Lee Kuan Yew. *The Singapore Story: Memoirs of Lee Kuan Yew*. Singapore: Prentice Hall, 1998.

Letchumanan, A. "Nagging Pains of Local Indians". In *Another Malaysia is Possible and Other Essays*, edited by M. Nadarajah. Kuala Lumpur: Nohd, 2004.

Liew Chin Tong. *Speaking for the Reformasi Generation*. Kuala Lumpur: Research for Social Advancement, 2009.

Lim Hong Hai. "The Public Service and Ethnic Restructuring under the New Economic Policy: The New Challenge of Correcting Selectivity and Excess". In *The New Economic Policy in Malaysia: Affirmative Action, Ethnic Inequalities and Social Justice*, edited by Edmund Terence Gomez and Johan Saravanamuttu. Singapore: NUS/Institute of Southeast Asian Studies, 2013.

Lim Kit Siang. *Time Bombs in Malaysia*. Petaling Jaya: Democratic Action Party, 1978.

Lim Pui Huen, Patricia. "War and Ambivalence: Monuments and Memorials in Johor". In *War and Memory in Malaysia and Singapore*, edited by Patricia Lim Pui Huen and Diana Wong. Singapore: Institute of Southeast Asian Studies, 2000.

Lim Pui Huen, Patricia and Diana Wong, eds. *War and Memory in Malaysia and Singapore*. Singapore: Institute of Southeast Asian Studies, 2000.

Lim Teck Ghee. "Introduction: Future Prospects". In *Multiethnic Malaysia: Past, Present and Future*, edited by Lim Teck Ghee, Alberto Gomes, and Azly Rahman. Petaling Jaya: Strategic Information and Research Development Centre, 2009.

———. "Introduction: Historical Roots of Identity in Malaysia". In *Multiethnic Malaysia: Past Present and Future*, edited by Lim Teck Ghee, Alberto Gomes, and Azly Rahman. Petaling Jaya: Strategic Information and Research Development Centre, 2009.

———. "Malaysia's Prospects: Rising to or in Denial of Challenges?". In *Multiethnic Malaysia: Past, Present and Future*, edited by Lim Teck Ghee, Alberto Gomes, and Azly Rahman. Petaling Jaya: Strategic Information and Research Development Centre, 2009.

Lim Teck Ghee and Alberto Gomes. "Culture and Development in Malaysia". In *Multiethnic Malaysia: Past, Present and Future*, edited by Lim Teck Ghee, Alberto Gomes, and Azly Rahman. Petaling Jaya: Strategic Information and Research Development Centre, 2009.

Lim Teck Ghee, Alberto Gomes, and Azly Rahman. "Introduction". In *Multi-ethnic Malaysia: Past, Present and Future*, edited by Lim Teck Ghee, Alberto Gomes, and Azly Rahman. Petaling Jaya: Strategic Information and Research Development Centre, 2009.

———, eds. *Multi-ethnic Malaysia: Past, Present and Future*. Petaling Jaya: Strategic Information and Research Development Centre, 2009.

Loh Kok Wah, Francis. *Beyond the Tin Mines: Coolies, Squatters and New Villagers in the Kinta Valley, Malaysia c1880–1980*. Singapore: Oxford University Press, 1990.

———. "From the Tin Mine Coolies to Agricultural Squatters: Socio-Economic

Change in the Kinta District during the Inter-War Years". In *The Underside of Malaysian History: Pullers, Prostitutes, Plantation Workers*, edited by Peter J. Rimmer and Lisa M. Allen. Singapore: Singapore University Press, 1990.

Loh Kok Wah, Francis and Joel S. Kahn. "Introduction: Fragmented Vision". In *Fragmented Vision: Culture and Politics in Contemporary Malaysia*, edited by Joel S. Kahn and Francis Loh Kok Wah. Sydney: Asian Studies Association of Australia/Allen and Unwin, 1992.

McKenzie, John M. *Propaganda and Empire: The Manipulation of British Public Opinion 1880–1960*. Manchester: Manchester University Press, 1985.

MacMillan, Margaret. *Women of the Raj*. London: Thames and Hudson, 1988.

McPherson, Kenneth. *'How Best do we Survive?': A Modern Political History of the Tamil Muslims*. New Delhi: Routledge, 2010.

Mackie, James. "The Formation of Malaysia (1961–3) and *Konfrontasi*". In *Dialogues with Chin Peng: New Light on the Malayan Communist Party*, edited by C.C. Chin and Karl Hack. Singapore: Singapore University Press, 2004.

Mahajani, Usha. *The Role of Indian Minorities in Burma and Malaya*. Bombay: Vora, 1960.

Maharaj, Brij. "Introduction: 'New Form of Slavery': Indentured Diaspora". In *Tracing an Indian Diaspora: Contexts, Memories, Representations*, edited by Parvati Raghuram, Ajaya Kumar Sahoo, Brij Maharaj, and Dave Sanga. New Delhi: Sage, 2008.

Mahathir bin Mohamad. *The Malay Dilemma*. Petaling Jaya: Federal, 1981.

Mahathir Mohamad. *A Doctor in the House: The Memoirs of Tun Mahathir Mohamad*. Petaling Jaya: MPH Publishing, 2011.

Mahizhnan, Arun. "Indian Interactions in East Asia". In *Rising India and Indian Communities in East Asia*, edited by K. Kesavapany, A. Mani, and P. Ramasamy. Singapore: Institute of Southeast Asian Studies, 2008.

Mahli, Amrita. "The PAS-BN Conflict in the 1990s: Islamism and Modernity". In *Malaysia: Islam, Society and Politics*, edited by Virginia Hooker and Norani Othman. Singapore: Institute of Southeast Asian Studies, 2003.

Makkal Sakthi: What Must we Do, 20 February 2008. (emailed anonymously to author).

Malaya: Registration and Control of Trade Unions, May–August 1940. London: File L/P&J/8/263, Collection 108/21F, Oriental and India Office Collection.

Malhotra, Rajiv and Aravindan Neelakandan. *Breaking India: Western Interventions in Dravidian and Dalit Faultlines*. New Delhi: Amaryllis, 2011.

Manderson, Leonore. "Colonial Mentality and Public Health in Early Twentieth Century Malaya". In *The Underside of Malaysian History: Pullers, Prostitutes, Plantation Workers*, edited by Peter J. Rimmer and Lisa M. Allen. Singapore: Singapore University Press, 1990.

Mangan, J.A. *The Games Ethic and Imperialism: Aspects of the Diffusion of an Ideal.* Harmondsworth: Viking, 1986.

Marimuthu, T. "The Plantation School as an Agent of Social Reproduction". In *Indian Communities in Southeast Asia*, edited by K.S. Sandhu and A. Mani. Singapore: Institute of Southeast Asian Studies, 1993.

Marjoribanks, N.G. and A.K.G. Ahmad Tambi Marrakayar. *Report on Indian Labour Emigrating to Ceylon and Malaya 1917.* London: File V/27/820/12, Oriental and India Office Collection.

Markendeya, Subodh. *Subhas Chandra Bose: Netaji's Passage to Immortality.* New Delhi: Arnold, 1990.

Marks, Shula and Peter Richardson, eds. *International Labour Migration: Historical Perspectives.* London: Maurice Temple Smith, 1984.

———. "Introduction". In *International Labour Migration: Historical Perspectives*, edited by Shula Marks and Peter Richardson. London: Maurice Temple Smith, 1984.

Martinez, Patricia A. "Is it always Islam versus Civil Society?". In *Islam in Southeast Asia: Political, Social and Strategic Challenges for the 21ˢᵗ Century*, edited by K.S. Nathan and Mohammad Hashim Kamali. Singapore: Institute of Southeast Asian Studies, 2005.

Maznah Mohamad. *Paradoxes of State Islamization in Malaysia: Routinization of Religious Charisma and Secularization of the Syariah*, Working Papers Series No. 129. Singapore: Asia Research Institute, 2009.

———. "Politics of the NEP and Ethnic Relations in Malaysia". In *Multiethnic Malaysia: Past, Present and Future*, edited by Lim Teck Ghee, Alberto Gomes, and Azly Rahman. Petaling Jaya: Strategic Information and Research Development Centre, 2009.

Means, Gordon P. *Political Islam in Southeast Asia.* Boulder, CO: Rienner, 2009.

Mehta, Ved. *Mahatma Gandhi and His Apostles.* Harmondsworth: Penguin Books, 1976.

Metcalf, Thomas R. *Ideologies of the Raj.* Cambridge: Cambridge University Press, 1977.

Milne, R.S and Diane K. Mauzy. *Politics and Government in Malaysia.* Singapore: Federal, 1978.

Milner, Anthony. *The Invention of Politics in Colonial Malaya.* Cambridge: Cambridge University Press, 1995.

———. *The Malays.* Chichester: Wiley Blackwell, 2011.

Misra, Maria. *Vishnu's Crowded Temple: India since the Great Rebellion.* London: Allen Lane, 2007.

Mohamed Abu Bakar. "Islam, Civil Society and Ethnic Relations in Malaysia". In *Islam and Civil Society in Southeast Asia*, edited by Nakamura Mitsuo, Sharon

Siddique, and Omar Farouk Bajunid. Singapore: Institute of Southeast Asian Studies, 2001.

Mohamed Amin and Malcolm Caldwell, eds. *Malaya: The Making of a Neo-Colony*. Nottingham: Spokesman, 1977.

Moore, Donald, ed. *Where Monsoons Meet: The Story of Malaya in the Form of an Anthology*. London: Harap, 1956.

Morais, J. Victor. *Hussein Onn: A Tryst with Destiny*. Singapore: Times Book International, 1981.

Morgan, Michael. "The Rise and Fall of Malayan Trade Unionism 1945–1950". In *Malaya: The Making of a Neo-Colony*, edited by Mohamed Amin and Malcolm Caldwell. Nottingham: Spokesman, 1977.

Muhammad Ikbal Said. "Ethnic Perspectives of the Left in Malaysia". In *Fragmented Vision: Culture and Politics in Contemporary Malaysia*, edited by Joel S. Kahn and Francis Loh Kok Wah. Sydney: Asian Studies Association of Australia/Allen and Unwin, 1992.

Muhammad Takiyuddin Ismail and Ahmad Fauzi Abdul Hamid. "Abdullah Ahmad Badawi and Malaysia's Neo-Conservative Intellectuals", *Pacific Affairs* 86, no. 1 (March 2013): 73–94.

Mukundan, K.A. *Annual Report of the Government of India in British Malaya, 1934*. Calcutta: Government of India Press, 1935.

———. *Annual Report of the Government of India in British Malaya, 1935*. Calcutta: Government of India Press, 1936.

———. *Annual Report of the Government of India in British Malaya, 1936*. Calcutta: Government of India Press, 1937.

Murfett, Malcolm H. "An Enduring Theme: The 'Singapore Strategy'". In *A Great Betrayal? The Fall of Singapore Revisited*, edited by Brian Farrell and Sandy Hunter. Singapore: Marshall Cavendish Editions, 2010.

Muzaffar, Chandra. *Islamic Resurgence in Malaysia*. Petaling Jaya: Penerbity Fajar Bakti, 1987.

———. "Political Marginalization in Malaysia". In *Indian Communities in Southeast Asia*, edited by K.S. Sandhu and A. Mani. Singapore: Institute of Southeast Asian Studies, 1993.

Nadaraja, K. "The Thondar Padai Movement of Kedah 1945–1947". *Malaysia in History* 24 (n.d.): 96–107.

Nadarajah, M., ed. *Another Malaysia is Possible and Other Essays; Writings on Culture and Politics for a Sustainable World*. Kuala Lumpur: Nohd, 2004.

Nadarajan, M. "The Nattukottai Chettiar Community and Southeast Asia". *International Conference Seminar of Tamil Studies*, Kuala Lumpur, 1966: 251–60.

Nadarajan, V. *Bujang Valley: The Wonder that was Ancient Kedah*. Sungai Petani: Dato V. Nadarajan, 2011.

Nagarajan, S. "Indians in Malaysia: Towards 2020". In *Rising India and Indian Communities in East Asia*, edited by K. Kesavapany, A. Mani, and P. Ramasamy. Singapore: Institute of Southeast Asian Studies, 2008.

———. "Marginalisation and Ethnic Relations: The Indian Malaysian Experience". In *Multiethnic Malaysia: Past, Present and Future*, edited by Lim Teck Ghee, Alberto Gomes, and Azly Rahman. Petaling Jaya: Strategic Information and Research Development Centre, 2009.

Nagarajan, S. and K. Arumugam. *Violence against an Indian Minority in Malaysia: Kampung Medan, 2001*. Petaling Jaya: Suram, 2012.

Nagata, Judith. *Malaysian Mosaic: Perspectives from a Poly-Ethnic Society*. Vancouver: University of Columbia Press, 1979.

———. *The Reflowering of Malaysian Islam: Modern Religious Radicals and Their Roots*. Vancouver: University of British Columbia Press, 1984.

———. "Religion and Ethnicity among the Indian Muslims of Malaysia". In *Indian Communities in Southeast Asia*, edited by K.S. Sandhu and A. Mani. Singapore: Institute of Southeast Asian Studies, 1993.

Nair, Sheila. "Constructing Civil Society in Malaysia: Nationalism, Hegemony and Resistance". In *Rethinking Malaysia*, edited by K.S. Jomo. Kuala Lumpur: Malaysian Social Science Association, 1999.

———. "Colonialism, Nationalism, Ethnicity: Constructing Identity and Difference". In *Multiethnic Malaysia: Past, Present and Future*, edited by Lim Teck Ghee, Alberto Gomes, and Azly Rahman. Petaling Jaya: Strategic Information and Research Development Centre, 2009.

Nakahara Michiko. "Labour Recruitment in Malaya under the Japanese Occupation: The Case of the Burma-Siam Railway". In *Rethinking Malaysia*, edited by K.S. Jomo. Kuala Lumpur: Malaysian Social Science Association, 1999.

Nakamura Mitsuo, Sharon Siddique, and Omar Farouk Bajunid, eds. *Islam and Civil Society in Southeast Asia*. Singapore: Institute of Southeast Asian Studies, 2001.

Nathan, K.S. and Mohammad Hashim Kamali, eds. *Islam in Southeast Asia: Political, Social and Strategic Challenges for the 21st Century*. Singapore: Institute of Southeast Asian Studies, 2005.

Netaji Subhas Bose — A Malaysian Perspective. Kuala Lumpur: Netaji Centre, 1992.

Nicolson, Juliet. *The Perfect Summer: Dancing into Shadow in 1911*. London: John Murray, 2007.

Noor Yahaya Hamzah. "Anything to do with Muslims, Hands-off Please". In *Religion under Siege? Lina Joy, The Islamic State and Freedom of Speech*, edited by Nathaniel Tan and John Lee. Kuala Lumpur: Kinibooks, 2008.

Nordin Hussin. *Trade and Society in the Straits of Melaka: Dutch Melaka and English Penang, 1780–1830*. Singapore: NUS Press, 2007.

North-Coombs, M.D. "From Slavery to Indenture: Forced Labour in the Political Economy of Mauritius 1834–1867". In *Indentured Labour in the British Empire 1834–1920*, edited by Kay Saunders. London: Croom Helm, 1984.

O'Donovan, Patrick. "For Fear of Weeping". In *Where Monsoons Meet: The Story of Malaya in the Form of an Anthology*, edited by Donald Moore. London: Harap, 1956.

Ong Puay Liu. "Identity Matters: Ethnic Perception and Concerns". In *Multiethnic Malaysia: Past, Present and Future*, edited by Lim Teck Ghee, Alberto Gomes, and Azly Rahman. Petaling Jaya: Strategic Information and Research Development Centre, 2009.

Ooi Kee Beng. "Bangsa Malaysia: Vision or Spin?". In *Malaysia: Recent Trends and Challenges*, edited by Saw Swee-Hock and K. Kesavapany. Singapore: Institute of Southeast Asian Studies, 2006.

———. *The Reluctant Politician: Tun Dr Ismail and His Time*. Singapore: Institute of Southeast Asian Studies, Singapore, 2006.

———. *Lost in Transition: Malaysia under Abdullah*. Petaling Jaya: Strategic Information and Research Development Centre/Singapore, Institute of Southeast Asian Studies, 2008.

———. *Arrested Reform: The Unmaking of Abdullah Badawi*. Kuala Lumpur: Research for Social Advancement, 2009.

———. "Beyond Ethnocentrism: Malaysia and the Affirmation of Hybridisation". In *Multiethnic Malaysia: Past, Present and Future*, edited by Lim Teck Ghee, Alberto Gomes, and Azly Rahman. Petaling Jaya: Strategic Information and Research Development Centre, 2009.

———. *Between UMNO and a Hard Place: The Najib Era Begins*. Kuala Lumpur: Research for Social Advancement/ Singapore: Institute of Southeast Asian Studies, 2010.

———. "The New Economic Policy and the Centralisation of Power". In *The New Economic Policy in Malaysia: Affirmative Action, Ethnic Inequalities and Social Justice*, edited by Edmund Terence Gomez and Johan Saravanamuttu. Singapore: NUS/Institute of Southeast Asian Studies, 2013.

Oorjitham, K.S. Susan. "Kinship Organization in Urban Tamil Working Class Families in West Malaysia". *Jurnal Penjagian India* (1983): 117–23.

———. "The Role of Religious Values in the South Indian Family Structure in West Malaysia". *Jurnal Penjagian India* 2 (1984): 171–80.

———. "Urban Indian Working Class Households". *Jurnal Pengajian India* 4 (1986): 66–79.

———. "Economic Profile of the Tamil Working Class in Peninsular Malaysia". *Jurnal Pengajian India* 5 (1993): 101–8.

———. "Urban Working-Class Indians in Malaysia". In *Indian Communities in Southeast Asia*, edited by K.S. Sandhu and A. Mani. Singapore: Institute of Southeast Asian Studies, 1993.

Orde-Brown, Major St J. *Report on Labour Conditions in Ceylon, Mauritius and Malaya 1942–1943*. London: Parliamentary Paper (HC) IX-659, CMB 6423, Oriental and India Office Collection.

Orwell, George. *Burmese Days*. Harmondsworth: Penguin Books, 1967 (1934).

Ota Koki. "Railway Operations in Japanese-occupied Malaya/Syonan, 1943–45". In *New Perspectives on the Japanese Occupation in Malaya and Singapore, 1941–1945*, edited by Akashi Yoji and Yoshimura Mako. Singapore: NUS Press, 2008.

Parmer, J. Norman. *Colonial Labor Policy and Administration: A History of Labor in the Rubber Plantation Industry in Malaya 1910–1941*. New York: Augustin, 1960.

––––––. "Health in the Federated Malay States in the 1920s". In *The Underside of Malaysian History: Pullers, Prostitutes, Plantation Workers*, edited by Peter J. Rimmer and Lisa M. Allen. Singapore: Singapore University Press, 1990.

Phua Kai Lit, ed. *Malaysia: Public Policy and Marginalized Groups*. Kajang: Persatuan Sains Sosial, 2007.

Pillai, Shanthini. *Colonial Visions, Post Colonial Revisions: Images of the Indian Diaspora in Malaysia*. Newcastle: Cambridge Scholars, 2007.

Poole, Philippa. *Of Love and War: The Letters and Diaries of Captain Adrian Curlewis and His Family*. Sydney: Landsdowne Press, 1982.

Potts, Lydia. *The World Labour Market: A History of Migration*, translated by Terry Bond. London: Zed Books, 1990.

Puthucheary, Mavis. "Indians in the Public Sector in Malaysia". In *Indian Communities in Southeast Asia*, edited by K.S. Sandhu and A. Mani. Singapore: Institute of Southeast Asian Studies, 1993.

Quigley, Declan. *The Interpretation of Caste*. Oxford: Clarendon Press, 1993.

Ragayah Haji Mat Zin. "The New Economic Policy and Poverty Eradication in Malaysia". In *The New Economic Policy in Malaysia: Affirmative Action, Ethnic Inequalities and Social Justice*, edited by Edmund Terence Gomez and Johan Saravanamuttu. Singapore: NUS/Institute of Southeast Asian Studies, 2013.

Raghavan, Nedyam. *India and Malaya: A Study*. Bombay: Indian Council of World Affairs/Orient Longman, 1954.

Raghuram, Parvati, Ajaya Kumar Sahoo, Brij Maharaj, and Dave Sangha, eds. *Tracing an India Diaspora: Contexts, Memories, Representations*. New Delhi: Sage, 2008.

Rai, Rajesh. "'Positioning' the Indian Diaspora: The Southeast Asian Experience". In *Tracing an Indian Diaspora: Contexts, Memories, Representations*, edited by Parvati Raghuram, Ajaya Kumar Sahoo, Brij Maharaj, and Dave Sangam. New Delhi: Sage, 2008.

Rajakrishnan, R. "Social Change and Group Identity among the Sri Lankan Tamils". In *Indian Communities in Southeast Asia*, edited by K.S. Sandhu and A. Mani. Singapore: Institute of Southeast Asian Studies, 1993.

Rajakrishnan Ramasamy. *Caste Consciousness among Indian Tamils in Malaysia*. Petaling Jaya: Pelanduk, 1984.

―――. "Indo-Ceylonese Relations in Malaysia". *Jurnal Pengajian India* 4 (1986): 88–106.

Rajeswary Amplavanar. *The Indian Minority and Political Change in Malaya 1945–1957*. Kuala Lumpur: Oxford University Press, 1981.

Rajeswary Amplavanar-Brown. "The Contemporary Indian Political Elite in Malaysia". In *Indian Communities in Southeast Asia*, edited by K.S. Sandhu and A. Mani. Singapore: Institute of Southeast Asian Studies, 1993.

Rajoo, R. "Indian Squatter Settlers: Rural-Urban Migration in West Malaysia". In *Indian Communities in Southeast Asia*, edited by K.S. Sandhu and A. Mani. Singapore: Institute of Southeast Asian Studies, 1993.

Ramachandra, G.P. "The Indian Independence Movement in Malaya 1942–45". MA dissertation, Universiti Malaya, 1970.

Ramachandran, C.P. "The Malaysian Indian in the New Millennium". *Keynote Address: The Malaysian Indian and the New Millennium Conference*, Kuala Lumpur, May 2002.

Ramasamy, P. "Socio-economic Transformation of Malaysian Plantation Workers". In *Indian Communities of Southeast Asia*, edited by K.S. Sandhu and A. Mani. Singapore: Institute of Southeast Asian Studies, 1993.

―――. *Plantation Labour, Unions, Capital and the State in Peninsular Malaysia*. New York: Oxford University Press, 1994.

―――. "Indian War Memory in Malaysia". In *War and Memory in Malaysia and Singapore*, edited by Patricia Lim Pui Huen and Diana Wong. Singapore: Institute of Southeast Asian Studies, 2000.

―――. "Politics of Indian Representation in Malaysia". In *Rising India and Indian Communities in East Asia*, edited by K. Kesavapany, A. Mani, and P. Ramasamy. Singapore: Institute of Southeast Asian Studies, 2008.

―――. "Ethnicity, Patronage and Legacy: Leadership Conflicts in UMNO". In *Multiethnic Malaysia: Past, Present and Future*, edited by Lim Teck Ghee, Alberto Gomes, and Azly Rahman. Petaling Jaya: Strategic Information and Research Development Centre, 2009.

Ramaswamy, Sumathi. *Passions of the Tongue: Language Devotion in Tamil India 1891–1970*. New Delhi: Munshiram Manoharlal, 1998.

Ramesar, Marianne D. "Indentured Labour in Trinidad 1880–1917". In *Indentured Labour in the British Empire 1834–1920*, edited by Kay Saunders. London: Croom Helm, 1984.

Ratnam, K.J. *Communalism and the Political Process in Malaya*. Kuala Lumpur and Singapore: University of Malaya Press, 1965.

Rehman Rashid. *A Malaysian Journey*. Petaling Jaya: Rehman Rashid, 1993.

Reid, Anthony. *Charting the Shape of Early Modern Southeast Asia*. Singapore: Institute of Southeast Asian Studies, 2000.

Representations of the Government of India in Malaya and Certain Other Colonial Territories in the Far East, October 1938–January 1950. London: CMD 6724, File L/P & J/8/261, Collection 108/21D, Oriental and India Office Collection.

Review of Important Events Relating to or Affecting Indians in Different Parts of the British Empire, July 1937, March 1946. London: File L/P &J/8/185, Collection 108/D, Oriental and India Office Collection.

Review of Important Events Relating to or Affecting Indians in Different Parts of the British Empire, 1936–1937, 1944–1945. London: File V/24/1190, Oriental and India Office Collection.

Ricklefs, M.C., Bruce Lockhart, Albert Lau, Portia Reyes, and Maitrii Aung-Thwin. *A New History of Southeast Asia.* Basingstoke: Palgrave Macmillan, 2010.

Rimmer, Peter J. and Lisa M. Allen, eds. *The Underside of Malaysian History: Pullers, Prostitutes, Plantation Workers.* Singapore University Press, 1990.

Rimmer, Peter J., Leonore Manderson, and Colin Barlow. "The Underside of Malaysian History". In *The Underside of Malaysian History: Pullers, Prostitutes, Plantation Workers,* edited by Peter J. Rimmer and Lisa M. Allen. Singapore: Singapore University Press, 1990.

Robins, Nick. *The Corporation that Changed the World: How the East India Company Shaped the Modern Multinational.* London: Pluto Press, 2006.

Rules Relating to the Emigration from the Port of Madras under the Provisions of Act VII of 1871. Madras: Government of Madras Presidency, 1874.

Rusalina Idris. "Left Behind: The Orang Asli under the New Economic Policy". In *The New Economic Policy in Malaysia: Affirmative Action, Ethnic Inequalities and Social Justice,* edited by Edmund Terence Gomez and Johan Saravanamuttu. Singapore: NUS/Institute of Southeast Asian Studies, 2013.

Russell, Lord. *The Knights of Bushido: A Short History of Japanese War Crimes.* London: Corgi, 1967 (1958).

Sabri Zain. *Face-Off: A Malaysian Reformasi Diary (1998–99).* Singapore: BigO Books, 2000.

Said, Edward. *Orientalism: Western Conceptions of the Orient.* London: Penguin, 1991.

Said, Edward W. *Culture and Imperialism.* London: Vintage, 1993.

Said Zahari. *Dark Clouds at Dawn: A Political Memoir.* Kuala Lumpur: Insan, 2001.

Sakhuja, Vijay and Sangeeta Sakhuja. "Rajendra Chola I's Naval Expedition to Southeast Asia: A Nautical Perspective". In *Nagapattinam to Suvarnadwipa: Reflections on the Chola Naval Expeditions to Southeast Asia,* edited by Hermann Kulke, K. Kesavapany, and Vijay Sakhuja. Singapore: Institute of Southeast Asian Studies, 2009.

Sandhu, Kernial Singh. "Tamils and Other Indian Convicts in the Straits Settlements 1790–1873". *International Conference Seminar of Tamil Studies,* Kuala Lumpur, 1966: 197–208.

———. *Indians in Malaya: Some Aspects of their Immigration and Settlement 1786–1957.* Cambridge: Cambridge University Press, 1969.

———. "The Coming of Indians to Malaysia". In *Indian Communities in Southeast Asia*, edited by K.S. Sandhu and A. Mani. Singapore: Institute of Southeast Asian Studies, 1993.

———. "Indian Immigration and Settlement in Singapore". In *Indian Communities in Southeast Asia*, edited by K.S. Sandhu and A. Mani. Singapore: Institute of Southeast Asian Studies, 1993.

Sandhu, K.S. and Mani, A., eds. *Indian Communities in Southeast Asia.* Singapore: Institute of Southeast Asian Studies, 1993.

Saravanamuttu, Johan. "The Great Middle Class Debate: Ethnicity, Politics or Lifestyle". In *Multiethnic Malaysia: Past, Present and Future*, edited by Lim Teck Ghee, Alberto Gomes, and Azly Rahman. Petaling Jaya: Strategic Information and Research Development Centre, 2009.

———. "The New Economic Policy, New Malay Middle Class and the Politics of Reform". In *The New Economic Policy in Malaysia: Affirmative Action, Ethnic Inequalities and Social Justice*, edited by Edmund Terence Gomez and Johan Saravanamuttu. Singapore: NUS/Institute of Southeast Asian Studies, 2013.

Sastri, Srinivasa. *Report: Conditions of Indian Labour in Malaya.* Calcutta: Government of India Press, 1937.

Saunders, Kay, ed. *Indentured Labour in the British Empire 1834–1920.* London: Croom Helm, 1984.

Saw Swee-Hock. "Population Trends and Patterns in Multiracial Malaysia". In *Malaysia: Recent Trends and Challenges*, edited by Saw Swee-Hock and K. Kesavapany. Singapore: Institute of Southeast Asian Studies, 2006.

Saw Swee-Hock and K. Kesavapany, eds. *Malaysia: Recent Trends and Challenges.* Singapore: Institute of Southeast Asian Studies, 2006.

Selvakumaran Ramachandran. *Indian Plantation Labour in Malaysia.* Kuala Lumpur: S. Abdul Majeed, 1994.

Sen, Amartya. *The Argumentative Indian: Writings on Indian History, Culture and Identity.* London: Allen Lane, 2005.

Sen, Tansen. "The Military Campaigns of Rajendra Chola and the Chola-Srivijaya-China Triangle". In *Nagapattinam to Suvaranadwipa: Reflections on the Chola Naval Expeditions to Southeast Asia*, edited by Hermann Kulke, K. Kesavapany, and Vijay Sakhuja. Singapore: Institute of Southeast Asian Studies, 2009.

Shaharuddin Ma'aruf. *Malay Ideas on Development: From Feudal Lord to Capitalist.* Singapore: Times Books International, 1988.

Shamsul A.B. *From British to Bumiputera Rule: Local Politics and Rural Development in Peninsular Malaysia.* Singapore: Institute of Southeast Asian Studies, Singapore, 2004 (1986).

Shan Ru-hong. *The War in the South: The Story of Negri Sembilan's Guerrillas.* Bangkok: Mental Health Publishing, 2003.

Sharifah Zaleha Syed Hassan. "Islamization and Emerging Civil Society: A Case Study". In *Islam in Civil Society in Southeast Asia*, edited by Nakamura Mitsuo, Sharon Siddique, and Omar Farouk Bajunid. Singapore: Institute of Southeast Asian Studies, 2001.

Shaw, William. *Tun Razak: His Life and Times*. Kuala Lumpur: Longman Malaysia, 1976.

Shennan, Margaret. *Out in the Midday Sun: The British in Malaya 1880–1960*. London: John Murray, 2004.

Short, Anthony. *The Communist Insurrection in Malaya 1948–1960*. London: Frederick Muller, 1975.

Singh, Giani Kesar. *Indian Independence Movement in East Asia*. Lahore: Singh Bros., 1947.

Sinha, Vineeta. "Hinduism in Contemporary Singapore". In *Indian Communities in Southeast Asia*, edited by K.S. Sandhu and A. Mani. Singapore: Institute of Southeast Asian Studies, 1993.

Sivachandralingam Sundara Raja. *Hindu Rights Action Force (Hindraf) from the Perspective of Utusan Malaysia*. Unpublished paper, not dated. (Copy presented to author in May 2010.)

———. "The London Dawn Raid and its Effect on Malaysian Plantation Workers", *Indonesia and the Malay World* 40, no. 116 (2012): 74–93.

Smyth, Sir John, V.C. *Percival and the Tragedy of Singapore*. London: McDonald, 1971.

Souden, David. "English Indentured Servants and the Transatlantic Colonial Economy". In *International Labour Migration: Historical Perspectives*, edited by Shula Marks and Peter Richardson. London: Maurice Temple Smith, 1984.

Srebrnik, Henry. "Indo-Fijians: Marooned without Land and Power in a South Pacific Archipelago". In *Tracing an Indian Diaspora: Contexts, Memories, Representations*, edited by Parvati Raghuram, Ajaya Kumar Sahoo, Brij Maharaj, and Dave Sangha. New Delhi: Sage, 2008.

Sreenivas, Mytheli. *Wives, Widows and Concubines: The Conjugal Family Ideal in Colonial India*. Bloomington: Indiana University Press, 2008.

Stein, Burton. *A History of India*. London: Blackwell, 1998.

Stenson, Michael R. *Repression and Revolt: The Origins of the 1948 Communist Insurrection in Malaya and Singapore*. Athens: Ohio University Press, 1969.

———. *Class, Race and Colonialism in West Malaysia: The Indian Case*. St. Lucia, University of Queensland Press, 1980.

Stewart, Brian. *Smashing Terrorism in the Malayan Emergency*. Subang Jaya: Pelanduk, 2004.

Stokes, Eric. *The English Utilitarians and India*. Oxford: Oxford University Press, 1959.

Stubbs, Richard. "Guerrilla Strategies and British Counter-Insurgency Strategies of the 1950s and 1960s: Why Was the War Lost?" In *Dialogues with Chin Peng:*

New Light on the Communist Party, edited by C.C. Chin and Karl Hack. Singapore: Singapore University Press, 2004.

Subbaya, R. *Annual Report of the Government of India in British Malaya, 1928*. Calcutta: Government of India Press, 1929.

———. *Annual Report of the Government of India in British Malaya, 1929*. Calcutta: Government of India Press, 1930.

———. *Annual Report of the Government of India in British Malaya, 1930*. Calcutta: Government of India Press, 1931.

Suryadinata, Leo, ed. *Admiral Zheng He and Southeast Asia*. Singapore: International Zheng He Society/Institute of Southeast Asian Studies, 2005.

Swettenham, Sir Frank. *British Malaya: An Account of the Origin and Progress of British Influence in Malaya*. Allen and Unwin, 1948.

Syed Muhammad Khairudin Aljunied. "Rethinking Riots in Colonial South East Asia: The Case of the Maria Hertogh Controversy in Singapore, 1950–54", *South East Asia Research* 18, no. 1 (2010): 105–31.

Takashi Inoguchi. "How to Assess World War II in World History: One Japanese Perspective". In *Legacies of World War II in South and East Asia*, edited by David Koh Wee Hock. Singapore: Institute of Southeast Asian Studies, 2007.

Tan, Nathaniel, ed. *Mahathir vs Abdullah: Covert Wars and Challenged Legacies*. Kuala Lumpur: Kinibooks, 2007.

Tan, Nathaniel and John Lee. "Introduction: Lina Joy". In *Religion Under Siege? Lina Joy, The Islamic State and Freedom of Faith*, edited by Nathaniel Tan and John Lee. Kuala Lumpur: Kinibooks, 2007.

———, eds. *Religion Under Siege? Lina Joy, The Islamic State and Freedom of Faith*. Kuala Lumpur: Kinibooks, 2008.

Tan Ta Sen. "Did Zheng He Set Out to Colonize Southeast Asia?". In *Admiral Zheng He and Southeast Asia*, edited by Leo Suryadinata. Singapore: International Zheng He Society/Institute of Southeast Asian Studies, 2005.

———. *Cheng Ho and Islam in Southeast Asia*. Singapore: Institute of Southeast Asian Studies, 2009.

Tan Tai Yong. *Creating 'Greater Malaysia': Decolonization and the Politics of Merger*. Singapore: Institute of Southeast Asian Studies, 2008.

Tan Yeok Seong. "Chinese Element in the Islamization of Southeast Asia: A Study of the Story of Njai Gede Pinatih, the Great Lady of Gresik". In *Admiral Zheng He and Southeast Asia*, edited by Leo Suryadinata. Singapore: International Zheng He Society/ Institute of Southeast Asian Studies, 2005.

Tarling, Nicholas. *Southeast Asia: Past and Present*. Melbourne: F.W. Cheshire, 1966.

Tate, Muzafar Desmond. *The Malaysian Indians: History, Problems and Future*. Petaling Jaya: Strategic Information Research Development Centre, 2008.

Thillainathan, R. "A Critical Review of Indian Economic Performance and Priorities for Action". In *Rising India and Indian Communities in East Asia*, edited by

K. Kesavapany, A. Mani, and P. Ramasamy. Singapore: Institute of Southeast Asian Studies, Singapore, 2008.

Thompson, Andrew. *The Empire Strikes Back? The Impact of Imperialism on Britain from the Mid-Nineteenth Century*. Harlow: Pearson Longman, 2005.

Thompson, Peter. *The Battle for Singapore: The True Story of the Greatest Catastrophe of World War II*. London: Portrait, 2005.

Thompson, Virginia. *Post-Mortem on Malaya*. New York: Macmillan, 1943.

Tinker, Hugh. *A New System of Slavery: The Export of Indian Labour Overseas 1830–1920*. London: Oxford University Press, 1974.

———. "Into Servitude: Indian Labour in the Sugar Industry". In *International Labour Migration: Historical Perspectives*, edited by Shula Marks and Peter Richardson. London: Maurice Temple Smith, 1984.

Tominga Shozo. "Qualifying as a Leader". In *Japan at War: An Oral History*, edited by Haruko Taya Cook and Theodore F. Cook. New York: The New Press, 1992.

Toye, Hugh. *The Springing Tiger: A Study of a Revolutionary*. London: Cassell, 1959.

Trautmann, Thomas R. *Aryans and British India*. Berkeley: University of California Press, 1997.

———. *Languages and Nations: The Dravidian Proof in Colonial Madras*. Berkeley: University of California Press, 2006.

Trocki, Carl A. *Prince of Pirates: The Temenggongs and the Development of Johor and Singapore 1784–1885*, 2nd ed. Singapore: NUS Press, 2007.

Uthayakumar, P. *Political Empowerment Strategy: The Way Forward*. Kuala Lumpur: P. Uthaykumar, 2009.

———. *Marginalization of Indians in Malaysia*. (Copy emailed to author on 6 April 2010.)

Van der Veer, Peter. *Religious Nationalism: Hindus and Muslims in India*. Berkeley: University of California Press, 1994.

Vasil, R.K. *Ethnic Politics in Malaysia*. New Delhi: Radiant, 1980.

Vasil, Raj K. *Tan Chee Khoon: An Elder Statesman*. Petaling Jaya: Pelanduk, 1987.

Venkatachar, C.S. *Report of the Agent of the Government of India in British Malaya for the Year 1937*. Calcutta: Government of India Press, 1938.

———. *Report of the Agent of the Government of India in British Malaya for the Year 1939*. Calcutta: Government of India Press, 1940.

Victor, Barbara. *The Last Crusade: Religion and the Politics of Misdirection*. London: Constable, 2005.

Viswanathan, Gauri. *The Masks of Conquest: Literary Study and British Rule in India*. New York: Columbia University Press, 1989.

Von Tunzelmann, Alex. *Indian Summer: The Secret History of the End of an Empire*. London: Simon and Schuster, 2007.

Wade, Geoff. *The Origins and Evolution of Ethnocracy in Malaysia*, Working Paper

Series No. 112. Singapore: Asia Research Institute, National University of Singapore, April 2009.

Wain, Barry. *Malaysian Maverick: Mahathir Mohamad in Turbulent Times*. Basingstoke: Palgrave MacMillan, 2009.

Wan Hashim. *Race Relations in Malaysia*. Kuala Lumpur: Heinemann Educational Books (Asia), 1983.

Wang Gungwu. "Memories of War: World War II in Asia". In *War and Memory in Malaysia and Singapore*, edited by Patricia Lim Pui Huen and Diana Wong. Singapore: Institute of Southeast Asian Studies, 2000.

——. "The First Three Rulers of Malacca". In *Admiral Zheng He and Southeast Asia*, edited by Leo Suryadinata. Singapore: International Zheng He Society/Institute of Southeast Asian Studies, 2005.

——. "The Opening of Relations between China and Malacca 1403–05". In *Admiral Zheng He and Southeast Asia*, edited by Leo Suryadinata. Singapore: International Zheng He Society/Institute of Southeast Asian Studies, 2005.

Warren, Alan. "The Indian Army and the Fall of Singapore Revisited". In *A Great Betrayal? The Fall of Singapore Revisited*, edited by Brian Farrell and Sandy Hunter. Singapore: Marshall Cavendish Editions, 2010.

Washbrook, David. "The Development of Caste Organization in South India 1880–1940". In *South India: Political Institutions and Political Change*, edited by C.J. Baker and D.A. Washbrook. Delhi: Macmillan, 1975.

Wazir Jahan Karim. "The Affairs of the Bogeyman: Migration and Class across Borders". In *Multiethnic Malaysia: Past, Present and Future*, edited by Lim Teck Ghee, Alberto Gomes, and Azly Rahman. Petaling Jaya: Strategic Information and Research Development Centre, 2009.

White, Jerry. *London in the Nineteenth Century*. London: Jonathan Cape, 2007.

Widido, Johannes. "A Celebration of Diversity: Zheng He and the Origin of the Pre-Colonial Coastal Urban Pattern in Southeast Asia". In *Admiral Zheng He and Southeast Asia*, edited by Leo Suryadinata. Singapore: International Zheng He Society/Institute of Southeast Asian Studies, 2005.

Wiebe, Paul W. and S. Mariappen. *Indian Malaysians: The View from the Plantation*. Delhi: Manohar, 1978.

Wilford, Andrew C. *Cage of Freedom: Tamil Identity and the Ethnic Fetish in Malaysia*. Ann Arbor: University of Michigan Press, 2006.

——. "Ethnic Clashes, Squatters and Historicity in Malaysia". In *Rising India and Indian Communities in East Asia*, edited by K. Kesavapany, A. Mani, and P. Ramasamy. Singapore: Institute of Southeast Asian Studies, 2008.

Wilson, A.N. *The Victorians*. London: Hutchinson, 2002.

——. *After the Victorians: The World Our Parents Knew*. London: Arrow Books, 2006.

——. *Our Times: The Age of Elizabeth II*. London: Hutchinson, 2008.

Wilson, C.E. *Annual Report of the Labour Department Malaya, 1936*. Kuala Lumpur: Government Press, 1937.

———. *Annual Report of the Labour Department, Malaya, 1938*. Kuala Lumpur: Government Press, 1939.

———. *Annual Report of the Labour Department Malaya, 1939*. Kuala Lumpur: Government Press, 1940.

Wilson, Sir Samuel. *Report: Visit to Malaya 1933*. London: CMD 4276, Oriental and India Office Collection.

Wingford-Stratford, Esme. *The Victorian Sunset*. London: Routledge, 1932.

Winstedt, Richard. *The Malays: A Cultural History*. London: Routledge and Kegan Paul, 1963.

Winzeler, Robert L. "Overseas Chinese Power, Social Organization and Ethnicity in Southeast Asia: An East Coast Malayan Example". In *Ethnicity and Ethnic Relations in Malaysia*, edited by Raymond L.M. Lee. Illinois: Northern Illinois University, Center for Southeast Asian Studies, 1986.

Wolters, O.W. *The Fall of Srivijaya in Malay History*. London: Lund Humphries, 1970.

Wong, Diana. "War and Memory in Malaysia and Singapore: An Introduction". In *War and Memory in Malaysia and Singapore*, edited by Patricia Lim Pui Huen and Diana Wong. Singapore: Institute of Southeast Asian Studies, 2000.

Wong Chin-Huat, James Wong, and Noraini Othman. "Malaysia: Towards a Topology of an Electoral One-Party State". *Democratization* 17, no. 5 (2010): 920–49.

Wong Wing On, James. *From Pacific War to Merdeka: Reminiscences of Abdullah C.D., Rashid Maidin, Suriani Abdulla and Abu Samah*. Petaling Jaya: Strategic Information Research Development Centre, 2005.

Yadav, K.C. and Akiko Seki. *Subhas Chandra Bose: The Last Days*. Gurgaon: Hope India, 2003.

Yoshimura Mako. "Japan's Economic Policy for Occupied Malaya". In *New Perspectives on the Japanese Occupation in Malaya and Singapore, 1941–1945*, edited by Akashi Yoji and Yoshimura Mako. Singapore: NUS Press, 2008.

Zaid Ibrahim. *In Good Faith: Articles, Essays and Interviews*. Kuala Lumpur: Zaid Ibrahim Publications, 2007.

Zainah Anwar. *Islamic Revivalism in Malaysia: Dakwah among the Students*. Petaling Jaya: Pelanduk, 1987.

———. "State Intervention in Personal Faith: The Case of Malaysia". In *Multiethnic Malaysia: Past, Present and Future*, edited by Lim Teck Ghee, Alberto Gomes, and Azly Rahman. Petaling Jaya: Strategic Information and Research Development Centre, 2009.

Zainal Kling. "UMNO and BN in the 2004 Election: The Political Culture of Complex Identities". In *Malaysia: Recent Trends and Challenges*, edited by

Saw Swee-Hock and K. Kesavapany. Singapore: Institute of Southeast Asian Studies, 2006.

Zawawi Ibrahim. "The New Economic Policy and the Identity Question of the Indigenous Peoples of Sabah and Sarawak". In *The New Economic Policy in Malaysia: Affirmative Action, Ethnic Inequalities and Social Justice*, edited by Edmund Terence Gomez and Johan Saravanamuttu. Singapore: NUS/Institute of Southeast Asian Studies, 2013.

Index

www.ingramcontent.com/pod-product-compliance
Lightning Source LLC
Chambersburg PA
CBHW072038020426
42334CB00017B/1318